THE BOOK ®

Rover 216 & 416
Service and Repair Manual

Mark Coombs

Models covered *(1830-9X2)*

All Rover 216 & 416 models, including special/limited editions, fitted with single overhead camshaft (SOHC) or double overhead camshaft (DOHC) 1590 cc engines

Covers major mechanical features of Cabriolet
Does not cover Diesel engine models

© Haynes Publishing 1995

A book in the **Haynes Service and Repair Manual Series**

ISBN 1 85960 148 0

British Library Cataloguing in Publication Data
A catalogue record for this book is available from the British Library.

ABCDE
FGHIJ
KL

Printed by **J H Haynes & Co. Ltd, Sparkford, Nr Yeovil, Somerset BA22 7JJ**

Haynes Publishing
Sparkford, Nr Yeovil, Somerset BA22 7JJ, England

Haynes North America, Inc
861 Lawrence Drive, Newbury Park, California 91320, USA

Editions Haynes S.A.
147/149, rue Saint Honoré, 75001 PARIS, France

Contents

Working on your car can be dangerous. This page shows just some of the potential risks and hazards, with the aim of creating a safety-conscious attitude.

General hazards

Scalding

• Don't remove the radiator or expansion tank cap while the engine is hot.
• Engine oil, automatic transmission fluid or power steering fluid may also be dangerously hot if the engine has recently been running.

Burning

• Beware of burns from the exhaust system and from any part of the engine. Brake discs and drums can also be extremely hot immediately after use.

Crushing

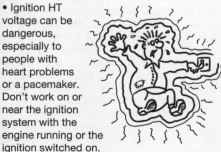

• When working under or near a raised vehicle, always supplement the jack with axle stands, or use drive-on ramps. *Never venture under a car which is only supported by a jack.*
• Take care if loosening or tightening high-torque nuts when the vehicle is on stands. Initial loosening and final tightening should be done with the wheels on the ground.

Fire

• Fuel is highly flammable; fuel vapour is explosive.
• Don't let fuel spill onto a hot engine.
• Do not smoke or allow naked lights (including pilot lights) anywhere near a vehicle being worked on. Also beware of creating sparks (electrically or by use of tools).
• Fuel vapour is heavier than air, so don't work on the fuel system with the vehicle over an inspection pit.
• Another cause of fire is an electrical overload or short-circuit. Take care when repairing or modifying the vehicle wiring.
• Keep a fire extinguisher handy, of a type suitable for use on fuel and electrical fires.

Electric shock

• Ignition HT voltage can be dangerous, especially to people with heart problems or a pacemaker. Don't work on or near the ignition system with the engine running or the ignition switched on.

• Mains voltage is also dangerous. Make sure that any mains-operated equipment is correctly earthed. Mains power points should be protected by a residual current device (RCD) circuit breaker.

Fume or gas intoxication

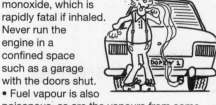

• Exhaust fumes are poisonous; they often contain carbon monoxide, which is rapidly fatal if inhaled. Never run the engine in a confined space such as a garage with the doors shut.
• Fuel vapour is also poisonous, as are the vapours from some cleaning solvents and paint thinners.

Poisonous or irritant substances

• Avoid skin contact with battery acid and with any fuel, fluid or lubricant, especially antifreeze, brake hydraulic fluid and Diesel fuel. Don't syphon them by mouth. If such a substance is swallowed or gets into the eyes, seek medical advice.
• Prolonged contact with used engine oil can cause skin cancer. Wear gloves or use a barrier cream if necessary. Change out of oil-soaked clothes and do not keep oily rags in your pocket.
• Air conditioning refrigerant forms a poisonous gas if exposed to a naked flame (including a cigarette). It can also cause skin burns on contact.

Asbestos

• Asbestos dust can cause cancer if inhaled or swallowed. Asbestos may be found in gaskets and in brake and clutch linings. When dealing with such components it is safest to assume that they contain asbestos.

Special hazards

Hydrofluoric acid

• This extremely corrosive acid is formed when certain types of synthetic rubber, found in some O-rings, oil seals, fuel hoses etc, are exposed to temperatures above 400ºC. The rubber changes into a charred or sticky substance containing the acid. *Once formed, the acid remains dangerous for years. If it gets onto the skin, it may be necessary to amputate the limb concerned.*
• When dealing with a vehicle which has suffered a fire, or with components salvaged from such a vehicle, wear protective gloves and discard them after use.

The battery

• Batteries contain sulphuric acid, which attacks clothing, eyes and skin. Take care when topping-up or carrying the battery.
• The hydrogen gas given off by the battery is highly explosive. Never cause a spark or allow a naked light nearby. Be careful when connecting and disconnecting battery chargers or jump leads.

Air bags

• Air bags can cause injury if they go off accidentally. Take care when removing the steering wheel and/or facia. Special storage instructions may apply.

Diesel injection equipment

• Diesel injection pumps supply fuel at very high pressure. Take care when working on the fuel injectors and fuel pipes.

⚠ *Warning: Never expose the hands, face or any other part of the body to injector spray; the fuel can penetrate the skin with potentially fatal results.*

Remember...

DO

• Do use eye protection when using power tools, and when working under the vehicle.

• Do wear gloves or use barrier cream to protect your hands when necessary.

• Do get someone to check periodically that all is well when working alone on the vehicle.

• Do keep loose clothing and long hair well out of the way of moving mechanical parts.

• Do remove rings, wristwatch etc, before working on the vehicle – especially the electrical system.

• Do ensure that any lifting or jacking equipment has a safe working load rating adequate for the job.

DON'T

• Don't attempt to lift a heavy component which may be beyond your capability – get assistance.

• Don't rush to finish a job, or take unverified short cuts.

• Don't use ill-fitting tools which may slip and cause injury.

• Don't leave tools or parts lying around where someone can trip over them. Mop up oil and fuel spills at once.

• Don't allow children or pets to play in or near a vehicle being worked on.

Roadside Repairs

Jacking, towing and wheel changing

Note: *On models fitted with side skirt/sill extension trim panels, the access panel must first be removed from the trim panel, to gain access to jacking points 2, 3, 4 and 5 (see accompanying illustration)*
To change a wheel, have the car parked on firm, level ground, apply the handbrake firmly, and select first or reverse gear. Remove the spare wheel, tools and jack from the luggage compartment.

Remove the roadwheel trim (where fitted), and slacken the roadwheel nuts through half to one turn each, working in a diagonal sequence. Using chalk or similar, mark the relationship of the roadwheel to the hub.

Place chocks (any blocks of wood, bricks or stones lying around will do) at the front and rear of the roadwheel diagonally opposite the one to be changed. Locate the jack head in the jacking point nearest to the wheel to be changed. For additional safety, it is worthwhile sliding the spare wheel under the side of the car, close to the jack, while the car is raised. When the spare wheel is required, put the punctured wheel under the car in its place. This will reduce the risk of personal injury (and of damage to the car), should the car slip off the jack.

Ensure that the jack base is located on firm ground, and jack up the car. When the wheel is clear of the ground, remove the nuts and lift off the wheel.

Check that the threads and the wheel-to-hub mating surfaces are clean and undamaged, and that the inside of the spare wheel is clean. The threads may be cleaned with a brass wire brush if rusty. Apply a thin smear of copper-based anti-seize compound to the threads and roadwheel-to-hub mating surfaces, to prevent the formation of corrosion. *Obviously, you are not likely to be able to do anything about this at the roadside, but it is worthwhile attending to it as soon as possible once the car is running again, or changing a wheel may be even more difficult next time!*

On refitting, align the marks made on removal (if the same roadwheel is being fitted), and tighten the nuts securely, but not yet fully while the car is still raised. Lower the car, then tighten the nuts fully, working in progressive stages and in a diagonal sequence, to the specified torque wrench setting if possible.

Refit the roadwheel trim (where applicable), and **check the tyre pressure.** With the spare wheel in position, remove the chocks, and stow the jack and tools. If a new roadwheel has been fitted, have it balanced as soon as possible. If the roadwheel nuts were tightened using the car's wheelbrace, check as soon as possible that they are tightened to the specified torque wrench setting.

When jacking up the car to carry out repair or maintenance tasks, position the jack as follows; see the accompanying illustration for details.

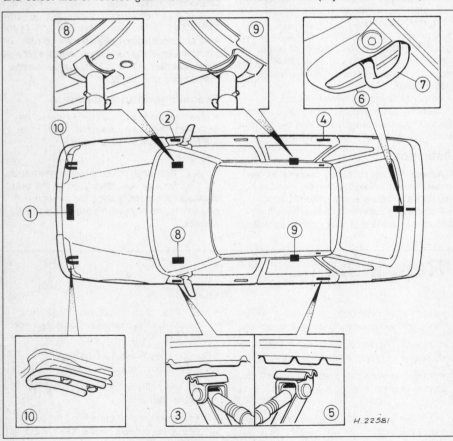

H.22581

Jacking towing and supporting points

1 Front central jack location pad
2 Right-hand sill front jacking/support point
3 Left-hand sill front jacking/support point
4 Right-hand sill rear jacking/support point
5 Left-hand sill rear jacking/support point
6 Rear reinforced jack location pad
7 Rear towing eye
8 Front underbody longitudinal support points
9 Rear underbody longitudinal support points
10 Front towing eyes

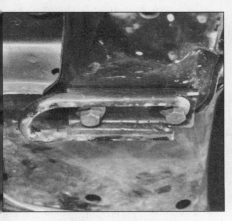

Front towing eye location

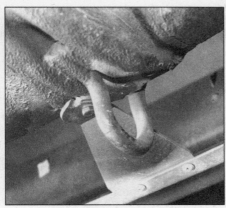

Rear towing eye location

If the front of the car is to be raised, firmly apply the handbrake, and place the jack head under point 1. Jack the car up, and position the axle stands either on the sills at points 2 and 3, or the underbody longitudinal supports at points 8.

To raise the rear of the car, chock the front wheels, and place the jack head under point 6, the reinforced location pad immediately in front of the rear towing hook. The axle stands should be placed either on the sills at points 4 and 5, or the underbody longitudinal supports at points 9.

To raise the side of the car, place the jack head under the sill at point 2 or 3 (as applicable) at the front, then jack up the car and position an axle stand under the underbody longitudinal support at point 8. Remove the jack, position it under point 4 or 5 (as applicable), then jack up the rear of the car and position an axle stand under the underbody longitudinal support at point 9.

Never work under, around or near a raised car, unless it is adequately supported in at least two places with axle stands. *Never use makeshift piles of narrow wooden blocks or house bricks, as they can easily topple (or in the case of house bricks, disintegrate under the weight of the car).*

The car may be towed for breakdown recovery purposes, but only using the towing eyes positioned at the front and rear of the vehicle (photos). These eyes are intended only for towing other vehicles (or being towed by them), and must not be used for lifting the car either directly or indirectly. On models with automatic transmission, the car must **never** be towed with its front wheels on the ground; *without the engine running, the transmission is not sufficiently lubricated, and extensive damage will be done.* On models with a manual gearbox, on no account should the car be towed with the front wheels on the ground if the transmission is faulty or the transmission oil level is low. If the car is being towed with its wheels on the ground, it must not be towed at speeds in excess of 30 mph (50 kmh), or for a distance in excess of 30 miles (50 km). **Note:** *If the car is being towed in an attempt to start it (flat battery), this is only permissible if the car does not have a catalytic converter fitted. Models with catalytic converters should not be tow- or push-started, as unburned fuel will enter the converter unit, causing it to overheat when the engine starts.*

Roadside Repairs

Booster battery (jump) starting

When jump-starting a car using a booster battery, observe the following precautions:

A) Before connecting the booster battery, make sure that the ignition is switched off.

B) Ensure that all electrical equipment (lights, heater, wipers, etc) is switched off.

C) Make sure that the booster battery is the same voltage as the discharged one in the vehicle.

D) If the battery is being jump-started from the battery in another vehicle, the two vehcles MUST NOT TOUCH each other.

E) Make sure that the transmission is in neutral (or PARK, in the case of automatic transmission).

HAYNES HiNT *Jump starting will get you out of trouble, but you must correct whatever made the battery go flat in the first place. There are three possibilities:*

1 *The battery has been drained by repeated attempts to start, or by leaving the lights on.*

2 *The charging system is not working properly (alternator drivebelt slack or broken, alternator wiring fault or alternator itself faulty).*

3 *The battery itself is at fault (electrolyte low, or battery worn out).*

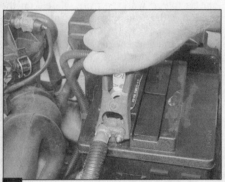

1 Connect one end of the red jump lead to the positive (+) terminal of the flat battery

2 Connect the other end of the red lead to the positive (+) terminal of the booster battery.

3 Connect one end of the black jump lead to the negative (-) terminal of the booster battery

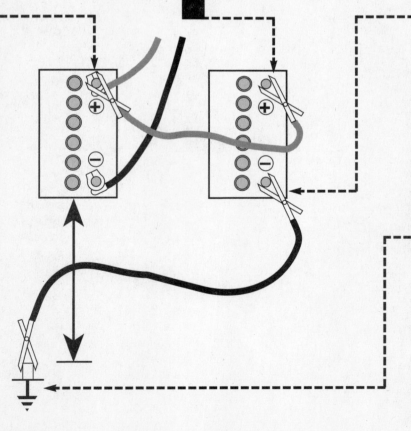

4 Connect the other end of the black jump lead to a bolt or bracket on the engine block, well away from the battery, on the vehicle to be started.

5 Make sure that the jump leads will not come into contact with the fan, drive-belts or other moving parts of the engine.

6 Start the engine using the booster battery, then with the engine running at idle speed, disconnect the jump leads in the reverse order of connection.

Identifying leaks

Puddles on the garage floor or drive, or obvious wetness under the bonnet or underneath the car, suggest a leak that needs investigating. It can sometimes be difficult to decide where the leak is coming from, especially if the engine bay is very dirty already. Leaking oil or fluid can also be blown rearwards by the passage of air under the car, giving a false impression of where the problem lies.

 Warning: Most automotive oils and fluids are poisonous. Wash them off skin, and change out of contaminated clothing, without delay.

 HAYNES HiNT *The smell of a fluid leaking from the car may provide a clue to what's leaking. Some fluids are distictively coloured. It may help to clean the car carefully and to park it over some clean paper overnight as an aid to locating the source of the leak.*
Remember that some leaks may only occur while the engine is running.

Sump oil

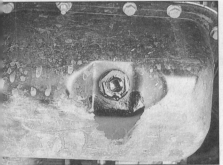

Engine oil may leak from the drain plug...

Oil from filter

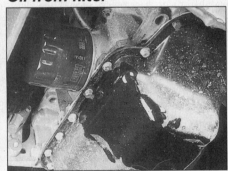

...or from the base of the oil filter.

Gearbox oil

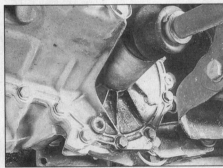

Gearbox oil can leak from the seals at the inboard ends of the driveshafts.

Antifreeze

Leaking antifreeze often leaves a crystalline deposit like this.

Brake fluid

A leak occurring at a wheel is almost certainly brake fluid.

Power steering fluid

Power steering fluid may leak from the pipe connectors on the steering rack.

Buying spare parts

Spare parts are available from many sources; for example, Rover garages, other garages and accessory shops, and motor factors. Our advice regarding spare part sources is as follows.

Officially-appointed Rover garages – This is the best source for parts which are peculiar to your car, and are not generally available (eg complete cylinder heads, internal gearbox components, badges, interior trim, etc.). It is also the only place at which you should buy parts if the vehicle is still under warranty. To be sure of obtaining the correct parts, it will be necessary to give the storeman your car's vehicle identification number, and if possible, take the old parts along for positive identification. Many parts are available under a factory exchange scheme – any parts returned should always be clean. It obviously makes good sense to go straight to the specialists on your car for this type of part, as they are best-equipped to supply you.

Other garages and accessory shops – These are often very good places to buy materials and components needed for the maintenance of your car (eg oil filters, spark plugs, bulbs, drivebelts, oils and greases, touch-up paint, filler paste, etc.). They also sell general accessories, usually have convenient opening hours, charge lower prices and can often be found not far from home.

Motor factors – Good factors will stock all the more important components which wear out comparatively quickly (eg exhaust systems, brake pads, seals and hydraulic parts, clutch components, bearing shells, pistons, valves, etc.). Motor factors will often provide new or reconditioned components on a part exchange basis – this can save a considerable amount of money.

Vehicle identification numbers

Modifications are a continuing and unpublicised process in vehicle manufacture, quite apart from major model changes. Spare parts manuals and lists are compiled upon a numerical basis, the individual vehicle identification numbers being essential to correct identification of the component concerned.

When ordering spare parts, always give as much information as possible. Quote the car model, year of manufacture, body and engine numbers as appropriate.

The *vehicle identification plate* is located the bottom of the passenger side door pillar (photo). It gives the VIN (vehicle identification number), vehicle weight information, and paint and trim colour codes.

The *vehicle identification number* is given on the vehicle identification plate and is repeated, stamped onto the centre of the engine compartment bulkhead (photo).

The *body number* is stamped into a plate fixed to the left-hand side of the spare wheel well, in the luggage compartment.

The *engine number* is stamped onto the front right-hand end of the cylinder block face, next to the transmission (photo).

The *transmission number* is stamped onto a label attached to the front face of the gearbox on models with a manual gearbox, and onto a plate attached to the underside of the gearbox on models with automatic transmission.

Vehicle identification plate on passenger door pillar

Vehicle identification number on engine compartment bulkhead

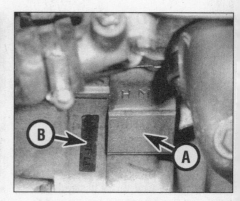
Engine number (A) on front of cylinder block/crankcase, and manual gearbox identification number (B)

This is a guide to getting your vehicle through the MOT test. Obviously it will not be possible to examine the vehicle to the same standard as the professional MOT tester. However, working through the following checks will enable you to identify any problem areas before submitting the vehicle for the test.

Where a testable component is in borderline condition, the tester has discretion in deciding whether to pass or fail it. The basis of such discretion is whether the tester would be happy for a close relative or friend to use the vehicle with the component in that condition. If the vehicle presented is clean and evidently well cared for, the tester may be more inclined to pass a borderline component than if the vehicle is scruffy and apparently neglected.

It has only been possible to summarise the test requirements here, based on the regulations in force at the time of printing. Test standards are becoming increasingly stringent, although there are some exemptions for older vehicles. For full details obtain a copy of the Haynes publication Pass the MOT! (available from stockists of Haynes manuals).

An assistant will be needed to help carry out some of these checks.

The checks have been sub-divided into four categories, as follows:

1 Checks carried out **FROM THE DRIVER'S SEAT**

2 Checks carried out **WITH THE VEHICLE ON THE GROUND**

3 Checks carried out **WITH THE VEHICLE RAISED AND THE WHEELS FREE TO TURN**

4 Checks carried out on **YOUR VEHICLE'S EXHAUST EMISSION SYSTEM**

---

1 Checks carried out **FROM THE DRIVER'S SEAT**

Handbrake

☐ Test the operation of the handbrake. Excessive travel (too many clicks) indicates incorrect brake or cable adjustment.
☐ Check that the handbrake cannot be released by tapping the lever sideways. Check the security of the lever mountings.

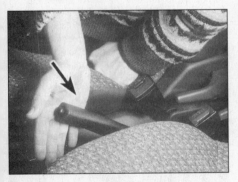

Footbrake

☐ Depress the brake pedal and check that it does not creep down to the floor, indicating a master cylinder fault. Release the pedal, wait a few seconds, then depress it again. If the pedal travels nearly to the floor before firm resistance is felt, brake adjustment or repair is necessary. If the pedal feels spongy, there is air in the hydraulic system which must be removed by bleeding.

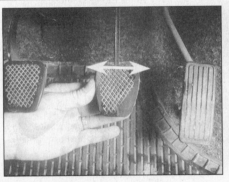

☐ Check that the brake pedal is secure and in good condition. Check also for signs of fluid leaks on the pedal, floor or carpets, which would indicate failed seals in the brake master cylinder.
☐ Check the servo unit (when applicable) by operating the brake pedal several times, then keeping the pedal depressed and starting the engine. As the engine starts, the pedal will move down slightly. If not, the vacuum hose or the servo itself may be faulty.

Steering wheel and column

☐ Examine the steering wheel for fractures or looseness of the hub, spokes or rim.
☐ Move the steering wheel from side to side and then up and down. Check that the steering wheel is not loose on the column, indicating wear or a loose retaining nut. Continue moving the steering wheel as before, but also turn it slightly from left to right.
☐ Check that the steering wheel is not loose on the column, and that there is no abnormal

movement of the steering wheel, indicating wear in the column support bearings or couplings.

Windscreen and mirrors

☐ The windscreen must be free of cracks or other significant damage within the driver's field of view. (Small stone chips are acceptable.) Rear view mirrors must be secure, intact, and capable of being adjusted.

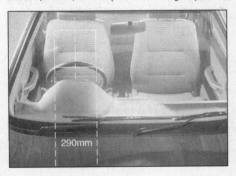

290mm

MOT Test Checks

Seat belts and seats

Note: *The following checks are applicable to all seat belts, front and rear.*

☐ Examine the webbing of all the belts (including rear belts if fitted) for cuts, serious fraying or deterioration. Fasten and unfasten each belt to check the buckles. If applicable, check the retracting mechanism. Check the security of all seat belt mountings accessible from inside the vehicle.

☐ The front seats themselves must be securely attached and the backrests must lock in the upright position.

Doors

☐ Both front doors must be able to be opened and closed from outside and inside, and must latch securely when closed.

2 Checks carried out WITH THE VEHICLE ON THE GROUND

Vehicle identification

☐ Number plates must be in good condition, secure and legible, with letters and numbers correctly spaced – spacing at (A) should be twice that at (B).

☐ The VIN plate (A) and homologation plate (B) must be legible.

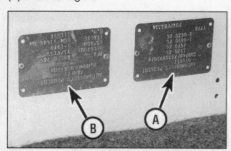

Electrical equipment

☐ Switch on the ignition and check the operation of the horn.

☐ Check the windscreen washers and wipers, examining the wiper blades; renew damaged or perished blades. Also check the operation of the stop-lights.

☐ Check the operation of the sidelights and number plate lights. The lenses and reflectors must be secure, clean and undamaged.

☐ Check the operation and alignment of the headlights. The headlight reflectors must not be tarnished and the lenses must be undamaged.

☐ Switch on the ignition and check the operation of the direction indicators (including the instrument panel tell-tale) and the hazard warning lights. Operation of the sidelights and stop-lights must not affect the indicators - if it does, the cause is usually a bad earth at the rear light cluster.

☐ Check the operation of the rear foglight(s), including the warning light on the instrument panel or in the switch.

Footbrake

☐ Examine the master cylinder, brake pipes and servo unit for leaks, loose mountings, corrosion or other damage.

☐ The fluid reservoir must be secure and the fluid level must be between the upper (A) and lower (B) markings.

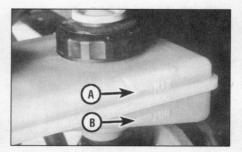

☐ Inspect both front brake flexible hoses for cracks or deterioration of the rubber. Turn the steering from lock to lock, and ensure that the hoses do not contact the wheel, tyre, or any part of the steering or suspension mechanism. With the brake pedal firmly depressed, check the hoses for bulges or leaks under pressure.

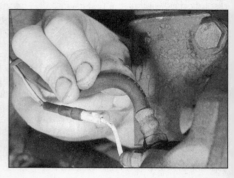

Steering and suspension

☐ Have your assistant turn the steering wheel from side to side slightly, up to the point where the steering gear just begins to transmit this movement to the roadwheels. Check for excessive free play between the steering wheel and the steering gear, indicating wear or insecurity of the steering column joints, the column-to-steering gear coupling, or the steering gear itself.

☐ Have your assistant turn the steering wheel more vigorously in each direction, so that the roadwheels just begin to turn. As this is done, examine all the steering joints, linkages, fittings and attachments. Renew any component that shows signs of wear or damage. On vehicles with power steering, check the security and condition of the steering pump, drivebelt and hoses.

☐ Check that the vehicle is standing level, and at approximately the correct ride height.

Shock absorbers

☐ Depress each corner of the vehicle in turn, then release it. The vehicle should rise and then settle in its normal position. If the vehicle continues to rise and fall, the shock absorber is defective. A shock absorber which has seized will also cause the vehicle to fail.

Exhaust system

☐ Start the engine. With your assistant holding a rag over the tailpipe, check the entire system for leaks. Repair or renew leaking sections.

3 Checks carried out **WITH THE VEHICLE RAISED AND THE WHEELS FREE TO TURN**

Jack up the front and rear of the vehicle, and securely support it on axle stands. Position the stands clear of the suspension assemblies. Ensure that the wheels are clear of the ground and that the steering can be turned from lock to lock.

Steering mechanism

☐ Have your assistant turn the steering from lock to lock. Check that the steering turns smoothly, and that no part of the steering mechanism, including a wheel or tyre, fouls any brake hose or pipe or any part of the body structure.
☐ Examine the steering rack rubber gaiters for damage or insecurity of the retaining clips. If power steering is fitted, check for signs of damage or leakage of the fluid hoses, pipes or connections. Also check for excessive stiffness or binding of the steering, a missing split pin or locking device, or severe corrosion of the body structure within 30 cm of any steering component attachment point.

Front and rear suspension and wheel bearings

☐ Starting at the front right-hand side, grasp the roadwheel at the 3 o'clock and 9 o'clock positions and shake it vigorously. Check for free play or insecurity at the wheel bearings, suspension balljoints, or suspension mountings, pivots and attachments.
☐ Now grasp the wheel at the 12 o'clock and 6 o'clock positions and repeat the previous inspection. Spin the wheel, and check for roughness or tightness of the front wheel bearing.

☐ If excess free play is suspected at a component pivot point, this can be confirmed by using a large screwdriver or similar tool and levering between the mounting and the component attachment. This will confirm whether the wear is in the pivot bush, its retaining bolt, or in the mounting itself (the bolt holes can often become elongated).

☐ Carry out all the above checks at the other front wheel, and then at both rear wheels.

Springs and shock absorbers

☐ Examine the suspension struts (when applicable) for serious fluid leakage, corrosion, or damage to the casing. Also check the security of the mounting points.
☐ If coil springs are fitted, check that the spring ends locate in their seats, and that the spring is not corroded, cracked or broken.
☐ If leaf springs are fitted, check that all leaves are intact, that the axle is securely attached to each spring, and that there is no deterioration of the spring eye mountings, bushes, and shackles.

☐ The same general checks apply to vehicles fitted with other suspension types, such as torsion bars, hydraulic displacer units, etc. Ensure that all mountings and attachments are secure, that there are no signs of excessive wear, corrosion or damage, and (on hydraulic types) that there are no fluid leaks or damaged pipes.
☐ Inspect the shock absorbers for signs of serious fluid leakage. Check for wear of the mounting bushes or attachments, or damage to the body of the unit.

Driveshafts (fwd vehicles only)

☐ Rotate each front wheel in turn and inspect the constant velocity joint gaiters for splits or damage. Also check that each driveshaft is straight and undamaged.

Braking system

☐ If possible without dismantling, check brake pad wear and disc condition. Ensure that the friction lining material has not worn excessively, (A) and that the discs are not fractured, pitted, scored or badly worn (B).

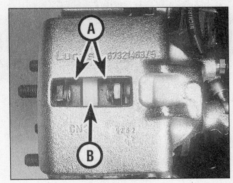

☐ Examine all the rigid brake pipes underneath the vehicle, and the flexible hose(s) at the rear. Look for corrosion, chafing or insecurity of the pipes, and for signs of bulging under pressure, chafing, splits or deterioration of the flexible hoses.
☐ Look for signs of fluid leaks at the brake calipers or on the brake backplates. Repair or renew leaking components.
☐ Slowly spin each wheel, while your assistant depresses and releases the footbrake. Ensure that each brake is operating and does not bind when the pedal is released.

□ Examine the handbrake mechanism, checking for frayed or broken cables, excessive corrosion, or wear or insecurity of the linkage. Check that the mechanism works on each relevant wheel, and releases fully, without binding.

□ It is not possible to test brake efficiency without special equipment, but a road test can be carried out later to check that the vehicle pulls up in a straight line.

Fuel and exhaust systems

□ Inspect the fuel tank (including the filler cap), fuel pipes, hoses and unions. All components must be secure and free from leaks.

□ Examine the exhaust system over its entire length, checking for any damaged, broken or missing mountings, security of the retaining clamps and rust or corrosion.

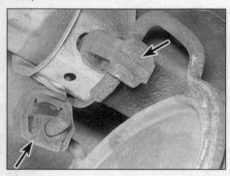

Wheels and tyres

□ Examine the sidewalls and tread area of each tyre in turn. Check for cuts, tears, lumps, bulges, separation of the tread, and exposure of the ply or cord due to wear or damage. Check that the tyre bead is correctly seated on the wheel rim, that the valve is

sound and properly seated, and that the wheel is not distorted or damaged.

□ Check that the tyres are of the correct size for the vehicle, that they are of the same size and type on each axle, and that the pressures are correct.

□ Check the tyre tread depth. The legal minimum at the time of writing is 1.6 mm over at least three-quarters of the tread width. Abnormal tread wear may indicate incorrect front wheel alignment.

Body corrosion

□ Check the condition of the entire vehicle structure for signs of corrosion in load-bearing areas. (These include chassis box sections, side sills, cross-members, pillars, and all suspension, steering, braking system and seat belt mountings and anchorages.) Any corrosion which has seriously reduced the thickness of a load-bearing area is likely to cause the vehicle to fail. In this case professional repairs are likely to be needed.

□ Damage or corrosion which causes sharp or otherwise dangerous edges to be exposed will also cause the vehicle to fail.

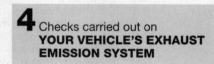

4 Checks carried out on **YOUR VEHICLE'S EXHAUST EMISSION SYSTEM**

Petrol models

□ Have the engine at normal operating temperature, and make sure that it is in good tune (ignition system in good order, air filter element clean, etc).

□ Before any measurements are carried out, raise the engine speed to around 2500 rpm, and hold it at this speed for 20 seconds. Allow the engine speed to return to idle, and

watch for smoke emissions from the exhaust tailpipe. If the idle speed is obviously much too high, or if dense blue or clearly-visible black smoke comes from the tailpipe for more than 5 seconds, the vehicle will fail. As a rule of thumb, blue smoke signifies oil being burnt (engine wear) while black smoke signifies unburnt fuel (dirty air cleaner element, or other carburettor or fuel system fault).

□ An exhaust gas analyser capable of measuring carbon monoxide (CO) and hydrocarbons (HC) is now needed. If such an instrument cannot be hired or borrowed, a local garage may agree to perform the check for a small fee.

CO emissions (mixture)

□ At the time or writing, the maximum CO level at idle is 3.5% for vehicles first used after August 1986 and 4.5% for older vehicles. From January 1996 a much tighter limit (around 0.5%) applies to catalyst-equipped vehicles first used from August 1992. If the CO level cannot be reduced far enough to pass the test (and the fuel and ignition systems are otherwise in good condition) then the carburettor is badly worn, or there is some problem in the fuel injection system or catalytic converter (as applicable).

HC emissions

□ With the CO emissions within limits, HC emissions must be no more than 1200 ppm (parts per million). If the vehicle fails this test at idle, it can be re-tested at around 2000 rpm; if the HC level is then 1200 ppm or less, this counts as a pass.

□ Excessive HC emissions can be caused by oil being burnt, but they are more likely to be due to unburnt fuel.

Diesel models

□ The only emission test applicable to Diesel engines is the measuring of exhaust smoke density. The test involves accelerating the engine several times to its maximum unloaded speed.

Note: *It is of the utmost importance that the engine timing belt is in good condition before the test is carried out.*

□ Excessive smoke can be caused by a dirty air cleaner element. Otherwise, professional advice may be needed to find the cause.

Chapter 1 Routine maintenance and servicing

Contents

Degrees of difficulty

| Easy, suitable for novice with little experience | | Fairly easy, suitable for beginner with some experience | | Fairly difficult, suitable for competent DIY mechanic | | Difficult, suitable for experienced DIY mechanic | | Very difficult, suitable for expert DIY or professional | |

Maintenance Schedule

Maintenance schedule

The maintenance intervals in this manual are provided with the assumption that you, not the dealer, will be carrying out the work. These are the minimum maintenance intervals recommended by the manufacturer for vehicles driven daily. Alongside each operation in the schedule is a reference which directs the reader to the Sections in this Chapter covering maintenance procedures or to other Chapters in the Manual, where the operations are described and illustrated in greater detail. If you wish to keep your vehicle in peak condition at all times, you may wish to perform some of these procedures more often. We encourage frequent maintenance because it enhances the efficiency, performance and resale value of your vehicle. If the vehicle is driven in dusty areas, used to tow a trailer, or driven frequently at slow speeds (idling in traffic) or on short journeys, more frequent maintenance intervals are recommended.

When the vehicle is new, it should be serviced by a factory-authorised dealer service depart-ment, in order to preserve the factory warranty.

If, from the time the vehicle is new, the routine maintenance schedule is followed closely, and frequent checks are made of fluid levels and high-wear items, as suggested throughout this manual, the engine will be kept in relatively good running condition, and the need for additional work will be minimised.

It is possible that there will be times when the engine is running poorly due to the lack of regular maintenance. This is even more likely if a used vehicle, which has not received regular and frequent maintenance checks, is purchased. In such cases, additional work may need to be carried out, outside of the regular maintenance intervals.

If engine wear is suspected, a compression test (Chapter 2) will provide valuable information regarding the overall performance of the main internal components. Such a test can be used as a basis to decide on the extent of the work to be carried out. If, for example, a compression test indicates serious internal engine wear, conventional maintenance as described in this Chapter will not greatly improve the performance of the engine, and may prove a waste of time and money, unless extensive overhaul work is carried out first.

Daily

- [ ] Check the operation of the horn, all lamps, the direction indicators and the wipers and washers (Section 2)
- [ ] Check the operation of the seat belts (Section 2)
- [ ] Check under the car for signs of fluid leaks on the ground
- [ ] Perform a road test (Section 2).

Every 250 miles or weekly (400 km)

- [ ] Check the engine oil level (Section 3)
- [ ] Check the washer system reservoir fluid level (Section 3)
- [ ] Check the engine for leaks and component security (Section 4)
- [ ] Visually examine the tyres for tread depth, wear or damage (Section 5)
- [ ] Check, and if necessary adjust, the tyre pressures (Section 5)

Every 1000 miles (1500 km) – or monthly whichever comes first

Carry out the daily and weekly checks, then check the following:
- [ ] Check the coolant level (Section 6)
- [ ] Check the brake fluid level (Section 6)
- [ ] Check the power steering fluid level (Section 6)
- [ ] Check the operation of all locks, hinges and latch mechanisms (Section 7)

Every 12 000 miles (20 000 km) or annually – whichever comes first

In addition to the items listed under the daily, weekly and monthly checks, carry out the following:
- [ ] Check and adjust the valve clearances (Section 9)
- [ ] Drain, flush and refill the cooling system, renewing the antifreeze (Section 10)˙
- [ ] Check the cooling system hoses (Section 11)
- [ ] Check and adjust the air conditioner compressor drivebelt (Section 12)
- [ ] Check the operation of the radiator cooling fan (Chapter 3)
- [ ] Check the base idle speed and exhaust gas CO content (Section 13)
- [ ] Check the operation of the lambda sensor – models with a catalytic converter (Chapter 4 and Section 14)
- [ ] Check the fuel system hoses, pipes and connections (Section 15)
- [ ] Check the exhaust system (Section 16)
- [ ] Check the distributor cap, ignition HT coil and the spark plug (HT) leads (Section 17)
- [ ] Check the operation of the clutch (Section 18)
- [ ] Check the transmission oil level (Sections 19 and 20)
- [ ] Check the driveshaft gaiters and CV joints (Section 21)
- [ ] Check the brake pads, calipers and discs (Sections 22 and 24)
- [ ] Check the rear brake shoes, wheel cylinders and drums – where fitted (Section 23)
- [ ] Adjust and lubricate the handbrake (Section 25)
- [ ] Check the braking system master cylinder, flexible hoses and metal pipes (Section 26)
- [ ] Check the tightness of the roadwheel nuts (Section 27)
- [ ] Check the front suspension (Section 28)
- [ ] Check the steering gear, the rubber gaiters and the track rod balljoints (Section 28)
- [ ] Check the power steering pump drivebelt (Sections 29)
- [ ] Check the rear suspension (Section 30)
- [ ] Check and lubricate all locks, hinges, latch mechanisms and the sunroof (Section 31)
- [ ] Check the paintwork and the body panels (Section 32)
- [ ] Check the underbody sealer (Section 33)
- [ ] Check the battery connections and electrolyte level (Section 34)
- [ ] Check and adjust the alternator drivebelt (Sections 35)
- [ ] Check headlamp beam alignment (Section 36)

˙If Rover-recommended antifreeze is used, this task need only be carried out after the first three years of the car's life, and every two years thereafter

... miles (40 000 km) or ... ichever comes first

... ms listed under the 12 000 mile service:

- ... nditioning system (Section 37)
- ... eaner filter element (Section 38)
- ... lter (Section 39)
- ... plugs (Section 40)
- ... n timing (Section 41)
- ☐ Renew th... al gearbox oil (Section 42)
- ☐ Renew the automatic transmission fluid (Section 43)
- ☐ Renew the braking system hydraulic fluid (Section 44)

Every 60 000 miles (100 000 km) or 5 years – whichever comes first

In addition to the items listed under the 12 000 mile service:

- ☐ Check the components of the evaporative emission control system models with a catalytic converter (Chapter 4)
- ☐ Renew the timing belt (Section 45)
- ☐ At this mileage interval or every **THREE** years – whichever comes first – the braking system master cylinder, brake calipers and (where necessary) rear wheel cylinders must be overhauled and their seals renewed. (Chapter 9)

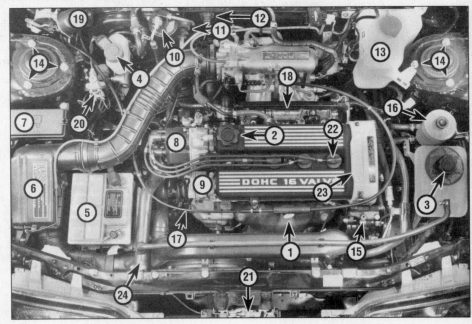

Engine compartment – SOHC engine

1. Engine oil level dipstick
2. Engine oil filler cap
3. Coolant expansion tank filler cap
4. Braking system fluid reservoir cap
5. Battery
6. Air cleaner housing
7. Engine compartment fusebox
8. Distributor
9. Cooling system bleed screw
10. Fuel filter
11. Clutch cable
12. Speedometer cable
13. Washer fluid reservoir
14. Front suspension strut mounting nuts
15. Right-hand engine/transmission mounting
16. Left-hand engine/transmission mounting
17. Accelerator cable
18. Fuel rail and injectors
19. Alternator
20. Windscreen wiper motor
21. Braking system pressure-regulating valve – models without anti-lock brakes (ALB)
22. Starter motor
23. Bonnet lock
24. Number 1 cylinder HT lead
25. Timing belt cover
26. Radiator top hose

Engine compartment – DOHC engine

1. Engine oil level dipstick
2. Engine oil filler cap
3. Coolant expansion tank filler cap
4. Braking system fluid reservoir cap
5. Battery
6. Air cleaner housing
7. Engine compartment fusebox
8. Distributor
9. Cylinder position sensor housing
10. Fuel filter
11. Clutch cable
12. Speedometer cable
13. Washer fluid reservoir
14. Front suspension strut mounting nuts
15. Power steering pump
16. Power steering fluid reservoir
17. Accelerator cable
18. Fuel rail and injectors
19. Windscreen wiper motor
20. Braking system pressure-regulating valve – models without anti-lock brakes (ALB)
21. Bonnet lock
22. Number 1 cylinder HT lead
23. Timing belt cover
24. Radiator top hose

Front underbody view – undercover panel removed for clarity

1 Engine oil drain plug
2 Oil filter
3 Transmission oil drain plug
4 Transmission oil level plug
5 Front engine/transmission mounting
6 Left-hand driveshaft inner constant velocity joint
7 Right-hand driveshaft inner constant velocity joint
8 Intermediate shaft
9 Front towing eye
10 Front suspension tie-bar

11 Front suspension lower arm
12 Anti-roll bar connecting link
13 Steering gear track rod balljoint
14 Anti-roll bar
15 Fuel lines
16 Gearchange mechanism selector rod
17 Gearchange mechanism steady rod
18 Front exhaust pipe shield
19 Intermediate exhaust pipe

Rear underbody view

1 Fuel tank
2 Left-hand handbrake cable
3 Fuel lines
4 Rear suspension left-hand front lateral link
5 Rear suspension left-hand trailing arm
6 Flexible brake hose
7 Rear suspension left-hand rear lower lateral link
8 Rear towing eye
9 Exhaust tailpipe

10 Rear suspension right-hand rear lower lateral link
11 Flexible brake hose
12 Rear suspension right-hand trailing arm
13 Right-hand handbrake cable
14 Rear suspension right-hand front lateral link
15 Intermediate exhaust pipe
16 Exhaust heatshield
17 Rear suspension anti-roll bar
18 Rear suspension anti-roll bar connecting link

Maintenance procedures

1 Introduction

This Chapter is designed to help the DIY owner maintain the Rover 216/416 with the goals of maximum economy, safety, reliability and performance in mind.

On the following pages is a master maintenance schedule, listing the servicing requirements, and the intervals at which they should be carried out as recommended by the manufacturers. Specifications for all the maintenance operations, together with a list of lubricants, fluids and capacities are provided at the end of this Chapter. Refer to the accompanying photographs of the engine compartment and the underbody of the car for the locations of the various components.

Servicing your car in accordance with the mileage/time maintenance schedule, using step-by-step procedures, will result in a planned maintenance programme that should give a long and reliable service life. Bear in mind that it is a comprehensive plan, so maintaining some items but not others at the specified intervals will not produce the same results.

The first step in this maintenance programme is to prepare yourself before the actual work begins. Read through all the procedures to be undertaken, then obtain all the parts, lubricants and any additional tools needed.

Daily checks

2 Operational checks

Horn, lamps, direction indicators, wipers and washers

1 Check the operation of all the electrical equipment. Refer to the appropriate Sections of Chapter 12 for details if any of the circuits are found to be inoperative.

2 Note that stop-lamp switch adjustment is described in Chapter 9.

3 Visually check all accessible wiring connectors, harnesses and retaining clips for security, and for signs of chafing or damage. Rectify any faults found.

4 Check the operation of the windscreen and rear window washers. Adjust the nozzles using a pin if necessary, aiming the spray to a point slightly above the centre of the swept area (remember that the airflow will tend to deflect the washer spray down, when the car is moving).

5 Check the condition of the wiper blades; if they are cracked or show any signs of deterioration, or if the glass swept area is smeared, renew them. For maximum clarity of vision, wiper blades should be renewed annually, as a matter of course.

6 To remove a wiper blade, pull the arm fully away from the glass until it locks. Swivel the blade through 90°, press the locking tab with your fingernail, and slide the blade out of the arm's hooked end (photo). On refitting, ensure that the blade locks securely into the arm.

Seat belts

7 All models are fitted with three-point lap and diagonal inertia reel seat belts, on both front and the rear outer seats. The rear centre seat has a two-point lap-type belt which is fixed (ie not inertia reel).

8 Belt maintenance is limited to regular inspection. Check the webbing for signs of fraying, cuts or other damage, pulling the belt out to its full extent to check its entire length. Check the operation of the buckles by fitting the belt tongue plate, and pulling hard to ensure that it remains locked, then check the retractor mechanism (inertia reel only) by pulling out the belt to the halfway point and jerking hard; the mechanism must lock immediately to prevent any further unreeling, but must allow free movement during normal driving. Finally, ensure that all mounting bolts are securely tightened. Note that the bolts are shouldered so that the belt anchor points are free to rotate.

9 If there is any sign of damage, or any doubt about a belt's condition, it must be renewed. If the car has been involved in a collision, any belts in use at the time must be renewed as a matter of course, and all other belts should be checked carefully.

10 Use only warm water and non-detergent soap to clean the belts. Never use any chemical cleaners, strong detergents, dyes or bleaches. Keep the belts fully extended until they have dried naturally; do not apply heat to dry them.

Road test

11 Check that the engine starts and warms up properly, that the oil pressure and ignition/battery charging warning lamps go out, that the throttle pedal movement is correct, and that the engine responds correctly to the throttle. When driving, check the operation of the clutch (where applicable), gearchange/gear selector mechanism and brakes; listen for noises, and pay particular attention for any roughness, vibrations or other faults from the engine and transmission, steering and suspension.

Weekly checks or every 250 miles

3 Fluid level checks

Engine oil

1 The engine oil level is checked with a dipstick, which extends through a tube and into the sump at the bottom of the engine. The dipstick is located at the centre of the front of the engine, where it extends from the exhaust manifold heatshield.

2 The oil level should be checked with the car standing on level ground, before it is driven, or at least 5 minutes after the engine has been switched off.

> **HAYNES HINT** *If the oil is checked immediately after driving the car, some of the oil will remain in the engine upper components and oil galleries, resulting in an inaccurate dipstick reading.*

3 Withdraw the dipstick from the tube, and wipe all the oil from its end with a clean rag or paper towel. Insert the clean dipstick back into the tube as far as it will go, then withdraw it once more. Note the oil level on the end of the dipstick. Add oil as necessary until the level is between the upper (MAX) and lower (MIN) marks on the dipstick (photo). Note that approximately half a litre of oil will be required to raise the level from the lower mark to the upper mark.

4 Always maintain the level between the two dipstick marks. If the level is allowed to fall below the lower mark, oil starvation may result, which could lead to severe engine damage. If the engine is overfilled by adding too much oil, this may result in oil-fouled spark plugs, oil leaks or oil seal failures.

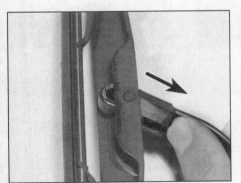

2.6 Depress the locking tab, and slide out wiper blade in direction of arrow

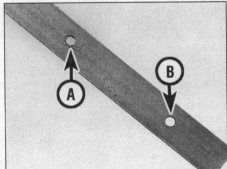

3.3 Engine oil dipstick marks MAX (A) and MIN (B) marks

3.5 Use only good quality oil of the specified grade when topping-up the engine (SOHC engine shown)

1

Weekly Checks

5 Oil is added to the engine after unscrewing the filler cap from the cylinder head cover. An oil can spout or funnel may help to reduce spillage. Always use the correct grade and type of oil, as shown in *'Lubricants, fluids and capacities'* (photo).

Washer fluid

6 The reservoir for the windscreen and rear window (where fitted) washer systems is located on the left-hand side of the engine compartment.
7 Check, and if necessary, top-up the washer fluid level in the reservoir. When topping-up the reservoir, a screenwash additive should be added in the quantities recommended on the bottle. It is permissible to use clean water only in Summer, but most screenwash additives can also be of use in removing dead insects from the windscreen. In Winter, mix the water either with methylated spirit, or with a screenwash additive which has antifreeze properties. Follow the screenwash manufacturer's instructions for the mixing ratio.
8 **Never** use strong detergents (washing-up liquids, etc.) or engine antifreeze in the washer fluid. Not only can they cause smearing of the glass, but they can also damage the car's paintwork.
9 Check the security of the pump wires and the washer tubing; if any of the jets is blocked, clear the obstruction using a thin wire probe.

4 Engine checks

1 Visually inspect the engine joint faces, gaskets and seals for any signs of water or oil leaks. Pay particular attention to the areas around the cylinder head cover, cylinder head, oil filter and sump joint faces. Bear in mind that, over a period of time, some very slight seepage from these areas is to be expected, but what you are really looking for is any indication of a serious leak. Should a leak be found, renew the offending gasket or oil seal by referring to the appropriate Chapters in this manual.
2 Also check the security and condition of all the engine-related pipes and hoses, particularly the crankcase breather hose(s) from the cylinder head cover, PCV valve and oil separator. Ensure that all cable ties or securing clips are in place, and in good condition. Clips which are broken or missing can lead to chafing of the hoses pipes or wiring, which could cause more serious problems in the future.

5 Wheel and tyre maintenance and tyre pressure checks

1 Periodically remove the wheels, and clean any dirt or mud from their inside and outside surfaces. Examine the wheel rims for signs of

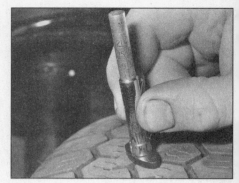

5.2 Checking tyre tread depth with a depth gauge

rusting, corrosion or other damage. Light alloy wheels are easily damaged by 'kerbing' whilst parking, and steel wheels may become similarly dented or buckled. Renewal of the wheel is very often the only course of remedial action possible.
2 The tyres originally fitted are equipped with tread wear indicators, which will appear flush with the surface of the tread, thus producing the effect of a continuous band of rubber across the width of the tyre, when the tread depth is reduced to approximately 1.6 mm (0.063 in); **at this point the tyre must be renewed immediately.** Tread wear can be monitored with a simple inexpensive device, known as a tread depth indicator gauge (photo).

Tyre Tread Wear Patterns (Fig. 1.1)

Shoulder Wear

Underinflation (wear on both sides)
Check and adjust pressures

Incorrect wheel camber (wear on one side)
Repair or renew suspension parts

Hard cornering
Reduce speed!

Centre Wear

Overinflation
Check and adjust pressures

If you sometimes have to inflate your car's tyres to the higher pressures specified for maximum load or sustained high speed, don't forget to reduce the pressures to normal afterwards.

Toe Wear

Incorrect toe setting
Adjust front wheel alignment

Note: The feathered edge of the tread which characterises toe wear is best checked by feel.

Uneven Wear

Incorrect camber or castor
Repair or renew suspension parts

Malfunctioning suspension
Repair or renew suspension parts

Unbalanced wheel
Balance tyres

Out-of-round brake disc/drum
Machine or renew

3 Note any abnormal tread wear with reference to Fig. 1.1. Tread pattern irregularities such as feathering, flat spots and more wear on one side than the other, are indications of front wheel alignment and/or wheel balance problems. If any of these conditions is noted, it should be rectified as soon as possible.

4 General tyre wear is influenced to a large degree by driving style harsh braking and acceleration, or fast cornering, will all result in rapid tyre wear. Interchanging of tyres may result in more even wear, but it is worth bearing in mind that if this is completely effective, the added expense is incurred of replacing simultaneously a complete set of tyres, which may prove financially restrictive for many owners.

5 Front tyres may wear unevenly as a result of wheel misalignment. The front wheels should always be correctly aligned according to the settings specified; refer to Chapter 10 for further information.

6 Regularly check the tyres for damage in the form of cuts or bulges, especially in the sidewalls. Remove any nails or stones embedded in the tread before they penetrate the tyre to cause deflation. If removal of a nail does reveal that the tyre has been punctured, refit the nail so that its point of penetration is marked, then immediately change the wheel and have the tyre repaired by a tyre dealer. Do not drive on a tyre in such a condition. In many cases, a puncture can be simply repaired by the use of an inner tube of the correct size and type. If you are in any doubt as to the possible consequences of any damage found, consult your local tyre dealer for advice.

7 Ensure that tyre pressures are checked regularly, and maintained correctly (photo). Checking should be carried out with the tyres cold, and not immediately after the car has been in use. If the pressures are checked with the tyres hot, an apparently-high reading will be obtained owing to heat expansion. Under no circumstances should an attempt be made to reduce the pressures to the quoted cold reading in this instance, or effective under-inflation will result.

8 Under-inflation will cause overheating of the tyre owing to excessive flexing of the casing, and the tread will not sit correctly on the road surface. This will cause a consequent loss of adhesion and excessive wear, not to mention the danger of sudden tyre failure due to heat build-up.

9 Over-inflation will cause rapid wear of the centre part of the tyre tread, coupled with reduced adhesion, harsher ride, and the danger of shock damage occurring in the tyre casing.

10 The balance of each wheel and tyre assembly should be maintained to avoid excessive wear, not only to the tyres but also to the steering and suspension components. Wheel imbalance is normally signified by vibration through the car's bodyshell, although in many cases it is particularly noticeable through the steering wheel. Conversely, it should be noted that wear or damage in suspension or steering components may cause excessive tyre wear. Out-of-round or out-of-true tyres, damaged wheels and wheel bearing wear also fall into this category. Balancing will not usually cure vibration caused by such wear.

11 Wheel balancing may be carried out with the wheel either on or off the car. If balanced on the car, ensure that the wheel-to-hub relationship is marked in some way prior to subsequent wheel removal, so that it may be refitted in its original position.

12 Legal restrictions apply to many aspects of tyre fitting and usage, and in the UK this information is contained in the Motor Vehicle Construction and Use Regulations. It is suggested that a copy of these regulations is obtained from your local police if in doubt as to current legal requirements with regard to tyre type and condition, minimum tread depth, etc.

Every 1000 miles or monthly

6 Fluid level checks

Coolant

⚠️ **Warning: DO NOT attempt to remove the expansion tank filler cap when the engine is hot, as there is a very great risk of scalding.**

1 All models are equipped with a sealed cooling system. A translucent expansion tank (located in the front left-hand corner of the engine compartment) is connected by hoses to the cooling system (see Chapter 3), and a continual flow of coolant passes through it, to purge any air from the system.

2 The coolant level in the expansion tank should be checked regularly. The level in the tank varies with the temperature of the engine. When the engine is cold, the coolant level should be between the COOLANT LEVEL (MAX) mark on the front of the of the expansion tank and the expansion tank ridge (MIN); when the engine is hot, the level will be slightly higher (photo).

3 If topping-up is necessary, wait until the engine is cold, then cover the expansion tank with a thick layer of rag, and unscrew the filler cap anti-clockwise until a hissing sound is heard; wait until the hissing ceases, indicating that all pressure is released, then slowly unscrew the filler cap until it can be removed. If more hissing sounds are heard, wait until they have stopped before unscrewing the cap completely. At all times, keep well away from the filler opening.

4 Add a mixture of water and antifreeze (see Section 10) through the expansion tank filler neck, until the coolant is up to the level mark (photo). Refit the cap, tightening it securely.

5 With this type of cooling system, the addition of coolant should only be necessary at very infrequent intervals. If frequent topping-up is required, it is likely there is a leak in the system. Check the radiator, all hoses and joint faces for any sign of staining or

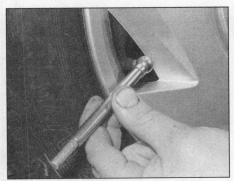

5.7 Checking the tyre pressures with a tyre pressure gauge

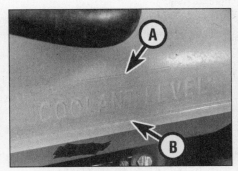

6.2 Coolant level must be between expansion tank MAX (A) and MIN (B) level marks

6.4 Use only the specified mixture to top-up the cooling system

Weekly Checks

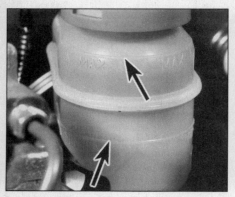

6.6 Brake fluid level must be maintained between the reservoir MAX and MIN level marks (arrowed) – non-ALB model shown

6.7 Use only good-quality brake fluid of the specified type when topping-up brake system fluid reservoir

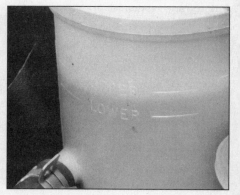

6.13 Power steering fluid level must be between the UPPER and LOWER level marks on the side of the reservoir

6.14 Top-up the power steering fluid with a good-quality fluid of the specified type

actual wetness, and rectify as necessary. If no leaks can be found, it is advisable to have the expansion tank filler cap and the entire system pressure-tested by a dealer or suitably-equipped garage, as this will often show up a small leak not previously visible.

Hydraulic fluid

6 The brake master cylinder and fluid reservoir are mounted on top of the vacuum servo unit in the engine compartment. On models with anti-lock brakes (ALB), there is also a second brake fluid reservoir situated just to the right of the master cylinder fluid reservoir; this is the ALB high-pressure system reservoir. The MAX and MIN level marks are indicated on the side of the reservoir(s), and the fluid level in both reservoirs must be maintained between these marks at all times (photo).
7 If topping-up is necessary, wipe the area around the filler cap with a clean rag. Unscrew the cap and remove it from the reservoir, taking care not to damage the sender unit (where fitted). When adding fluid, pour it carefully into the reservoir – avoid spilling it on surrounding painted surfaces. Be sure to use only the specified brake hydraulic fluid, since mixing different types of fluid can cause damage to the system; see 'Lubricants, fluids and capacities' at the end of this Chapter (photo).

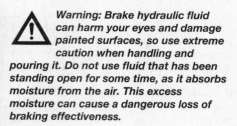

⚠️ **Warning: Brake hydraulic fluid can harm your eyes and damage painted surfaces, so use extreme caution when handling and pouring it. Do not use fluid that has been standing open for some time, as it absorbs moisture from the air. This excess moisture can cause a dangerous loss of braking effectiveness.**

8 When adding fluid, it is a good idea to inspect the reservoir for contamination. The system should be drained and refilled if deposits, dirt particles or contamination are seen in the fluid. *Note: If the ALB high-pressure system is contaminated, the car must be taken to a Rover dealer for the fluid to be changed. Bleeding of the system requires special Rover electrical test equipment, refer to Chapter 9 for further information.*
9 After filling the reservoir to the proper level, make sure that the cap is refitted securely, to avoid leaks and the entry of foreign matter, and reconnect the fluid level wiring connector.
10 The fluid level in the master cylinder reservoir will drop slightly as the brake pads and shoes wear down during normal operation. If the reservoir requires repeated topping-up to maintain the proper level, this is an indication of an hydraulic leak somewhere in the system, which should be investigated **immediately.**

Power steering fluid

11 The power steering fluid reservoir is located on the left-hand side of the engine compartment, just behind the cooling system expansion tank.
12 For the check, the vehicle should be parked on level ground, with the front wheels pointing straight-ahead and the engine stopped. Note that for the check to be accurate, the steering **must not** be operated once the engine has been stopped.
13 The fluid level is visible through the translucent material of the reservoir, and should be between the UPPER (maximum)

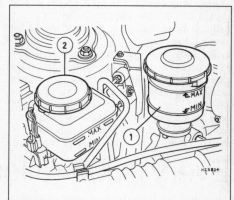

Fig. 1.2 Braking system reservoirs and markings – models with anti-lock brakes (ALB) (Sec 6)

1 Main braking system master cylinder reservoir
2 ALB high-pressure hydraulic system reservoir

and LOWER (minimum) level lines cast on the side of the reservoir (photo).
14 If necessary, wipe the area around the reservoir cap clean, then remove the cap and top-up to the UPPER mark, using the specified type of fluid (photo). Take great care not to allow any dirt or foreign matter to enter the hydraulic system, and do not overfill the reservoir. When the level is correct, refit the cap. Note that the need for frequent topping-up of the system indicates a leak, which should be investigated immediately.

7 Hinge and lock check

1 Check carefully the security and operation of all hinges, latches and locks, adjusting them where required. Check the operation of the central locking system (if fitted).

Every 6000 miles or 6 months

8 Engine oil and filter renewal

1 Frequent oil and filter changes are the most important preventative maintenance procedures that can be undertaken by the DIY owner. As engine oil ages, it becomes diluted and contaminated, which leads to premature engine wear.

2 Before starting this procedure, gather together all the necessary tools and materials. Also make sure that you have plenty of clean rags and newspapers handy, to mop up any spills. Ideally, the engine oil should be warm – it will drain better, and more built-up sludge will be removed with it. Take care however, not to touch the exhaust or any other hot parts of the engine when working under the car. To avoid any possibility of scalding, and to protect yourself from possible skin irritants and other harmful contaminants in used engine oils, it is advisable to wear gloves when carrying out this work.

3 Remove the oil filler cap. The engine oil drain plug is located on the rear of the sump, and is easily reached without having to raise the car. Use a spanner, or preferably a suitable socket and bar, to slacken the drain plug about half a turn. Position the draining container under the drain plug, then remove the plug completely. If possible, try to keep the plug pressed into the sump while unscrewing it by hand the last couple of turns. As the plug releases from the threads, move the plug away sharply so the stream of oil issuing from the sump runs into the container, not up your sleeve.

4 Allow some time for the old oil to drain, noting that it may be necessary to reposition the container as the flow of oil slows to a trickle; work can be speeded-up by removing the oil filter, as described below, while the oil is draining.

5 After all the oil has drained, wipe off the drain plug with a clean rag, and renew its sealing washer. Clean the area around the drain plug opening, and refit the plug. Tighten the plug securely, preferably to the specified torque using a torque wrench.

6 Move the container into position under the oil filter, which is located above the drain plug on the rear of the engine.

7 Use an oil filter removal tool to slacken the filter initially (if necessary), then unscrew it by hand the rest of the way (photo). Empty the oil in the old filter into the container, and allow any residual oil to drain out of the engine.

8 Use a clean rag to remove all oil, dirt and sludge from the filter sealing area on the engine. Check the old filter to make sure that the rubber sealing ring has not stuck to the engine. If it has, carefully remove it.

9 Apply a light coating of clean engine oil to the new filter's sealing ring (photo), and screw the filter into position on the engine until it seats, then tighten it through a further half-turn; tighten the filter by hand only, **do not use any tools**.

10 Remove the old oil and all tools from under the car.

11 Refill the engine with fresh oil, using the correct grade and type of oil. Pour in half the specified quantity of oil first, then wait a few minutes for the oil to fall to the sump. Continue adding oil, a small quantity at a time, until the level is up to the lower mark on the dipstick. Adding approximately a further half a litre will bring the level up to the upper mark on the dipstick.

12 Start the engine and run it for a few minutes, and check for leaks around the oil filter seal and the sump drain plug.

13 Switch off the engine, and wait a few minutes for the oil to settle in the sump once more. Now the new oil has circulated and the filter is completely full, recheck the level on the dipstick, adding more oil as necessary.

14 Dispose of the used engine oil safely with reference to *'General repair procedures'* in the Reference Sections of this Manual.

OIL CARE FOLLOW THE CODE

OIL BANK LINE
0800 66 33 66

Note: It is antisocial and illegal to dump oil down the drain. To find the location of your local oil recycling bank, call this number free.

Every 12 000 miles or annually

9 Valve clearance adjustment

Note: *Valve clearances must be checked and adjusted with the engine cold (cylinder head below 38°C).*

SOHC engines

1 Position the number 1 piston at TDC, then remove the cylinder head cover and upper timing belt cover as described in the relevant Sections of Chapter 2. With number 1 piston at TDC, the lower mark on the camshaft sprocket will be aligned with the mark on the upper inner timing belt cover, and the UP mark on the sprocket will be at the top (photos).

2 With the engine in this position, check that the clearances of number 1 cylinder's four valves are as given in the Specifications at the start of this Chapter. Clearances are checked by inserting a feeler gauge of the correct thickness between the valve stem and the rocker adjusting screw. If adjustment is necessary, slacken the adjusting screw locknut, and turn the screw as necessary until the feeler blade is a light sliding fit (photo). Once the correct clearance is obtained, hold the adjusting screw and tighten the locknut to the specified torque. Recheck the valve clearance, and adjust again if necessary.

3 Once all number 1 cylinder valves are correctly adjusted, rotate the crankshaft 180°

8.7 Using an oil filter removal tool to slacken the filter

8.9 Apply a light coat of clean oil to the oil filter sealing ring before fitting

9.1A On SOHC engine, with number 1 cylinder at TDC, UP mark (arrowed) on the camshaft sprocket is at the top ...

9.1B ... and lower mark aligns with pointer on timing belt inner cover (arrowed)

9.2 Adjusting a valve clearance on SOHC engine

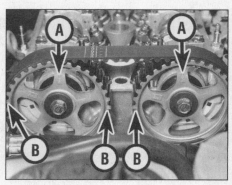

9.7 On DOHC engine, with number 1 cylinder at TDC, UP marks (A) on camshaft sprockets are at the top, and lines (B) on sprockets align with the cylinder head surface

in an anti-clockwise direction to bring number 3 cylinder to TDC. Note that the UP mark on the camshaft will move through 90°, and will now be on the exhaust side of the sprocket. Check and, if necessary, adjust the clearances of number 3 cylinder's four valves as described above in paragraph 2.

4 Once all number 3 cylinder valves are correctly adjusted, rotate the crankshaft a further 180°, again in an anti-clockwise direction, to bring number 4 cylinder to TDC; the UP mark on the camshaft sprocket will move a further 90°, and will now be at the bottom. Check and, if necessary, adjust the clearances of number 4 cylinder's four valves as described above in paragraph 2.

5 Once all number 4 cylinder valves are correctly adjusted, rotate the crankshaft a further 180°, again in an anti-clockwise direction, to bring number 2 cylinder to TDC. The UP mark will again move through a further 90°, and will now be on the inlet side of the sprocket. Check and, if necessary, adjust the clearances of number 2 cylinder's four valves as described above in paragraph 2.

6 Once all the valve clearances have been checked, refit the cylinder head cover and upper timing belt cover as described in Chapter 2.

DOHC engines

7 Position the number 1 piston at TDC, and remove the cylinder head cover as described in the relevant Sections of Chapter 2. With

number 1 piston at TDC, the UP marks on the camshaft sprockets will be in the 12 o'clock (uppermost) position, and the index marks on each sprocket will align with the upper cylinder head mating surface in the 9 o'clock and 3 o'clock positions (photo).

8 With the engine in this position, check the clearances of number 1 cylinder's four valves as described above in paragraph 2, noting that the feeler blade should be inserted between the camshaft lobe and rocker arm bearing surface (photo).

9 Once all number 1 cylinder valves are correctly adjusted, rotate the crankshaft 180° in an anti-clockwise direction to bring number 3 cylinder to TDC. Note that the UP marks on the camshaft sprockets will move through 90°, and will now be aligned with the cylinder head mating surface on the exhaust side of each sprocket. Check and, if necessary, adjust the clearances of number 3 cylinder's four valves as described above in paragraph 2.

10 Once all number 3 cylinder valves are correctly adjusted, rotate the crankshaft a further 180°, again in an anti-clockwise direction, to bring number 4 cylinder to TDC; the UP marks on the camshaft sprocket will move a further 90°, and will now be in the 6 o'clock (lowest) position. Check and, if necessary, adjust the clearances of number 4 cylinder's four valves as described above in paragraph 2.

11 Once all number 4 cylinder valves are correctly adjusted, rotate the crankshaft a

further 180°, again in an anti-clockwise direction, to bring number 2 cylinder to TDC; the UP marks will again move through a further 90°, and will now be aligned with the cylinder head mating surface on the inlet side of each sprocket. Check and, if necessary, adjust the clearances of number 2 cylinder's four valves as described above in paragraph 2.

12 Once all the valve clearances have been checked, refit the cylinder head cover as described in Chapter 2.

10 Coolant renewal

Draining

⚠ **_Warning: Wait until the engine is cold before starting this procedure. Do not allow antifreeze to come in contact with your skin or painted surfaces of the car. Rinse off spills immediately with plenty of water. Never leave antifreeze lying around in an open container, or in a puddle in the driveway or on the garage floor. Children and pets are attracted by its sweet smell, but antifreeze is fatal if ingested._**

1 To drain the system, remove the expansion tank filler cap, then move the heater air temperature control to the maximum heat position. On some models, a drain tap is fitted to the bottom right-hand corner of the radiator, and the coolant can be drained via this tap. On models where the radiator is not fitted with a drain tap, it will be necessary to drain the coolant by slackening the retaining clip and disconnecting the bottom hose from the radiator.

2 Place a large drain tray beneath the coolant drain tap or bottom hose, then either open the tap or disconnect the hose (as appropriate), and allow the coolant to drain into the container. To drain the system completely, it will also be necessary to slacken and remove the engine coolant drain plug, situated on the right-hand side of the front face of the block (photo). This will drain any remaining coolant

9.8 Adjusting a valve clearance on DOHC engine

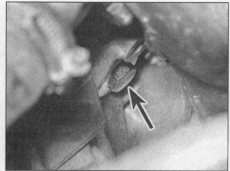

10.2 Cylinder block coolant drain plug (viewed from above)

10.12A Slacken the cooling system bleed screw (arrowed) to allow trapped air to escape while filling the cooling system (SOHC engine shown)

from the cylinder block. Once the system had drained completely, securely close the tap (or reconnect the hose and tighten its retaining clip securely), then refit the drain plug to the cylinder block, and tighten it to the specified torque.

Flushing

3 With time, the cooling system may gradually lose its efficiency, due to the radiator core having become choked with rust, scale deposits from the water, and other sediment. To minimise this, use only good-quality antifreeze and clean soft water, and flush the system as follows whenever the coolant is renewed.

4 With the coolant drained, ensure the drain tap is closed (or hose reconnected), then refill the system with fresh water. Refit the expansion tank filler cap, start the engine and warm it up to normal operating temperature, then stop it and (after allowing it to cool down completely) drain the system again. Repeat as necessary until only clean water can be seen to emerge, then refill finally with the specified coolant mixture.

5 If the specified coolant mixture has been used, and has been renewed at the specified intervals, the above procedure will be sufficient to keep clean the system for a considerable length of time. If, however, the system has been neglected, a more thorough operation will be required, as follows.

6 First drain the coolant, then disconnect the radiator top and bottom hoses from the radiator. Insert a garden hose into the radiator top hose outlet, and allow water to circulate through the radiator until it runs clean from the bottom outlet.

7 To flush the engine, insert the garden hose into the top hose, and allow water to circulate until it runs clear from the bottom hose. If, after a reasonable period, the water still does not run clear, the cooling system should be flushed with a good proprietary cleaning agent.

8 In severe cases of contamination, reverse-flushing of the radiator may be necessary. To do this, remove the radiator as described in

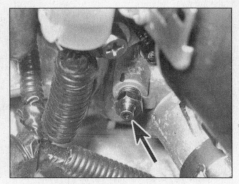

10.12B Cooling system bleed screw (arrowed) – DOHC engine

Chapter 3, invert it and insert a garden hose into the bottom outlet. Continue flushing until clear water runs from the top hose outlet. If necessary, a similar procedure can be used to flush the heater matrix.

9 The use of chemical cleaners should be necessary only as a last resort; the regular renewal of the coolant will prevent excessive contamination of the system.

Filling

10 With the cooling system drained and flushed, ensure that the drain tap (where fitted) is securely closed, and that all disturbed hose unions are correctly secured.

11 Prepare a sufficient quantity of the specified coolant mixture (see below); allow for a surplus, so as to have a reserve supply for topping-up.

12 Slacken the bleed screw, situated on the engine top hose coolant outlet elbow (located at the front right-hand corner of the cylinder head on SOHC engines, and the rear right-hand corner of the cylinder head on DOHC engines), to allow any trapped air to escape during refilling, then remove the expansion tank filler cap (photos).

13 Fill the system slowly through via the expansion tank. When coolant can be seen emerging from the bleed screw in a steady stream, tighten the bleed screw securely. Continue filling until the coolant reaches the expansion tank COOLANT LEVEL (MAX) mark, then refit the filler cap. Wash off any spilt coolant from the engine compartment and bodywork.

14 Start the engine, running it at no more than idle speed until it has warmed up to normal operating temperature and the radiator electric cooling fan has cut in; watch the temperature gauge to check for signs of overheating.

15 Stop the engine, allow it to cool down **completely**, then remove the expansion tank filler cap and top-up the tank to the correct level. Refit the filler cap, and wash off all the spilt coolant from the engine compartment and bodywork.

16 After refilling, always check all components of the system (especially any unions disturbed during draining and flushing) carefully for signs of coolant leaks; fresh

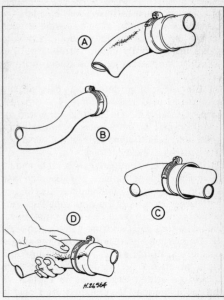

Fig. 1.3 Coolant hose inspection (Sec 10)

A *Check hose for chafing or burning; these may lead to sudden and costly failure*
B *A soft hose indicates internal deterioration, leading to contamination of the cooling system and clogging of the radiator*
C *A hardened hose can fail at any time; tightening the clamps will not seal the joint or prevent leaks*
D *A swollen hose, or one with oil-soaked ends, indicates contamination from oil or grease. Cracks and breaks can easily be seen by squeezing the hose*

antifreeze has a searching action, which will rapidly expose any weak points in the system.

17 Note: *If, after draining and refilling the system, symptoms of overheating are found which did not occur previously, then the fault is almost certainly due to trapped air at some point in the system causing an air-lock and restricting the flow of coolant, usually, the air is trapped because the system was refilled too quickly. In some cases, air-locks can be released by tapping or squeezing the various hoses. If the problem persists, stop the engine and allow it to cool down completely before unscrewing the bleed screw to allow the trapped air to escape.*

Antifreeze mixture

18 The antifreeze should always be renewed at the specified intervals. This is necessary not only to maintain the antifreeze properties, but also to prevent corrosion which would otherwise occur as the corrosion inhibitors (present in good-quality antifreeze) become progressively less effective.

19 Always use an ethylene glycol-based antifreeze which is suitable for use in mixed-metal cooling systems. The type of antifreeze and levels of protection afforded are indicated in the Specifications. To give the recommended 50% concentration, 2.75 litres

1

of antifreeze must be mixed with 2.75 litres of clean, soft water; this should provide enough to refill the complete system, but it is best to make up a slightly larger amount, so that a supply is available for subsequent topping-up.

20 Before adding antifreeze, the cooling system should be completely drained, preferably flushed, and all hoses checked for condition and security; fresh antifreeze has a searching action which will rapidly find any weaknesses in the system.

21 After filling with antifreeze, a label should be attached to the radiator or expansion tank stating the type and concentration of antifreeze used, and the date installed. Any subsequent topping-up should be made with the same type and concentration of antifreeze.

22 Do not use engine antifreeze in the screen washer system, as it will damage the car's paintwork. A screen wash additive should be added to the washer system, in the recommended quantities stated on the bottle.

11 Cooling system checks

1 The engine should be cold for the cooling system checks, so perform the following procedure before driving the car, or wait until it has been shut off for at least three hours.

2 Remove the expansion tank filler cap, and clean it thoroughly inside and out with a rag. Also clean the filler neck on the expansion tank. The presence of rust or corrosion in the filler neck indicates that the coolant should be changed. The coolant inside the expansion tank should be relatively clean and transparent. If it is rust-coloured, drain and flush the system, and refill with a fresh coolant mixture.

3 Carefully check the radiator hoses and heater hoses along their entire length. Renew any hose which is cracked, swollen or deteriorated. Cracks will show up better if the hose is squeezed. Pay close attention to the hose clips that secure the hoses to the cooling system components. Hose clips can pinch and puncture hoses, resulting in cooling system leaks. If wire type hose clips are used, it may be a good idea to replace them with screw-type hose clips.

4 Inspect all the cooling system components (hoses, joint faces, etc.) for leaks. A leak in the cooling system will usually show up as white or rust-coloured deposits on the area adjoining the leak. Where any problems of this nature are found on system components, renew the component or gasket with reference to Chapter 3.

5 Clean the front of the radiator with a soft brush to remove all insects, leaves, etc., imbedded in the radiator fins. Be extremely careful not to damage the radiator fins or cut your fingers on them.

12 Air conditioning system compressor drivebelt

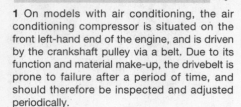

1 On models with air conditioning, the air conditioning compressor is situated on the front left-hand end of the engine, and is driven by the crankshaft pulley via a belt. Due to its function and material make-up, the drivebelt is prone to failure after a period of time, and should therefore be inspected and adjusted periodically.

Check and adjustment

2 Apply the handbrake, then jack up the front of the vehicle and support it on axle stands. Remove the left-hand front roadwheel.

3 From underneath the front of the vehicle, slacken and remove the three bolts securing the bumper flange to the body. Remove the seven bolts securing the front undercover panel to the body, and remove the panel.

4 Check the drivebelt for cracks, splitting, fraying or damage, rotating the crankshaft using a suitable spanner applied to the crankshaft pulley retaining bolt, so that the entire length of the belt is examined. Check also for signs of glazing (shiny patches), and for separation of the belt plies. Renew the belt if worn or damaged.

5 The drivebelt's tension is checked by measuring the amount of deflection that takes place when a force equivalent to 10 kg is applied (using a spring balance, or similar) midway between the crankshaft and air conditioning compressor pulleys on the belt's lower run; a rough check can be made using firm finger pressure. If the deflection measured is any more or less than that specified, the drivebelt must be adjusted as follows.

6 Slacken the drivebelt adjuster (idler) pulley spindle nut and bolt, then rotate the adjuster bolt (situated on the upper side of the pulley assembly) clockwise or anti-clockwise as required to obtain the correct belt tension.

7 When the correct tension is achieved, tighten the adjuster pulley spindle bolt and nut to the specified torque setting, and rotate the crankshaft several times to settle the drivebelt. Recheck the belt tension, repeating the adjustment procedure if necessary.

8 Refit the undercover panel and roadwheel, and lower the car to the ground.

Renewal

9 Carry out the operations in paragraphs 2 and 3. If the car is also equipped with power steering, remove the power steering pump drivebelt, as described in Section 29.

10 Slacken the drivebelt adjuster (idler) pulley spindle nut and bolt, then slacken the adjuster bolt until the drivebelt can be slipped off the pulleys and removed from the car.

11 Clean the belt pulleys carefully, removing all traces of oil or grease, and checking that the grooves are clear. Fit the new belt to the pulleys, tighten the adjuster bolt until the tension is approximately correct, then check

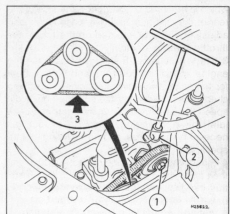

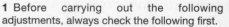

Fig. 1.4 Air conditioning compressor drivebelt adjustment (Sec 12)

1 Adjuster (idler) pulley spindle bolt
2 Adjuster bolt
3 Drivebelt tension checking point

and adjust the tension as described above. Refit the power steering pump drivebelt, and adjust it as described in Section 29.

12 Start the engine, and allow it to idle at the specified speed for approximately 10 minutes to settle the drivebelt in position. Stop the engine, then recheck the drivebelt tension as described above and, if necessary, repeat the adjustment procedure.

13 Refit the undercover panel and roadwheel, then lower the car to the ground.

13 Base idle speed and mixture adjustments

1 Before carrying out the following adjustments, always check the following first.

(a) *Check that the ignition timing is set accurately (Section 41).*

(b) *Check that the spark plugs are in good condition and correctly gapped (Section 40).*

(c) *Check that the throttle cable is correctly adjusted (Chapter 4).*

(d) *Check that the crankcase breather hoses are sound, with no leaks, kinks, or blockages.*

(e) *Check that the air cleaner filter element is clean, and that the exhaust system is in good condition.*

(f) *If the engine is running very roughly, check the compression pressures as described in Chapter 2, and adjust the valve clearances as described in Section 9.*

(g) *Check that the PGM-Fi warning lamp/engine management ECU LED are not flashing (Chapter 4).*

Base idle speed

2 Start the engine, warm it up to normal operating temperature, then switch it off and disconnect the wiring connector from the idle speed electronic air control valve (EACV), which is mounted on the right-hand side of the rear of the inlet manifold. The base idle speed adjusting screw is situated on the top of the throttle housing (photos).

3 Start the engine, then slowly increase the engine speed to 2000 rpm, and hold it there for ten seconds. Allow the engine to idle, and check that it is idling at the specified base idle speed. If adjustment is required, turn the base idle speed adjusting screw in or out (as necessary) until the engine is idling at the specified base idle speed.

4 Slowly raise the engine speed to 1000 rpm, then allow the engine to idle again, and check that the engine speed returns to the specified base idle speed, adjusting again if necessary.

5 Once the base idle speed is correctly set, stop the engine. Remove the hazard warning lamp fuse from the engine compartment fusebox for ten seconds, to erase the EACV fault code from the engine management ECU memory.

6 Reconnect the EACV wiring connector, start the engine and raise the engine speed to 2000 rpm for ten seconds. Allow the engine to idle, and check that it idles smoothly within the specified idle speed limits given in the Specifications. Switch on the heated rear window, and check that the idle speed remains within the specified limits. If all is well, switch off the engine. If the idle speed is not as specified, there is a fault in the engine management (fuel injection/ignition) system, and the car must be taken to a Rover dealer for inspection using the special diagnostic equipment.

Idle mixture CO content check and adjustment – models without a catalytic converter

7 The idle mixture is set at the factory, and should require no further adjustment. However, over time, carbon build-up and cylinder bore wear will change the engine characteristics (as will a major engine overhaul), so the mixture becomes incorrect and has to be reset. Note, however, that an exhaust gas analyser (CO meter) will be required to check the mixture, and to set it with the necessary standard of accuracy; if this is not available, the car **must** be taken to a

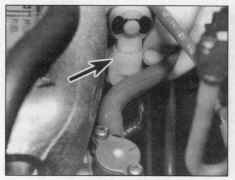

13.2A To adjust the base idle speed, first disconnect the wiring connector (arrowed) from the EACV, which is mounted on the rear of the inlet manifold

Rover dealer for the work to be carried out. If an exhaust gas analyser is available, first check the base idle speed as described above, then check the mixture CO content as follows.

8 Take the car on a journey of sufficient length to warm it up to normal operating temperature, then connect the exhaust gas analyser using the equipment manufacturer's instructions. **Note:** *Adjustment should be carried out immediately on return from the warm-up journey, without stopping the engine. Adjustment must also be carried out while the radiator cooling fan is not operating. If at any time the cooling fan cuts in, wait for it to stop, then increase the engine speed to 2000 rpm for ten seconds Release the throttle, and allow the engine to return to its specified idle speed before continuing with the following procedure.*

9 With the engine idling within the specified speed range, check that the exhaust gas CO content is within the specified limits. If adjustment is necessary, peel back the passenger footwell carpet, then undo the four ECU cover retaining bolts and remove the cover. Unclip the idle mixture (IMA) sensor from the ECU, and turn the sensor around to gain access to the mixture adjusting screw. Adjust the mixture by rotating the screw a small amount at a time, either anti-clockwise to lessen the CO content or clockwise to increase the CO content, allowing time for the analyser

13.2B Base idle speed adjusting screw (arrowed) is situated on the top of the throttle housing

readings to stabilise between adjustments (photos). Once the CO content is correct, increase the engine speed to 2000 rpm, and hold there for ten seconds before allowing the engine to idle again. Recheck the CO content, and adjust again if necessary.

10 Once the CO content is correct, switch off the engine and disconnect the exhaust analyser. Turn the sensor around, and clip it securely in position on the ECU. Refit the ECU cover, tightening its retaining nuts securely, then refit the passenger footwell carpet.

Idle mixture CO content check – models with a catalytic converter

11 On models with a catalytic converter, the exhaust gases are constantly measured by the lambda sensor (see below), which then informs the ECU of the exhaust gas content. The ECU then alters the fuel system settings as required, so that the CO content of the gases is at the optimum level whatever the operating conditions. For this reason, it should never be necessary to adjust the idle mixture. However, the exhaust gas CO content must still be checked at the specified intervals, as described above, to ensure that the system is functioning correctly. If the exhaust gas CO content is not within the specified range, there is a fault in the engine management (fuel injection/ignition) system or the catalytic converter, and the car must be taken to a Rover dealer for further inspection using special diagnostic equipment.

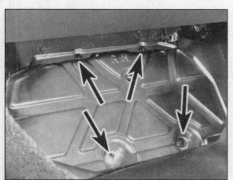

13.9A Undo the ECU cover retaining nuts (arrowed), then remove the cover ...

13.9B ... and unclip the IMA sensor from the ECU

13.9C Adjusting the idle mixture CO content

14 Lambda sensor operational check

1 This task (outlined in Chapter 4, Part B) can only be carried out using Rover diagnostic equipment; see the preceding Section. Do not neglect to have this check made at the specified intervals, especially as the car's mileage increases, as it is the only means of checking (in conjunction with a CO level check) whether the catalytic converter's closed-loop control system is working properly or not. Lambda sensors are delicate components working under arduous conditions, and they do not last forever; if the sensor is no longer effective, it must be renewed.

15 Fuel system checks

1 The fuel system is most easily checked with the car raised on a hoist (or suitably supported on axle stands), so that the components underneath are readily visible and accessible.
2 If the smell of petrol is noticed while driving or after the car has been parked in the sun, the system should be thoroughly inspected immediately.
3 Remove the petrol tank filler cap, and check for damage, corrosion and an unbroken sealing imprint on the gasket. Renew the cap if necessary.
4 With the car raised, inspect the petrol tank and filler neck for punctures, cracks and other damage. The connection between the filler neck and tank is especially critical. Sometimes a rubber filler neck or connecting hose will leak due to loose retaining clamps or deteriorated rubber.
5 Carefully check all rubber hoses and metal fuel lines leading away from the petrol tank. Check for loose connections, deteriorated hoses, crimped lines and other damage. Pay particular attention to the vent pipes and hoses which often loop up around the filler neck, and can become blocked or crimped. Follow the lines to the front of the car, carefully inspecting them all the way. Renew damaged sections as necessary.
6 From within the engine compartment, check the security of all fuel hose attachments, and inspect the fuel hoses and vacuum hoses for kinks, chafing and deterioration. Where an evaporative emission control system is fitted, check its hoses and the security of the purge control valve wiring, as well as checking the physical condition of the charcoal canister.
7 Check the operation of the throttle linkage, and lubricate the linkage components with a few drops of light oil.

16 Exhaust system check

1 With the engine cold (or at least an hour after the car has been driven), check the complete exhaust system from the engine to the end of the tailpipe. Ideally, the inspection should be carried out with the car on a hoist to permit unrestricted access. If a hoist is not available, raise and support the car on axle stands.
2 Check the exhaust pipes and connections for evidence of leaks, severe corrosion, or damage. Make sure that all brackets and mountings are in good condition and tight. Leakage at any of the joints or in other parts of the system will usually show up as a black sooty stain in the vicinity of the leak.
3 Rattles and other noises can often be traced to the exhaust system, especially the brackets and mountings. Try to move the pipes and silencers. If the components can come into contact with the body or suspension parts, secure the system with new mountings, or if possible, separate the joints and twist the pipes as necessary to provide additional clearance.

17 Spark plug (HT) leads, distributor cap and rotor arm check and renewal

1 The spark plug (HT) leads should be checked whenever new spark plugs are installed in the engine.
2 Ensure that the leads are numbered before removing them, to avoid confusion when refitting. Pull the leads from the plugs by gripping the end fitting, not the lead, otherwise the lead connection may be fractured.
3 Check inside the end fitting for signs of corrosion, which will look like a white crusty powder. Push the end fitting back onto the spark plug, ensuring that it is a tight fit on the plug (there should be a soft 'click' as the lead is connected). If not, remove the lead again, and use pliers to carefully crimp the metal connector inside the end fitting until it fits securely on the end of the spark plug.
4 Using a clean rag, wipe the entire length of the lead to remove any built-up dirt and grease. Once the lead is clean, check for burns, cracks and other damage. Do not bend the lead excessively or pull the lead lengthwise – the conductor inside might break.
5 Disconnect the other end of the lead from the distributor cap. Again, pull only on the end fitting. Check for corrosion and a tight fit in the same manner as the spark plug end. If an ohmmeter is available, check the resistance of the lead by connecting the meter between the spark plug end of the lead and the segment inside the distributor cap. Refit the lead securely on completion.
6 Check the remaining leads one at a time, in the same way.

7 If new spark plug (HT) leads are required, purchase a set for your specific car and engine, referring to a Rover dealer in the first instance.
8 Unscrew its retaining screws, then remove the distributor cap. Wipe it clean, and carefully inspect it inside and out for signs of cracks, carbon tracks (tracking) and worn, burnt or loose contacts. Check that the cap's carbon brush is unworn, free to move against spring pressure, and making good contact with the rotor arm. Also inspect the cap seal for signs of wear or damage, and renew if necessary. Similarly, slacken the rotor arm retaining grub screw (photo), and remove the arm from the distributor shaft for inspection. If checking components with a meter, note that the rotor arm has an in-built resistor. Renew any components which are found to be faulty. It is common practice to renew the cap and rotor arm whenever new spark plug (HT) leads are fitted. On refitting, tighten the rotor arm grub screw and the cap retaining screws securely.

> **HAYNES HINT** *When fitting a new cap, remove the leads from the old cap one at a time, and fit them to the new cap in the exact same location – do not simultaneously remove all the leads from the old cap, or firing-order confusion may occur.*

9 Even with the ignition system in first class condition, some engines may still occasionally experience poor starting, attributable to damp ignition components. To disperse moisture, use a water-repelling aerosol spray.

18 Clutch checks

1 Check that the clutch pedal moves smoothly and easily through its full travel, and that the clutch itself functions correctly, with no trace of slip or drag. Adjust the clutch cable as described in Chapter 6. If excessive effort is required to operate the clutch, check first that the cable is correctly routed and undamaged, then remove the pedal to ensure that its pivot is properly greased. Refer to Chapter 6 for further information.

17.8 Distributor rotor arm is retained by a grub screw (arrowed)

19.3A Manual gearbox is refilled/topped-up via the filler/level plug hole (arrowed) ...

19.3B ... oil level is correct when oil has just stopped trickling from filler/level plug hole

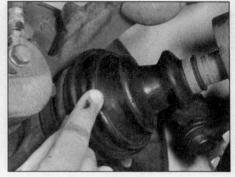

21.1 Checking driveshaft outer CV joint rubber gaiter

19 Manual gearbox oil level check

1 Even though this makes access awkward, the oil level must be checked with the car standing on its wheels on level ground. Also, the level must be checked before the car is driven, or after waiting at least 5 minutes after the engine has been switched off. If the oil is checked immediately after driving the car, some of the oil will remain distributed around the transmission components, resulting in an inaccurate level reading.

2 Wipe clean the area around the filler/level plug, which is located at the rear of the transmission, next to the right-hand driveshaft inner constant velocity joint. Unscrew the plug and clean it; discard the sealing washer.

3 The oil level should reach the lower edge of the filler/level hole. A certain amount of oil will have gathered behind the filler/level plug, and will trickle out when it is removed; this does not necessarily indicate that the level is correct. To ensure that a true level is established, wait until the initial trickle has stopped, then add oil as necessary until a trickle of new oil can be seen emerging (photos). The level will be correct when the flow ceases; use only good-quality oil of the specified type.

4 **Note:** *Refilling the transmission is an extremely awkward operation; above all, allow plenty of time for the oil level to settle properly before checking it. If a large amount had to be added to the transmission and a large amount flows out on checking the level, refit the filler/level plug and take the vehicle on a short journey so that the new oil is distributed fully around the transmission components, then recheck the level when it has settled again.*

5 If the transmission has been overfilled so that oil flows out as soon as the filler/level plug is removed, check that the car is completely level (front-to-rear and side-to-side), and allow the surplus to drain off into a suitable container.

6 When the level is correct, fit a new sealing washer to the filler/level plug, and tighten the plug to the specified torque wrench setting. Wash off any spilt oil.

20 Automatic transmission fluid level check

1 Take the vehicle on a short journey to warm the transmission up to normal operating temperature, then park the vehicle on level ground. The fluid level is checked using the dipstick located at the front of the transmission unit, next to the transmission unit fluid cooler hoses. Note that the fluid level must be checked within one minute of returning from the warm-up journey.

2 Withdraw the dipstick from the tube, and wipe all the fluid from its end with a clean rag or paper towel. Insert the clean dipstick back into the tube as far as it will go, then withdraw it once more. Note the oil level on the end of the dipstick. Add fluid as necessary until the level is between the upper (MAX) and lower (MIN) marks on the dipstick (Fig. 1.5).

3 If topping-up is necessary, add the required quantity of the specified fluid to the transmission via the dipstick tube. Use a funnel with a fine mesh gauze, to avoid spillage and to ensure that no foreign matter enters the transmission.

4 After topping-up, take the vehicle on a short run to distribute the fresh fluid, then recheck the oil level again, topping-up if necessary.

5 Always maintain the level between the two dipstick marks. If the level is allowed to fall below the lower mark, fluid starvation may result which could lead to severe transmission damage.

21 Driveshaft rubber gaiter and CV joint check

1 With the car raised and securely supported on axle stands, turn the steering onto full lock, then slowly rotate the roadwheel. Inspect the condition of the outer constant velocity (CV) joint rubber gaiters, squeezing the gaiters to open out the folds (photo). Check for signs of cracking, splits or deterioration of the rubber, which may allow the grease to escape and lead to the entry of water and grit into the joint. Also check the security and condition of the retaining clips. Repeat these checks on the

inner CV joints. If any damage or deterioration is found, the gaiters should be renewed as described in Chapter 8.

2 At the same time, check the general condition of the CV joints themselves by first holding the driveshaft and attempting to rotate the roadwheel. Repeat this check by holding the inner joint and attempting to rotate the driveshaft. Any appreciable movement indicates wear in the joints or in the driveshaft splines, or a loose driveshaft nut.

22 Front brake pad, caliper and disc check

1 Firmly apply the handbrake, then jack up the front of the car and support it securely on axle stands. Remove the front roadwheels.

2 For a quick check, the thickness of friction material remaining on each brake pad can be

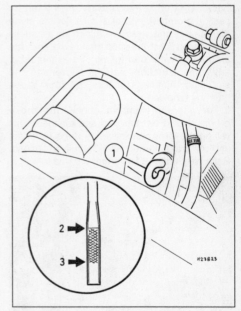

Fig. 1.5 Automatic transmission dipstick location and markings (Sec 20)

1 Dipstick
2 Upper (MAX) mark
3 Lower (MIN) mark

22.2 Front brake pad friction material (arrowed) can be checked through slot in caliper body

measured through the slot in the caliper body (photo). If any pad's friction material is worn to the specified thickness or less, **all four** pads must be renewed as a set.

3 For a comprehensive check, the brake pads should be removed and cleaned. This will permit the operation of the caliper to be checked, and the brake disc itself to be fully examined on both sides. Refer to Chapter 9 for further information.

23 Rear brake shoe, wheel cylinder and drum check

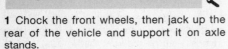

1 Chock the front wheels, then jack up the rear of the vehicle and support it on axle stands.

2 For a quick check, the thickness of friction material remaining on one of the brake shoes can be measured through the slot in the brake backplate that is exposed by prising out its sealing grommet (photo). If a rod of the same diameter as the specified minimum thickness is placed against the shoe friction material, the amount of wear can quickly be assessed; if any shoe's friction material is worn to the specified thickness or less, **all four** shoes must be renewed.

3 For a comprehensive check, the brake drums should be removed and cleaned. This will permit the wheel cylinders to be checked, and the brake drum itself to be fully examined. Refer to Chapter 9 for further information.

23.2 Remove grommet to check rear brake shoe friction material thickness on drum brake models

24 Rear brake pad, caliper and disc check

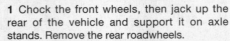

1 Chock the front wheels, then jack up the rear of the vehicle and support it on axle stands. Remove the rear roadwheels.

2 For a quick check, the thickness of friction material remaining on each brake pad can be measured through the slot in the caliper body. If any pad's friction material is worn to the specified thickness or less, **all four** pads must be renewed as a set.

3 For a comprehensive check, the brake pads should be removed and cleaned. This will permit the operation of the caliper to be checked, and the brake disc itself to be fully examined on both sides. Refer to Chapter 9 for further information.

25 Handbrake check and adjustment

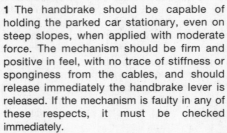

1 The handbrake should be capable of holding the parked car stationary, even on steep slopes, when applied with moderate force. The mechanism should be firm and positive in feel, with no trace of stiffness or sponginess from the cables, and should release immediately the handbrake lever is released. If the mechanism is faulty in any of these respects, it must be checked immediately.

2 To check the setting, first apply the footbrake firmly several times to establish correct shoe-to-drum/pad-to-disc clearance. Applying normal, moderate pressure, pull the handbrake lever to the fully-applied position, counting the number of clicks emitted from the handbrake ratchet mechanism. If the adjustment is correct, there should be between 8 and 10 clicks before the handbrake is fully applied; if this is not the case, adjustment is required.

3 To adjust the handbrake, chock the front wheels, then jack up the rear of the vehicle and support it on axle stands.

4 Lift out the ashtray, situated between the two front seats, from the rear of the centre console to gain access to the handbrake

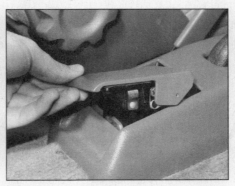

25.4A Remove the ashtray from the centre console ...

adjusting nut (photos). Apply the handbrake, check that the equalizer and cables move freely and smoothly, then set the lever on the first notch of the ratchet mechanism. With the lever in this position, rotate the handbrake lever adjusting nut until only a slight drag can be felt when the rear wheels are turned. Once this is so, fully release the handbrake lever, and check that the wheels rotate freely. Check the adjustment by applying the handbrake fully, counting the clicks emitted from the handbrake ratchet and, if necessary, re-adjust.

5 Once the adjustment is correct, refit the ashtray and lower the car to the ground.

26 Braking system checks

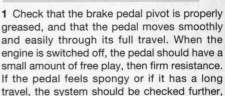

1 Check that the brake pedal pivot is properly greased, and that the pedal moves smoothly and easily through its full travel. When the engine is switched off, the pedal should have a small amount of free play, then firm resistance. If the pedal feels spongy or if it has a long travel, the system should be checked further, as described in Chapter 9.

2 The brake hydraulic system consists of a number of metal hydraulic pipes, which run from the master cylinder around the engine compartment to the front brakes and pressure-regulating valves, and along the underbody to the rear brakes. Flexible hoses are fitted at front and rear to cater for steering and suspension movement.

3 When checking the system, first look for signs of leakage at the pipe or hose unions, then examine the flexible hoses for signs of cracking, chafing or deterioration of the rubber. Bend them sharply between the fingers (but do not actually bend them double, or the casing may be damaged), and check that this does not reveal previously-hidden cracks, cuts or splits. Check that all pipes and hoses are securely fastened in their clips.

4 Carefully work along the length of the metal hydraulic pipes, looking for dents, kinks, damage of any sort or corrosion. Corrosion should be polished off; if the depth of pitting is significant, the pipe must be renewed.

25.4B ... to gain access to the handbrake cable adjuster nut and equalizer mechanism

28.2 Checking one of the steering gear rubber gaiters

28.4 Rocking the roadwheel to check steering/suspension wear

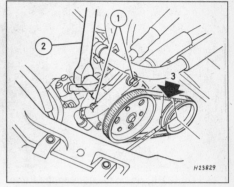

Fig. 1.6 Adjusting power steering pump drivebelt on SOHC engine (Sec 29)

1 Pump mounting bolts
2 Socket and extension bar fitted to rear of pump
3 Drivebelt tension checking point

27 Roadwheel nut check

1 To check that the roadwheel nuts are securely fastened, remove the roadwheel trim (where fitted), then slacken each nut in turn through one-quarter of a turn, and tighten it to the specified torque wrench setting. Refit the trim, where applicable.

28 Front suspension and steering check

1 Raise the front of the car, and securely support it on axle stands.
2 Visually inspect the balljoint dust covers and the steering gear rubber gaiters for splits, chafing or deterioration (photo). Any wear of these components will cause loss of lubricant, and will permit the entry of dirt and water, resulting in rapid deterioration of the balljoints or steering gear.
3 On vehicles with power steering, check the fluid hoses for chafing or deterioration, and the pipe and hose unions for fluid leakage. Turning the steering onto full-lock will generate maximum pressure in the system for leakage checks, but do not hold the steering in this position for more than a few seconds. Also check for signs of fluid leakage under pressure from the steering gear rubber gaiters, which would indicate failed fluid seals within the steering gear.
4 Grasp the roadwheel at the 12 o'clock and 6 o'clock positions, and try to rock it (photo). Very slight free play may be felt, but if the movement is appreciable, further investigation is necessary to determine the source. Continue rocking the wheel while an assistant depresses the brake pedal. If the movement is now eliminated or significantly reduced, it is likely that the hub bearings are at fault. If the free play is still evident with the brake pedal depressed, then there is wear in the suspension joints or mountings.
5 Now grasp the roadwheel at the 9 o'clock and 3 o'clock positions, and try to rock it as before. Any movement felt now may again be caused by wear in the hub bearings, or in the track rod balljoints. If a balljoint is worn, the visual movement will be obvious. If the inner joint is suspect, it can be felt by placing a hand over the steering gear rubber gaiter and gripping the track rod. If the wheel is now rocked, movement will be felt at the inner joint if wear has taken place.
6 Using a large screwdriver or flat bar, check for wear in the suspension mounting bushes by levering between the relevant suspension component and its attachment point. Some movement is to be expected, as the mountings are made of rubber, but excessive wear should be obvious. Also check the condition of any visible rubber bushes, looking for splits, cracks or contamination of the rubber.
7 With the car standing on its wheels, have an assistant turn the steering wheel back and forth, about an eighth of a turn each way. There should be very little, if any, lost movement between the steering wheel and the roadwheels. If this is not the case, closely observe the joints and mountings previously described, but in addition, check for wear of the steering column universal joint and the steering gear itself.

29 Power steering pump drivebelt check, adjustment and renewal

1 On models with power-assisted steering, the power steering pump is situated on the front left-hand end of the engine, and is driven by the crankshaft pulley via a belt. Due to its function and material make-up, the drivebelt is prone to failure after a period of time, and should therefore be inspected and adjusted periodically.

Check

2 Apply the handbrake, then jack up the front of the vehicle and support it on axle stands. Remove the left-hand front roadwheel.
3 From underneath the front of the vehicle, slacken and remove the three bolts securing the bumper flange to the body. Remove the seven bolts securing the front undercover panel to the body, and remove the panel.
4 Check the drivebelt for cracks, splitting, fraying or damage, rotating the crankshaft using a suitable spanner applied to the crankshaft drive pulley bolt, so that the entire length of the belt is examined. Check also for signs of glazing (shiny patches), and for separation of the belt plies. Renew the belt if worn or damaged.
5 The drivebelt's tension is checked by measuring the amount of deflection that takes place when a force equivalent to 10 kg is applied (using a spring balance, or similar) midway between the crankshaft and power steering pump pulleys on the belt's upper run. A rough check can be made using firm finger pressure. If the deflection measured is any more or less than that specified, the drivebelt must be adjusted as follows.

Adjustment – SOHC engines

6 Release the air conditioning hose (where fitted) from its bracket on the power steering pump, then slacken the two bolts which secure the pump to its mounting bracket.
7 Using a spanner (or extension bar and suitable socket) fitted to the rear of the pump, rotate the pump in a clockwise direction to tension the belt. When the correct tension is obtained, tighten the pump mounting bolts to the specified torque setting. Start the engine, and allow it to idle for a few minutes while turning the steering from lock-to-lock a few times to settle the drivebelt in position. Stop the engine and recheck the belt tension, repeating the adjustment procedure if necessary.
8 Refit the undercover panel and roadwheel, and lower the car to the ground.

Adjustment – DOHC engines

9 Where necessary, undo the bolt securing the air conditioning hose to the top of the power steering pump, then slacken the three bolts securing the pump to its mounting bracket (photo).

1

29.9 On DOHC engines, slacken the three pump mounting bolts (arrowed) ...

29.10 ... and rotate the adjuster bolt (arrowed) to tension the power steering pump drivebelt

10 Drivebelt tension is adjusted by rotating the adjusting bolt situated on the top of the pump mounting bracket; rotate the bolt clockwise to tension the belt, or anti-clockwise to slacken the belt (photo). Once the belt tension is correct, tighten the pump mounting bolts to the specified torque setting. Start the engine, and allow it to idle for a few minutes while turning the steering from lock-to-lock a few times to settle the drivebelt in position. Stop the engine and recheck the belt tension, repeating the adjustment procedure if necessary.
11 Refit the undercover panel and roadwheel, and lower the car to the ground.

Renewal
12 Carry out the operations in paragraphs 2 and 3.
13 Slacken the power steering pump mounting bolts and, on DOHC engines, the pump adjusting bolt, until the drivebelt can be slipped off the pulleys and removed from the car.
14 Clean the belt pulleys carefully, removing all traces of oil or grease, and check that the grooves are clear. Fit the new belt to the pulleys, then adjust the drivebelt tension as described above.
15 Start the engine, and allow it to idle for approximately 10 minutes while turning the steering from lock-to-lock several times to settle the drivebelt in position. Stop the engine, then recheck the drivebelt tension as described above and, if necessary, repeat the adjustment procedure.
16 Refit the undercover panel and roadwheel, then lower the car to the ground.

30 Rear suspension check

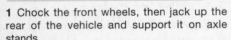

1 Chock the front wheels, then jack up the rear of the vehicle and support it on axle stands.
2 Working as described above for the front suspension, check the rear hub bearings and the trailing arm and lateral link bushes for wear.

31 Hinge and lock lubrication

1 Lubricate the hinges of the bonnet, doors and tailgate with a light machine oil.
2 Lightly lubricate the bonnet release mechanism and cable with the specified type of grease.
3 The door and tailgate latches, strikers and locks must be lubricated using only the special Rover Door Lock and Latch Lubricant supplied in 25 gram sachets under Part Number VWN 10075; inject 1 gram into each lock and wipe off any surplus, then apply a thin film to the latches and strikers. **Do not** lubricate the steering lock mechanism with oil or any other lubricant which might foul the ignition switch contacts; if the lock is stiff, try to introduce a graphite-based powder into the mechanism.
4 Check the condition and operation of the tailgate struts, renewing them if either is leaking or is no longer able to support the tailgate securely when raised.

32 Exterior paintwork and body panels check

1 Once the car has been washed, and all tar spots and other surface blemishes have been cleaned off, check carefully all paintwork, looking closely for chips or scratches; check with particular care vulnerable areas such as the front (bonnet and spoiler), and around the wheel arches. Any damage to the paintwork must be rectified as soon as possible, to comply with the terms of the manufacturer's cosmetic and anti-corrosion warranties; check with a Rover dealer for details.
2 If a chip or (light) scratch is found that is recent and still free from rust, it can be touched-up using the appropriate touch-up pencil; these can be obtained from Rover dealers. Any more serious damage, or rusted stone chips, can be repaired as described in the relevant sub-section of Chapter 11, Section 4, but if damage or corrosion is so severe that a panel must be renewed, seek professional advice as soon as possible.

3 Always check that the door and ventilator opening drain holes and pipes are completely clear, so that water can be drained out.

33 Underbody sealer check

1 The wax-based underbody protective coating should be inspected annually, preferably just prior to winter, when the underbody should be washed down as thoroughly (but as gently) as possible. Any damage to the coating can be repaired using a suitable sealant; if any of the body panels are disturbed for repair or are renewed, do not forget to replace the coating, and to inject wax into door panels, sills, box sections, etc., to maintain the level of protection provided by the car's manufacturer.
2 Check carefully that the wheel arch liners and undercover panel are in place and securely fastened, and that there is no sign of underbody damage or of developing corrosion; if any is found, seek immediate professional advice.
3 If a sunroof is fitted, lubricate very sparingly the seal lip with Rover's Non-Staining Grease (Corning No. 7) available under Part Number BAU 5812.

34 Battery check and maintenance

Caution: *Before carrying out any work on the car battery, read through the precautions given in 'Safety first!' at the beginning of this manual.*
1 A 'maintenance-free' (sealed-for-life) battery is standard equipment on all cars covered by this manual. Although this type of battery has many advantages over the older refillable type and should never require the addition of distilled water, it should still be routinely checked according to the following procedure.
2 The battery is located on the right-hand side of the engine compartment. The exterior of the battery should be inspected periodically for damage such as a cracked case or cover, and should be kept clean and dry.
3 The electrolyte level can be seen through the battery's translucent case; although it should not alter in normal use, if the level has lowered (for example, due to electrolyte having boiled away as a result of overcharging) it is permissible to gently prise up the cell cover(s) and to top-up the level as described in paragraphs 10 and 11 below.
4 If regular topping-up becomes necessary and the battery case is not fractured, the battery is being over-charged, and the voltage regulator will have to be checked. Refer to Chapter 12, Section 5 for further information.
5 Check the tightness of the battery terminal clamps to ensure good electrical connections and check the entire length of each cable for cracks and frayed conductors. Remove the fusible link box cover (situated on the right-hand side of the engine compartment, just in

35.5 Insert a suitable lever (arrowed), lever the alternator rearwards until the drivebelt tension is correct, then tighten the adjusting link bolts

front of the suspension turret), and check the security of the link connections; refit the cover on completion.

6 If corrosion (visible as white, fluffy deposits) is evident on the battery terminals, remove the cables from the battery terminals, clean them with a small wire brush, then refit them. Corrosion can be kept to a minimum by applying a layer of petroleum jelly to the clamps and terminals after they are reconnected.

7 Make sure that the battery tray is in good condition, and the battery retaining clamp is tight.

8 Corrosion on the retaining clamp and the battery itself can be removed with a solution of water and baking soda. Thoroughly rinse all cleaned areas with plain water.

9 Any metal parts of the car damaged by corrosion due to contact with battery electrolyte should be treated with a water/baking soda solution or with household ammonia, to neutralise the acid. The area should then be flushed with plain water, dried thoroughly and coated with a zinc-based primer before repainting.

10 If a conventional battery has been fitted as a replacement, the electrolyte level of each cell should be checked every month and, if necessary, topped-up until the separators are just covered. On some batteries, the case is translucent and incorporates minimum and maximum level marks. The check should be made more often if the car is operated in high ambient temperature conditions.

11 If necessary, top-up the level with distilled or de-ionized water (not tap water), after removing the cell plug(s) or cover(s) from the top of the casing; it should be noted that this should not often be necessary under normal operating conditions.

12 Further information on the battery, charging and jump-starting can be found in Chapter 12, and in the preliminary sections of this manual.

35 Alternator drivebelt check, adjustment and renewal

1 The alternator is located on the rear left-hand side of the engine unit, below the inlet manifold, and is driven by the crankshaft pulley via a belt. Due to the drivebelt's function and construction, it is subject to wear, and will cause poor battery charging, or may even break, if not checked and adjusted at regular intervals.

Check and adjustment

2 Apply the handbrake, then jack up the front of the vehicle and support it on axle stands. Remove the left-hand front roadwheel.

3 From underneath the front of the vehicle, slacken and remove the three bolts securing the bumper flange to the body. Remove the seven bolts securing the front undercover panel to the body, and remove the panel.

4 Check the drivebelt for cracks, splitting, fraying or damage, rotating the crankshaft using a suitable spanner applied to the crankshaft pulley bolt, so that the entire length of the belt is examined. Check also for signs of glazing (shiny patches), and for separation of the belt plies. Renew the belt if worn or damaged. If necessary, adjust as follows.

5 Slacken the upper alternator adjusting link bolt and the lower pivot bolt. Carefully insert a suitable lever between the alternator and cylinder block, and lever the alternator outwards until the correct belt tension is obtained. Hold the alternator in this position, and tighten its pivot and adjusting link bolts to the specified torque (photo). Start the engine, and allow it to idle for a few minutes to settle the drivebelt in position, then recheck the belt tension and adjust if necessary.

6 Refit the undercover panel and roadwheel, and lower the car to the ground.

Renewal

7 Carry out the operations in paragraphs 2 and 3, if not already having done so.

8 If the car is equipped with air conditioning and/or power steering, remove the air conditioning and/or power steering pump drivebelt(s) as described in Sections 12 and 29 (as applicable).

9 Slacken the upper alternator adjusting link bolt and the lower pivot bolt, then move the alternator towards the engine and slip the drivebelt off its pulleys.

10 Clean the belt pulleys carefully, removing all traces of oil or grease, and check that the grooves are clear. Fit the new belt to the pulleys, and adjust the tension as described above.

11 Where necessary, refit the air conditioning and/or power steering pump drivebelt(s) as described in Sections 12 and 29 (as applicable).

12 Start the engine, and allow it to idle for approximately 10 minutes to settle the drivebelt in position. Stop the engine, then recheck the drivebelt tension as described above and, if necessary, repeat the adjustment procedure.

13 Refit the undercover panel and roadwheel, then lower the car to the ground.

36 Headlamp beam alignment – general information

1 Accurate adjustment of the headlamp beam is only possible using optical beam-setting equipment, and this work should therefore be carried out by a Rover dealer or workshop with the necessary facilities.

2 For reference, the headlamps can be adjusted by using a suitably-sized crosshead screwdriver to rotate the two adjuster assemblies fitted to the rear of the lamp (see Fig. 1.7). Access to the lower adjuster can be gained through the hole in the bonnet lock platform.

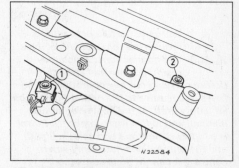

Fig. 1.7 Headlamp unit adjusters (Sec 11)

1 Vertical adjuster   2 Horizontal adjuster

Every 24 000 miles or 2 years

37 Air conditioner refrigerant check

1 The refrigerant condition and level is checked via the sightglass on the top of the receiver drier. The receiver drier is situated in the engine compartment, just to the left of the radiator.

2 Start the engine, then switch on the air conditioning system and allow the engine to idle for a couple of minutes whilst observing the sightglass. If the air conditioning system is operating normally, occasional bubbles should be visible through the sightglass.

3 If a constant stream of bubbles is visible, the refrigerant level is low and must be topped-up. If the sightglass has become clouded or streaked, there is a fault in the system. If either condition is present, the vehicle must be taken to a Rover dealer or suitable professional refrigeration specialist for the air conditioning system to be checked further and overhauled.

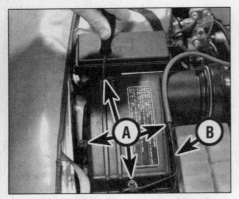

38.1 Remove the air cleaner housing cover screws (A), and position the resonator vacuum pipe and hose (B) clear of housing

38.2 Remove the cover, and lift out the filter element

39.2 Use two spanners when slackening fuel filter inlet union

38 Air cleaner filter element renewal

1 Disconnect the intake hose from the air cleaner housing, then slacken and remove the four housing cover retaining screws. Position the resonator vacuum pipe and hose clear of the cover, then lift off the cover (photo).

2 Lift out the air cleaner filter element, and discard it (photo). Wipe clean the inside of the assembly and the cover then check that there is no foreign matter visible either in the air cleaner intake duct or in the inlet tract.

3 Place the new element in the air cleaner assembly, ensure that it is correctly seated, and refit the housing cover. Position the resonator vacuum pipe on the side of the housing, then refit the cover retaining screws and tighten them securely.

39 Fuel filter renewal

⚠️ **Warning: Certain procedures require the removal of fuel lines and connections, which may result in some fuel spillage.**
Before carrying out any operation on the fuel system, refer to the precautions given in 'Safety first!' at the beginning of this manual, and follow them implicitly. Petrol is a highly dangerous and volatile liquid and the precautions necessary when handling it cannot be overstressed.

1 Depressurise the fuel system as described in Chapter 4. Position wads of rag beneath the fuel filter to catch any spilled fuel.

2 Using two spanners to prevent damage to any of the fuel system pipes or components, unscrew the fuel filter inlet and outlet union nut and bolt (photo), and disconnect the pipes from the filter. Slacken and remove the bolt securing the fuel filter to its mounting bracket, and withdraw the filter from the engine compartment.

3 Fit the new filter, and tighten its mounting bolt to the specified torque setting. Connect the fuel pipes to the filter, using new sealing

washers on the union bolt. Tighten the connections securely, noting the specified torque wrench settings. Start the engine, and check carefully for any signs of fuel leaks from any of the disturbed components.

Dispose of the old filter safely; it will be highly flammable, and may explode if thrown on a fire.

40 Spark plug renewal

1 The correct functioning of the spark plugs is vital for the correct running and efficiency of the engine. It is essential that the plugs fitted are appropriate for the engine (the suitable type is specified at the beginning of this Chapter). If this type is used and the engine is in good condition, the spark plugs should not need attention between scheduled replacement intervals. Spark plug cleaning is rarely necessary, and should not be attempted unless specialised equipment is available, as damage can easily be caused to the firing ends (photo).

2 If the marks on the original-equipment spark plug (HT) leads cannot be seen, mark the leads 1 to 4, according to which number cylinder the lead serves (number 1 cylinder is at the timing belt end of the engine). Pull the leads from the plugs by gripping the end fitting, not the lead, otherwise the lead connection may be fractured.

3 It is advisable to remove the dirt from the

spark plug recesses using a clean brush, vacuum cleaner or compressed air before removing the plugs, to prevent dirt dropping into the cylinders.

4 Unscrew the plugs using a spark plug spanner, suitable box spanner, or a deep socket and extension bar. Keep the socket aligned with the spark plug, otherwise if it is forcibly moved to one side, the ceramic insulator may be broken off.

5 Examination of the spark plugs will give a good indication of the condition of the engine. If the insulator nose of the spark plug is clean and white, with no deposits, this is indicative of a weak mixture or too hot a plug (a hot plug transfers heat away from the electrode slowly, a cold plug transfers heat away quickly).

6 If the tip and insulator nose are covered with hard black-looking deposits, then this is indicative that the mixture is too rich. Should the plug be black and oily, then it is likely that the engine is fairly worn, as well as the mixture being too rich.

7 If the insulator nose is covered with light tan to greyish-brown deposits, then the mixture is correct and it is likely that the engine is in good condition.

8 The spark plug electrode gap is of considerable importance as, if it is too large or too small, the size of the spark and its efficiency will be seriously impaired. The gap should be set to the value given in the Specifications at the end of this Chapter.

9 To set it, measure the gap with a feeler gauge (photo), and then bend the outer plug

40.1 Tools required for removing, refitting and adjusting spark plugs

40.9 Measuring the spark plug electrode gap using a feeler gauge

40.10A Measuring the spark plug electrode gap using a special wire gauge tool

40.10B Adjusting the spark plug electrode gap using a special tool

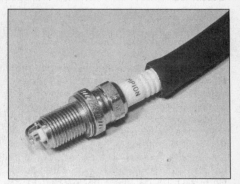

40.12 Using a short length of rubber hose to guide spark plugs into position on refitting

electrode open or closed until the correct gap is achieved. The centre electrode should never be bent, as this may crack the insulator and cause plug failure, if nothing worse.

10 Specialised spark plug electrode gap measuring and adjusting tools are available from most motor accessory shops (photos).

11 Before fitting the spark plugs, check that the threaded connector sleeves on the plug tops are tight, and that the plug exterior surfaces and threads are clean. To make removal of the plugs easier for next time, apply a smear of copper-based brake grease to the plug threads.

12 It is very often difficult to insert spark plugs into their holes without cross-threading them. To avoid this possibility, fit a short length of 5/16 inch internal diameter rubber hose over the end of the spark plug (photo). The flexible hose acts as a universal joint, to help align the plug with the plug hole. Should the plug begin to cross-thread, the hose will slip on the spark plug, preventing thread damage to the aluminium cylinder head. Remove the rubber hose, and tighten the plug to the specified torque using the spark plug socket and a torque wrench. Refit the remaining spark plugs in the same manner.

13 Check the spark plug (HT) leads, then reconnect them in their correct order, and refit all the components which were removed for access.

41 Ignition timing check and adjustment

> **Warning: Voltages produced by an electronic ignition system are considerably higher than those produced by conventional ignition systems. Extreme care must be taken when working on the system with the ignition switched on. Persons with surgically-implanted cardiac pacemaker devices should keep well clear of the ignition circuits, components and test equipment.**

1 Position the front wheels on full left-hand lock, then remove the rubber grommet from the left-hand side of the undercover panel to gain access to the crankshaft pulley bolt. Using a socket and extension bar, fit a socket onto the crankshaft pulley bolt.

2 Rotate the crankshaft pulley anti-clockwise, and clean the pulley rim; the timing marks are as follows. The pulley has a total of four notches; a small group of three, then a single notch just to the right of the group of three. The single notch is the TDC indicator. The pulley marks align with a pointer, in the form of a set of 'sights', which are cast into the lower timing belt cover. The sights work in the same

way as the sights on a rifle do; the upper pointer aligns with a lower notch on the lower timing belt. With the single notch aligned with the pointer, the engine is at TDC with either number 1 or number 4 cylinders on compression. The group of three notches are the ignition timing marks; when the centre notch, which should highlighted with red paint, is aligned with the pointer on the lower timing belt cover, the crankshaft is the specified ignition timing position (see Specifications) for cylinders 1 and 4; the two marks on either side of centre mark indicate the 2° ignition timing tolerance (photo).

3 To check the ignition timing, first warm the engine up to normal operating temperature (until the cooling cuts in), then switch it off. Remove the yellow cap from the ignition timing adjuster wiring terminal (situated beside the windscreen washer reservoir pump), and connect the two terminal wires together using a short piece of wire or a split pin (photo). Connect a timing light to the number 1 cylinder (nearest the timing belt end of the engine) HT lead, as described in the equipment manufacturer's instructions.

4 Start the engine, and allow it to idle at the specified speed. Aim the timing light at the crankshaft pulley, and check that the centre one of the three crankshaft pulley timing notches (which is highlighted in red), or one of the tolerance notches, aligns with the pointer on the timing belt lower cover.

5 If adjustment is required, slacken the distributor mounting bolts until the distributor body is just able to rotate, then turn the body clockwise (viewed from the car's right-hand side) to retard the ignition timing, or anti-clockwise to advance it, until the centre timing mark is aligned with the timing belt cover pointer. Tighten the bolts to their specified torque wrench setting, then recheck the ignition timing to ensure that it has not altered.

6 When the ignition timing is correctly set, turn off the engine and disconnect the timing light. Remove the wire from the timing adjuster terminal, and refit the terminal cap. Refit the grommet to the undercover panel.

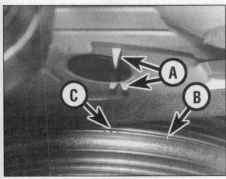

41.2 Timing belt cover pointer (A), crankshaft pulley TDC notch (B), and crankshaft pulley ignition timing marks (C)

41.3 To adjust ignition timing, connect the ignition timing adjuster terminals together using a split pin or piece of spare wire

1

42 Manual gearbox oil renewal

1 This operation is much quicker and more efficient if the car is first taken on a journey of sufficient length to warm the engine/transmission up to normal operating temperature.

2 Park the car on level ground, then switch off the ignition and apply the handbrake firmly. For improved access, jack up the front of the car and support it securely on axle stands. Note that the car must be lowered to the ground and level (to ensure accuracy) when refilling and checking the oil level.

3 Unscrew the filler/level plug. Position a suitable container under the drain plug at the rear of the transmission, below the right-hand driveshaft inner constant velocity joint, and unscrew the plug.

4 Allow the oil to drain completely into the container. If the oil is hot, take precautions against scalding. Clean both the filler/level and the drain plugs, being especially careful to wipe any metallic particles off the magnetic inserts. Discard the original sealing washers; they should be renewed whenever they are disturbed.

5 When the oil has finished draining, clean the drain plug threads and those of the transmission casing, then refit the drain plug, using a new sealing washer and tightening the plug to the specified torque wrench setting. It the car was raised for the draining operation, now lower it to the ground.

6 Refilling the transmission is an extremely awkward operation. Above all, allow plenty of time for the oil level to settle properly before checking it. Note that the car must be parked on flat level ground when checking the oil level.

7 Refill the transmission with the exact amount of the specified type of oil, then check the oil level as described above; if the correct

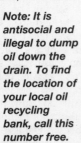

Note: It is antisocial and illegal to dump oil down the drain. To find the location of your local oil recycling bank, call this number free.

amount was poured into the transmission, but a large amount flows out on checking the level, refit the filler/level plug and take the car on a short journey so that the new oil is distributed fully around the transmission components, then check the level again.

8 Dispose of the old oil safely; **do not** pour it down a drain (see *'General repair procedures'* at the end of this manual).

43 Automatic transmission fluid renewal

1 Take the vehicle on a short run to warm the transmission up to normal operating temperature.

2 Park the car on level ground, then switch off the ignition and apply the handbrake firmly. For improved access, jack up the front of the car and support it securely on axle stands. Note that the car must be lowered to the ground and level (to ensure accuracy) when refilling and checking the fluid level.

3 Remove the transmission fluid dipstick. Position a suitable container under the drain plug at the rear of the transmission, below the right-hand driveshaft inner constant velocity joint, and unscrew the plug.

4 Allow the fluid to drain completely into the container. If the fluid is hot, take precautions against scalding. Clean the drain plug, being especially careful to wipe any metallic particles off the magnetic insert. Discard the original sealing washer; this should be renewed whenever it is disturbed.

5 When the fluid has finished draining, clean the drain plug threads and those of the transmission casing, then refit the drain plug, using a new sealing washer and tightening the plug to the specified torque wrench setting. If the car was raised for the draining operation, now lower it to the ground.

6 Refilling the transmission is an extremely awkward operation, adding the specified type of fluid to the transmission a little at a time via the dipstick tube.

 Use a funnel with a fine mesh gauze, to avoid spillage and to ensure that no foreign matter enters the transmission. Allow plenty of time for the level to settle properly before checking it. Note that the car must be parked on flat level ground when checking the level.

7 Once the fluid level is up to the MAX mark on the dipstick, refit the dipstick, then start the engine and allow it to idle for a few minutes. Switch the engine off, then recheck the fluid level, topping-up if necessary. Take the car on a short run to fully distribute the new fluid around the transmission, and recheck the fluid level.

44 Brake fluid renewal

Note: *This procedure covers only the main braking system. On models equipped with anti-lock brakes (ALB) renewal of the ALB high-pressure system fluid must be entrusted to a Rover dealer who will have access to the necessary special equipment necessary to bleed the system on completion. Refer to Chapter 9 for further information.*

1 The procedure is similar to that for the bleeding of the hydraulic system described in Chapter 9, except that the brake fluid reservoir should be emptied by syphoning, using a clean poultry baster or syringe before starting, and allowance should be made for the old fluid to be expelled when bleeding a section of the circuit.

2 Working as described in Chapter 9, open the first bleed nipple in the sequence, and pump the brake pedal gently until nearly all the old fluid has been emptied from the master cylinder reservoir. Top-up to the MAX level with new fluid, and continue pumping until only the new fluid remains in the reservoir, and new fluid can be seen emerging from the bleed nipple. Tighten the nipple, and top the reservoir level up to the MAX level line.

3 Old hydraulic fluid is invariably much darker in colour than the new, making it easy to distinguish the two.

4 Work through all the remaining nipples in the sequence, until new fluid can be seen at all of them. Be careful to keep the master cylinder reservoir topped-up to above the MIN level at all times, or air may enter the system and greatly increase the length of the task.

5 When the operation is complete, check that all nipples are securely tightened (do not over-tighten, however) and that their dust caps are refitted. Wash off all traces of spilt fluid, and recheck the master cylinder reservoir fluid level.

6 Check the operation of the brakes before taking the car on the road.

Every 60 000 miles or 5 years

45 Timing belt renewal

1 The timing belt **must** be renewed as a matter of course at the specified interval, following the procedure given in Section 7 of Chapter 2. If the belt is not renewed as

directed, it may break while the engine is running, which will result in serious (and expensive) engine damage.

Specifications

Engine

Oil filter type	Champion F208
Valve clearances:	
SOHC engine:	
Inlet	0.17 to 0.22 mm
Exhaust	0.22 to 0.27 mm
DOHC engine:	
Inlet	0.13 to 0.17 mm
Exhaust	0.15 to 0.19 mm

Cooling, heating and ventilation systems

Antifreeze properties – 50 % antifreeze (by volume):	
Commences freezing	–36°C
Frozen solid	–48°C
Air conditioning compressor drivebelt deflection	9 to 11 mm @ 10 kg force

Fuel system

Idle speed – nominal value given for reference purposes only:	800 ± 50 rpm
Base idle speed – EACV disconnected	550 ± 50 rpm
CO level at idle speed – engine at normal operating temperature:	
Models without catalytic converter	
SOHC engines	0.2 to 1.0%
DOHC engines	0.2 to 0.8%
Models with catalytic converter	0.1% maximum
Recommended fuel – minimum octane rating:	
Models without catalytic converter	95 RON unleaded or 97 RON leaded ('4-star')
Models with catalytic converter:	
SOHC engines	91 RON unleaded (not available in UK; 95 RON unleaded nearest available – **do not use leaded petrol**
DOHC engines	95 RON unleaded – **do not use leaded petrol**

Ignition system

Firing order	1-3-4-2 (No 1 cylinder at timing belt end)
Direction of crankshaft rotation	Anti-clockwise (viewed from left-hand side of car)
Direction of distributor rotor arm rotation	Clockwise (viewed from right-hand side of car)
Ignition timing (at specified idle speed):	
SOHC engines	18° + 2° BTDC
DOHC engines	16° + 2° BTDC
Spark plugs:	
Type:	
SOHC engines	Champion RC9YCC or RC9YC4
DOHC engines	Champion RC7YCC or RC7YC4
Electrode gap	1.0 mm
Spark plug (HT) leads:	
Maximum resistance per lead	25 000 ohms

Braking system

Front and rear brake pad friction material minimum thickness	3.0 mm
Rear brake shoe friction material minimum thickness	2.0 mm

Suspension and steering

Power steering pump drivebelt deflection	9 to 12 mm @ 10 kg force

Tyre pressures (tyres cold)

	Front	Rear
175/65 HR 14 and 185/60 HR 14 tyres:		
Normal driving conditions	2.1 bars (30 lbf/in²)	2.1 bars (30 lbf/in²)
Speeds in excess of 100 mph	2.5 bars (36 lbf/in²)	2.5 bars (36 lbf/in²)
185/55 VR 15 tyres:		
Normal driving conditions	2.2 bars (32 lbf/in²)	2.2 bars (32 lbf/in²)
Speeds in excess of 100 mph	2.7 bars (39 lbf/in²)	2.7 bars (39 lbf/in²)

Note: Pressures apply only to original equipment tyres, and may vary if any other make or type is fitted; check with the tyre manufacturer or supplier for correct pressures if necessary.

Electrical system

Alternator drivebelt deflection	9 to 11 mm @ 10 kg force
Wiper blades – front and rear	Champion X-4503

Specifications

Torque wrench settings

	Nm	lbf ft
Engine oil drain plug	45	33
Rocker adjusting screw locknut	14	10
Cylinder block coolant drain plug	45	33
Air conditioning compressor drivebelt adjuster pulley spindle bolt	48	35
Fuel filter:		
Mounting bolt	10	7
Outlet union nut	35	26
Inlet union nut	40	30
Distributor mounting bolts	22	16
Spark plugs	18	13
Manual gearbox oil filler/level and drain plugs	45	33
Automatic transmission oil drain plug	40	30
Power steering pump:		
Upper mounting bolt	45	33
Lower mounting bolt(s)	25	18
Alternator pivot and adjusting link bolts	45	33
Roadwheel nuts	100	74

Lubricants and fluids

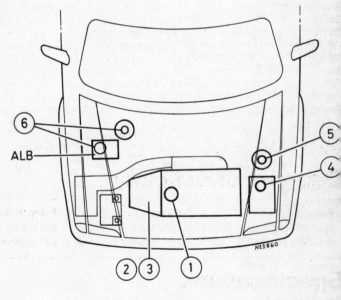

Component or system	Lubricant type/specification
1 Engine	SAE 10W/40 multigrade engine oil meeting specifications API-SG or SG/CD, CCMC G4, or RES.22.OL.G4
2 Manual gearbox	SAE 10W/30 or 10W/40 multigrade engine oil
3 Automatic transmission	
Topping-up only	Automatic transmission fluid (ATF) meeting Dexron II D specification
Drain and refill	Unipart Transmatic ATF
4 Cooling system	Ethylene glycol-based antifreeze with non-phosphate corrosion inhibitors, suitable for mixed-metal engines, containing no methanol, and meeting specifications BS6580 and BS5117
5 Power steering system	Automatic Transmission Fluid (ATF) meeting Dexron II D specification
6 Braking system	Hydraulic fluid meeting specification SAE J1703 or DOT 4
General greasing	Multi-purpose lithium-based grease, NLGI consistency No. 2

Capacities

Engine oil
Total capacity (including filter) . . . . 3.4 litres
Difference between dipstick MAX and MIN marks . . . 0.5 litre (approx)

Cooling system . . . . 5.5 litres

Power steering reservoir . . . . 1.2 litres

Fuel tank . . . . 55 litres

Manual gearbox . . . . 1.8 litres

Automatic transmission
Refill capacity . . . . 2.4 litres
Capacity when dry (eg. after rebuild) . . . . 5.8 litres

Washer system reservoir . . . . 3.1 litres

Chapter 2 Engine

Contents

2

Degrees of difficulty

| Easy, suitable for novice with little experience | | Fairly easy, suitable for beginner with some experience | | Fairly difficult, suitable for competent DIY mechanic | | Difficult, suitable for experienced DIY mechanic | | Very difficult, suitable for expert DIY or professional | |

Specifications

Engine (general)

Type	Sixteen-valve four-cylinder in-line, four-stroke, water-cooled
Designation	D16
Number of cylinders	4
Bore	75.00 mm
Stroke	90.00 mm
Capacity	1590 cc
Firing order	1 -3-4-2 (No 1 cylinder at timing belt end)
Direction of crankshaft rotation	Anti-clockwise (viewed from the left-hand side of car)
Compression ratio:	
SOHC engine	9.1: 1
DOHC engine	9.5: 1
Minimum compression pressure	10.3 bars
Maximum compression pressure difference between cylinders	1.4 bars
Maximum power (EEC):	
SOHC engine	116 PS (85 kW) @ 6300 rpm
DOHC engine with automatic transmission	124 PS (91 kW) @ 6800 rpm
DOHC engine with manual gearbox	130 PS (96 kW) @ 6800 rpm

Note: *All the above figures are for non-catalyst models. Figures for models with catalytic converters not available at the time of writing.*

Cylinder block

Material . . . . Aluminium alloy
Cylinder bore diameter:
  Standard . . . . 75.00 to 75.02 mm
  Service limit . . . . 75.07 mm
  1st oversize (0.25 mm) . . . . 75.25 to 75.27 mm
  2nd oversize (0.50 mm) . . . . 75.50 to 75.52 mm
Maximum cylinder bore ovality . . . . N/A
Maximum cylinder bore taper . . . . 0.05 mm
Maximum gasket face distortion . . . . 0.10 mm

Crankshaft

Number of main bearings 5
Main bearing journal running clearance:
  Standard:
    Numbers 1, 2, 4 and 5 journals . . . . 0.024 to 0.042 mm
    Number 3 journal . . . . 0.030 to 0.048 mm
  Service limit (all journals) . . . . 0.050 mm
Maximum difference between main bearing journal running clearances 0.010 mm
Crankpin (big-end) journal running clearance:
  Standard . . . . 0.020 to 0.038 mm
  Service limit . . . . 0.050 mm
Maximum difference between crankpin (big-end) journal running
clearances . . . . 0.030 mm
Crankshaft endfloat (side play):
  Standard . . . . 0.10 to 0.35 mm
  Service limit . . . . 0.45 mm
Maximum difference between journal diameters (ovality/taper limit):
  Standard . . . . 0.0025 mm
  Service limit . . . . 0.010 mm
Crankshaft main bearing journal run-out:
  Standard . . . . 0.03 mm
  Service limit . . . . 0.06 mm

Pistons and piston rings

Piston diameter:
  Standard . . . . 74.98 to 74.99 mm
  Service limit . . . . 74.97 mm
  1st oversize (0.25 mm) . . . . 75.23 to 75.24 mm
  2nd oversize (0.50 mm) . . . . 75.48 to 75.49 mm
Piston-to-bore clearance:
  By direct measurement:
    Standard . . . . 0.01 to 0.04 mm
    Service limit . . . . 0.05 mm
  Using feeler gauge (see text) . . . . 0.08 mm
Piston ring end gaps (fitted in bore):
  Top compression ring:
    Standard . . . . 0.015 to 0.030 mm
    Service limit . . . . 0.6 mm
  Second compression ring:
    Standard . . . . 0.30 to 0.45 mm
    Service limit . . . . 0.6 mm
  Oil control ring:
    Standard . . . . 0.2 to 0.6 mm
    Service limit . . . . 0.8 mm
Piston ring-to-groove clearance:
  Top compression ring:
    Standard . . . . 0.03 to 0.06 mm
    Service limit . . . . 0.13 mm
  Second compression ring:
    Standard . . . . 0.030 to 0.055 mm
    Service limit . . . . 0.6 mm
  Oil control ring . . . . N/A

Gudgeon pins

Diameter:
  Standard . . . . 18.994 to 19.000 mm
  Oversize . . . . 18.997 to 19.003 mm
Maximum gudgeon pin-to-piston clearance . . . . 0.010 mm
Fit in connecting rod . . . . Interference

Connecting rods
Big-end cap endfloat (side play):
    Standard . . . .   0.15 to 0.30 mm
    Service limit . . . .   0.4 mm

Cylinder head
Material . . . .   Aluminium alloy
Minimum acceptable height after machining:
    SOHC engine . . . .   94.8 mm
    DOHC engine . . . .   131.8 mm
Maximum acceptable gasket face distortion . . . .   0.05 mm
Valve seat angle . . . .   45°
Valve seat width:
    Standard:
        SOHC engine inlet valve . . . .   0.85 to 1.15 mm
        SOHC engine exhaust valve . . . .   1.25 to 1.55 mm
        DOHC engine (inlet and exhaust valves) . . . .   1.25 to 1.55 mm
    Service limit:
        SOHC engine inlet valve . . . .   1.6 mm
        SOHC engine exhaust valve . . . .   2.0 mm
        DOHC engine (inlet and exhaust valves) . . . .   2.0 mm
Seat cutter correction angle:
    Upper . . . .   30°
    Lower . . . .   60°
Valve guide protrusion . . . .   16.2 mm

Rocker shaft (SOHC engine) running clearance . . . . . .   0.08 mm

Valves
Length (new):
    Inlet:
        SOHC engine . . . .   114.82 to 115.12 mm
        DOHC engine . . . .   105.18 to 105.48 mm
    Exhaust:
        SOHC engine . . . .   118.60 to 118.90 mm
        DOHC exhaust . . . .   104.47 to 104.77 mm
Head diameter (new):
    Inlet:
        SOHC engine . . . .   28.9 to 29.1 mm
        DOHC engine . . . .   29.9 to 30.1 mm
    Exhaust:
        SOHC engine . . . .   24.9 to 25.1 mm
        DOHC engine . . . .   26.9 to 27.1 mm
Head thickness:
    Inlet – SOHC engine:
        Standard . . . .   0.85 to 1.15 mm
        Service limit . . . .   0.65 mm
    Inlet – DOHC engine:
        Standard . . . .   1.05 to 1.35 mm
        Service limit . . . .   1.00 mm
    Exhaust – SOHC engine:
        Standard . . . .   1.05 to 1.35 mm
        Service limit . . . .   0.95 mm
    Exhaust – DOHC engine:
        Standard . . . .   1.65 to 1.95 mm
        Service limit . . . .   1.45 mm
Stem diameter:
    Inlet – SOHC engine:
        Standard . . . .   5.48 to 5.49 mm
        Service limit . . . .   5.45 mm
    Inlet – DOHC engine:
        Standard . . . .   6.58 to 6.59 mm
        Service limit . . . .   6.55 mm
    Exhaust – SOHC engine:
        Standard . . . .   5.45 to 5.46 mm
        Service limit . . . .   5.42 mm
Stem diameter:

2

Valves (continued)

Exhaust – DOHC engine:
  Standard .... 6.55 to 6.56 mm
  Service limit .... 6.52 mm
Stem-to-guide clearance:
  Inlet:
    Standard .... 0.02 to 0.05 mm
    Service limit .... 0.08 mm
  Exhaust:
    Standard .... 0.05 to 0.08 mm
    Service limit .... 0.11 mm
Valve head movement when installed in guide (see text):
  Inlet:
    Standard .... 0.04 to 0.10 mm
    Service limit .... 0.16 mm
  Exhaust:
    Standard .... 0.10 to 0.16 mm
    Service limit .... 0.24 mm
Valve stem fitted height:
  Inlet – SOHC engine:
    Standard .... 46.985 to 47.455 mm
    Service limit .... 47.705 mm
  Inlet – DOHC engine:
    Standard .... 45.780 mm
    Service limit .... 46.625 mm
  Exhaust – SOHC engine:
    Standard .... 48.965 to 49.435 mm
    Service limit .... 49.685 mm
  Exhaust DOHC engine:
    Standard .... 44.970 mm
    Service limit .... 45.455 mm
Valve clearances .... See Chapter 1

Camshaft(s)

Drive .... Toothed belt
Number of bearings 6
Bearing journal running clearance:
  Standard .... 0.050 to 0.089 mm
  Service limit .... 0.15 mm
Lobe height (new):
  Inlet:
    SOHC engine .... 36.957 mm
    DOHC engine .... 33.021 mm
  Exhaust:
    SOHC engine .... 36.996 mm
    DOHC engine .... 32.382 mm
Camshaft run-out:
  Standard .... 0.03 mm
  Service limit .... 0.06 mm
Camshaft endfloat (side play):
  Standard .... 0.05 to 0.15 mm
  Service limit .... 0.50 mm

Lubrication system

System pressure (engine idling) .... 1.4 bars
Oil pump type .... Eccentric rotor, driven off crankshaft left-hand end
Oil pump clearances:
  Rotor endfloat:
    Standard .... 0.03 to 0.08 mm
    Service limit .... 0.15 mm
  Outer rotor-to-body clearance:
    Standard .... 0.100 to 0.175 mm
    Service limit .... 0.2 mm
  Rotor lobe clearance:
    Standard .... 0.04 to 0.14 mm
    Service limit .... 0.2 mm
Oil pressure warning lamp switch opening pressure .... Below 0.3 to 0.5 bars
Pressure relief valve operating pressure .... 4.5 bars

Torque wrench settings

	Nm	lbf ft
Sump drain plug	45	33
Manual gearbox drain plug	45	33
Automatic transmission drain plug	40	30
Automatic transmission torque converter mounting bolts	12	9
Intermediate shaft bearing housing mounting bolts	40	33
Cylinder head cover nuts	10	7
Timing belt cover bolts	10	7
Crankshaft pulley retaining bolt	165	122
Air conditioning drivebelt adjuster (idler) pulley mounting plate bolts	24	18
Timing belt tensioner pulley bolt	45	33
Camshaft sprocket retaining bolt	38	28
Camshaft bearing cap bolts:		
SOHC engine	22	16
DOHC engine	12	9
Cylinder head bolts:		
Stage 1	30	22
Stage 2	65	48
Oil pump pick-up/strainer pipe:		
Mounting bolts	11	8
Mounting nuts	24	18
Flywheel retaining bolts	120	89
Driveplate retaining bolts	75	55
Flywheel/driveplate cover nuts and bolts	12	9
Anti-twisting bracket:		
Bracket-to-transmission bolts	40	30
Bracket-to-cylinder block bolt	2	18
Sump retaining nuts and bolts	12	9
Oil pump:		
Pump-to-cylinder block bolts	11	8
Cover retaining screws	7	5
Relief valve piston threaded plug	30	22
Oil cooler centre bolt DOHC engine	10	7
Sump retaining nuts	12	9
Right-hand crankshaft seal housing bolts	12	9
Connecting rod big-end bearing cap nuts	32	24
Main bearing cap bolts	67	49
Engine/transmission front mounting:		
Through-bolt	60	44
Mounting-to-engine/transmission bolts	55	41
Mounting-to-crossmember bolts	55	41
Engine/transmission rear mounting:		
Through-bolt	60	44
Mounting bracket-to-engine/transmission bolts	55	41
Engine/transmission right-hand mounting:		
Through-bolt	60	44
Mounting plate-to-transmission bolts	39	29
Mounting-to-mounting plate nuts and bolts	55	41
Engine/transmission left-hand mounting:		
Through-bolt	55	41
Mounting-to-mounting bracket nut and bolt	39	29
Mounting bracket-to-engine bolts	45	33

Part A: In-car engine repair procedures

1 General information

How to use this Chapter

This Part of Chapter 2 describes those repair procedures that can reasonably be carried out on the engine while it remains in the car. If the engine has been removed from the car and is being dismantled as described in Part B, any preliminary dismantling procedures can be ignored.

Note that, while it may be possible physically to overhaul items such as the piston/connecting rod assemblies while the engine is in the car, such tasks are not usually carried out as separate operations, and usually require the execution of several additional procedures (not to mention the cleaning of components and of oilways); for this reason, all such tasks are classed as major overhaul procedures, and are described in Part B of this Chapter.

Part B describes the removal of the engine/transmission unit from the car, and the full overhaul procedures that can then be carried out.

For ease of reference, all specifications are given in the one Specifications Section at the beginning of the Chapter.

Engine description

The engine is a four-cylinder, in-line unit, mounted transversely at the front of the car, with the clutch and transmission on its right-hand end. The engine is available in two forms, a single overhead camshaft (SOHC) sixteen-valve engine, and a double overhead camshaft (DOHC) sixteen-valve engine. The DOHC engine is fitted to the 416 GTi and 216 GTi Twin Cam models, whereas all other models are equipped with the SOHC engine. Apart from the different cylinder head designs, both engines are of identical construction.

The aluminium alloy cylinder block is of the dry-liner type, which can be rebored to accept pistons up to 0.5 mm oversize. The crankshaft is supported within the cylinder block on five shell-type main bearings. Thrustwashers are fitted to number 4 main bearing, to control crankshaft endfloat.

The connecting rods are attached to the crankshaft by horizontally split shell-type big-end bearings, and to the pistons by interference-fit gudgeon pins. The aluminium alloy pistons are of the slipper type, and are fitted with three piston rings, comprising two compression rings and a scraper-type oil control ring.

The camshaft(s) is/are mounted directly in the cylinder head, and driven by the crankshaft via a toothed rubber timing belt (which also drives the water pump). The camshaft operates each valve via a rocker arm. On the SOHC engine, the rocker arms are mounted on a shaft above the camshaft; on DOHC engines, the rocker arms are located below the camshafts, and are mounted directly into the cylinder head via a balljoint type arrangement.

Lubrication is by pressure-feed from a gear-type oil pump, which is mounted on the left-hand end of the crankshaft. It draws oil through a strainer located in the sump, and then forces it through an externally mounted full-flow cartridge-type filter. The oil flows into galleries in the main bearing cap bridge arrangement and cylinder block/crankcase, from where it is distributed to the crankshaft (main bearings) and camshaft(s). The big-end bearings are supplied with oil via internal drillings in the crankshaft, while the camshaft bearings also receive a pressurised supply. The camshaft lobes and valves are lubricated by splash, as are all other engine components. On DOHC engines, an oil cooler is mounted between the oil filter and cylinder block, to cool the oil as it passes through the filter. The oil cooler is supplied with engine coolant, taken from the metal coolant pipe which runs along the rear of the cylinder block.

Repair operations possible with the engine in the car

The following work can be carried out with the engine in the car.
(a) Compression pressure – testing.
(b) Cylinder head cover – removal and refitting.
(c) Crankshaft pulley – removal and refitting.
(d) Timing belt covers – removal and refitting.
(e) Timing belt – removal, refitting and adjustment.
(f) Timing belt tensioner and sprockets – removal and refitting.
(g) Camshaft oil seal(s) – renewal.
(h) Camshaft(s) and rocker arms – removal, inspection and refitting.
(i) Cylinder head – removal and refitting.
(j) Cylinder head and pistons – decarbonising.
(k) Sump – removal and refitting.
(l) Oil pump – removal, overhaul and refitting.
(m) Oil cooler – removal and refitting (DOHC engines only).
(n) Crankshaft oil seals – renewal.
(o) Engine/transmission mountings – inspection and renewal.
(p) Flywheel – removal, inspection and refitting.

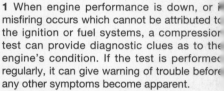

2 Compression test – description and interpretation

1 When engine performance is down, or misfiring occurs which cannot be attributed to the ignition or fuel systems, a compression test can provide diagnostic clues as to the engine's condition. If the test is performed regularly, it can give warning of trouble before any other symptoms become apparent.
2 The engine must be fully warmed-up to normal operating temperature, the battery must be fully charged, and the spark plugs must be removed (see Chapter 1). The aid of an assistant will also be required.
3 Disable the ignition system by removing the engine management/ignition system fuse (number 14) from the passenger compartment fusebox.
4 Fit a compression tester to the number 1 cylinder spark plug hole the type of tester which screws into the plug thread is to be preferred (photo).
5 Have the assistant hold the throttle wide open and crank the engine on the starter motor; after one or two revolutions, the compression pressure should build up to a maximum figure, and then stabilise. Record the highest reading obtained.
6 Repeat the test on the remaining cylinders, recording the pressure in each.
7 All cylinders should produce very similar pressures; any difference greater than that specified indicates the existence of a fault. Note that the compression should build up quickly in a healthy engine; low compression on the first stroke, followed by gradually-increasing pressure on successive strokes, indicates worn piston rings. A low compression reading on the first stroke, which does not build up during successive strokes, indicates leaking valves or a blown head gasket (a cracked head could also be the cause). Deposits on the undersides of the valve heads can also cause low compression.
8 If the pressure in any cylinder is reduced to the specified minimum or less, carry out the following test to isolate the cause. Introduce a teaspoonful of clean oil into that cylinder through its spark plug hole, and repeat the test.
9 If the addition of oil temporarily improves the compression pressure, this indicates that bore or piston wear is responsible for the

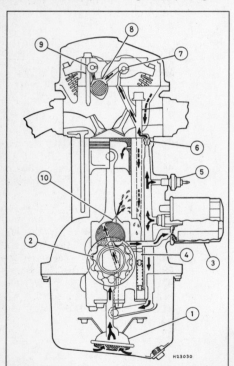

Fig. 2.1 Engine lubrication system – SOHC engine (DOHC engine similar) (Sec 1)

1 Oil pump pick-up/strainer pipe
2 Oil pump
3 Oil filter
4 Oil pressure relief valve
5 Oil pressure switch
6 Oil control jet
7 Inlet rocker arm shaft
8 Camshaft
9 Exhaust rocker arm shaft
10 Connecting rod oil hole

2.4 Measuring compression pressure

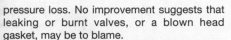

3.6 Crankshaft pulley TDC notch (arrowed) aligned with timing belt cover pointer

4.2 Release the retaining clip, and disconnect the cylinder head cover breather hose (SOHC engine shown)

4.4 Removing the upper timing belt cover – DOHC engine

4.8 Ensure gasket and sealing rings are correctly located in cylinder head cover grooves (SOHC engine shown)

pressure loss. No improvement suggests that leaking or burnt valves, or a blown head gasket, may be to blame.

10 A low reading from two adjacent cylinders is almost certainly due to the head gasket having blown between them; the presence of coolant in the engine oil will confirm this.

11 If one cylinder is about 20 per cent lower than the others, and the engine has a slightly rough idle, a worn camshaft lobe could be the cause.

12 If the compression reading is unusually high, the combustion chambers are probably coated with carbon deposits. If this is the case, the cylinder head should be removed and decarbonised.

13 On completion of the test, refit the spark plugs, and refit the engine management/ignition fuse to the fusebox.

3 Top Dead Centre (TDC) for number 1 piston locating

Note: If the crankshaft pulley bolt slackens while the crankshaft is being rotated, it must be tightened to the specified torque (referring to Section 5 for further information) before proceeding further.

1 In its travel up and down its cylinder bore, Top Dead Centre (TDC) is the highest point that each piston reaches as the crankshaft rotates. While each piston reaches TDC both at the top of the compression stroke and again at the top of the exhaust stroke, for the purpose of timing the engine, TDC refers to the piston position (usually number 1) at the top of its compression stroke.

2 Number 1 piston (and cylinder) is at the left-hand (timing belt) end of the engine, and its TDC position is located as follows. Note that the crankshaft rotates anti-clockwise when viewed from the left-hand side of the car.

3 Disconnect the battery negative terminal, and remove all the spark plugs as described in Chapter 1.

4 Trace number 1 spark plug (HT) lead from the plug back to the distributor cap, and use chalk or similar to mark the distributor body or engine casting nearest to the cap's number 1

terminal. Undo the distributor cap retaining screws, and remove the cap and HT leads.

5 Turn the steering onto full left lock, then remove the grommet from the front undercover panel to gain access to the crankshaft pulley retaining bolt.

6 Using a socket and extension bar applied to the crankshaft pulley bolt, rotate the crankshaft anti-clockwise until the single TDC notch on the crankshaft pulley rim is aligned with the pointer on the timing belt lower cover (see Chapter 1, ignition timing check and adjustment, for details of the crankshaft pulley marks) (photo).

7 With the crankshaft in this position, numbers 1 and 4 cylinders are now at TDC, one of them on the compression stroke. If the distributor rotor arm is pointing at (the previously-marked) number 1 terminal, then number 1 cylinder is correctly positioned; if the rotor arm is pointing at number 4 terminal, rotate the crankshaft one full turn (360°) anti-clockwise until the arm points at the marked terminal. Number 1 cylinder will then be at TDC on the compression stroke.

8 Once number 1 cylinder has been positioned at TDC on the compression stroke, TDC for any of the other cylinders can then be located by rotating the crankshaft anti-clockwise 180° at a time and following the firing order (see Specifications).

4 Cylinder head cover – removal and refitting

Removal

1 Disconnect the battery negative terminal.

2 Using a suitable pair of pliers, release the retaining clip, and disconnect the breather hose from the rear of the cylinder head cover (photo).

3 Carefully disconnect the ignition HT leads from the spark plugs, then free the leads from their retaining clips, and position them clear of the cylinder head cover.

4 On DOHC engines, undo the two retaining bolts and remove the upper timing belt cover (photo), noting the correct fitted position of its

seal, the accelerator cable retaining clip, and the earth lead.

5 On SOHC engines, free the accelerator cable from its retaining clips on the front edge of the cylinder head cover.

6 On all engines, slacken and remove the cylinder head cover retaining nuts, and remove all the sealing washers, noting the earth lead which is fitted to the front left-hand stud. On DOHC engines also note the accelerator cable retaining clip which is fitted the front right-hand stud, and the HT lead retaining clips fitted to the centre studs.

7 Carefully lift off the cylinder head cover, and remove it from the engine.

Refitting

8 Inspect the cover gasket, spark plug hole sealing rings and cover retaining nut sealing washers for signs of wear or damage, and renew as required. If renewal of the gasket and/or sealing rings is necessary, remove the old gasket and/or sealing rings from the cover, then remove all traces of dirt and oil from the cover grooves. Fit the new gasket and/or sealing rings to the cover (photo).

9 Ensure the cylinder head mating surface, gasket and sealing rings are clean and free from all traces of oil, and that all gaskets are securely located in the head cover. On DOHC engines, apply a smear of suitable sealant to

4.9 On DOHC engine, apply a smear of sealant to the areas of the cover gasket on either side of the camshaft cutout

4.10 Fit the cylinder head cover, ensuring gasket and sealing rings remain in position (SOHC engine shown)

4.11A On SOHC engine, do not forget to fit earth lead beneath left-hand front cover retaining nut

4.11B On DOHC engine, ensure HT lead clips (A), accelerator cable clip (B) and earth lead (C) are fitted beneath the correct cover retaining nuts

the cylinder head cover gasket on each side of all the camshaft cut-outs (photo).

10 On all engines, refit the cylinder head cover to the engine, taking great care to ensure that gasket and sealing rings remain in position on the cover (photo).

11 Once the cover is correctly seated, refit all the sealing washers and retaining nuts (not forgetting to position the accelerator cable retaining clip and/or earth lead, as applicable, beneath the relevant cover nuts), and tighten them to the specified torque (photos).

12 On DOHC engines, ensure that the upper timing belt cover seal is in position, then refit the timing belt cover. Position the accelerator cable retaining clip and earth lead under the front retaining bolts, and tighten both bolts to the specified torque.

13 Reconnect the HT leads to the relevant plugs, then refit the leads to all their retaining clips. Refit the accelerator cable to its retaining clips on the front of the head cover.

14 Reconnect the breather hose to the rear of the cylinder head cover, ensuring it is securely held in position by its retaining clip, and reconnect the battery negative terminal.

5 Crankshaft pulley – removal and refitting

Removal

1 Apply the handbrake, then jack up the front of the car and support it on axle stands. Remove the left-hand roadwheel.

2 From underneath the front of the vehicle, slacken and remove the three bolts securing the bumper flange to the body. Remove the seven bolts securing the front undercover panel to the body, and remove the panel.

3 If necessary, rotate the crankshaft until the relevant timing marks align.

4 Referring to Chapter 1 for further information, remove the power steering pump, air conditioning compressor and/or alternator drivebelt(s) (as applicable).

5 To prevent crankshaft rotation while the pulley bolt is unscrewed, select top gear and have an assistant apply the brakes hard. Alternatively, a holding tool similar to that shown (photo) can be fabricated from two strips of steel and a few bolts (see Section 8, paragraph 7 for details). If the engine has been removed from the car, lock the flywheel using the arrangement shown in photo 17.8.

6 Slacken and remove the pulley retaining bolt and washer, noting that the washer is fitted with its tapered surface outermost, then withdraw the pulley from the crankshaft. Remove the Woodruff key from the crankshaft groove, and store it with the pulley for safe keeping.

Refitting

7 Refit the Woodruff key to the crankshaft groove, then align the crankshaft pulley centre notch with the key, and slide the pulley onto the crankshaft end. Apply a few drops of oil to the pulley retaining bolt threads, then refit the bolt and washer, ensuring that the washer is fitted with its tapered surface outermost (photos).

8 Lock the crankshaft by the method used on removal, and tighten the pulley retaining bolt to the specified torque setting (photo).

5.5 Using fabricated tool to retain crankshaft pulley while retaining bolt is slackened

5.7A Refit Woodruff key (arrowed), then install crankshaft pulley, ensuring pulley notch engages correctly with key

5.7B Refit the retaining bolt and special washer ...

5.8 ... and tighten it to the specified torque setting

6.3 Removing the upper timing belt cover – SOHC engine

6.8 Removing the lower timing belt cover – SOHC engine

9 Refit the power steering pump, air conditioning compressor and/or alternator drivebelt(s) (as applicable), and adjust them as described in Chapter 1.

10 Refit the undercover panel and roadwheel, and lower the car to the ground.

6 Timing belt covers –
removal and refitting

Removal

Upper cover – SOHC engine

1 Remove the cylinder head cover, as described in Section 4.

2 On models with power steering, slacken and remove the bolts securing the power steering pump to its mounting bracket. Undo the bolt which secures the pipe retaining clamp to the top of the pump, and remove the clamp. Release the pump hoses from any relevant retaining clips, then free the pump pulley from its drivebelt, and position the pump and hoses clear of the timing belt cover.

3 On all models, remove the two retaining bolts and withdraw the upper cover from the engine, along with its sealing strip (photo).

Upper cover – DOHC engine

4 Free the accelerator cable from its retaining clip, then slacken and remove the two upper timing belt cover retaining bolts along with the

cable clip, noting the correct fitted position of the earth lead.

5 Remove the upper cover from the engine, noting the correct fitted position of its sealing strip.

Lower cover – SOHC engine

6 Remove the crankshaft pulley as described in Section 5, and the upper timing belt cover as described above.

7 On models with air conditioning, undo the two bolts securing the air conditioning compressor drivebelt adjuster (idler) pulley mounting plate to the engine, and remove the plate assembly.

8 On all models, slacken and remove the four lower cover retaining bolts, and withdraw the cover along with is sealing strip (photo).

Lower cover DOHC engine

9 Remove the crankshaft pulley as described in Section 5, and the upper timing belt cover as described above.

10 On models with air conditioning, slacken and remove the bolt securing the air conditioning hose to the top of the power steering pump. Undo the two bolts securing the air conditioning compressor drivebelt adjuster (idler) pulley mounting plate to the engine, and remove the plate assembly. Undo the bolt which secures the air conditioning pipe retaining clamp to the top of the pump, and remove the clamp.

11 On models with power steering, unscrew

the pump adjusting bolt from the top of the pump mounting bracket, then slacken and remove the bolts securing the pump to its mounting bracket. Position the pump clear of the bracket. Undo the five pump mounting bracket retaining bolts, and remove the brackets from the engine, noting the seal which is fitted behind the left-hand bracket (photos).

12 Slacken and remove the four lower cover retaining bolts, and withdraw the cover along with its sealing strip (photo).

Refitting

Upper cover – SOHC engine

13 Refitting is a reversal of the removal procedure, noting that the cover sealing strip must be renewed if it is damaged, and the cover retaining bolts should be tightened to their specified torque. On models with power steering, on completion, adjust the power steering pump drivebelt as described in Chapter 1.

Upper cover – DOHC engine

14 Refitting is a reverse of the removal procedure, noting that the cover sealing strip must be renewed if damaged, and the cover retaining bolts should be tightened to the specified torque setting.

Lower cover – SOHC engine

15 Refitting is a reverse of the removal

6.11A On DOHC engine models with power steering, remove the pump mounting bracket from the engine ...

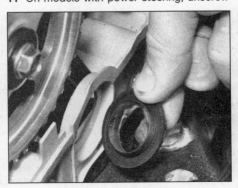

6.11B ... noting the seal which is fitted behind it

6.12 Removing the lower cover – DOHC engine

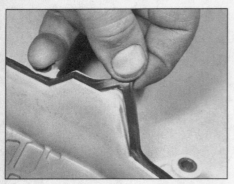

6.15 Renew timing belt cover sealing strips if damaged

procedure, ensuring that the lower cover edge engages correctly with the inner cover. Note that the cover sealing strip must be renewed if damaged (photo). Tighten the cover retaining bolts and, where necessary, the air conditioning drivebelt idler pulley mounting plate bolts, to their specified torque settings.

Lower cover – DOHC engine

16 Refitting is a reverse of the removal sequence, ensuring that the cover edge engages correctly with the inner cover. Note that the cover sealing strip must be renewed if damaged, and all nuts and bolts should be tightened to their specified torque settings.

7 Timing belt – removal, refitting and adjustment

Removal

1 Disconnect the battery negative terminal, and remove the cylinder head cover as described in Section 4.
2 Position number 1 cylinder at TDC on its compression stroke, then remove the upper and lower timing belt covers as described in Section 6. Check that the camshaft and crankshaft sprocket marks align as described in paragraph 8. On DOHC engines, the

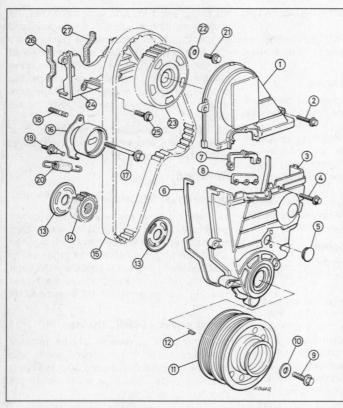

Fig. 2.2 Timing belt, sprockets and covers – SOHC engine (Secs 6, 7 and 8)

1 Timing belt upper cover
2 Bolt – upper cover-to-cylinder head
3 Timing belt lower cover
4 Bolt – lower cover-to-cylinder block
5 Tensioner pulley access grommet
6 Lower cover seal
7 Seal – upper cover
8 Seal – lower cover
9 Crankshaft pulley retaining bolt
10 Washer
11 Crankshaft pulley
12 Woodruff key
13 Timing belt outer guide plate
14 Crankshaft sprocket
15 Timing belt
16 Timing belt tensioner pulley assembly
17 Tensioner pulley retaining bolt
18 Tensioner locating stud
19 Pillar bolt
20 Tensioner pulley spring
21 Camshaft sprocket retaining bolt
22 Washer
23 Camshaft sprocket
24 Timing belt inner cover
25 Bolt – inner cover-to-cylinder head
26 Inner cover seal
27 Inner cover seal

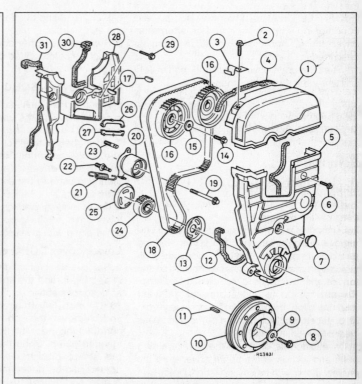

Fig. 2.3 Timing belt, sprockets and covers – DOHC engine (Secs 6, 7 and 8)

1 Timing belt upper cover
2 Bolt – upper cover-to-cylinder head
3 Accelerator cable retaining clip
4 Upper cover seal
5 Timing belt lower cover
6 Bolt – lower cover-to-cylinder block
7 Tensioner pulley access grommet
8 Crankshaft pulley retaining bolt
9 Washer
10 Crankshaft pulley
11 Woodruff key
12 Lower cover seal
13 Timing belt outer guide plate
14 Camshaft sprocket retaining bolt
15 Washer
16 Camshaft sprocket
17 Camshaft sprocket Woodruff keys
18 Timing belt
19 Tensioner pulley retaining bolt
20 Tensioner pulley assembly
21 Spring
22 Pillar bolt
23 Tensioner locating stud
24 Crankshaft sprocket
25 Timing belt inner guide plate
26 Seal – upper cover
27 Seal – lower cover
28 Timing belt inner cover
29 Bolt – inner cover-to-cylinder head
30 Inner cover seal
31 Inner cover seal

7.2 On DOHC engine, peg the camshafts in position to prevent them moving under valve spring pressure when the timing belt is removed

7.3 Remove the outer timing belt guide plate from the crankshaft, noting which way around it is fitted

7.6A On SOHC engines, remove the left-hand mounting and front mounting bracket ...

camshafts can be held in the correct position by inserting two suitably-sized pegs or bolts through the holes in the top of the left-hand end camshaft bearing caps and into the camshafts; this will prevent the shafts moving under valve spring pressure when the timing belt is removed (photo).

3 Slide the outer timing belt guide plate off the end of the crankshaft, noting that it is fitted with its concave surface facing outwards (away from the engine) (photo).

4 Slacken the timing belt tensioner pulley bolt through half a turn, and pull the pulley assembly downwards to remove all the tension from the timing belt. Hold the tensioner pulley in this position, and retighten the pulley bolt securely.

5 If the timing belt is to be re-used, use white paint or similar to mark the direction of rotation on the belt, then slip the belt off its sprocket(s). **Do not** rotate the crankshaft until the timing belt has been refitted.

6 If the belt is to be removed fully from the engine, it will be necessary to split the left-hand engine mounting as follows. Place a jack with interposed block of wood beneath the engine sump, and gently raise the jack until it is supporting the weight of the engine. Undo the left-hand engine/transmission mounting through-bolt, then slacken and remove the nut and bolt securing the mounting to its engine bracket, and remove the mounting block. On SOHC engines, slacken and remove the bolts

securing the power steering pump mounting bracket or mounting bracket (as applicable) to the front of the cylinder block and side mounting, and remove the bracket. The belt can then be removed from the engine (photos).

7 Check the timing belt carefully for any signs of uneven wear, splitting or oil contamination, and renew it if there is the slightest doubt about its condition. If the engine is undergoing an overhaul and has covered more than 60 000 miles (100 000 km) since the original belt was fitted, renew the belt as a matter of course, regardless of its apparent condition. If signs of oil contamination are found, trace the source of the oil leak and rectify it, then wash down the engine timing belt area and all related components to remove all traces of oil.

Refitting and adjustment

8 On reassembly, thoroughly clean the timing belt sprockets, and check that they are aligned as follows (photos).

(a) *Camshaft sprocket – SOHC engine – the UP mark on the sprocket must be at the top, and the line at the bottom of the sprocket must be aligned with the pointer on the inner timing belt cover.*

(b) *Camshaft sprockets – DOHC engine – both the UP arrow marks on each*

7.6B ... to allow the timing belt to be fully removed from engine

7.8A On SOHC engine, ensure UP mark on camshaft sprocket (arrowed) is at the top ...

7.8B ... and lower mark (arrowed) aligns with pointer on timing belt inner cover

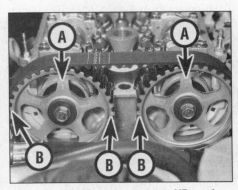

7.8C On DOHC engine, ensure UP marks on camshaft sprockets (A) are at the top, and lines on sprockets (B) align with the cylinder head surface

7.8D Ensure line on crankshaft sprocket is aligned with arrow cast onto oil pump surface

2

7.9 Belt lower run (viewed from underneath)

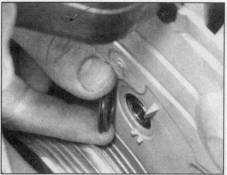

7.14A Remove the rubber grommet from the lower timing belt cover, to gain access to tensioner pulley bolt

7.14B Tension timing belt as described in text, then tighten the tensioner pulley bolt to the specified torque

sprocket must be in the 12 o'clock position (pointing directly upwards), with the index lines on each sprocket being directly aligned with the cylinder head upper mating surface in the 3 o'clock and 9 o'clock positions

(c) Crankshaft sprocket – the line scribed on the outer edge of the sprocket must be aligned with the arrow cast onto the face of the oil pump body.

9 Fit the timing belt over the crankshaft and camshaft sprockets, ensuring that the belt front run (and, on DOHC engines, the top run) is taut (ie, all slack is on the tensioner pulley side of the belt), then fit the belt over the water pump sprocket and tensioner pulley (photo). Do not twist the belt sharply while refitting it. Ensure that the belt teeth are correctly seated centrally in the sprockets, and that the timing marks remain in alignment. If a used belt is being refitted, ensure that the arrow mark made on removal points in the normal direction of rotation, as before.

10 Slacken the tensioner pulley bolt, and check that the tensioner pulley moves to tension the belt; if the tensioner assembly is not free to move under spring tension, rectify the fault, or the timing belt will not be correctly tensioned. On DOHC engines, remove the camshaft retaining pins/bolts from the camshaft bearing caps.

11 Where removed, refit the power steering pump mounting bracket or bracket (SOHC engines only), then reassemble the left-hand engine/transmission mounting, tightening all nuts and bolts to their specified torque settings.

12 Refit the outer timing belt guide to the crankshaft, ensuring its concave surface is facing outwards (away from the engine).

13 Refit the lower timing belt cover, and install the crankshaft pulley as described in Sections 6 and 5, but do not install the undercover panel or roadwheel.

14 Once the pulley is correctly installed, check that the single TDC groove on the pulley rim is aligned with the pointer on the lower timing belt cover, and that the camshaft sprocket marks are still positioned as described in paragraph 8. If all is well, rotate

the crankshaft through 90° in an anticlockwise direction to tension the timing belt correctly. Remove the rubber grommet from the lower timing cover to gain access to the tensioner pulley bolt, and tighten the pulley bolt to the specified torque (photos). Carry on rotating the pulley anti-clockwise until number 1 piston is back at TDC on compression, and make a final check that the sprocket marks are correctly positioned. If all is well, refit the tensioner bolt grommet to the lower cover.

15 Refit the upper timing belt cover and cylinder head cover, as described in Sections 6 and 4. Once all components are correctly installed, refit the undercover panel and roadwheel, and lower the car to the ground.

8 Timing belt tensioner and sprockets – removal, inspection and refitting

Removal

1 Firmly apply the handbrake, then jack up the front of the car and support it on axle stands. Remove the left-hand roadwheel.

2 From underneath the front of the vehicle, slacken and remove the three bolts securing the bumper flange to the body. Remove the seven bolts securing the front undercover panel to the body, and remove the panel.

3 Position number 1 cylinder at TDC on its compression stroke as described in Section 3, then proceed as described under the relevant subheading.

Camshaft sprocket – SOHC engine

4 Remove the upper timing belt cover as described in Section 6, and check that the camshaft sprocket marks are positioned as described in paragraph 8 of Section 7.

5 Remove the rubber grommet from the lower timing belt cover, to gain access to the timing belt tensioner pulley bolt, and slacken the bolt through half a turn. Using a long flat-bladed screwdriver, carefully push down on the tensioner pulley mounting plate from above, to move the pulley away from the belt and relieve the timing belt tension. Hold the pulley in this position while an assistant tightens the pulley

retaining bolt securely. **Note:** To avoid damaging the timing belt ensure the screwdriver is resting on the tensioner assembly and not the timing belt, before exerting any pressure on the screwdriver.

6 Disengage the belt from the camshaft sprocket, taking care not to twist it too sharply; use the fingers only to handle the belt. Do not rotate the crankshaft until the timing belt is refitted.

7 Slacken the camshaft sprocket retaining bolt, while holding the sprocket with Rover service tool 18G 1521 to prevent the sprocket from rotating. If this is not available, an acceptable substitute can be fabricated from two lengths of steel strip (one long, the other short) and three nuts and bolts; one nut and bolt forming the pivot of a forked tool, with the remaining two nuts and bolts at the tips of the 'forks' to engage with the sprocket spokes, as shown in photo 8.21B.

8 Remove the sprocket retaining bolt and washer, and slide the sprocket off the end of the camshaft (photo).

Camshaft sprockets – DOHC engine

9 Remove the cylinder head cover, as described in Section 4.

10 Check the camshaft sprocket marks are positioned as described in paragraph 8 of Section 7.

11 Remove the rubber grommet from the lower timing belt cover, to gain access to the

8.8 Remove the retaining bolt and washer, and slide the sprocket off the camshaft end – SOHC engine

8.11 On DOHC engines, push on the upper run of timing belt midway between camshaft pulleys to relieve timing belt tension

8.12 Using an open-ended spanner, return camshafts to their original positions, and peg them in place with a suitable tool (arrowed)

8.14A Slacken the camshaft sprocket retaining bolt while holding the camshaft with an open-ended spanner (arrowed)

8.14B Slide the sprocket off the camshaft end ...

8.14C ... and remove the Woodruff key

timing belt tensioner pulley bolt, and slacken the bolt through half a turn. To relieve the timing belt tension, press firmly down on the belt at the mid-point between the two camshaft sprockets until maximum belt free play is obtained (photo). Hold the belt in this position while an assistant tightens the pulley retaining bolt securely.

12 Using a suitable open-ended spanner fitted to the hexagonal section of the camshaft, return both shafts to their previously-noted positions (paragraph 10). Insert two suitably-sized pegs or bolts through the holes in the top of the left-hand end camshaft bearing caps and into the camshafts; this will prevent the camshafts from moving under valve spring pressure when the timing belt is removed (photo).

13 Disengage the belt from the camshaft sprockets, taking care not to twist it too sharply; use the fingers only to handle the belt. **Do not** rotate the crankshaft until the timing belt is refitted.

14 Using a suitable open-ended spanner fitted to the hexagonal section of the camshaft, hold the camshaft and slacken the camshaft sprocket retaining bolt. Remove the bolt and washer, and slide the sprocket off the camshaft end. Remove the Woodruff key from the camshaft groove, and store it with the sprocket for safe keeping (photos). If required, repeat the procedure for the remaining sprocket.

Crankshaft sprocket

15 Remove the timing belt, as described in Section 7.

16 Slide the crankshaft sprocket off the end of the crankshaft and, if necessary, remove the inner timing belt guide, noting that it is fitted with its concave surface facing inwards (towards the engine) (photos).

Tensioner assembly

17 Remove the timing belt, as described in Section 7.

18 Slacken and remove the pulley retaining bolt, then unhook the tensioner spring from its pillar bolt, and slide the tensioner assembly off its locating stud.

Inspection

19 Clean thoroughly the camshaft/crankshaft sprockets, and renew any that show signs of wear, damage or cracks.

20 Clean the tensioner assembly, but do not use any strong solvent which may enter the pulley bearing. Check that the pulley rotates freely, with no sign of stiffness or of free play. Renew the assembly if there is any doubt about its condition, or if there are any obvious signs of wear or damage; the same applies to the tensioner spring, which should be checked with great care, as its condition is critical for the correct tensioning of the timing belt.

Refitting

Camshaft sprocket – SOHC engine

21 Refit the sprocket to the camshaft end, so that its timing marks are facing outwards, and install the retaining bolt and washer. Tighten the camshaft sprocket retaining bolt to the specified torque while using the method employed on removal to retain the sprocket (photos).

22 Ensure the TDC notch on the crankshaft pulley is still aligned with the pointer on the lower timing belt cover, then position the camshaft sprocket so the timing marks are as described in paragraph 8 of Section 7.

23 Fit the timing belt over the camshaft sprocket, ensuring that the belt front run is

8.16A Remove the crankshaft sprocket ...

8.16B ... and slide off the inner timing belt guide plate, noting which way around it is fitted

2

8.21A Refit the camshaft sprocket ...

8.21B ... and tighten the sprocket retaining bolt to the specified torque (fabricated sprocket holding tool shown in use)

8.27 Refit the Woodruff key to the camshaft, and slide the sprocket into position DOHC engine

taut (ie, all slack is on the tensioner pulley side of the belt). Do not twist the belt sharply while refitting it. Ensure that the belt teeth are correctly seated centrally in the sprockets, and that the timing marks remain in alignment.

24 Slacken the tensioner pulley retaining bolt, and check that the tensioner pulley moves to tension the belt; if the tensioner assembly is not free to move under spring tension, rectify the fault, or the timing belt will not be correctly tensioned.

25 If all is well, rotate the crankshaft through 90° in an anti-clockwise direction to tension the timing belt correctly, then tighten the tensioner pulley bolt to the specified torque. Carry on rotating the pulley anti-clockwise until number 1 piston is back at TDC on compression, and make a final check that the sprocket marks are correctly positioned. If all is well, refit the tensioner bolt grommet to the lower cover.

26 Refit the upper timing belt cover and cylinder head cover, as described in Sections 6 and 4. Once all components are correctly installed, refit the undercover panel and roadwheel, and lower the car to the ground.

Camshaft sprockets – DOHC engine

27 Refit the Woodruff key to the groove in the camshaft, then slide the sprocket onto the camshaft (photo), ensuring that the sprocket markings are facing outwards. Refit the sprocket retaining bolt and washer, and

tighten it to the specified torque while holding the camshaft with an open-ended spanner.

28 Check that the crankshaft pulley TDC notch is still aligned with pointer on the lower timing belt cover, then fit the timing belt over the camshaft sprockets. Ensure that the belt front and top runs are taut (ie, all slack is on the tensioner pulley side of the belt). Do not twist the belt sharply while refitting it. Ensure that the belt teeth are correctly seated centrally in the sprockets, and that the timing marks remain in alignment.

29 Slacken the tensioner pulley retaining bolt, and check that the tensioner pulley moves to tension the belt; if the tensioner assembly is not free to move under spring tension, rectify the fault, or the timing belt will not be correctly tensioned. Check that the crankshaft pulley notch is correctly aligned, then remove the locating pins or bolts from the camshaft bearing caps.

30 Rotate the crankshaft through 90° in an anti-clockwise direction to tension the timing belt correctly, then tighten the tensioner pulley bolt to the specified torque. Carry on rotating the pulley anti-clockwise until number 1 piston is back at TDC on compression, and make a final check that the sprocket marks are correctly positioned. If all is well, refit the tensioner bolt grommet to the lower cover.

31 Refit the cylinder head and upper timing belt cover as described in Section 4, then refit the undercover panel and roadwheel, and lower the car to the ground.

Crankshaft sprocket

32 Fit the inner timing belt guide onto the crankshaft, ensuring that its concave surface is facing inwards (towards the engine). Offer up the crankshaft sprocket, ensuring that its timing mark is facing outwards, then align the sprocket key with the crankshaft groove, and slide the sprocket into position.

33 Refit the timing belt, as described in Section 7.

Tensioner assembly

34 Align the hole in the tensioner backplate with its locating stud, and slide the tensioner assembly into position. Hook the spring over its pillar bolt, and refit the tensioner pulley bolt. Pull the pulley fully downwards, and tighten its retaining bolt securely to hold it in this position (photos).

35 Refit the timing belt, as described in Section 7.

9 Camshaft oil seal(s) – renewal

Note: If an oil seal is to be renewed with the timing belt still in place, check first that the belt is free from oil contamination (renew the belt as a matter of course if signs of oil contamination are found; see Section 7). Cover the belt to protect it from contamination by oil while work is in progress, and ensure that all traces of oil are removed from the area before the belt is refitted.

1 Remove the camshaft sprocket, as described in Section 8.

2 Punch or drill two small holes opposite each other in the oil seal. Screw a self-tapping screw into each, and pull on the screws with pliers to extract the seal.

3 Clean the seal housing, and polish off any burrs or raised edges which may have caused the seal to fail in the first place.

4 Lubricate the lips of the new seal with clean engine oil, and drive it into position until it seats on its locating shoulder, using a suitable tubular drift (such as a socket) which bears only on the hard outer edge of the seal (photo). Take care not to damage the seal lips during

8.34A On refitting, ensure hole in tensioner backplate is correctly engaged with its locating stud (arrowed) ...

8.34B ... and spring is correctly located on its pillar bolt (arrowed)

9.4 Fitting a camshaft oil seal (DOHC engine shown)

10.6 On SOHC engines, remove the camshaft bearing cap/rocker arm assembly ...

10.7 ... and lift out the camshaft

fitting; note that the seal lips should face inwards. On DOHC engines, if necessary, repeat the above procedure for the remaining oil seal.

5 Refit the camshaft sprocket(s), as described in Section 8.

10 Camshaft(s) and rocker arms – removal, inspection and refitting

Removal

SOHC engine

1 Remove the distributor, as described in Chapter 5.

2 Remove the camshaft sprocket, as described in Section 8.

3 Slacken all the rocker arm adjusting screw locknuts, then unscrew the adjusting screws until all valve spring pressure has been relieved from the camshaft.

4 Set up a dial gauge on one end of the camshaft, and measure the camshaft endfloat

while moving the camshaft to and fro. If the endfloat exceeds the specified service limit, expert advice should be sought from a Rover dealer or an engine repair specialist.

5 Working in a reverse of the tightening sequence (Fig. 2.5), evenly and progressively slacken the sixteen camshaft bearing cap retaining bolts. **Note:** *Fully unscrew all the bolts from the cylinder head, but do not remove any bolts from the bearing caps.* There is no need to disturb the distributor bearing cap on the right-hand end of the cylinder head.

6 Lift the camshaft bearing cap/rocker arm assembly clear of the cylinder head, ensuring that all retaining bolts remain in position in the caps (photo). Remove the O-rings from the underside of the bearing caps, and discard them; new ones **must** be used on refitting. Note the correct fitted positions of bearing cap locating dowels, and remove any that are loose.

7 Lift the camshaft out of the cylinder head (photo), and discard the oil seal; a new one must be used on refitting.

8 If necessary, the camshaft bearing cap/rocker arm assembly can be dismantled by removing the retaining bolts one at a time, and sliding the various components off the end of the shafts (photos). Keeping all components in their correct fitted order, make a note of each component's correct fitted position as it is removed, to ensure it is positioned correctly on reassembly. Note that each bearing cap has an identification number, 1 to 6, cast onto its upper surface, and each rocker arm has an identification letter, A or B, cast onto its side (see Fig. 2.4).

DOHC engine

9 Remove the distributor and cylinder position sensor housing, as described in Chapter 5.

10 Remove the camshaft sprockets, as described in Section 8.

11 Remove the locating pins or bolts from the left-hand bearing caps, then slacken all the rocker arm adjusting screw locknuts, and unscrew the adjusting screws until all valve spring pressure is relieved from the camshafts.

12 Set up a dial gauge on one end of the inlet camshaft, and measure the camshaft endfloat

Fig. 2.4 Exploded view of the rocker arms and shafts – SOHC engine (Sec 10)

1 Short inlet rocker arm shaft
2 Long inlet rocker arm shaft
3 Wave washer
4 Inlet rocker arm (B)
5 Inlet rocker arm (A)
6 Number 1 camshaft bearing cap
7 Number 2 camshaft bearing cap
8 Number 3 camshaft bearing cap
9 Number 4 camshaft bearing cap
10 Number 5 camshaft bearing cap
11 Number 6 camshaft bearing cap
12 Short exhaust rocker arm spring
13 Exhaust rocker arm (A)
14 Long exhaust rocker arm spring
15 Exhaust rocker shaft
16 Exhaust rocker arm (B)

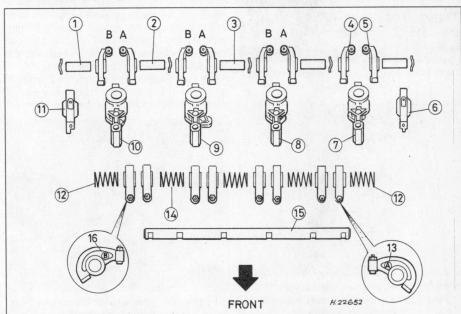

10.8A On SOHC engines, remove the camshaft bearing cap bolts ...

10.8B ... and slide off the bearing caps, springs ...

10.8C ... and rocker arms, keeping all components in their correct fitted positions

while moving the camshaft to and fro. Repeat the procedure and measure the exhaust camshaft endfloat (photo). If the endfloat of either camshaft exceeds the specified service limit, expert advice should be sought from a Rover dealer or an engine repair specialist.

13 Evenly and progressively slacken all the inlet camshaft bearing cap retaining bolts, then remove the bearing caps from the cylinder head, noting the identification marks cast onto the top surface of each cap (see paragraph 33). To avoid confusion on refitting, store the retaining bolts with their relevant bearing caps. Note the locating dowels which are fitted to each cap; remove any that are loose, and store them with the bearing caps for safe keeping.

10.12 Measuring camshaft endfloat (DOHC engine shown)

1015 On DOHC engines, the camshafts are marked to avoid confusion (exhaust camshaft shown)

14 Lift the inlet camshaft out of the cylinder head, and store it with the bearing caps. Discard the camshaft oil seal; a new one **must** be used on refitting.

15 Repeating the operations in paragraphs 13 and 14, remove the exhaust camshaft and bearing caps. Note that the inlet and exhaust camshafts are not interchangeable, and must be kept separate; the shafts are marked to avoid confusion (photo).

16 Take a small box and divide it into sixteen separate compartments, or make up a cardboard template of the cylinder head. Remove each rocker arm from the cylinder head one at a time (photo), and store it in its correct fitted position in the container or template (as applicable). This is necessary to ensure that the rocker arms are refitted to their original positions on reassembly; if the rocker arms are interchanged, the rate of wear between the rocker arms and camshaft will be dramatically increased.

Inspection

17 Examine the camshaft bearing surfaces and cam lobes for signs of wear ridges and scoring. Renew the camshaft if any of these conditions are apparent. Examine the condition of the bearing surfaces both on the camshaft journals and in the cylinder head. If the head bearing surfaces are worn excessively, the cylinder head will need to be renewed.

18 If the necessary measuring equipment is available, measure the outside diameter of each camshaft journal, then bolt the camshaft

10.16 Rocker arms can simply be lifted out of the cylinder head

bearing caps onto the cylinder head and measure the inside diameter of the camshaft bearing journals. Subtract the camshaft journal outside diameter from the bearing inside diameter, and calculate the camshaft journal running clearance. Also measure the height of each cam lobe (photo). If any of the measurements exceed the wear limits given in the Specifications, renew the camshaft and/or cylinder head.

19 Support the camshaft end journals on V-blocks, and measure the run-out at the centre journal using a dial gauge. If the run-out exceeds the specified limit, the camshaft should be renewed.

20 Examine the rocker arm bearing surfaces which contact the camshaft lobes for wear ridges and scoring. Renew any rocker arms on which these conditions are apparent.

21 On SOHC engines, if the camshaft bearing cap/rocker arm assembly has been dismantled, examine the rocker arm and shaft bearing surfaces for wear ridges and scoring. If the necessary measuring equipment is available, measure the inside diameter of the rocker arm and the outside diameter of the rocker shaft at the point where the rocker pivots, and calculate the running clearance. If the clearance exceeds the figure given in the Specifications at the start of this Chapter (or if there are obvious signs of wear), the rocker arm and/or shaft must be renewed.

22 On DOHC engines, inspect the rocker arm adjusting screw pivots for signs of wear or

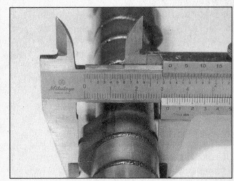

10.18 Measuring cam lobe height

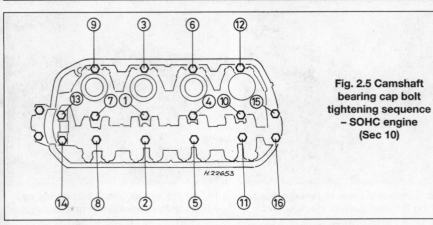

Fig. 2.5 Camshaft
bearing cap bolt
tightening sequence
– SOHC engine
(Sec 10)

H.22653

10.23A On SOHC engines, reassemble the camshaft bearing cap/rocker arm assembly using the rocker arm ...

10.23B ... and bearing cap identification marks (arrowed) to ensure components are correctly positioned

damage. If wear is found, then the adjusting screw must be renewed, along with its pivot seat, which is a screw fit in the cylinder head.

Refitting

SOHC engine

23 If the camshaft bearing cap/rocker arm assembly was dismantled, reassemble it by reversing the dismantling sequence, noting that the exhaust rocker shaft oilways must be facing downwards. If difficulties arise, refer to Fig. 2.4 and use the rocker arm and bearing cap identification marks for reference. Prior to reassembly, apply a smear of clean engine oil to the shaft and rocker arm bearing surfaces (photos).

24 Ensure the cylinder head and camshaft bearing surfaces are clean, then liberally oil the camshaft bearings and lobes, and refit the camshaft. Position the shaft so that its sprocket keyway is in the 12 o'clock position (uppermost).

25 Check that all bearing cap locating dowels are in position, and fit new O-rings to the recesses in the base of the camshaft bearing caps. Carefully refit the camshaft bearing cap/rocker arm assembly to the cylinder head, taking great care to ensure that the O-rings remain in position on the bearing caps (photo). Once the assembly is correctly seated, refit the camshaft bearing cap bolts, tightening them all by hand only.

26 Working in the sequence in Fig. 2.5,

tighten the camshaft bearing cap retaining bolts evenly and progressively to their specified torque setting.

27 Lubricate the lips of a new camshaft oil seal with clean engine oil, and drive it into position until it seats on its locating shoulder; use a suitable tubular drift (such as a socket) which bears only on the hard outer edge of the seal. Take care not to damage the seal lips during fitting; note that the seal lips should face inwards.

28 Refit the camshaft sprocket as described in Section 8, noting that the valve clearances must be adjusted as described in Chapter 1 before the upper timing belt and cylinder head covers are installed.

29 Refit the distributor, as described in Chapter 5.

DOHC engine

30 Apply a drop of oil to the rocker arm adjusting screw pivots, then refit all the rocker arms to their original locations in the cylinder head. Once installed, ensure all the rocker arm grooves are correctly engaged with the valve stem ends.

31 Ensure the cylinder head and camshaft bearing surfaces are clean, then liberally oil the camshaft bearings and lobes. Refit both the camshafts to the cylinder head, ensuring that the inlet and exhaust camshafts are not transposed, and position each shaft so that its sprocket keyway is in the 12 o'clock position (uppermost) (photo).

32 Ensure all the locating dowels are in position, and that the cylinder head and camshaft bearing cap mating surfaces are clean and dry.

33 The bearing caps are marked for identification '11' to '16', and 'E1' to 'E6'; the caps marked '1' are the inlet camshaft bearing caps, and the caps marked 'E' are the exhaust camshaft bearing caps. For both sets of caps, number 1 cap is the left-hand cap and number 6 the right-hand bearing cap (ie. bearing cap 11 is the left-hand inlet camshaft cap, and cap E6 is the right-hand exhaust camshaft cap). All caps must be installed with the arrow cast on the top of the cap (next to the

2

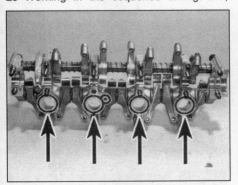

10.25 On SOHC engines, fit new O-rings (arrowed) to recesses in base of camshaft bearing caps

10.31 Refitting the exhaust camshaft – DOHC engine

10.33 Use the identification marks to ensure all camshaft bearing caps are correctly positioned on refitting

10.34A Apply a smear of sealant to mating surfaces of specified bearing caps (see text) ...

10.34B ... then refit them to cylinder head, ensuring locating dowels are in position (arrowed)

10.34C Tighten all camshaft bearing cap bolts to the specified torque setting, working in a diagonal sequence

identification mark) pointing towards the timing belt (left-hand) end of the engine (photo).

34 Apply a smear of suitable sealant to the mating surfaces of number 1 and number 6 bearing caps (both inlet and exhaust), then, using the identification marks, refit the caps and bolts to their original positions. Once all caps are correctly seated, work in a diagonal sequence, and tighten the cap retaining bolts to the specified torque setting (photos).

35 Lubricate the lips of a new inlet camshaft oil seal with clean engine oil, and drive it into position until it seats on its locating shoulder; use a suitable tubular drift (such as a socket) which bears only on the hard outer edge of the seal. Take care not to damage the seal lips during fitting; note that the seal lips should face inwards. Fit a new exhaust camshaft oil seal in the same way.

36 Using an open-ended spanner on the hexagonal section of each camshaft, position both shafts so that their sprocket keyways are in the 12 o'clock position, then insert two suitably-sized pegs or bolts through the holes in the left-hand bearing caps and into the camshafts, to hold the shafts in this position.

37 Refit the camshaft sprockets as described in Section 8, noting that the valve clearances must be adjusted as described in Chapter 1 before the cylinder head cover is installed.

38 Refit the distributor and cylinder position sensor housing, as described in Chapter 5.

11 Cylinder head – removal and refitting

Removal

1 Disconnect the battery negative terminal.

2 Drain the cooling system and remove the spark plugs, as described in Chapter 1.

3 Using a pair of pliers, release the retaining clip, and disconnect the vacuum pipe from the throttle housing end of the air intake hose. Slacken the retaining clamp which secures the intake hose to the throttle housing, and disconnect the intake hose. Working along the length of the intake hose, release the vacuum hoses from their retaining clips, then disconnect the intake hose from the air

cleaner housing, and remove it from the engine compartment.

4 Note that the following text assumes that the cylinder head will be removed with both inlet and exhaust manifolds attached; this is easier, but makes it a bulky and heavy assembly to handle. If it is wished first to remove the manifolds, proceed as described in the relevant Sections of Chapter 4.

5 On SOHC engines, remove the upper timing belt cover as described in Section 6, then disengage the timing belt from the camshaft sprocket as described in paragraphs 1 to 6 of Section 8. Remove the distributor as described in Chapter 5.

6 On DOHC engines, remove the timing belt as described in Section 7, and the camshafts and rocker arms as described in Section 10. Undo the single bolt securing the inner timing belt cover to the cylinder head, and slide the cover along the mounting bracket to free it from the cylinder head.

7 On all engines, working as described in Section 16 of Chapter 4, carry out the following operations.

(a) Depressurise the fuel system, then disconnect the outlet hose from the fuel filter and the return hose from the fuel pressure regulator.

(b) Disconnect the accelerator cable.

(c) Disconnect the kickdown cable (automatic transmission only).

(d) Disconnect the injector wiring connectors.

(e) Disconnect the PCV valve hose from the oil separator.

(f) Disconnect all the relevant coolant and vacuum hoses.

(g) Disconnect all the relevant wiring connectors.

(h) Remove the inlet manifold support bracket

8 Working as described in Section 17 of Chapter 4, carry out the following operations.

(a) Remove the intake duct.

(b) Disconnect the exhaust front pipe from the manifold.

(c) Remove the lambda sensor (catalytic converter models).

(d) Remove the exhaust manifold support bracket

9 Slacken the retaining clips, and disconnect

the heater and radiator top hose from the right-hand side of the cylinder head.

10 Disconnect the wiring connectors from the coolant temperature (TW) sensor, and the coolant temperature gauge sender unit fitted to the right-hand end of the cylinder head.

11 Working in the **reverse** of the sequence shown in photo 11.25A or 11.25B, progressively slacken the ten cylinder head bolts by half a turn at a time. Remove each bolt in turn, along with its washer, and store it in its correct fitted order by pushing it through a clearly-marked cardboard template.

12 Once all the cylinder head bolts are removed, gently rock the head to break the gasket joint. When the joint is broken, lift the cylinder head away; use assistance if possible as it is a heavy assembly, especially if it is removed complete with the manifolds. Remove the gasket and discard it. Note the fitted positions of the two locating dowels, and remove them for safe keeping if they are loose. Carefully remove the oil control jet from the rear of the cylinder block mating surface, noting which way around it is fitted, and discard its sealing O-ring; the O-ring **must** be renewed whenever it is disturbed (photo).

13 On SOHC engines, if the cylinder head is to be dismantled, remove the rocker arms and camshaft as described in Section 10.

Refitting

14 The mating faces of the cylinder head and cylinder block/crankcase must be perfectly clean before refitting the head. Use a hard plastic or wood scraper to remove all traces of gasket and carbon; also clean the piston crowns. Take particular care, as the soft aluminium alloy is easily damaged. Also, make sure that the carbon is not allowed to enter the oil and water passages – this is particularly important for the lubrication system, as carbon could block the oil supply to any of the engine's components. Using adhesive tape and paper, seal the water, oil and bolt holes in the cylinder block/crankcase.

HAYNES HINT *To prevent carbon entering the gap between the pistons and bores, smear a little grease in the gap.*

11.12 Remove the oil control jet from the cylinder block, noting which way around it is fitted

After cleaning each piston, use a small brush to remove all traces of grease and carbon from the gap, then wipe away the remainder with a clean rag. Clean all the pistons in the same way.

15 Check the mating surfaces of the cylinder block/crankcase and the cylinder head for nicks, deep scratches and other damage. If slight, they may be removed carefully with a file, but if excessive, machining may be the only alternative to renewal.

16 If warpage of the cylinder head gasket surface is suspected, use a straight-edge to check it for distortion. Refer to Part B of this Chapter for further information.

17 Clean out all the bolt holes in the block using a cloth rag and screwdriver. Make sure that all oil is removed, otherwise there is a possibility of the block being cracked by hydraulic pressure when the bolts are tightened.

18 Examine the bolt threads and the threads in the cylinder block for damage. Renew any cylinder head bolts which have damaged threads and, if necessary, use the correct-size tap to chase out the threads in the block. If it is thought likely that the head has been removed before, consider renewing all the head bolts as a matter of course.

19 Position number 1 piston at TDC, and wipe clean the mating faces of the head and block.

20 Check that the two locating dowels are in position at each end of the cylinder block/crankcase surface.

21 Fit a new O-ring to the oil control jet, then apply a smear of clean engine oil to the jet, and (ensuring it is the correct way around) fit it to the cylinder block.

22 Fit a new cylinder head gasket to the block, ensuring that all the coolant passages and oilways align correctly with those of the gasket (photo).

23 Carefully refit the cylinder head, locating it on the dowels (photo).

24 Make sure that, if the head bolts are being re-used (see paragraph 18), they are refitted in their original locations. Wash all the bolts in a suitable solvent, then wipe them dry, leaving them to dry fully before oiling and fitting. Very

Fig. 2.6 Exploded view of the cylinder head and associated components – SOHC engine (Secs 4, 9, 10 and 11)

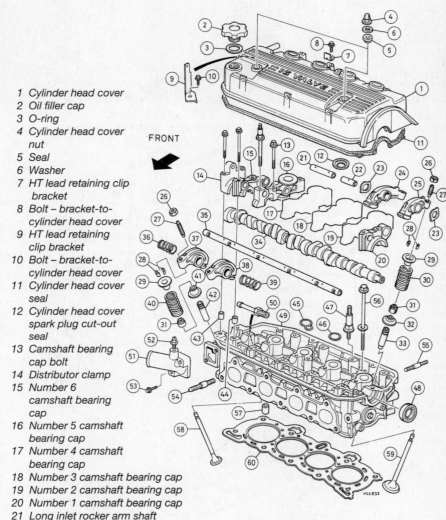

1 Cylinder head cover
2 Oil filler cap
3 O-ring
4 Cylinder head cover nut
5 Seal
6 Washer
7 HT lead retaining clip bracket
8 Bolt – bracket-to-cylinder head cover
9 HT lead retaining clip bracket
10 Bolt – bracket-to-cylinder head cover
11 Cylinder head cover seal
12 Cylinder head cover spark plug cut-out seal
13 Camshaft bearing cap bolt
14 Distributor clamp
15 Number 6 camshaft bearing cap
16 Number 5 camshaft bearing cap
17 Number 4 camshaft bearing cap
18 Number 3 camshaft bearing cap
19 Number 2 camshaft bearing cap
20 Number 1 camshaft bearing cap
21 Long inlet rocker arm shaft
22 Short inlet rocker arm shaft
23 Rocker arm wave washer
24 Inlet rocker arm (B)
25 Inlet rocker arm (A)
26 Rocker arm adjusting screw locknut
27 Rocker arm adjusting screw
28 Collets
29 Spring retainer
30 Inlet valve spring
31 Inlet valve spring seat
32 Inlet valve stem oil seal
33 Inlet valve guide
34 Camshaft
35 Exhaust rocker shaft
36 Short exhaust rocker arm spring
37 Exhaust rocker arm (B)
38 Exhaust rocker arm (A)
39 Long exhaust rocker arm spring
40 Exhaust valve spring
41 Exhaust valve stem oil seal
42 Exhaust valve guide
43 Distributor clamp dowel
44 Camshaft bearing cap dowel
45 Camshaft bearing cap O-ring
46 Camshaft bearing cap O-ring
47 Cylinder head cover stud
48 Camshaft oil seal
49 Cylinder head
50 Coolant hose adaptor union
51 Coolant top hose elbow
52 Cooling system bleed screw
53 Top hose elbow retaining bolt
54 Exhaust manifold stud
55 Inlet manifold stud
56 Cylinder head bolt
57 Cylinder head dowel
58 Exhaust valve
59 Inlet valve
60 Cylinder head gasket

Fig. 2.7 Exploded view of the cylinder head and associated components – DOHC engines (Secs 4, 9, 10 and 11)

FRONT

H25844

1 Cylinder head cover	13 Inlet camshaft	26 Inlet manifold stud
2 Cylinder head cover nut	14 Exhaust camshaft bearing cap	27 Inlet valve
3 Seal	15 Exhaust camshaft	28 Inlet valve collets
4 Oil filler cap	16 Camshaft oil seal	29 Inlet valve spring retainer
5 O-ring	17 Rocker arm adjusting screw locknut	30 Inlet valve spring
6 Accelerator cable clip	18 Rocker arm	31 Inlet valve stem oil seal
7 HT lead retaining bracket and clip	19 Rocker arm adjusting screw and pivot	32 Inlet valve spring
8 Cylinder head cover seal	20 Cylinder head bolt	33 Inlet valve guide
9 Cylinder head cover spark plug cutout seal	21 Camshaft bearing cap bolt/ cylinder head cover stud	34 Exhaust valve
10 Inlet camshaft bearing cap	22 Cylinder head	35 Exhaust valve collets
11 Camshaft bearing cap retaining bolts	23 Cylinder head gasket	36 Exhaust valve spring retainer
12 Camshaft bearing cap dowels	24 Cylinder head dowel	37 Exhaust valve spring
	25 Exhaust manifold stud	38 Exhaust valve stem oil seal
		39 Exhaust valve spring
		40 Exhaust valve guide

11.22 Ensure the locating dowels (arrowed) are in position, and fit a new cylinder head gasket

11.23 Refitting the cylinder head – SOHC engine

11.25A Cylinder head bolt tightening sequence – SOHC engine

lightly oil under the head and on the threads of each bolt, then carefully insert them into their original holes (**do not drop**) and screw them in, finger-tight only at this stage.

25 Working progressively and in the sequence shown in photo 11.25A or 11.25B (as appropriate), first tighten all the cylinder head bolts to the stage 1 torque setting given in the Specifications Section of this Chapter. Once all bolts have been tightened to the stage 1 torque, again working in the sequence shown, progressively tighten all the bolts to the stage 2 torque setting (photos).

26 Reconnect the top hose and heater hose

11.25B Cylinder head bolt tightening sequence – DOHC engine

11.25C Tighten cylinder bolts to the specified torque as described in text (SOHC engine shown)

12.5 Undo the retaining bolts (arrowed) and remove the anti-twisting bracket

to the cylinder head, and tighten their retaining clips securely. Reconnect the wiring to the coolant temperature sender and engine coolant temperature (TW) sensor.

27 Working as described in the relevant Sections of Chapter 4, connect or refit all disturbed wiring, hoses and control cable(s) to the inlet manifold and fuel system components, then adjust the throttle cable (and the kickdown cable, where necessary).

28 Working as described in Chapter 4, reconnect the exhaust system front pipe to the manifold, and refit the manifold support bracket. Refit the lambda sensor (where applicable), and refit the intake duct and hose.

29 On SOHC engines, refit the camshaft and rocker arms (if removed) as described in Chapter 10, or refit the timing belt to the camshaft sprocket as described in paragraphs 21 to 25 of Section 8. Refit the distributor as described in Chapter 5.

30 On DOHC engines, slide the inner timing belt cover into position on the cylinder head, and tighten its retaining bolt securely. Refit the rocker arms and camshafts as described in Chapter 10, and the timing belt as described in Section 7.

31 Reconnect the battery negative terminal, then refit the spark plugs and refill the cooling system as described in Chapter 1.

12 Sum – removal and refitting

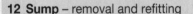

Removal

1 Disconnect the battery negative terminal.
2 Drain the engine oil, then clean and refit the engine oil drain plug, tightening it to the specified torque wrench setting. If the engine is nearing its service interval when the oil and filter are due for renewal, it is recommended that the filter is also removed and a new one fitted. After reassembly, the engine can then be replenished with fresh engine oil. Refer to Chapter 1 for further information.
3 Apply the handbrake, then jack up the front of the car and support it on axle stands.
4 Remove the exhaust front pipe, as described in Chapter 4.

5 Undo the three bolts securing the anti-twisting bracket to engine/ transmission, and remove the bracket from the underside of the cylinder block (photo).
6 Slacken and remove the flywheel/driveplate cover retaining nuts and/or bolts (as applicable), and remove the cover (photo).
7 Progressively slacken and remove all the sump retaining nuts and bolts. Break the sump joint by striking the sump with the palm of the hand, then lower the sump away from the engine and withdraw it. Remove the gasket and discard it (photos).
8 While the sump is removed, take the opportunity to unbolt the oil pump pick-

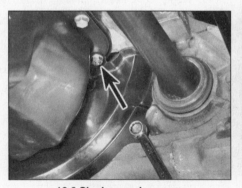

12.6 Slacken and remove flywheel/driveplate cover retaining nuts/bolts (upper nut arrowed), and remove the cover (manual gearbox shown)

12.7B ... and remove the sump from the engine

up/strainer pipe (photo), and clean it using a suitable solvent. Inspect the strainer mesh for signs of clogging or splitting, and renew if necessary.

Refitting

9 Clean all traces of gasket from the mating surfaces of the cylinder block/crankcase and sump, then use a clean rag to wipe out the sump and the engine's interior. If the oil pump pick-up/strainer pipe was removed, fit a new gasket to its end (photo) and refit the pipe, tightening its retaining nuts and bolts to their specified torque settings.
10 Apply a suitable sealant to the areas of the

12.7A Undo sump retaining nuts and bolts ...

12.8 Unbolt the oil pump pick-up pipe/strainer, and remove it from the engine, the strainer can then be easily cleaned

12.9 On refitting, use a new oil pump pick-up pipe/strainer gasket

12.10 Apply sealant to the sump and gasket upper surface on either side of the crankshaft cut-outs

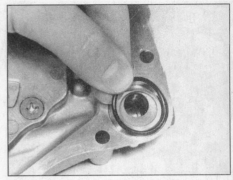

13.5 Fit a new O-ring to the oil pump recess

sump on each side of the semi-circular crankshaft cut-outs, then fit a new gasket to the sump (photo). Apply the sealant to the same areas of the gasket upper surface.

11 Offer up the sump to the cylinder block/crankcase, then refit the sump retaining nuts and bolts, noting that on models fitted with a manual gearbox, it will not be necessary to refit the two right-hand sump nuts until the flywheel cover plate is installed.

12 Working out from the centre in a diagonal sequence, progressively tighten the sump retaining nuts and bolts to their specified torque setting.

13 Refit the flywheel/driveplate cover, and tighten its retaining nuts and/ or bolts to the specified torque setting.

14 Install the anti-twisting bracket, and tighten its retaining bolts to their specified torque settings.

15 Refit the front exhaust pipe as described in Chapter 4, then lower the car to the ground and replenish the engine oil as described in Chapter 1.

13 Oil pump – removal and refitting

Removal

1 Remove the crankshaft sprocket, as described in Section 8.

2 Remove the sump and oil pump pick-up/strainer pipe, as described in Section 12.

3 Slacken and remove the four bolts securing the oil pump assembly to the cylinder block, then slide the pump off the end of the crankshaft, noting its two locating dowels. Remove the O-ring from the cylinder block and discard it; it **must** be renewed whenever it is disturbed.

Refitting

4 Remove all traces of gasket sealant from the mating surfaces of the oil pump and cylinder block, and ensure the surfaces are clean and dry.

5 Apply a thin bead of suitable sealant to the centre of the mating surface of the oil pump, and fit a new O-ring to the recess in the oil pump (photo).

13.7 Apply a thin bead of sealant to oil pump mating surface, then fit the pump to the engine, ensuring locating dowels (arrowed) are in position

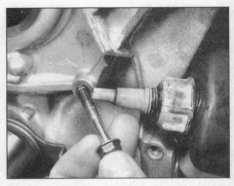

13.8 Apply thread-locking compound to oil pump bolts, and tighten them to the specified torque

6 Note that, whether the original pump is refitted or a new pump is installed, it is essential that the pump is primed before installation by injecting oil into it and turning it by hand.

7 Ensure that the locating dowels are in position, then apply a smear of oil to the lip of the pump oil seal, and locate the pump on the end of the crankshaft. Locate the pump inner gear on the crankshaft flats, and push the

pump fully into position (photo).

8 Apply a few drops of thread-locking compound to the threads of each oil pump retaining bolt, then install the bolts and progressively tighten them to the specified torque setting (photo).

9 Refit the oil pump pick-up/strainer pipe and sump as described in Section 12.

10 Remove all traces of oil, then refit the crankshaft sprocket as described in Section 8.

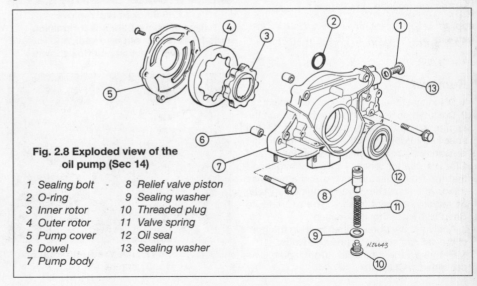

Fig. 2.8 Exploded view of the oil pump (Sec 14)

1 Sealing bolt
2 O-ring
3 Inner rotor
4 Outer rotor
5 Pump cover
6 Dowel
7 Pump body
8 Relief valve piston
9 Sealing washer
10 Threaded plug
11 Valve spring
12 Oil seal
13 Sealing washer

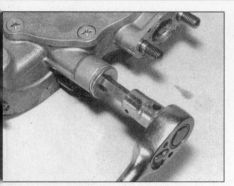

14.4A Unscrew the threaded plug ...

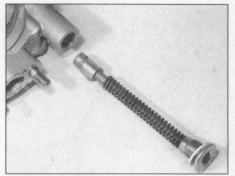

14.4B ... and withdraw the spring and oil pressure relief valve piston, noting which way around it is fitted

14.6A Measuring oil pump outer rotor-to-body clearance

14 Oil pump – dismantling, inspection and reassembly

Dismantling

1 Remove the oil pump as described in Section 13.
2 Undo the six pump cover retaining screws, and remove the cover from the pump body.
3 Using a suitable marker pen, mark the outer surface of both the inner and outer rotors, then remove them from the pump body.
4 The oil pressure relief valve can be dismantled, if required, without disturbing the pump cover. To dismantle the valve, unscrew the threaded plug, and recover the valve spring and plunger (Fig. 2.8). Discard the plug's sealing washer (photos).

Inspection

5 Inspect the rotors for obvious signs of wear or damage, and renew if necessary; if the pump body or cover plate is scored or damaged, the complete oil pump assembly must be renewed. If all appears to be well, refit the rotors to the pump, and check the following.
6 Using feeler gauge blades of the appropriate thickness, measure the clearance between the outer rotor and the pump body,

and between the tips of the inner and outer rotor lobes (photos).
7 Using feeler gauge blades and a straight-edge placed across the top of the pump body and the rotors, measure the rotor endfloat (photo).
8 If any measurement is outside the specified limits, the complete pump assembly must be renewed.
9 If the pressure relief valve plunger is scored, or if it does not slide freely in the pump body bore, the oil pump must be renewed as an assembly.
10 The oil pump oil seal should be renewed as a matter of course. The old oil seal can be carefully levered out of position using a suitable flat-bladed screw, and the new seal tapped into position using a suitable tubular drift (such as a socket) which bears only on the hard outer edge of the seal. Fit the seal with its sealing lip facing inwards, and tap it into the pump body until it seats on its locating shoulder (photos).

Reassembly

11 Lubricate the rotors with clean engine oil, and refit them to the pump body, using the marks made on dismantling to ensure they are fitted the correct way around.
12 Ensure the pump body and cover mating surfaces are clean and dry, then refit the cover. Apply a few drops of thread-locking compound

14.6B Measuring oil pump rotor tip clearance

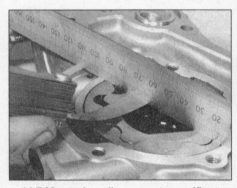

14.7 Measuring oil pump rotor endfloat

2

14.10A Carefully lever the oil pump seal out with a flat-bladed screwdriver ...

14.10B ... and tap the new one into position using a suitable tubular drift

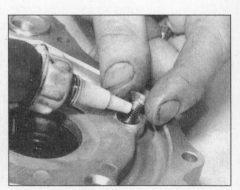

14.12 Apply thread-locking compound to the pump cover screws, and tighten them to the specified torque

16.10 Use a feeler blade to check right-hand oil seal-to-housing clearance

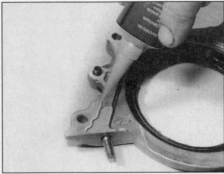

16.12 Apply sealant to the oil seal housing mating surface ...

16.13 ... and refit the housing to the engine, ensuring the locating dowels (arrowed) are correctly positioned

to the threads of each cover retaining screw, then install the screws and tighten them to the specified torque setting (photo).

13 Check that the pump rotors are free to turn smoothly, then prime the pump by injecting oil into its passages and rotating it; if the pump is not to be refitted to the engine immediately, prime it again before installation.

14 Lubricate the relief valve piston with clean engine oil, then refit the piston, ensuring that it is the correct way up (Fig. 2.8), and install the spring. Fit a new sealing washer to the threaded plug, and tighten the plug to its specified torque setting.

15 Oil cooler – removal and refitting (DOHC engines only)

Removal

1 Apply the handbrake, then jack up the front of the car and support it on axle stands.

2 Position a suitable container beneath the oil filter, then remove the filter as described in Chapter 1. If the engine is nearing its service interval when the oil and filter are due for renewal, it is recommended that the engine oil is also drained. After reassembly, the engine can then be replenished with fresh engine oil, and a new oil filter fitted. Refer to Chapter 1 for further information.

3 Either drain the cooling system as described in Chapter 1, or be prepared for some coolant spillage during the following operation. Release the retaining clips and disconnect the coolant hoses from the oil cooler. Plug both the hose ends to prevent the entry of dirt into the cooling system. Work quickly to minimise coolant loss if the system has not been drained.

4 Unscrew the oil cooler centre bolt, and remove the cooler from the rear of the cylinder block. Remove the oil cooler O-ring and discard it; it must be renewed whenever it is disturbed.

Refitting

5 Fit a new O-ring to the recess in the oil cooler, and apply a smear of clean engine oil to the O-ring.

6 Offer up the oil cooler, then refit the centre bolt and tighten it to the specified torque setting.

7 Refit the coolant hoses to the oil cooler, and secure them in position with their retaining clips. Work quickly again to minimise coolant loss if the cooling system was not drained. Top-up or refill the cooling system as described in Chapter 1.

8 Working as described in Chapter 1, fit the oil filter, then lower the car to the ground and top-up or refill (as applicable) the cooling system and engine oil.

16 Crankshaft oil seals – renewal

Left-hand oil seal

1 Remove the crankshaft sprocket, as described in Section 8.

2 Punch or drill two small holes opposite each other in the seal. Screw a self-tapping screw into each, and pull on the screws with pliers to extract the seal.

3 Clean the seal housing, and polish off any burrs or raised edges which may have caused the seal to fail in the first place.

4 Lubricate the lips of the new seal with clean engine oil, and drive it into position until it seats on its locating shoulder, using a suitable tubular drift (such as a socket) which bears only on the hard outer edge of the seal. Take care not to damage the seal lips during fitting; use either grease or a thin layer of insulating tape to protect the seal lips from the edges of the crankshaft flats, but be careful to remove all traces of tape and to lubricate the seal lips if the second method is used. Note that the seal lips should face inwards.

5 Wash off any traces of oil, then refit the crankshaft sprocket as described in Section 8.

Right-hand oil seal

Note: *Although it is possible to renew the oil seal with the housing in position on the engine, the position of the oil seal in its housing is critical. Without access to Rover special tool 18G 1485 to install the new seal it will be very*

difficult to ensure that the seal is correctly positioned. For this reason, it is recommended that the oil seal housing is removed from the engine for oil seal renewal.

6 Remove the flywheel/driveplate, as described in Section 17.

7 Remove the sump, as described in Section 12.

8 Slacken and remove the four bolts securing the oil seal housing to the cylinder block, and slide the housing off the end of the crankshaft, noting its two locating dowels.

9 Using a large flat-bladed screwdriver, carefully lever the old seal out of the housing. Clean the seal housing, and polish off any burrs or raised edges which may have caused the seal to fail in the first place.

10 Lubricate the outer edge of the new seal, and tap the seal gently into place in the housing until the chamfer of the seal outer surface is correctly lined up with the inner chamfer of the oil seal housing. Note that its

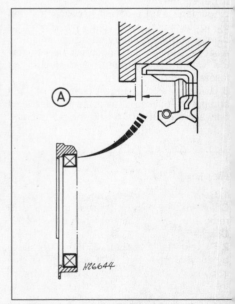

Fig. 2.9 Crankshaft right-hand oil seal installation – ensure gap 'A' between seal inner edge and cover is 0.2 to 0.5 mm (Sec 16)

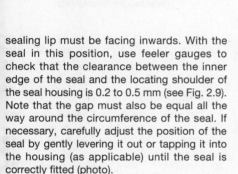

17.4 Removing the flywheel

17.5 Tap flywheel centre bearing into position using a hammer and suitable tubular drift

17.8 Use fabricated tool as shown (arrowed) to lock flywheel/driveplate while slackening or tightening the retaining bolts

sealing lip must be facing inwards. With the seal in this position, use feeler gauges to check that the clearance between the inner edge of the seal and the locating shoulder of the seal housing is 0.2 to 0.5 mm (see Fig. 2.9). Note that the gap must also be equal all the way around the circumference of the seal. If necessary, carefully adjust the position of the seal by gently levering it out or tapping it into the housing (as applicable) until the seal is correctly fitted (photo).

11 Remove all traces of sealant from the cylinder block and housing mating surfaces, and ensure the surfaces are clean and dry.

12 Apply a thin coating of a suitable sealant to the housing mating surface (photo), and lubricate the oil seal lip with a smear of engine oil.

13 Check that the locating dowels are in position, then carefully ease the oil seal housing over the crankshaft end, and push it fully into position on the cylinder block. Refit the housing retaining bolts, and tighten them to the specified torque setting (photo).

14 Refit the sump as described in Chapter 12.

15 Refit the flywheel/driveplate as described in Section 17.

17 Flywheel/driveplate –
removal, inspection and refitting

Removal

1 Remove the transmission, as described in Chapter 7. On manual gearbox models, also remove the clutch assembly, as described in Chapter 6.

2 Prevent the flywheel/driveplate from turning by locking the ring gear teeth as shown in photo 17.8, or by bolting a strap between the flywheel and the cylinder block/crank-case.

3 Mark the relationship between the flywheel/driveplate and crankshaft, then slacken and remove the flywheel/driveplate retaining bolts. On automatic transmission

models, also remove the driveplate retaining bolt spacer.

4 Remove the flywheel/driveplate (photo). Do not drop it – it is very heavy.

Inspection

5 On manual gearbox models, examine the flywheel for scoring of the clutch face, and for wear or chipping of the ring gear teeth. If the clutch face is scored, the flywheel may be machined until flat, but renewal is preferable. If the ring gear is worn or damaged, the flywheel must be renewed, as it is not possible to renew the ring gear separately. Inspect the centre bearing for signs of free play, and check that its inner race rotates smoothly without any sign of roughness. If necessary, the bearing can be renewed individually; the old bearing can be drifted out of position and the new one tapped into place using a suitable tubular drift (such as a socket) which bears only on the bearings outer race (photo).

6 On automatic transmission models, check the torque converter driveplate carefully for signs of distortion, and for any hairline cracks around the bolt holes or radiating outwards from the centre. Inspect the ring gear teeth for signs of wear or chipping. If any sign of wear or damage is found, the driveplate must be renewed.

Refitting

7 Ensure the mating surfaces of the flywheel/driveplate and crankshaft are clean, then refit the flywheel/driveplate, using the marks made on removal to ensure it is correctly positioned.

8 Refit the flywheel retaining bolts or the driveplate retaining bolts and spacer (as applicable), tightening them to the specified torque setting while using the method employed on dismantling to retain the flywheel/ driveplate (photo).

9 Refit the clutch (manual gearbox) as described in Chapter 6, then remove the locking tool and refit the transmission as described in Chapter 7.

18 Engine/transmission mountings –
inspection and renewal

Inspection

1 If improved access is required, raise the front of the car and support it securely on axle stands.

2 Check the mounting rubber to see if it is cracked, hardened or separated from the metal at any point; renew the mounting if any such damage or deterioration is evident.

3 Check that all the mounting s fasteners are securely tightened; use a torque wrench to check if possible.

4 Using a large screwdriver or a pry bar, check for wear in the mounting by carefully levering against it to check for free play; where this is not possible, enlist the aid of an assistant to move the engine/transmission unit back and forth, or from side to side, while you watch the mounting. While some free play is to be expected even from new components, excessive wear should be obvious. If excessive free play is found, check first that the fasteners are correctly secured, then renew any worn components as described below.

Renewal

Right-hand mounting

5 Disconnect the battery negative terminal. Firmly apply the handbrake, then jack up the front of the car and support it on axle stands.

6 To improve access to the mounting, using a pair of pliers, release the retaining clip, then disconnect the vacuum pipe from the throttle housing end of the air intake hose. Slacken the retaining clamp which secures the intake hose to the throttle housing, and disconnect the intake hose. Working along the length of the intake hose, release the vacuum hoses from their retaining clips, then disconnect the intake hose from the air cleaner housing, and remove it from the engine compartment.

7 Support the weight of the engine/ transmission using a trolley jack, with a

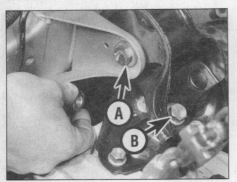

18.7A Slacken and remove the right-hand mounting through-bolt (A) and mounting-to-mounting plate bolt (B) ...

18.7B ... and the two mounting plate retaining nuts (viewed from underneath)

18.7C Right-hand mounting plate is retained by three bolts

wooden spacer to prevent damage to the sump, then slacken and remove the mounting through-bolt. Undo the two nuts (accessed from underneath) and the single bolt which secure the mounting to its mounting plate, then lower the engine/ transmission slightly and remove the mounting. If necessary, undo the three mounting plate retaining bolts, and remove the plate from the top of the transmission (photos).

8 Check all components for signs of wear or damage, and renew as necessary.

9 On reassembly, refit the mounting plate (where removed) to the top of the transmission, and tighten its retaining bolts to the specified torque setting. Refit the mounting to the mounting plate and tighten its retaining nuts and bolt to the specified torque.

10 Using the trolley jack to position the engine/transmission unit at the correct height, then refit the through-bolt and tighten it to the specified torque setting.

11 Remove the trolley jack from underneath the car, and lower the car to the ground.

12 Refit the air intake hose, and securely tighten its retaining clamp. Ensure the vacuum pipe and hoses are properly routed and retained by all the necessary clips. Reconnect the battery.

Left-hand mounting

13 Disconnect the battery negative terminal.

14 Support the weight of the engine/transmission using a trolley jack, with a wooden spacer to prevent damage to the sump. Slacken and remove the mounting through-bolt, then undo the nut and bolt securing the mounting to its engine mounting bracket (photo), and remove the mounting from the car.

15 To dismantle the engine mounting bracket, first remove the lower timing belt cover as described in Section 6. The bracket assembly can then be unbolted from the cylinder block.

16 Check all components for signs of wear or damage, and renew as necessary.

17 On reassembly, refit the engine mounting bracket assembly (if removed), tightening all its fasteners to the specified torque, and refit the timing belt covers as described in Section 6.

18 Manoeuvre the mounting into position, then refit its retaining nut and bolt, and tighten them to the specified torque setting.

19 Use the trolley jack to raise the engine to the correct height, then refit the mounting through-bolt, tightening it to the specified torque setting.

20 Lower the car to the ground, then remove the trolley jack and reconnect the battery.

Rear mounting

21 Disconnect the battery negative terminal, then apply the handbrake, then jack up the front of the car and support it securely on axle stands.

22 Support the weight of the engine/transmission using a trolley jack, with a wooden spacer to prevent damage to the transmission casing, then slacken and remove the three bolts securing the rear mounting bracket to the transmission. Undo the mounting through-bolt, and manoeuvre the mounting bracket out of position (photos).

23 Undo the three bolts securing the mounting to the rear crossmember, and remove the mounting from the car.

24 Check all components for signs of wear or damage, and renew as necessary.

25 On reassembly, fit the mounting to the crossmember, and tighten its retaining bolts to the specified torque.

26 Manoeuvre the mounting bracket into position, then install the through-bolt, tightening it by hand only. Refit the three mounting bracket-to-transmission bolts, tighten them to the specified torque, then

18.14 Left-hand mounting through-bolt (A), and mounting retaining nut and bolt (B)

18.22A Slacken and remove the three bolts securing the rear mounting to the transmission (arrowed} ...

18.22B ... then undo the mounting through-bolt and withdraw the mounting bracket (manual gearbox model shown)

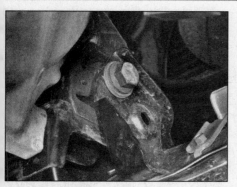

18.30 Front engine/transmission mounting viewed from underneath

tighten the mounting through-bolt to the specified torque.

27 Lower the car to the ground, and reconnect the battery.

Front mounting

28 Disconnect the battery negative terminal. With the handbrake firmly applied, jack up the front of the car and support it securely on axle stands.

29 From underneath the front of the vehicle, slacken and remove the three bolts securing the bumper flange to the body. Remove the seven bolts securing the front undercover panel to the body, and remove the panel.

30 Support the weight of the engine/

transmission using a trolley jack, with a wooden spacer to prevent damage to the transmission casing, then slacken and remove the front mounting through-bolt. Undo the two bolts securing the mounting to the cylinder block, and remove it from under the car (photo).

31 Check the mounting for signs of wear or deterioration, and renew if necessary.

32 Offer up the mounting, then refit the two bolts which secure it to the cylinder block, and tighten them to the specified torque. Install the through- bolt, tightening it to the specified torque setting.

33 Refit the undercover panel, then lower the car to the ground and reconnect the battery.

Part B: Engine removal and general overhaul procedures

19 General information

Included in this part of Chapter 2 are details of removing the engine/ transmission unit from the car, and general overhaul procedures for the cylinder head, cylinder block/crankcase and all other engine internal components.

The information given ranges from advice concerning preparation for an overhaul and the purchase of replacement parts, to detailed step-by-step procedures covering removal, inspection, renovation and refitting of engine internal components.

After Section 23, all instructions are based on the assumption that the engine has been removed from the car. For information concerning in-car engine repair, as well as the removal and refitting of those external components necessary for full overhaul, refer to Part A of this Chapter and to Section 23. Ignore any preliminary dismantling operations described in Part A that are no longer relevant once the engine has been removed from the car.

All specifications relating to engine overhaul are at the beginning of this Chapter.

20 Engine overhaul – general information

It is not always easy to determine when, or if, an engine should be completely overhauled, as a number of factors must be considered.

High mileage is not necessarily an indication that an overhaul is needed, while low mileage does not preclude the need for an overhaul. Frequency of servicing is probably the most important consideration; an engine which has had regular and frequent oil and filter changes, as well as other required maintenance, should give many thousands of miles of reliable service. Conversely, a neglected engine may require an overhaul very early in its life.

Excessive oil consumption is an indication that piston rings, valve seals and/or valve

guides are in need of attention. Make sure that oil leaks are not responsible before deciding that the rings and/or guides are worn. Perform a compression test, as described in Section 2, to determine the likely cause of the problem.

Check the oil pressure with a gauge fitted in place of the oil pressure switch and compare it with that specified. If it is extremely low, the main and big-end bearings and/or the oil pump are probably worn out.

Loss of power, rough running, knocking or metallic engine noises, excessive valve gear noise and high fuel consumption may also point to the need for an overhaul, especially if they are all present at the same time. If a complete service does not remedy the situation, major mechanical work is the only solution.

An engine overhaul involves restoring all internal parts to the specification of a new engine. During an overhaul, the pistons and the piston rings are renewed and, if necessary, the cylinder block is rebored. New main and big-end bearings are generally fitted and if necessary, the crankshaft may be renewed to restore the journals. The valves are also serviced as well, since they are usually in less-than-perfect condition at this point. While the engine is being overhauled, other components, such as the distributor, starter and alternator, can be overhauled as well. The end result should be an as-new engine that will give many trouble-free miles. **Note:** *Critical cooling system components such as the hoses, thermostat and water pump should be renewed when an engine is overhauled. The radiator should be checked carefully to ensure that it is not clogged or leaking. Also, it is a good idea to renew the oil pump whenever the engine is overhauled.*

Before beginning the engine overhaul, read through the entire procedure to familiarize yourself with the scope and requirements of the job. Overhauling an engine is not difficult if you follow carefully all of the instructions, have the necessary tools and equipment, and pay close attention to all specifications; however, it can be time-consuming. Plan on the car being

off the road for a minimum of two weeks, especially if parts must be taken to an engineering works for repair or reconditioning. Check on the availability of parts, and make sure that any necessary special tools and equipment are obtained in advance. Most work can be done with typical hand tools, although a number of precision measuring tools are required for inspecting parts to determine if they must be renewed. Often the engineering works will handle the inspection of parts, and offer advice concerning reconditioning and renewal. **Note:** *Always wait until the engine has been completely dismantled, and all components, especially the cylinder block/crankcase, the cylinder liners and the crankshaft have been inspected before deciding what service and repair operations must be performed by an engineering works. Since the condition of these components will be the major factor to consider when determining whether to overhaul the original engine or buy a reconditioned unit, do not purchase parts or have overhaul work done on other components until they have been thoroughly inspected. As a general rule, time is the primary cost of an overhaul, so it does not pay to fit worn or substandard parts.*

As a final note, to ensure maximum life and minimum trouble from a reconditioned engine, everything must be assembled with care, in a spotlessly-clean environment.

21 Engine/transmission removal – methods and precautions

If you have decided that the engine must be removed for overhaul or major repair work, several preliminary steps should be taken.

Locating a suitable place to work is extremely important. Adequate work space, along with storage space for the car, will be needed. If a shop or garage is not available, at the very least a flat, level, clean work surface is required.

Cleaning the engine compartment and engine/transmission before beginning the

Fig. 2.10 Exploded view of the engine bottom end (Sec 19)

1 Oil pump housing
2 Oil pump inner rotor
3 Oil pump outer rotor
4 Oil pump cover
5 Oil pump dowel
6 Bolt – oil pump-to-cylinder block
7 O-ring
8 Sealing bolt
9 Sealing washer
10 Crankshaft left-hand oil seal
11 Oil pump relief valve piston
12 Oil pump relief valve spring
13 Sealing washer
14 Threaded plug
15 Stud
16 Gasket – oil pump- to-pick-up/strainer
17 Oil pick-up/strainer pipe
18 Nut – pick-up/strainer pipe-to-oil pump
19 Bolt – pick-up/strainer pipe-to-main
   bearing bridge
20 Water pump
21 Dowel
22 O-ring
23 Bolt – water pump-to-cylinder block
24 O-ring
25 Coolant pipe – thermostat housing-to-
   water pump
26 O-ring
27 Thermostat housing
28 Bolt – thermostat housing-to-cylinder
   block
29 Bolt – thermostat housing-to-cylinder
   block
30 Thermostat
31 Thermostat seal
32 Thermostat housing cover
33 Bolt – thermostat cover-to-housing
34 Cylinder block
35 Oil control jet
36 O-ring
37 Breather cover plate
38 Bolt – breather cover plate-to-cylinder
   block
39 Coolant drain plug
40 Sealing washer
41 Right-hand crankshaft oil seal housing
42 Stud
43 Bolt – oil seal housing-to-cylinder block
44 Right-hand crankshaft oil seal
45 Piston and connecting rod assembly
46 Top compression ring
47 Second compression ring
48 Oil control ring
49 Connecting rod big-end cap bolt
50 Connecting rod big-end bearing shell
51 Connecting rod big-end bearing cap
52 Connecting rod big-end bearing cap nut
53 Crankshaft
54 Crankshaft main bearing shell
55 Crankshaft thrustwashers
56 Flywheel/driveplate
57 Bolt flywheel/driveplate-to-crankshaft
58 Main bearing caps

59 Main bearing cap bridge
60 Dowel
61 Dowel
62 Dowel
63 Dowel
64 O-ring
65 Threaded plug
66 Threaded plug
67 Main bearing cap bolt
68 Main bearing cap bolt
69 Dipstick tube
70 Dipstick
71 Sump gasket

72 Sump
73 Stud
74 Nut – sump-to-cylinder block
75 Bolt – sump-to-cylinder block
76 Sump drain plug
77 Sealing washer
78 Oil separator
79 O-ring
80 Bolt oil separator-to-cylinder block
81 Oil cooler – DOHC engine only
82 Oil cooler centre bolt – DOHC engine only
83 O-ring – DOHC engine only
84 Oil filter

FRONT

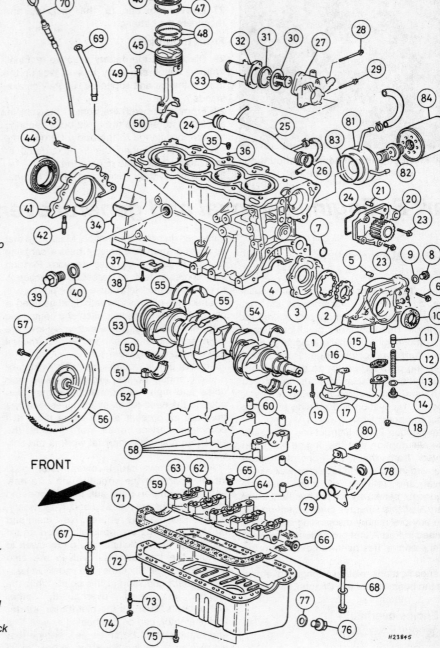

H23845

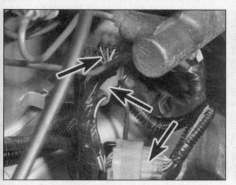

22.11A Release the three engine harness wiring connectors from their mounting bracket in right-hand corner of the engine compartment ...

22.11B ... and disconnect them from the main loom

22.12 Undo the retaining screw, and disconnect the battery lead to the fusebox terminal

removal procedure will help keep tools clean and organized.

An engine hoist or A-frame will also be necessary. Make sure the equipment is rated well in excess of the combined weight of the engine and transmission (350 lb/160 kg approximately). Safety is of primary importance, considering the potential hazards involved in lifting the engine/transmission out of the car.

If the engine/transmission is being removed by a novice, a helper should be available. Advice and aid from someone more experienced would also be helpful. There are many instances when one person cannot simultaneously perform all of the operations required when lifting the engine out of the car.

Plan the operation ahead of time. Before starting work, arrange for the hire of (or obtain) all of the tools and equipment you will need. Some of the items necessary to perform engine/transmission removal and installation safely and with relative ease are (in addition to an engine hoist) a heavy-duty trolley jack, a complete set of spanners and sockets as described in the front of this manual, wooden blocks, and plenty of rags and cleaning solvent for mopping-up spilled oil, coolant and fuel. If the hoist must be hired, make sure that you arrange for it in advance, and perform all of the operations possible without it

beforehand. This will save you money and time.

Plan for the car to be out of use for quite a while. An engineering works will be required to perform some of the work which the do-it-yourselfer cannot accomplish without special equipment. These places often have a busy schedule, so it would be a good idea to consult them before removing the engine in order to accurately estimate the amount of time required to rebuild or repair components that may need work.

Always be extremely careful when removing and refitting the engine/transmission. Serious injury can result from careless actions. Plan ahead and take your time, and a job of this nature, although major, can be accomplished successfully.

22 Engine/transmission – removal and refitting

Removal

Note: *The engine can be removed from the car only as a complete unit with the transmission; the two are then separated for overhaul.*
1 Park the vehicle on firm, level ground, then remove the bonnet as described in Chapter 11.
2 If the engine is to be dismantled, working as described in Chapter 1, drain the oil and

remove the oil filter, then clean and refit the drain plug, tightening it to its specified torque setting.
3 Firmly apply the handbrake, then jack up the front of the car and support it securely on axle stands. Remove both front roadwheels.
4 From underneath the front of the vehicle, slacken and remove the three bolts securing the bumper flange to the body. Remove the seven bolts securing the front undercover panel to the body, and remove the panel.
5 Drain the transmission oil, as described in Chapter 1, then clean and refit the drain plug, tightening it to its specified torque setting.
6 Drain the cooling system as described in Chapter 1.
7 Working as described in Chapter 12, remove the battery, battery tray and support bracket.
8 Slacken and remove the two bolts securing the intake duct to the bonnet locking platform, and release the expansion tank hose from its duct retaining clips. Disconnect the duct from the intake hose, then free its lower retaining clip from the radiator, and remove the duct from the engine compartment.
9 Remove the starter motor, as described in Chapter 12.
10 Remove the distributor, as described in Chapter 5.
11 Trace the engine wiring harness back from the engine to the right-hand corner of the engine compartment, and undo the bolt securing the harness retaining clip to the body. Disconnect the three engine harness wiring connectors, and release them from the mounting bracket so that the engine harness is free to be removed with the engine/transmission unit (photos).
12 Unclip the engine compartment fusebox lid, and remove the fusible link cover plate. Slacken and remove the screw which secures the battery lead to the fusebox terminal, and remove the lead from the underside of the box. Refit the screw loosely to the fusebox terminal for safe keeping (photo).
13 Undo the retaining screw, and free the earth lead from the bonnet locking platform.
14 Working as described in Chapter 4, depressurise the fuel system, then unscrew

22.14A Slacken the union bolt, and disconnect the outlet hose from the fuel filter. Note sealing washers (arrowed)

22.14B Release the retaining clip, and disconnect the return hose from the fuel pressure regulator

2

the fuel filter outlet union bolt and disconnect the outlet hose from the filter; discard the union sealing washers, as they **must** be renewed whenever they are disturbed. Using pliers, release its retaining clip, then disconnect the return hose from the base of the fuel pressure regulator (photos). Plug all fuel unions, to minimise the loss of fuel and prevent the entry of dirt into the fuel system.

15 Disconnect the accelerator cable from the throttle housing, as described in Chapter 4. Free the cable from all of its retaining clips, and place it clear of the engine/transmission unit so that it will not hinder the removal process.

16 On SOHC engine models with power steering, undo the bolt securing the power steering pump hose retaining bracket to the pump, and remove the bracket. Undo the three pump mounting bolts, then disengage the drivebelt from the pump pulley and remove it from the engine. Release the hoses from any retaining clips, and place the pump clear of the engine.

17 On DOHC engines with power steering, where necessary, slacken and remove the bolt securing the air conditioning pipe to the pump mounting bracket. Unscrew the pump adjusting bolt, then slacken and remove the pump mounting bolts and remove the power steering pump drivebelt. Release the pump hoses from any retaining clips, and place the pump clear of the engine.

18 On all models with air conditioning, slacken the drivebelt adjuster (idler) pulley centre bolt, then slacken the adjuster bolt until the drivebelt can be slipped off the pulleys and removed. Undo the four bolts securing the air conditioning compressor to the engine, then place the compressor clear of the engine, tying it to the body so that it will not hinder engine/transmission removal.

19 On manual gearbox models, slide the gearbox selector shaft gaiter towards the gearbox, then remove the roll pin retaining clip from the gearbox end of the gearchange selector rod. Using a hammer and suitable punch, tap the roll pin out of the selector rod, and disconnect the rod from the gearbox. Slacken and remove the bolt which secures the steady rod to its gearbox mounting bracket, and free the rod from the bracket. Turn the clutch cable adjusting nut anti-clockwise to obtain maximum clutch cable free play, then raise the gearbox clutch release lever and disconnect the cable from the lever. Free the cable from its bracket, and place it clear of the gearbox.

20 On automatic transmission models, disconnect the selector cable from the transmission as described in Section 12 of Chapter 7. Disconnect the wiring connector from the transmission lock-up control solenoid, which is situated on the top surface of the transmission. Where necessary, slacken the two fluid cooler hose retaining clips, and disconnect both hoses from the transmission. Plug both the hose and transmission pipe

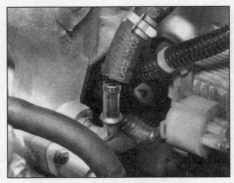

22.23 Disconnect the braking system vacuum servo hose from the manifold

ends to prevent the entry of dirt into the hydraulic system.

21 On all models, remove the gaiter from the lower end of the speedometer cable, and slide the gaiter up the cable. Carefully remove the cable retaining clip, and withdraw the cable from the drivegear housing.

22 Working as described in Chapter 4, remove the exhaust front pipe and (where fitted) the lambda sensor.

23 Disconnect the resonator vacuum hose from the manifold, and the MAP sensor vacuum hose from the top of the throttle housing. Using pliers, release the retaining clip, and disconnect the brake vacuum servo unit hose from the left-hand side of the inlet manifold (photo).

24 Trace the engine wiring harness back to the injector resistor pack, which is mounted onto the left-hand side of the engine compartment bulkhead, and disconnect the two wiring connectors. Free the engine harness from any relevant retaining clips or ties, so that it is free to be removed with the engine/transmission unit.

25 Slacken the retaining clips, and disconnect the heater hose and the radiator top hose from the right-hand end of the cylinder head.

26 Slacken and remove the bolt and washer securing the anti-roll bar connecting link to the right-hand lower suspension arm, and the two bolts securing the tie-bar to the lower suspension arm.

27 Extract the split pins, and undo the nuts securing the steering gear track rod end balljoint and the right-hand lower suspension arm balljoint to the swivel hub. Remove the nuts, and release the balljoint tapered shanks using a universal balljoint separator.

28 Insert a suitable flat bar between the right-hand inner constant velocity joint and transmission housing, then carefully lever the joint out of position, taking great care not to damage the transmission housing.

29 Withdraw the right-hand inner constant velocity joint from the transmission, and support the driveshaft to avoid damaging the constant velocity joints or gaiters.

30 Repeating the operations described in paragraphs 26 to 29, disengage the left-driveshaft from the intermediate shaft.

22.38 Lifting out the engine/transmission unit (SOHC engine shown)

31 The cylinder head has a tapped hole provided at the left-hand rear end. Using a suitable 10 mm bolt, attach a lifting bracket to the cylinder head at this point, noting that a suitable spacer of approximately 20 mm in length should be positioned between the lifting bracket and the cylinder head; the spacer will prevent the lifting chains contacting the cylinder head cover as the engine is lifted. The second lifting bracket is already installed on the top surface of the transmission. Attach the lifting chains to the brackets, then take the weight of the engine/transmission on the hoist while checking that the chains do not come into contact with any other components.

32 Slacken and remove the two bolts securing the front mounting bracket to the engine/transmission unit. **Note:** *Do not slacken the mounting through-bolt, as the mounting is stepped and, if left in its original position, is very useful to use as an alignment point when lowering the engine/ transmission unit back into the car.*

33 On manual gearbox models, undo the three bolts which secure the rear mounting bracket to the engine/transmission unit. Slacken and remove the mounting through-bolt, then manoeuvre the mounting bracket out of position and away from the gearbox.

34 On automatic transmission models, undo the three bolts securing the rear mounting bracket to the top of the transmission unit. Slacken the mounting through-bolt, and pivot the bracket upwards and away from the transmission so that it will not hinder removal.

35 On all models, slacken and remove the right-hand mounting through-bolt, then lower the engine/transmission unit slightly. Undo the two nuts and single bolt which secure the mounting to its mounting plate, then remove the mounting. Undo the three mounting plate retaining bolts, then remove the plate from the top of the transmission, and raise the unit back to its original height.

36 Slacken and remove the left-hand mounting through-bolt, then undo the nut and bolt which secure the mounting to its engine bracket. Remove the mounting from the engine.

37 Make a final check that all components that will prevent the removal of the engine/transmission from the car have been removed or disconnected, and ensure that all components are positioned clear of the unit so that they will not hinder removal.

38 Lift the engine/transmission out of the car, ensuring that nothing is trapped or damaged. Once the engine is high enough, lift it out over the front of the body, and lower the unit to the ground (photo).

39 If the engine and transmission are to be separated for overhaul, first undo the three bolts securing the intermediate shaft bearing housing to the cylinder block, then carefully lever the shaft out of the transmission, taking great care not damage the transmission oil seal.

40 On manual gearbox models, undo the two bolts which secure the anti-twisting bracket to the underside of the cylinder block, and the single bolt which secures it to the gearbox, then remove the bracket. Undo the flywheel lower cover plate retaining nuts and bolt, and remove the plate from the gearbox. Slacken and remove the remaining bolts securing the gearbox housing to the engine unit, noting the correct fitted positions of the bolts to use as a reference on refitting. Move the gearbox squarely away from the engine unit to release it from its locating dowels, and separate the two. If necessary, also remove the clutch as described in Chapter 6.

41 On automatic transmission models, first disconnect the kickdown cable from the transmission and throttle housing, as described in Chapter 7. Slacken and remove the visible bolt(s) which secure the torque converter to the driveplate. Using a spanner or socket and extension bar on the crankshaft pulley bolt, rotate the engine anti-clockwise, and undo the remaining bolts as they become accessible through the lower cover plate aperture, noting that there are eight in total. Undo the remaining bolts securing the transmission housing to the engine unit, noting the correct fitted positions of the bolts to use as a reference on refitting. Move the transmission squarely away from the engine unit to release it from its locating dowels, and separate the two, ensuring that the torque converter remains in position on the transmission.

Refitting

42 Refitting is the reverse of removal, following where necessary the instructions given in the other Chapters of this manual. Note the following additional points.

(a) On manual gearbox models, prior to assembling the engine and transmission, overhaul and lubricate the clutch components as described in Chapter 6.

(b) On automatic transmission models, when assembling the engine and transmission, note that the torque converter mounting bolts must be tightened to the specified torque setting in a diagonal sequence.

(c) Once the intermediate shaft is installed and its bearing housing bolts have been

tightened to the specified torque, lift the engine/transmission unit into position. Lower it into the engine compartment, and align it with the front mounting bracket. Install the front mounting bracket bolts first, then refit the remaining engine/transmission mountings.

(d) Tighten all nuts and bolts to their specified torque wrench settings.

(e) Ensure all hoses/pipes are securely reconnected to their original positions, and (where necessary) are securely held in position with their retaining clips.

(f) Adjust the accelerator cable as described in Chapter 4.

(g) On automatic transmission models, adjust the kickdown cable as described in Chapter 7.

(h) On completion, working as described in Chapter 1, refill the engine and transmission with the specified type and amount of oil. and refill the cooling system.

23 Engine overhaul – dismantling sequence

1 It is much easier to dismantle and work on the engine if it is mounted on a portable engine stand. These stands can often be hired from a tool hire shop. Before the engine is mounted on a stand, the flywheel/driveplate should be removed, as described in Section 17, so that the stand bolts can be tightened into the end of the cylinder block/crankcase.

2 If a stand is not available, it is possible to dismantle the engine with it blocked up on a sturdy workbench, or on the floor. Be extra careful not to tip or drop the engine when working without a stand.

3 If you are going to obtain a reconditioned engine, all external components must be removed first to be transferred to the replacement engine (just as they will if you are doing a complete engine overhaul yourself). These components include the following.

(a) Alternator mounting brackets (Chapter 12).

(b) Power steering pump and air conditioning compressor brackets (where fitted).

(c) Oil separator (photo).

(d) Thermostat housing (photo) and coolant rail (Chapter 3).

(e) All electrical switches and sensors.

(f) Inlet and exhaust manifolds (Chapter 4).

(g) Oil cooler – DOHC engine only (Section 15).

(h) Engine mounting brackets (Section 18).

(i) Flywheel/driveplate (Section 17).

Note: When removing the external components from the engine, pay close attention to details that may be helpful or important during refitting.

Note the fitted position of gaskets, seals, spacers, pins, washers, bolts and other small items.

4 If you are obtaining a 'short' engine (which consists of the engine cylinder block/crankcase, crankshaft, pistons and connecting rods all assembled), then the cylinder head, sump, oil pump, and timing belt will have to be removed also.

5 If you are planning a complete overhaul, the engine can be dismantled and the internal components removed in the following order.

(a) Inlet and exhaust manifolds (Chapter 4).

(b) Timing belt, sprockets, tensioner and timing belt inner cover (Sections 6, 7 and 8).

(c) Cylinder head (Section 11).

(d) Flywheel/driveplate (Section 17).

(e) Sump (Section 12).

(f) Oil pump (Section 13).

(g) Crankshaft (Section 27).

(h) Piston/connecting rod assemblies (Section 28).

6 Before beginning the dismantling and overhaul procedures, make sure that you have all of the correct tools necessary. Refer to 'Tools and working facilities' at the end of this manual for further information.

24 Cylinder head – dismantling

Note: New and reconditioned cylinder heads are available from the manufacturer, and from engine overhaul specialists. Bearing in mind that several specialist tools are required for the dismantling and inspection procedures, and that new components may not be readily available, it may be more practical and

23.3A Removing the oil separator ...

23.3B ... and thermostat housing

24.3 Compress the valve spring, and remove the collets

24.6 Use a labelled plastic bag to keep together and identify valve components

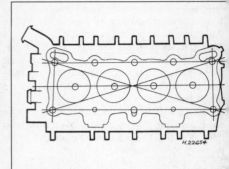

Fig. 2.11 Check the cylinder head for warpage along the lines shown (Sec 25)

economical for the home mechanic to purchase a reconditioned head rather than dismantle, inspect and recondition the original head.

1 Remove the camshaft(s) and rocker arms, as described in Section 10.

2 Remove the cylinder head, as described in Section 11.

3 Using a valve spring compressor, compress each valve spring in turn until the split collets can be removed (photo). Release the compressor, and lift off the spring retainer and spring, then use a pair of pliers to extract the stem seal and remove the lower spring seat.

> **HAYNES HINT** If, when the valve spring compressor is screwed down, the spring retainer refuses to free and expose the split collets, gently tap the top of the tool, directly over the retainer, with a light hammer. This will free the retainer.

4 Withdraw the valve through the combustion chamber.

5 It is essential that each valve is stored together with its collets, retainer and spring, and that all valves are in their correct sequence, unless they are so badly worn that they are to be renewed. If they are going to be kept and used again, place each valve assembly in a labelled polythene bag or similar small container (photo).

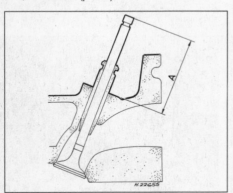

Fig. 2.12 Check valve seat wear by measuring valve stem installed height 'A' (Sec 25)

25 Cylinder head and valves – cleaning and inspection

1 Thorough cleaning of the cylinder head and valve components, followed by a detailed inspection, will enable you to decide how much valve service work must be carried out during the engine overhaul. **Note:** *If the engine has been severely overheated, it is best to assume that the cylinder head is warped and to check carefully for signs of this.*

Cleaning

2 Scrape away all traces of old gasket material and sealing compound from the cylinder head; see Section 11 for details.

3 Scrape away the carbon from the combustion chambers and ports, then wash the cylinder head thoroughly with paraffin or a suitable solvent.

4 Scrape off any heavy carbon deposits that may have formed on the valves, then use a power-operated wire brush to remove deposits from the valve heads and stems.

Inspection

Note: *Be sure to perform all the following inspection procedures before concluding that the services of a machine shop or engine overhaul specialist are required. Make a list of all items that require attention.*

Cylinder head

5 Inspect the head very carefully for cracks, evidence of coolant leakage, and other

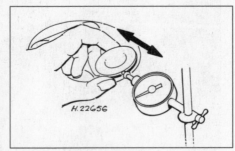

Fig. 2.13 Checking valve guide wear using a dial gauge (Sec 25)

damage. If cracks are found, a new cylinde head should be obtained.

6 Use a straight-edge (placed as shown i Fig. 2.11) and feeler gauge blade to check tha the cylinder head surface is not distorted. If is, it may be possible to resurface it, provide that the specified reface limit is not exceede in so doing, or that the cylinder head is n reduced to less than the specified height.

7 Examine the valve seats in each of th combustion chambers. If they are severe pitted, cracked or burned, then they will nee to be renewed or recut by an engine overha specialist. If they are only slightly pitted, th can be removed by grinding-in the valv heads and seats with fine valve-grindin compound, as described below. To chec whether they are excessively worn, refit th valve and measure the installed height of i stem tip above the cylinder head uppe surface (Fig. 2.12); if the measurement i above the specified limit, repeat the test usin a new valve. If the measurement is st excessive, the valve seat is excessively wor and the cylinder head must be renewed.

8 If the valve guides are worn (indicated by side-to-side motion of the valve, an accompanied by excessive blue smoke in th exhaust when running) new guides must b fitted. Measure the diameter of the existin valve stems (see below) and the bore of th guides, then calculate the clearance an compare the result with the specified value. A alternative method is to measure the amou of side play there is with the valve installed i its guide using a dial gauge. To do this, ret the valve to its original position in the cylind head, and hold it approximately 10 mm abov the cylinder head surface. Position the di gauge on the edge of the valve head, an measure the side play while moving the valv to and fro (Fig. 2.13). If either method show valve stem/guide wear to be excessive, rene the valves or guides as necessary.

9 The renewal of valve guides is best carrie out by an engine overhaul specialist. If th work is to be carried out at home, howeve use a stepped, double-diameter drift to dri out the worn guide towards the combustio chamber. On fitting the new guide, place it fir in a deep-freeze for one hour, then drive it in

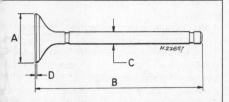

Fig. 2.14 Valve measurement points (Sec 25)

A *Head diameter*　　C *Stem diameter*
B *Length*　　　　　D *Head thickness*

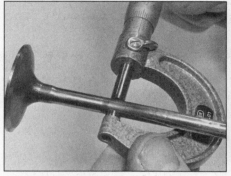

25.12 Measuring valve stem diameter

26.2A Fit the valve spring seat ...

its cylinder head bore from the camshaft side until it projects the specified amount above the cylinder head surface.

10 If the valve seats are to be re-cut this must be done only after the guides have been renewed.

Valves

11 Examine the head of each valve for pitting, burning, cracks and general wear, and check the valve stem for scoring and wear ridges. Rotate the valve, and check for any obvious indication that it is bent. Look for pitting and excessive wear on the tip of each valve stem. Renew any valve that shows any such signs of wear or damage.

12 If the valve appears satisfactory at this stage, using a micrometer and vernier calipers, measure the dimensions of the valve as shown in Fig. 2.14, noting that the valve stem diameter should be measured at several points along its length (photo). If any of the measurements obtained exceed the specified service limit, or are significantly different to the measurements for a new valve, the valve(s) must be renewed.

13 If the valves are in satisfactory condition, they should be ground (lapped) into their respective seats, to ensure a smooth gas-tight seal. If the seat is only lightly pitted, or if it has been re-cut, fine grinding compound **only** should be used to produce the required finish. Coarse valve-grinding compound should **not** be used unless a seat is badly burned or deeply pitted; if this is the case, the cylinder head and valves should be inspected by an

expert to decide whether seat re-cutting, or even the renewal of the valve or seat insert, is required.

14 Valve grinding is carried out as follows. Place the cylinder head upside-down on a bench.

15 Smear a trace of the appropriate grade of valve-grinding compound on the seat face, and press a suction grinding tool onto the valve head. With a semi-rotary action, grind the valve head to its seat, lifting the valve occasionally to redistribute the grinding compound. A light spring placed under the valve head will greatly ease this operation.

16 If coarse grinding compound is being used, work only until a dull, matt even surface is produced on both the valve seat and the valve, then wipe off the used compound and repeat the process with fine compound. When a smooth unbroken ring of light grey matt finish is produced on both the valve and seat, the grinding operation is complete. **Do not** grind in the valves any further than absolutely necessary, or the seat will be prematurely sunk into the cylinder head.

17 To check that the seat has not been over-ground, measure the valve stem installed height, as described in paragraph 7 above.

18 When all the valves have been ground-in, carefully wash off all traces of grinding compound using paraffin or a suitable solvent before reassembly of the cylinder head.

Valve components

19 Examine the valve springs for signs of

damage and discoloration; if possible; also compare the existing spring free length with new components.

20 Stand each spring on a flat surface, and check it for squareness. If any of the springs are damaged, distorted or have lost their tension, obtain a complete new set of springs.

26 Cylinder head – reassembly

2

1 Lubricate the stems of the valves, and insert them into their original locations. If new valves are being fitted, insert them into the locations to which they have been ground.

2 Working on the first valve, refit the lower spring seat. Dip the correct valve stem seal in fresh engine oil, then carefully locate it over the valve and onto the guide. **Note:** *The inlet and exhaust valve stem oil seals are different (not interchangeable); the inlet valve seals are fitted with a white spring and the exhaust valve seals are fitted with a black spring.* Take care not to damage the seal as it is passed over the valve stem. Use a suitable socket or metal tube to press the seal firmly onto the guide (photos).

3 Locate the spring on the seat, ensuring its closest-wound coils are at the bottom, and fit the spring retainer (photos).

4 Compress the valve spring and locate the split collets in the recess in the valve stem.

26.2B ... then fit the valve stem oil seal

26.3A Fit the valve spring, ensuring its closest-wound coils are at the bottom ...

26.3B ... and install the spring retainer (SOHC engine shown)

26.4 Use a little grease to hold the collets in place

Use a little grease to hold the collets in place (photo). Release the compressor, then repeat the procedure on the remaining valves.

5 With all the valves installed, place the cylinder head flat on the bench and, using a hammer and interposed block of wood, tap the end of each valve stem to settle the components.

27 Crankshaft – removal

1 Remove the timing belt, timing belt tensioner and crankshaft sprocket, as described in Sections 7 and 8.
2 Remove the camshaft(s) and rocker arms, as described in Section 10.
3 Remove the oil pump, as described in Section 13.
4 Undo the four bolts securing the right-hand (rear) oil seal housing to the cylinder block, and carefully slide the housing off the end of the crankshaft.
5 Check the crankshaft endfloat, as described in Section 31.
6 Rotate the crankshaft so that number 2 and 3 cylinders are at BDC (Bottom Dead Centre), then progressively slacken the ten main bearing cap retaining bolts by half a turn at a time. Remove the bolts along with their washers, and store them in their original fitted positions in a cardboard template.
7 Carefully free the main bearing cap bridge from the caps, and remove it from the engine,

27.9 Always mark big-end caps and connecting rods prior to removal (see text)

noting the fitted positions of its locating dowels. Remove the O-ring from the centre of the bridge, and discard it; the O-ring **must** be renewed whenever it is disturbed.
8 Note the identification marks on each of the main bearing caps, then carefully remove each cap from the cylinder block, ensuring that the lower main bearing shell remains in position in the cap. Note the fitted positions of the cap locating dowels; remove any that are loose, and store them with the relevant cap for safe keeping.
9 Using a hammer and centre-punch, or quick-drying paint, mark each connecting rod big-end bearing cap with its respective cylinder number, on the machined-flat surface provided; if the engine has been dismantled before, note carefully any identifying marks made previously (photo). Note that number 1 cylinder is at the timing belt end of the engine.
10 Before removing the connecting rod big-end caps, use a feeler gauge to check the amount of side play (endfloat) between the caps and crankshaft webs (photo). If the clearance exceeds the service limit given in the Specifications, the connecting rod must be renewed (see Section 30).
11 Slacken and remove the big-end bearing cap nuts, then withdraw the cap, complete with the lower bearing shell, from each of the four connecting rods. Push the connecting rods up and off their crankpins, then remove the upper bearing shell. Keep the cap, nuts and (if they are to be refitted) the bearing shells together in their correct sequence.
12 Lift the crankshaft out of the cylinder block, and withdraw the two thrustwashers from the number 4 main bearing upper location. Remove the upper main bearing shells, which must be kept with their correct respective main bearing cap and lower shell, so that all shells can be identified and (if necessary) refitted in their original locations.

28 Piston/connecting rod assembly – removal

1 Remove the timing belt and timing belt tensioner, as described in Sections 7 and 8.
2 Remove the cylinder head, as described in Section 11.

27.10 Checking connecting rod big-end side play

3 Remove the crankshaft, as described in Section 27.
4 Push each piston/connecting rod assembly up, and remove it from the top of the bore. Remove the ridge of carbon from the top of each cylinder bore, and ensure that the connecting rod big-ends do not mark the cylinder bore walls. Immediately refit the bearing cap, shells and nuts to each piston/connecting rod assembly, so that they are all kept together as a matched set.

29 Cylinder block/crankcase – cleaning and inspection

1 For complete cleaning, remove all external components and electrical switches/sensors.
2 Scrape all traces of gasket from the cylinder block/crankcase, taking great care not to damage the gasket/sealing surfaces.
3 Remove all oil gallery plugs (where fitted). The plugs are usually very tight – they may have to be drilled out and the holes re-tapped. Use new plugs when the engine is reassembled.
4 If any of the castings are extremely dirty, all should be steam-cleaned.
5 After the castings are returned, clean all oil holes and oil galleries one more time. Flush all internal passages with warm water until the water runs clear, then dry thoroughly and apply a light film of oil to all cylinder bore surfaces to prevent rusting. If you have access to compressed air, use it to speed up the drying process, and to blow out all the oil holes and galleries.

 Warning: Wear eye protection when using compressed air!

6 If the castings are not very dirty, you can do an adequate cleaning job with hot (as hot as you can stand!), soapy water and a stiff brush. Take plenty of time, and do a thorough job.

> **HAYNES HINT** *Regardless of the cleaning method used, be sure to clean all oil holes and galleries very thoroughly, and to dry all components well; protect the cylinder bores to prevent rusting.*

7 All threaded holes must be clean to ensure accurate torque readings during reassembly. To clean all threads, run the proper size tap into each of the holes to remove rust, corrosion, thread sealant or sludge, and to restore damaged threads. If possible, use compressed air to clear the holes of debris produced by this operation; a good alternative is to inject aerosol-applied water-dispersant lubricant into each hole, using the long spout usually supplied.

 Warning: Wear eye protection when cleaning out these holes in this way!

Apply suitable sealant to the new oil gallery plugs, and insert them into the holes in the block. Tighten them securely.

If the engine is not going to be reassembled right away, cover it with a large plastic bag to keep it clean; protect the cylinder bores as described above to prevent rusting.

Inspection

0 Visually check the castings for cracks and corrosion. Look for stripped threads in the threaded holes. If there has been any history of internal water leakage, it may be worthwhile having an engine overhaul specialist check the cylinder block/crankcase with special equipment. If defects are found, have them repaired if possible, or renew the assembly.

1 Check the bore of each cylinder liner for scuffing and scoring.

2 Measure the diameter of each cylinder bore at the top (just below the wear ridge), centre and bottom of the bore, both parallel to the crankshaft axis and at right angles to it, so that a total of six measurements are taken.

3 Compare the results with the Specifications at the beginning of this Chapter; if any measurement exceeds the service limit specified, the cylinder block must be rebored if possible, or renewed and new piston assemblies fitted.

4 Measure the piston diameter at right angles to the gudgeon pin axis, 16 mm up from the bottom of the skirt; compare the results with the Specifications at the beginning of this Chapter.

30.1 Measuring piston diameter

15 To measure the piston-to-bore clearance, either measure the bore and piston skirt as described above and subtract the skirt diameter from the bore measurement, or insert each piston into its original bore, then select a feeler gauge blade and slip it into the bore along with the piston. The piston must be aligned exactly in its normal attitude, and the feeler gauge blade must be between the piston and bore, on one of the thrust faces, approximately 20 mm up from the bottom of the bore.

16 If the clearance is excessive, a new piston will be required. If the piston binds at the lower end of the bore and is loose towards the top, the bore is tapered. If tight spots are encountered as the piston/feeler gauge blade is rotated in the bore, the bore is out-of-round.

17 Repeat this procedure for the remaining pistons and cylinder bores.

18 If the cylinder bores are badly scuffed or scored, or if they are excessively worn, out-of-round or tapered, the cylinder block must be rebored (if possible) or renewed; new pistons will also be required.

19 If the bores are in reasonably good condition and not worn to the specified limits, and if the piston-to-bore clearances can be maintained properly, then it may only be necessary to renew the piston rings.

20 If this is the case, the bores should be honed to allow the new rings to bed in correctly and provide the best possible seal. The conventional type of hone has spring-loaded stones, and is used with a power drill. You will also need some paraffin (or honing oil) and rags. The hone should be moved up and down the bore to produce a crosshatch pattern, and plenty of honing oil should be used. Ideally, the crosshatch lines should intersect at approximately a 60° angle. Do not take off more material than is necessary to produce the required finish. If new pistons are being fitted, the piston manufacturers may specify a finish with a different angle, so their instructions should be followed. Do not withdraw the hone from the bore while it is still being turned – stop it first. After honing a bore, wipe out all traces of the honing oil. If equipment of this type is not available, or if you are not sure whether you are competent to

undertake the task yourself, an engine overhaul specialist will carry out the work at moderate cost.

30 Piston/connecting rod assembly – inspection

1 Examine the pistons for ovality, scoring and scratches, and for wear of the piston ring grooves. Use a micrometer to measure the pistons (photo).

2 If the pistons or connecting rods are to be renewed, it is necessary to have this work carried out by a Rover dealer or suitable engine overhaul specialist, who will have the necessary tooling to remove and install the gudgeon pins.

3 If new rings are to be fitted to the original pistons, expand the old rings over the top of the pistons. The use of two or three old feeler gauge blades will be helpful in preventing the rings dropping into empty grooves (photo).

4 When the original piston rings have been removed, ensure that the ring grooves in the piston are free of carbon by cleaning them using an old ring. Break the ring in half to do this.

5 Check the ring-to-groove clearance by inserting each ring from the outside together with a feeler gauge blade between the ring's top surface and the piston land. Check the ring end gaps by inserting each ring into the cylinder bore, pushing it in with the piston crown to ensure that it is square in the bore, 15 to 20 mm from the top; use feeler gauges to measure the gap (photos).

6 Note that each piston should be considered as being matched to its respective bore, and they must not be interchanged.

31 Crankshaft – inspection

Checking crankshaft endfloat

1 If the crankshaft endfloat is to be checked, this must be done when the crankshaft is still installed in the cylinder block/crankcase, but is free to move (see Section 27).

2 Check the endfloat using a dial gauge in

2

30.3 Removing piston rings using feeler blades

30.5A Measuring piston ring-to-groove clearance

30.5B Measuring piston ring end gap

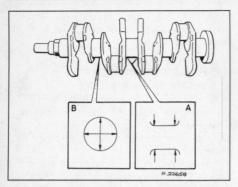

Fig. 2.15 Crankshaft journal measurement – measure the diameter at each edge of the journal (A) then repeat at a point 90° away from the first measurement (B) (Sec 31)

31.2 Checking crankshaft endfloat using a dial gauge

31.3 Checking crankshaft endfloat using feeler blades

contact with the end of the crankshaft. Push the crankshaft fully one way, and then zero the gauge. Push the crankshaft fully the other way, and check the endfloat. The result can be compared with the specified amount, and will give an indication as to whether new thrustwashers are required (photo).

3 If a dial gauge is not available, feeler gauges can be used. First push the crankshaft fully towards the flywheel end of the engine, then use feeler gauges to measure the gap between the web of number 4 crankpin and the thrustwasher (photo).

Inspection

4 Clean the crankshaft, and dry it with compressed air, if available.

 Warning: Wear eye protection when using compressed air! Be sure to clean the oil holes with a pipe cleaner or similar probe.

5 Check the main and crankpin (big-end) bearing journals for uneven wear, scoring, pitting and cracking.

6 Rub a penny across each journal several times (photo). If a journal picks up copper from the penny, it is too rough.

7 Remove any burrs from the crankshaft oil holes with a stone, file or scraper.

8 Using a micrometer, measure the diameter of each main bearing and crankpin (big-end) journal, at each edge of the journal at the same point. Measure the same journal at each edge again, but at a point 90° away from the

31.6 Using a penny to check the condition of a crankshaft journal

first point of measurement (see Fig. 2.15) (photo). Use the measurements to calculate the journal taper at both points, and the ovality of the journal. Compare the results with the Specifications at the beginning of this Chapter.

9 If the crankshaft journals are damaged, tapered or out-of-round (oval), the crankshaft must be renewed, unless an engine overhaul specialist can be found who will regrind it, and supply the necessary undersize bearing shells.

10 Check the oil seal journals at each end of the crankshaft for wear and damage. If either seal has worn an excessive groove in its journal, consult an engine overhaul specialist, who will be able to advise whether a repair is possible or whether a new crankshaft is necessary.

11 Set the crankshaft up in V-blocks, and position a dial gauge on the top of the crankshaft number 1 main bearing journal.

31.8 Measuring the diameter of a crankshaft journal

Zero the dial gauge, then slowly rotate the crankshaft through two complete revolutions, noting the journal run-out. Repeat the procedure on the remaining four main bearing journals, so that a run-out measurement is available for all main bearing journals. If the difference between the run-out of any two journals exceeds the service limit given in the Specifications, the crankshaft must be renewed.

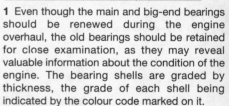

32 Main and big-end bearings – inspection

1 Even though the main and big-end bearings should be renewed during the engine overhaul, the old bearings should be retained for close examination, as they may reveal valuable information about the condition of the engine. The bearing shells are graded by thickness, the grade of each shell being indicated by the colour code marked on it.

2 Bearing failure can occur due to lack of lubrication, the presence of dirt or other foreign particles, overloading the engine, or corrosion. Regardless of the cause of bearing failure, it must be corrected (where appropriate) before the engine is reassembled, to prevent it from happening again.

3 When examining the bearing shells, remove them from the cylinder block/crankcase along with the main bearing caps, the connecting rods and the connecting rod big-end bearing caps, and lay them out on a clean surface in

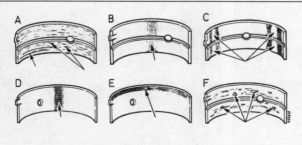

Fig. 2.16 Typical bearing shell failures (Sec 32)

A Scratched by dirt; dirt embedded into bearing material
B Lack of oil; overlay wiped out
C Improper seating; bright (polished) sections
D Tapered journal; overlay gone from entire surface
E Radius ride
F Fatigue failure; craters or pockets

the same general position as their location in the engine. This will enable you to match any bearing problems with the corresponding crankshaft journal. Do not touch any shell's bearing surface with your fingers while checking it, or the delicate surface may be scratched.

Dirt and other foreign particles get into the engine in a variety of ways. Dirt may be left in the engine during assembly, or it may pass through filters or the crankcase ventilation system. It may get into the oil, and from there into the bearings. Metal chips from machining operations and normal engine wear are often present. Abrasives are sometimes left in engine components after reconditioning, especially when parts are not thoroughly cleaned using the proper cleaning methods. Whatever the source, these foreign objects often end up embedded in the soft bearing material, and are easily recognized. Large particles will not embed in the bearing, and will score or gouge the bearing and journal. The best prevention for this cause of bearing failure is to clean all parts thoroughly, and to keep everything spotlessly-clean during engine assembly. Frequent and regular engine oil and filter changes are also recommended.

Lack of lubrication (or lubrication breakdown) has a number of interrelated causes. Excessive heat (which thins the oil), overloading (which squeezes the oil from the bearing face) and oil leakage (from excessive bearing clearances, worn oil pump or high engine speeds) all contribute to lubrication breakdown. Blocked oil passages, which usually are the result of misaligned oil holes in a bearing shell, will also oil-starve a bearing and destroy it. When lack of lubrication is the cause of bearing failure, the bearing material is wiped or extruded from the steel backing of the bearing. Temperatures may increase to the point where the steel backing turns blue from overheating.

Driving habits can have a definite effect on bearing life. Full-throttle, low-speed operation (labouring the engine) puts very high loads on bearings, which tends to squeeze out the oil film. These loads cause the bearings to flex, which produces fine cracks in the bearing face

(fatigue failure). Eventually, the bearing material will loosen in pieces and tear away from the steel backing. Short-distance driving leads to corrosion of bearings, because insufficient engine heat is produced to drive off the condensed water and corrosive gases. These products collect in the engine oil, forming acid and sludge. As the oil is carried to the engine bearings, the acid attacks and corrodes the bearing material.

7 Incorrect bearing installation during engine assembly will lead to bearing failure as well. Tight-fitting bearings leave insufficient bearing running clearance, and will result in oil starvation. Dirt or foreign particles trapped behind a bearing shell result in high spots on the bearing which lead to failure. Do not touch any shell's bearing surface with your fingers during reassembly; there is a risk of scratching the delicate surface, or of depositing particles of dirt on it.

33 Engine overhaul – reassembly sequence

1 Before reassembly begins, ensure that all new parts have been obtained, and that all necessary tools are available. Read through the entire procedure to familiarise yourself with the work involved, and to ensure that all items necessary for reassembly of the engine are at hand. In addition to all normal tools and materials, a thread-locking compound will be needed. A tube of liquid sealant will also be required for the joint faces that are fitted without gaskets.
2 In order to save time and avoid problems, engine reassembly can be carried out in the following order.
(a) Crankshaft (Section 36).

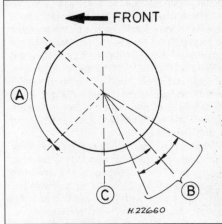

FRONT

H.22660

Fig. 2.18 Piston ring end gap spacing (Sec 34)

A Top and second compression ring end gaps – spaced approximately 90° apart
B Oil control ring end – outer rail end gaps should be positioned on either side of the centre ring
C Gudgeon pin axis

(b) Piston/connecting rod assemblies (Section 35).
(c) Oil pump (Section 13).
(d) Sump (Section 12).
(e) Flywheel/driveplate (Section 17).
(f) Cylinder head (Section 11).
(g) Timing belt tensioner and sprockets, and timing belt (Sections 6, 7 and 8).
(h) Engine external components.
3 At this stage, all engine components should be absolutely clean and dry, (with all faults repaired) and should be laid out (or placed in individual containers) on a completely-clean work surface.

34 Piston rings – refitting

1 Before installing new piston rings, check the ring end gaps and the ring-to-groove clearance, as described in Section 30.
2 When measuring new rings, lay out each piston set with a piston/connecting rod assembly, and keep them together as a matched set from now on.
3 If the end gap of a new ring is found to be too large or too small, double-check to ensure that you have the correct rings before proceeding. If the end gap is still too small, it must be opened up by careful filing of the ring ends using a fine file; if it is too large, this is not as serious, unless the specified service limit is exceeded, in which case very careful checking is required of the dimensions of **all** components, as well as of the new parts.
4 Once all rings have been checked, they can be installed; ensure that each ring is refitted only to its matched piston and bore.
5 Install the new rings by fitting them over the top of the piston, starting with the oil control ring spring. Note that the compression rings must be fitted with the manufacturer's markings uppermost (photo). The second compression ring is easily identifiable from the top ring, due to its chamfered outer edges (Fig. 2.17).
6 With all the rings in position, space the ring gaps as shown in Fig. 2.18, noting that the end gaps must **not** be positioned on the thrust side of the piston, or in line with the gudgeon pin axis.

2

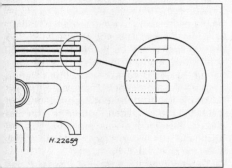

H.22659

Fig. 2.17 Ensure the compression rings are correctly installed, second ring is easily identified due to its chamfered outer edges (Sec 34)

34.5 Compression rings must be fitted to piston so that their markings are uppermost

35.2 Connecting rod big-end journal identification number

35.3 Crankshaft big-end journal identification letter (arrowed)

35.11 Lay the length of Plastigage on the journal to be measured, parallel to the crankshaft centre-line

35 Piston/connecting rod assembly – refitting, and big-end bearing running clearance check

Selection of bearing shells

1 The big-end bearing running clearance is controlled in production by selecting one of seven grades of bearing shell. The grades are indicated by a colour-coding marked on the edge of each shell which governs the shell's thickness. In order, from the thinnest to the thickest, the shell grades are: Red, Pink, Yellow, Green, Brown, Black and Blue.

2 If the bearing shells are to be renewed, first check and record the number stamped across one face of each big-end bearing cap and connecting rod. The number, between 1 and 4, is the size code of the connecting rod big-end bore inside diameter; '1' indicates the smallest-possible inside diameter, and '4' the largest (photo).

3 Secondly, check and record the crankpin/big-end journal code letters stamped on the crankshaft's web on the left-hand side of each big-end journal. The letter, between A and D, indicates the outside diameter of the crankpin/big-end journal; 'A' indicates the largest-possible outside diameter, and 'D' the smallest (photo).

4 Match the relevant connecting rod code with its crankshaft code, and select a new set of bearing shells using the following table. The crankshaft codes are listed down the left-hand side, and the connecting rod codes along the top; the required bearing grade is indicated in the box where the two columns intersect.

	1	2	3	4
A	Red	Pink	Yellow	Green
B	Pink	Yellow	Green	Brown
C	Yellow	Green	Brown	Black
D	Green	Brown	Black	Blue

Big-end bearing running clearance check

5 Refit the upper main bearing shells to the cylinder block, and temporarily lay the crankshaft in position.

6 Clean the backs of the bearing shells, and the bearing locations in both the connecting rod and bearing cap.

7 Press the bearing shells into their locations, ensuring that the tab on each shell engages in the notch in the connecting rod/bearing cap, and taking care not to touch any shell's bearing surface with your fingers.

8 The big-end bearing running clearance should be checked if there is any doubt about crankshaft wear. The running clearance should also be checked if the crankshaft has been reground and is to be refitted with non-genuine undersized bearing shells, or if non-genuine bearing shells are to be fitted. If the original crankshaft or a genuine Rover replacement part is to be installed, the shell selection procedure given above will produce the correct clearances, and a further check will not be necessary. If the clearance is to be checked, it can be done in either of two ways.

9 One method (which will be difficult to achieve without a range of internal micrometers or internal/external expanding calipers) is to refit the big-end bearing cap to the connecting rod, with the bearing shells in place. With the cap retaining nuts tightened to the specified torque, use an internal micrometer or vernier caliper to measure the inside diameter of each assembled pair of bearing shells. If the diameter of each corresponding crankshaft journal is measured and then subtracted from the bearing inside diameter, the result will be the big-end bearing running clearance.

10 The second (and more accurate) method is to use an American product known as 'Plastigage'. This consists of a fine thread of perfectly-round plastic which is compressed between the bearing shell and the crankpin/journal. When the shell is removed, the plastic is deformed, and can be measured with a special card gauge supplied with the kit. The running clearance is determined from this gauge. Plastigage is sometimes difficult to obtain, but enquiries at one of the larger specialist quality motor factors should produce the name of a stockist in your area. The procedure for using Plastigage is as follows.

35.12 Using the scale provided to check the width of the crushed Plastigage (at its widest point), giving the bearing running clearance

11 Cut several lengths of the appropriate size Plastigage, slightly shorter than the width of the crankpin/journal. Place a strand of Plastigage on each (cleaned) crankpin journal, and refit the (clean) piston/connecting rod assemblies, shells and big-end bearing caps (photo). Tighten the bearing cap nuts to the specified torque wrench setting, ensuring that the crankshaft does not rotate. Take care not to disturb the Plastigage. Slacken the bearing cap nuts and remove the connecting rod assemblies, again taking great care not to rotate the crankshaft.

12 Compare the width of the crushed Plastigage on each journal against the scale printed on the Plastigage envelope to obtain the big-end bearing running clearance (photo).

13 If the clearance is not as specified, the bearing shells may be the wrong grade (or excessively worn, if the original shells are being re-used). Before deciding that different grade shells are needed, make sure that no dirt or oil was trapped between the bearing shells and the connecting rod or bearing cap when the clearance was measured. If the Plastigage was wider at one end than at the other, the journal may be tapered.

14 Carefully scrape away all traces of the Plastigage material from the crankpin/journal and bearing shells, using a fingernail or other object which is unlikely to score the shells. Remove the crankshaft and bearing shells,

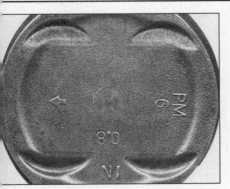

35.19A Piston/connecting rod assemblies must be installed so that arrow on piston crown points towards timing belt end of engine ...

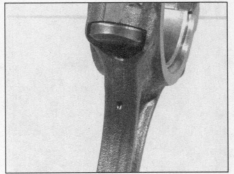

35.19B ... and connecting rod oilway is facing the rear

35.19C Use a piston ring compressor to clamp rings in position, then gently tap pistons into the cylinder bores

... taking great care to keep the shells in their original positions.

Final piston/connecting rod assembly refitting

15 Clean the backs of the bearing shells, and the bearing recesses in both the connecting rod and the big-end bearing cap. If new shells are being fitted, ensure that all traces of the protective grease are cleaned off, using paraffin. Wipe the shells and connecting rods dry with a lint-free cloth.

16 Press the bearing shells into their locations, ensuring that the tab on each shell engages in the notch in the connecting rod or big-end bearing cap, and taking care not to touch any shell's bearing surface with your fingers.

17 Lubricate the cylinder bores, the pistons and piston rings, then lay out each piston/connecting rod assembly in its respective position.

18 Starting with assembly number 1, make sure that the piston rings are still spaced as shown in Fig. 2.18, then clamp them in position with a piston ring compressor.

19 Insert the piston/connecting rod assembly into the top of bore number 1, ensuring that the arrow on the piston crown faces the timing belt end of the engine; note that the oilway on the connecting rod shaft should face the rear

(oil filter side) of the engine. Using a block of wood or hammer handle against the piston crown, tap the assembly into the liner until the piston crown is flush with the top of the liner (photos).

20 Repeat the procedure for the remaining three piston/connecting rod assemblies, then refit the crankshaft as described in Section 36.

36 Crankshaft – refitting, and main bearing running clearance check

Selection of bearing shells

1 The main bearing running clearance is controlled in production by selecting one of seven grades of bearing shell. The grades are indicated by a colour-coding marked on the edge of each shell which governs the shell's thickness. In order, from the thinnest to the thickest, the shell grades are: Red, Pink, Yellow, Green, Brown, Black and Blue.

2 If the bearing shells are to be renewed, first check and record the number stamped on the crankshaft adjacent to each main bearing journal. The number, between 1 and 4, is the size code of the adjacent main bearing journal outside diameter; '1' indicates the largest-possible outside diameter, and '4' the smallest. Number 1 (timing belt end of the engine) bearing code is situated to the right of

the journal, whereas all other codes are on the left-hand side of the relevant journal (photo).

3 Secondly, check and record the main bearing journal code letters which are stamped on the right-hand end of the cylinder block, just below the block upper mating surface. Reading the letters with the block inverted, number 1 main bearing's code is at the top, with the remainder following in order from the timing belt end of the engine. The letter, between A and D, indicates the main bearing bore inside diameter; 'A' indicates the smallest-possible inside diameter, and 'D' the largest (photo).

4 Match the relevant main bearing bore code with its crankshaft journal code, and select a new set of bearing shells using the table in Section 35. The crankshaft codes are listed down the left-hand side, and the main bearing bore codes along the top; the required bearing grade is indicated in the box where the two columns intersect.

Main bearing running clearance check

5 Clean the backs of the bearing shells, and the bearing locations in both the cylinder block/crankcase and the main bearing caps.

6 Press the bearing shells into their locations, ensuring that the tab on each shell engages in the notch in the cylinder block/crankcase or main bearing cap location (photo), and taking

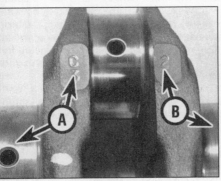

36.2 Crankshaft main bearing journal identification numbers. Number (A) is for left-hand end journal, and (B) is for journal on right of number (see text)

36.3 Cylinder block main bearing journal identification letters. Left-hand letter is for number 1 bearing, right-hand letter for number 5 bearing (see text)

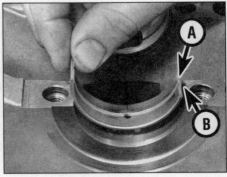

36.6 When fitting bearing shells, ensure tab (A) is correctly located in cylinder block notch (B)

36.13A Fit thrustwashers to cylinder block/crankcase, ensuring their grooved oilways (arrowed) are facing outwards

36.13B Liberally lubricate the upper main bearing shells with clean engine oil ...

36.13C ... and lay the crankshaft in position

care not to touch any shell's bearing surface with your fingers. If the original bearings are being re-used, ensure they are refitted to their original positions.

7 The main bearing running clearance should be checked if there is any doubt about crankshaft wear. The running clearance should also be checked if the crankshaft has been reground and is to be refitted with non-genuine undersize bearing shells, or if non-genuine bearing shells are to be fitted. If the original crankshaft or a genuine Rover replacement part is to be installed, the shell selection procedure given above will produce the correct clearances, and a further check will not be necessary. If the clearance is to be checked, it can be done in either of two ways.

8 One method (which will be difficult to achieve without a range of internal micrometers or internal/external expanding calipers) is to refit the main bearing caps to the cylinder block/crankcase, with bearing shells in place, and refit the bearing cap bridge. With the bearing cap retaining bolts tightened to the specified torque, measure the inside diameter of each assembled pair of bearing shells. If the diameter of each corresponding crankshaft journal is measured and then subtracted from the bearing inside diameter, the result will be the main bearing running clearance.

9 The second (and more accurate) method is to use Plastigage (see Section 35, para-

graph 10). Ensure the bearing surfaces and crankshaft journals are perfectly clean, then, with all the upper bearing shells in position in the cylinder block, carefully lay the crankshaft in position. Place a strand of Plastigage on each crankshaft main bearing journal, and refit the bearing caps and shells to their original positions. Refit the bearing cap bridge, and tighten the retaining bolts to their specified torque setting, ensuring that the crankshaft does not rotate. Once all the bolts are tight, undo them again, and carefully remove the bearing cap bridge and bearing caps. Take great care not to turn the crankshaft, or to disturb the Plastigage, and again store all caps and bearings in their fitted positions. Compare the width of the crushed Plastigage on each journal to the scale printed on the Plastigage envelope to obtain the main bearing running clearance. On completion of the measurement, carefully scrape off all traces of Plastigage from the journal and shells, using a fingernail or other object which will not score the components.

10 If the clearance is not as specified, the bearing shells may be the wrong grade (or excessively worn, if the original shells are being re-used). Before deciding that different grade shells are needed, make sure that no dirt or oil was trapped between the bearing shells and the connecting rod or bearing cap when the clearance was measured. If the

Plastigage (if used) was wider at one end than at the other, the journal may be tapered.

11 Remove the crankshaft and main bearing shells from the cylinder block, again taking great care to ensure that the shells are stored in their correct fitted positions.

Final crankshaft refitting

12 Install the bearing shells as described above in paragraphs 5 and 6. If new shells are being fitted, ensure that all traces of the protective grease are cleaned off, using paraffin. Where necessary, also refit the upper bearing shells to their correct fitted positions in the connecting rods.

13 Using a little grease, stick the thrustwashers to each side of the number 4 main bearing upper location; ensure that the oilway grooves on each thrustwasher face outwards. Wipe the shells and crankshaft journals dry with a lint-free cloth. Liberally lubricate each bearing shell in the cylinder block/crankcase, then lower the crankshaft into position so that numbers 1 and 4 cylinder crankpins are at TDC (photos).

14 Ensure that the connecting rod bearing shell is still correctly installed. Taking care not to mark the cylinder bores, liberally lubricate the crankpin and both bearing shells, then pull the piston/connecting rod assembly down its bore and onto the crankpin. Noting that the faces with the stamped marks must match, refit the big-end bearing cap, and fit both its retaining nuts. Progressively tighten the big-end bearing cap retaining nuts to the specified torque setting, then repeat the procedure for the three remaining piston/connecting rod assemblies (photos).

15 Ensure that the locating dowels and bearing shells are in their correct fitted positions in the main bearing caps, then, using the identification marks, refit the bearing caps to their original positions. With the exception of the centre cap, the caps are numbered 1 to 5 (number 1 being at the timing belt end of the engine), and all the arrows on the caps must point towards the timing belt end of the engine (photos). The centre cap is easily identifiable, and must be fitted with its large dowel hole at the rear.

36.14A Push the connecting rods down onto the big-end journals, then fit the bearing caps, using the marks made on removal (arrowed)

36.14B Fit bearing cap nuts, and progressively tighten them to the specified torque

36.15A Ensure the locating dowels (arrowed) and bearing shell are correctly located ...

36.15B ... then refit the main bearing caps using the identification marks (arrowed) to ensure they are correctly positioned (see text)

36.16A Fit a new O-ring to the recess in the main bearing cap bridge ...

36.16B ... and refit bridge to the main bearing caps, ensuring O-ring remains in position (arrowed)

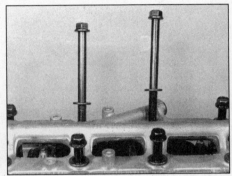

36.17A Refit the main bearing cap bolts, noting the two longer bolts are fitted to the centre bearing cap ...

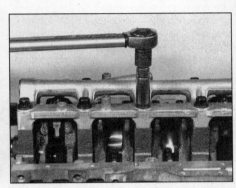

36.17B ... and tighten them to the specified torque setting, as described in text

2

16 Fit a new O-ring to the recess in the centre of the main bearing cap bridge, using a smear of grease to hold it in position. Ensure all the locating dowels are correctly positioned, then refit the bridge to the bearing caps, taking great care to ensure that the O-ring remains firmly seated in its recess (photos).

17 Apply a smear of clean engine to oil to the threads and underneath the heads of the main bearing cap bolts. Refit the bolts and washers to their original positions, noting the two longer bolts are fitted to the centre bearing cap, and tighten them all by hand. Working in a diagonal sequence from the centre outwards, progressively tighten the main bearing cap bolts to the specified torque setting (photos). Check that the crankshaft is free to rotate smoothly; if excessive pressure is required to turn the crankshaft, investigate the cause before proceeding further.

18 Renew the right-hand crankshaft oil seal, and refit the seal housing as described in Section 16.

19 Refit the oil pump and sump, as described in Sections 12 and 13.

20 Refit the cylinder head (where removed), camshaft(s) and rocker arms as described in Sections 10 and 11, then refit the crankshaft sprocket timing belt tensioner and timing belt, as described in Sections 7 and 8.

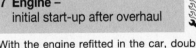

37 Engine –
initial start-up after overhaul

1 With the engine refitted in the car, double-check the engine oil and coolant levels. Make a final check that everything has been reconnected, and that there are no tools or rags left in the engine compartment.

2 With the spark plugs removed and the ignition system disabled by removing the engine management/ignition system fuse (number 14) from the passenger compartment fusebox, turn the engine over on the starter until the oil pressure warning lamp goes out.

3 Refit the spark plugs and connect all the spark plug (HT) leads, referring to Chapter 1 for further information. Refit fuse number 14.

4 Start the engine, noting that this may take a little longer than usual, due to the fuel system components being empty.

5 While the engine is idling, check for fuel, water and oil leaks. Don't be alarmed if there are some odd smells and smoke from parts getting hot and burning off oil deposits.

6 Keep the engine idling until hot water is felt circulating through the top hose. Check the ignition timing, base idle speed and mixture (as appropriate), then switch it off.

7 After a few minutes, recheck the oil and coolant levels as described in Chapter 1, and top-up as necessary.

8 If they were tightened as described, there is no need to re-tighten the cylinder head bolts once the engine has first run after reassembly.

9 If new pistons, rings or crankshaft bearings have been fitted, the engine must be run-in for the first 500 miles (800 km). Do not operate the engine at full-throttle, nor allow it to labour in any gear during this period. It is recommended that the oil and filter be changed at the end of this period.

Notes

Chapter 3
Cooling, heating and ventilation systems

Contents

Degrees of difficulty

Easy, suitable for novice with little experience		Fairly easy, suitable for beginner with some experience		Fairly difficult, suitable for competent DIY mechanic		Difficult, suitable for experienced DIY mechanic		Very difficult, suitable for expert DIY or professional	

Specifications

System type .... Pressurised, pump-assisted thermo-syphon, with front-mounted radiator and thermostatically-controlled electric cooling fan

Thermostat
Type .... Wax
Start-to-open temperature .... 72 to 76°C
Fully-open temperature .... 78°C (value stamped in unit end)
Full-lift height .... 9.0 mm

Expansion tank cap pressure .... 0.9 to 1.0 bar

Cooling fan operating temperature .... 88 to 92°C

System capacity .... 5.5 litres

Antifreeze properties and quantities
50% antifreeze (by volume):
    Commences freezing .... –36°C
    Frozen solid .... –48°C
    Quantities (system refill) .... 2.75 litres antifreeze, 2.75 litres water
Antifreeze type .... See Chapter 1

Torque wrench settings

	Nm	lbf ft
Thermostat housing cover bolts	12	9
Radiator cooling fan motor nuts	5	4
Coolant temperature gauge sender unit	9	7
Water pump retaining bolts	12	9
Heater lower mounting nut	21	15
Heater blower motor mounting bolts	10	7
Air conditioning compressor mounting bolts	25	18
Air conditioning pipe union nuts:		
Condenser unions	17	13
Evaporator inlet union (from receiver drier)	17	13
Evaporator outlet union	33	24
Receiver drier union	17	13
Dual-pressure switch	12	9

1 General information and precautions

The cooling system is of the pressurised, pump-assisted thermo-syphon type. It consists of the front-mounted radiator (made of copper/brass, with moulded plastic side tanks), a translucent expansion tank mounted on the right-hand inner wing, a thermostatically-controlled electric cooling fan mounted on the rear of the radiator, a thermostat, a centrifugal water pump, and the various connecting hoses. The water pump is driven by the engine's timing belt. On models with automatic transmission, a transmission fluid cooler is incorporated into the left-hand end of the radiator.

The locations of the system components, and the direction of coolant flow, are shown in Figs. 3.1 and 3.2.

The system is of the bypass type, allowing coolant to circulate around the engine while the thermostat is closed. When the engine is cold, the thermostat closes off the coolant feed from the bottom radiator hose. The coolant is then drawn into the engine via the heater matrix, inlet manifold, and from the top of the cylinder block. This allows some heat transfer (by convection) to the radiator through the top hose, while retaining the majority of heat within the cylinder block.

The siting of the thermostat in the intake rather than the outlet side of the system ensures that the engine warms up quickly, by circulating a small amount of coolant around a shorter tract. This also prevents temperature build-up in the cylinder head prior to the thermostat opening.

When the coolant reaches a predetermined temperature, the thermostat opens, and the coolant is allowed to flow freely through the top hose to the radiator. As the coolant circulates through the radiator, it is cooled by the inrush of air when the car is in forward motion. Airflow is supplemented by the action of the electric cooling fan when necessary. By the time it reaches the bottom of the radiator, the coolant is cooled and the cycle is repeated.

When the engine is at normal operating temperature, the coolant expands, and some of it is displaced into the expansion tank. This coolant collects in the tank, and is returned to the radiator when the system cools.

The electric cooling fan mounted behind the radiator is controlled by a thermostatic switch which is fitted to the rear of the cylinder block. At a pre-determined coolant temperature, the switch contacts close, thus actuating the fan.

On models with air conditioning, it is necessary to observe special precautions whenever dealing with any part of the system, its associated components, and any items which necessitate disconnection of the system. If for any reason the system must be disconnected, entrust this task to your Rover dealer or a refrigeration engineer. The layout of the air conditioning system is shown in Fig. 3.3.

Warning: The air conditioning refrigeration circuit contains a potentially-harmful liquid refrigerant (Freon) and it is therefore dangerous to disconnect any part of the system without specialised knowledge and equipment. The refrigerant must not be allowed to come in contact with a naked flame, otherwise a poisonous gas will be created. Do not allow the fluid to come in contact with the skin or eyes.

Warning: Do not attempt to remove the expansion tank filler cap for to disturb any part of the cooling system) while the engine is hot, as there is a very great risk of scalding. If the expansion tank filler cap must be removed before the engine and radiator have fully cooled down (even though this is not recommended), the pressure in the cooling system must first be released. Cover the cap with a thick layer of cloth, to avoid scalding, and slowly unscrew the filler cap until a hissing sound can be heard. When the hissing has stopped, showing that pressure is released slowly unscrew the filler cap until it can be removed. If more hissing sounds are heard, wait until they have stopped before unscrewing the cap completely. At all times, keep well away from the filler opening.

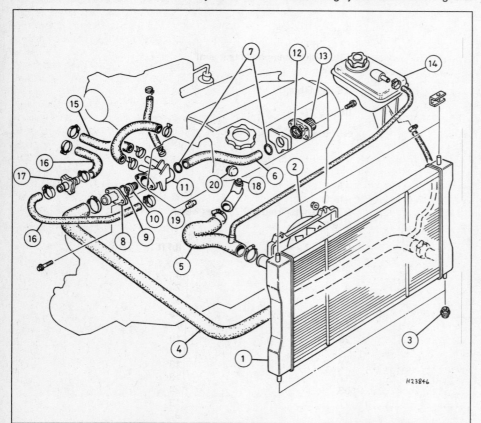

H23846

Fig. 3.1 Cooling system components – SOHC engine (DOHC engine similar) (Sec 1)

1 Radiator
2 Cooling fan and cowling
3 Radiator mounting rubbers
4 Bottom hose
5 Top hose
6 Coolant pipe – thermostat housing-to-water pump
7 O-ring
8 Thermostat housing cover
9 Seal
10 Thermostat
11 Thermostat housing
12 O-ring
13 Water pump
14 Expansion tank
15 Hose – heater matrix-to-thermostat housing return
16 Hose – heater temperature control valve-to-heater matrix feed
17 Heater temperature control valve
18 Cooling system bleed screw
19 Coolant temperature gauge sender unit
20 Cooling system cylinder block drain plug

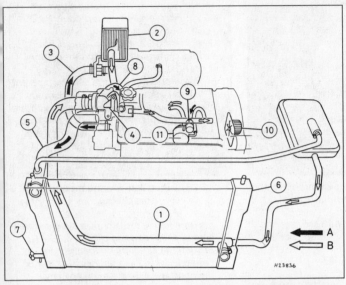

Fig. 3.2 Direction of coolant flow – DOHC engine (SOHC engine similar) (Sec 1)

1 Bottom hose	5 Top hose	9 Coolant pipe –
2 Heater matrix	6 Radiator	thermostat housing-
3 Hose – cylinder	7 Radiator drain plug	to-water pump
head-to-heater	(where fitted)	10 Water pump
control valve	8 Hose – thermostat	A Engine hot
4 Thermostat housing	housing-to-cylinder	B Engine cold
	head	

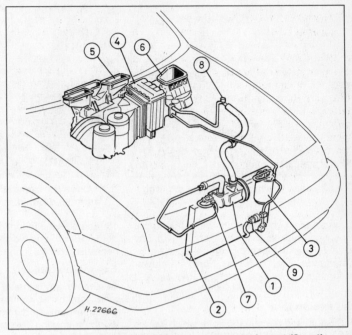

Fig. 3.3 Air conditioning system component layout (Sec 1)

1 Compressor	5 Heater unit	8 Low-pressure
2 Condenser	6 Blower unit	servicing connection
3 Receiver drier	7 High-pressure	9 Dual-pressure
4 Evaporator	servicing connection	switch

⚠️ *Warning: Do not allow antifreeze to come in contact with your skin, or with the painted surfaces of the vehicle. Rinse off spills immediately with plenty of water. Never leave antifreeze lying around in an open container, or in a puddle in the driveway or on the garage floor. Children and pets are attracted by its sweet smell but antifreeze is fatal if ingested.*

⚠️ *Warning: If the engine is hot, the radiator cooling fan may start rotating even if the engine is not running, so be careful to keep hands, hair and loose clothing well clear when working in the engine compartment.*

2 Radiator and expansion tank – removal, inspection and refitting

Note: *Refer to the warnings given in Section 1 before proceeding further.*

Removal
Radiator

Note: *Minor leaks from the radiator can be cured without removing the radiator, using a suitable product..*

1 Drain the cooling system, as described in Chapter 1.

2 On models with air conditioning, remove the condenser fan as described in Section 11.

3 Slacken and remove the two bolts securing the intake duct to the bonnet locking platform, and free the expansion tank hose from its duct

retaining clips (photo). Disconnect the duct from the intake hose, then free its retaining stud from the radiator and remove the duct.

4 Disconnect the radiator cooling fan wiring connector (photo), then slacken and remove the bolt securing the earth leads to the bonnet platform.

5 Slacken the top and bottom hose retaining clips, and disconnect both hoses from the radiator (photos).

6 On models with automatic transmission, position a suitable container beneath the fluid cooler unions on the left-hand end of the radiator. Working quickly, unscrew the pipe union nuts from the cooler, then plug both the pipe ends and cooler unions, to minimise the loss of fluid and prevent dirt entering the hydraulic system. Free both the pipes from their retaining clips on the bottom of the radiator.

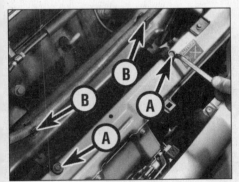

2.3 Undo the intake duct retaining bolts (A), and free the expansion tank hose from its duct retaining clips (B)

2.4 Disconnecting the cooling fan wiring connector

2.5A Slacken the retaining clips, and disconnect the bottom ...

2.5B ... and top hoses from the radiator

2.7A Undo the radiator mounting bolts and earth lead retaining bolt (arrowed) ...

2.7B ... then remove the mounting brackets ...

7 Undo the two bolts securing the upper mounting brackets to the bonnet platform, and remove the brackets from the radiator. Disengage the radiator from its lower mounting points, and carefully manoeuvre it out of the engine compartment (photos).

Expansion tank

8 Slacken and remove the bolts which secure the expansion tank to the body. Unscrew the expansion tank cap, and tip out its contents into a suitable container.

9 Slacken the retaining clips, then disconnect both the hoses from the expansion tank, and remove the tank from the vehicle. Mop up any spilt coolant immediately.

Inspection

Radiator

10 If the radiator was removed because of clogging (causing overheating), then try reverse-flushing or, in severe cases, use a radiator cleanser strictly in accordance with the manufacturer's instructions; ensure that the cleanser is suitable for use in a copper/brass radiator. Refer to Chapter 1 for further information.

11 Using a soft brush, and an air line or garden hose, clear the radiator matrix of leaves, insects, etc.

12 If the radiator is suffering major leaks or extensive damage, it should be repaired by a specialist, or the radiator should be renewed (or exchanged for a reconditioned unit).

13 Examine the mounting rubbers for signs of damage or deterioration, and renew if necessary (photo).

Expansion tank

14 Empty any remaining coolant from the tank, and flush it with fresh water to clean it. If the tank is leaking, it must be renewed, but it is worth attempting a repair using a proprietary sealant or suitable adhesive.

15 The expansion tank cap should be cleaned and checked whenever it is removed. Check that its sealing surfaces and threads are clean and undamaged, and that they mate correctly with those of the expansion tank.

16 The cap's performance can only be checked using a cap pressure-tester (cooling system tester) with a suitable adaptor. On applying pressure, the cap's pressure relief valve should hold until the specified pressure is reached, at which point the valve should open.

17 If there is any doubt about the cap's performance, it must be renewed; ensure that the replacement is of exactly the correct type and rating.

Refitting

Radiator

18 Refitting is the reverse of the removal procedure, noting the following points.
(a) *Ensure that the radiator is seated correctly, without placing any strain on its mountings.*

(b) *Ensure that the radiator hoses are securely held by their retaining clips.*
(c) *Ensure that all wiring connectors are correctly routed so that they are clear of the cooling fan, and retained by any necessary clips or ties.*
(d) *On models with automatic transmission, tighten the cooler pipe union nuts securely, and top-up the transmission fluid as described in Chapter 1.*
(e) *Refill the cooling system as described in Chapter 1.*

Expansion tank

19 Refitting is the reverse of the removal procedure, noting the following points.
(a) *Ensure that the hoses are correctly routed with no kinks or sharp bends, and securely held by their retaining clips.*
(b) *Top-up the coolant level as described in Chapter 1.*

3 Thermostat – removal, testing and refitting

Note: *Refer to the warnings given in Section 1 before proceeding further.*

Removal

1 Drain the cooling system, as described in Chapter 1.

2 Slacken the hose retaining clip, and disconnect the bottom radiator hose from the thermostat housing.

3 Slacken and remove the two thermostat housing cover retaining bolts, then remove the housing cover and withdraw the thermostat. Remove the thermostat seal, and discard it.

Testing

4 If the thermostat remains in the open position at room temperature, it is faulty and must be renewed as a matter of course.

5 To test it fully, suspend the (closed) thermostat on a length of string in a container of cold water, with a thermometer beside it; ensure that neither touches the side of the container (Fig. 3.4).

6 Heat the water, and check the temperature at which the thermostat begins to open; compare this value with that specified.

2.7C ... and manoeuvre the radiator assembly out of the engine compartment

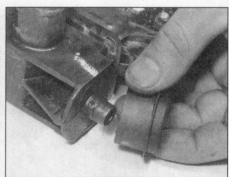

2.13 Inspect the radiator mounting rubbers for signs of wear, and renew if necessary

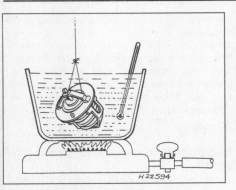

Fig. 3.4 Testing the thermostat (Sec 3)

3.6 Note temperature specification stamped in thermostat end (arrowed)

Continue to heat the water until the thermostat is fully open; the temperature at which this should happen is stamped in the end of the thermostat (photo). Remove the thermostat, measure the height of the fully-opened valve, then allow the thermostat to cool down, and check that it closes fully.

7 If the thermostat does not open and close as described, if it sticks in either position, or if it does not open at the specified temperature, it must be renewed.

Refitting

8 Fit a new seal to the thermostat, and install the thermostat in the housing.

9 Ensure the thermostat housing and cover mating surfaces are clean, then refit the cover and tighten its retaining bolts to the specified torque.

10 Refit the bottom hose to the thermostat housing, and securely tighten its retaining clip.

11 Refill the cooling system, as described in Chapter 1.

4 Radiator cooling fan – testing, removal and refitting

Testing

1 The cooling fan motor is supplied with current via the thermostatic switch which is screwed into the rear face of the cylinder block. The switch is the left-hand of the two switches in the block, the right-hand switch being the oil pressure switch (photo). The switch is fed with current via the ignition switch and fuse number 15. **Note:** *On models with air conditioning, there is also a cooling fan relay – see Section 11 for further information.*

2 If the fan does not appear to work, first check that the fuse is in good condition and has not blown. Run the engine until normal operating temperature is reached (or preferably, take the car for a drive of several miles), then allow it to idle. If the fan does not cut in within a few minutes (or before the temperature gauge enters the 'Hot' section), switch off the ignition, and disconnect the two wires from the thermostatic switch. Bridge these two wires with a length of spare wire,

and switch on the ignition. If the fan now operates, the thermostatic switch is probably faulty, and must be tested further as described in Section 5.

3 If the fan still fails to operate, check that full battery voltage is available at the switch's light green and grey wire terminal; if not, check the feed for a blown fuse or other fault such as a broken wire. If the feed is good, check for continuity between the fan motor's black wire terminal and a good earth point on the body; if there is no continuity, then the earth connection is faulty and must be remade. The circuit earth connection is one of those at earth header 7, attached to the bonnet locking platform.

4 If the switch and wiring are in good condition, the fault must be in the motor itself. This can be checked by disconnecting it from the wiring loom and connecting a 12-volt supply directly to it. If the motor does not work, it must be renewed.

Removal

Note: *Refer to the warnings given in Section 1 of this Chapter before starting work.*

5 Slacken and remove the two bolts securing the intake duct to the bonnet locking platform, and free the expansion tank hose from its duct retaining clips. Disconnect the duct from the resonator and intake hoses, then free its retaining stud from the radiator, and remove the duct.

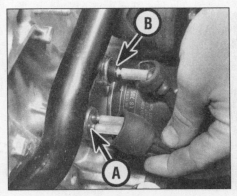

4.1 Cooling fan switch (A) is screwed into the rear of the cylinder block. Switch (B) is the oil pressure switch

6 Disconnect the cooling fan wiring connector, then slacken and remove the four nuts securing the fan cowling to the rear of radiator, and manoeuvre the fan assembly out of the engine compartment. If greater access to the lower cowling nuts is required, firmly apply the handbrake, then jack up the front of the car and support it firmly on axle stands. Slacken and remove the three bolts securing the bumper flange to the body. Remove the seven bolts securing the front undercover panel to the body, and remove the panel. The cowling nuts can then easily be reached from underneath the car.

7 To dismantle the assembly, first prise off the fan retaining circlip, then lift the fan off the motor spindle. Undo the three nuts which secure the motor assembly to the cowling (photo), then release the motor wiring and connector, and separate the motor and cowling.

Refitting

8 Refitting is a reversal of the removal procedure, ensuring that the motor wiring is correctly routed and retained by the cowling clips.

5 Cooling system electrical switches – testing, removal and refitting

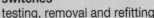

Testing

Radiator cooling fan thermostatic switch

1 Refer to Section 4 for details of a quick test which should eliminate most faulty switches. If the switch is to be renewed, or to be tested thoroughly, it must be removed.

2 To carry out a thorough test of the switch, use two spare wires to connect to it either a multimeter (set to the resistance function) or a battery and bulb test circuit. Suspend the switch in a pan of water which is being heated. Measure the temperature of the water with a thermometer. Do not let either the switch or

4.7 Cooling fan motor retaining nuts (arrowed)

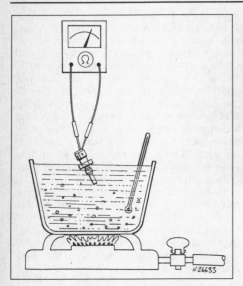

Fig. 3.5 Testing the cooling system electrical switches (Sec 5)

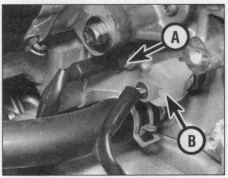

5.6 Coolant temperature sender gauge unit (A) location. (B) is the coolant temperature (TW) sensor (DOHC engine shown)

the thermometer touch the pan (see Fig. 3.5).

3 The switch contacts should close to the 'on' position (ie, continuity should exist) when the water reaches the temperature specified. Allow the water to cool down; the switch contacts should open at the same temperature or just below.

4 If the switch's performance is significantly different from that specified, or if it does not work at all, it must be renewed.

Coolant temperature gauge sender unit

5 The coolant temperature gauge mounted in the instrument panel is fed with a stabilised 10-volt supply from the instrument panel feed (via the ignition switch and fuse 1), its earth being controlled by the sender unit.

6 The sender unit is screwed into the right-hand end of the cylinder head, and is situated just below the distributor (photo). **Note:** *Do not confuse the temperature gauge sender with the fuel injection system coolant temperature (TW) sensor. The temperature gauge sender unit sits further back, and has only a single wire connected to it.* The sender contains a thermistor (the electrical resistance of which decreases at a predetermined rate as its temperature rises); thus when the coolant is cold, the sender's resistance is high, current flow through the gauge is reduced, and the gauge needle points to the 'C' (cold) end of the scale. If the unit is faulty, it must be renewed.

7 If the gauge develops a fault, check first the other instruments; if they do not work at all, check the instrument panel feed. If the readings are erratic, there may be a fault in the voltage stabiliser, which will necessitate the renewal of the gauge unit or printed circuit (see Chapter 12). If the fault is in the temperature gauge alone, check it as follows.

8 If the gauge needle remains at the 'C' end of the scale, disconnect the sender unit wire, and

earth it to the cylinder head; if the needle then deflects when the ignition is switched on, the sender unit is proven faulty, and must be renewed. If the needle still does not move, remove the instrument panel as described in Chapter 12, and check the continuity of the green/blue wire between the gauge and the sender unit and the feed to the gauge unit. If continuity is shown, and the fault still exists, then the gauge is faulty and the gauge unit must be renewed.

9 If the gauge needle remains at the 'H' end of the scale, disconnect the sender unit wire; if the needle then returns to the 'C' end of the scale when the ignition is switched on, the sender unit is proven faulty, and must be renewed. If the needle still does not move, check the remainder of the circuit as described above.

Removal

Radiator cooling fan thermostatic switch

10 Firmly apply the handbrake, then jack up the front of the vehicle and support it on axle stands. Access to the thermostatic switch (which is situated just above and to the left of the oil filter) can then be gained from underneath the car. As mentioned before, the cooling fan switch is the left-hand of the two switches with two wires connected to it, and should not be confused with the oil pressure switch (see photo 4.1). Either drain the cooling system as described in Chapter 1, or be prepared for some loss of coolant as the switch is unscrewed.

11 Remove the rubber cover, and disconnect the wiring connectors from the switch.

12 Unscrew the switch from the rear of the cylinder block, then withdraw it, along with its sealing washer. Plug the switch opening to prevent the entry of dirt; if the cooling system has not been drained, work quickly to minimise coolant loss.

Coolant temperature gauge sender unit

13 Either drain the cooling system as described in Chapter 1, or be prepared for

some loss of coolant as the sender unit is unscrewed.

14 Disconnect the wiring connector, then unscrew the sender unit from the cylinder head and withdraw it. Plug the opening to prevent the entry of dirt; if the cooling system has not been drained, work quickly to minimise coolant loss.

Refitting

Radiator cooling fan thermostatic switch

15 Prior to refitting, inspect the switch sealing washer for wear or damage, and renew as necessary. Apply a smear of grease to the washer, then screw the switch into position on the cylinder block. If the cooling system was not drained, work quickly to minimise coolant loss.

16 Tighten the switch securely, then reconnect its wiring connectors and slide the rubber cover back into position.

17 Lower the car to the ground, and refill the cooling system or check the coolant level (as applicable), as described in Chapter 1.

Coolant temperature gauge sender unit

18 Ensure the sender unit is clean, then apply a smear of suitable sealant to the unit threads. Screw the unit into position on the cylinder head, working quickly if the cooling system was not fully drained. Tighten the sender unit it to its specified torque wrench setting, and reconnect its wiring connector. On completion, refill the cooling system or check the coolant level (as applicable), as described in Chapter 1.

6 Water pump – removal and refitting

Note: *Refer to the warnings given in Section 1 before proceeding further.*

Removal

1 Water pump failure is usually indicated by coolant leaking from the gland behind the pump's bearing, or by rough and noisy operation, usually accompanied by excessive pump spindle play. If the pump shows any of these symptoms, it must be renewed as follows.

2 Drain the cooling system, as described in Chapter 1.

3 Remove the timing belt, as described in Chapter 2.

4 Slacken and remove the bolt securing the alternator adjusting link to the water pump, and position the link clear of the pump (photo).

5 Undo the four water pump retaining bolts, and remove the pump from the engine unit, along with its O-ring (photos).

Refitting

6 Refitting is a reverse of removal, noting the following points.

6.4 Remove the alternator adjusting link bolt, and position the link clear of the water pump

6.5B ... and remove the pump from the cylinder block. Note the O-ring fitted to the pump groove (arrowed)

(a) Ensure the pump and cylinder block mating surfaces are clean, and fit a new O-ring to the rear of the water pump
(b) Ensure the pump locating dowels are in position.
(d) Refit the timing belt, as described in Chapter 2.
(e) On completion, refill the cooling system as described in Chapter 1.

7 Cooling system hoses – renewal

Note: *Refer to the warnings given in Section 1 before proceeding further.*

1 If the checks described in Chapter 1 reveal a faulty hose, it must be renewed as follows.
2 First drain the cooling system, as described in Chapter 1; if the antifreeze is not due for renewal, the drained coolant may be re-used if it is collected in a clean container.
3 To disconnect any hose, use a screwdriver to slacken its retaining clips, then move them along the hose clear of the outlet. Carefully work the hose off its outlets. Whilst the hoses can be removed with relative ease when new or hot, **do not** attempt to disconnect any part of the system when it is still hot (see Section 1).
4 Note that the radiator hose outlets are fragile; do not use excessive force when attempting to remove the hoses. If a hose proves stubborn, try to release it by rotating it on its outlets before attempting to work it off. A hose which is stuck fast may be released by carefully prising or levering the end of the hose with a screwdriver, but do not use excessive force. If all else fails, cut the hose with a sharp knife, then slit it so that it can be peeled off in two pieces. While expensive, this is preferable to buying a new radiator.
5 When refitting a hose, first slide the clips onto the hose, then work the hose onto its outlets.

HAYNES HiNT *If the hose is stiff, use soap (washing-up liquid is ideal) as a lubricant, or soften it by first soaking it in boiling water, but take care to avoid scalding.*

6.5A Undo the four water pump retaining bolts (arrowed) ...

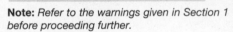

6.6 Fit a new O-ring to the water pump, and ensure the locating dowels are in position

6 Work each hose end fully onto its outlet, check that the hose is settled correctly and is properly routed, then slide each retaining clip along the hose until it is behind the outlet flared end before tightening it securely (photo).
7 Refill the system with coolant, as described in Chapter 1.
8 Check carefully for leaks as soon as possible after disturbing any part of the cooling system.

8 Heater components – removal and refitting

Note: *Refer to the warnings given in Section 1 before proceeding further.*

Removal

Heater unit

1 Drain the cooling system, as described in Chapter 1.
2 Working in the engine compartment, slacken their hose clips, then disconnect the heater feed and return hoses from the matrix outlets on the bulkhead. Disconnect the inner cable from the heater valve, and free the outer cable from its retaining clip. Slacken and remove the heater lower mounting nut which is situated just to the left of the matrix outlets (photos).
3 Remove the facia, as described in Chapter 11.
4 Slacken and remove its two retaining

7.6 Ensure all hose retaining clips are securely tightened

8.2A Disconnect the heater feed and return hoses ...

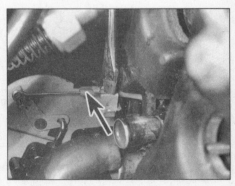

8.2B ... and free the heater valve cable (arrowed) from its retaining clip

3

8.2C Slacken and remove the heater unit lower mounting nut

8.4 Remove the blower motor-to-heater unit duct

8.5A Undo the right-hand duct retaining screw (arrowed) ...

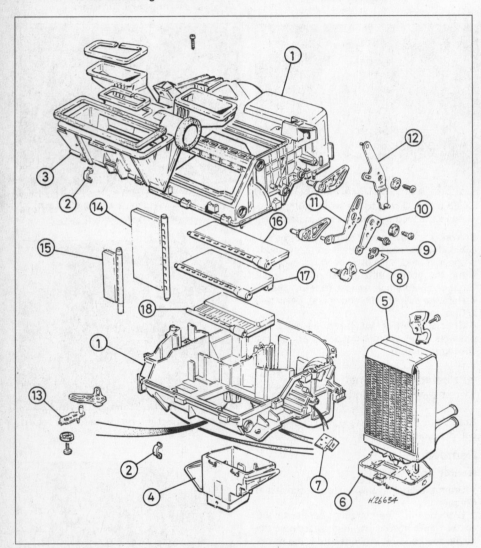

Fig. 3.6 Heater unit components (Sec 8)

1 Heater case
2 Heater case clip
3 Face level/windscreen duct
4 Floor level duct
5 Heater matrix
6 Heater matrix cover
7 Cable retaining clip
8 Floor level flap operating lever
9 Clip
10 Floor level flap idler lever
11 Face level flap idler lever
12 Flap operating lever
13 Air mix flap operating lever
14 Air mix flap
15 Ambient air flap – centre console vents
16 Distribution flap – windscreen
17 Distribution flap – face level vents
18 Distribution flap – floor level vents

8.5B ... and disengage the duct from the heater unit

screws, then remove the blower motor-to-heater unit duct (photo). **Note:** *On models with air conditioning, the evaporator unit is fitted in place of the duct. It may be possible to gain the necessary clearance required to disengage the evaporator from the heater unit by removing its mounting brackets and nuts, but if not, the evaporator must be removed. Refer to the warnings on air conditioning in Section 1, and to Section 11 for further information.*

5 Undo the screw securing the right-hand heater duct to its mounting bracket, then move the duct to the right to disengage it from the heater unit (photos).

6 Undo the fuel cut-off inertia switch retaining nut, and disengage the switch from the steering column support bracket.

7 Release the wiring block connector from the right-hand end of the steering column support bracket, and undo the fusebox retaining nut. Slacken and remove the five support bracket retaining bolts, and remove the bracket from the car (photos).

8 Disconnect the air recirculation cable inner cable from the flap, and free the outer cable from the blower motor.

9 Prise out the stud securing the rear heater duct sleeve to the bottom of the heater unit, and slide the sleeve down to disengage it from the unit (photo).

10 Disconnect the wiring connectors from the heater control panel, then remove the two upper heater unit retaining nuts, and carefully manoeuvre the heater unit out of the car (photos).

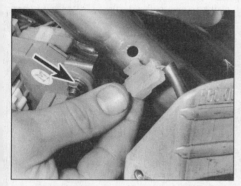

8.7A Release the wiring connector from the steering column support bracket and remove the fusebox nut (arrowed)

8.7B Remove its mounting bolts, then manoeuvre the steering column mounting bracket out of position

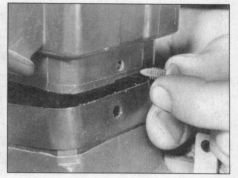

8.9 Remove the retaining stud, and disengage the rear heater duct sleeve from the heater unit

8.10A Disconnect the wiring from the heater control panel ...

8.10B ... and remove the heater upper retaining nuts

8.12 Undo the retaining screw, and remove the matrix outlet pipe bracket

3

Heater matrix

11 Remove the heater unit, as described above.

12 Undo the screw securing the matrix outlet pipe bracket to the heater unit, and remove the bracket (photo).

13 Slacken and remove the two matrix cover retaining screws, then remove the cover and withdraw the matrix from the heater unit (photos).

14 If the matrix is leaking, it is best to obtain a new or reconditioned unit; home repairs are seldom successful. If it is blocked, it can sometimes be cleared by reverse-flushing with a garden hose, using a proprietary radiator cleaning product if absolutely necessary. Refer to Chapter 1 for further information.

Heater blower motor

15 Undo the two glovebox retaining screws, then partially withdraw the glovebox until access can be gained to the glovebox damper-to-facia screw. Undo the damper screw, and remove the glovebox and damper (photo).

16 Slacken and remove the four glovebox support rail mounting bolts, and remove the rail (photo).

17 Slacken and remove its two retaining screws, then remove the blower motor-to-heater unit duct (photo). **Note:** *On models with air conditioning, the evaporator unit is fitted in place of the duct It may be possible to gain the*

8.13A Undo the two matrix cover retaining screws ...

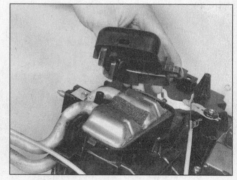

8.13B ... then remove the cover ...

8.13C ... and withdraw the matrix from the heater unit

8.15 Glovebox damper retaining screw (arrowed)

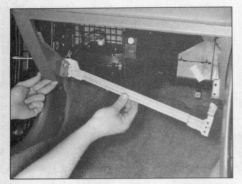

8.16 Remove the glovebox support rail ...

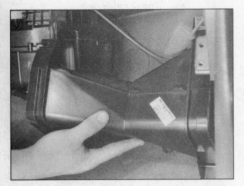

8.17 ... then remove the blower motor-to-heater unit duct

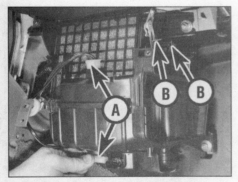

8.18 Disconnect the motor wiring connectors (A). Air recirculation cable already removed here, but note attachment peg and clip (B)

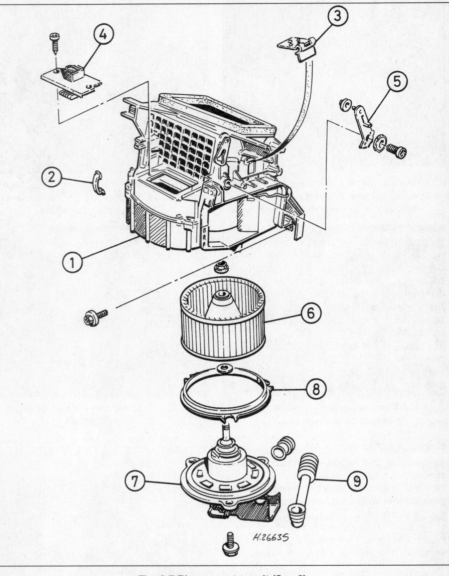

Fig. 3.7 Blower motor unit (Sec 8)

1 Blower motor case
2 Blower motor case clip
3 Cable retaining clip
4 Blower motor resistor
5 Recirculation flap operating lever
6 Fan
7 Blower motor
8 Seal
9 Breather tube

8.19A Undo the three blower motor mounting bolts (arrowed) ...

8.19B ... and remove the unit from behind the facia

8.20A Remove the motor cover retaining screws (arrowed) ...

8.20B ... and disconnect the breather hose

8.20C Undo the motor retaining bolts, and withdraw the motor from the unit

8.20D Remove the fan retaining nut ...

necessary clearance required to disengage the evaporator and remove the blower motor by removing its mounting brackets and nuts, but if not, the evaporator must be removed. Refer to the air conditioning warnings in Section 1, and to Section 11 for further information.

18 Disconnect the air recirculation inner cable from the flap, and free the outer cable from the blower motor. Disconnect the two blower motor wiring connectors (photo).
19 Slacken and remove the three blower motor mounting bolts, and manoeuvre the blower unit out from underneath the facia (photos).
20 To remove the motor from the unit, undo the four motor cover retaining screws, then disconnect the breather hose and lift off the cover. Slacken and remove the three motor retaining bolts, and withdraw the motor assembly from the blower unit. Undo the fan retaining nut, and separate the fan and motor, noting the seal which is fitted between the two components (photos).

Heater blower motor resistor

21 Remove the glovebox, as described above in paragraphs 15 and 16.
22 Disconnect the wiring connector, then undo its two retaining screws, and remove the resistor from the front of the motor assembly.

Heater valve

23 Using a pair of pliers, release the retaining clip and disconnect the vacuum pipe from the throttle housing end of the air intake hose. Slacken the retaining clip which secures the intake hose to the throttle housing, and disconnect the intake hose. Working along the length of the intake hose, release the vacuum hoses from their retaining clips, then disconnect the intake hose from the air cleaner housing, and remove it from the engine compartment.
24 Working in the engine compartment, disconnect the inner cable from the heater valve, and free the outer cable from its retaining clip.
25 Slacken and remove the bolt securing the heater valve mounting bracket and the clutch cable support bracket to the engine compartment bulkhead.

8.20E ... and lift off the fan, noting the seal (arrowed)

26 Either drain the cooling system as described in Chapter 1, or clamp the coolant hoses on each side of the coolant valve, to minimise the loss of coolant.
27 Slacken the hose retaining clips (photo), then disconnect both hoses from the coolant valve, and remove the valve from the engine compartment. Mop up any spilt coolant immediately.

Refitting

Heater unit

28 Refitting is a reverse of the removal procedure, noting the following points.
(a) Ensure that the heater ducts are securely connected to the unit, so that there are no air leaks or gaps.
(b) Check the operation of all heater cables before refitting the facia, ensuring that the relevant components move smoothly from the fully-open to the fully-closed position. If necessary, adjustments can be made by releasing the relevant cable retaining clip and repositioning the outer cable.
(c) Ensure that the heater hoses are correctly reconnected, and securely held by their retaining clips.
(d) Tighten the lower heater mounting nut to the specified torque setting.
(e) Refill the cooling system, as described in Chapter 1.

Heater matrix

29 Refitting is a reverse of the removal procedure.

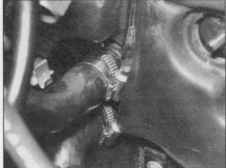
8.27 Slackening heater feed and return hose clamps – ensure they are securely tightened when refitting

Heater blower motor

30 Refitting is a reversal of the removal sequence, noting the following points.
(a) Ensure that the foam rubber seal is refitted correctly, so that the blower motor to bulkhead aperture is closed off.
(b) Tighten the blower motor mounting bolts to the specified torque setting.
(c) Ensure that the air recirculation cable and flap functions correctly before refitting the glovebox. If necessary, adjust by releasing the cable retaining clip and repositioning the outer cable.

Heater blower motor resistor

31 Refitting is a reversal of the removal procedure.

Heater valve

32 Refitting is a reversal of the removal procedure. On completion, check that the heater cable operates smoothly, and top-up or refill (as applicable) the cooling system, as described in Chapter 1.

9 Heater ducts and vents – removal and refitting

Removal

Facia ducts

1 Remove the facia, as described in Chapter 11.

3

2 The ducts are mounted onto the facia assembly, and can be removed individually once their retaining screws have been removed.

Heater unit ducts

3 The left-hand heater unit-to-blower motor duct is removed as described in paragraphs 15 to 17 of Section 8.

4 To remove the right-hand duct, remove the facia as described in Chapter 11. Slacken and remove the retaining screw which secures the right-hand end of the duct to its mounting bracket, and release the radio aerial from its retaining clips on the underside of the duct. The duct can then be manoeuvred out of position.

5 Removal of the lower ducts which supply air to the rear passenger footwells is a complex job, requiring the removal of the front seats, centre console and the various trim panels so that the floor carpet can be peeled back. This job is therefore not recommended, unless absolutely necessary.

Centre console vents

6 Remove the centre console, as described in Chapter 11.

7 The vents can then be unclipped from the rear of the front console section and removed.

Facia vents

8 The adjustable face-level vents can be removed by prising them gently out of the facia until their clips are released, taking care not to mark the facia.

9 The door window demister vents, fitted to the sides of the facia, can also be prised out of position, with the relevant door open.

Refitting

10 Refitting is a reverse of the removal procedure.

10 Heater controls – removal, refitting and adjustment

Removal

1 Remove the heater unit, as described in Section 8.

2 Disconnect the heater control cables from the heater unit, and unclip the control panel. Remove the panel assembly, complete with cables (photos).

Refitting and adjustment

3 Refit the heater control panel to the heater unit, and reconnect the necessary control cables to their original positions.

4 Check the operation of the control cables, ensuring that they operate smoothly and move the necessary component from the fully-open to the fully-closed position. Adjustments can be made by releasing the cable retaining clip and repositioning the outer cable.

5 Once the necessary control cables are

functioning correctly, refit the heater unit as described in Section 8.

11 Air conditioning system components – removal and refitting

⚠️ **Warning: The system should be professionally discharged before any of the air conditioning hoses are disconnected. Cap or plug the pipe lines as soon as they are disconnected, to prevent the entry of moisture. Refer to the precautions given in Section 1 before proceeding.**

Compressor

Removal

1 Remove the air conditioning compressor drivebelt, as described in Chapter 1.

2 Undo the single bolt which secures each air conditioning hose union to the compressor, and disconnect both hoses. Discard the hose union O-rings; they **must** be renewed whenever they are disturbed.

3 Disconnect the compressor switch wiring connector, then slacken and remove the four bolts securing the compressor to the engine, and remove the compressor downwards and away from the engine.

Refitting

4 Refitting is a reversal of the removal procedure, noting the following.

(a) Tighten the compressor mounting bolts to the specified torque.

(b) Fit new O-rings to the air conditioning hose unions, and tighten their retaining bolts securely.

(c) On completion, have the air conditioning system recharged by a refrigeration specialist or Rover dealer.

Condenser

Removal

5 Remove the front bumper, as described in Chapter 11.

6 Slacken and remove the bolts securing the power steering fluid cooler to the body, then

undo the bonnet lock mounting bracket bolts, and position the lock assembly clear of the condenser unit.

7 Unscrew the air conditioning pipe union nuts from the condenser unit, then disconnect the pipes. Discard the union pipe O-rings, as these **must** be renewed whenever they are disturbed.

8 Slacken and remove the four retaining bolts, and withdraw both the condenser upper mounting brackets. Release the condenser from its lower mounting points, and manoeuvre it away from the car.

Refitting

9 Prior to refitting, check the condenser lower mounting rubbers for signs of damage or deterioration, and renew as necessary. Renew the pipe union O-rings as a matter of course.

10 Refitting is a direct reversal of the removal procedure, tightening the pipe union nuts to the specified torque setting. On completion, have the air conditioning system recharged by a refrigeration specialist or Rover dealer.

Condenser cooling fan

Removal

11 Slacken and remove the two bolts securing the intake duct to the bonnet locking platform, and free the expansion tank hose from its duct retaining clips. Disconnect the duct from the resonator and intake hoses, then free its retaining stud from the radiator, and remove the duct.

12 Undo the bolt securing the air conditioning pipe to the bonnet locking platform, and disconnect the condenser fan wiring connector.

13 Slacken and remove the four nuts securing the fan cowling to the rear of radiator, and manoeuvre the fan assembly out of the engine compartment. If greater access to the lower cowling nuts is required, firmly apply the handbrake, then jack up the front of the car and support it firmly on axle stands. Slacken and remove the three bolts securing the bumper flange to the body. Remove the seven bolts securing the front undercover panel to the body, and remove the panel. The cowling nuts can then easily be reached from underneath the car.

10.2A Disconnect the control cables from the heater unit ...

10.2B ... and remove the heater control panel and cables as an assembly

14 To dismantle the assembly, slacken and remove the fan retaining nut and washer, and remove the fan from the motor spindle. Free the motor wiring from the cowling retaining clips. Undo the three motor retaining screws, then lift off the motor cover, and separate the motor and cowling.

Refitting

15 Refitting is a reversal of the removal procedure, ensuring that the motor wiring connector is securely retained by the cowling clips and is clear of the fan rotor.

Evaporator

Removal

16 Undo the three bolts which secure the washer system reservoir to the engine compartment bulkhead, and move the reservoir to gain access to the two evaporator union nuts. Slacken both the union nuts, and disconnect the pipes from the evaporator. Remove the O-rings from the union nuts, and discard them.

17 Working from inside the car, undo the two glovebox retaining screws, then partially withdraw the glovebox until access can be gained to the glovebox damper-to-facia screw. Undo the damper screw, and remove the glovebox and damper.

18 Slacken and remove the four glovebox support rail mounting bolts, and remove the rail.

19 Undo the two evaporator bracket retaining bolts, and remove both the brackets.

20 Disconnect the wiring connector from the right-hand side of the evaporator.

21 Slacken and remove the two evaporator mounting nuts, and manoeuvre the unit out of position.

Refitting

22 Refitting is a reverse of the removal procedure, noting the following points:

(a) *Ensure that the evaporator is correctly joined to the heater unit and blower*

motor, so that there are no air leaks or gaps, then tighten its retaining nuts and bracket bolts securely.

(b) *Fit new O-rings to the pipe unions, and tighten the union nuts to the specified torque setting.*

(c) *On completion, have the system recharged by a refrigeration specialist or Rover dealer.*

Receiver drier

Note: *The receiver drier unit unions must be capped immediately after they are disconnected, and must remain capped until they are to be reconnected. If the receiver drier unit is left uncapped for any period of time, it must be renewed.*

Removal

23 Remove the left-hand headlamp, as described in Chapter 12. On models with power steering, also free the power steering reservoir from its mounting bracket and, ensuring that it remains upright, position it clear of the air conditioning pipe.

24 Undo the bolt securing the air conditioning pipe to the body.

25 Slacken the union nuts, and disconnect the pipes from the receiver drier, noting the O-rings which are fitted to the pipe unions; discard the O-rings, as they **must** be renewed whenever they are disturbed.

26 Slacken the receiver drier clamp bolt, then slide the unit out of its retaining clamp, and remove it from the engine compartment.

Refitting

27 Refitting is a direct reversal of the removal sequence, tightening the pipe union nuts to the specified torque setting. On completion, have the system recharged by a refrigeration specialist or Rover dealer.

Dual-pressure switch

Removal

28 Remove the front bumper, as described in Chapter 11.

29 Disconnect the wiring connector, and unscrew the switch from the air conditioning pipe. Remove the O-ring from the switch, and discard it.

Refitting

30 Refitting is a reversal of the removal procedure. Fit a new O-ring to the switch, and tighten it to the specified torque setting. On completion, have the system recharged by a refrigeration specialist or Rover dealer.

Air conditioning relays and diode pack

Removal

31 The air conditioning relays and diode pack are all mounted onto a single bracket, which is situated directly beneath the battery tray. With the bracket in place in the car, the relays are as follows from front to rear; radiator cooling fan relay, compressor clutch relay, and condenser fan relay, with the diode pack mounted on the rear of the bracket. The bracket assembly is removed as follows.

32 Remove the battery and battery tray, as described in Chapter 12.

33 Slacken and remove the two bolts securing the intake duct to the bonnet locking platform, and free the expansion tank hose from its duct retaining clips. Disconnect the duct from the resonator and intake hoses, then free its retaining stud from the radiator and remove the duct.

34 Disconnect the rubber intake hose from the base of the air cleaner housing, and remove it to gain access to the relay mounting bracket assembly.

35 Undo the bolt securing the relay mounting bracket to the body, then disconnect the wiring connectors, and remove the bracket assembly from the car. Refer to Chapter 12 for further information on relays.

Refitting

36 Refitting is a reverse of the removal procedure.

3

Notes

Chapter 4
Fuel, exhaust and emission control systems

Contents

Degrees of difficulty

| Easy, suitable for novice with little experience | | Fairly easy, suitable for beginner with some experience | | Fairly difficult, suitable for competent DIY mechanic | 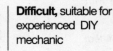 | Difficult, suitable for experienced DIY mechanic | | Very difficult, suitable for expert DIY or professional | |

Specifications

| System type . . . . | Honda PGM-Fi engine management system, using ECU-controlled multi-point fuel injection |

PGM-Fi system data

Fuel pump type . . . .   Electric, immersed in fuel tank
Fuel pump pressure:
  Maximum – at 16 volts . . . .   4.1 bars
  Regulated constant pressure . . . .   2.3 to 3.0 bars
Idle speed – nominal value given for reference purposes only . . . .   800 + 50 rpm
CO level at idle speed – engine at normal operating temperature:
  Models without catalytic converter:
    SOHC engines . . . .   0.2 to 1.0%
    DOHC engines . . . .   0.2 to 0.8%
  Models with catalytic converter . . . .   0.1 % maximum

Accelerator cable deflection/free play . . . .   10 to 12 mm (measured at throttle linkage)

Recommended fuel

Minimum octane rating:
  Models without catalytic converter . . . .   95 RON unleaded or 97 RON leaded ('4-star')
  Models with catalytic converter:
    SOHC engines . . . .   91 RON unleaded (not yet available in the UK, 95 RON unleaded is the nearest equivalent) – **do not use leaded petrol**
    DOHC engines . . . .   95 RON unleaded – **do not use leaded petrol**

Torque wrench settings

	Nm	lbf ft
Fuel system bleed screw	12	9
Fuel pump retaining nuts	9	7
Vent valve and hose retaining nuts	9	7
Throttle housing retaining nuts and bolt	22	16
Fuel rail retaining nuts	10	7
Injector wiring connector cover nuts	10	7

Torque wrench settings (continued)

	Nm	lbf ft
Fuel pressure regulator retaining bolts	10	7
Fuel filter outlet hose union bolt	35	26
Lambda sensor	45	33
Inlet manifold:		
Retaining nuts	45	33
Support bracket bolts	25	18
Exhaust manifold:		
Retaining nuts	45	33
Support bracket bolts	25	18
Heatshield retaining screws	6	4
Exhaust system joint nuts and bolts:		
Manifold-to-front pipe joint	50	37
Front pipe-to-intermediate pipe/catalytic converter bolts	22	16
Catalytic converter-to-intermediate pipe nuts	34	25
Intermediate pipe-to-tailpipe bolts	22	16
Exhaust front pipe mounting nuts/bolts	15	11

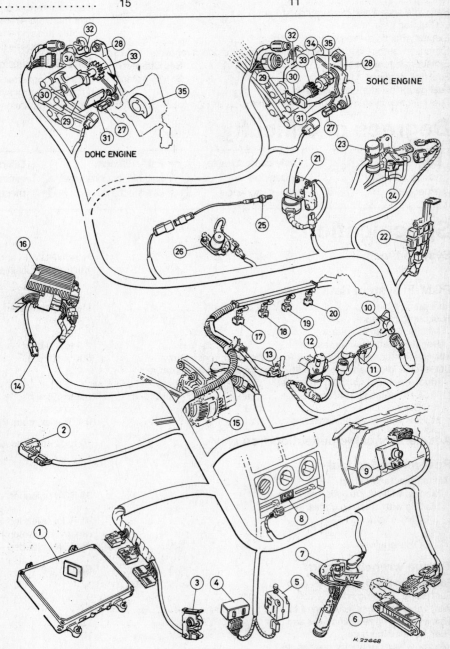

Fig. 4.1 Location of engine management (fuel/ignition) system components (Sec 1)

1 Electronic control unit (ECU)
2 Atmospheric pressure (AP) sensor
3 Idle mixture (IMA) sensor
4 Fuel pump relay
5 Fuel cut-off inertia switch
6 Starter inhibitor switch models with automatic transmission
7 Fuel pump
8 Air conditioner switch (where fitted)
9 Vehicle speed sensor
10 Throttle angle sensor
11 Electronic air control valve (EACV)
12 Fast idle speed solenoid valve – SOHC and later DOHC engines
13 Intake air temperature (TA) sensor
14 Ignition timing inspection/adjuster wiring terminal
15 Alternator
16 Injector resistor pack
17 Number 1 cylinder injector
18 Number 2 cylinder injector
19 Number 3 cylinder injector
20 Number 4 cylinder injector
21 Two-stage resonator control solenoid
22 Compressor clutch relay – models with air conditioning
23 Purge control valve – models with catalytic converter
24 Manifold absolute pressure (MAP) sensor
25 Lambda sensor – models with catalytic converter
26 Lock-up control solenoid – models with automatic transmission
27 Engine coolant temperature (TW) sensor
28 Distributor
29 Distributor cap
30 Rotor arm
31 Igniter unit
32 Ignition HT coil
33 Crankshaft position sensor
34 TDC sensor
35 Cylinder position sensor

H.22668

Part A: Fuel injection system

1 General information and precautions

The fuel system consists of a fuel tank mounted under the rear of the car with an electric fuel pump immersed in it, a fuel filter, and the fuel feed and return lines. The fuel pump supplies fuel to the fuel rail, which acts as a reservoir for the four fuel injectors which inject fuel into the inlet tracts. A fuel filter is incorporated in the feed line from the pump to the fuel rail, to ensure that the fuel supplied to the injectors is clean.

The air cleaner contains a disposable paper filter element. An intake air system is incorporated into the air cleaner intake to minimise the intake noise of the engine (see Section 3).

The ECU fully controls both the ignition system and the fuel injection system, integrating the two in a complete engine management system; refer to Section 7 for information regarding the fuel injection system, and Chapter 5 for information on the ignition side of the system.

The exhaust system consists of three sections; the front pipe and front silencer box, the intermediate pipe and middle silencer box, and the tailpipe and main silencer box. The system is suspended throughout its entire length by rubber mountings. If a catalytic converter is fitted, the exhaust system consists of four sections, the catalytic converter being situated between the front pipe and the (much shorter) intermediate pipe.

⚠️ **Warning: Many of the procedures in this Chapter require the removal of fuel lines and connections which may result in some fuel spillage. Before carrying out any operation on the fuel system refer to the precautions given in Safety first! at the beginning of this Manual and follow them implicitly. Petrol is a highly dangerous and volatile liquid and the precautions necessary when handling it cannot be overstressed.**

Note: *Residual pressure will remain in the fuel lines long after the vehicle was last used; before disconnecting any fuel line, depressurise the fuel system as described in Section 8.*

2 Air cleaner housing assembly – removal and refitting

Removal

1 Remove the battery, as described in Chapter 12.
2 Using a pair of pliers, release the retaining clip and disconnect the vacuum pipe from the throttle housing end of the air intake hose. Slacken the retaining clip which secures the intake hose to the throttle housing, and disconnect the intake hose. Working along the length of the intake hose, release the vacuum hoses from their retaining clips, then disconnect the intake hose from the air cleaner housing and remove it from the engine compartment (photos).
3 Undo the two bolts securing the resonator vacuum pipe to the top of the air cleaner housing, and position the pipe clear of the working area.
4 Slacken and remove the three bolts securing the air cleaner housing to the body, then disconnect the rubber intake hose from the front of the assembly, and manoeuvre the housing assembly out of position.

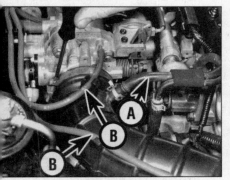

2.2A Slacken the retaining clip, then disconnect the vacuum pipe (A) and free the vacuum hoses (B) ...

2.2B Removing the intake hose

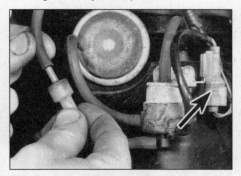

3.5 Disconnect the control valve solenoid wiring connector (arrowed), and the vacuum reservoir pipe from the check valve

5 If necessary, undo the two bolts securing the intake duct to the bonnet locking platform. Disconnect the intake duct from the intake hose, then free the expansion tank hose from the top of the duct and remove the duct assembly from the car.

Refitting

6 Refitting is a reverse of the removal procedure, ensuring that all hoses and ducts are correctly reconnected, and that all bolts are securely tightened.

3 Air intake system – general information, component removal and refitting

General information

1 The intake air system is fitted to reduce the amount of induction noise (see Fig. 4.2). The system operates as follows.
2 Air is drawn into the air cleaner housing via the duct which is mounted onto the bonnet locking platform, behind the radiator. Linked to the intake duct is a two-stage resonator, which is controlled by the ECU via a vacuum solenoid valve and a diaphragm unit. A vacuum reservoir is connected to the inlet manifold via a long hose, and to the electrically-operated control valve; the check valve is fitted to the hose between the reservoir and manifold, to allow air to pass only from the reservoir to the manifold. The control valve is connected to the vacuum diaphragm unit, which in turn operates the resonator aperture flap. Below 3000 rpm, the control valve is closed and the vacuum diaphragm unit is isolated from the inlet manifold vacuum which is present in the vacuum reservoir. With no vacuum acting on the diaphragm unit, the resonator aperture flap is closed. At engine speeds above 3000 rpm the ECU energises the control valve solenoid and the valve opens. The inlet manifold vacuum which is present in the reservoir then acts on the vacuum diaphragm unit, which in turn opens up the two-stage resonator flap. This increases the resonator aperture opening, and so keeps induction noise to a minimum. When the engine speed returns to below 3000 rpm, the ECU shuts the control valve, isolating the diaphragm unit from the inlet manifold vacuum, and the resonator aperture flap closes again.
3 All the system components are mounted onto the two-stage resonator, and are removed as follows.

Removal

4 Remove the front bumper, as described in Chapter 11.
5 Disconnect the wiring connector from the control valve solenoid, and disconnect the vacuum pipe from the vacuum reservoir check valve (photo).

4

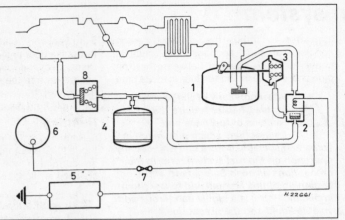

Fig. 4.2 Air cleaner intake system components (Sec 3)

1 Two-stage resonator
2 Resonator control valve
3 Vacuum diaphragm unit
4 Vacuum reservoir
5 Engine management ECU
6 Ignition switch
7 Fuse number 14
8 Check valve

3.7 Note the correct fitted positions of resonator vacuum pipes before disconnecting them

6 Slacken and remove the three bolts securing the resonator assembly to the body, release it from the intake duct, and remove it from the car, noting the rubber mountings and spacers. If necessary, with the resonator removed, the various system components can then be removed as follows.

7 Make a note of the correct fitted positions of the various vacuum pipes (photo), then disconnect the vacuum reservoir pipe from the control valve, and unclip the reservoir from the resonator. Disconnect the control valve vacuum pipes from the diaphragm unit and resonator, then undo the two valve retaining screws and remove the valve. Unhook the diaphragm rod from the resonator flap, then undo the two diaphragm retaining screws and

remove the diaphragm. If necessary, remove the joint rubber from the resonator intake.

Refitting

8 Refitting is a reversal of the removal procedure, noting the following.
(a) If the resonator assembly was dismantled use the notes made to ensure all vacuum pipes are reconnected to their original positions.
(b) Tighten all retaining bolts and screws securely.

4 Accelerator cable – removal, refitting and adjustment

Removal

1 Slacken the accelerator cable locknuts, and free the outer cable from its mounting bracket on the throttle housing. Release the inner cable from the throttle cam (photos).
2 Work back along the length of the outer cable, and release it from any relevant retaining clips and ties. Rotate the cable retainer a quarter of a turn anti-clockwise to release it from the engine compartment bulkhead. If necessary, remove the four windscreen wiper motor mounting bolts to free the motor from the engine compartment bulkhead, and pivot the motor away from the retainer to improve access.
3 Working inside the car, undo the five right-hand lower facia panel retaining screws, and remove the panel.

4 On models with a manual gearbox, remove the retaining clip from the pedal mounting bracket, and disconnect the cable from the upper end of the pedal.
5 On models with automatic transmission, lift the cable retaining bracket upwards, and detach the cable from the upper end of the accelerator pedal.
6 On all models, return to the engine compartment and remove the cable from the car.

Refitting and adjustment

7 Refitting is the reverse of the removal procedure, ensuring that the cable is correctly routed and retained by all the necessary clips. Where necessary, tighten the windscreen wiper motor retaining bolts to the specified torque (see Chapter 12), then loosely tighten the cable locknuts and adjust the cable as follows.
8 Warm the engine up to normal operating temperature, then switch it off and disconnect the battery negative terminal. Disconnect the throttle control dashpot vacuum pipe, and connect a hand-operated vacuum pump to the dashpot.
9 Apply vacuum to the dashpot diaphragm so that the pullrod is drawn into the diaphragm, and check the amount of free play present in the accelerator cable. If access to a vacuum pump cannot be gained, the cable free play can be checked with the dashpot pullrod manually pushed into the diaphragm (photo). If the amount of cable deflection is not as given in the Specifications, adjust it by repositioning the locknuts as required to obtain the correct amount of cable free play. Once the cable is correctly adjusted, have an assistant depress the accelerator pedal, and check that the throttle valve opens fully and returns to the at-rest position smoothly. If all is well, tighten the cable locknuts securely. Disconnect the vacuum pump (where used), then reconnect the vacuum hose to the dashpot and reconnect the battery negative terminal. **Note:** On models with automatic transmission, check the kickdown cable adjustment as described in Chapter 7 before disconnecting the vacuum pump.

4.1A Slacken the accelerator cable locknuts ...

4.1B ... and free the inner cable from the throttle cam

4.9 In the absence of a vacuum pump, check accelerator cable free play (arrows) while manually pushing the pullrod into the dashpot

5 Accelerator pedal – removal and refitting

Removal

1 Working from inside the car, undo the five right-hand lower facia panel retaining screws, and remove the panel.

2 On manual gearbox models, remove the retaining clip from the pedal mounting bracket, and disconnect the cable from the upper end of the pedal.

3 On models with automatic transmission, lift the cable retaining bracket upwards, and detach the cable from the upper end of the accelerator pedal.

4 On all models, prise off the circlip from the pedal pivot, and withdraw the accelerator pedal from the mounting bracket.

Refitting

5 Refitting is a reverse of the removal procedure, applying a smear of multi-purpose grease to the pedal pivot. On completion, adjust the accelerator cable as described in Section 4.

6 Unleaded petrol – general information and usage

Note: *The information given in this Chapter is correct at the time of writing, but applies only to petrol currently available in the UK. If updated information is thought to be required, check with a Rover dealer. If travelling abroad, consult one of the motoring organisations (or a similar authority) for advice on the petrol available and its suitability for your vehicle.*

1 The fuel recommended by Rover for the 216/416 models is given in the Specifications Section of this Chapter.

2 RON and MON are different testing standards; RON stands for Research Octane Number (also written as RM), while MON stands for Motor Octane Number (also written as MM).

3 Rover 216/416 models with the SOHC engine and a catalytic converter are designed to run on 91 (RON) octane unleaded petrol (which is not available in the UK, 95 RON unleaded being the nearest equivalent). All other models are designed to run on 95 (RON) octane unleaded petrol. Super/Super Plus (98 RON unleaded) petrols can be used without modification, if nothing else is available. Four-star (leaded) petrol can **only** be used if the car is **not** fitted with a catalytic converter, using leaded petrol will destroy a catalyst unit, and these are expensive! Refer to Section 21 for more information on catalytic converters.

7 Fuel injection system – general information

Rover 216/416 models are equipped with a Honda PGM-Fi engine management system

which controls both the ignition and fuel injection systems. The ignition side of the system is explained in Chapter 5, and the fuel side of the system consists of three sub-systems; the fuel delivery system, the air metering system, and the electrical control system.

The fuel delivery system incorporates the fuel tank, which houses an electric fuel pump immersed in a swirl pot inside it to prevent aeration of the fuel. When the ignition is switched on, the pump is supplied with current via the fuel pump relay, under the control of the ECU; the pump feeds petrol via a non-return valve (to prevent fuel draining out of the system components and back to the tank when the pump is not working) to the fuel filter, and from the filter to the fuel rail. Fuel pressure is controlled by the pressure regulator (mounted on the fuel rail), which lifts to allow excess fuel to return to the tank swirl pot where a venturi causes the returning fuel to draw cool fuel from the tank into the swirl pot. In the event of extreme deceleration, such as happens during an accident, the inertia switch cuts off the power to the pump, so that the risk of fire is minimised from fuel spraying out of broken fuel lines under pressure.

The air metering system includes the air intake system (see Section 3) and the air cleaner, but its main components are the throttle housing and the idle speed control system. The throttle housing contains the throttle valve. A throttle angle sensor is fitted to the throttle valve spindle, to inform the ECU of the throttle valve opening, and hence the airflow to the engine. The idle speed is electronically controlled by the ECU, via the electronic air control valve (EACV) which is mounted onto the rear of the inlet manifold. When the throttle valve is closed, the ECU varies the current supplied to the EACV windings, which in turn opens and closes a throttle valve bypass passage by the appropriate amount. This then controls the amount of air flowing through the manifold, therefore altering the idle speed. **Note:** *Apart from the base idle speed adjustment (see Chapter 1), there is no provision for idle speed adjustment. When checking the idle speed remember that it will vary constantly under control of the ECU.*

On SOHC engines, (and DOHC engines from June 1990 onwards), a fast idle system is also incorporated; this is controlled by the fast idle speed control valve, which is also mounted onto the rear of the inlet manifold. When the engine coolant temperature is below –10°C, the ECU energises the fast idle speed control valve solenoid, which then opens a second throttle valve bypass passage. This then supplements the operation of the EACV until the engine warms up.

The electrical control system consists of the ECU, with all the sensors that provide it with information and the actuators by which it controls the whole system's operation. The ECU has the basic injector opening times for

the various engine speeds and manifold pressures programmed into its memory. The ECU then alters this basic setting, using the inputs from the various sensors on and around the engine, and provides the correct ignition and injector (duration) timing to suit those conditions. The manifold absolute pressure (MAP) sensor informs it of the load on the engine, and the intake air temperature (TA) sensor gives it the ambient air temperature. The atmospheric pressure (AP) sensor gives it the altitude at which the vehicle is operating, while the crankshaft position, cylinder position and TDC sensors inform it of engine speed and crankshaft position. The coolant temperature (TW) sensor indicates the engine temperature, the throttle angle sensor gives it information on throttle valve opening, and on models with catalytic converters, the lambda sensor informs it of the composition of the exhaust gases. In addition, the ECU senses battery voltage, and modifies the injector pulse width to suit.

If there is an abnormality in any of the readings obtained from the sensors, the ECU has a back-up facility, which assumes a pre-programmed value to allow the engine to continue running at reduced efficiency. When this occurs, the ECU will illuminate the PGM-Fi warning lamp on the instrument panel, informing the driver of the fault, and will store the relevant fault code in the ECU memory. The ECU has an LED which will then flash this fault code repeatedly; a trained Rover mechanic can then interpret this code, and quickly trace and rectify the fault. If necessary, a more complete test of the engine management system can be carried out by a Rover dealer, using a special electronic diagnostic test unit which is simply plugged into the system. Once rectified, the fault code can be erased from the ECU by cutting the electrical supply to the ECU; this is achieved simply by removing the hazard warning lamp fuse from the engine compartment fusebox for 10 seconds.

8 Fuel system – depressurisation

Note: *Refer to the warning note in Section 1 before proceeding.*

⚠️ *Warning: The following procedure will merely relieve the pressure in the fuel system – remember that fuel will still be present in the system components and take precautions accordingly before disconnecting any of them.*

1 The fuel system referred to in this Section is defined as the tank-mounted fuel pump, the fuel filter, the fuel rail, pressure regulator and injectors, and the metal pipes and flexible hoses of the fuel lines between these components. All these contain fuel, which will be under pressure while the engine is running and/or while the ignition is switched on. The

4

8.3 Tightening the fuel bleed screw after depressurising the fuel system

pressure will remain for some time after the ignition has been switched off, and must be relieved before any of these components is disturbed for servicing work.

2 The fuel system is depressurised via the bleed screw which is fitted to the head of the fuel filter outlet pipe union bolt.

3 Position wads of rag around the union to catch the spilled fuel, and slowly slacken the bleed screw. Once all the pressure has been released, mop up any spilt fuel and tighten the bleed screw to the specified torque setting (photo).

9 Fuel system pressure check

Note: *Refer to the warning note in Section 1 before proceeding.*

1 The following procedure is based on the use of the Rover pressure gauge and adaptor (Service Tool Numbers 18G 1500 and 18G 1500/3).

2 Depressurise the fuel system, as described in Section 8.

3 Remove the bleed screw, then screw the adaptor and fuel pressure gauge into its position.

4 Turn the engine over on the starter motor; the pressure should reach the specified value.

5 If the pressure first recorded was too high, renew the pressure regulator as described in Section 15.

6 If the pressure first recorded was too low, or if it falls too quickly, check the system carefully for leaks. If no leaks are found, first renew the fuel filter (to check that the filter was not blocked), then recheck the pressure. If this does not cure the fault, check the pump by substituting a new one (see Section 10) and recheck the pressure. If this still does not improve the pressure, it is likely that the pressure regulator is at fault, this can also be checked by substitution (see Section 15).

10 Fuel pump – removal and refitting

Note: *Refer to the warning note in Section 1 before proceeding.*

Removal

1 Remove the fuel tank, as described in Section 12.

2 Release the clips securing the tank vent hose to the fuel tank breather and fuel cut-off valve, and disconnect the hose. Undo the vent hose and valve retaining nuts, then disconnect the vent valve hose from the fuel pump, and remove the vent hose and valve assembly from the tank.

3 Disconnect the wiring connector from the fuel pump.

4 Slacken and remove the six fuel pump retaining nuts, then carefully withdraw the fuel pump assembly from the tank, and remove the pump seal.

Refitting

5 Refitting is a reversal of the removal sequence, noting the following points.

(a) Renew the pump seal if there is any doubt as to its condition.

(b) Tighten all the retaining nuts to the specified torque setting.

(c) Ensure that the vent hoses are correctly connected, and securely held by any necessary retaining clips.

11 Fuel gauge sender unit – removal and refitting

Note: *Refer to the warning note in Section 1 before proceeding.*

Removal

1 Disconnect the battery negative lead.

2 On 216 models, open up the tailgate and remove the parcel tray shelf. Fold the rear seats fully forwards, then raise the luggage compartment carpet to gain access to the fuel sender unit access cover.

3 On 416 models, open up the boot lid and lift up the luggage compartment carpet to gain access to the fuel sender unit access cover.

4 On all models, undo the three screws and remove the access cover from the floor (photos).

5 Remove the sender unit wiring connector rubber cover, and disconnect the connector from the sender.

6 Unscrew the sender unit retaining ring by turning it in an anti-clockwise direction, and remove it from the fuel tank.

 HAYNES HiNT *In the absence of the special Rover ring spanner (Service Tool Number 18G 1595), a pair of slip-jointed pliers will serve as an adequate substitute to slacken the ring.*

7 Carefully lift out the sender unit, taking great care not to bend or damage the sender float, and remove the sealing ring. Examine the sealing ring, and renew it if it is worn or damaged.

Refitting

8 Refitting is the reverse of the removal procedure, ensuring that the tab on the sender unit is correctly engaged with the cutout in the fuel tank.

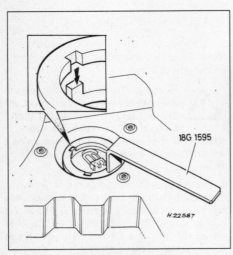

Fig. 4.3 Using Rover special tool to remove fuel gauge sender unit (Sec 11)

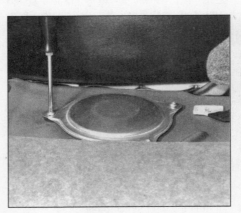

11.4A Undo the three screws ...

11.4B ... and remove the access cover to reach fuel gauge sender unit

12.3 Remove cover retaining bolt and screw retaining plugs, and remove the fuel tank cover

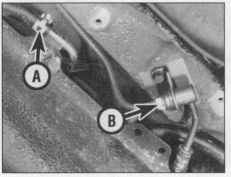

12.4 Fuel tank return pipe retaining clip (A) and feed pipe union nut (B)

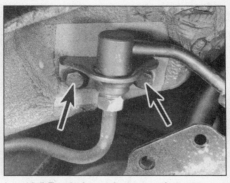

12.5 Feed pipe union mounting nuts (arrowed)

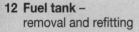
12 Fuel tank –
removal and refitting

Note: *Refer to the warning note in Section 1 before proceeding.*

Removal

1 Before removing the fuel tank, all fuel must be drained from the tank. Since a fuel tank drain plug is not provided, it is therefore preferable to carry out the removal operation when the tank is nearly empty. Before proceeding, disconnect the battery negative lead, and syphon or hand-pump the remaining fuel from the tank. Also depressurise the fuel system, as described in Section 8.
2 Chock the front wheels, then jack up the rear of the car and support it on axle stands. Remove the left-hand rear roadwheel.
3 Undo the bolt, then slacken and remove the two screws securing the cover fitted to the left-hand side of the fuel tank. Prise out the screw retaining plugs, and remove the cover to gain access to the fuel tank feed and return pipes (photo).
4 Using a suitable pair of pliers, release the retaining clip and disconnect the small section of return pipe hose from the fuel tank (photo).
5 Slacken the fuel feed pipe union nut, and disconnect the pipe from its union. Undo the two union mounting bolts, and free the union from the body (photo).
6 Disconnect the fuel tank wiring block connector from the main wiring harness (photo). If the block connector cannot yet be reached, it can be disconnected as the tank is lowered out of position.
7 Slacken the clip securing the filler neck hose to the tank, and use a pair of pliers to release the filler neck breather pipe retaining clip (photo). Disconnect both the filler neck hose and breather pipe from the fuel tank.
8 Release the fuel tank breather, situated directly above the filler neck hose, from the vehicle body.
9 Slacken the tank retaining strap locknuts, then unscrew the lower locknuts and remove the straps while supporting the tank (photo).
10 Lower the fuel tank, and remove it from under the car.

11 If the tank is contaminated with sediment or water, remove the sender unit as described in Section 11, and swill the tank out with clean fuel. If the tank is damaged or leaks, it should be repaired by a specialist or alternatively renewed. Do not under any circumstances attempt to solder or weld a fuel tank.

Refitting

12 Refitting is the reverse of the removal procedure; tighten all nuts and bolts to their specified torque wrench settings, and ensure that all hoses are correctly routed and securely fastened – never forget the danger of fuel leakage.

13 Throttle housing –
removal and refitting

Removal

1 Disconnect the battery negative terminal.
2 Slacken the air intake hose retaining clip, and disconnect the hose from the throttle housing.
3 Slacken the accelerator cable locknuts, and free the outer cable from its mounting bracket. Release the inner cable from the throttle cam.
4 On models with automatic transmission, slacken the kickdown cable locknuts, then free the outer cable from its mounting bracket and disconnect the inner cable from the throttle cam.
5 Disconnect the vacuum hose from the throttle housing dashpot (photo), then remove the hose from the top of the housing itself.

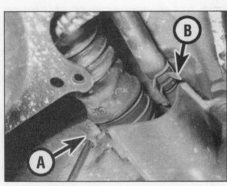

12.6 Fuel tank wiring harness block connector

12.7 Slacken the filler neck hose retaining clamp (A), and disconnect the breather pipe (B)

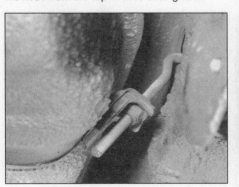

12.9 Fuel tank mounting strap retaining locknut

13.5 Disconnect the vacuum hose from the throttle housing dashpot ...

13.6 ... and disconnect the wiring connector from the throttle angle sensor

13.7 Slide the throttle housing off its mounting studs, then disconnect the coolant hoses (arrowed)

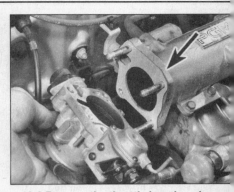

13.8 Remove the throttle housing along with its gasket (arrowed)

6 Disconnect the wiring connector from the throttle angle sensor, and free the wiring from its retaining clip on the base of the throttle housing (photo).

7 Slacken and remove the throttle housing retaining nuts and bolt, and slide the housing off its retaining studs. Position a suitable container beneath the housing, then, using a pair of pliers, release the retaining clips and quickly disconnect the coolant hoses from the base of the throttle housing (photo). Plug both hose ends, to minimise the loss of coolant and to prevent the possible entry of dirt into the cooling system.

8 Remove the throttle housing from the car, along with its gasket (photo).

Refitting

9 Refitting is a reverse of the removal procedure, noting the following points.

(a) *Ensure the throttle housing and inlet manifold mating surfaces are clean, and fit a new gasket.*

(b) *Tighten the throttle housing retaining nuts and bolt to the specified torque setting.*

(c) *Adjust the accelerator cable as described in Section 4 and (where necessary) the kickdown cable as described in Chapter 7.*

(d) *On completion, using the information in Chapter 1, top-up the cooling system, then check and if necessary adjust the base idle speed and mixture setting.*

14 Fuel injection system components – testing

1 If a fault appears in the engine management (ignition/fuel injection) system, first ensure that the fault is not due to poor maintenance; ie, check that the air cleaner filter element is clean, the spark plugs are in good condition and correctly gapped, that the engine breather hoses are clear and undamaged, referring to Chapter 1 for further information. Also check that the accelerator cable is correctly adjusted, as described in Section 4. If the engine is running very roughly, check the compression pressures as described in Chapter 2, and the valve clearances as described in Chapter 1.

2 If these checks fail to reveal the cause of the problem, the vehicle should be taken to a Rover dealer for testing. A wiring block connector is incorporated in the engine management circuit, into which a special electronic diagnostic tester can be plugged. The tester will locate the fault quickly and simply, alleviating the need to test all the system components individually, which is a time-consuming operation that carries a high risk of damaging the ECU.

3 If necessary, the system wiring and wiring connectors can be checked as described in Chapter 12, ensuring that the ECU wiring connectors have first been disconnected.

15 Fuel injection system components – removal and refitting

Note: *Refer to the warning note in Section 1 before proceeding.*

Fuel injectors

Removal

1 Depressurise the fuel system, as described in Section 8.

2 Undo the two fuel injector wiring connector cover retaining nuts, then lift up the cover and disconnect the four injector wiring connectors (photos).

3 Release the accelerator cable from its manifold retaining brackets, then position

15.2A Remove the two injector wiring cover retaining nuts (arrowed) ...

15.2B ... then lift up the cover, and disconnect the four injector wiring connectors (arrowed)

15.4A Fuel rail retaining nut locations (arrowed)

15.4B Lift off the fuel rail ...

15.4C ... and remove the three fuel rail spacers (arrowed)

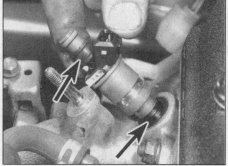

15.5 Removing an injector; note the upper and lower seals (arrows)

15.11 Release the retaining clip, and disconnect the return hose from the fuel pressure regulator

wads of rag underneath and around the fuel rail to absorb any spilt fuel. Release the retaining clip, and disconnect the fuel return hose from the fuel pressure regulator.

4 Slacken and remove the three fuel rail retaining nuts, then carefully lift off the rail and position it clear of the injectors, noting the seal which is fitted to the top of each injector. The seals should be discarded, and new ones fitted, whenever they are disturbed. Withdraw the three fuel rail mounting spacers (photos).

5 Carefully remove the injector(s) from the inlet manifold, and remove the lower seal from each (photo).

Refitting

6 Carefully fit a new lower seal to each of the injectors removed. Lubricate the seals with a smear of engine oil, then carefully install the injector(s) in the inlet manifold. Ensure all the injectors are correctly positioned, with their wiring connectors pointing directly upwards.

7 Ensure the injector and fuel rail mating surfaces are clean, and fit a new seal to the top of each injector. Apply a smear of engine oil to each injector seal, and refit the fuel rail spacers to their studs. Carefully locate the fuel rail with the four injectors, noting that the centreline on each injector wiring connector should align with corresponding mark on the fuel rail. Push the fuel rail fully onto the injectors, then refit its retaining nuts and tighten them to the specified torque setting.

8 Reconnect the injector wiring connectors,

and refit the accelerator cable to its retaining bracket. Reconnect the return hose to the pressure regulator, and secure it with its retaining clip.

9 Refit the injector wiring connector cover, tightening its retaining nuts to the specified torque, and reconnect the battery.

Fuel pressure regulator

Removal

10 Depressurise the fuel system as described in Section 8, and disconnect the battery negative terminal.

11 Position a wad of rag beneath the pressure regulator, then, using a pair of pliers, release the retaining clip and disconnect the return hose from the regulator (photo). Plug the end of the hose, to minimise the loss of fuel and prevent the possible entry of dirt into the system.

12 Disconnect the vacuum hose from the top of the pressure regulator.

13 Undo the two retaining bolts, and remove the pressure regulator from the fuel rail (photo), noting its O-ring. Plug the fuel rail orifice, to minimise fuel loss and prevent dirt entry.

Refitting

14 Refitting is a reversal of the removal procedure, using a new O-ring and tightening the regulator retaining bolts to the specified torque.

Throttle angle sensor

15 The throttle angle sensor is available only as part of the throttle housing assembly. See Section 13 for removal and refitting details.

Engine management (ignition/fuel injection) ECU and idle mixture (IMA) sensor

Removal

16 Disconnect the battery negative terminal.

17 From inside the car, peel back the carpet from the front passenger's footwell to gain access to the ECU cover. Undo the four cover retaining nuts, and remove the cover (photo).

18 To remove the ECU alone, slide the unit

15.13 Disconnect the vacuum hose (arrow) and undo the two fuel pressure regulator retaining bolts

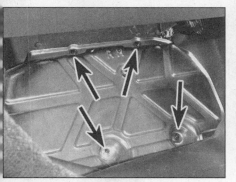

15.17 ECU cover is retained by four nuts (arrowed)

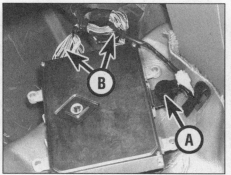

15.18 Unclip IMA sensor (A), then disconnect wiring connectors (B) and remove ECU

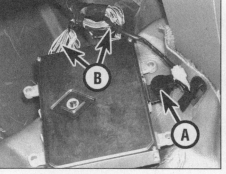

15.19 Removing the IMA sensor

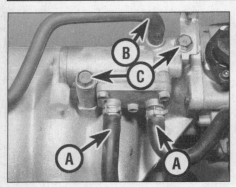

15.22 EACV coolant hoses (A), vacuum hose (B) and retaining bolts (C) – shown with manifold removed for clarity

15.25 Fast idle solenoid valve is fitted to left-hand rear face of inlet manifold (shown with manifold removed for clarity)

15.28 Manifold absolute pressure (MAP) sensor is mounted on the engine compartment bulkhead

out of its retaining studs, and carefully disconnect its wiring connectors. Unclip the IMA sensor, and remove the ECU (photo).

19 To remove the IMA sensor alone, disconnect the sensor wiring connector, then unclip the sensor from the ECU and remove it from the car (photo).

Refitting

20 Refitting is a reverse of the removal procedure, ensuring that the wiring connectors are secure.

Idle speed electronic air control valve (EACV)

Removal

21 Disconnect the battery earth lead, and disconnect the wiring connector from the idle speed EACV (which is mounted on the right-hand side of the rear of the inlet manifold).

22 Position a suitable container beneath the valve, then, using a pair of pliers, compress the retaining clips and disconnect the coolant hoses from the underside of the EACV. Plug the hose ends to minimise coolant loss. Disconnect the vacuum hose from the top of the valve (photo).

23 Undo the two EACV retaining bolts, then remove the valve from the manifold, along with its seal.

Refitting

24 Refitting is a reverse of the removal sequence, noting the following points.

15.33 Removing the atmospheric pressure (AP) sensor

(a) Ensure the EACV and manifold mating surfaces are clean, and fit a new seal to the valve. Tighten the EACV retaining bolts securely.

(b) On completion, top-up the cooling system, and adjust the base idle speed as described in Chapter 1.

Fast idle speed solenoid valve – SOHC and later DOHC engines

Removal

25 Disconnect the battery negative terminal, and disconnect the wiring connector from the fast idle solenoid valve (which is mounted on the left-hand rear face of the inlet manifold) (photo).

26 Disconnect the vacuum hose from the valve, then undo its two retaining bolts and remove the valve and its O-ring from the manifold.

Refitting

27 Refitting is a reverse of removal, using a new O-ring.

Manifold absolute pressure (MAP) sensor

Removal

28 The MAP sensor is mounted onto the left-hand side of the engine compartment

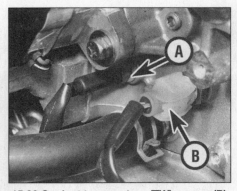

15.36 Coolant temperature (TW) sensor (B) is located on right-hand end of cylinder head. Do not confuse it with temperature gauge sender unit (A)

bulkhead (photo). Prior to removing it, first disconnect the battery negative terminal.

29 Disconnect the MAP sensor wiring connector, and slacken and remove its retaining bolt. Disconnect the vacuum hoses from the base of the sensor, and remove it from the car. If necessary, remove the two screws and separate the sensor and mounting bracket.

Refitting

30 Refitting is a reverse of the removal sequence.

Atmospheric pressure (AP) sensor

Removal

31 Disconnect the battery negative terminal.

32 Working from inside the car, undo the two glovebox retaining screws, then partially withdraw the glovebox until access can be gained to the glovebox damper-to-facia screw. Undo the damper screw, and remove the glovebox and damper to gain access to the AP sensor.

33 Disconnect the sensor wiring connector, then undo the retaining bolt and remove the sensor from the car (photo).

Refitting

34 Refitting is a reverse of removal.

Coolant temperature (TW) sensor

Removal

35 The coolant temperature sensor is situated just below the distributor. Either drain the cooling system as described in Chapter 1, or be prepared for some loss of coolant as the switch is unscrewed.

36 Disconnect the battery negative terminal, and disconnect the TW sensor wiring connector (photo). Note: Do not confuse the coolant temperature (TW) sensor with the temperature gauge sender unit The TW sensor sits further forward, and has two wires connected to it.

37 Unscrew the sensor from the cylinder head and withdraw it, then plug the opening to prevent the entry of dirt; if the cooling system has not been drained, work quickly to minimise coolant loss.

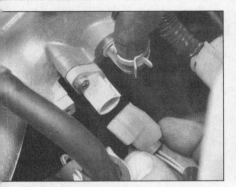

15.41 Disconnecting the wiring connector from the intake air (TA) sensor

15.44 Injector resistor pack is mounted on the engine compartment bulkhead

15.47 Reset the fuel cut-off inertia switch by depressing the plunger

Refitting

38 Wipe the threads of the sensor and those of the cylinder head clean. If a sealing washer is fitted, renew it whenever it is disturbed, to prevent leaks; if no sealing washer is fitted, apply a smear of sealant to the sensor threads.

39 Refit the sensor, working quickly if the cooling system was not drained, and tighten it securely. Reconnect the wiring connector.

40 Refill or top-up the cooling system, as described in Chapter 1.

Intake air temperature (TA) sensor

Removal

41 Disconnect the battery negative lead, and disconnect the wiring connector from the TA sensor (which is mounted on the left-hand end of the inlet manifold) (photo).

42 Slacken and remove the two sensor retaining screws and washers, then remove the sensor along with its O-ring.

Refitting

43 Refitting is a reverse of removal, using a new O-ring.

Injector resistor pack

Removal

44 Disconnect the battery negative terminal, then disconnect the wiring connectors from the injector resistor pack (which is mounted on the left-hand side of the engine compartment bulkhead) (photo). If necessary, to improve

access to the resistor pack, remove the washer system reservoir as described in Chapter 12.

45 Release the wiring harness from its retaining clip on the resistor pack, then undo the bracket retaining nut, and remove the bracket and resistor pack assembly from the car. If necessary, undo the two screws and separate the resistor pack and mounting bracket.

Refitting

46 Refitting is a reversal of the removal procedure.

Fuel cut-off inertia switch

47 The fuel cut-off inertia switch is located behind the centre console, where it is mounted onto the steering column support bracket. If the switch has tripped, it can be reset by pressing in the plunger situated at the top of the switch (photo).

Removal

48 Remove the centre console, as described in Chapter 11.

49 Disconnect the wiring connector, then undo the switch mounting bracket retaining nut and remove the switch (photos).

Refitting

50 Refitting is a reverse of the removal sequence. Before installing the centre console, reset the inertia switch by pressing in the plunger.

Relays

51 Refer to Chapter 12 for further information.

16 Inlet manifold – removal and refitting

Note: *Refer to the warning note in Section 1 before proceeding.*

Removal

1 Disconnect the battery negative terminal, and drain the cooling system as described in Chapter 1.

2 Remove the alternator adjusting link as described in Section 6 of Chapter 12. This will be necessary, to gain access to the lower centre manifold retaining nut.

3 Depressurise the fuel system, as described in Section 8. Position wads of rag beneath the fuel filter, then slacken and remove the filter outlet union bolt. Disconnect the hose union from the filter, and recover the sealing washer positioned on each side of union; discard the washers, as they **must** be renewed whenever they are disturbed (photo). Plug the hose end and filter union, to minimise fuel loss and prevent the entry of dirt.

4 Using a pair of pliers, release the retaining clip, and disconnect the vacuum pipe from the throttle housing end of the air intake hose. Slacken the retaining clip which secures the intake hose to the throttle housing, and

15.49A Undo the retaining nut ...

15.49B ... and remove the inertia switch

16.3 Remove the union bolt, and disconnect the outlet hose from the fuel filter. Note sealing washers (arrowed)

16.5 Release the retaining clip, and disconnect the return hose from the fuel pressure regulator

16.10A Disconnect the thermostat coolant hose (arrowed) ...

16.10B ... and brake servo vacuum hose from the inlet manifold

disconnect the intake hose. Working along the length of the intake hose, release the vacuum hoses from their retaining clips, then disconnect the intake hose from the air cleaner housing and remove it from the engine compartment.

5 Position a wad of rag beneath the pressure regulator, then, using a pair of pliers, release the retaining clip and disconnect the return hose from the regulator (photo). Plug the end of the hose and the pressure regulator union, to minimise the loss of fuel and prevent the possible entry of dirt into the fuel system.

6 Slacken the accelerator cable locknuts, and free the outer cable from its mounting bracket. Release the inner cable from the throttle cam. Work back along the cable, and free it from all its retaining clips on the inlet manifold.

7 On models with automatic transmission, slacken the kickdown cable locknuts, then free the outer cable from its mounting bracket, and disconnect the inner cable from the throttle cam.

8 Undo the two fuel injector wiring connector cover retaining nuts, then remove the cover and disconnect the four injector wiring connectors. Undo the bolt which secures the injector wiring harness to the left-hand side of manifold, and position the wiring clear of the working area.

9 Trace the PCV valve hose back from the underside of the valve, (which is fitted into the manifold between the inlet tracts for cylinder numbers 1 and 2), and disconnect the hose end from the oil separator sealing grommet.

10 Make a note of the correct fitted positions of the vacuum hoses, then, using pliers to compress their retaining clips (where fitted), disconnect the following hoses from the manifold (photos).

(a) Thermostat housing-to-manifold coolant hose.
(b) Brake servo vacuum hose.
(c) Manifold absolute pressure (MAP) sensor vacuum hose.

11 Disconnect the wiring connectors from the following components, and free the relevant wiring from any retaining clips on the manifold.

(a) Intake air temperature (TA) sensor.
(b) Throttle angle sensor.
(c) Idle speed electronic air control valve (EACV).
(d) Fast idle speed control valve – SOHC and later DOHC engines.

12 Undo the two bolts which secure the manifold support bracket to the cylinder block/crankcase, and the two bolts which secure the bracket to the underside of the inlet manifold, then remove the bracket (photo).

13 Make a final check that all the necessary vacuum hoses have been disconnected from the manifold, then slacken (evenly and progressively) the nuts securing the manifold to the cylinder head. Manoeuvre the manifold out of the engine compartment, and discard the manifold gasket (photos).

Refitting

14 Refitting is a reversal of the removal procedure, noting the following points.

(a) Ensure the manifold and cylinder head mating surfaces are clean and dry, and fit a new manifold gasket.
(b) Tighten the manifold retaining nuts evenly and progressively, to the specified torque setting.
(c) Tighten the manifold support bracket retaining bolts to the specified torque.
(d) Ensure that all hoses are reconnected to their original positions and securely held (where necessary) by their retaining clips.
(e) Refit the alternator adjusting link, using the information given in paragraphs 10 and 11 of Section 6 in Chapter 12.
(f) Fit a new sealing washer to each side of the fuel filter outlet hose union, and tighten the union bolt to the specified torque setting.
(g) Adjust the accelerator cable as described in Section 4, and (where necessary) the kickdown cable as described in Chapter 7.
(h) On completion, using the information in Chapter 1, top-up the cooling system, then check and, if necessary, adjust the base idle speed and mixture setting.

16.12 Manifold support bracket-to-cylinder block bolts (arrowed) – viewed from underneath

16.13A Remove the inlet manifold from the engine ...

16.13B ... along with its gasket

17.4A Undo the exhaust manifold heatshield retaining bolts (remaining three arrowed) ...

17.4B ... and remove the heatshield

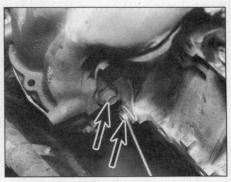

17.6 Undo the exhaust manifold support bracket retaining bolts (arrowed), and remove the bracket

17 Exhaust manifold – removal and refitting

Removal

1 Disconnect the battery negative terminal, then firmly apply the handbrake and chock the rear wheels. Jack up the front of the car, and support it on axle stands.

2 Undo the two bolts securing the accelerator cable mounting brackets to the cylinder head cover, and position the cable clear of the working area. Remove the engine oil dipstick.

3 Slacken and remove the two bolts securing the intake duct to the bonnet locking platform, and free the expansion tank hose from its retaining clips on the duct. Free the duct from the resonator and intake hoses, then release its lower retaining clip and remove it from the engine compartment.

4 Undo the four exhaust manifold heatshield retaining bolts, and remove the shield from the engine compartment (photos).

5 On models with a catalytic converter, disconnect the lambda sensor wiring connector, and free the wiring from its retaining bracket. Carefully unscrew the sensor, and remove it from the manifold along with its sealing washer. **Note:** *The lambda sensor is delicate, and will not function correctly if it is dropped, knocked or damaged in any way.*

6 Slacken and remove the two exhaust manifold support bracket mounting bolts, and remove the bracket from the left-hand side of the manifold (photo).

7 From underneath the car, undo the two nuts or bolts (as applicable) securing the exhaust front pipe to its mounting bracket. Undo the three nuts securing the front pipe to the exhaust manifold, then disconnect the pipe and collect the gasket.

8 Evenly and progressively slacken and remove the nine nuts securing the exhaust manifold to the cylinder head, then carefully manoeuvre the manifold out of the engine compartment. Remove the manifold gasket, and discard it (photos).

9 Examine all the exhaust manifold studs for signs of damage and corrosion; remove all traces of corrosion, and repair or renew any damaged studs.

Refitting

10 Refitting is the reverse of the removal procedure, noting the following points.

(a) *Ensure that the manifold and cylinder head sealing faces are clean and flat, and fit a new manifold gasket*

(b) *Working in the sequence shown in Fig. 4.4, tighten the manifold retaining nuts evenly to the specified torque wrench setting.*

(c) *Fit a new sealing washer to the lambda sensor (where fitted), and tighten it to the specified torque.*

(d) *Tighten all other disturbed nuts and bolts securely, or to their specified torque wrench settings (where given).*

18 Exhaust system – general information and component renewal

Note: *If a catalytic converter is fitted, remember that it is FRAGILE – do not use hammers, mallets, etc., to strike any part of the system, and take care not to drop it or strike it against anything else while handling it.*

General information

1 The exhaust system components are shown in Figs. 4.5 and 4.6. On models without a catalytic converter, the exhaust system is in three sections; the front pipe and front silencer box, the intermediate pipe and middle silencer boxes, and the tailpipe and main silencer box. All exhaust sections are joined by a flanged joint. If a catalytic converter is fitted, it is situated between the front pipe and the (much shorter) intermediate pipe, with a flanged joint at each end.

2 The system is suspended throughout its entire length by rubber mountings.

Removal

3 Each exhaust section can be removed individually. Alternatively, the complete system

4

17.8A Slacken the manifold retaining nuts ...

17.8B ... then remove the manifold along with its gasket

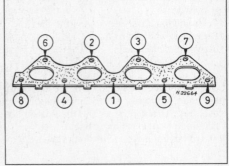

Fig. 4.4 Exhaust manifold fastener tightening sequence (Sec 17)

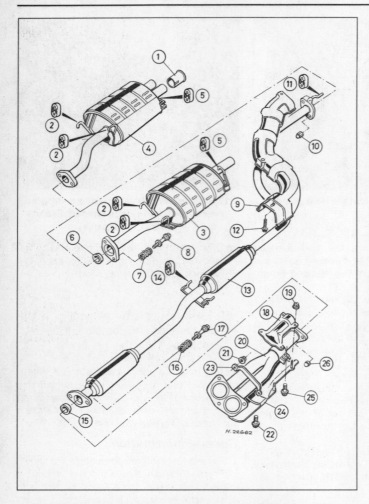

Fig. 4.5 Exhaust system components models without catalytic converter (DOHC engine shown, SOHC engine similar) (Sec 18)

1 Tailpipe trim
2 Mounting rubber
3 Tailpipe – SOHC engines
4 Tailpipe – DOHC engines
5 Mounting rubber
6 Gasket – intermediate pipe-to-tailpipe
7 Spring
8 Bolt – intermediate pipe-to-tailpipe
9 Heatshield
10 Nut – intermediate pipe-to-tailpipe
11 Mounting rubber
12 Bolt – heatshield-to-body
13 Intermediate pipe
14 Mounting rubber
15 Gasket – front pipe-to-intermediate pipe
16 Spring
17 Bolt – intermediate pipe-to-front pipe
18 Upper front pipe heatshield
19 Heatshield retaining nut
20 Front pipe
21 Heatshield retaining nut
22 Heatshield retaining bolt
23 Bracket
24 Lower front pipe heatshield
25 Bolt – front pipe-to-mounting bracket

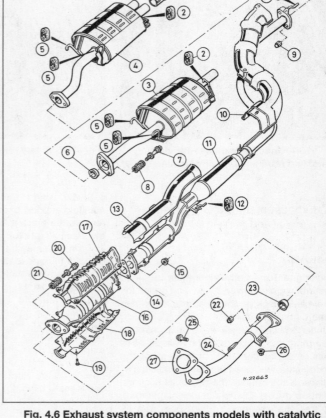

Fig. 4.6 Exhaust system components models with catalytic converter (SOHC engine shown, DOHC engine similar) (Sec 18)

1 Tailpipe trim
2 Mounting rubber
3 Tailpipe – SOHC engines
4 Tailpipe – DOHC engines
5 Mounting rubber
6 Gasket – intermediate pipe-to-tailpipe
7 Bolt – intermediate pipe-to-tailpipe
8 Spring
9 Nut – intermediate pipe-to-tailpipe
10 Heatshield
11 Intermediate pipe
12 Mounting rubber
13 Heatshield
14 Gasket – intermediate pipe-to-catalytic converter
15 Nut – intermediate pipe-to-catalytic converter
16 Catalytic converter
17 Upper catalytic converter heatshield
18 Lower catalytic converter heatshield
19 Heatshield retaining bolt
20 Bolt – catalytic converter-to-front pipe
21 Spring
22 Nut – catalytic converter-to-front pipe
23 Gasket – catalytic converter-to-front pipe
24 Front pipe
25 Bolt – front pipe-to-mounting bracket
26 Nut – front pipe-to-mounting bracket
27 Gasket – front pipe-to-manifold

can be removed as a unit, once the front pipe has been unbolted from the manifold (as described in paragraph 5), and the system has been freed from all its mounting rubbers.

4 To remove the system or part of the system, first jack up the front or rear of the car, and support it on axle stands. Alternatively, position the car over an inspection pit or on car ramps.

Front pipe

5 Remove the three nuts securing the front pipe flange joint to the manifold, and the two nuts or bolts (as appropriate) securing the front pipe to its mounting bracket. Separate the flange joint, and collect the gasket (photo).
6 Slacken and remove the two nuts, then withdraw the bolts and springs which secure

the front pipe to the intermediate pipe/catalytic converter (as applicable), and manoeuvre the front pipe out from under the vehicle (photo).

Catalytic converter (where fitted)

7 Slacken and remove the three nuts securing the catalytic converter to the intermediate pipe, then separate the flange joint and recover the gasket.

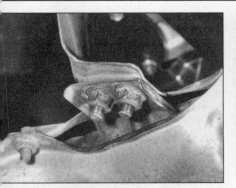

18.5 Exhaust front pipe-to-bracket mounting nuts (DOHC engine shown)

18.6 Exhaust front pipe-to-intermediate pipe joint

18.14A On refitting, renew all exhaust gaskets (front pipe to intermediate joint shown) ...

8 Slacken and remove the two nuts, then withdraw the two bolts and springs securing the converter to the front pipe, and remove it from the vehicle.

Intermediate pipe

9 Slacken the two nuts securing the tailpipe flange joint to the intermediate pipe, and separate the flange joint.
10 Slacken and remove the two nuts, then withdraw the two bolts and springs securing the intermediate pipe to the front pipe, or the three nuts securing the pipe to the catalytic converter (as applicable).
11 Free the intermediate pipe from all its mounting rubbers, and manoeuvre it out from under the car.

Tailpipe

12 Remove the two nuts, then withdraw the two bolts and springs securing the tailpipe

flange joint to the intermediate pipe. Separate the joint.
13 Unhook the tailpipe from its three mounting rubbers, and remove it from the vehicle.

Refitting

14 Each section is refitted by a reverse of the removal sequence. Note that where new sections are to be installed, transfer the heatshield (where fitted) from the original component to the new one before installing it on the vehicle; this also applies to the tailpipe trims fitted on some models. Ensure that all traces of corrosion have been removed from the flanges, and renew all necessary gaskets. Inspect the rubber mountings for signs of damage or deterioration, and renew as necessary. Tighten all nuts and bolts by hand only to locate the disturbed section in position, then ensure all exhaust system rubber mountings are correctly seated (photos).

18.14B ... and ensure all rubber mountings are correctly seated

Check that there is adequate clearance between the exhaust system and vehicle underbody before tightening all the disturbed nuts and bolts to the specified torque.

Part B: Emission control systems

19 General information

All models have the ability to use unleaded petrol, and various features which help to minimise emissions are built into the fuel system. All models are equipped with a crankcase emission control system, and the throttle control system described under the exhaust emission heading. Models equipped with a catalytic converter are also fitted with the evaporative emission control system; the operation of the catalytic converter is also described under the exhaust emission heading.

Crankcase emission control system

The purpose of this system is to reduce the emission of unburnt hydrocarbons (mainly engine oil vapour) from the crankcase into the atmosphere. The engine is sealed, and the blow-by gases and oil vapour are drawn from the crankcase, through an oil separator which is bolted onto the rear face of the cylinder

block, into the inlet tract, to be burned by the engine during normal combustion. A positive crankcase ventilation (PCV) valve is fitted to the hose which links the oil separator and inlet manifold, to ensure the gases can only flow one way (from the separator to the manifold). A single breather hose connects the cylinder head cover to the air intake hose, just upstream of the throttle housing, to supply the fresh air into the engine necessary to create the airflow which draws the blow-by gases out.

Under conditions of high manifold depression (idling or deceleration), the gases will be sucked positively out of the crankcase. Under conditions of low manifold depression (acceleration or full-throttle running) the gases are forced out of the crankcase by the higher crankcase pressure. If the engine is worn, the raised crankcase pressure (due to increased blow-by) will cause some of the flow to return under all manifold conditions.

Evaporative emission control system

To minimise the escape into the atmosphere of unburnt hydrocarbons (fuel vapour), an

evaporative emission control system is fitted to models equipped with a catalytic converter. The fuel tank filler cap is sealed, and a charcoal canister is mounted in the engine compartment to collect the petrol vapours generated in the tank when the car is parked. It stores them until the engine reaches a pre-determined temperature, then they are released from the canister (under the control of the fuel-injection/ignition system ECU, via the purge control valve) into the inlet tract, to be burned by the engine during normal combustion.

Exhaust emission control system

To minimise the amount of pollutants which escape into the atmosphere, all models are equipped with a throttle control system. The system consists of a vacuum-operated dashpot which is connected to the inlet manifold; the dashpot pullrod is connected to the throttle cam. When the throttle is released during gearchanging or deceleration, a depression is created in the inlet manifold which acts on the dashpot diaphragm. The diaphragm then retracts the dashpot pullrod,

4

which in turn causes the throttle valve to close momentarily. This then increases the airflow into the engine, causing the exhaust gases to burn more completely, so reducing the exhaust emissions.

Some models are also equipped with a closed-loop catalytic converter in the exhaust system. The closed-loop system is controlled by the lambda sensor which is screwed into the exhaust manifold. The sensor provides the fuel injection/ignition system ECU with constant feedback on the content of the exhaust gases, enabling the ECU to adjust the fuel mixture to provide the best possible conditions for the converter to operate in. The sensor's tip is sensitive to oxygen, and sends the ECU a varying voltage depending on the amount of oxygen in the exhaust gases; if the intake air/fuel mixture is too rich, the exhaust gases are low in oxygen, and the sensor sends a high-voltage signal; the voltage lowers as the mixture weakens and the amount of oxygen rises in the exhaust gases. Peak conversion efficiency of all major exhaust pollutants occurs if the intake air/fuel mixture is maintained at the chemically-correct ratio for the complete combustion of petrol, which is 14.7 parts (by weight) of air to 1 part of fuel (the 'stoichiometric' ratio). The sensor output voltage alters in a large step at this point, the ECU using the signal change as a reference point, and correcting the intake air/fuel mixture accordingly by altering the fuel injector pulse width (injection duration).

20 Emission control system components – testing and renewal

Crankcase emission control system

Testing

1 Apart from the checks described in Chapter 1, the components of this system require no attention other than to check that the hose(s) are clear. If the PCV valve is thought to be faulty, it must be renewed as follows.

20.2 Positive crankcase ventilation (PCV) valve viewed from above

Positive crankcase ventilation (PCV) valve – renewal

2 The PCV valve is situated between the inlet tracts of numbers 1 and 2 cylinders, directly below the fuel pressure regulator (photo). To remove the valve, trace the centre of the three upper inlet manifold hoses back to the valve, and carefully pull the valve out of its lower hose. Using a pair of pliers, release the valve upper retaining clip, then disconnect the valve from its upper hose and remove it from the engine. Fit the new valve to the upper hose, ensuring it is fitted the correct way around, and secure it in position with the retaining clip. Carefully ease the valve into position in the lower hose.

Evaporative emission control system

Testing

3 If the system is thought to be faulty, disconnect the hoses from the charcoal canister and purge control valve, and check that they are clear by blowing through them. If the purge control valve or charcoal canister are thought to be faulty, they must be renewed.

Charcoal canister – renewal

4 Disconnect the battery negative terminal.
5 Make a note of the correct fitted positions of the canister hoses, then use a suitable pair of pliers to release the retaining clips (where fitted), and disconnect all the hoses from the canister (which is mounted on the engine compartment bulkhead).
6 Lift the canister up to free it from its mounting bracket, then remove it from the engine compartment.
7 Refitting is the reverse of the removal procedure, ensuring that all the hoses are correctly refitted and, where necessary, securely held by their retaining clips.

Purge valve – renewal

8 Disconnect the battery negative terminal, then disconnect the wiring connector from the purge valve (which is mounted onto the engine compartment bulkhead, on the same bracket as the MAP sensor).

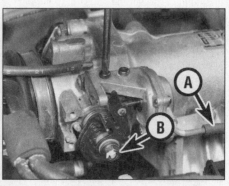

20.14 Undo the dashpot retaining screws, then disconnect the vacuum hose (A) and remove the throttle cam nut (B)

9 Release their retaining clips, then disconnect the inlet and outlet hoses from the valve. The purge valve can then be lifted off its mounting bracket and removed from the car. Remove the filter from the top of the valve; check it for signs of clogging, and renew if necessary.
10 Refitting is a reverse of the removal procedure.

Exhaust emission control system

Testing – throttle control system

11 To test the operation of the throttle control system, disconnect the vacuum hose from the dashpot, and connect a hand-operated vacuum pump. Apply a vacuum to the dashpot diaphragm, and check that the pullrod retracts into the dashpot. Release the vacuum, and check that the pullrod extends quickly and smoothly under pressure of the return spring. If this is not the case, the dashpot must be renewed as described below, but if all is well, reconnect the vacuum hose.

Testing – catalytic converter and lambda sensor

12 If the CO level at the tailpipe is too high (see Chapter 1), the car must be taken to a Rover dealer so that the engine management system can be checked thoroughly, using special Rover diagnostic equipment. This equipment will test the operation of the complete system, including the lambda sensor. If the system is checked and is free from faults, the fault must be in the catalytic converter, which must be renewed.

Throttle control system dashpot – renewal

13 Disconnect the battery negative terminal, and disconnect the dashpot vacuum hose.
14 Slacken and remove the throttle cam retaining nut and washers, and undo the two dashpot mounting screws and washers (photo).
15 Slide the dashpot and lever assembly off the throttle valve spindle, and remove it from the engine. Separate the lever and dashpot, and examine the lever bushes for wear and damage, renewing if necessary.
16 Fit the bushes to the lever, and engage the lever with the dashpot pullrod. Locate the lever on the throttle valve spindle, and slide the assembly into position.
17 Refit the dashpot mounting screws and the throttle cam retaining nut and washers, and tighten them securely.
18 Adjust the throttle cable as described in Section 4 and, on models with automatic transmission, adjust the kickdown cable as described in Chapter 7.

Catalytic converter – renewal

19 Refer to Section 18.

Lambda sensor – renewal

Note: *The lambda sensor is delicate, and will not work if it is dropped or knocked, if its* power supply is disrupted, or if any cleaning materials are used on it.

20 Disconnect the battery negative terminal, and remove the engine oil dipstick.

21 Slacken and remove the two bolts securing the intake duct to the bonnet locking platform, and free the expansion tank hose from its retaining clips on the duct. Free the duct from the resonator and intake hoses, then release its lower retaining clip and remove it from the engine compartment.

22 Undo the four exhaust manifold heatshield retaining bolts, and remove the shield from the engine compartment.

23 Disconnect the lambda sensor wiring connector, and free the wiring from its retaining bracket. Carefully unscrew the sensor, and remove it from the manifold along with its sealing washer.

24 Refitting is a reversal of the removal procedure, using a new sealing washer and tightening the sensor to the specified torque.

21 Catalytic converter – general information and precautions

The catalytic converter is a reliable and simple device which needs no maintenance in itself, but there are some facts of which an owner should be aware if the converter is to function properly for its full service life. Bearing in mind that a replacement converter is highly expensive, it is worth noting carefully the points listed below.

(a) *DO NOT use leaded petrol (known in the UK as 4-star) in a car equipped with a catalytic converter – the lead will coat the precious metals, reducing their converting efficiency, and will eventually destroy the converter. At the time of writing, unleaded petrol of 95 RON and 98 RON (super unleaded) octane ratings is available in the UK. Either type may safely be used on models with a catalytic converter and indeed, on ALL models).*

(b) *Always keep the ignition and fuel systems well-maintained in accordance with the manufacturer's schedule (see Chapter 1) particularly, ensure that the air cleaner filter element, the fuel filter and the spark plugs are renewed at the correct intervals. If the intake air/fuel mixture is allowed to become too rich due to neglect, the unburned surplus will enter and burn in the catalytic converter, overheating the element and eventually destroying the converter.*

(c) *If the engine develops a misfire, do not drive the car at all (or at least as little as possible) until the fault is cured – the misfire will allow unburned fuel to enter the converter, which will result in its overheating, as noted in (b) above.*

(d) *DO NOT push- or tow-start the car – this will soak the catalytic converter in unburned fuel causing it to overheat when the engine does start – see (b) above.*

(e) *DO NOT switch off the ignition at high engine speeds – in other words, do not blip the throttle immediately before switching off the engine. If the ignition is switched off at anything above idle speed, unburned fuel will enter the (very hot) catalytic converter, with the possible risk of its igniting on the element and damaging the converter.*

(f) *DO NOT use fuel or engine oil additives – these may contain substances harmful to the catalytic converter.*

(g) *DO NOT continue to use the car if the engine burns oil to the extent of leaving a visible trail of blue smoke – the unburned carbon deposits will clog the converter passages and reduce its efficiency; in severe cases, the element will overheat.*

(h) *Remember that the catalytic converter operates at very high temperatures – hence the heatshields on the car's underbody and the casing will become hot enough to ignite combustible materials which brush against it. DO NOT, therefore, park the car in dry undergrowth, over long grass or piles of dead leaves.*

(I) *Remember that the catalytic converter is FRAGILE – do not strike it with tools during servicing work, and take great care when working on the exhaust system. Ensure that the converter is well clear of any jacks or other lifting gear used to raise the car, and do not drive the car over rough ground, road humps, etc., in such a way as to ground the exhaust system.*

(j) *In some cases, particularly when the car is new and/or is used for stop/start driving, a sulphurous smell (like that of rotten eggs) may be noticed from the exhaust This is common to many catalytic converter-equipped cars, and seems to be due to the small amount of sulphur found in some petrols reacting with hydrogen in the exhaust to produce hydrogen sulphide (H_2S) gas. While this gas is toxic, it is not produced in sufficient amounts to be a problem. Once the car has covered a few thousand miles, the problem should disappear – in the meantime, a change of driving style or of the brand of petrol used may effect a solution.*

(k) *The catalytic converter, used on a well-maintained and well-driven car, should last between 50 000 and 100 000 miles. From this point on, careful checks should be made at all specified service intervals of the CO level, to ensure that the converter is still operating efficiently – if the converter is no longer effective, it must be renewed.*

4

Notes

Chapter 5 Ignition system

Contents

Degrees of difficulty

Easy, suitable for novice with little experience	**Fairly easy,** suitable for beginner with some experience	**Fairly difficult,** suitable for competent DIY mechanic	**Difficult,** suitable for experienced DIY mechanic	**Very difficult,** suitable for expert DIY or professional

Specifications

General

System type	Electronic (breakerless), constant-energy inductive type
Firing order	1-3-4-2
Location of number 1 cylinder	Timing belt (left-hand) end of engine

Distributor

Type	Spark distribution only (ignition timing totally controlled by ECU). Contains ignition HT coil and igniter unit
Direction of rotor arm rotation	Clockwise
Distributor cap:	
SOHC engines	GDC 346
DOHC engines	GDC 347
Rotor arm	GRA 2287 (resistive type)

Ignition coil

Type	GCL 161
Current consumption – average	0.25 to 0.75 amps @ idle speed
Primary resistance	0.3 to 0.5 ohms @ 20°C
Secondary resistance	5000 to 15 000 ohms @ 20°C

Torque wrench settings

	Nm	lbf ft
Distributor mounting bolts	22	16
Cylinder position sensor housing mounting bolts – DOHC engines	12	9

1 General information and precautions

The fully-electronic ignition system consists of the distributor, spark plugs, HT leads, ignition coil and associated wiring, and the Electronic Control Unit (ECU) situated beneath the passenger footwell carpet. The system is divided into two circuits; primary (low tension/LT) and secondary (high tension/HT). The primary circuit consists of the battery, ignition switch, ignition HT coil primary windings, ECU and wiring. The secondary circuit consists of the ignition HT coil secondary windings, the distributor cap and rotor arm, the spark plugs and the HT leads.

The two main system components are the ECU and the distributor. On single overhead camshaft (SOHC) engines, the distributor houses the igniter unit and ignition HT coil, as well as three sensors; a crankshaft position sensor, a cylinder position sensor, and a TDC sensor. The distributor is mounted on the right-hand end of the camshaft. On double overhead camshaft (DOHC) engines, the distributor (which is mounted on the right-hand end of the inlet camshaft) is very similar in construction to that of SOHC engines, except that there is no cylinder position sensor incorporated in the distributor; the cylinder position sensor is housed separately, and is fitted on the right-hand end of the exhaust camshaft.

The ECU controls both the ignition system and the fuel injection system, integrating the two in a complete engine management system; refer to Chapter 4 for information on any part of the system not given here.

As far as the ignition system is concerned, the ECU receives information in the form of electrical impulses or signals from the crankshaft position and cylinder position sensors. The crankshaft position sensor detects engine speed and the position of number 1 cylinder, as a base for the injection/ignition sequence, and the cylinder position sensor determines the injection timing for each cylinder. Besides these, the coolant temperature sensor and intake air temperature sensor provide engine and ambient air temperature information, the throttle angle sensor provides throttle valve position information, and the manifold absolute pressure (MAP) sensor detects the load on the engine. All these signals are compared by the ECU, using digital techniques, with set values pre-programmed (mapped) into its memory; based on this information, the ECU selects the ignition timing appropriate to those values, and controls the ignition HT coil accordingly. Should the crankshaft position and cylinder number sensors fail, or produce abnormal readings, the ECU will then use the TDC sensor as a back-up. When an abnormal signal is sent from any other sensor, the ECU ignores that signal and assumes a pre-programmed value that allows the engine to continue to run.

Note that this means that the distributor, apart from housing the various sensors, is just that – a distributor of the HT pulse to the appropriate spark plug; it has no effect whatsoever on the ignition timing. An unusual feature of the system is that the ignition timing is adjustable (see Chapter 1, Section 4).

3.1A Slacken the distributor cap retaining screws, then remove the cap and leads as an assembly ...

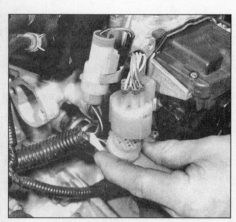

3.1B ... and disconnect the distributor wiring connectors

> **Warning:** The voltages produced by the electronic ignition system are considerably higher than those produced by conventional systems. Extreme care must be taken when working on the system with the ignition switched on. Persons with surgically-implanted cardiac pacemaker devices should keep well clear of the ignition circuits, components and test equipment.

2 Ignition system – testing

1 If a fault appears in the engine management (ignition/fuel) system, first ensure that the fault is not due to poor maintenance; ie, check that the air cleaner filter element is clean, the spark plugs are in good condition and correctly gapped, and that the engine breather hoses are clear and undamaged (refer to Chapter 1 for further information). Also check that the throttle cable is correctly adjusted, as described in Chapter 4. If the engine is running very roughly, check the compression pressures as described in Chapter 2, and the valve clearances as described in Chapter 1.

2 If these checks fail to reveal the cause of the problem, the vehicle should be taken to a suitably-equipped Rover dealer for testing. A wiring block connector is incorporated in the engine management circuit, into which a special electronic diagnostic tester can be plugged. The tester will locate the fault quickly and simply, alleviating the need to test all the system components individually, which is a time-consuming operation that carries a high risk of damaging the ECU.

3 The only ignition system checks which can be carried out by the home mechanic are those described in Chapter 1, relating to the spark plugs, HT leads, rotor arm and distributor cap, and the ignition coil test described in this Chapter. If necessary, the system wiring and wiring connectors can be checked as described in Chapter 12, ensuring that the ECU wiring connectors have first been disconnected.

3.4 Fit a new O-ring to the distributor body

3 Distributor – removal and refitting

Removal

1 Disconnect the HT leads from the spark plugs, and free the leads from their retaining clips. Slacken the three distributor cap screws, and remove the cap and leads as an assembly, noting the cap seal. Disconnect the wiring block connectors from the side of the distributor (photos).

2 On models with a catalytic converter, remove the tamperproof cap from the upper distributor mounting bolt.

3 Using a scriber or suitable marker pen, mark the relationship of the distributor body to the cylinder head. Slacken and remove the three mounting bolts, and withdraw the distributor from the cylinder head. Remove the O-ring from the end of the distributor body, and discard it; a new O-ring must be used on refitting.

Refitting

4 Lubricate the new O-ring with a smear of engine oil, and fit it to the groove in the distributor body (photo). Examine the distributor cap seal for wear or damage, and renew if necessary.

5 Align the distributor rotor shaft drive coupling key with the slots in the camshaft end, noting that the slots are offset to ensure that the distributor can only be fitted in one position (photo). Carefully insert the distributor into the cylinder head, rotating the rotor arm slightly to ensure the coupling is correctly engaged. Align the marks made on removal, then install the distributor mounting bolts, tightening them lightly only at this stage.

6 Ensure that the seal is correctly located in its groove, then refit the cap assembly to the distributor, and tighten its retaining screws securely. Reconnect the HT leads to their respective spark plugs, and clip the leads into position in all their relevant retaining clips.

7 Check and, if necessary, adjust the ignition timing as described in Chapter 1. Tighten the distributor mounting bolts to the specified

3.5 Align the drive coupling key (arrowed) with the camshaft slots, and refit the distributor to the cylinder head

4.3 Slacken the LT wiring retaining screws, and disconnect the wiring from the coil

4.4A Undo the four HT coil retaining screws (arrowed) ...

4.4B ... and remove coil from the distributor

torque, and (where necessary) refit the tamperproof cap to the upper retaining bolt.

4 Ignition HT coil – removal, testing and refitting

Removal

1 Disconnect the HT leads from the spark plugs, and free the leads from their retaining clips. Slacken the three distributor cap screws, and remove the cap and leads as an assembly, noting the cap seal.
2 Unclip the rotor shaft cover, and remove it from the distributor.
3 Make a note of the fitted positions of the coil LT wiring connectors, then undo the retaining screws, remove the sealing grommet and disconnect the wiring from the coil (photo).
4 Slacken and remove the four ignition HT coil mounting screws, and lift the coil away from the distributor (photos).

Testing

5 Testing of the coil consists of using a multimeter set to its resistance function, to check the primary winding (LT '+' to '–' terminals) and secondary winding (LT ' + ' to HT lead terminal) for continuity. If the meter is used, the resistance of either winding can be checked and compared with the specified

value. Note the resistance of the coil windings will vary slightly according to the coil temperature; the results in the Specifications are approximate values, and are accurate only when the coil is at 20°C.
6 Using an ohmmeter or continuity tester, check that there is no continuity between the HT lead terminal and the coil body.
7 If the coil is thought to be faulty, have your findings confirmed by a Rover dealer before renewing the coil.

Refitting

8 Refitting is the reverse of the removal procedure, using the notes made on removal to ensure the LT wires are connected to the correct terminals.

5 Igniter unit – removal and refitting

⚠️ **Warning: Do not attempt to open or repair the igniter unit, if it is faulty, it must be renewed.**

Removal

1 Disconnect the HT leads from the spark plugs, and free the leads from their retaining clips. Slacken the three distributor cap screws, and remove the cap and leads as an assembly, noting the cap seal.

2 Unclip the rotor shaft cover, and remove it from the distributor (photo).
3 Undo the single screw securing the wiring clip to the igniter unit, and remove the clip.
4 Make a note of the correct fitted positions of the four igniter unit wiring connections, then disconnect them from the igniter (photo).
5 Slacken and remove the two igniter retaining screws, and withdraw the unit from the distributor (photo). If necessary, remove the screws and separate the igniter and mounting bracket.
6 No test information is available for the igniter unit, so a faulty unit can only be identified by substitution of a new unit.

Refitting

7 Refitting is a reverse of removal, using the notes made on removal to ensure the wires are connected to the correct terminals.

6 Cylinder position sensor housing (DOHC engines) – removal and refitting

Removal

1 Undo the bolt which secures the wiring retaining clamp to the underside of the housing cover, and remove the clip. Undo the

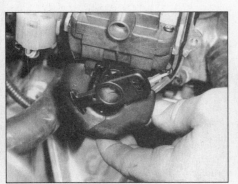

5.2 Removing the rotor shaft cover

5.4 Note the correct fitted positions of the igniter wiring connectors prior to disconnecting them

5.5 Igniter unit retaining screws are situated on the bottom of the distributor. Note wiring clip retaining screw (arrowed)

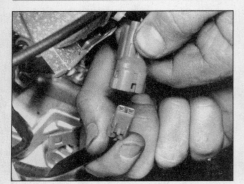

6.2 Disconnect the wiring connector ...

6.3A ... then undo the housing retaining screws ...

6.3B ... and remove the cylinder position sensor housing from the cylinder head – DOHC engines (O-ring seal arrowed)

cylinder position sensor housing cover retaining bolts and remove the cover, noting its seal. The HT lead bracket can be left attached to the leads.

2 Disconnect the sensor wiring connector (photo).

3 Slacken and remove the two mounting bolts, and remove the sensor housing from the cylinder head. Remove the O-ring from the end of the housing, and discard it; a new O-ring must be used on refitting (photos).

Refitting

4 Lubricate the new O-ring with a smear of engine oil, and fit it to the groove in the sensor housing. Examine the housing cover seal for wear or damage, and renew if necessary.

5 Align the sensor shaft drive coupling key with the slots in the camshaft end, noting that the slots are offset to ensure that the sensor housing can only be fitted in one position. Carefully insert the housing into the cylinder head, rotating the sensor slightly to ensure the

coupling is correctly engaged. Refit the sensor housing mounting bolts, and tighten them to the specified torque setting.

6 Ensure that the seal is correctly located in its groove, then refit the housing cover. Refit the cover retaining bolts, not forgetting to fit the HT lead mounting bracket to the rear bolt, and tighten them all securely.

7 Reconnect the sensor wiring connector, then refit the wiring retaining clip, and secure it in position with its retaining bolt.

Chapter 6 Clutch

Contents

Degrees of difficulty

Easy, suitable for novice with little experience	Fairly easy, suitable for beginner with some experience	Fairly difficult, suitable for competent DIY mechanic	Difficult, suitable for experienced DIY mechanic	Very difficult, suitable for expert DIY or professional

Specifications

Type	Single dry plate with diaphragm spring, cable-operated, manual adjustment

Friction plate

Diameter . .229 mm	
Lining thickness:	
New plate	8.4 to 8.9 mm
Service limit	5.9 mm
Minimum rivet depth distance from friction material surface to rivet head:	
New plate	1.3 mm
Service limit	0.2 mm
Maximum run-out	1.0 mm

Pressure plate

Maximum warpage of machined surface	0.15 mm
Maximum wear of diaphragm spring fingers	1.0 mm

Clutch adjustment

Free play:	
Measured at clutch release lever tip	3.5 to 4.5 mm
Measured at clutch pedal pad	15 to 20 mm

Torque wrench settings

	Nm	lbf ft
Pressure plate-to-flywheel bolts	26	19
Release fork retaining bolt	29	21

1 General information

The clutch consists of a friction plate, a pressure plate assembly, a release bearing and the release mechanism; all of these components are contained in the large cast aluminium alloy bellhousing, sandwiched between the engine and the transmission. The clutch release mechanism is mechanical, operated by a cable.

The friction plate is fitted between the engine flywheel and the clutch pressure plate, and is allowed to slide on the transmission input shaft splines. It consists of two circular facings of friction material riveted in position to provide the clutch bearing surface, and a spring-cushioned hub to damp out transmission shocks.

The pressure plate assembly is bolted to the engine flywheel, and is located by three dowel pins; it comprises the clutch cover, the diaphragm spring, and the pressure plate. When the engine is running, drive is transmitted from the crankshaft via the flywheel and clutch cover to the friction plate (these last three components being clamped securely together by the pressure plate and diaphragm spring), and from the friction plate to the transmission input shaft.

To interrupt the drive, the spring pressure must be relaxed. This is achieved by a sealed release bearing fitted concentrically around the transmission input shaft; when the driver depresses the clutch pedal, the release bearing is pressed against the fingers at the centre of the diaphragm spring. Since the spring is held by rivets between two annular fulcrum rings, the pressure at its centre causes it to deform so that it flattens, thus releasing the clamping force it exerts, at its periphery, on the pressure plate.

Depressing the clutch pedal pulls the control cable inner wire, and this in turn rotates the release fork by acting on the lever at the fork's upper end, above the bellhousing. The fork itself is clipped to the left of the release bearing.

As the friction plate facings wear, the pressure plate moves towards the flywheel; this causes the diaphragm spring fingers to push against the release bearing, thus reducing the clearance which must be present in the mechanism. To ensure correct operation, the clutch cable must be regularly adjusted.

6

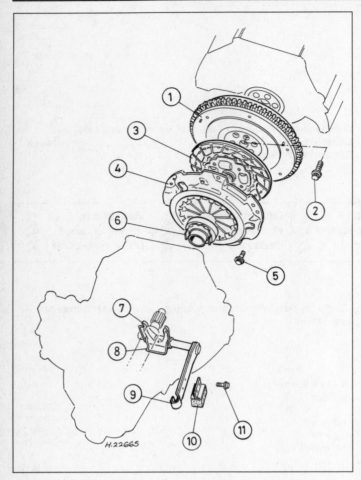

Fig. 6.1 Clutch components (Sec 1)

1 Flywheel
2 Flywheel bolt
3 Friction plate
4 Pressure plate assembly
5 Pressure plate bolt
6 Release bearing
7 Release fork
8 Release fork spring
9 Release lever
10 Release lever damper
11 Damper bolts

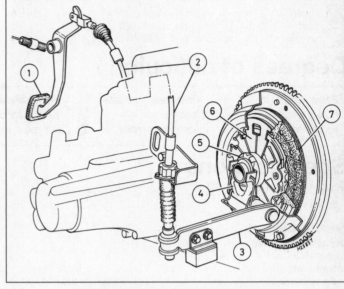

Fig. 6.2 Clutch release mechanism (Sec 1)

1 Clutch pedal
2 Clutch cable
3 Release lever
4 Release fork
5 Release bearing
6 Diaphragm spring
7 Friction plate

2 Clutch cable – removal, refitting and adjustment

Removal

1 Working in the engine compartment, rotate the clutch adjusting nut in anti-clockwise direction to obtain maximum cable free play. Release the inner cable from the clutch release lever, and free the outer cable from its mounting bracket (photos).

2 Work back along the length of the cable, and free it from its support bracket and any other relevant ties or clamps. Free the cable sealing grommet from the bulkhead.

3 Working inside the car, undo the five retaining screws, and remove the right-hand lower facia panel.

4 Unhook the cable from the pedal upper end (photo).

5 Return to the engine compartment, and withdraw the cable forwards through the bulkhead.

6 Examine the cable, looking for worn end fittings or a damaged outer casing, and also for signs of fraying of the inner wire. Check the cable's operation; the inner wire should move smoothly and easily through the outer casing, but remember that a cable which appears serviceable when tested off the car may well be much heavier in operation when compressed into its working position. Renew the cable if it shows any signs of excessive wear or damage.

Refitting and adjustment

7 Apply a thin smear of multi-purpose grease to the cable end fittings, then pass the cable

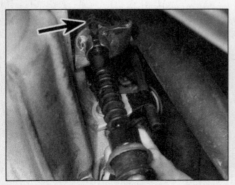

2.1A Rotate the adjusting nut (arrowed) to obtain maximum free play, then disconnect the inner cable from the clutch release lever ...

2.1B ... and free the outer cable from the transmission bracket

2.4 Disconnect the clutch cable (arrowed) from the clutch pedal hook

through the engine compartment bulkhead. Engage the inner cable slot with the pedal hook, then refit the right-hand lower facia panel.
8 Ensuring that the cable is correctly routed, pass the lower end through the mounting bracket, and engage the inner cable with the clutch release lever. Locate the cable in its support bracket, and secure it with any relevant ties or clamps. Fit the cable sealing grommet to the engine compartment bulkhead. Adjust the cable as follows.
9 The clutch cable adjustment is set by measuring the free play present either at the tip of the clutch release lever or at the clutch pedal pad (Fig. 6.3). Rotate the adjusting nut as necessary, until the specified amount of free play is present at either point.

3 Clutch pedal – removal, inspection and refitting

Removal

1 Working in the engine compartment, rotate the clutch adjusting nut in anti-clockwise direction to obtain maximum clutch cable free play.
2 Working inside the car, undo the five retaining screws, and remove the right-hand lower facia panel.
3 Unhook the cable from the pedal upper end, then, using a pair of pliers, carefully unhook the clutch pedal return spring from the pedal (photo).
4 Slacken and remove the clutch pedal pivot nut, and slide the pedal off its pivot.

Inspection

5 Carefully clean all components, and renew any that are worn or damaged; check the bearing surfaces of the pivot bushes and the shaft with particular care; the bushes can be renewed separately if worn.

Refitting

6 Refitting is the reverse of the removal procedure, but apply a thin smear of multi-purpose grease to the pedal pivot bearing surfaces. On completion, adjust the clutch cable as described in Section 2.

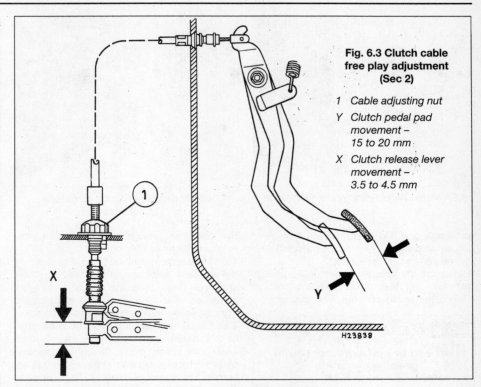

Fig. 6.3 Clutch cable free play adjustment (Sec 2)

1 Cable adjusting nut
Y Clutch pedal pad movement – 15 to 20 mm
X Clutch release lever movement – 3.5 to 4.5 mm

3.3 Clutch pedal return spring and pivot nut (arrowed)

4 Clutch assembly – removal, inspection and refitting

⚠️ **Warning: Dust created by clutch wear and deposited on the clutch components may contain asbestos, which is a health hazard. DO NOT blow it out with compressed air, or inhale any of it. DO NOT use petrol or petroleum-based solvents to clean off the dust. Brake system cleaner or methylated spirit should be used to flush the dust into a suitable receptacle. After the clutch components are wiped clean with rags, dispose of the contaminated rags and cleaner in a sealed, marked container. Although some friction materials may no longer contain asbestos, it is safest to assume that they do, and to take precautions accordingly.**

4.4 Note locating dowels (two arrowed) and which way around friction plate is fitted on removing clutch components

Removal

1 Unless the complete engine/transmission unit is to be removed from the car and separated for major overhaul (see Chapter 2), the clutch can be reached by removing the transmission as described in Chapter 7.
2 Before disturbing the clutch, use chalk, white paint, or a felt-tip pen to mark the relationship of the pressure plate assembly to the flywheel.
3 Working in a diagonal sequence, slacken the pressure plate bolts by half a turn at a time, until the spring pressure is released and the bolts can be unscrewed by hand.
4 Prise the pressure plate assembly off its locating dowels, and collect the friction plate, noting which way round the friction plate is fitted (photo).

Inspection

Note: *Due to the amount of work necessary to remove and refit the clutch components, it is usually considered good practice to renew the clutch friction plate, pressure plate assembly and release bearing as a matched set, even if only one of these is actually worn enough to require renewal. The release bearing in particular is often overlooked, and will give trouble when worn.*

5 Remove the clutch assembly.
6 When cleaning clutch components, first read the warning at the beginning of this Section; remove any dust using a clean, dry cloth, and work in a well-ventilated atmosphere.
7 Check the friction plate facings for signs of wear, damage or oil contamination. If the friction material is cracked, burnt, scored or

6

4.8A Measuring friction plate rivet depth

4.8B Measuring friction plate total thickness

4.20 Using a clutch-aligning tool (arrowed) to centralise the friction plate while tightening pressure plate bolts to specified torque

damaged, or if it is contaminated with oil or grease (shown by shiny black patches), the friction plate must be renewed.

8 Measure the total thickness of the friction material, and the depth from the friction material surface to all of the rivets (photos).

 HAYNES HiNT *If the specialised vernier tools shown are not available, a ruler (and a tyre tread depth gauge or the tip of a screwdriver, for rough depth measurements) will suffice.*

If the thickness of the plate or the depth of any of the rivets is worn to, or even close to, the specified service limits, the friction plate must be renewed.

9 If the friction material is still serviceable, check that the centre boss splines are unworn, that the torsion springs are in good condition and securely fastened, and that all the rivets are tightly fastened. If any wear or damage is found, the friction plate must be renewed.

10 If the friction material is fouled with oil, this must be due to an oil leak from the crankshaft left-hand oil seal, from the sump-to-cylinder block joint, or from the transmission input shaft. Renew the seal or repair the joint, as appropriate, as described in Chapter 2 or 7 before installing the new friction plate; if you don't, the new plate will quickly suffer the same fate as the old.

11 Check the pressure plate assembly for obvious signs of wear or damage; shake it to check for loose rivets and for worn or damaged fulcrum rings, and check that the drive straps securing the pressure plate to the cover do not show signs (such as a deep yellow or blue discoloration) of overheating. If the diaphragm spring is worn or damaged, or if its pressure is in any way suspect, the pressure plate assembly should be renewed.

12 To check the condition of the diaphragm spring, place a circular piece of flat plate across the tips of the spring fingers, and use feeler gauges to measure the clearance between each finger's tip and the plate. If any finger is worn or distorted so that the clearance between its tip and the plate is at

the specified service limit or greater, the pressure plate must be renewed.

13 Examine the machined bearing surfaces of the pressure plate and of the flywheel; they should be clean, completely flat and free from scratches or scoring. If either is discoloured from excessive heat, or shows signs of cracks, it should be renewed; however, minor damage of this nature can sometimes be polished away using emery paper. Check the pressure plate surface using a straight-edge, placed across the pressure plate surface at four different points, and feeler gauges. Compare any warpage found with the specified service limit.

14 Check the release bearing as described in Section 5 of this Chapter.

Refitting

15 On reassembly, ensure that the bearing surfaces of the flywheel and pressure plate are completely clean, smooth, and free from oil or grease. Use solvent to remove any protective grease from new components.

16 Fit the friction plate so that the longer part of its central, splined, boss is towards the flywheel, and so that its spring hub assembly faces away from the flywheel; there may also be a marking showing which way round the plate is to be refitted.

17 Refit the pressure plate assembly, aligning the marks made on dismantling (if the original pressure plate is re-used), and locating the pressure plate on its three locating dowels. Fit the pressure plate bolts, but tighten them only finger-tight, so that the friction plate can still be moved.

18 The friction plate must now be centralised, so that when the transmission is refitted, its input shaft will pass through the splines at the centre of the friction plate.

19 Centralisation can be achieved by passing a screwdriver or other long bar through the friction plate and into the hole in the crankshaft; the friction plate can then be moved around until it is centred on the crankshaft hole. Alternatively, a clutch-aligning tool can be used to eliminate the guesswork; these can be obtained from most car accessory shops, or can be made up from a length of metal rod or wooden dowel which fits

closely inside the crankshaft hole with insulating tape wound around it to match the diameter of the friction plate splined hole.

20 When the friction plate is centralised, tighten the pressure plate bolts evenly and in a diagonal sequence to the specified torque setting (photo).

21 Apply a thin smear of molybdenum disulphide grease to the splines of the friction plate and the transmission input shaft, and also to the release bearing bore and release fork shaft. Do not apply an excessive amount, or it may find its way onto the friction plate surfaces.

22 Refit the transmission as described in Chapter 7.

5 Clutch release mechanism – removal, inspection and refitting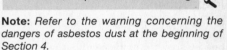

Note: *Refer to the warning concerning the dangers of asbestos dust at the beginning of Section 4.*

Removal

1 Unless the complete engine/transmission unit is to be removed from the car and separated for major overhaul (see Chapter 2), the clutch release mechanism can be reached only by removing the transmission, as described in Chapter 7.

2 Slacken and remove the clutch release fork retaining bolt, then withdraw the release lever from the gearbox, while retaining the release bearing. The release bearing and fork assembly can then be also removed.

3 Make a note of the correct fitted position of the spring, then unhook it from the release bearing, and separate the spring, bearing and fork assembly.

Inspection

4 Check the release mechanism, renewing any component which is worn or damaged. Carefully check all bearing surfaces and points of contact.

5 When checking the release bearing itself, note that it is often considered worthwhile to renew it as a matter of course. Check that the

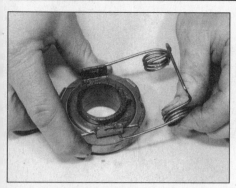

5.7A Ensure the spring ends are correctly located in the release bearing slots ...

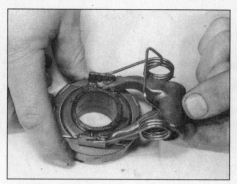

5.7B ... then slide the release fork into position

5.8A Offer up the bearing and fork assembly, and insert the release lever

contact surface rotates smoothly and easily, with no sign of noise or roughness, and that the surface itself is smooth and unworn, with no signs of cracks, pitting or scoring. If there is any doubt about its condition, the bearing must be renewed. The release fork spring must be renewed, regardless of its apparent condition.

6 Note that when cleaning clutch components, do not use solvents on the release bearing; it is packed with grease, which may be washed out if care is not taken.

Refitting

7 Using the notes made on dismantling to ensure the components are correctly positioned, fit the bearing to the release fork, and locate the spring ends in the release bearing slots. Apply a smear of molybdenum disulphide grease to the centre of the release bearing, and to the shaft of the release lever (photos).

8 Position the release bearing and fork assembly in the gearbox housing, and insert the release lever. Ensure the release lever shaft passes through the spring coils, then align the release fork hole with that of the release lever shaft. Refit the fork retaining bolt, and tighten it to the specified torque setting (photos).

9 Move the release lever up and down to check the operation of the release fork spring, before refitting the transmission as described in Chapter 7.

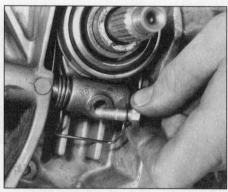

5.8B Align the release lever shaft hole with that of the fork, and refit the bolt

6

Notes

Chapter 7 Transmission

Contents

Degrees of difficulty

Easy, suitable for novice with little experience	**Fairly easy,** suitable for beginner with some experience	**Fairly difficult,** suitable for competent DIY mechanic	**Difficult,** suitable for experienced DIY mechanic	**Very difficult,** suitable for expert DIY or professional

Specifications

Part A: Manual gearbox

Type . . . .   Five forward speeds (all synchromesh) and reverse. Final drive differential integral with main gearbox

Identification

Gearbox code number:
  Single overhead camshaft (SOHC) engine . . . .   P7 (PP 7A-S3)
  Double overhead camshaft (DOHC) engine . . . .   P7 (PP 7A-M4)

Ratios

	SOHC engine	DOHC engine
Final drive	4.437 : 1	4.250 : 1
1st	3.250 : 1	3.250 : 1
2nd	1.894 : 1	1.944 : 1
3rd	1.259 : 1	1.345 : 1
4th	0.937 : 1	1.033 : 1
5th	0.771 : 1	0.848 : 1
Reverse	3.153 : 1	3.153 : 1

Recommended gearchange linkage grease . . . .   Rover grease containing 3% molybdenum disulphide – part number AFU 1500.1509

Part B: Automatic transmission

Type . . . .   Four forward speeds and reverse. Final drive differential integral with transmission

Identification

Transmission code number:
  Single overhead camshaft (SOHC) engine . . . .   P6 (PP 6A-E4)
  Double overhead camshaft (DOHC) engine . . . .   P6 (PP 6A-E5)

Ratios

	SOHC engine	DOHC engine
Final drive	4.214 : 1	4.214 : 1
1st	2.705 : 1	2.705 : 1
2nd	1.560 : 1	1.560 : 1
3rd	1.027 : 1	1.085 : 1
4th	0.780 : 1	0.825 : 1
Reverse	1.954 : 1	1.954 : 1

7

Torque wrench settings

	Nm	lbf ft
Manual gearbox models		
Gearbox oil filler/level and drain plugs	45	33
Gearchange mechanism steady rod-to-gearbox bracket bolt	35	26
Intermediate shaft bearing housing mounting bolts	40	30
Gearbox housing-to-engine bolts	60	44
Flywheel lower cover plate retaining bolts	12	9
Automatic transmission models		
Transmission fluid drain plug	40	30
Selector cable retaining clamp-to-transmission bolt	27	20
Selector cable-to-selector lever housing bolts	10	7
Torque converter lower cover plate retaining bolts	12	9
Torque converter-to-driveplate bolts	12	9
Transmission housing-to-engine bolts	58	43
All models		
Anti-twisting bracket:		
Bracket-to-transmission bolt	40	30
Bracket-to-cylinder block bolts	24	18
Engine/transmission front mounting:		
Through-bolt	60	44
Mounting-to-engine/transmission bolts	55	41
Engine/transmission rear mounting:		
Through-bolt	60	44
Mounting bracket-to-engine/transmission bolts	55	41
Engine/transmission right-hand mounting:		
Through-bolt	60	44
Mounting plate-to-transmission bolts	39	29
Mounting-to-mounting plate nuts and bolts	55	41

Part A – Manual gearbox

1 General information

The transmission is contained in a cast aluminium alloy casing, which is bolted to the engine's right-hand end. The transmission consists of the gearbox and final drive differential, and is often called a 'transaxle'.

Drive is transmitted from the crankshaft (via the clutch and flywheel) to the input shaft, which has a splined extension to accept the clutch friction plate, and which rotates in sealed ball-bearings; from the input shaft, drive is transmitted to the output shaft, which rotates in a roller bearing at its right-hand end, and a sealed ball-bearing at its left-hand end. From the output shaft, the drive is transmitted to the differential crownwheel, which rotates with the differential case and planetary gears, thus driving the sun gears and driveshafts. The rotation of the planetary gears on their shaft allows the inner roadwheel to rotate at a slower speed than the outer roadwheel when the car is cornering.

The input and output shafts are arranged side by side, parallel to the crankshaft and driveshafts, so that their gear pinion teeth are in constant mesh. In the neutral position, the output shaft gear pinions rotate freely, so that drive cannot be transmitted to the crownwheel.

Gear selection is via a floor-mounted lever and selector rod assembly. The selector rod causes the appropriate selector fork to move its respective synchro-sleeve along the shaft, to lock the gear pinion to the synchro-hub. Since the synchro-hubs are splined to the output shaft, this locks the pinion to the shaft so that drive can be transmitted. To ensure that gear changing can be made quickly and quietly, a synchro-mesh system is fitted to all forward gears, consisting of baulk rings and spring-loaded fingers, as well as the gear pinions and synchro-hubs; the synchromesh cones are formed on the mating faces of the baulk rings and gear pinions.

2 Gearchange linkage/mechanism – removal, overhaul and refitting

Removal

1 Park the car on level ground, then switch off the ignition, check that the transmission is in neutral and apply the handbrake firmly. Jack up the front of the car, and support it securely on axle stands.

2 Slide the gearbox selector shaft gaiter towards the gearbox, then remove the roll pin retaining clip from the gearbox end of the gearchange selector rod. Using a hammer and suitable punch, tap the roll pin out of the selector rod, and disconnect the rod from the gearbox. Slacken the nut and bolt which secure the selector rod to the gearchange lever, then withdraw the bolt, and collect the washers fitted between the selector rod and gearchange lever (photos). Manoeuvre the selector rod out from under the car, and withdraw the spacer from the base of the gearchange lever.

3 From inside the car, remove the centre console as described in Chapter 11.

4 Working again from under the car, slacken and remove the two nuts and bolts which secure the gearchange lever ball holder to the steady rod. Remove the holder, and withdraw the gearchange lever (photos).

5 To remove the steady rod, undo the bolt which secures the front end of the rod to the gearbox. Slacken and remove the two steady rod rear mounting assembly retaining bolts, then remove the mounting clamp and rubber, along with the spacers. The steady rod can then be manoeuvred out from under the car, noting the correct fitted positions of the gearchange lever gaiter and holder.

6 If necessary, undo the six gearchange lever plate retaining nuts, and remove the plate assembly and seal from inside the car.

Overhaul

7 Thoroughly clean all components and check them for wear or damage, paying particular attention to the bushes and renewing all worn or faulty items. Note that all bushes can be renewed separately if necessary.

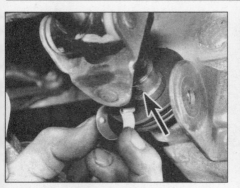

2.2A Slide back the gaiter and remove the roll pin retaining clip from the selector shaft (roll pin arrowed)

2.2B Tap out the roll pin and disconnect the selector shaft from the gearbox ...

2.2C ... then remove the gearchange lever lower bolt and remove selector shaft

2.4A Undo the two gearchange lever ball holder retaining nuts ...

2.4B ... and withdraw the gearchange lever

8 Check the selector rod universal joint for signs of wear, and check that its bearings move freely, without any trace of roughness. If the bearing is damaged, the selector rod must be renewed as a complete unit, since the joint is not available separately.

9 Examine all rubber gaiters and seals for signs of damage or deterioration, and renew as necessary.

Refitting

10 Refitting is the reverse of the removal procedure, noting the following points.
(a) Apply a smear of the specified grease (refer to the Specifications at the start of this Chapter) to all gearchange linkage pivot and bearing surfaces.
(b) Tighten all nuts and bolts securely, or to the specified torque (where given).

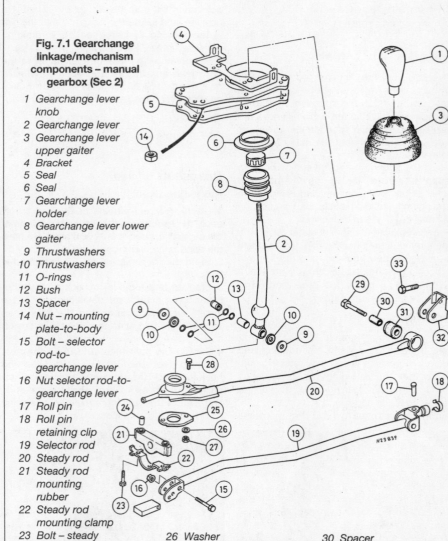

Fig. 7.1 Gearchange linkage/mechanism components – manual gearbox (Sec 2)

1 Gearchange lever knob
2 Gearchange lever
3 Gearchange lever upper gaiter
4 Bracket
5 Seal
6 Seal
7 Gearchange lever holder
8 Gearchange lever lower gaiter
9 Thrustwashers
10 Thrustwashers
11 O-rings
12 Bush
13 Spacer
14 Nut – mounting plate-to-body
15 Bolt – selector rod-to-gearchange lever
16 Nut selector rod-to-gearchange lever
17 Roll pin
18 Roll pin retaining clip
19 Selector rod
20 Steady rod
21 Steady rod mounting rubber
22 Steady rod mounting clamp
23 Bolt – steady rod mounting clamp-to-body
24 Spacer
25 Gearchange lever ball holder
26 Washer
27 Nut – ball holder-to-steady rod
28 Bolt – ball holder-to-steady rod
29 Bolt – steady rod-to-gearbox
30 Spacer
31 Mounting bush
32 Steady rod gearbox mounting bracket
33 Bolt – mounting bracket-to-gearbox

7

3.2 Remove the retaining bolt, then lift off the lockplate and withdraw the speedometer drive

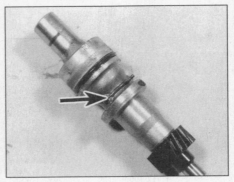

3.3 Remove the retaining clip (arrowed), and withdraw the speedometer drivegear

3.5 Apply a smear of oil to speedometer drive O-ring (arrowed), to aid refitting

3 Speedometer drive – removal and refitting

Removal

1 Working in the engine compartment, carefully remove the gaiter from the transmission end of the speedometer cable, and slide the gaiter up the cable. Remove the retaining clip from the speedometer drivegear housing, and disconnect the cable from the transmission.

2 Hold the speedometer drive assembly, to prevent it from falling down into the transmission, then slacken and remove the retaining bolt and lockplate (photo), and lift the assembly out of the transmission.

3 If required, with the speedometer drive on a bench, remove the retaining clip and separate the drivegear and housing (photo). Remove the housing O-ring and discard it. Note that a new housing O-ring and drivegear retaining clip will be required on refitting.

Refitting

4 Apply a smear of grease to the drivegear shaft, then fit the gear to the housing and secure it in position with a new retaining clip. Ensure that the retaining clip is securely located in the drivegear groove, and fit the new O-ring to the housing.

5 Apply a smear of oil to the O-ring, then ease the speedometer gear assembly back into position in the transmission (photo). Hold it in position, and locate the lockplate with the slot in the housing. Refit the lockplate retaining bolt, and tighten it securely.

6 Reconnect the speedometer cable to the drivegear, and secure it in position with its retaining clip. Slide the gaiter back down into position over the speedometer gear housing.

4 Oil seals – renewal

Driveshaft oil seal

Right-hand seal

1 Chock the rear wheels of the car, firmly apply the handbrake, then jack up the front of the car and support it on axle stands. Remove the appropriate front roadwheel.

2 Drain the transmission oil, as described in Chapter 1.

3 Slacken and remove the bolt and washer securing the anti-roll bar connecting link to the lower suspension arm, and the two bolts securing the tie-bar to the lower suspension arm.

4 Extract the split pins, and undo the nuts securing the steering gear track rod end balljoint and the lower suspension arm balljoint to the swivel hub. Remove the nuts, and release the balljoint tapered shanks using a universal balljoint separator.

5 Insert a suitable flat bar between the inner constant velocity joint and transmission housing, then carefully lever the joint out of position, taking great care not to damage the transmission housing (photo).

6 Withdraw the inner constant velocity joint from the transmission, and support the driveshaft to avoid damaging the constant velocity joints or gaiters.

7 Carefully prise the oil seal out of the transmission with a large flat-bladed screwdriver (photo).

8 Remove all traces of dirt from the area around the oil seal aperture, then apply a smear of grease to the outer lip of the new oil seal. Fit the new seal into its aperture, and drive it squarely into position using a suitable tubular drift (such as a socket) which bears only on the hard outer edge of the seal (photo), until it abuts its locating shoulder.

9 Prior to refitting the driveshaft, check that the inner constant velocity joint seal shoulder is undamaged, and free of burrs and scratches. Small burrs or scratches can be removed using emery cloth, but larger imperfections may require the renewal of joint. Regardless of its apparent condition, renew the circlip which is fitted to the groove in the inner constant velocity joint splines.

10 Thoroughly clean the driveshaft splines, then apply a thin film of grease to the oil seal lips, and to the inner constant velocity joint splines and shoulder.

11 Ensure that the new circlip is located

4.5 Levering right-hand constant velocity joint out of position

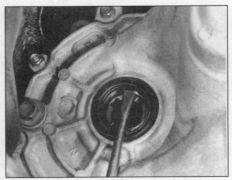

4.7 Carefully lever out the old seal using a large flat-bladed screwdriver ...

4.8... and install the new one using a hammer and suitable tubular drift

4.27 Selector shaft oil seal can be levered out of position with a flat-bladed screwdriver

4.30 Secure the selector shaft in position with the roll pin

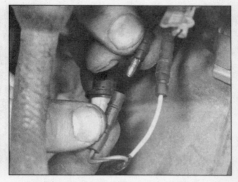

5.3 Disconnecting the reversing lamp switch wiring connectors

securely in its groove, then locate the joint splines with those of the differential sun gear, taking great care not to damage the oil seal. Push the joint fully into the transmission, and check that it is securely retained by the circlip by pulling the hub assembly outwards.

12 Insert the lower suspension arm and track rod balljoints into their respective locations in the swivel hub, and tighten their retaining nuts to the specified torque (Chapter 10). Secure both nuts in position with new split pins.

13 Refit the bolts securing the trailing arm and anti-roll bar connecting link to the lower suspension arm, and tighten them to the specified torque (Chapter 10).

14 Refit the roadwheel, then lower the car to the ground and tighten the wheel nuts to the specified torque (Chapter 10).

15 Refill the transmission with the correct type and quantity of lubricant, as described in Chapter 1.

Left-hand seal

16 Carry out the operations described in paragraphs 1 to 6, noting that all references to the transmission should be replaced by references to the intermediate shaft.

17 Slacken and remove the three bolts securing the intermediate shaft bearing housing to the cylinder block. Rotate the shaft so its mounting flange is pointing downwards, then carefully withdraw the shaft assembly from the transmission.

18 Renew the oil seal as described in paragraphs 7 and 8.

19 Prior to refitting, check that the intermediate shaft seal shoulder is undamaged, and free of burrs and scratches. Small burrs or scratches can be removed using emery cloth, but larger imperfections may require the renewal of shaft. Regardless of its apparent condition, renew the circlip which is fitted to the groove in the driveshaft inner constant velocity joint splines.

20 Thoroughly clean the intermediate shaft splines, then apply a thin film of grease to the oil seal lips, and to the intermediate shaft splines and shoulder.

21 With the mounting flange pointing downwards, carefully locate the shaft splines with those of the differential sun gear, taking

great care not to damage the transmission oil seal lips.

22 Keeping the intermediate shaft square at all times, align the mounting flange holes with those on the cylinder block, then refit the bearing housing mounting bolts, and tighten them to the specified torque setting.

23 Ensure that the new circlip is located securely in its groove in the driveshaft inner constant velocity joint, then locate the joint splines with those of the intermediate shaft, taking great care not to damage the oil seal. Push the joint fully into position, and check that it is securely retained by the circlip by pulling the hub assembly outwards.

24 The remainder of the refitting procedure is as described above in paragraphs 12 to 15.

Selector shaft oil seal

25 Park the car on level ground, then switch off the ignition, check that the transmission is in neutral, and apply the handbrake firmly. Jack up the front of the car, and support it securely on axle stands.

26 Slide the gearbox selector shaft gaiter towards the gearbox, then remove the roll pin retaining clip from the gearbox end of the gearchange selector rod. Using a hammer and suitable punch, tap the roll pin out of the selector rod, and disconnect the rod from the gearbox.

27 Remove the selector shaft gaiter, then, using a suitable flat-bladed screwdriver, carefully lever the seal out of the housing, and slide it off the end of the shaft (photo).

28 Before fitting a new seal, check the selector shaft's seal rubbing surface for signs of burrs, scratches or other damage which may have caused the seal to fail in the first place. It may be possible to polish away minor faults of this sort using fine abrasive paper, but more serious defects will require the renewal of the input shaft.

29 Apply a smear of grease to the new seal's outer edge and sealing lip, then carefully slide the seal along the selector rod. Press the seal fully into position in the gearbox housing, then refit the gaiter, ensuring that it is correctly located with the seal shoulder.

30 Reconnect the selector rod to the shaft,

and align the roll pin holes. Tap the roll pin into position using a suitable hammer and punch (photo), and refit the retaining clip. Lower the car to the ground.

5 Reversing lamp switch – testing, removal and refitting

Testing

1 The reversing lamp circuit is controlled by a plunger-type switch that is screwed into the top of the transmission casing, situated directly below the distributor. If a fault develops in the circuit, first ensure that the circuit fuse has not blown.

2 To test the switch, trace the wiring back from the switch to its wiring connectors. Disconnect the wiring connectors, and use a multimeter (set to the resistance function) or a battery and bulb test circuit, to check that there is continuity between the switch terminals only when reverse gear is selected. If this is not the case, and there are no obvious breaks or other damage to the wires, the switch is faulty, and must be renewed.

Removal

3 To remove the switch, disconnect its wiring connector(s) (photo) and unscrew it.

Refitting

4 On refitting, apply a smear of sealant to the switch threads, and tighten it securely – take care not to overtighten it, however. Reconnect its wiring connectors, and test the operation of the circuit.

6 Manual gearbox – removal and refitting

Removal

1 Drain the gearbox oil as described in Chapter 1, then refit the drain and filler plugs, and tighten them to the specified torque.

2 Remove the battery and battery tray, as described in Chapter 12.

3 Remove the starter motor, as described in Chapter 12.

7

6.9 Remove the bolt and disconnect the earth lead from the gearbox

6.11 Undo the bolt and disconnect the gearchange linkage steady rod from the gearbox

6.15 Remove the anti-twisting bracket ...

4 Carefully remove the gaiter from the transmission end of the speedometer cable, and slide the gaiter up the cable. Remove the retaining clip from the speedometer drivegear housing, and disconnect the cable from the gearbox.

5 Release the retaining clip securing the intake duct to the rear of the radiator, then release the expansion tank hose from its retaining clips on the duct. Undo the two bolts securing the duct to the bonnet locking platform, and remove the duct.

6 Firmly apply the handbrake and chock the rear wheels, then jack up the front of the car and support it on axle stands. Remove both front roadwheels.

7 From underneath the front of the vehicle, slacken and remove the three bolts securing the bumper flange to the body. Remove the seven bolts securing the front undercover panel to the body, and remove the panel.

8 Release the radiator bottom hose from its gearbox retaining clip, then disengage the clip from its mounting, and remove the mounting from the car.

9 Undo the bolt securing the earth lead to the top of the gearbox, and position the lead clear of the working area (photo). Trace the wiring back from the reversing lamp switch, and disconnect it at its wiring connectors.

10 Turn the clutch cable adjusting nut anti-clockwise to obtain maximum clutch cable

free play, then raise the gearbox clutch release lever and disconnect the cable from the lever. Release the cable from its mounting bracket, then undo the two retaining bolts and remove the bracket from the gearbox. Position the cable clear of the gearbox so that it does not hinder the removal process.

11 Slide the gearbox selector shaft gaiter towards the gearbox, then remove the roll pin retaining clip from the gearbox end of the gearchange selector rod. Using a hammer and suitable punch, tap the roll pin out of the selector rod, and disconnect the rod from the gearbox. Slacken and remove the bolt which secures the gearchange linkage steady rod to the gearbox, and free the rod from its mounting bracket (photo) .

12 Remove the exhaust front pipe, as described in Chapter 4.

13 Remove the right-hand front suspension tie-bar, as described in Chapter 10.

14 Release the right-hand driveshaft inner constant velocity joint from the gearbox, as described in paragraphs 1 to 6 of Section 4.

15 Undo the two bolts which secure the anti-twisting bracket to the underside of the cylinder block, and the single bolt which secures it to the gearbox, then remove the bracket (photo).

16 Undo the flywheel lower cover plate retaining nuts and bolt, and remove the plate from the gearbox (photo).

17 Place a jack with interposed block of wood beneath the engine, to take the weight of the engine. Alternatively, attach a couple of lifting eyes to the engine, and fit a hoist or support bar to take the weight of the engine.

18 Place a jack and block of wood beneath the gearbox, to take the weight of the gearbox.

19 Slacken and remove the front gearbox mounting through-bolt and nut, then undo the two mounting bracket retaining bolts, and remove the bracket from the gearbox.

20 Remove the three bolts which secure the rear mounting bracket to the gearbox. Slacken and remove the mounting through-bolt, then manoeuvre the mounting bracket out of position and away from the gearbox.

21 Slacken and remove the right-hand mounting through-bolt. Undo the two nuts and single bolt which secure the mounting to its mounting plate, then remove the mounting. Undo the three mounting plate retaining bolts, and remove the plate from the top of the gearbox.

22 With the jack positioned beneath the gearbox and taking its weight, slacken and remove the five remaining bolts securing the gearbox housing to the engine unit. Note the correct fitted positions of the bolts to use as a reference on refitting, then make a final check that all necessary components have been disconnected.

23 With the bolts removed, move the trolley jack and gearbox to the right, to free it from its locating dowels. At the same time, carefully disengage the intermediate shaft from the left-hand side of the gearbox, taking great care not to damage the oil seal.

24 Once the transmission is free, lower the jack and manoeuvre the unit out from under the car. If the locating dowels are loose, remove them from the gearbox or engine unit, and keep them in a safe place.

Refitting

25 The gearbox is refitted using a reversal of the removal procedure, bearing in mind the following points.

(a) Apply a little high-melting-point grease to the splines of the transmission input shaft.

6.16... and the flywheel lower cover plate

6.25 Prior to refitting the gearbox, check that the locating dowels are in position

Fig. 7.2 Exploded view of manual gearbox (Sec 7)

1 Washer
2 Drain plug
3 Sealing bolt
4 Driveshaft oil seal
5 Filler/level plug
6 Washer
7 Gearbox housing
8 Reversing lamp switch
9 Clutch cable bracket
10 Breather tube
11 1st/2nd gear selector fork
12 1st/2nd gear selector fork shaft
13 Detent spring
14 Steel ball
15 Roll pin
16 Snap ring
17 Nut
18 Washer
19 Ball bearing
20 Needle roller bearing
21 Countershaft 5th gear pinion
22 Countershaft 4th gear pinion
23 Countershaft 3rd gear pinion
24 Countershaft 2nd gear pinion
25 Needle roller bearing
26 Spacer
27 Synchro-ring
28 Synchro-spring
29 Reverse gear
30 Synchro-hub
31 Synchro-spring
32 Synchro-spring
33 Countershaft 1st gear pinion
34 Needle roller bearing
35 Countershaft
36 Needle roller bearing
37 Oil guide plate
38 5th/reverse gear selector shaft
39 Roller
40 5th gear detent spring
41 5th gear selector fork
42 Oil guide plate
43 Thrust shim
44 Ball bearing
45 Synchro-hub
46 Synchro-sleeve
47 Synchro-spring
48 Synchro-ring
49 Mainshaft 5th gear pinion
50 Needle roller bearing
51 3rd/4th gear selector fork
52 Shift piece
53 Roll pin
54 Spacer/bush
55 Mainshaft 4th gear pinion
56 Needle roller bearing
57 Synchro-ring
58 Synchro-spring
59 Synchro-hub
60 Synchro-sleeve
61 Synchro-spring
62 Synchro-ring

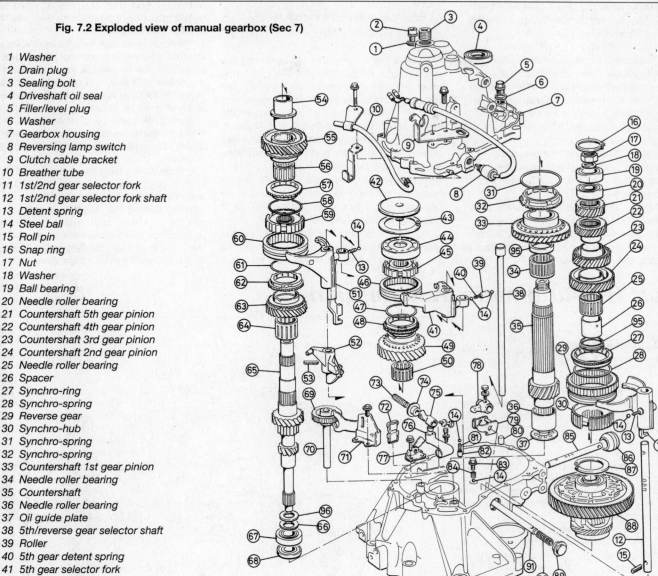

63 Mainshaft 3rd gear pinion
64 Needle roller bearing
65 Mainshaft
66 Spring washer
67 Ball bearing
68 Oil seal
69 Reverse gear idler pinion
70 Reverse gear idler pinion shaft
71 Reverse gear shift holder
72 Magnet
73 Reverse gear selector spring
74 Reverse gear return selector
75 Selector arm
76 Selector arm
77 Reverse gear locking cam
78 Selector arm
79 Interlock

80 Dowel pin
81 Spring
82 Spring collar
83 Spring bolt
84 Spring
85 Selector shaft
86 Gaiter
87 Thrust shim
88 Differential assembly
89 Plug
90 1st/2nd gear selector spring
91 Selector arm shaft
92 Oil seal
93 Clutch housing
94 Interlock guide bolt
95 Friction damper
96 Flat washer

7

Do not apply too much, otherwise there is a possibility of the grease contaminating the clutch friction plate.

(b) *Make sure the dowels are correctly positioned prior to installation (photo). Ensure that the intermediate shaft splines engage with those of the differential sun wheel when refitting the gearbox to the engine unit. Take great care not to damage the oil seal when refitting the gearbox.*

(c) *Renew the driveshaft inner constant velocity joint circlip, and install the driveshaft as described in Section 4, paragraphs 10 to 14.*

(d) *Tighten all nuts and bolts securely, or to the specified torque (where given).*

(e) *On completion, refill the gearbox with the specified type and quantity of lubricant as described in Chapter 1.*

7 Manual gearbox overhaul – general information

Overhauling a manual transmission unit is a difficult and involved job for the DIY home mechanic. In addition to dismantling and reassembling many small parts, clearances must be precisely measured and, if necessary, changed by selecting shims and spacers. Internal transmission components are also often difficult to obtain, and in many instances, are extremely expensive. Because of this, if the transmission develops a fault or becomes noisy, the best course of action is to have the unit overhauled by a specialist repairer, or to obtain an exchange reconditioned unit.

Nevertheless, it is not impossible for the more experienced mechanic to overhaul the transmission, provided the special tools are available, and that the job is done in a deliberate step-by-step manner so that nothing is overlooked.

The tools necessary for an overhaul include internal and external circlip pliers, bearing pullers, a slide hammer, a set of pin punches, a dial test indicator, and possibly a hydraulic press. In addition, a large, sturdy workbench and a vice will be required.

During dismantling of the transmission, make careful notes of how each component is fitted, to make reassembly easier and accurate.

Before dismantling the transmission, it will help if you have some idea which area is malfunctioning. Certain problems can be closely related to specific areas in the gearbox, which can make component examination and replacement easier. Refer to the *'Fault diagnosis'* Section at the beginning of this manual for more information.

Part B – Automatic transmission

8 General information

Most models in the 216/416 range are offered with the option of a four-speed fully-automatic transmission, consisting of a torque converter, an epicyclic geartrain, hydraulically-operated clutches and brakes, and an electronic control unit.

The torque converter provides a fluid coupling between engine and transmission, which acts as an automatic clutch, and also provides a degree of torque multiplication when accelerating.

The epicyclic geartrain provides each of the four forward and one reverse gear ratios, according to which of its component parts are held stationary or allowed to turn. The components of the geartrain are held or released by brakes and clutches, which are activated by a hydraulic control unit. An oil pump within the transmission provides the necessary hydraulic pressure to operate the brakes and clutches.

Driver control of the transmission is by a six-position selector lever. The transmission has two drive options, and a hold position on the second gear ratio. The first option 'D4' provides automatic changing on all four gears throughout the range, and is the one to select for normal driving. The second option 'D3' is very similar, but only uses the first three gears of the transmission; for this reason, 'D3' must never be selected while the vehicle is travelling at over 95 mph (150 kmh). The '2' position locks the transmission in the second gear position. This position can be used to provide engine braking while travelling down steep gradients, but the '2' position must never be selected while the vehicle is travelling at over 60 mph (95 kmh).

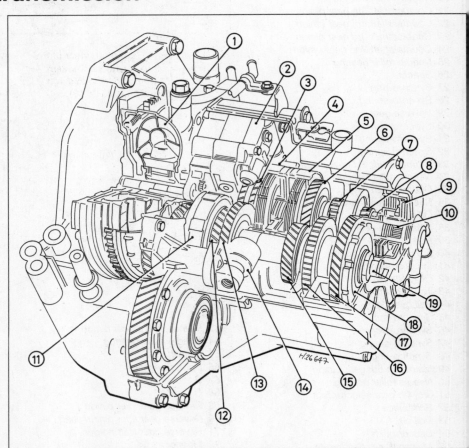

Fig. 7.3 Cutaway view of the automatic transmission (Sec 8)

1 Torque converter	8 Mainshaft 1st gear	14 Governor
2 Valve body	9 1st clutch	15 Countershaft 4th gear
3 Mainshaft 2nd gear	10 Mainshaft	16 Countershaft reverse gear
4 2nd clutch	11 3rd clutch	17 Countershaft 1st gear
5 4th clutch	12 Countershaft 3rd gear	18 Parking gear
6 Mainshaft 4th gear	13 Countershaft 2nd gear	19 Countershaft
7 Mainshaft reverse gear		

Due to the complexity of the automatic transmission, any repair or overhaul work must be left to a Rover dealer with the necessary special equipment for fault diagnosis and repair. The contents of the following Sections are therefore confined to supplying general information, and any service information and instructions that can be used by the owner.

9 Kickdown cable – adjustment

1 Adjust the accelerator cable as described in Chapter 4, and leave the vacuum pump attached to the dashpot.
2 Trace the kickdown cable back from the throttle cam to the transmission, then slacken the two adjuster locknuts securing the cable to its mounting bracket.

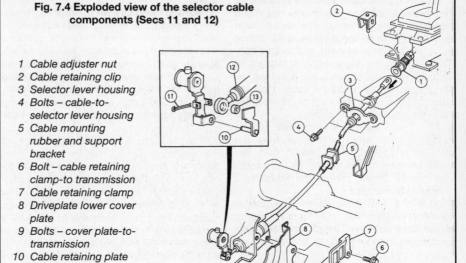

Fig. 7.4 Exploded view of the selector cable components (Secs 11 and 12)

1 Cable adjuster nut
2 Cable retaining clip
3 Selector lever housing
4 Bolts – cable-to-selector lever housing
5 Cable mounting rubber and support bracket
6 Bolt – cable retaining clamp-to transmission
7 Cable retaining clamp
8 Driveplate lower cover plate
9 Bolts – cover plate-to-transmission
10 Cable retaining plate
11 Split pin
12 Cable end fitting
13 Collar

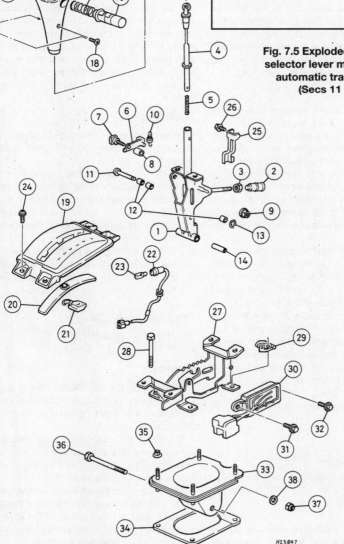

Fig. 7.5 Exploded view of the selector lever mechanism – automatic transmission (Secs 11 to 13)

1 Selector lever
2 Selector cable adjuster nut
3 Adjuster locknut
4 Pushrod
5 Spring
6 Selector lever detent arm
7 Bolt – detent arm-to-lever
8 Spacer
9 Nut – detent arm-to-lever
10 Detent arm spring
11 Pin
12 Collars
13 Circlip
14 Selector lever pivot bush
15 Selector lever knob
16 Selector lever detent release button
17 Spring
18 Grub screws
19 Selector lever position indicator panel
20 Selector lever cover
21 Indicator
22 Position indicator bulbholder
23 Bulb
24 Screw – indicator panel- to bracket
25 Wiring guide
26 Screw – wiring guide-to-selector
27 Lever mounting bracket
28 Bolt – mounting bracket-to-body
29 Wiring clamp
30 Starter inhibitor/reversing lamp switch
31 Bolt – inhibitor switch-to-bracket
32 Bolt – inhibitor switch-to-bracket
33 Selector lever pivot bracket
34 Seal
35 Nut – pivot bracket-to-body
36 Bolt – selector lever-to-pivot bracket
37 Nut – selector lever-to-pivot bracket
38 Washer

7

3 With vacuum still applied to the dashpot, or the pullrod pushed manually into the diaphragm, press down on the transmission kickdown lever so the lever is at its lowest point. With the lever held in this position, lightly tighten the upper adjuster nut until it contacts the cable mounting bracket and all free play is removed from the cable. Hold the upper adjuster nut in this position, then tighten the lower adjuster nut securely.

4 With the vacuum still applied to the dashpot, have an assistant depress the accelerator pedal, and check that the kickdown lever moves the instant the throttle cam moves. If not, repeat the adjustment procedure as necessary.

5 Once the kickdown cable is correctly adjusted, disconnect the vacuum pump (where used) from the dashpot, and reconnect the dashpot vacuum hose.

10 Kickdown cable – removal and refitting

Removal

1 Slacken the locknuts securing the upper end of the kickdown cable to the throttle housing, and release the cable from its mounting bracket. Disconnect the inner cable from the throttle cam.

2 Work back along the length of the cable, and free it from any relevant retaining clips or ties.

3 Slacken the two adjuster locknuts which secure the lower end of the cable to its mounting bracket. Free the outer cable from its mounting bracket, then disconnect the inner cable from the transmission kickdown lever, and remove the cable from the engine compartment.

Refitting

4 Manoeuvre the cable into position, then connect the lower end inner cable to the transmission kickdown lever, and locate the outer cable with the mounting bracket. Tighten the adjuster locknuts finger-tight only at this stage.

5 Connect the upper end of the inner cable to the throttle cam, and locate the outer cable with its mounting bracket. Tighten the upper cable locknuts securely.

6 Ensure that the cable is correctly routed and retained by any relevant ties or clips, then adjust the kickdown cable as described in Section 9.

11 Selector cable/mechanism – checking and adjustment

Checking

1 With the selector lever in the 'N' position, check that the index line on the 'N' position window aligns with the index line on the green band. Note that if only one index mark is visible, it may be that the marks are already aligned. To check this, move the selector lever slightly, and check that the lower mark is exposed. If the marks are not aligned, remove the centre console as described in Chapter 11. With the selector lever in the 'N' position, slacken the four indicator panel retaining screws, then move the panel as required. Once the index marks are correctly aligned, tighten the panel retaining screws securely. Once the indicator panel is known to be correctly positioned, check the selector cable adjustment as follows.

2 With the transmission in the 'N' position and the handbrake applied, start the engine. Firmly apply the footbrake, then slowly move the selector lever forwards into the 'R' position while observing the position of the green band in 'R' position window. Approximately three-quarters of the green band should be visible in the window when engagement of reverse gear is felt. Move the selector lever back to the 'N' position, then move it slowly rearwards into the 'D4' position again, while observing the position of the green band in the 'D4' position window. Again, approximately three-quarters of the green band should be visible in the window when engagement of first gear is felt. If the green band is not positioned as described, the selector cable must be adjusted as described below. If adjustment is not required, refit the centre console assembly (where removed).

Adjustment

3 If not already done, remove the centre console as described in Chapter 11.

4 Position the selector lever in the 'N' position, then remove the retaining clip which secures the selector cable to the base of the lever.

5 Selector cable adjustment is checked by passing a rod with a diameter of 4 mm through the selector lever and cable retaining pin holes. If resistance is felt as the rod is passed through, the cable requires adjustment as follows.

6 Remove the rod, then slacken the selector lever adjuster locknut. Rotate the adjuster clockwise if the cable is too short, or anti-clockwise if it is too long, until the rod passes cleanly through the cable and lever holes. Leave the pin in position, then move the selector lever through its complete working range and back to the 'N' position. Recheck that the rod passes freely through the holes, adjusting again if necessary, then hold the adjuster and tighten the locknut securely. Remove the rod, and refit the cable retaining clip.

7 Refit the centre console, as described in Chapter 11.

12 Selector cable – removal and refitting

Removal

1 Firmly apply the handbrake, then jack up the front of the vehicle and support it on axle stands.

2 Remove the exhaust front pipe, as described in Chapter 4.

3 Working from underneath the car, undo the two bolts securing the anti-twisting bracket to the underside of the cylinder block, and the single bolt securing it to the transmission, and remove the bracket.

4 Slacken and remove the three remaining driveplate ('flywheel') cover plate retaining bolts, and withdraw the plate from the transmission.

5 Undo the selector cable retaining clamp bolt, and remove the clamp from the transmission.

6 Extract the split pin from the transmission shift lever, and withdraw the selector cable retaining plate. Free the selector cable from the lever, and remove the collar from the cable end fitting.

7 Free the cable mounting rubber from its support bracket, then withdraw the cable from the transmission.

8 Working inside the car, remove the centre console as described in Chapter 11. Position the selector lever in the 'N' position, then remove the retaining clip which secures the selector cable to the base of the lever.

9 Underneath the vehicle, undo the two bolts securing the rear of the cable to the selector lever housing. Withdraw the cable from the housing, and remove it from underneath the vehicle.

Refitting

10 Refitting is a reversal of the removal procedure, bearing in mind the following points.

(a) Ensure the collar is fitted to the front selector cable end fitting, and secure the cable retaining plate in position with a new split pin.

(b) Tighten all nuts and bolts to the specified torque setting.

(c) Prior to refitting the centre console assembly, check and if necessary adjust the selector cable, as described in Section 11.

13 Selector lever – removal and refitting

Removal

1 Firmly apply the handbrake, then jack up the front of the car and support it on axle stands.

2 Remove the centre console, as described in Chapter 11.

3 Slacken the two selector lever handle grub screws, and lift the handle off the lever. Withdraw the pushrod and spring from the centre of the selector lever.

4 Undo the four screws which secure selector lever indicator panel to the lever mounting bracket. Lift up the panel, disengage the bulbholder from its underside, and lift the panel up and off the selector lever.

5 Remove the retaining clip which secures the

selector cable to the base of the lever, and free the cable from the selector lever.

6 Undo the two nuts and two bolts securing the selector lever mounting bracket to the floor.

7 From underneath the vehicle, withdraw the selector cable mounting plate from the body, noting its rubber seal, to gain access to the selector lever pivot bolt. Slacken and remove the selector lever pivot nut and bolt, then working inside the car, remove the selector lever and mounting bracket assembly, noting the pivot bush which is fitted to the base of the lever.

8 Inspect the selector lever pivot bush and selector cable housing seal for signs of damage, and renew as necessary.

Refitting

9 Refitting is a reversal of the removal procedure, bearing in mind the following points.

(a) Prior to installation, apply a smear of grease to the selector lever pivot bush and detent mechanism.

(b) Tighten all nuts and bolts securely.

(c) Prior to refitting the centre console, adjust the position of the indicator panel and the selector cable, as described in Section 11.

14 Starter inhibitor/reversing lamp switch – general information, removal and refitting

General information

1 The starter inhibitor/reversing lamp switch is a dual-function switch which is fitted to the selector lever assembly. The inhibitor function of the switch ensures that the engine can only be started when the selector lever is in either the 'N' or 'P' positions, thus preventing the engine being started while the transmission is in gear. This is achieved by the switch cutting the supply to the starter motor solenoid. If at any time it is noted that the engine can be started whilst the selector lever is in any position other than 'P' or 'N', then it is likely that the inhibitor function of the switch is faulty. The switch also performs the function of the reversing lamp switch, illuminating the reversing lamps whenever the selector lever is in the 'R' position. If either function of the switch is faulty, the complete switch must be renewed as a unit.

Removal

2 Remove the centre console, as described in Chapter 11.

3 Slacken and remove the two bolts which secure the inhibitor switch to the right-hand side of the selector lever mounting bracket, then disconnect the wiring connector and remove the switch from the car.

Refitting

4 Connect the wiring connector, then fit the switch to the selector lever mounting bracket, and tighten its retaining screws by hand.

5 Turn on the ignition, and check the operation of both the inhibitor and reversing lamp functions of the switch. If necessary, slight adjustments can be made by slackening the switch retaining bolts, and repositioning the switch as necessary. Once the switch is correctly positioned, tighten its retaining bolts securely, and refit the centre console as described in Chapter 11.

15 Speedometer drive – removal and refitting

Refer to Part A, Section 3.

16 Oil seals – renewal

Driveshaft oil seal

1 Refer to Part A, Section 4.

Input shaft oil seal

2 Remove the transmission as described in Section 18.

3 Carefully punch or drill two small holes opposite each other in the oil seal. Screw a self-tapping screw into each, and pull on the screws with pliers to extract the seal.

4 Clean the seal housing, and polish off any burrs or raised edges which may have caused the seal to fail in the first place.

5 Lubricate the lips of the new seal with clean engine oil, and drive it into position until it seats on its locating shoulder, using a suitable tubular drift which bears only on the hard outer edge of the seal. Note that the seal lips should face inwards; take care not to damage them during fitting.

6 Refit the transmission as described in Section 18.

17 Automatic transmission fluid cooler – general information

On models with automatic transmission, a transmission fluid cooler is available as an optional extra; the fluid cooler is considered virtually essential equipment for models which are to be used for towing. Where fitted, the fluid cooler is an integral part of the radiator assembly, located on the left-hand end of the radiator matrix. The transmission and fluid cooler are linked by two metal pipes (which are screwed into the cooler, and run along the bottom of the radiator), and two hoses which connect the pipes to the transmission. Regularly inspect the pipes and hoses for signs of leakage or damage, and renew

components as required. As mentioned before, the fluid cooler is an integral part of the radiator, and cannot be removed, or renewed, separately. If the cooler is damaged. the complete radiator assembly must be renewed. Refer to Chapter 3 for details of radiator removal and refitting.

18 Automatic transmission – removal and refitting

Removal

1 Firmly apply the handbrake and chock the rear wheels, then jack up the front of the car and support it on axle stands. Remove both front roadwheels.

2 Drain the transmission fluid as described in Chapter 1, then refit the drain plug and tighten it to the specified torque.

3 Remove the battery and battery tray, as described in Chapter 12.

4 Remove the starter motor, as described in Chapter 12.

5 Carefully remove the gaiter from the transmission end of the speedometer cable, and slide the gaiter up the cable. Remove the retaining clip from the speedometer drivegear housing, and disconnect the cable from the transmission.

6 Release the retaining clip securing the intake duct to the rear of the radiator, then release the expansion tank hose from its retaining clips on the duct. Undo the two bolts securing the duct to the bonnet locking platform, and remove the duct.

7 From underneath the front of the vehicle, slacken and remove the three bolts securing the bumper flange to the body. Remove the seven bolts securing the front undercover panel to the body, and remove the panel.

8 Slacken the two adjuster locknuts which secure the lower end of the kickdown cable to its mounting bracket. Free the outer cable from its mounting bracket, then disconnect the inner cable from the transmission kickdown lever, and place the cable clear of the transmission.

9 Undo the bolt securing the earth lead to the top of the transmission next to the kickdown cable mounting bracket, and disconnect the wiring connector from the transmission lock-up control solenoid. Free both the wiring leads from any relevant retaining clips, and place them clear of the working area.

10 Where necessary, slacken the two fluid cooler hose retaining clips, and disconnect both hoses from the transmission. Plug both the hose and transmission pipe ends to prevent the entry of dirt into the hydraulic system.

11 Remove the exhaust front pipe, as described in Chapter 4.

12 Remove the right-hand front suspension tie-bar, as described in Chapter 10.

13 Release the right-hand driveshaft inner constant velocity joint from the transmission,

7

as described in paragraphs 1 to 6 of Section 4 earlier in this Chapter.

14 Release the left-hand driveshaft and remove the intermediate shaft, using the information given in paragraphs 16 and 17 of Section 4 earlier in this Chapter.

15 Release the radiator bottom hose from its transmission retaining clip, then disengage the clip from its mounting, and remove the clip from the car.

16 Undo the two bolts which secure the anti-twisting bracket to the underside of the cylinder block, and the single bolt which secures it to the transmission, then remove the bracket.

17 Undo the three remaining driveplate ('flywheel') lower cover plate retaining bolts, and remove the plate from the transmission.

18 Undo the selector cable retaining clamp bolt, and remove the clamp from the transmission. Extract the split pin from the transmission shift lever, and withdraw the selector cable retaining plate. Free the selector cable from the lever, and remove the collar from the cable end fitting. Free the cable mounting rubber from its support bracket, then withdraw the cable from the transmission.

19 Slacken and remove the visible bolt(s) which secure the torque converter to the driveplate. Using a spanner or socket and extension bar on the crankshaft pulley bolt, rotate the engine anti-clockwise, and undo the remaining bolts as they become accessible through the lower cover plate aperture, noting that there are eight in total. **Note:** *If the crankshaft pulley bolt slackens while the crankshaft is being rotated it must be tightened to the specified torque, referring to Chapter 2 for further information, before proceeding further.*

20 Place a jack with interposed block of wood beneath the engine, to take the weight of the engine. Alternatively, attach a couple of lifting eyes to the engine, and fit a hoist or support bar to take the weight of the engine.

21 Place a jack and block of wood beneath the transmission, to take the weight of the transmission.

22 Slacken and remove the front transmission mounting through-bolt and nut, then undo the two mounting bracket retaining bolts, and remove the bracket from the transmission.

23 Remove the three bolts which secure the rear mounting to the top of the transmission, then slacken the mounting through-bolt, and pivot the mounting plate upwards and away from the transmission.

24 Slacken and remove the right-hand mounting through-bolt. Undo the three mounting plate retaining bolts, and remove the plate from the top of the transmission.

25 With the jack positioned beneath the transmission taking its weight, slacken and remove the five remaining bolts securing the transmission housing to the engine unit. Note the correct fitted positions of the bolts to use as a reference on refitting, then make a final check that all necessary components have been disconnected.

26 With the bolts removed, move the trolley jack and transmission to the right, to free it from its locating dowels. Once the transmission is free, lower the jack and manoeuvre the unit out from under the car, ensuring that the torque converter stays in position on the transmission shaft. If the locating dowels are loose, remove them from the transmission or engine unit, and keep them in a safe place.

Refitting

27 The transmission is refitted using a reversal of the removal procedure, bearing in mind the following points.

(a) *Apply a little high-melting-point grease to the splines of the transmission input shaft. Do not apply too much, otherwise there is a possibility of the grease contaminating the torque converter.*

(b) *Make sure the dowels are correctly positioned prior to refitting the transmission to the engine unit.*

(c) *Install all the torque converter-to-driveplate bolts, tightening them first by hand only, then tighten them to the specified torque in a diagonal sequence.*

(d) *Renew the driveshaft inner constant velocity joint circlip, then install the right-hand driveshaft as described in Section 4, paragraphs 10 to 14.*

(e) *Refit the intermediate shaft and left-hand driveshaft, using the information given in paragraphs 19 to 24 of Section 4.*

(f) *Ensure the collar is fitted to the front selector cable end fitting, and secure the cable retaining plate in position with a new split pan.*

(g) *Connect the kickdown cable to the transmission, and adjust it as described in Section 9.*

(h) *Tighten all nuts and bolts securely, or to the specified torque (where given).*

(l) *On completion, refill the transmission with the specified type and quantity of lubricant, as described in Chapter 1.*

19 Automatic transmission
overhaul – general information

In the event of a fault occurring on the transmission, it is first necessary to determine whether it is of an electrical, mechanical or hydraulic nature, and to do this, special test equipment is required. It is therefore essential to have the work carried out by a Rover dealer if a transmission fault is suspected.

Don't be too quick to remove the transmission from the car for possible repair before professional fault diagnosis has been carried out, since most tests require the transmission to be in the vehicle.

Chapter 8 Driveshafts

Contents

Degrees of difficulty

Easy, suitable for novice with little experience	Fairly easy, suitable for beginner with some experience	Fairly difficult, suitable for competent DIY mechanic	Difficult, suitable for experienced DIY mechanic	Very difficult, suitable for expert DIY or professional

Specifications

Type . . . . Equal-length solid steel shafts, splined to inner and outer constant velocity joints, dynamic damper on both shafts. Intermediate shaft fitted between left-hand driveshaft inner end and transmission

Lubrication (overhaul only – see text)

Lubricant type/specification . . . . Use only special grease supplied in sachets with gaiter kits – joints are otherwise pre-packed with grease and sealed

Torque wrench settings	Nm	lbf ft
Driveshaft retaining nut	185	137
Intermediate shaft bearing housing mounting bolts	40	33
Roadwheel nuts	100	74

1 General information

Drive is transmitted from the differential to the front wheels by means of two solid steel driveshafts and an intermediate shaft. The intermediate shaft is fitted between the left-hand driveshaft inner end and the transmission, to allow driveshafts of equal length to be used.

Both driveshafts are splined at their outer ends to accept the wheel hubs, and are threaded so that each hub can be fastened by a large nut. The inner end of each driveshaft is splined to accept the differential sun gear/intermediate shaft (as applicable), and has a groove to accept the circlip which retains the driveshaft in position.

Constant velocity (CV) joints are fitted to each end of the driveshafts, to ensure the smooth and efficient transmission of drive at all the angles possible as the roadwheels move up and down with the suspension, and as they turn from side to side under steering. The outer constant velocity joints are of the ball-and-cage type, and the inner constant velocity joints are of the tripod type.

A dynamic damper is fitted to both the left- and right-hand driveshafts, to reduce harmonic vibrations and resonance.

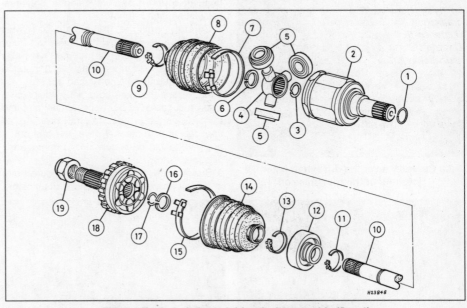

Fig. 8.1 Exploded view of driveshaft assembly (Sec 1)

1 Circlip
2 Inner tripod joint outer member
3 Circlip
4 Tripod joint
5 Bearings
6 Stopper ring
7 Large gaiter retaining clip
8 Gaiter
9 Small gaiter retaining clip
10 Driveshaft
11 Damper clip
12 Dynamic damper
13 Small gaiter retaining clip
14 Gaiter
15 Large gaiter retaining clip
16 Stopper ring
17 Circlip
18 Outer joint assembly
19 Driveshaft retaining nut

8

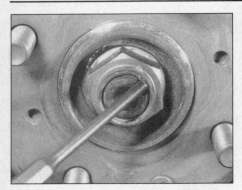

2.3 Use a hammer and suitable punch to tap up the driveshaft nut staking

2.6 Balljoint shanks can be released using a universal balljoint separator

2.7 Pull the swivel hub outwards and disengage the driveshaft outer CV joint

2 Driveshafts –
removal and refitting

Removal

1 Chock the rear wheels, firmly apply the handbrake, then jack up the front of the car and support it on axle stands. Remove the appropriate front roadwheel.

2 If the right-hand driveshaft is to be removed, drain the transmission oil as described in Chapter 1.

3 Using a hammer and suitable chisel-nosed tool, tap up the staking (notch) securing the driveshaft retaining nut to the groove in the constant velocity joint (photo).

2.8 Carefully lever the driveshaft inner CV joint out of the transmission

4 Have an assistant firmly depress the brake pedal to prevent the front hub from rotating, then using a socket and extension bar, slacken and remove the driveshaft retaining nut. *Be sure that the car is adequately supported, as considerable force will be required to undo the nut.* Discard the nut, as a new driveshaft retaining nut must be obtained for reassembly.

5 Slacken and remove the bolt and washer securing the anti-roll bar connecting link to the lower suspension arm, and the two bolts securing the tie-bar to the lower suspension arm.

6 Extract the split pins, and undo the nuts securing steering gear track rod end balljoint and the lower suspension arm balljoint to the swivel hub. Remove the nuts, and release the balljoint tapered shanks using a universal balljoint separator (photo).

7 Carefully pull the swivel hub assembly outwards, and withdraw the driveshaft outer constant velocity joint from the hub assembly (photo). If necessary, the shaft can be tapped out of the hub using a soft-faced mallet.

8 To release the inner constant velocity joint, insert a suitable flat bar between the joint and transmission/intermediate shaft housing (as applicable), then carefully lever the joint out of position, taking great care not to damage the oil seal (photo).

9 Support the inner constant velocity joint while withdrawing it from the transmission/

intermediate shaft (as applicable), to ensure that the oil seal is not damaged, and remove the driveshaft from the vehicle.

Refitting

10 Before installing the driveshaft, examine the transmission/intermediate shaft housing oil seal for signs of damage or deterioration, and renew it if necessary, referring to Chapter 7 or Section 5 of this Chapter (as appropriate) for further information. Similarly inspect the oil seal which is fitted to the outer constant velocity joint for damage or deterioration, and renew if necessary. Regardless of its apparent condition, renew the circlip which is fitted to the groove in the inner constant velocity joint splines as a matter of course (photos).

11 Thoroughly clean the driveshaft splines and the apertures in the transmission/ intermediate shaft (as applicable) and hub assembly, then apply a thin film of grease to the oil seal lips and to the driveshaft splines and shoulders. Check that all gaiter clips are securely fastened.

12 Ensure that the circlip fitted to the inner constant velocity is located securely in its groove, then locate the joint splines with those of the differential sun gear or intermediate shaft (as applicable). Taking great care not to damage the oil seal, push the joint fully into position (photo). To check that the joint is securely retained by the circlip, try pulling the shaft outwards.

2.10A Inspect the outer CV joint seal (arrowed) for signs of wear, and renew if necessary

2.10B Inner CV joint circlip (arrowed) must be renewed as a matter of course

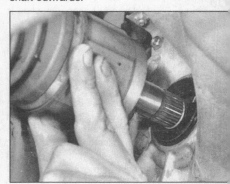

2.12 Refit the driveshaft inner CV joint to the transmission, taking care not to damage the driveshaft oil seal ...

2.13 ... and engage the outer CV joint with the swivel hub

2.16A Tighten the driveshaft retaining nut to the specified torque ...

2.16B ... and stake it firmly into the CV joint groove

13 Locate the outer constant velocity joint splines with those of the swivel hub, and slide the joint back into position in the hub (photo).
14 Insert the lower suspension arm and track rod balljoints into their respective locations in the swivel hub, and tighten their retaining nuts to the specified torque. Secure both nuts in position using new split pins.
15 Refit the bolts securing the trailing arm and anti-roll bar connecting link to the lower suspension arm, and tighten them to the specified torque.
16 Fit the new driveshaft retaining nut, and tighten it to the specified torque setting while an assistant firmly depresses the brake pedal. Be sure that the car is adequately supported, as considerable force will be required to secure the nut. Release the brake, check that the hub rotates freely, then stake the nut firmly into the groove on the constant velocity joint using a suitable punch (photos).
17 Refit the roadwheel, then lower the car to the ground and tighten the wheel nuts to the specified torque.
18 If the right-hand shaft was removed, refill the transmission with the correct type and quantity of lubricant, as described in Chapter 1.

3 Driveshaft rubber gaiters – renewal

Outer joint

1 Remove the driveshaft from the car, as described in Section 2.
2 Secure the driveshaft in a vice equipped with soft jaws, then release the two rubber gaiter retaining clips by raising the locking tangs with a screwdriver, and then raising the end of the clip with pliers. If necessary, the gaiter retaining clips can be cut to release them (photo).
3 Slide the rubber gaiter down the shaft to expose the outer constant velocity joint.
4 Using a soft-faced mallet, sharply strike the inner member of the joint to drive it off the end of the shaft (photo). The outer joint is retained on the driveshaft by a circlip, and striking the joint in this manner forces the circlip into its groove, so allowing the joint to slide off.

5 Once the joint assembly has been removed, remove the circlip from the groove in the driveshaft splines and discard it. A new circlip must be fitted on reassembly.
6 Withdraw the rubber gaiter from the driveshaft.
7 With the constant velocity joint removed from the driveshaft, thoroughly clean the joint using paraffin (or other suitable solvent), and dry it thoroughly. Carry out a visual inspection of the joint.
8 Move the inner splined driving member from side to side, to expose each ball in turn at the top of its track. Examine the balls for cracks, flat spots or signs of surface pitting.
9 Inspect the ball tracks on the inner and outer members. If the tracks have widened, the balls will no longer be a tight fit. At the same time, check the ball cage windows for wear or cracking between the windows. Check the driveshaft dynamic damper for signs of damage and deterioration, and renew if necessary.
10 If on inspection any of the constant velocity joint components are found to be worn or damaged, it will be necessary to renew the complete joint assembly, since no components are available separately. If the joint is in satisfactory condition, obtain a repair kit consisting of a new gaiter, retaining clips, and the correct type and quantity of grease.
11 If driveshaft damper renewal is necessary, release the damper retaining clip and slide off the old damper. Position the new damper as shown in Fig. 8.2, and secure it in position with a new retaining clip.

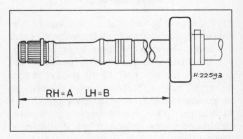

Fig. 8.2 Position the dynamic damper the specified distance from the outer end of the driveshaft (Sec 3)
Right-hand driveshaft (A) – 220 to 224 mm
Left-hand driveshaft (B) – 301 to 305 mm

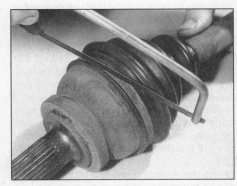

3.2 It may be necessary to cut gaiter clips to release them

3.4 Driving outer constant velocity joint off driveshaft end

3.12 Ensure stopper ring and new circlip are correctly located before refitting outer constant velocity joint

8

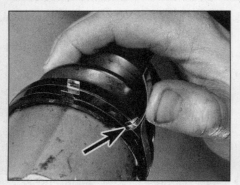

3.17A Locate the clip inner tab with the hook (arrow) ...

3.17B ... then press the clip down, and bend down the tangs to lock the clip in position

3.24 Using a two-legged puller to draw the tripod joint off the driveshaft end

12 Tape over the splines on the end of the driveshaft, then carefully slide the gaiter onto the shaft. Remove the tape, then, ensuring that the stopper ring is securely located in its groove, fit a new circlip to the groove in the driveshaft splines (photo). Engage the help of an assistant for the following operations.

13 Position the constant velocity joint over the splines on the driveshaft until it abuts the circlip.

14 Using two small screwdrivers placed either side of the circlip, compress the clip, and at the same time have your assistant firmly strike the end of the joint with a soft-faced mallet. This should not require an undue amount of force. if the joint does not spring into place, remove it, reposition the circlip, and try again. Do not force the joint, otherwise the circlip will be damaged.

15 Check that the circlip holds the joint securely on the driveshaft end, then pack the joint with the grease supplied. Work the grease well into the ball tracks whilst twisting the joint, and fill the rubber gaiter with any excess.

16 Ease the gaiter over the joint, and place the large retaining clip in position. Ensure that the gaiter is correctly located in the grooves on both the driveshaft and constant velocity joint.

17 Fit the large retaining clip, and fold it around the gaiter. Lift the end of the clip, and locate the inner tab on the inside of the clip, with the hook adjacent to the outer locating

tangs. Press the clip down so that it clips into position with the two raised tangs, and holds the gaiter firmly in position. Bend the raised tangs over to lock the clip in position. Fit the small retaining clip using the same procedure (photos).

18 Check that the constant velocity joint moves freely in all directions, then refit the driveshaft to the car as described in Section 2.

Inner joint

19 Remove the driveshaft from the car, as described in Section 2.

20 Secure the driveshaft in a vice equipped with soft jaws, then release the two rubber gaiter retaining clips by raising the locking tangs with a screwdriver, and then raising the end of the clip with pliers. If necessary, the gaiter retaining clips can be cut to release them.

21 Slide the rubber gaiter down the shaft to expose the inner constant velocity joint.

22 Remove all excess grease from inside the joint. Using a dab of quick-drying white paint or a suitable marker pen, make suitable alignment marks between the driveshaft and tripod joint, and between each of the three tripod joint bearings and the outer member.

23 Slide the outer member off the end of the shaft, and remove the three bearings from the tripod joint.

24 Carefully prise the circlip out of its groove in the end of the driveshaft, then draw the tripod joint off the driveshaft end using a

suitable two- or three-legged bearing puller (photo).

25 Remove the stopper ring from the driveshaft splines, and slide off the gaiter.

26 With the constant velocity joint components removed, thoroughly clean all the components using paraffin (or other suitable solvent), and dry them thoroughly; take great care not to remove the alignment marks made on dismantling. Carry out a visual inspection of the joint.

27 Check the tripod joint bearings and joint outer member for signs of wear, pitting or scuffing on their bearing surfaces. Refit the bearings to the tripod joint, and check that they rotate smoothly and easily, with no traces of roughness.

28 If on inspection the tripod joint or outer member reveals signs of wear or damage, it will be necessary to renew the complete joint as an assembly, since no components are available separately. If the joint components are in satisfactory condition, obtain a repair kit consisting of a new gaiter, retaining clips, and the correct type and quantity of grease.

29 Tape over the splines on the end of the driveshaft, then carefully slide the gaiter onto the shaft (photo).

30 Remove the tape, then refit the stopper ring, ensuring that it is securely located in its groove (photo).

31 Align the marks made on dismantling, and engage the tripod joint with the driveshaft splines. Use a hammer and soft metal drift to

3.29 Slide on the gaiter ...

3.30 ... then fit the stopper ring to its driveshaft groove

3.31A Engage the tripod joint with the driveshaft splines, and tap it into position using a suitable hammer and drift

3.31B Secure the joint in position with the circlip

3.32A Lubricate the bearings with the grease supplied in the repair kit ...

3.32B ... then pack the remainder into the joint outer member ...

tap the joint onto the shaft, taking great care not to damage the driveshaft splines. Once the joint abuts the stopper ring, secure it in position with the circlip (photos).

32 Apply a smear of the grease supplied with the repair kit to the tripod joint stems and bearings, then refit the bearings to the joint. Pack the remainder of the grease into the outer member (photos).

33 Align the joint outer member aligning marks with those made on the bearings, and slide the outer member over the tripod joint (photo).

34 Ease the gaiter over the joint outer member, and secure in position as described above in paragraphs 16 to 18 above.

4 Driveshaft overhaul – general information

1 If any of the checks described in Chapter 1 reveal wear in any driveshaft joint, first remove the roadwheel trim or centre cap (as appropriate). If the staking (notch) is still effective, the driveshaft nut should be correctly tightened; if in doubt, use a torque wrench to check that the nut is securely fastened, re-stake the nut, then refit the centre cap or trim. Repeat this check on the remaining driveshaft nut. Refer to Section 2 for further information.

2 Road test the vehicle, and listen for a metallic clicking from the front as the vehicle is driven slowly in a circle on full lock. If a clicking noise is heard, this indicates wear in the outer constant velocity joint. This means that the joint must be renewed; reconditioning is not possible.

3 If vibration, consistent with road speed, is felt through the car when accelerating, there is a possibility of wear in the inner constant velocity joints.

4 To check the joints for wear, remove the driveshafts, then dismantle them as described in Section 3; if any wear or free play is found, the affected joint must be renewed as an assembly.

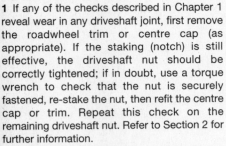

3.33 ... and slide the outer member onto the driveshaft

5 Intermediate shaft – removal and refitting

Removal

1 Disengage the left-hand driveshaft from the intermediate shaft, as described in Section 4 of Chapter 7 (photo).

2 Slacken and remove the three bolts securing the intermediate shaft bearing housing to the cylinder block (photo).

3 Rotate the shaft so its mounting flange is pointing downwards, then carefully withdraw the shaft assembly from the transmission. Note that the shaft must be withdrawn squarely, to prevent the transmission oil seal being damaged (photo).

4 Inspect the shaft and mounting flange assembly for signs of wear or damage, paying particular attention to the bearing housing oil seals, and check that the shaft bearing rotates freely and easily, without any trace of roughness. Worn components must be renewed. **Note**: *Dismantling of the intermediate shaft assembly for bearing renewal, etc., is a complex task, requiring the use of several special-shaped mandrels and a hydraulic press, and should therefore be entrusted to a Rover dealer. The only task which can comfortably be carried out by the home mechanic is the renewal of the bearing housing outer oil seal. This can be simply levered out of position using a suitable flat-bladed screwdriver (photo), the new seal being*

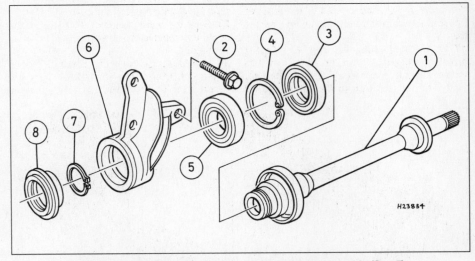

Fig. 8.3 Exploded view of the intermediate shaft assembly (Sec 5)

1 Intermediate shaft	3 Inner seal	6 Bearing housing
2 Bearing housing mounting bolts	4 Circlip	7 Small circlip
	5 Bearing	8 Outer seal

8

5.1 Disengage the driveshaft from the intermediate shaft ...

5.2 ... then undo the three intermediate shaft mounting bolts (two arrowed, one hidden) ...

5.3 ... and carefully remove the intermediate shaft as described in text

tapped into position using a suitable tubular drift, such as a socket, which bears only on the hard outer edge of the seal.

Refitting

5 Prior to refitting, check the transmission oil seal for signs of wear and, if necessary, renew it as described in Chapter 7.

6 Remove all traces of dirt from the transmission housing aperture and the intermediate shaft inner splines, then apply a thin smear of grease to the transmission oil seal lip and shaft splines. With the mounting flange pointing downwards, carefully locate the shaft splines with those of the differential sun gear, taking great care not to damage the transmission oil seal lips.

7 Keeping the intermediate shaft square at all times, align the mounting flange holes with those on the cylinder block, then refit the bearing housing mounting bolts and tighten them to the specified torque setting.

8 Refit the left-hand driveshaft as described in Chapter 7, Section 4.

5.4 Intermediate shaft bearing housing outer seal can be levered out of position with a flat-bladed screwdriver

Chapter 9 Braking system

Contents

Degrees of difficulty

Easy, suitable for novice with little experience | **Fairly easy,** suitable for beginner with some experience | **Fairly difficult,** suitable for competent DIY mechanic | **Difficult,** suitable for experienced DIY mechanic | **Very difficult,** suitable for expert DIY or professional

Specifications

System type . . . . Dual hydraulic circuit, split diagonally. Disc front brakes. Drum rear brakes or disc rear brakes, depending on model and specification. Anti-lock braking (ALB) system on some models. Vacuum servo assistance on all models; cable-operated handbrake on rear brakes

Front brakes

Type . . . . Disc, with single-piston sliding caliper
Disc diameter . . . . 262 mm
Disc thickness:
 New . . . . 21.60 mm
 Minimum thickness after machining . . . . 19.00 mm
Maximum disc run-out . . . . 0.02 mm
Brake pad friction material minimum thickness . . . . 3.0 mm

Rear brakes

Type:
 Si, SLi and later GSi models, without anti-lock brakes . . . . Single leading-shoe drum
 All other models . . . . Disc, with single-piston sliding caliper
Drum brakes:
 Drum diameter:
  New . .200 mm
  Maximum diameter after machining . . . . 204 mm
 Maximum drum ovality . . . . 0.012 mm
 Brake shoe friction material minimum thickness . . . . 2.0 mm
Disc brakes:
 Disc diameter . . . . 239 mm
 Disc thickness:
  New . .10 mm
  Minimum thickness after machining . . . . 8 mm
 Maximum disc run-out . . . . 0.06 mm
 Brake pad friction material minimum thickness . . . . 3.0 mm

9

Torque wrench settings

	Nm	lbf ft
Brake hose union bolt	38	28
Brake pipe union nuts	20	15
Master cylinder-to-servo unit nuts	17	13
Brake caliper guide pin bolt	32	24
Brake disc retaining screws	12	9
Front brake caliper bracket-to-hub bolts	80	59
Rear brake drum retaining screws	10	7
Rear wheel cylinder-to-backplate bolts	10	7
Rear brake caliper bracket-to-trailing arm bolts	40	30
Handbrake cable-to-underbody retaining bolts	22	16
ALB wheel sensor retaining bolts	10	7
ALB wheel sensor wiring bracket bolts	10	7
ALB rear wheel sensor cover and cover strap bolts	10	7
Roadwheel nuts	100	74

1 General information

The braking system is of the servo-assisted, dual-circuit hydraulic type. The arrangement of the hydraulic system is such that each circuit operates one front and one rear brake from a tandem master cylinder. Under normal circumstances, both circuits operate in unison; however, in the event of hydraulic failure in one circuit, full braking force will still be available at two wheels. On models not equipped with anti-lock brakes (ALB), a pressure-regulating valve is also incorporated in the hydraulic circuit, to regulate the pressure applied to the rear brakes, and thus reduce the possibility of the rear wheels locking under heavy braking.

All models are fitted with front disc brakes. The disc brakes are actuated by single-piston sliding type calipers, which ensures that equal pressure is applied to each disc pad.

All GTi models and early GSi models have rear disc brakes, regardless of whether anti-lock braking is fitted. On Si, SLi and later GSi models, only those models equipped with anti-lock brakes (ALB) are also fitted with rear disc brakes. The disc brakes are actuated by a single-piston sliding caliper, which incorporates a mechanical handbrake mechanism. Models (other than those mentioned above) which are not equipped with anti-lock brakes are fitted with rear drum brakes, which incorporate leading and trailing shoes, actuated by twin-piston wheel cylinders. A self-adjust mechanism is incorporated to automatically compensate for brake shoe wear. As the brake shoe linings

wear, footbrake operation automatically operates the adjuster mechanism quadrant, which effectively lengthens the shoe strut and repositions the brake shoes, to reduce the lining-to-drum clearance.

On all models, the handbrake provides an independent mechanical means of rear brake application.

Note: *When servicing any part of the system, work carefully and methodically; also observe scrupulous cleanliness when overhauling any part of the hydraulic system. Always renew components (in axle sets, where applicable) if in doubt about their condition, and use only genuine Rover replacement parts, or at least those of known good quality. Note the warnings given in 'Safety first!' and at the relevant points in this Chapter, concerning the dangers of asbestos dust and hydraulic fluid.*

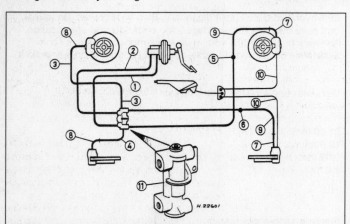

Fig. 9.1 Layout of braking system components – models without anti-lock brakes (Sec 1)

1 Primary hydraulic circuit
2 Secondary hydraulic circuit
3 Brake pipe – pressure-regulating valve-to-right-hand front hose
4 Brake pipe – pressure-regulating valve-to-left-hand front hose
5 Brake pipe – pressure-regulating valve-to-right-hand rear hose
6 Brake pipe – pressure-regulating valve-to-left-hand rear hose
7 Brake pipe – hose to rear wheel cylinder
8 Brake flexible hose – brake pipe to front brake caliper
9 Brake flexible hose – rear wheel
10 Handbrake cable
11 Pressure regulating valve

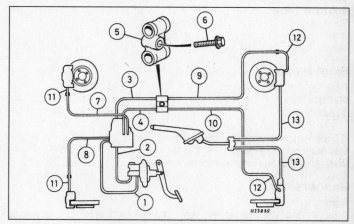

Fig. 9.2 Layout of braking system components – models with anti-lock brakes (ALB) (Sec 1)

1 Primary hydraulic circuit
2 Secondary hydraulic circuit
3 Brake pipe – modulator-to-adaptor union
4 Brake pipe – modulator-to-adaptor union
5 Adaptor union
6 Adaptor union mounting bolt
7 Brake pipe – modulator-to-right-hand front hose
8 Brake pipe – modulator-to-left-hand front hose
9 Brake pipe – modulator-to-right-hand rear hose
10 Brake pipe – modulator-to-left-hand rear hose
11 Brake flexible hose – brake pipe-to-front brake caliper
12 Brake flexible hose – brake pipe-to-rear brake caliper
13 Handbrake cable

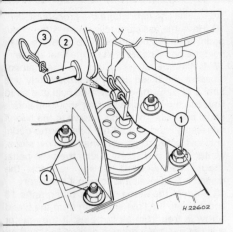

Fig. 9.3 Vacuum servo unit and pushrod fixings (Sec 3)

1 Servo unit mounting nuts   3 R-clip
2 Pushrod clevis pin

2 Brake pedal – removal and refitting

Removal

1 Working from inside the car, undo the five screws, and remove the right-hand lower facia panel.
2 Extract the R-clip and clevis pin securing the servo unit pushrod to the brake pedal.
3 Using pliers, carefully unhook the brake pedal return spring from the pedal, to release all the spring tension.
4 Slacken and remove the nut and washers (as applicable) from the brake pedal pivot bolt, then withdraw the pivot bolt, and remove the brake pedal and return spring.
5 Examine all brake pedal components for signs of wear, paying particular attention to the pedal bushes and the pivot bolt and return spring, and renew as necessary.

Refitting

6 Refitting is a reverse of the removal, but lubricate the bushes, pivot bolt and clevis pin with a multi-purpose grease. On completion, check the operation of the pedal, and ensure it returns smoothly to the at-rest position under the pressure of the return spring.

3 Vacuum servo unit – testing, removal and refitting

Testing

1 To test the operation of the servo unit, depress the footbrake several times to exhaust the vacuum, then start the engine, keeping the pedal firmly depressed. As the engine starts, there should be a noticeable 'give' in the brake pedal as the vacuum builds up. Allow the engine to run for at least two minutes, then switch it off. If the brake pedal is

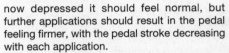

3.8 Removing the fuel filter to enable removal of the servo

now depressed it should feel normal, but further applications should result in the pedal feeling firmer, with the pedal stroke decreasing with each application.
2 If the servo does not operate as described, inspect the servo unit check valve, as described in Section 4.
3 If the servo unit still fails to operate satisfactorily, the fault lies within the unit itself. Repairs to the unit are possible, but special tools are required, and the work should be entrusted to a suitably-equipped Rover dealer.

Removal

4 Remove the master cylinder, as described in Section 7.
5 Using a suitable pair of pliers, release the retaining clip, and disconnect the vacuum hose from the servo unit.
6 Working from inside the car, undo the five retaining screws, and remove the right-hand lower facia panel.
7 Extract the R-clip and clevis pin securing the servo unit pushrod to the brake pedal, then slacken and remove the four nuts securing the servo unit to the engine compartment bulkhead.
8 Working in the engine compartment, to gain the necessary clearance to remove the servo unit, remove the two bolts securing the fuel filter to the bulkhead, and position the filter clear of the servo unit (photo). Manoeuvre the servo out of position, noting the gasket which is fitted to the rear of the unit.

Refitting

9 Fit a new gasket to the rear of the servo unit, and reposition the unit in the engine compartment.
10 From inside the car, ensure the servo unit pushrod is correctly engaged with the brake pedal, then refit the servo unit mounting nuts, and tighten them securely.
11 Refit the servo unit pushrod-to-brake pedal clevis pin, and secure it in position with the R-clip.
12 Refit the right-hand lower facia panel, tightening its retaining screws securely.
13 From inside the engine compartment, connect the vacuum hose to the servo unit, and secure it in position with its retaining clip.

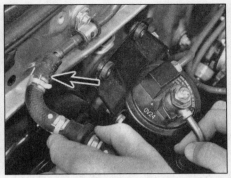

4.2 Disconnecting servo vacuum hose (arrowed)

4.5 Vacuum servo unit check valve, showing fitted direction marking

Refit the fuel filter mounting bolts, and tighten them securely.
14 Refit the master cylinder, as described in Section 7 of this Chapter.
15 On completion, start the engine and check the operation of the braking system.

4 Vacuum servo unit check valve – removal, testing and refitting

Removal

1 To remove the check valve and its connecting hoses, first slacken and remove the two bolts securing the fuel filter to the engine compartment bulkhead, and carefully position the filter clear of the hose.
2 Using a suitable pair of pliers, release the retaining clips, then disconnect the vacuum hoses from the servo and vacuum pipe (photo), and remove the hose and check valve assembly from the engine compartment.
3 If necessary, the vacuum pipe and the hose which connects the vacuum pipe to the inlet manifold can be also removed, once the pipe mounting bolts have been undone and the hose is disconnected from its manifold union.

Testing

4 Examine the vacuum pipe and hoses for damage, splits, cracks or general deterioration, and renew as necessary. Make

sure that the check valve is working correctly by blowing through the hose from the servo unit end. Air should flow in this direction, but not when blown through from the inlet manifold vacuum pipe end. Renew the check valve if at all suspect.

Refitting

5 Refitting is a reversal of the removal procedure, noting the following points.
(a) *Ensure that the check valve is installed so that its arrow points towards the inlet manifold vacuum pipe (photo).*
(b) *Ensure that all vacuum hoses are securely held in position by their retaining clips.*
(c) *On completion, start the engine and check the operation of the servo unit as described in Section 3.*

5 Hydraulic system – bleeding

Note: *Hydraulic fluid is poisonous; wash off immediately and thoroughly in the case of skin contact, and seek immediate medical advice if any fluid is swallowed or gets into the eyes. Certain types of hydraulic fluid are inflammable, and may ignite when allowed into contact with hot components; when servicing any hydraulic system it is safest to assume that the fluid is inflammable, and to take the same precautions against the risk of fire as you would with petrol. Finally, it is hygroscopic (it absorbs moisture from the air) – old fluid stored for several months may be contaminated and unfit for further use. When topping-up or renewing the fluid, always use the recommended type, and ensure that it comes from a freshly-opened sealed container.*

 HAYNES HiNT *Hydraulic fluid is an effective paint stripper, and will attack plastics; if any is spilt, it should be washed off immediately, using copious quantities of fresh water.*

General

1 The correct operation of any hydraulic system is only possible after removing all air from the components and circuit; this is achieved by bleeding the system.
2 During the bleeding procedure, add only clean, unused hydraulic fluid of the recommended type; never re-use fluid that has already been bled from the system. Ensure that sufficient fluid is available before starting work.
3 If there is any possibility of incorrect fluid being in the system already, the brake components and circuit must be flushed completely with uncontaminated, correct fluid, and new seals should be fitted to the various components.

4 If hydraulic fluid has been lost from the system, or air has entered because of a leak, ensure that the fault is cured before proceeding further.
5 Park the car on level ground, switch off the engine and select first or reverse gear, then chock the wheels and release the handbrake.
6 Check that all pipes and hoses are secure, that fluid unions are tight and bleed screws closed. Clean any dirt from around the bleed screws.
7 Unscrew the master cylinder reservoir cap and top the master cylinder reservoir up to the 'MAX' level line; refit the cap loosely. Remember to maintain the fluid level at least above the 'MIN' level line throughout the following procedure, or there is a risk of further air entering the system.
8 There are a number of one-man, do-it-yourself brake bleeding kits currently available from motor accessory shops. It is recommended that one of these kits is used whenever possible, as they greatly simplify the bleeding operation, and also reduce the risk of expelled air and fluid being drawn back into the system. If such a kit is not available, the basic (two-man) method must be used, which is described in detail below.
9 If a one-man kit is to be used, prepare the car as described previously, and follow the kit manufacturer's instructions in the first instance (the procedure may vary slightly according to the type being used; generally, they are as outlined below in the relevant sub-section).
10 Whichever method is used, the same sequence must be followed (paragraphs 11 and 12) to ensure the removal of all air from the system.

Bleeding sequence

11 If the system has been only partially disconnected, and suitable precautions were taken to minimise fluid loss, it should be necessary only to bleed that part of the system (ie the primary or secondary circuit).
12 If the complete system is to be bled, then it should be done working in the following sequence.
(a) *Left-hand front brake.*
(b) *Right-hand rear brake.*
(c) *Right-hand front brake.*
(d) *Left-hand rear brake.*

Bleeding – basic (two-man) method

13 Collect a clean glass jar, a suitable length of plastic or rubber tubing which is a tight fit over the bleed screw, and a ring spanner to fit the screw. The help of an assistant will also be required.
14 Remove the dust cap from the first screw in the sequence. Fit the spanner and tube to the screw, place the other end of the tube in the jar and pour sufficient fluid into the jar to cover the open end of the tube.
15 Ensure that the master cylinder reservoir fluid level is maintained at least above the

'MIN' level line throughout the procedure.
16 Have the assistant fully depress the brake pedal several times to build up pressure, then hold the pedal depressed on the final stroke.
17 While pedal pressure is maintained, unscrew the bleed screw (approximately one turn) and allow the compressed fluid and air to flow into the jar. The assistant should maintain pedal pressure, following it down to the floor if necessary, and should not release the pedal until instructed to do so. When the flow stops, tighten the bleed screw again, **then** the pedal should be released slowly, recheck the reservoir fluid level, and top-up if necessary.
18 Repeat the steps given in paragraphs 16 and 17 until the fluid emerging from the bleed screw is free from air bubbles. If the master cylinder has been drained and refilled, and air is being bled from the first screw in the sequence, allow approximately five seconds between cycles for the master cylinder passages to refill.
19 When no more air bubbles appear, tighten the bleed screw securely, remove the tube and spanner, and refit the dust cap. Do not overtighten the bleed screw.
20 Repeat the procedure on the remaining screws in the sequence, until all air is removed from the system and the brake pedal feels firm again.

Bleeding – using a one-way valve kit

21 As their name implies, these kits consist of a length of tubing with a one-way valve fitted, to prevent expelled air and fluid being drawn back into the system; some kits include a translucent container, which can be positioned so that the air bubbles can be more easily seen flowing from the end of the tube (photo).
22 The kit is connected to the bleed screw, which is then opened. The user returns to the driver's seat, and depresses the brake pedal with a smooth, steady stroke and slowly releases it; this is repeated until the expelled fluid is clear of air bubbles.
23 Note that these kits simplify work so much that it is easy to forget to top-up the master cylinder reservoir fluid level; ensure that this is maintained at least above the 'MIN' level line at all times.

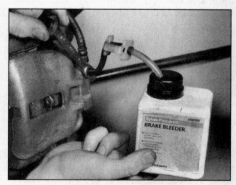

5.21 Bleeding the braking system using a typical one-way valve kit

Bleeding – using a pressure-bleeding kit

24 These kits are usually operated by the reservoir of pressurised air contained in the spare tyre – although note that it will probably be necessary to reduce the pressure to lower than normal; refer to the instructions supplied with the kit.

25 By connecting a pressurised, fluid-filled container to the master cylinder reservoir, bleeding can be carried out simply by opening each screw in turn (in the specified sequence) and allowing the fluid to flow out, until no more air bubbles can be seen in the expelled fluid.

26 This method has the advantage that the large reservoir of fluid provides an additional safeguard against air being drawn into the system during bleeding.

27 Pressure-bleeding is particularly effective when bleeding 'difficult' systems, or when bleeding the complete system at the time of routine fluid renewal.

All methods

28 When bleeding is complete and firm pedal feel is restored, wash off any spilt fluid, tighten the bleed screws securely and refit their dust caps.

29 Check the hydraulic fluid level, and top-up if necessary (refer to Chapter 1).

30 Discard any hydraulic fluid that has been bled from the system; it will definitely not be fit for re-use.

31 Check the feel of the brake pedal. If it feels at all spongy, air must still be present in the system, and further bleeding is required. Failure to bleed satisfactorily after a reasonable repetition of the bleeding procedure may be due to worn master cylinder seals.

6 Hydraulic pipes and hoses – renewal

Note: *Before starting work, refer to the note at the beginning of Section 5 concerning the dangers of hydraulic fluid.*

1 If any pipe or hose in the main braking system is to be renewed, minimise fluid loss by first removing the master cylinder reservoir cap, and then tightening it down onto a piece of polythene (taking care not to damage the sender unit) to obtain an airtight seal. Alternatively, the flexible hoses can be sealed, if required, using a proprietary brake hose clamp (photo). Metal brake pipe unions can be plugged (care must be taken not to allow dirt into the system) or capped, immediately they are disconnected. Place a wad of rag under any union that is to be disconnected, to catch any spilt fluid.

2 If a flexible hose is to be disconnected, unscrew the brake pipe union nut before removing the spring clip which secures the hose to its mounting bracket.

3 To unscrew the union nuts, it is preferable to obtain a brake pipe spanner of the correct

6.1 Using a brake hose clamp to minimise the loss of fluid when flexible hoses are disconnected

size; these are available from most large motor accessory shops (photo). Failing this, a close-fitting open-ended spanner will be required – though if the nuts are tight or corroded, their flats may be rounded-off if the spanner slips. In such a case, a self-locking wrench is often the only way to unscrew a stubborn union, but it follows that the pipe and the damaged nuts must be renewed on reassembly. Always clean a union and the surrounding area before disconnecting it. If disconnecting a component with more than one union, make a careful note of the connections before disturbing any of them.

4 If a brake pipe is to be renewed, it can be obtained, cut to length and with the union nuts and end flares in place, from Rover dealers. All that is then necessary is to bend it to shape, following the line of the original, before fitting it to the car. Alternatively, most motor accessory shops can make up brake pipes from kits, but this requires very careful measurement of the original to ensure that the replacement is of the correct length. The safest answer is usually to take the original to the shop as a pattern.

6.3 Using a brake pipe spanner to unscrew a union nut

5 On refitting, do not overtighten the union nuts. The specified torque wrench settings (where given) are not high, and it is not necessary to exercise brute force to obtain a sound joint. When refitting flexible hoses, always renew any sealing washers used; again, note the torque settings specified.

6 Ensure that the pipes and hoses are correctly routed, with no kinks, and that they are secured in the clips or brackets provided. After fitting, remove the polythene from the reservoir, and bleed the hydraulic system as described in Section 5. Wash off any spilt fluid, and check carefully for fluid leaks.

7 Master cylinder – removal, overhaul and refitting

Note: *Before starting work, refer to the note at the beginning of Section 5 concerning the dangers of hydraulic fluid.*

Removal

1 Remove the master cylinder reservoir cap, having disconnected the sender unit wiring

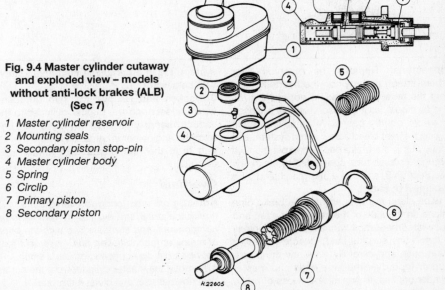

Fig. 9.4 Master cylinder cutaway and exploded view – models without anti-lock brakes (ALB) (Sec 7)

1 Master cylinder reservoir
2 Mounting seals
3 Secondary piston stop-pin
4 Master cylinder body
5 Spring
6 Circlip
7 Primary piston
8 Secondary piston

9

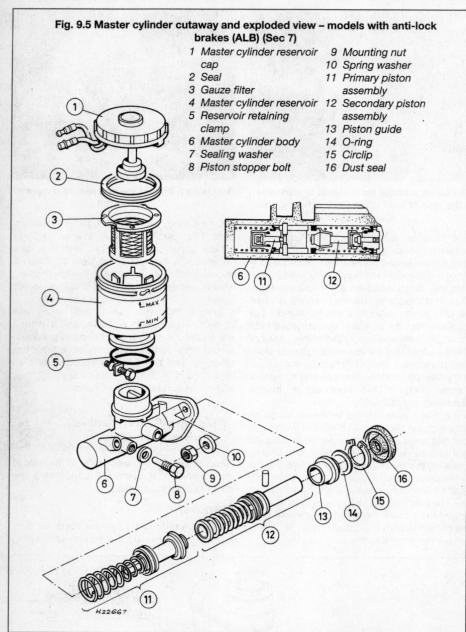

Fig. 9.5 Master cylinder cutaway and exploded view – models with anti-lock brakes (ALB) (Sec 7)

1 Master cylinder reservoir cap	9 Mounting nut
2 Seal	10 Spring washer
3 Gauze filter	11 Primary piston assembly
4 Master cylinder reservoir	12 Secondary piston assembly
5 Reservoir retaining clamp	13 Piston guide
6 Master cylinder body	14 O-ring
7 Sealing washer	15 Circlip
8 Piston stopper bolt	16 Dust seal

connector(s). Remove the reservoir filter (where fitted), and syphon the hydraulic fluid from the reservoir. **Note:** *Do not syphon the fluid by mouth, as it is poisonous; use a syringe or an old poultry baster.* Alternatively, open any convenient bleed screw in the system, and gently pump the brake pedal to expel the fluid through a plastic tube connected to the screw (see Section 5, and use a one-man bleed tube or bottle if possible).

2 Wipe clean the area around the brake pipe unions on the side of the master cylinder, and place absorbent rags beneath the pipe unions to catch any surplus fluid. Unscrew the two union nuts, and carefully withdraw the pipes. Plug or tape over the pipe ends and master cylinder orifices, to minimise the loss of brake fluid and to prevent the entry of dirt into the

system. Wash off any spilt fluid immediately with cold water.

3 Slacken and remove the two nuts and washers securing the master cylinder to the vacuum servo unit, then withdraw the unit from the engine compartment. Remove the O-ring from the rear of master cylinder, and discard it.

Overhaul

Note: *Before attempting to overhaul the unit, check the price and availability of individual components, and compare this with the price of a new or reconditioned unit – overhaul may not be viable, on economic grounds alone.*

4 Remove the master cylinder from the car as described above, and clean it thoroughly.

5 Prepare a clean working surface, and

proceed as described under the relevant sub-heading.

Models without anti-lock brakes

6 Carefully prise the reservoir from the master cylinder body, and remove the two mounting seals.

7 Using a wooden dowel, press the primary piston in as far as possible, extract the secondary piston stop-pin from the reservoir inlet port, then remove the retaining circlip.

8 Noting the order of removal and the direction of fitting of each component, then withdraw the piston assemblies with their springs and seals, tapping the body on to a clean wooden surface to dislodge them. If necessary, clamp the master cylinder body in a vice (fitted with soft jaw covers), and use compressed air (applied through the secondary circuit fluid port) to assist the removal of the secondary piston assembly.

9 Thoroughly clean all components, using only methylated spirit, isopropyl alcohol or clean hydraulic fluid. Never use mineral-based solvents such as petrol or paraffin, which will attack the hydraulic system's rubber components. Dry the components immediately using compressed air or a clean, lint-free cloth.

10 Check all components, and renew any that are worn or damaged. Check particularly the cylinder bores and pistons; the complete assembly should be renewed if these are scratched, worn or corroded. If there is any doubt about the condition of the assembly or of any of its components, renew it. Check that the body's inlet and bypass ports are clear.

11 If the assembly is fit for further use, obtain a repair kit. Renew all seals and sealing O-rings disturbed on dismantling as a matter of course; these should never be re-used. Renew also any other items included in the repair kit.

12 On reassembly, soak the pistons and the new seals In clean hydraulic fluid, and smear clean fluid in the cylinder bore.

13 Fit the new seals to their pistons, using only your fingers (no tools) to manipulate them into the grooves.

14 Insert the pistons into the bore, using a twisting motion to avoid trapping the seal lips. Ensure that all components are refitted in the correct order and the right way round.

15 Press the secondary piston assembly fully up into the bore using a clean wooden dowel, then refit the stop-pin.

16 Refit the primary piston assembly, securing it in position with a new circlip.

17 Press the new mounting seals into the master cylinder body, and carefully refit the reservoir, ensuring that it is pressed fully into position.

Models equipped with anti-lock brakes (ALB)

18 Slacken the retaining clamp, and remove the reservoir from the master cylinder body. Carefully remove the dust seal from the rear of the master cylinder.

8.2A Remove the lower caliper guide pin bolt ...

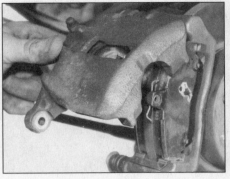

8.2B ... and pivot the caliper away from the disc

8.3 Remove the circular shim from the caliper piston

19 Using a wooden dowel, press the secondary piston in as far as possible, and extract the circlip from the master cylinder bore. With the circlip removed, withdraw the O-ring, piston guide and secondary piston assembly, noting the small locating pin which is fitted to the piston.

20 Use the wooden dowel to press the primary piston into the master cylinder, then slacken and remove the piston stopper bolt and washer from the side of the master cylinder body. With the bolt removed, withdraw the primary piston and spring assembly from the master cylinder bore.

21 Examine and overhaul the master cylinder components as described above in paragraphs 9 to 14.

22 Fit the spring to the primary piston assembly, and carefully insert the assembly into the master cylinder bore. Use a clean wooden dowel to press the piston fully into the bore, then refit the piston stopper bolt and washer, and tighten it securely. Remove the wooden dowel, and check that the stopper bolt is correctly located with the piston.

23 Fit the secondary piston assembly to the master cylinder, then install the piston guide and a new O-ring. Secure the piston assembly and associated components in position with the circlip, ensuring that it is correctly located in its groove in the master cylinder bore, and fit the dust seal.

24 Refit the reservoir to the master cylinder, and tighten its retaining clamp securely.

Refitting

25 Remove all traces of dirt from the master cylinder and servo unit mating surfaces, and fit a new O-ring to the groove on the master cylinder body.

26 Fit the master cylinder to the servo unit, ensuring that the servo unit pushrod enters the master cylinder bore centrally. Refit the master cylinder washers and mounting nuts, and tighten them to the specified torque.

27 Wipe clean the brake pipe unions, then refit them to the master cylinder ports and tighten them to the specified torque setting.

28 Refill the master cylinder reservoir with new fluid, and bleed the hydraulic system as described in Section 5.

8 Front brake pads – renewal

⚠️ **Warning: Renew both sets of front brake pads at the same time – never renew the pads on only one wheel, as uneven braking may result. Note that the dust created by wear of the pads may contain asbestos, which is a health hazard. Never blow it out with compressed air, and don't inhale any of it. An approved filtering mask should be worn when working on the brakes. DO NOT use petroleum-based solvents to clean brake parts – use brake cleaner or methylated spirit only.**

1 Chock the rear wheels, firmly apply the handbrake, then jack up the front of the car and support it on axle stands. Remove both front roadwheels.

2 Remove the lower caliper guide pin bolt, if necessary using a slim open-ended spanner to prevent the guide pin itself from rotating. Pivot the caliper away from the disc to gain access to the brake pads, and tie it to the suspension strut using a piece of wire (photos).

3 Remove the circular shim which is fitted to the caliper piston (photo).

4 Remove the brake pads from the caliper mounting bracket, noting the correct fitted position of the pad retainer springs and pad shims (photo).

5 First measure the thickness of friction material remaining on each brake pad (photo). If either pad is worn at any point to the specified minimum thickness or less, all four pads must be renewed. The pads should also be renewed if any are fouled with oil or grease; there is no satisfactory way of degreasing friction material once contaminated. If any of the brake pads is worn unevenly, or fouled with oil or grease, trace and rectify the cause before reassembly. New brake pad kits are available from Rover dealers, and include new shims and pad retainer springs.

6 If the brake pads are still serviceable, carefully clean them using a clean, fine wire brush or similar, paying particular attention to the sides and back of the metal backing. Clean out the grooves in the friction material

9

8.4 Remove the pads, noting the correct position of the pad springs and shims

8.5 Measuring thickness of brake pad friction material

8.7 Check condition of guide pins and gaiters before refitting pads

8.8 Fit the pad retainer springs to the caliper bracket ...

8.9 ... and install the shims on the pads

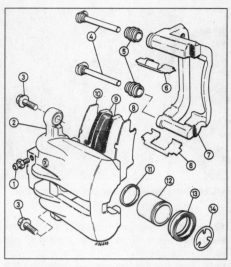

Fig. 9.6 Exploded view of the front brake caliper (Sec 9)

1 Bleed screw
2 Caliper body
3 Guide pin bolt
4 Guide pin
5 Gaiter
6 Pad retainer spring
7 Caliper mounting
  bracket
8 Inner pad shim
9 Brake pads
10 Outer pad shim
11 Piston seal
12 Piston
13 Dust seal
14 Circular shim

(where applicable), and pick out any large embedded particles of dirt or debris. Carefully clean the pad retainer springs, and the pad locations in the caliper body and mounting bracket.

7 Prior to fitting the pads, check that the guide pins are free to slide easily in the caliper bracket, and check that the rubber guide pin gaiters are undamaged (photo). Brush the dust and dirt from the caliper and piston, but do not inhale it as it is injurious to health. Inspect the dust seal around the piston for damage, and the piston for evidence of fluid leaks, corrosion or damage. If attention to any of these components is necessary, refer to Section 9.

8 On refitting, first fit the pad retainer springs to the caliper mounting bracket (photo).

9 Apply a thin smear of high-temperature brake grease (silicone- or PBC/Poly Butyl Cuprysil-based) or anti-seize compound to the sides and back of each pad's metal backing, and to those surfaces of the caliper body and mounting bracket which bear on the pads. Fit the shims to the back of both pads, and apply a thin smear of lubricant to the back of each shim (photo). Do not allow the lubricant to foul the friction material.

10 Install the brake pads in the caliper mounting bracket, ensuring that the friction material is against the disc.

11 If new brake pads have been fitted, the caliper piston must be pushed back into the cylinder to make room for them. Either use a G-clamp or similar tool, or use suitable pieces of wood as levers. Provided that the master cylinder reservoir has not been overfilled with hydraulic fluid, there should be no spillage, but keep a careful watch on the fluid level while retracting the piston. If the fluid level rises above the 'MAX' level line at any time, the surplus should be syphoned off or ejected via a plastic tube connected to the bleed screw (see Section 7, paragraph 1).

12 Apply a thin smear of the recommended lubricant (see paragraph 9) to the circular shim, and fit the shim to the caliper piston. Pivot the caliper body down over the brake pads, then refit the bottom guide pin bolt, and tighten it to the specified torque wrench setting.

13 Check that the caliper body slides smoothly in the mounting bracket, then depress the brake pedal repeatedly until the pads are pressed into firm contact with the brake disc, and normal (non-assisted) pedal pressure is restored.

14 Repeat the above procedure on the remaining front brake caliper.

15 Refit the roadwheels, then lower the car to the ground, and tighten the roadwheel nuts to the specified torque setting.

16 Check the hydraulic fluid level as described in Chapter 1.

9 Front brake caliper – removal, overhaul and refitting

Note: *Before starting work, refer to the note at the beginning of Section 5 concerning the dangers of hydraulic fluid, and to the warning at the beginning of Section 8 concerning the dangers of asbestos dust.*

Removal

1 Chock the rear wheels, firmly apply the handbrake, then jack up the front of the car and support on axle stands. Remove the appropriate front roadwheel.

2 Minimise fluid loss by first removing the master cylinder reservoir cap, and then tightening it down onto a piece of polythene sheet to obtain an airtight seal (taking care not to damage the sender unit). Alternatively, use a brake hose clamp, a G-clamp or a similar tool to clamp the flexible hose.

3 Clean the area around the union, then undo the brake hose union bolt and disconnect the hose from the caliper. Plug the end of the hose and the caliper orifice to prevent dirt entering the hydraulic system. Discard the sealing washers; they must be renewed whenever disturbed.

4 Unscrew the two caliper guide pin bolts, if necessary using a slim open-ended spanner to prevent the guide pins themselves from rotating.

5 Carefully lift the caliper assembly off the brake pads, and remove the circular shim from the caliper piston. Note that the brake pads need not be disturbed, and can be left in position in the caliper mounting bracket.

Overhaul

6 With the caliper on the bench, wipe away all traces of dust and dirt, but *avoid inhaling the dust, as it is injurious to health.*

7 Withdraw the partially-ejected piston from the caliper body, and remove the dust seal. The piston can be withdrawn by hand, or if necessary pushed out by applying compressed air to the union bolt hole. Only low pressure should be required, such as that generated by a bicycle pump or car footpump.

8 Using a small screwdriver, extract the piston hydraulic seal, taking great care not to damage the caliper bore.

9 Withdraw the guide pins from the caliper mounting bracket, and remove the guide pin gaiters.

10 Thoroughly clean all components using only methylated spirit, isopropyl alcohol or clean hydraulic fluid. Never use mineral-based solvents such as petrol or paraffin, which will attack the hydraulic system's rubber components. Dry the components immediately, using compressed air or a clean, lint-free cloth. Use compressed air to blow clear the fluid passages.

11 Check all components, and renew any that are worn or damaged. Check particularly the cylinder bore and piston; these should be renewed if they are scratched, worn or corroded in any way (note that this means the renewal of the complete body assembly). Similarly check the condition of the guide pins and their bores in the mounting bracket; both guide pins should be undamaged and (when cleaned) should be a reasonably tight sliding fit in the mounting bracket bores. If there is any doubt about the condition of any component, renew it.

12 If the assembly is fit for further use, obtain

10.3 Using a micrometer to measure brake disc thickness

10.4 Using a dial gauge to check brake disc run-out

10.6 Remove the caliper assembly ...

the appropriate repair kit; the components are available from Rover dealers in various combinations.

13 Renew all rubber seals, dust covers and caps, and also the sealing washers disturbed on dismantling, as a matter of course; these should never be re-used.

14 On reassembly, ensure that all components are absolutely clean and dry.

15 Soak the piston and the new piston (fluid) seal in clean hydraulic fluid, and smear clean fluid on the cylinder bore surface.

16 Fit the new piston (fluid) seal, using only your fingers (no tools) to manipulate it into the cylinder bore groove. Fit the new dust seal to the piston, refit it to the cylinder bore using a twisting motion, and ensure that the piston enters squarely into the bore. Press the piston fully into the bore, then secure the dust seal to the caliper body.

17 Apply the grease supplied in the repair kit, or a good quality high-temperature brake grease (silicone- or PBC/Poly Butyl Cuprysil-based) or anti-seize compound to the guide pins, and fit the new gaiters. Fit the guide pins to the caliper mounting bracket, ensuring that the gaiters are correctly located in the grooves on both the guide pin and mounting bracket.

Refitting

18 Refit the circular shim to the piston, and carefully slide the caliper into position over the brake pads. Refit the caliper guide pin bolts, and tighten them to the specified torque setting.

19 Position a new sealing washer on each side of the hose union, and refit the brake hose union bolt. Ensure that the brake hose union is correctly positioned between the lugs on the caliper, then tighten the union bolt to the specified torque setting.

20 Remove the brake hose clamp, where fitted, and bleed the hydraulic system as described in Section 5. Note that, providing the precautions described were taken to minimise brake fluid loss, it should only be necessary to bleed the relevant front brake.

21 Refit the roadwheel, then lower the car to the ground and tighten the roadwheel nuts to the specified torque.

10 Front brake disc – inspection, removal and refitting

Note: *Before starting work, refer to the warning at the beginning of Section 8 concerning the dangers of asbestos dust.*

Inspection

Note: *If either disc requires renewal both should be renewed at the same time, to ensure even and consistent braking.*

1 Chock the rear wheels, firmly apply the handbrake, then jack up the front of the car and support on axle stands. Remove the appropriate front roadwheel.

2 Slowly rotate the brake disc so that the full area of both sides is checked; remove the brake pads, as described in Section 8, if better access is required to the inboard surface. Light scoring is normal in the area swept by the brake pads, but if heavy scoring is found, the disc must be renewed. The only alternative to this is to have the disc surface-ground until it is flat again, but this must not reduce the disc to less than the minimum thickness specified.

3 It is normal to find a lip of rust and brake dust around the disc's perimeter; this can be scraped off if wished. If, however, a lip has formed due to excessive wear of the brake pad swept area, then the disc's thickness must be measured using a micrometer (photo). Take measurements at four places around the

disc, at the inside and outside of the pad swept area; if the disc has worn at any point to the specified minimum thickness or less, or if any measurement differs from the others by more than the maximum specified variation, the disc must be renewed.

4 If the disc is thought to be warped, it can be checked for run-out (6 mm in from the disc's outer edge) either using a dial gauge mounted on any convenient fixed point, while the disc is slowly rotated (photo). Alternatively, use feeler gauges (at several points all around the disc) to measure the clearance between the disc and a fixed point, such as the caliper mounting bracket. If the measurements obtained are at the specified maximum or beyond, the disc is excessively warped, and must be renewed; however it is worth checking first that the hub bearing is in good condition (Chapters 1 and/or 10). Also try the effect of removing the disc and turning it through 180° to reposition it on the hub; if run-out is still excessive, the disc must be renewed.

5 Check the disc for cracks (especially around the stud holes), and for any other wear or damage. Renew it if any of these are found.

Removal

6 Unscrew the two bolts securing the caliper mounting bracket to the swivel hub, and slide the caliper assembly off the disc (photo). Using a piece of wire or string, tie the caliper to the front suspension coil spring, to avoid placing any strain on the hydraulic brake hose.

10.7A ... and remove the disc retaining screws note jacking holes (arrowed)

10.7B If tight the disc can be drawn off using two 8 mm bolts

9

11.2 Pressure-regulating valve – in the event of failure, fluid will seep from plug (arrowed)

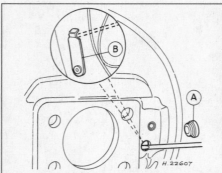

Fig. 9.7 Releasing the handbrake mechanism stop lever (Sec 12)

Remove the rubber grommet (A) and use a small screwdriver to depress the handbrake lever stop (B)

12.3 Removing brake drum retaining screws – note jacking holes (arrowed)

7 Use chalk or paint to mark the relationship of the disc to the hub, then remove the two screws securing the brake disc to the hub, and remove the disc. If the disc is a tight fit on the hub, it can be drawn off by screwing two bolts into the jacking holes provided (photos).

Refitting

8 Refitting is the reverse of the removal procedure, noting the following points.
(a) Ensure that the mating surfaces of the disc and hub are clean and flat.
(b) Align the marks made on removal (if applicable).
(c) If a new disc has been fitted, use a suitable solvent to wipe any preservative coating from the disc before refitting the caliper.
(d) Tighten the disc retaining screws, caliper bracket bolts and roadwheel nuts to their specified torque wrench settings.

11 Pressure-regulating valve (models without anti-lock brakes) – testing, removal and refitting

Testing

1 On models not equipped with anti-lock brakes (ALB), a pressure-regulating valve is incorporated in the hydraulic braking circuit, to regulate the pressure applied to the rear brakes

and reduce the risk of the rear wheels locking under heavy braking. The pressure-regulating valve is mounted on the right-hand side of the bulkhead in the engine compartment.
2 Specialist equipment is required to check the performance of the valve, therefore if the valve is thought to be faulty, the car should be taken to a suitably-equipped Rover dealer for testing. However, in the event of an internal failure, brake fluid will seep from the plug on the front face of the valve which is situated directly above the lower two hose unions (photo). Repairs are not possible, and if faulty, the valve must be renewed.

Removal

Note: *Before starting work, refer to the note at the beginning of Section 5 concerning the dangers of hydraulic fluid.*
3 Disconnect the sender unit wiring connector, and unscrew the master cylinder reservoir filler cap. Place a piece of polythene over the filler neck, and securely refit the cap (taking care not to damage the sender unit) this will minimise brake fluid loss during subsequent operations. As an added precaution, place absorbent rags beneath the pressure-regulating valve brake pipe unions.
4 Wipe clean the area around the brake pipe unions on the pressure regulating valve, then make a note of how the pipes are arranged, to use as a reference on refitting. Unscrew the

union nuts, and carefully withdraw the pipes. Plug or tape over the pipe ends and valve orifices, to minimise the loss of brake fluid, and to prevent the entry of dirt into the system. Wash off any spilt fluid immediately with cold water.
5 Slacken the two bolts which secure the valve to the bulkhead, and remove it from the engine compartment.

Refitting

6 Refit the pressure-regulating valve to the bulkhead, and tighten its mounting bolts securely.
7 Wipe the brake pipe unions clean, then refit them to the valve, using the notes made on dismantling to ensure they are correctly positioned. Tighten the union nuts to the specified torque.
8 Remove the polythene from the master cylinder reservoir filler neck, and bleed the complete hydraulic system as described in Section 5.

12 Rear brake drum – removal, inspection and refitting

Note: *Before starting work, refer to the warning at the beginning of Section 13 concerning the dangers of asbestos dust.*

Removal

1 Chock the front wheels, then jack up the rear of the car and support it on axle stands. Remove the appropriate rear wheel.
2 Use chalk or paint to mark the relationship of the drum to the hub.
3 With the handbrake firmly applied to prevent drum rotation, unscrew the drum retaining screws (photo). Fully release the handbrake cable, and withdraw the drum.
4 If the drum will not pull away, first check that the handbrake is fully released. If the drum will still not come away, remove the grommet from the rear of the backplate and, using a small screwdriver, disengage the handbrake lever stop from behind the lever to increase the shoe-to-drum clearance (see Fig. 9.7). If removal still proves troublesome, the brake drum can be drawn off by screwing two bolts into the jacking holes provided (photos).

12.4A Disengage the handbrake lever stop to increase shoe-to-drum clearance

12.4B If necessary, the drum can be drawn off using two 8 mm bolts

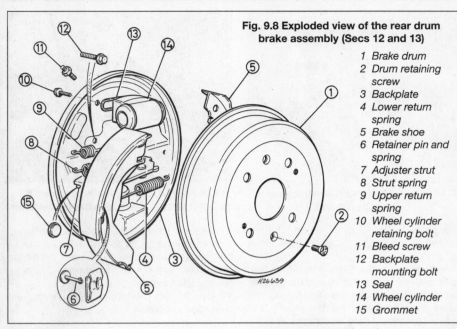

Fig. 9.8 Exploded view of the rear drum brake assembly (Secs 12 and 13)

1 Brake drum
2 Drum retaining screw
3 Backplate
4 Lower return spring
5 Brake shoe
6 Retainer pin and spring
7 Adjuster strut
8 Strut spring
9 Upper return spring
10 Wheel cylinder retaining bolt
11 Bleed screw
12 Backplate mounting bolt
13 Seal
14 Wheel cylinder
15 Grommet

13 Rear brake shoes – renewal

Warning: Brake shoes must be renewed on both rear wheels at the same time – never renew the shoes on only one wheel, as uneven braking may result. Also, the dust created by wear of the shoes may contain asbestos, which is a health hazard. Never blow it out with compressed air, and don't inhale any of it. An approved filtering mask should be worn when working on the brakes. DO NOT use petroleum-based solvents to clean brake parts – use brake cleaner or methylated spirit only.

1 Remove the brake drum, as described in Section 12.
2 Working carefully (refer to the warning above), remove all traces of brake dust from the brake drum, backplate and shoes.
3 Measure the thickness of friction material remaining on each brake shoe at several points; if either shoe is worn at any point to the specified minimum thickness or less, all four shoes must be renewed as a set. Also, the shoes should be renewed if any are fouled with oil or grease; there is no satisfactory way of degreasing friction material once contaminated. Replacement shoes from Rover dealers are only available as an axle set.
4 If any of the brake shoes is worn unevenly, or fouled with oil or grease, trace and rectify the cause before reassembly.
5 To remove the brake shoes, first remove the shoe retainer springs and pins, using a pair of pliers to press in each retainer clip until it can be rotated through 90° and released. Ease the shoes out one at a time from the lower pivot point, to release the tension of the return spring, then disconnect the lower return spring from both shoes. Ease the upper end of both shoes out from their wheel cylinder locations, taking great care not to damage the wheel cylinder seals, and disconnect the handbrake cable from the trailing shoe. The brake shoe and adjuster strut assembly can then be manoeuvred out of position and away from the

Inspection

Note: *If either drum requires renewal, both should be renewed at the same time, to ensure even and consistent braking.*

5 Carefully remove all traces of brake dust from the drum, but avoid inhaling the dust, as it is injurious to health.
6 Scrub clean the outside of the drum, and check it for obvious signs of wear or damage (such as cracks around the roadwheel stud holes); renew the drum if necessary.
7 Examine carefully the inside of the drum. Light scoring of the friction surface is normal, but if heavy scoring is found, the drum must be renewed. It is usual to find a lip on the drum's inboard edge, which consists of a mixture of rust and brake dust; this should be scraped away to leave a smooth surface which can be polished with fine (120 to 150 grade) emery paper. If, however, the lip is due to the friction surface being recessed by excessive wear, then the drum must be renewed.
8 If the drum is thought to be excessively worn, or oval, its internal diameter must be measured at several points using an internal

micrometer. Take measurements in pairs, the second at right angles to the first, and compare the two to check for signs of ovality. It may be possible to have the drum refinished by skimming or grinding (provided that it does not enlarge the drum to beyond the specified maximum diameter); if this is not possible, the drums on both sides must be renewed.

Refitting

9 Refitting is the reverse of the removal procedure, noting the following points.
(a) *When fitting a new brake drum, use a suitable solvent to remove any preservative coating that may have been applied to its interior.*
(b) *Use a clean wire brush to remove all traces of dirt, brake dust and corrosion from the mating surfaces of the drum and the hub flange.*
(c) *Align the marks made on removal (if applicable).*
(d) *Tighten the drum retaining screws and the road wheel nuts to their specified torque wrench settings*

9

13.5A Remove the brake shoe retainer springs ...

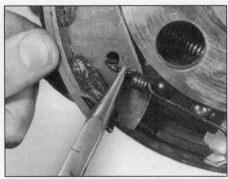

13.5B ... then unhook the lower return spring ...

13.5C ... and manoeuvre the shoe and adjuster strut assembly away from the backplate

13.6 Correct fitted positions of adjuster strut and springs

13.10 Ensure the handbrake stop lever is correctly located

13.14 Prior to refitting the drum, reset the adjuster strut to the fully-retracted position

backplate (photos). Do not depress the brake pedal until the brakes are reassembled; wrap a strong elastic band around the wheel cylinder pistons to retain them.

6 With the brake shoe assembly on a bench, make a note of the fitted positions of the adjuster strut and springs, to use as a guide on reassembly (photo). Carefully ease the adjuster strut from its slot in the trailing shoe, and remove the short spring which secures the two components together. Detach the upper return spring, and separate the shoes and strut.

7 Examine the adjuster strut assembly for signs of wear or damage, paying particular attention to the adjuster quadrant and knurled wheel. If damaged, the strut assembly must be renewed. Renew all the brake shoe return springs, regardless of their apparent condition.

8 Peel back the rubber protective caps, and check the wheel cylinder for fluid leaks or other damage; also check that both cylinder pistons are free to move easily. Refer to Section 14, if necessary, for information on wheel cylinder overhaul.

9 Prior to installation, clean the backplate and apply a thin smear of high-temperature brake grease (silicone- or PBC/Poly Butyl Cuprysil-based) or anti-seize compound to all those surfaces of the backplate which bear on the shoes, particularly the adjuster and the wheel cylinder pistons. Do not allow the lubricant to foul the friction material.

10 Ensure the handbrake lever stop on the

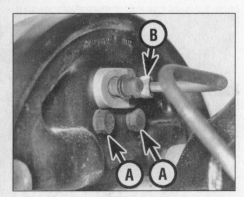

14.3 Wheel cylinder retaining bolts (A) and brake pipe union nut (B)

trailing shoe is correctly engaged with the lever, and is pressed tight against the brake shoe (photo).

11 Fully extend the adjuster strut quadrant, and fit the leading brake shoe into the adjuster strut slot, ensuring that the strut spring and knurled wheel are situated on the underside of the strut assembly. Using a screwdriver, move the quadrant away from the knurled wheel, and set it in the minimum-adjustment (fully-retracted) position.

12 Fit the upper return spring to its respective location on the leading shoe. Fit the trailing shoe to the upper return spring, and carefully ease the shoe into position in the adjuster strut slot. Once in position, fit the small spring which secures the trailing shoe to the strut assembly.

13 Remove the elastic band fitted to the wheel cylinder, and manoeuvre the shoe and strut assembly into position on the backplate. Locate the upper end of both shoes with the wheel cylinder pistons, and fit the handbrake cable to the trailing shoe operating lever. Fit the lower return spring to both shoes, and ease the shoes into position on the lower pivot point.

14 Tap the shoes to centralise them with the backplate, then refit the shoe retainer pins and springs, and secure them in position with the retainer clips. Check that the adjuster quadrant is still in the minimum-adjustment position, and if necessary reset as follows. Place a block of wood between the trailing shoe and hub, to prevent the shoe moving forwards, then lever the leading shoe away from the hub to release the brake shoe return spring pressure on the adjuster quadrant. With the shoe held in this position, reset the quadrant to the minimum-adjustment (fully-retracted) setting (photo). Once adjuster strut is correctly set, ease the leading shoe back into position, then remove the block of wood, and check that the shoes are still central.

15 Refit the brake drum as described in Section 12, then repeat the above operations on the other rear brake assembly.

16 On completion, apply the footbrake repeatedly, to set the shoe-to-drum clearance, until normal (non-assisted) brake pedal operation returns.

17 Check the handbrake cable operation and, if necessary, adjust as described in Chapter 1.

18 Refit the roadwheels, then lower the car to the ground and tighten the roadwheel nuts to the specified torque.

19 Check the hydraulic fluid level, as described in Chapter 1.

14 Rear wheel cylinder (drum brake models) – removal, overhaul and refitting

Note: *Before starting work, refer to the note at the beginning of Section 5 concerning the dangers of hydraulic fluid, and to the warning at the beginning of Section 13 concerning the dangers of asbestos dust.*

Removal

1 Remove the brake shoes as described in Section 13, paragraphs 1 to 5.

2 Minimise fluid loss by first removing the master cylinder reservoir cap, and then tightening it down onto a piece of polythene to obtain an airtight seal (taking care not to damage the sender unit). Alternatively, use a brake hose clamp, a G-clamp or a similar tool to clamp the flexible hose.

3 Wipe away all traces of dirt around the brake pipe union at the rear of the wheel cylinder, and unscrew the union nut (photo). Carefully ease the pipe out of the wheel cylinder, plugging or taping its end to reduce fluid loss and to prevent the entry of dirt.

4 Unscrew the two wheel cylinder retaining bolts from the rear of the backplate, then remove the cylinder, noting the rubber sealing ring which is fitted between the cylinder and backplate.

Overhaul

Note: *Before attempting to overhaul the unit, check the price and availability of individual components, compared to the price of a new or reconditioned unit – overhaul may not be viable, on economic grounds alone.*

5 Remove the wheel cylinder from the car, and clean it thoroughly.

6 Mount the wheel cylinder in a soft-jawed

15.2 Removing the rear caliper shield bolts (arrowed)

15.3A Remove the caliper guide pin bolts (arrowed) ...

15.3B ... and lift the caliper away – note upper pad spring (arrowed)

vice, and remove the rubber protective caps. Extract the piston assemblies.

7 Thoroughly clean all components using only methylated spirit, isopropyl alcohol or clean hydraulic fluid. Never use mineral-based solvents such as petrol or paraffin, which will attack the hydraulic system's rubber components. Dry the components immediately, using compressed air or a clean, lint-free cloth.

8 Check all components, and renew any that are worn or damaged. Check particularly the cylinder bore and pistons; the complete assembly must be renewed if these are scratched, worn or corroded. If there is any doubt about the condition of the assembly or of any of its components, renew it. Remove the bleed screw, and check that the fluid entry port and bleed screw passages are clear.

9 If the assembly is fit for further use, obtain a repair kit. Renew the rubber protective caps, dust caps and seals disturbed on dismantling as a matter of course; these should never be re-used. Renew also any other items included in the repair kit.

10 On reassembly, soak the pistons and the new seals in clean hydraulic fluid, and smear clean fluid on the cylinder bore surface.

11 Fit the new seals to their pistons, using only your fingers (no tools) to manipulate them into the grooves. Ensure that all components are refitted in the correct order and the right way round.

12 Insert the pistons into the bore, using a twisting motion to avoid trapping the seal lips. Apply a smear of rubber lubricant to each piston before fitting the new rubber protective caps.

Refitting

13 Fit a new sealing ring to the rear of the wheel cylinder, and place the cylinder in position on the backplate.

14 Refit the wheel cylinder retaining bolts, and tighten them to the specified torque.

15 Tighten the brake pipe union nut to the specified torque and, where applicable, remove the clamp from the brake hose.

16 Refit the brake shoes as described in Section 13.

17 Bleed the hydraulic braking system as

described in Section 5, noting that, if precautions were taken to minimise fluid loss, it should only be necessary to bleed the relevant rear brake. On completion, check that both the footbrake and handbrake function correctly before taking the car on the road.

15 Rear brake pads – renewal

⚠️ **Warning: Renew both sets of rear brake pads at the same time – never renew the pads on only one wheel, as uneven braking may result. Note that the dust created by wear of the pads may contain asbestos, which is a health hazard. Never blow it out with compressed air, and don't inhale any of it. An approved filtering mask should be worn when working on the brakes. DO NOT use petroleum-based solvents to clean brake parts – use brake cleaner or methylated spirit only.**

1 Chock the front wheels, then jack up the rear of the car and support on axle stands. Remove the rear roadwheels.

2 Undo the two bolts securing the caliper shield in position, and remove the shield from the rear of the caliper (photo).

3 Remove both the caliper guide pin bolts, if necessary using a slim open-ended spanner to prevent the guide pins from rotating. Lift the

caliper away from the disc, noting the upper pad spring which is fitted to the roof of the caliper (photos). Tie the caliper to the suspension strut using a piece of wire, to avoid straining the hydraulic hose.

4 Remove the brake pads from the caliper mounting bracket, noting the correct fitted positions of the brake pads, pad retainer springs and pad shims (photo).

5 Inspect the pads (and brake caliper) as described in paragraphs 5 to 7 of Section 8 and, if necessary, renew the pads as a complete axle set.

6 When refitting, first fit the pad retainer springs to the caliper mounting bracket.

7 Apply a thin smear of Molykote M77 compound to the sides and back of each pad's metal backplate, and to those surfaces of the caliper body and mounting bracket which bear on the pads. In the absence of this compound, a good quality high-temperature brake grease (silicone-or PBC/Poly Butyl Cuprysil- based) or anti-seize compound may be used. Fit the shims to the back of both pads, noting that the smaller shim must be fitted to the piston-side pad, and apply a thin smear of lubricant to the back of each shim (photo). Do not allow the lubricant to foul the friction material.

8 Install the brake pads in the caliper mounting bracket, ensuring that the friction material is against the disc, and that the pad with the smaller shim attached is fitted on the inside.

9 If new pads have been fitted, it will be

15.4 Removing the brake pads

15.7 Refitting the smaller piston-side pad shim

9

15.9 Using a pair of circlip pliers to retract the piston

necessary to retract the piston fully into the caliper bore, by rotating it in a clockwise direction. This can be achieved using a suitable pair of circlip pliers as a peg spanner, or by fabricating a peg spanner for the task (photo). Provided that the master cylinder reservoir has not been overfilled with hydraulic fluid, there should be no spillage, but keep a careful watch on the fluid level while retracting the piston. If the fluid level rises above the 'MAX' level line at any time, the surplus should be syphoned off or ejected via a plastic tube connected to the bleed screw (see Section 7, paragraph 1, and use a one-man bleed tube or bottle if possible).

10 Ensure the upper pad spring is still in position in the caliper, then slide the caliper into position in its mounting bracket. When fitting the caliper, ensure that the lug on the rear of the piston side pad is located in one of the piston slots. Refit the caliper guide pin bolts, and tighten them to the specified torque setting.

11 Depress the footbrake to bring the piston into contact with the pads, then check that the lug on the piston-side pad is located in one of the piston slots. If necessary, remove the caliper and adjust the piston position as described above. Refit the shield to the rear of the caliper, and tighten its bolts securely.

12 Repeat the above procedures on the other rear brake caliper.

13 Once both sets of pads have been renewed, repeatedly depress the brake pedal until normal (non-assisted) pedal operation returns, then repeatedly apply the handbrake to set the handbrake adjustment. Check the operation of the handbrake and, if necessary, adjust the cable as described in Chapter 1.

14 Refit the roadwheels, then lower the car to the ground and tighten the roadwheel nuts to the specified torque.

15 Check the hydraulic fluid level, as described in Chapter 1.

16 Rear brake caliper – removal, overhaul and refitting

Note: *Before starting work, refer to the note at the beginning of Section 5 concerning the dangers of hydraulic fluid, and to the warning at the beginning of Section 15 concerning the dangers of asbestos dust.*

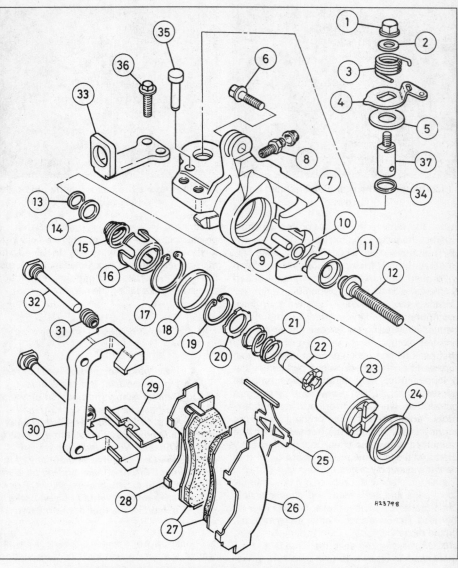

Fig. 9.9 Exploded view of the rear brake caliper (Secs 15 and 16)

1 Handbrake lever retaining nut	14 Spring seat	27 Brake pads
2 Washer	15 Spring	28 Outer pad shim
3 Return spring	16 Spring cover	29 Pad spring
4 Handbrake operating lever	17 Circlip	30 Caliper mounting bracket
5 Dust seal	18 Piston seal	31 Gaiter
6 Guide pin bolt	19 Circlip	32 Guide pin
7 Caliper body	20 Thrust washer	33 Handbrake cable mounting
8 Bleed screw	21 Spring	bracket
9 Pushrod	22 Adjuster nut	34 Cam washer
10 O-ring	23 Piston	35 Pin
11 Adjusting bolt piston	24 Dust seal	36 Bolt
12 Adjusting bolt	25 Pad spring	37 Handbrake mechanism
13 Bearing	26 Inner pad shim	cam

Removal

1 Chock the front wheels, then jack up the rear of the car and support on axle stands. Remove the rear wheel.

2 Undo the two bolts securing the caliper shield in position, and remove the shield from the rear of the caliper.

3 Extract the spring clip and clevis pin securing the handbrake cable to the caliper han dbrake lever, then remove the clip securing the outer cable to its mounting bracket, and detach the handbrake cable from the caliper (photos).

4 Minimise fluid loss by first removing the master cylinder reservoir cap, and then tightening it down onto a piece of polythene to

16.3A Extract the spring clip ...

16.3B ... and the clevis pin securing the handbrake cable to the caliper handbrake lever

16.3C Handbrake outer cable securing clip (arrowed)

obtain an airtight seal (taking care not to damage the sender unit). Alternatively, use a brake hose clamp, a G-clamp or a similar tool to clamp the flexible hose.

5 Clean the area around the hose union, then undo the brake hose union bolt and disconnect the hose from the caliper. Plug the end of the hose and the caliper orifice to prevent dirt entering the hydraulic system. Discard the sealing washers; they must be renewed whenever disturbed.

6 Remove both the caliper guide pin bolts, if necessary using a slim open-ended spanner to prevent the guide pins from rotating. Lift the caliper away from the disc, noting the upper pad spring which is fitted to the roof of the caliper. Note that the brake pads need not be disturbed, and can be left in position in the caliper mounting bracket.

Overhaul

7 With the caliper on the bench, wipe away all traces of dust and dirt, but *avoid inhaling the dust, as it is injurious to health.*

8 Using a small screwdriver, carefully prise out the dust seal from the caliper bore.

9 Remove the piston from the caliper bore by rotating it in an anti-clockwise direction. This can be achieved using a suitable pair of circlip pliers as a peg spanner, or by fabricating a peg spanner for the task. Once the piston turns freely but does not come out any further, the piston can be withdrawn by hand, or if necessary pushed out by applying compressed air to the union bolt hole. Only low pressure should be required, such as that generated by a bicycle pump or car footpump.

10 With the piston removed, extract the circlip from inside the piston, and withdraw the thrustwasher, spring and adjuster nut.

11 Remove the piston (fluid) seal, taking great care not to scratch the caliper bore.

12 Extract the circlip from the caliper bore, and withdraw the spring cover, spring, spring seat, bearing and adjusting bolt. Remove the adjusting bolt piston, noting the O-ring fitted to the rear of the piston, and withdraw the small pushrod.

13 Slacken and remove the handbrake lever

retaining nut and washer, and remove the return spring, lever and dust seal. Withdraw the handbrake mechanism cam from the caliper, and remove the cam washer.

14 Withdraw the guide pins from the caliper mounting bracket, and remove the guide pin gaiters.

15 Inspect all the caliper components as described in Section 9, paragraphs 10 to 13, and renew as necessary.

16 On reassembly, ensure that all components are absolutely clean and dry.

17 Apply a good quality high-temperature brake grease (silicone- or PBC/Poly Butyl Cuprysil-based) or anti-seize compound to the handbrake mechanism cam, and refit the cam washer and cam to the caliper. Fit the dust seal, lever, return spring and washer, and tighten the handbrake lever retaining nut securely.

18 Fit a new O-ring to the adjusting bolt piston, then insert the small pushrod into the rear of the piston, and install the adjusting bolt piston assembly in the caliper bore. Operate the handbrake lever, check that the piston is free to move smoothly, then refit the adjusting bolt, followed by the bearing and spring seat. Fit the spring with its tapered end innermost, then install the spring cover. Secure all the above components in position with the circlip, ensuring that it is correctly seated in its groove in the caliper bore.

19 Locate the adjusting nut with the cutout on the inside of the caliper piston, and refit the spring, thrustwasher and circlip. Ensure the circlip is correctly located in its groove.

20 Soak the piston and the new piston (fluid) seal in clean hydraulic fluid, and smear clean fluid in the cylinder bore.

21 Fit the new piston (fluid) seal, using only your fingers (no tools) to manipulate it into the cylinder bore groove, and refit the piston assembly. Turn the piston clockwise, using the method employed on dismantling (paragraph 9), until it is fully retracted into the caliper bore.

22 Fit the dust seal to the caliper, ensuring that it is correctly located in the caliper and also in the groove on the piston.

23 Apply the grease supplied in the repair kit, or a good quality high-temperature brake

grease (silicone- or PBC/Poly Butyl Cuprysil-based) or anti-seize compound to the guide pins, and fit the new gaiters. Fit the guide pins to the caliper mounting bracket, ensuring that the gaiters are correctly located in the grooves on both the guide pin and mounting bracket.

Refitting

24 Ensure the upper pad spring is still in position in the caliper, then slide the caliper into position in the mounting bracket. When fitting the caliper, ensure that the lug on the rear of the piston-side pad is located in the centre of the caliper piston, at the point where the two piston slots cross. Refit the caliper guide pin bolts, and tighten them to the specified torque setting.

25 Position a new sealing washer on each side of the hose union, and refit the brake hose union bolt. Ensure that the brake hose union is correctly positioned between the lugs on the caliper, then tighten the union bolt to the specified torque setting.

26 Remove the brake hose clamp, where fitted, and bleed the hydraulic system as described in Section 5. Note that, providing the precautions described were taken to minimise brake fluid loss, it should only be necessary to bleed the relevant rear brake.

27 Refit the handbrake outer cable to its mounting bracket, and secure it in position with the retaining clip. Ensure the return spring is located in the groove in the operating lever, then refit the handbrake cable-to-lever clevis pin, and secure it in position with the spring clip.

28 Depress the brake pedal several times until normal (non-assisted) operation returns, then check and if necessary adjust the handbrake cable, as described in Chapter 1.

29 Refit the shield to the rear of the caliper, and tighten its retaining bolts securely.

30 Refit the roadwheel, then lower the vehicle to the ground and tighten the roadwheel nuts to the specified torque.

31 Check the hydraulic fluid level, as described in Chapter 1.

9

17 Rear brake disc – inspection, removal and refitting

Note: *Before starting work, refer to the warning at the beginning of Section 15 concerning the dangers of asbestos dust.*

Inspection

Note: *If either disc requires renewal, both should be renewed at the same time, to ensure even and consistent braking.*

1 Chock the front wheels, then jack up the rear of the car and support on axle stands. Remove the appropriate rear roadwheel.
2 Inspect the disc as described in Section 10, paragraphs 2 to 5.

Removal

3 Undo the two caliper shield retaining bolts, and remove the shield from the rear of the caliper.
4 Undo the two bolts securing the caliper mounting bracket to the trailing arm assembly, and slide the caliper assembly off the disc. Using a piece of wire or string, tie the caliper to the rear suspension coil spring, to avoid placing any strain on the hydraulic brake hose.
5 Use chalk or paint to mark the relationship of the disc to the hub, then remove the two screws securing the brake disc to the hub, and remove the disc. If the disc is a tight fit on the hub, it can be drawn off by screwing two bolts into the jacking holes provided.

Refitting

6 Refitting is the reverse of the removal procedure, noting the following points.
(a) Ensure that the mating surfaces of the disc and hub are clean and flat.
(b) Align the marks made on removal (if applicable).
(c) If a new disc has been fitted, use a suitable solvent to wipe any preservative coating from the disc before refitting the caliper.
(d) Tighten the disc retaining screws, caliper bracket bolts and roadwheel nuts to their specified torque wrench settings.

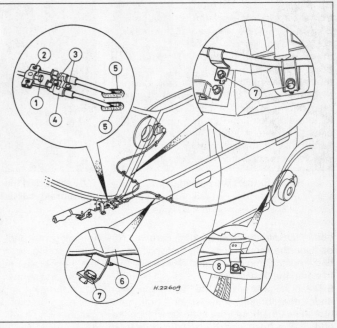

Fig. 9.10 Handbrake mechanism layout (Secs 18 and 19)

1 Handbrake cable adjuster nut
2 Equalizer plate
3 Bolts
4 Cable retaining plate
5 Grommet
6 Exhaust heatshield
7 Bolts – cable-to-body
8 Bolts – cable-to-trailing arm

18 Handbrake lever – removal and refitting

Removal

1 With the car parked on level ground, chock the roadwheels so that the car cannot move.
2 From inside the car, prise out the cover from the top of the rear centre console section, to gain access to the two retaining screws. Undo the two screws, and remove the rear console section.
3 Remove the handbrake lever rubber gaiter, and disconnect the wiring connector from the handbrake warning lamp switch (photo).
4 Slacken and remove the handbrake cable adjusting nut from the rear of the lever, and undo the bolts securing the handbrake lever assembly to the floorpan.
5 Lift the handbrake assembly out of position, noting the spring which is fitted to the lever adjusting rod.

Refitting

6 Refitting is a direct reversal of the removal procedure. Prior to refitting the handbrake lever rubber gaiter, adjust the handbrake cable as described in Chapter 1.

19 Handbrake cables – removal and refitting

Removal

1 Firmly chock the front wheels, then jack up the rear of the vehicle and support it on axle stands. The handbrake cable consists of two sections, a right- and left-hand section, which are linked to the lever assembly by an equalizer plate; each section can be removed individually.
2 From inside the car, prise out the cover from the top of the rear centre console section, to gain access to the two retaining screws. Undo the two screws, and remove the rear console section.
3 Slacken and remove the handbrake cable adjusting nut from the rear of the lever, and disconnect the equalizer plate, noting the spring which is fitted to the lever adjusting rod.
4 Undo the two bolts securing the outer cable retaining plate to the floorpan (photo). Remove the retaining plate, then detach the relevant inner cable from the equalizer plate and release the cable grommet from the floorpan.
5 On models with rear disc brakes, working from underneath the car, remove the two brake caliper shield retaining bolts, and remove the shield from the caliper. Extract the spring clip and clevis pin securing the handbrake cable to the caliper handbrake lever, then remove the clip securing the outer cable to its mounting bracket, and detach the handbrake cable from the caliper.

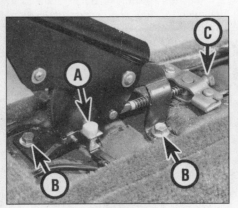

18.3 Handbrake lever switch (A), mounting bolts (B) and adjuster nut (C)

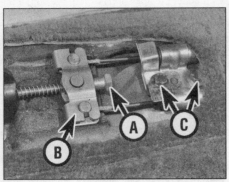

19.4 Handbrake cable adjusting nut (A), equalizer plate (B) and outer cable retaining plate bolts (C)

6 On models with rear drum brakes, remove the relevant rear brake drum, as described in Section 12. Remove the trailing shoe retainer spring and pin, using a pair of pliers to press in the retainer clip until it can be rotated through 90° and released. Ease the trailing shoe out of the lower pivot point to release the tension of the return spring, then disconnect the lower return spring from both shoes. Disconnect the handbrake cable from the trailing shoe, then use a 12 mm spanner to compress the handbrake cable retaining tangs, and withdraw the cable from the rear of backplate (photo).

7 On all models, release the main silencer from its three rubber mountings, and carefully lower the tailpipe section to gain access to the heat shield. Undo the three heat shield retaining bolts, and remove the shield from the vehicle underbody.

8 Work along the length of the cable section, and remove all the bolts securing the outer cable to the vehicle underbody and trailing arm. Once free, withdraw the cable from underneath the vehicle, and if necessary repeat the procedure for the remaining cable section.

Refitting

9 Refitting is a reversal of the removal

19.6 Use a 12 mm spanner to compress outer cable retaining tangs, and withdraw cable from backplate

sequence, noting the following points.
(a) Lubricate all exposed linkages and cable pivots with a good quality multi-purpose grease.
(b) Ensure the outer cable grommet is correctly located in the floorpan, and that all retaining bolts are tightened to the specified torque.
(c) On models with drum brakes, relocate the trailing shoe and refit the brake drum as described in Section 12.
(d) On all models, prior to refitting the rear

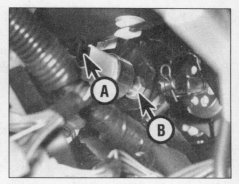

20.2 Stop-lamp switch wiring connector (A) and locknut (B)

centre console section, adjust the handbrake cable as described in Chapter 1.

20 Stop-lamp switch – removal, refitting and adjustment

Removal

1 Working from inside the car, undo the five screws and remove the right-hand lower facia panel.
2 Disconnect the wiring connector from the stop-lamp switch (photo).
3 Slacken the stop-lamp switch locknut, and unscrew the switch from its mounting bracket.

Refitting and adjustment

4 Screw the switch back into position in the mounting bracket.
5 Connect an ohmmeter across the stop-lamp switch terminals, and screw the switch in until an open-circuit is present between the switch terminals. Gently depress the pedal, and check that continuity exists between the switch terminals as soon as the pedal is depressed. If necessary, reposition the switch until it operates as specified.
6 Once the stop-lamp switch is correctly adjusted, hold the switch stationary and tighten the locknut securely.
7 Connect the wiring connector to the switch, and refit the lower facia panel.

21 Anti-lock braking system (ALB) – general information

ALB is available as an option on all models covered in this manual. The purpose of the system is to prevent wheel(s) locking during heavy braking, and this is achieved by controlling the pressure applied to the brakes when they are on the point of locking. When a wheel is about to lock, hydraulic pressure to that brake is momentarily reduced, so that the wheel keeps turning, and pressure is then re-applied – this 'cycle' can take place several times a second under heavy braking.

The system is comprised of an Electronic Control Unit (ECU), four roadwheel sensors

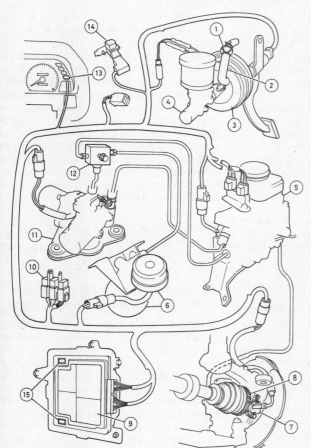

Fig. 9.11 ALB system components (Sec 21)

1 Servo unit check valve
2 Vacuum hose
3 Vacuum servo unit
4 Master cylinder
5 Modulator assembly
6 Accumulator and pressure switch
7 Wheel sensor
8 Reluctor ring
9 Electronic control unit (ECU)
10 ALB relays
11 ALB pump and motor unit
12 Three-way joint
13 ALB system warning lamp
14 Handbrake lever switch
15 ECU fault indicator LED

9

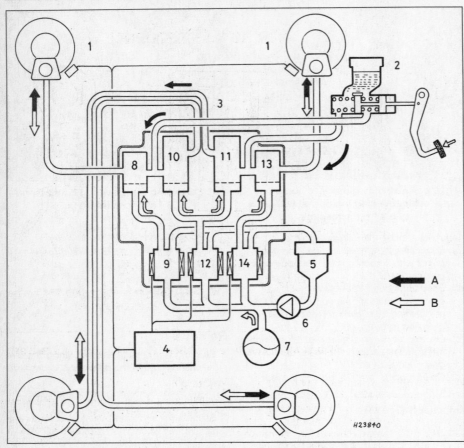

Fig. 9.12 Schematic layout of the ALB system components (Sec 21)

1 *Wheel sensor and reluctor ring*
2 *Master cylinder*
3 *Modulator assembly*
4 *Electronic control unit (ECU)*
5 *ALB reservoir*
6 *Pump*
7 *Accumulator*
8 *Front left-hand modulator valve*
9 *Front left-hand solenoid valve*
10 *Rear right-hand modulator valve*
11 *Rear left-hand modulator valve*
12 *Rear solenoid valve*
13 *Front right-hand modulator valve*
14 *Front right-hand solenoid valve*
A *Flow through main braking system*
B *Flow through ALB controlled system*

Note: *Dotted line passing through components 8, 10, 11 and 13 indicates the dividing line between the ALR high-pressure hydraulic system (below the line) and the main braking hydraulic system (above the line).*

(one fitted to each wheel), the modulator block which contains the modulator valves and solenoid control valves, the ALB pump and motor unit, and the accumulator unit. The latter components are all linked via a high-pressure hydraulic circuit. The master cylinder is connected to the modulator valves; the valves then distribute the main braking hydraulic system to the brake caliper. **Note:** *The ALB high-pressure hydraulic control circuit is a sealed circuit, and is completely separate from the main hydraulic braking system; the two hydraulic circuits are not linked in any way.*

The ALB system is controlled by the ECU which itself receives signals from the four wheel sensors (one fitted on each hub), which monitor the speed of rotation of each wheel. By comparing these speed signals from the four wheels, the ECU can determine the speed at which the vehicle is travelling. It can then use this information to determine when a wheel is decelerating at an abnormal rate compared to the speed of the vehicle, and can therefore predict when a wheel is about to lock.

During normal operation, the system functions in the same way as a normal braking system does, with the modulator valves having no effect on the braking system. At this stage, the modulator valves are fully open, and are isolated by the solenoid control valves from the ALB pump pressure which is present in the accumulator unit (Fig. 9.13).

If the ECU senses that a wheel is about to lock, the ECU will gradually open the relevant solenoid valve in the modulator block. This then allows the hydraulic pressure present in

the accumulator unit through to the relevant modulator valve. The cut-off valve within the modulator valve then closes, which isolates the relevant brake caliper from the master cylinder, effectively sealing-in the hydraulic pressure.

If the speed of rotation of the wheel continues to decrease at an abnormal rate, the ECU then opens the solenoid valve further. This increases the pressure present in chamber C of the modulator valve, and causes the valve to rise further (Fig. 9.14). As it rises, the pressure in chamber A of the valve decreases, which draws the fluid back from the relevant brake caliper, effectively reducing the pressure in the main braking system and releasing the relevant brake. At the same time, the pressure in chamber B of the modulator valve is increased, and fluid is forced back into the master cylinder reservoir, causing pulses in the main braking hydraulic system. This pulsing can be felt through the brake pedal.

Once the speed of rotation of the wheel returns to an acceptable rate, the ECU operates the solenoid valve to fully exhaust the hydraulic pressure present in chamber C of the modulator valve. The modulator valve then falls again, the cut-off valve opens, and normal operation of the braking system returns.

The ECU completes a self-checking sequence each time the engine is started, and will illuminate the ALB warning lamp on the instrument panel. If the system is functioning correctly and no fault is found, the warning lamp will go out after a few seconds. Should a fault be present in the system, the ALB warning lamp will remain lit. If this is the case, the car must immediately be taken to a Rover dealer for inspection. The ECU is fitted with a LED fault indicator. When a fault is detected, the ECU flashes the LED and reveals the appropriate fault code. A Rover dealer will be able to interpret this code, and will quickly be able to diagnose the fault. Note that whilst the ALB warning lamp is on, the ALB system is not functioning, and the braking system functions in exactly the same way as a normal non-anti-lock braking system would.

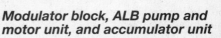
22 Anti-lock braking system (ALB) components – removal and refitting

Modulator block, ALB pump and motor unit, and accumulator unit

1 These components are all linked by the ALB system high-pressure hydraulic system. **Note:** *Under no circumstances should any of the ALB high-pressure hydraulic pipes be disconnected. This is due to the fact that once the pipes are reconnected, the system will require bleeding before it can be used. Bleeding is a complex operation, carried out with the ALB system under pressure, and requiring the use of several Rover service tools, including an electronic test unit.*

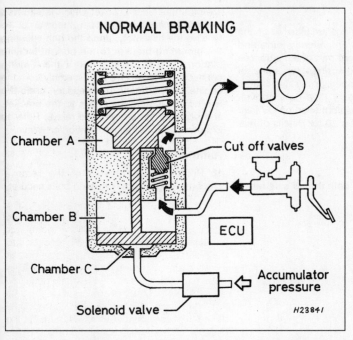

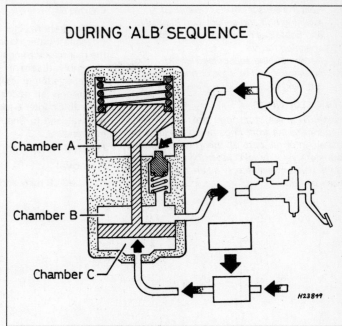

Fig. 9.13 Modulator valve operation during normal braking (Sec 21)   **Fig. 9.14 Modulator valve operation during ALB sequence (Sec 21)**

Removal and refitting of the modulator block, ALB pump and motor unit or accumulator unit must therefore be entrusted to a Rover dealer who has access to the relevant service tools to bleed the system on completion. For reference only, the modulator block is situated in the right-hand rear corner of the engine compartment (just in front of the master cylinder), the ALB pump and motor unit and accumulator unit are situated in the front right-hand corner of the engine compartment (behind the right-hand headlamp), with the accumulator unit directly above the pump unit.

Electronic Control Unit (ECU)
Removal

2 On 216 models, open up the tailgate, then prise out the screw caps (where necessary) and undo the luggage compartment rear inner trim panel screws; remove the panel from the car. Remove the rear window parcel shelf, and fold down the rear seat back. Closely examine the luggage compartment right-hand side trim panel, and remove any relevant retaining screws. Prise the luggage compartment lamp out of the right-hand trim panel, disconnect its wiring and remove the lamp. Carefully prise the trim panel away from the body, and remove it from the luggage compartment. Undo the three ECU retaining nuts, then manoeuvre the unit out of position and disconnect its wiring connectors. If necessary, undo the four cover bolts, and separate the ECU and cover.
3 On 416 models, open up the boot lid to gain access to the ECU, which is mounted on the underside of the rear window parcel shelf. Loosen the three cover retaining bolts, noting that there is no need to fully remove them,

then slide the cover towards the rear of the car, and remove it from the ECU. Loosen the three ECU retaining nuts, again noting that there is no need to fully remove them, then slide the ECU towards the rear of the car to disengage it from its mounting studs. Disconnect its wiring connectors, and remove the ECU from the luggage compartment.

Refitting

4 Refitting is a reversal of the relevant removal sequence.

Front wheel sensor
Removal

5 Chock the rear wheels, firmly apply the handbrake, then jack up the front of the vehicle and support it on axle stands. Remove the appropriate front roadwheel.
6 Working in the engine compartment, disconnect the wheel sensor wiring connector. The left-hand sensor connector is mounted onto the left-hand suspension turret, and the right-hand sensor connector is mounted onto the right-hand suspension turret, where it is situated directly below the air cleaner housing intake duct. Note that it may be necessary to disconnect the intake duct from the air cleaner housing to gain access to the right-hand sensor wiring connector.
7 From underneath the car, remove the sensor lead grommet, and pull the wiring connector through the wing valance. Undo the sensor lead bracket retaining bolts, and remove the brackets.
8 Slacken and remove the two bolts securing the sensor unit itself to the wheel hub, then remove the sensor and lead assembly.

Refitting

9 Refitting is a direct reversal of the removal procedure, noting the following points.
(a) *Ensure that the sensor and hub sealing faces are clean, then refit the sensor, and tighten its retaining bolts to the specified torque.*
(b) *Ensure the sensor wiring is correctly routed, and that all bracket retaining bolts are tightened to the specified torque.*

Rear wheel sensor
Removal

10 Chock the front wheels, then jack up the rear of the vehicle and support it on axle stands. Remove the appropriate roadwheel.
11 Trace the wiring back from the sensor to the wiring connector, then free the connector from its retaining clips and disconnect it.
12 Undo the sensor lead bracket retaining bolts, and remove the brackets.
13 Slacken and remove the bolt securing the strap to the sensor cover, then undo the sensor cover retaining bolts and remove the cover.
14 Undo the two bolts securing the sensor to the rear hub assembly, and remove it from the car, along with the shim which is fitted behind it.

Refitting

15 Refitting is the direct reversal of the removal sequence, bearing in mind the following points.
(a) *Ensure the sensor and hub sealing faces are clean, then install the sensor and shim, and tighten the sensor retaining bolts to the specified torque.*

9

(b) Refit the sensor cover, cover strap retaining bolt and sensor lead brackets, and tighten all retaining bolts to the specified torque.

(c) Reconnect the sensor lead wiring connector, and refit the connector to its retaining clip.

Reluctor rings

Note: *The reluctor rings are not available separately; the front rings being available only as an integral part of the driveshaft outer constant velocity joint assembly, and the rear rings being available only as an integral part of the rear hub.*

General

16 The front reluctor rings are situated on the driveshaft outer constant velocity joint, and the rear reluctor rings are part of the stub axle assembly. Examine the rings for signs of damage (such as chipped or missing teeth), and renew as necessary (see note above). Refer to Chapter 8 for information on CV joint renewal, and to Chapter 10 for details of rear hub renewal.

Relays

Removal

17 The ALB relay and both the fail-safe relays are mounted on a bracket which is situated directly behind the right-hand headlamp. To remove the assembly, undo the bolt securing the mounting bracket to the bonnet locking platform, then disconnect the wiring connectors and remove the assembly from the engine compartment. If necessary, undo the two bolts securing the relays to the bracket, and separate the bracket and relays. Refer to Chapter 12 for further information on relays.

Refitting

18 Refitting is a reverse of the removal procedure; tighten the retaining bolts securely.

Chapter 10 Suspension and steering

Contents

Degrees of difficulty

Easy, suitable for novice with little experience	Fairly easy, suitable for beginner with some experience	Fairly difficult, suitable for competent DIY mechanic	Difficult, suitable for experienced DIY mechanic	Very difficult, suitable for expert DIY or professional

Specifications

Front suspension

Type . . . . Fully-independent by MacPherson struts, with coil springs and integral shock absorbers. Anti-roll bar mounted on both lower suspension arms

Rear suspension

Type . . . . Fully-independent, double wishbone type, by trailing arms with transverse lateral links, and suspension struts with coil springs and integral shock absorbers. Anti-roll bar mounted on both rear lower lateral links

Steering

Type . . . . Rack and pinion power-assisted steering fitted as standard on most GTi models and available as an option on all other models

Turns lock-to-lock:
Manual steering 4.0
Power-assisted steering 3.4

Wheel alignment and steering angles

Note: *All measurements are with car at kerb weight (see 'General dimensions and weights')*

Toe-out in turns . . . . Inside roadwheel 17° 17', outside roadwheel 16° 21' ± 2'
Camber angle:
Front . . . . 0° 20' negative ± 0° 10'
Rear . . . . 0° 50' negative to 0° 50' positive
Castor angle:
Front . . . . 1° 59' positive ± 0° 30'
Rear . . . . N/A
Steering axis inclination (SAI) or kingpin inclination (KPI) . . . . 12 °
Toe setting:
Front . . . . 0° 10' ± 0° 15' toe-out
Rear . . . . 0° 11 ' ± 0° 7.5' toe-in (each wheel)

10

Roadwheels

Size and type:
Si and SLi models	5 x 14 steel wheels

GSi models:
Standard	5 x 14 steel wheels
Optional	5.5 x 14 alloy wheels

216 GTi 3-door models:
Standard	5.5 x 14 steel wheels
Optional	6 x 15 alloy wheels
216 GTi 5-door and 416 GTi models	5.5 x 14 alloy wheels
216 GTi Twin Cam models	6 x 15 alloy wheels

Tyres

Type	Tubeless, steel-braced radial

Size:
Models with 5 x 14 wheels	175/65 HR 14
Models with 5.5 x 14 wheels	185/60 HR 14
Models with 6 x 15 wheels	185/55 VR 15

Pressures (cold) – 175/65 HR 14 and 185/60 HR 14 tyres:	**Front**	**Rear**
Normal driving conditions	2.1 bars (30 lb/in^2)	2.1 bars (30 lb/in^2)
Speeds in excess of 100 mph	2.5 bars (36 lbf/in^2)	2.5 bars (36 lbf/in^2)
Pressures (cold) – 185/55 VR 15 tyres:	**Front**	**Rear**
Normal driving conditions	2.2 bars (32 lbf/in^2)	2.2 bars (32 lb/in^2)
Speeds in excess of 100 mph	2.7 bars (39 lbf/in^2)	2.7 bars (39 lb/in^2)

Note: *Pressures apply only to original-equipment tyres, and may vary if any other make or type is fitted; check with the tyre manufacturer or supplier for correct pressures if necessary*

Torque wrench settings

	Nm	lbf ft
Front suspension		
Front suspension strut:		
Upper mounting nuts	32	24
Swivel hub pinch-bolt	80	59
Brake hose clamp bolt	25	18
Upper mounting plate retaining nut	40	30
Anti-roll bar:		
Mounting clamp bolts	15	11
Connecting link bolts	45	33
Tie-bar:		
Lower suspension arm bolts	80	59
Retaining nut	55	41
Lower arm:		
Balljoint retaining nut	60	44
Body pivot bolt	45	33
Rear suspension		
Hub nut	185	137
Drum brake backplate-to-trailing arm bolts	65	48
Disc brake shield-to-trailing arm bolts	15	11
Brake hose bracket-to-trailing arm bolts	15	11
Handbrake cable-to-trailing arm bolts	22	16
Stub axle:		
Retaining nut	170	125
Mounting plate Torx bolts	55	41
Anti-roll bar:		
Mounting clamp bolts	15	11
Connecting link to lower arm	45	33
Connecting link to anti-roll bar	15	11
Suspension strut:		
Upper mounting nuts	32	24
Lower mounting bolt	45	33
Upper mounting plate retaining nut	30	22
Lateral link pivot bolts	45	33
Trailing arm mounting bolts	85	63
Steering		
Steering wheel nut	52	38
Steering column:		
Lower mounting bolt and nut	22	16
Upper mounting bolts	22	16
Upper mounting nuts	13	10

Torque wrench settings (continued)

	Nm	lbf ft
Universal joint pinch-bolts	30	22
Steering gear mounting nuts and bolts	42	31
Power-assisted steering gear:		
Feed pipe union nut	39	29
Return pipe union nut	31	23
Track rod balljoint:		
Retaining nut	44	32
Locknut	55	41
Power steering pump:		
Upper mounting bolt	45	33
Lower mounting bolt(s)	25	18
Outlet pipe union nut	55	41
Pulley retaining bolts	9	7
Power steering fluid cooler mounting bolts	9	7
Roadwheels		
Roadwheel nuts	100	74

1 General information

The independent front suspension is of the MacPherson strut type, incorporating coil springs and integral telescopic shock absorbers. The MacPherson struts are located by transverse lower suspension arms, which utilise rubber inner mounting bushes, and incorporate a balljoint at their outer ends, and forward-facing longitudinal tie-bars. Both lower suspension arms are connected to an anti-roll bar via a small connecting link. The front swivel hubs, which carry the wheel bearings, brake calipers and the hub/disc assemblies, are bolted to the MacPherson struts, and connected to the lower arms via the balljoints.

The independent rear suspension is of the double wishbone type, utilising pressed-steel trailing arms which have the roadwheel stub axles bolted into their rear ends. These are located longitudinally on the vehicle underbody, via a large rubber bush which is situated towards the centre of each arm. Each trailing arm assembly is located transversely by three lateral links, which utilise rubber mounting bushes at both their inner and outer ends. Both trailing arms are connected to a rear anti-roll bar via a small connecting link. The rear suspension struts incorporate coil springs and integral telescopic shock

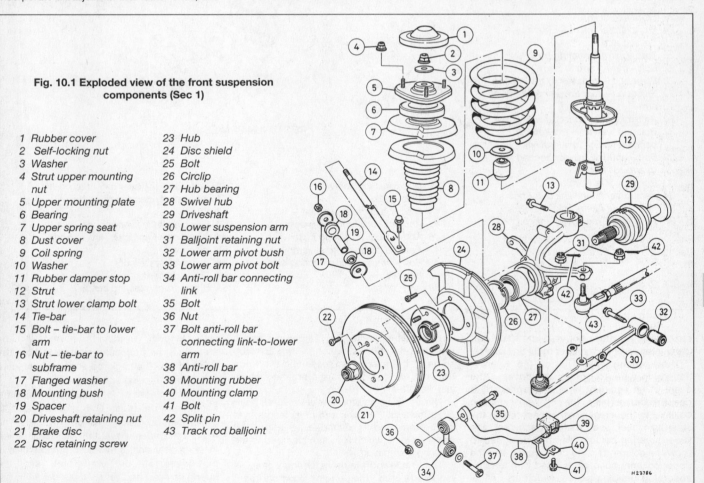

Fig. 10.1 Exploded view of the front suspension components (Sec 1)

1 Rubber cover
2 Self-locking nut
3 Washer
4 Strut upper mounting nut
5 Upper mounting plate
6 Bearing
7 Upper spring seat
8 Dust cover
9 Coil spring
10 Washer
11 Rubber damper stop
12 Strut
13 Strut lower clamp bolt
14 Tie-bar
15 Bolt – tie-bar to lower arm
16 Nut – tie-bar to subframe
17 Flanged washer
18 Mounting bush
19 Spacer
20 Driveshaft retaining nut
21 Brake disc
22 Disc retaining screw
23 Hub
24 Disc shield
25 Bolt
26 Circlip
27 Hub bearing
28 Swivel hub
29 Driveshaft
30 Lower suspension arm
31 Balljoint retaining nut
32 Lower arm pivot bush
33 Lower arm pivot bolt
34 Anti-roll bar connecting link
35 Bolt
36 Nut
37 Bolt anti-roll bar connecting link-to-lower arm
38 Anti-roll bar
39 Mounting rubber
40 Mounting clamp
41 Bolt
42 Split pin
43 Track rod balljoint

10

H23786

Fig. 10.2 Exploded view of the rear suspension components (Sec 1)

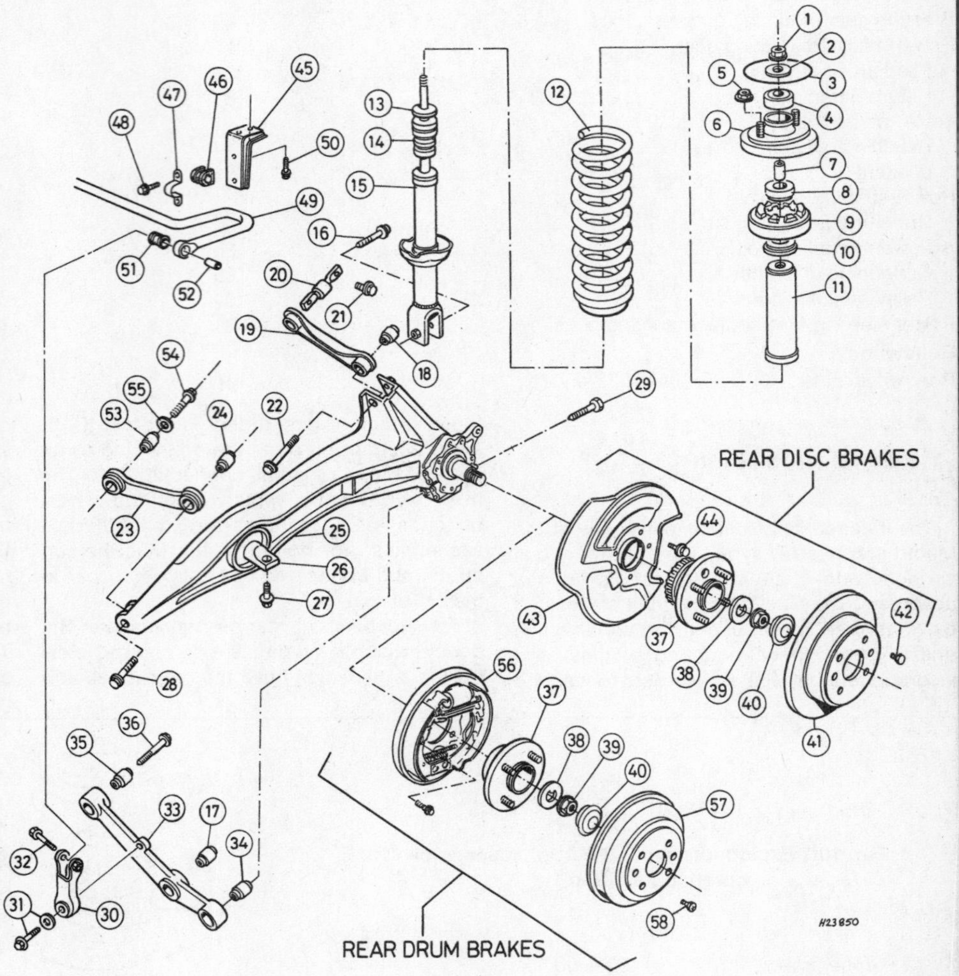

1 Self-locking nut
2 Washer
3 Seal
4 Mounting rubber
5 Strut upper mounting nut
6 Upper mounting plate
7 Spacer
8 Mounting rubber
9 Rubber damper
10 Dust seal
11 Dust cover
12 Coil spring
13 Stop-plate
14 Rubber stop
15 Strut
16 Strut lower mounting bolt
17 Strut lower mounting bush
18 Rear upper later link outer bush
19 Rear upper lateral link
20 Rear upper lateral link inner bush
21 Bolt – rear upper link to body
22 Pivot bolt – rear upper link to trailing arm
23 Front lateral link
24 Front lateral link outer bush
25 Trailing arm
26 Trailing arm mounting bush
27 Bolt – trailing arm to body
28 Pivot bolt – front link to trailing arm
29 Pivot bolt – rear lower link to trailing arm
30 Anti-roll bar connecting link
31 Bolt and washer – anti-roll bar connecting link to lateral link
32 Bolt – anti-roll bar connecting link to anti-roll bar
33 Rear lower later link
34 Rear lower lateral link outer bush
35 Rear lower lateral link inner bush
36 Pivot bolt – rear lower link to body
37 Rear hub
38 Toothed washer
39 Rear hub retaining nut
40 Hub cap
41 Brake disc
42 Disc retaining screw
43 Disc shield
44 Disc shield mounting bolt
45 Anti-roll bar mounting bracket
46 Anti-roll bar mounting bush
47 Anti-roll bar mounting clamp
48 Bolt – anti-roll bar mounting clamp to bracket
49 Anti-roll bar
50 Bolt – anti-roll bar bracket to body
51 Anti-spacer bar mounting bush
52 Spacer
53 Front lateral link inner bush
54 Pivot bolt – front lateral link to body
55 Washer
56 Backplate assembly
57 Brake drum
58 Brake drum retaining screw

REAR DISC BRAKES

REAR DRUM BRAKES

H23850

absorbers, and are mounted onto the rear lower lateral link via a rubber mounting bush.

The steering wheel is of the energy-absorbing type, to protect the driver in the event of an accident, and is attached by a deeply-recessed nut to the collapsible steering column. In the event of an impact hitting the steering wheel, such as in an accident, the lower steering column clamp is designed to allow the column to slide downwards, and the upper column mounting is fitted with energy-absorbing bending plates, which also allow the column to move downwards. The

downwards movement of the column bends the mounting plates, which in turn absorbs some of the energy, so lessening the force transmitted to driver via the steering wheel (see Fig. 10.4).

The steering column has a universal joint fitted towards the lower end of its length, and its bottom end is clamped to a second universal joint, which is in turn clamped to the steering gear pinion.

The rack-and-pinion steering gear is mounted onto the engine compartment bulkhead, and is connected by two track rods,

with balljoints at their outer ends, to the steering arms projecting rearwards from the hub carriers. The track rod ends are threaded, to facilitate tracking adjustments.

Power steering is fitted as standard equipment on most GTi models, and is available as an option on all other models. The main components are the rack-and-pinion steering gear unit, a hydraulic pump which is belt-driven off the crankshaft, and the hydraulic feed and return lines between the pump and steering gear.

Fig. 10.3 Exploded view of the steering column (Sec 1)

1 Horn button assembly
2 Steering wheel retaining nut
3 Steering wheel
4 Horn contact ring
5 Snap-ring
6 Upper shroud
7 Guide rails
8 Bending plate guide
9 Bending plate spring
10 Bending plate base
11 Upper column holder
12 Bending plate
13 Column hanger spring
14 Tilt adjusting bolt and washers
15 Tilt lockplate
16 Tilt lockbolt and washers
17 Tilt lever and spring
18 Steering column
19 Bush and retainer
20 Circlip
21 Washer
22 Spring washer
23 Bearing
24 Circlip
25 Steering shaft
26 Shaft bush
27 Horn pick-up
28 Indicator self-cancelling cam
29 Combination switch assembly
30 Ignition switch
31 Retaining clips
32 Lower cover
33 Lower shroud
34 Shroud retaining screw

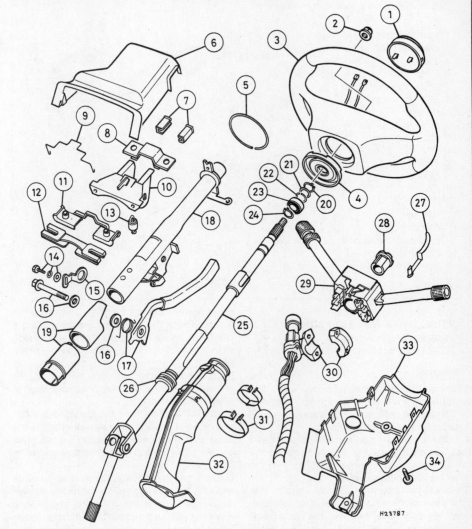

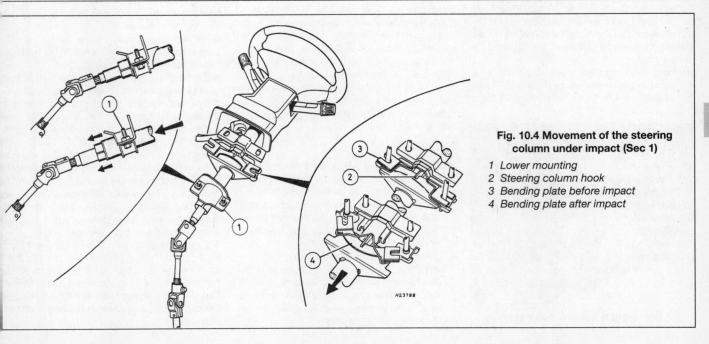

10

Fig. 10.4 Movement of the steering column under impact (Sec 1)

1 Lower mounting
2 Steering column hook
3 Bending plate before impact
4 Bending plate after impact

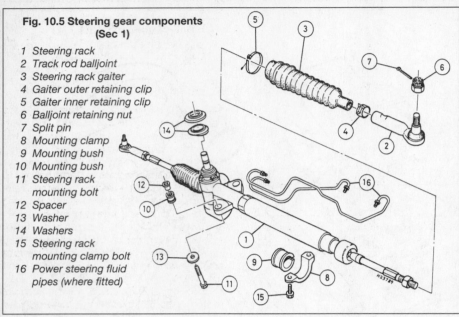

Fig. 10.5 Steering gear components (Sec 1)

1 Steering rack
2 Track rod balljoint
3 Steering rack gaiter
4 Gaiter outer retaining clip
5 Gaiter inner retaining clip
6 Balljoint retaining nut
7 Split pin
8 Mounting clamp
9 Mounting bush
10 Mounting bush
11 Steering rack mounting bolt
12 Spacer
13 Washer
14 Washers
15 Steering rack mounting clamp bolt
16 Power steering fluid pipes (where fitted)

2 Front swivel hub assembly – removal and refitting

Removal

1 Chock the rear wheels, firmly apply the handbrake, then jack up the front of the vehicle and support it on axle stands. Remove the appropriate front roadwheel.
2 Using a hammer and suitable chisel-nosed tool, tap up the staking (notch) securing the driveshaft retaining nut to the groove in the outer constant velocity joint.
3 Have an assistant firmly apply the footbrake, then using a socket and extension bar, slacken and remove the driveshaft retaining nut – *take care to ensure that the vehicle is adequately supported, as considerable force will be needed to undo the nut.* Discard the nut once removed, as a new driveshaft retaining nut **must** be obtained for reassembly.
4 If the hub bearings are to be disturbed, remove the brake disc as described in Chapter 9, Section 10. If not, undo the two bolts

2.8 Removing the swivel hub assembly

securing the caliper mounting bracket to the hub, and slide the caliper off the disc. Using a piece of wire, tie the caliper to the suspension strut, to avoid placing any strain on the brake hose.
5 On models with anti-lock brakes (ALB), remove the front wheel sensor as described in Chapter 9, Section 22.
6 Slacken and remove the bolt and washer securing the anti-roll bar connecting link to the lower suspension arm, and undo the two bolts securing the tie-bar to the lower suspension arm.
7 Extract the split pins, then undo the nuts securing the steering gear track rod and lower suspension arm balljoints to the swivel hub. Release both the balljoints from the swivel hub using a suitable balljoint separator, taking great care not to damage the balljoint gaiters.
8 Slacken the swivel hub-to-suspension strut clamp bolt, then carefully ease the hub off the end of the strut. Once it is free, pull the hub outwards to free it from the constant velocity joint splines, and remove it from the car (photo). While the hub is removed from the car, support the driveshaft by tying it to the suspension strut, to avoid damaging the inner constant velocity joint or gaiter.

Refitting

9 The swivel hub is refitted by a reversal of the removal procedure, noting the following points.
(a) Ensure that the lug on the base of the suspension strut correctly engages with the slot in the swivel hub assembly clamp.
(b) Tighten all nuts and bolts to the specified torque.
(c) Where necessary, refit the brake disc and/or ALB wheel sensor, as described in the relevant Section of Chapter 9.
(d) Use new split pins to secure the track rod and lower suspension arm balljoint retaining nuts in position.

(e) When fitting the new driveshaft retaining nut tighten it to the specified torque, then stake it firmly into the groove in the constant velocity joint, using a suitable punch.

3 Front hub bearings – removal and refitting

Note: *The double-row roller type bearing is sealed, pre-adjusted and pre-lubricated, and is intended to last the car's entire service life without maintenance or attention. Do not attempt to remove the bearing unless absolutely necessary, as it will probably be damaged during the removal operation. Never over-tighten the driveshaft nut beyond the specified torque wrench setting, in an attempt to 'adjust' the bearing.*

Note: *A press will be required to dismantle and rebuild the assembly; if such a tool is not available, a large bench vice and suitable spacers (such as large sockets) will serve as an adequate substitute. The service tool numbers for the special Rover mandrels are given in the accompanying figures. Also, the bearing's inner races are an interference fit on the hub; if the outboard inner race remains on the hub when it is pressed out of the hub carrier, a proprietary knife-edged bearing puller will be required to remove it.*

Removal

1 Remove the swivel hub assembly as described in Section 2, then undo the brake disc shield retaining screws, and remove the shield from the hub.
2 Press the hub out of the swivel hub, using a tubular spacer (Fig. 10.6). If the bearing's outboard inner race remains on the hub, remove it using a suitable bearing puller (see second note above).
3 Extract both circlips from the swivel hub, and discard them; they should be renewed whenever they are disturbed.
4 Press the bearing out of the swivel hub, using a suitable tubular spacer (Fig. 10.7).
5 Thoroughly clean the hub and swivel hub, removing all traces of dirt and grease, and polishing away any burrs or raised edges which might hinder reassembly. Check both components for cracks or any other signs of wear or damage, and renew them if necessary. As noted above, the bearing and its circlips must be renewed whenever they are disturbed. Note that a replacement bearing kit is available from Rover dealers, which consists of the bearing and both circlips.
6 Check the condition of the roadwheel studs in the hub flange. If any are sheared off, stretched or have damaged threads, they can be pressed out of the hub, providing that its flange is fully supported; on refitting, support the hub flange, and press in the new stud until it seats fully.

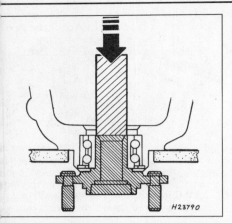

Fig. 10.6 Pressing out hub from the swivel hub (Sec 3)

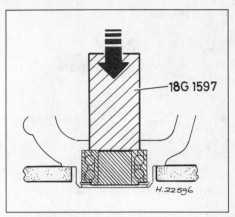

Fig. 10.7 Pressing hub bearing out of swivel hub (Sec 3)

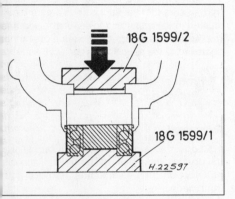

Fig. 10.8 Pressing new hub bearing into swivel hub (Sec 3)

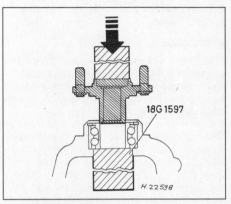

Fig. 10.9 Pressing hub into swivel hub – note support for bearing inner race (Sec 3)

Refitting

7 On reassembly, check (as far as is possible) that the new bearing is packed with grease, and fit the new circlip to the swivel hub outboard groove. Apply a light film of oil to the bearing inner and outer races, and to their matching surfaces in the hub and swivel hub, to aid installation of the bearing.

8 Support the swivel hub outboard face and, using a suitable tubular spacer which bears only on the bearing's outer race, press in the new bearing until it seats against the circlip (Fig. 10.8). Secure the bearing in position by

fitting the second new circlip to the swivel hub's inboard groove.

9 Supporting the bearing's inner race fully, press the hub into the bearing and swivel hub, until the hub shoulder seats against the bearing's inner race (Fig. 10.9). Wipe off any surplus oil or grease.

10 Refit the brake disc shield to the swivel hub, and tighten its retaining screws securely.

11 Refit the swivel hub assembly as described in Section 2.

4.4 Remove the bolt securing the brake hose to the suspension strut

4.6A Prior to removal of the strut, remove rubber cover and mark relative positions of strut and body. Upper mounting nuts arrowed – *do not* remove central nut

4 Front suspension strut – removal and refitting

Removal

1 Chock the rear wheels, firmly apply the handbrake, then jack up the front of the car and support it on axle stands. Remove the appropriate front roadwheel.

2 Extract the split pin, and undo the nut securing the steering gear track rod balljoint to the swivel hub. Release the balljoint shank using a suitable balljoint separator tool, taking care not to damage the balljoint gaiter.

3 Slacken and remove the bolt and washer securing the anti-roll bar connecting link to the lower suspension arm, and undo the two bolts securing the tie-bar to the lower suspension arm.

4 Undo the bolt securing the brake hose retaining clamp to the strut (photo), then remove the clamp and free the flexible hose. On models equipped with anti-lock brakes (ALB), where necessary, also undo the bolt(s) securing the front wheel sensor lead to the suspension strut.

5 Slacken the swivel hub-to-suspension strut clamp bolt, then carefully ease the swivel hub assembly off the end of the strut.

6 Working in the engine compartment, remove the rubber suspension strut cover, and use chalk or a dab of paint to mark the relative positions of the suspension strut upper mounting to the body. Undo the three suspension strut upper mounting nuts, and manoeuvre the strut out from under the wheel arch (photos), noting the seal which is fitted between the upper mounting plate and vehicle body.

Refitting

7 Refitting is by a reversal of the removal procedure, noting the following points.
(a) Ensure that the marks made on removal are aligned when installing the strut.
(b) Ensure that the lug on the base of the

10

4.6B Removing a front suspension strut

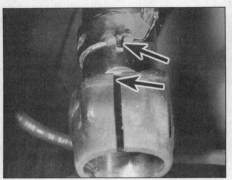

4.7A Align suspension strut lug with slot in swivel hub (arrowed)

4.7B Tightening swivel hub clamp bolt

5.2 Compress the coil spring with a suitable pair of spring compressors ...

suspension strut engages correctly with the slot in the swivel hub assembly (photo).

(c) Tighten all nuts and bolts to the specified torque (photo).

(d) Use a new split pin to secure the track rod balljoint retaining nut in position.

5 Front suspension strut – dismantling, inspection and reassembly

Note: *Before attempting to dismantle the front suspension strut, a suitable tool to hold the coil spring in compression must be obtained. Adjustable coil spring compressors are readily available, and are recommended for this operation. Any attempt to dismantle the strut without such a tool is likely to result in damage or personal injury.*

Dismantling

1 With the strut removed from the car as described in Section 4, clean away all external dirt, then mount it upright in a vice.

2 Fit the spring compressor, and compress the coil spring until all tension is relieved from the upper mounting plate (photo).

3 Slacken the upper mounting retaining nut, while holding the strut piston with an Allen key (photo).

4 Remove the nut and washer, followed by the mounting plate, bearing and upper spring

seat. Lift off the coil spring and damper piston dust cover, and separate the two components. Slide the washer and rubber damper stop off the strut piston.

Inspection

5 With the strut assembly now completely dismantled, examine all the components for wear, damage or deformation, and check the bearing for smoothness of operation. Renew any suspect components as necessary.

6 Examine the strut for signs of fluid leakage. Check the strut piston for signs of pitting along its entire length, and check the strut body for signs of damage. To test the operation of the strut, hold it in an upright position, then move the piston through a full stroke, and then through short strokes of 50 to 100 mm. In both cases, the resistance felt should be smooth and continuous. If the resistance is jerky or uneven, or if there is any visible sign of wear or damage to the strut, renewal is necessary.

7 If any doubt exists about the condition of the coil spring, carefully remove the spring compressors and check the spring for distortion and signs of cracking. Since no minimum free length is specified by Rover, the only way to check the tension of the spring is to compare it with a new component. Renew the spring if it is damaged or distorted, or there is any doubt as to its condition.

8 Inspect all other components for signs of damage or deterioration, and renew any that are suspect.

Reassembly

9 Reassembly is a reversal of dismantling, making sure that the spring ends are correctly located in the upper and lower seats, and that the upper mounting plate retaining nut is tightened to the specified torque.

6 Front anti-roll bar – removal and refitting

Removal

1 Chock the rear wheels, firmly apply the handbrake, then jack up the front of the car and support it on axle stands. Remove both front roadwheels.

2 From underneath the car, on manual gearbox models, undo the bolts securing the gearchange steady-rod rear rubber mounting to the vehicle underbody. Remove the rubber mounting assembly and bolts, noting the correct fitted positions of the mounting rubber spacers and mounting plate.

3 Slacken and remove the nuts and washers securing each end of the anti-roll bar to the connecting links, and remove the bolts (photo).

4 Mark the location of the clamp bushes on the bar, then undo the mounting clamp retaining bolts and remove the clamps. Make a note of the fitted position of the rubber bush splits, to ensure that they are positioned correctly on refitting (photo). Manoeuvre the

5.3... and remove the upper mounting nut, holding the piston with an Allen key

6.3 Slacken and remove the anti-roll bar-to-connecting link bolts

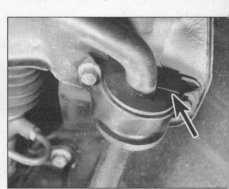

6.4 Prior to removal, note the position of anti-roll bar mounting bush split (arrowed)

anti-roll bar out over the gearchange linkage and exhaust system, and remove it from the right-hand side of the vehicle.

5 Carefully examine the anti-roll bar components for signs of wear, damage or deterioration, paying particular attention to the mounting rubbers. Also inspect the gearchange steady-rod mounting rubber for signs of wear or deterioration. Renew worn components as necessary.

Refitting

6 Manoeuvre the anti-roll bar into position from the right-hand side of the car, and refit the connecting link bolts. Refit the washers, and tighten the nuts finger-tight only at this stage.

7 Lubricate the mounting clamp bushes with a solution of soapy water, then lever the bar down and slide them into position on the anti-roll bar. Ensure that the splits are on the correct side of the bushes, then align them with the marks made on dismantling.

8 Refit the anti-roll bar mounting clamps, and tighten their retaining bolts to the specified torque setting, then tighten the anti-roll bar-to-connecting link bolts to the specified torque.

9 Apply a smear of grease to the gearchange steady-rod mounting rubber, and refit it to the steady-rod. Tighten the mounting bolts to the specified torque setting, and check that the gearchange mechanism operates smoothly.

10 Refit the roadwheels, then lower the car to the ground and tighten the roadwheel nuts to the specified torque.

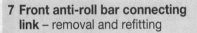

7 Front anti-roll bar connecting link – removal and refitting

Removal

1 Chock the rear wheels, firmly apply the handbrake, then jack up the front of the car and support it on axle stands. Remove the appropriate front roadwheel.

2 From underneath the car, slacken and remove the bolt and washer securing the connecting link to the lower suspension arm (photo).

3 Remove the nut and washer securing the connecting link to the anti-roll bar, then withdraw the bolt and remove the connecting link from under the vehicle.

8.5 Renew tie-bar mounting bushes if damaged (arrowed)

7.2 Anti-roll bar connecting link (arrowed)

4 Inspect the connecting link rubber mounting bushes for signs of damage, and renew them if they are cracked, worn, split or perished. The bushes are a press fit in the connecting link; they can be removed and refitted using a vice and two suitably-sized tubular drifts, such as sockets (one which bears on the hard outer edge of the bush, and another which bears against the edge of the connecting link).

Refitting

5 Refitting is the reverse of the removal sequence, tightening both the connecting link bolts to the specified torque setting.

8 Front suspension tie-bar – removal and refitting

Removal

1 Chock the rear wheels, firmly apply the handbrake, then jack up the front of the car and support it on axle stands. Remove the appropriate front roadwheel.

2 From underneath the front of the vehicle, slacken and remove the three bolts securing the bumper flange to the body. Remove the seven bolts securing the front undercover panel to the body, and remove the panel.

3 Undo the nut securing the front of the tie-bar to the front subframe, then remove the flanged washer, noting which direction the flange is facing, and the mounting bush (photo).

4 Undo the two bolts securing the tie-bar to the lower suspension arm (photo), then remove the rod from the car, and slide the

8.6 Fit flange washer, spacer and mounting bush onto tie-bar ...

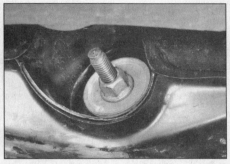

8.3 Tie-bar retaining nut is accessed from front of subframe

8.4 Tie-bar-to-lower suspension arm bolts (arrowed)

spacer, mounting bush and flanged washer off the tie-bar.

5 Examine all the components for signs of wear or damage, paying particular attention to the mounting bushes and tie-bar threads, and renew components as necessary (photo).

Refitting

6 Slide the flange washer, mounting bush and spacer onto the tie-bar threads, ensuring that the flange of the washer is facing away from the mounting bush, and that the rounded surface of the bush is facing the washer (photo).

7 Refit the tie-bar to the front subframe, and fit the second mounting bush and flanged washer. Ensure the flat surface of the mounting bush is facing the subframe, and that the flange of the washer is facing away from the mounting bush (photo), then refit the tie-bar nut, tightening it finger-tight only at this stage.

8.7 ... then refit tie-bar to subframe, and install second mounting bush and flange washer

10

8 Refit the tie-bar-to-lower suspension arm bolts, tighten them to the specified torque, then tighten the tie-bar retaining nut to the specified torque setting.
9 Refit the front undercover panel, and tighten all the panel and bumper flange bolts securely.
10 Refit the roadwheel, then lower the car to the ground and tighten the roadwheel nuts to the specified torque.

9 Front suspension lower arm – removal, overhaul and refitting

Removal

1 Chock the rear wheels, firmly apply the handbrake, then jack up the front of the car and support it on axle stands. Remove the appropriate front roadwheel.
2 Slacken and remove the bolt and washer securing the anti-roll bar connecting link to the lower suspension arm, and undo the two bolts securing the tie-bar to the lower suspension arm.
3 Extract the split pin, and undo the nut securing the lower arm balljoint to the swivel hub. Release the balljoint shank using a suitable balljoint separator tool, taking care not to damage the balljoint gaiter.
4 Undo the lower suspension arm-to-body pivot bolt, and withdraw the lower arm from the vehicle (photos).

Overhaul

Note: *The lower arm balljoint is an integral part of the lower arm assembly, and is not available separately. If renewal of the balljoint is necessary, the complete lower arm assembly must be renewed.*

5 Thoroughly clean the lower arm and the area around the arm mountings, removing all traces of dirt (and of underseal if necessary), then check carefully for cracks, distortion or any other signs of wear or damage. Check that the lower arm balljoint moves freely, without any sign of roughness, and that the balljoint gaiter shows no sign of deterioration, cracks, or splits. Examine the shank of the pivot bolt for signs of wear or scoring. Renew worn components as necessary.
6 Check the lower arm inner pivot bush; if it is

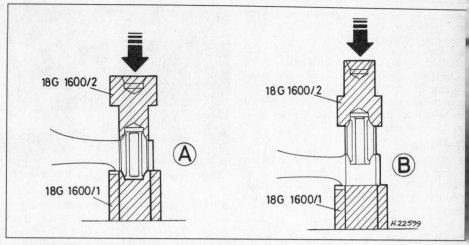

Fig. 10.10 Using special Rover mandrels to renew lower suspension arm bush (Sec 9)

A Removing old bush   B Fitting new bush

worn, cracked, split or perished, it must be renewed. The renewal of the bush is best left to a Rover dealer, as a press, a special bush removal/refitting mandrel, and a support are required (Rover Service Tool Numbers 18G 1600/2 and 18G 1600/1 respectively). While the old bush can be extracted using a strong bench vice and suitable sockets, it is unlikely that new bushes can be installed successfully without the shaped mandrel (see Fig. 10.10).

Refitting

7 Offer up the lower arm, and fit the arm-to-body pivot bolt. Tighten the bolt by hand only at this stage.
8 Insert the lower arm balljoint shank into the swivel hub, and tighten its retaining bolt to the specified torque. Secure the balljoint nut in position with a new split pin.
9 Refit the tie-bar and anti-roll bar connecting link-to-lower arm bolts, and tighten them to the specified torque.
10 Refit the roadwheel, then lower the car to the ground and tighten the roadwheel nuts to the specified torque.
11 With the car standing on its wheels, rock the suspension to settle the lower arm bush in position, then tighten the lower arm-to-body pivot bolt to the specified torque setting.

12 Check and if necessary adjust the front wheel alignment, as described in Section 27.

10 Rear hub and bearings – removal and refitting

Note: *The double-row tapered-roller type bearing is sealed, pre-adjusted and pre-lubricated, and is intended to last the car's entire service life without maintenance or attention. Never over-tighten the hub nut beyond the specified torque wrench setting, in an attempt to 'adjust' the bearings.*
Note: *The bearing is an integral part of the hub, and cannot be purchased separately. If renewal of the bearing is necessary, the complete hub assembly must be renewed as a unit. The only components which are available separately are the roadwheel studs.*

Removal

1 Chock the front wheels, then jack up the rear of the vehicle and support it on axle stands. Remove the appropriate rear roadwheel.
2 Prise out the cap from the centre of the hub assembly (photo) and, using a hammer and suitable chisel-nosed tool, tap up the staking (notch) securing the hub retaining nut to the groove in the stub axle.

9.4A Release balljoint from the swivel hub assembly ...

9.4B ... then remove pivot bolt (arrowed), and withdraw lower suspension arm

10.2 Prise off centre cap to gain access to rear hub nut

10.9A Refit the hub ...

10.9B ... and washer, ensuring its tooth engages with stub axle groove

10.11A Tighten hub retaining nut to the specified torque ...

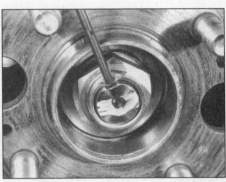

10.11B ... then stake it firmly into the stub axle groove

3 Have an assistant firmly apply the footbrake, then using a socket and extension bar, slacken, but do not remove, the hub retaining nut – *take care to ensure that the vehicle is adequately supported, as considerable force will be needed to undo the nut.*

4 Remove the brake drum or disc (as applicable), as described in the relevant Section of Chapter 9.

5 Once the brake drum/disc has been removed, remove the hub nut and toothed washer, and pull the hub assembly off the stub axle. If necessary, the hub can be drawn off the stub axle using a three-legged puller. Discard the nut once removed, as a new hub retaining nut must be obtained for reassembly.

6 Check that there is no sign of free play in the hub bearing, and that the bearing inner race rotates smoothly and easily, without any sign of roughness. If there is any sign of wear or damage to the hub assembly or bearing, the complete hub assembly must be renewed as a unit.

7 Check the condition of the roadwheel studs in the hub flange. If any are sheared off, stretched or have damaged threads, they can be pressed out of the hub, providing that its flange is fully supported. On refitting, support the hub flange, and press in the new stud until it seats fully.

Refitting

8 Prior to refitting the hub, inspect the stub axle for signs of wear or scoring and, if necessary, renew it as described in Section 11.

9 Apply a thin smear of grease to the hub bearing seal, and refit the hub assembly. Refit the toothed washer, ensuring that its tooth locates with the groove in the stub axle, and install the new hub nut (photos). Tighten the hub nut by hand only at this stage.

10 Refit the brake drum or disc (as applicable), as described in the relevant Section of Chapter 9, but do not refit the roadwheel.

11 Have an assistant firmly apply the footbrake, then tighten the hub retaining nut to the specified torque. Release the footbrake, and check that the hub rotates smoothly, then

stake the hub retaining nut fully into the stub axle groove (photos). Refit the hub centre cap.

12 Refit the roadwheel, then lower the car to the ground and tighten the roadwheel nuts to the specified torque.

13 Check and if necessary adjust the rear wheel alignment, as described in Section 27.

11 Rear stub axle – removal and refitting

Removal

1 Remove the rear hub assembly, as described in Section 10.

2 On models with rear drum brakes, remove the lower brake shoe return spring, then disconnect the handbrake cable from the trailing shoe, referring to Chapter 9, Section 13 for further information. Undo the bolts securing the handbrake cable and brake hose brackets to the trailing arm, then use a 12 mm ring spanner to compress the handbrake cable retaining clip, and withdraw the cable from the backplate. Remove the four bolts securing the backplate to the trailing arm, and carefully ease the backplate assembly outwards and off the end of the stub axle (photos). Position the backplate assembly out of the way of the stub axle, and tie it to the rear suspension unit coil spring using a piece of wire.

3 On models with rear disc brakes, undo the four disc shield retaining bolts, and remove the shield from the trailing arm.

4 On all models, using a socket and extension bar, undo the large stub axle retaining nut from the rear of the trailing arm assembly (photo).

5 Slacken and remove the four Torx bolts securing the stub axle mounting plate to the trailing arm assembly, then withdraw the stub axle and remove it from the vehicle.

6 Examine the stub axle spindle and mounting plate for signs of wear or damage, such as scoring or cracking. If damaged, the stub axle must be renewed.

11.2A On models with rear drum brakes, use a 12 mm spanner to compress handbrake cable retaining tangs

11.2B Backplate retaining bolts (arrowed) rear drum brake models

 10

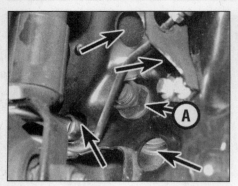

11.4 Stub axle retaining nut (A). Torx bolts are accessed via four holes (arrowed)

12.3 On 416 models, remove the luggage compartment side trim to gain access to strut upper mounting nuts

12.4 Removing rear suspension strut

Refitting

7 Refitting is a reverse of the removal sequence, bearing in mind the following points.
(a) Tighten all the nuts and bolts to the specified torque settings.
(b) Refit the hub as described in Section 10.

12 Rear suspension strut – removal and refitting

Removal

1 Chock the front wheels, then jack up the rear of the vehicle and support it on axle stands. Remove the appropriate rear roadwheel.
2 Slacken and remove both the pivot bolts securing the rear lower lateral link to the body and trailing arm. On models with anti-lock brakes (ALB), undo the bolts securing the wheel sensor wiring lead bracket to the lower arm, and release the wiring. On all models, undo the lower suspension strut mounting bolt, and remove the rear lower lateral link.
3 From inside the luggage compartment, on 216 models, prise off the trim cap to gain access to the rear suspension strut upper mounting nuts; on 416 models, remove the relevant luggage compartment side trim panel (photo).
4 Remove the rubber cover, and use chalk or a dab of paint to mark the relative positions of the suspension strut upper mounting to the body. Undo the two suspension strut upper mounting nuts (do not attempt to undo the central nut), and manoeuvre the strut out from under the wheel arch (photo), noting the seal which is fitted between the upper mounting plate and vehicle body.

Refitting

5 Prior to refitting, examine the rear lower lateral link mounting bushes as described in Section 15, and renew any which are worn or damaged.
6 Ensure the rubber seal is in position on the upper mounting plate, then refit the suspension strut, aligning the marks made on

removal (where necessary), and refit the upper mounting nuts. Tighten the nuts to the specified torque setting, then refit the rubber cover and trim cap/panel.
7 Offer up the lower lateral link, and refit the lower suspension strut mounting bolt, followed by both the lower lateral link pivot bolts. Tighten the bolts only loosely at this stage. On models with anti-lock brakes (ALB), refit the wheel sensor wiring bracket retaining bolts, and tighten them to the specified torque.
8 Refit the roadwheel, then lower the car to the ground and tighten the roadwheel nuts to the specified torque.
9 With the car standing on its wheels, rock the car to settle the disturbed components into position, then tighten the lower lateral link pivot bolts and the lower suspension strut mounting bolt to the specified torque.

13 Rear suspension strut – dismantling, inspection and reassembly

Note: Before attempting to dismantle the rear suspension strut, a suitable tool to hold the coil spring in compression must be obtained. Adjustable coil spring compressors are readily available, and are recommended for this operation. Any attempt to dismantle the strut without such a tool is likely to result in damage or personal injury.

Dismantling

1 With the strut removed from the car as described in Section 12, clean away all external dirt, then mount it upright in a vice.
2 Fit the spring compressor, and compress the coil spring until all tension is relieved from the upper mounting plate.
3 Slacken the upper mounting retaining nut, while holding the strut piston with an Allen key.
4 Remove the nut and washer, followed by the mounting plate assembly, noting the correct fitted positions of the mounting rubbers and spacer, and the upper spring rubber damper. Remove the coil spring, then lift the dust seal and cover off the damper, and slide the damper stop plate and rubber stop off the strut piston.

Inspection

5 Examine all the rear suspension strut components using the information given for the front suspension strut in Section 5.

Reassembly

6 Reassembly is a direct reversal of the dismantling sequence, ensuring that the spring ends are correctly located in the upper and lower seats, and that the upper mounting plate retaining nut is tightened to the specified torque setting.

14 Rear anti-roll bar – removal and refitting

Removal

1 Chock the front wheels, then jack up the rear of the vehicle and support it on axle stands. Remove both rear roadwheels.
2 Slacken and remove the bolt and washer which secures each anti-roll bar connecting link to each rear lower lateral link (photo).
3 Undo the bolts securing the left- and right-hand anti-roll bar mounting brackets to the vehicle underbody, then manoeuvre the anti-roll bar assembly out from under the vehicle.
4 Remove the connecting link retaining bolts, then separate the anti-roll bar and link, and withdraw the spacer and mounting bush from the anti-roll bar. The mounting bracket assemblies can also be dismantled, once their

14.2 Rear anti-roll bar connecting link (arrowed)

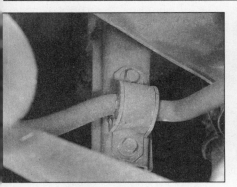

14.4 Rear anti-roll bar mounting clamp

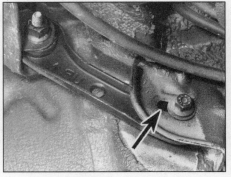

15.2 Front lateral link-to-body bolt mounting (arrowed) is slotted, for adjusting rear wheel alignment

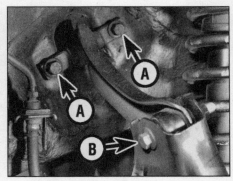

15.4 Rear upper lateral link-to-body bolts (A) and trailing arm pivot bolt (B)

clamp bolts have been undone (photo). Carefully examine the anti-roll bar components for signs of wear, damage or deterioration, paying particular attention to the mounting rubbers, and renew components as necessary.

Refitting

5 Lubricate the anti-roll bar bushes and locations with a solution of soapy water, then refit the mounting brackets and clamps. Fit the bushes to the anti-roll bar ends, then insert the spacers and refit the connecting links. Tighten the mounting clamp and connecting link bolts finger-tight only at this stage.

6 Manoeuvre the anti-roll bar assembly into position, and align the mounting brackets with their holes on the vehicle underbody. Refit the bracket bolts, and tighten them to the specified torque setting.

7 Refit the connecting link-to-rear lower lateral link bolts, then tighten both the connecting link-to-lateral link, and connecting link-to-anti-roll bar bolts to their specified torque settings.

8 Once all other bolts are correctly tightened, tighten the anti-roll bar mounting clamp bolts to their specified torque setting.

9 Refit the roadwheels, then lower the car to the ground and tighten the roadwheel nuts to the specified torque.

to the trailing arm, and remove the link from the vehicle.

Rear upper lateral link

4 Slacken and remove the pivot bolt securing the rear upper lateral link to the trailing arm assembly (photo).

5 Undo the two bolts securing the inner mounting to the vehicle body, and remove the link assembly from the car.

Rear lower lateral link

6 Slacken and remove both the pivot bolts securing the lower rear lateral link to the body and trailing arm, and the bolt securing the rear anti-roll bar to the lateral link. On models with anti-lock brakes (ALB), undo the bolts securing the wheel sensor wiring lead bracket to the lower arm, and release the wiring. On all models, undo the lower suspension mounting bolt, and remove the rear lower lateral link (photo).

Inspection

7 Examine the lateral link for signs of cracking, check the mounting bushes for signs of wear or deterioration, and renew as necessary (photo). The bushes are a press fit in the link; they can be removed and refitted using a vice and two suitably-sized tubular drifts, such as sockets (one which bears on the hard outer edge of the bush, and another

which bears against the edge of the lateral link). **Note:** *When renewing the inner bush on the rear upper lateral link, mark the position of the bush mounting plate in relation to the lateral link before removing the worn bush. Fit the new bush so that the mounting plate is in the same position in relation to the lateral link. This avoids placing any undue strain on the rubber bush when the link is refitted to the vehicle.*

8 Examine the pivot bolt shanks for signs of wear or damage such as scoring, and renew as necessary.

Refitting

9 Refitting is the reverse of the removal sequence, bearing in mind the following points.

(a) *Refit the pivot bolts, and tighten them only loosely.*

(b) *When refitting the front lateral link, align the inner pivot bolt using the marks made on dismantling.*

(c) *With the car standing on its wheels, rock the suspension to settle the all disturbed components into position, then tighten all the disturbed pivot bolts to the specified torque.*

(d) *Check and, if necessary, adjust the rear wheel alignment as described in Section 27.*

15 Rear suspension lateral links – removal, inspection and refitting

Removal

1 Chock the front wheels, then jack up the rear of the car and support it on axle stands. Remove the appropriate rear roadwheel.

Front lateral link

2 Mark the position of the lateral link-to-body pivot bolt in relation to the body – this mark can then be used as a guide on refitting (photo).

3 Slacken and remove the pivot bolts securing the front lateral link to the body and

15.6 Removing rear lower lateral link

15.7 Examine lateral link bushes for signs of wear, and renew if necessary

10

16.3 Remove retaining clip, and free the brake hose from the trailing arm

16.8 Trailing arm mounting bolts (arrowed)

17.2A Remove the horn button from the steering wheel ...

16 Rear suspension trailing arm – removal and refitting

Removal

1 Chock the front wheels, then jack up the rear of the vehicle and support it on axle stands. Remove the appropriate rear roadwheel, then follow the procedure under the relevant sub-heading.

Models with rear drum brakes
2 Remove the rear hub assembly, as described in Section 10.
3 Undo the bolts and remove the clips securing the handbrake cable and brake hose brackets to the trailing arm (photo). Remove the four bolts securing the backplate to the trailing arm, and carefully ease the backplate assembly outwards and off the end of the stub axle. Position the backplate assembly out of the way of the stub axle, and tie it to the rear suspension unit coil spring using a piece of wire.

Models with rear disc brakes
4 Remove the two brake caliper shield retaining screws, and remove the shield from the caliper.
5 Slacken and remove the bolts securing the handbrake cable and brake hose retaining clamps to the trailing arm. Undo the two bolts securing the caliper mounting bracket to the trailing arm, and slide the caliper off the disc. Tie the caliper to the rear suspension strut coil spring, to avoid placing any strain on the hydraulic hose or handbrake cable.
6 On models fitted with anti-lock brakes, remove the ALB rear wheel sensor as described Section 22 of Chapter 9.

All models
7 Slacken and remove the three pivot bolts securing the front lateral link, rear lower lateral link and rear upper lateral link to the trailing arm.
8 Remove the two bolts securing the trailing arm mounting bracket to the vehicle body, then manoeuvre the trailing arm assembly out of position and away from the vehicle (photo).
9 Inspect the trailing arm for signs of damage such as cracks, paying particular attention to

the areas around the mounting bolt holes, and examine the mounting bush for signs of damage and deterioration. If either the arm or bush show signs of wear or damage, the trailing arm and bush assembly must be renewed as a unit, since neither component is available separately.

Refitting

10 Refitting is reverse of the removal sequence, noting the following points.
(a) *Manoeuvre the trailing arm into position, and tighten its bush mounting bolts to the specified torque.*
(b) *Refit all the pivot bolts, but tighten them only loosely.*
(c) *On models with rear drum brakes, tighten the backplate retaining bolts to the specified torque, and refit the hub as described in Section 10.*
(d) *On models with rear disc brakes, tighten the brake caliper mounting bracket bolts to the specified torque, and (where necessary) refit the ALB wheel sensor, as described in Section 22 of Chapter 9.*
(e) *With the car standing on its wheels, rock the suspension to settle all the suspension components into position, then tighten all the disturbed pivot bolts to their specified torque settings.*
(f) *Check and, if necessary, adjust the rear wheel alignment as described in Section 27.*

17 Steering wheel – removal and refitting

Removal

1 Set the front wheels in the straight-ahead position. The steering wheel spokes should be horizontal.
2 Carefully prise out the horn button assembly from the centre of the steering wheel, then disconnect the wires from the horn terminals, and remove the horn button assembly (photos).
3 Using a socket, unscrew and remove the steering wheel retaining nut.
4 Mark the steering wheel and steering column shaft in relation to each other, then lift the steering wheel off the column splines. If it is tight, tap it upwards near the centre, using the palm of your hand, or twist it from side to side, pulling upwards to release it from the shaft splines.

Refitting

5 On refitting, check that the steering column splines are clean. Refit the wheel, engaging the cut-outs on its lower surface with the direction indicator cancelling cam tabs, and aligning the marks made on dismantling; this should leave the wheel positioned as described in paragraph 1 above (photos).

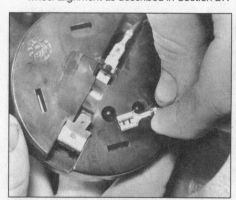

17.2B ... and disconnect the wiring from the button terminals

17.5A On refitting, ensure steering wheel cut-outs are correctly engaged with indicator cancelling cam tabs (arrowed)

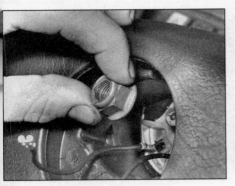

17.5B ... then refit retaining nut

18.3A Prise off the snap-ring ...

18.3B ... then undo the lower shroud retaining screws (arrowed) ...

6 Tighten the steering wheel nut to the specified torque setting, then reconnect the horn wiring to the horn terminals, and press the horn button into position in the centre of the wheel.

18 Steering column – removal and refitting

Removal

1 Insert the ignition key, and ensure the steering column is unlocked, then release the column tilt lever and position the steering wheel at the lowest possible position. Remove the steering wheel as described in Section 1 7.
2 Disconnect the battery negative terminal, then undo the five right-hand lower facia panel retaining screws, and remove the panel from the facia.
3 Prise the large snap-ring which secures the two halves of the steering column shroud together out from the top of the shrouds, and remove the ignition key. Undo the three retaining screws securing the lower shroud to the steering column, and remove both the upper and lower steering column shrouds (photos).
4 Lift the indicator self-cancelling cam off the steering column, and disconnect the wiring connectors from the rear of the steering column combination switch assembly.
5 Undo the two combination switch retaining screws, and slide the assembly off the end of the steering column (photo).

6 Trace the ignition switch wiring back to its wiring connectors, and disconnect the connectors from the main wiring loom.
7 Pull back the driver's footwell carpet and remove the two studs securing the lower steering column cover to the floor. Remove the two retaining clips from the upper end of the cover, and withdraw the cover (photos).
8 Using a hammer and punch (or white paint), mark the exact relationship between the steering column shaft and the shaft-to-steering gear universal joint, then slacken and remove the pinch-bolt securing the joint to the column shaft.
9 Undo the nut and bolt which hold the lower steering column mounting clamp in position, and remove the clamp (photo). Slacken and remove the two nuts and two bolts securing the upper mounting assembly to the vehicle, then disengage the column from its mounting studs and the universal joint, and remove it from the vehicle.

Refitting

10 Before refitting the steering column, closely examine the upper mounting assembly for signs of damage or misalignment, as described in Section 19.
11 Align the marks made on dismantling, and engage the steering column shaft splines with those of the universal joint.
12 Locate the upper mounting bracket assembly over its mounting studs, and refit the upper mounting nuts and bolts. Refit the lower

18.3C ... and remove both lower and upper shrouds

18.5 Combination switch assembly is retained by two screws (arrowed)

10

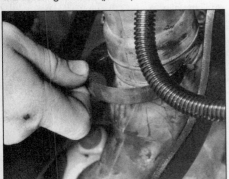

18.7A Remove the retaining clips ...

18.7B ... and withdraw the lower steering column cover

18.9 Steering column lower mounting clamp components

18.14 Ensure that the indicator self-cancelling cam is correctly engaged with the combination switch assembly

mounting clamp, tighten its retaining nut and bolt to the specified torque setting, then tighten the upper mounting nuts and bolts to their specified torque settings.

13 Refit the universal joint-to-steering column pinch-bolt, and tighten it to the specified torque. Refit the lower cover over the steering column, and secure it in position with its retaining clips and studs.

14 Refit the combination switch to the column, and tighten its screws securely. Refit the indicator self-cancelling cam to the steering column, ensuring that it is correctly located with the switch assembly (photo), and reconnect the combination and ignition switch wiring connectors. Ensure that the wiring is correctly routed and secured by the relevant clips.

15 Offer up the two halves of the steering column shroud, and refit the three retaining screws to the lower shroud. Ensure the shroud halves are clipped firmly together, then refit the snap-ring to its groove.

16 Refit the lower facia panel, tightening its retaining screws securely, then refit the steering wheel as described in Section 17.

19 Steering column – overhaul

1 With the steering column removed from the car as described in Section 18, fit the ignition key, and check that the steering lock is released. Remove the circlip from the upper end of the column shaft, and lift off the washer and spring washer.

2 Carefully withdraw the steering shaft from the lower end of the steering column, noting the inner circlip which is fitted to the shaft upper end.

3 Inspect the steering shaft for straightness, and for signs of impact and damage to the collapsible portion. Check for signs of wear (such as scoring) on the shaft bush; check the steering shaft universal joint for signs of damage, and or roughness in the joint bearings. If any damage or wear is found on the steering shaft, shaft bush or universal joint, the shaft must be renewed as an assembly.

4 Inspect the steering column for signs of

damage, and renew if necessary. Closely examine the column upper mounting and the tilt assembly for signs of damage or distortion, paying particular attention to the upper mounting lower bending plate and its spring retainer. The bending plate is designed to distort in the event of an impact hitting the steering wheel, and must be renewed, along with its spring retainer, if it is not completely straight. Renew other components as necessary.

5 If renewal of any of the upper mounting or steering column tilt assembly components is necessary, make a note of the correct fitted positions of all components before dismantling the assembly. Use this as a guide when reassembling all the components, to ensure they are correctly fitted. Ensure that the ends of the bending plate spring retainer are correctly located in the holes in the mounting bracket, and that the retainer is hooked over the claw situated in the centre of the bracket (photo).

6 Apply a smear of grease to the steering shaft and column bearing surfaces, and to the shaft bush. If a new steering shaft is being installed, transfer the inner circlip from the old shaft onto the second groove in the upper end of the new shaft.

7 Insert the steering shaft into position in the steering column, and refit the spring washer and flat washer to the upper end of the steering shaft, securing them in position with the circlip. Ensure that the circlip is correctly located in its groove, and check that the shaft rotates freely in the column. Remove the ignition key, and check that the steering lock functions correctly.

8 Before installing the column assembly, check the steering shaft-to-steering gear universal joint for signs of wear or damage, and for smoothness of operation. If there is any sign of roughness in the joint bearings, the joint must be renewed before refitting the steering column as described in Section 18.

20 Steering lock/ignition switch – removal and refitting

Removal

1 Remove the steering column from the car, as described in Section 18.

2 Securely clamp the column assembly in a vice equipped with soft jaws, *taking great care not to over-tighten the vice*, which would distort the steering column.

3 Centre-punch the two steering lock shear-bolts, then drill off the heads of the bolts. Note that new shear-bolts must be obtained for refitting.

4 Withdraw the steering lock/ignition switch, then unscrew the remains of the shear-bolts using a self-locking wrench or similar on the exposed ends.

19.5 Fitted positions of upper mounting assembly components

Refitting

5 On refitting, carefully align the assembly on the steering column, lightly tighten the bolts, and check that the steering lock works smoothly.

6 Tighten the shear-bolts evenly, until their heads shear off.

7 Refit the steering column as described in Section 18.

21 Steering gear rubber gaiters – renewal

1 Remove the track rod balljoint as described in Section 26, and unscrew the locknut from the track rod end.

2 Using a pair of pliers, release the outer steering gear gaiter retaining clip, and slide it off the track rod end. Remove the inner gaiter retaining clip by cutting it, then slide the gaiter off the end of the track rod.

3 Thoroughly clean the track rod and the steering gear housing, using fine abrasive paper to polish off any corrosion, burrs or sharp edges which might damage the new gaiter's sealing lips on installation. Repair kits which consist of new gaiters and retaining clips are available from Rover dealers.

4 Fit the new rubber gaiter, ensuring that it is correctly seated in the grooves in the steering gear housing and track rod.

5 Check that the gaiter is not twisted or dented, then secure it in position using new retaining clips.

6 Refit the locknut and balljoint onto the track rod end, as described in Section 26.

22 Steering gear – removal, overhaul and refitting

Removal

1 Chock the rear wheels, firmly apply the handbrake, then jack up the front of the car and support it on axle stands. Remove the appropriate front roadwheel.

2 Working from inside the car, peel back the driver's footwell carpet, and remove the studs securing the lower steering column cover to

22.3 Steering column universal joint pinch-bolts (arrowed)

22.8 Power steering pipes and steering gear right-hand mounting bolts (arrowed)

23.2 Undo the retaining bolt and remove the pipe clamp

the floor. Remove the two retaining clips from the upper end of the cover, and withdraw the cover.

3 Mark the relative positions of the steering gear pinion and joint to use as a guide on refitting, then slacken and remove the two universal joint pinchbolts (photo). Slide the universal joint up the steering column shaft splines until it is free from the steering gear pinion.

4 Extract the split pins, and undo the nuts securing the steering gear track rod balljoints to the swivel hubs. Release the balljoint shanks using a suitable balljoint separator tool, taking care not to damage the balljoint gaiters.

5 On all models, undo the two nuts securing the exhaust front pipe to the intermediate pipe, and remove the two bolts and springs. Separate the exhaust joint, and recover the sealing ring (gasket). Free the intermediate pipe from its mounting rubbers, and lower the exhaust system.

6 On manual gearbox models, slide the gearbox selector shaft gaiter towards the gearbox, then remove the roll pin retaining clip from the gearbox end of the gearchange selector rod. Using a hammer and suitable punch, tap the roll pin out of the selector rod, and disconnect the rod from the gearbox. Slacken and remove the bolt securing the gearchange steady-rod to the gearbox, and free the rod from its mounting bracket.

7 On automatic transmission models, undo the bolt which secures the selector cable retaining clamp to the transmission, and remove the clamp. Undo the bolt securing the selector cable mounting bracket to the subframe, then pull the cable fully rearwards to increase steering gear removal clearance.

8 On models with power steering, from underneath the car, undo the three steering rack cover retaining bolts, and remove the cover. Also slacken and remove the bolt securing the power steering hydraulic pipes to the subframe. Mark the pipe union nuts to ensure they are correctly positioned on reassembly, then unscrew the pipe-to-steering gear union nuts (photo). Be prepared for fluid spillage, and position a suitable container beneath the pipes while unscrewing the union

nuts. This fluid must be disposed of, and new fluid of the specified type used when refilling. Plug the pipe ends and steering gear orifices, to prevent excessive fluid leakage and the entry of dirt into the hydraulic system.

9 On all models, fully extend the left-hand track rod, then undo the two left-hand steering gear mounting bolts and remove the mounting bracket. Undo the two right-hand mounting bolts, noting the mounting bushes and spacers, and free the steering gear pinion from its cut-out.

10 Initially move the steering gear to the left, to free the right-hand track rod from the subframe, then manoeuvre the assembly out from the right hand side of the vehicle. Remove the washers from the steering gear pinion.

Overhaul

11 Examine the steering gear assembly for signs of wear or damage, and check that the rack moves freely throughout the full length of its travel, with no signs of roughness or excessive free play between the steering gear pinion and rack. The steering gear is available only as a complete assembly, with no individual components (apart from the track rod balljoints and rubber gaiters) being available separately. Therefore, if worn, the complete assembly must be renewed. Track rod balljoint and rubber gaiter renewal are covered in Sections 21 and 26 of this Chapter.

12 Inspect the steering gear mounting bushes for signs of damage or deterioration, and renew as necessary.

Refitting

13 Refit the washers to the pinion and, with the left-hand track rod fully extended, manoeuvre the steering gear into position from the right-hand side of the vehicle. Once both the track rods are in located in the subframe cut-outs, refit the mounting clamp and bolts, ensuring that the mounting bushes and spacers are correctly positioned, and tighten the mounting bolts to the specified torque.

14 Centralise the steering gear rack so that both track rods are protruding by an equal distance.

15 On models equipped with power steering,

wipe clean the feed and return pipe unions, then refit them to their respective positions on the steering gear, and tighten the union nuts to the specified torque. Refit the bolt securing the pipe retaining bracket to the subframe, and tighten it securely. Install the steering gear cover, and tighten its retaining bolts securely.

16 The remainder of the refitting procedure is a direct reversal of removal, noting the following points.

(a) Tighten all nuts and bolts to their specified torque settings.

(b) Secure the track rod balljoint retaining nuts in position with new split pins.

(c) When refitting the universal joint to the steering gear pinion splines, ensure that the front wheels are pointing in the straight-ahead direction, then, if necessary, align the marks made on dismantling and check that the steering wheel spokes are horizontal.

(d) On completion, check and if necessary adjust the front wheel alignment, as described in Section 27.

(e) On models equipped with power steering, bleed the hydraulic system as described in Section 25.

23 Power steering pump – removal and refitting

Removal

1 Remove the power steering pump drivebelt as described in Chapter 1.

2 Undo the inlet hose and outlet pipe clamp retaining bolts, and remove the clamp (photo).

3 On DOHC engines equipped with air conditioning, undo the bolt securing the air conditioning hose retaining clamp to the pump mounting bracket, and remove the clamp. Fully unscrew and remove the pump adjuster bolt from the top of the pump mounting bracket (photo) .

4 On all engines, position a suitable container beneath the power steering pump to catch any spilt fluid, then release the inlet hose retaining clip, and disconnect the hose from the top of the steering pump. Unscrew the outlet pipe union nut, and disconnect the pipe from the

10

23.3 On DOHC engines, slacken and remove the pump adjuster bolt

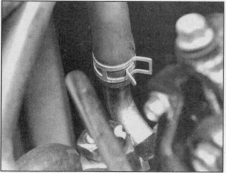

23.4A Release the retaining clip, and disconnect the inlet hose from the power steering pump ...

23.4B ... then slacken the outlet pipe union nut, and disconnect the pipe (DOHC engine shown)

pump, noting the O-ring which is fitted to the pipe union (photos). Plug the hose, the pipe ends and the pump unions, to prevent excessive fluid loss and the possible entry of dirt into the system.
5 Slacken and remove the nuts and bolts securing the power steering pump to its mounting bracket, and remove the pump from the engine.
6 The power steering pump is a sealed unit, and cannot be repaired. If faulty the pump assembly must be renewed. If a new pump is to be installed, it will be necessary to remove the pulley and transfer it to the new pump as follows.
7 Make an identification mark on the front face of the pulley, then prise out the rubber plug from the centre of the pump spindle. Slacken and remove the pulley retaining bolts, while preventing the pulley from rotating by retaining the pump spindle with a suitable Allen key (photo). Remove the pulley from the old pump and transfer it to the new one, using the mark made prior to removal to ensure that it is installed the correct way around. Tighten the pulley retaining bolts to the specified torque, again retaining the pump spindle with the Allen key, and refit the rubber plug.

Refitting

8 Refitting is a reverse of the removal procedure, noting the following points.
(a) *Tighten the pump mounting bolts to the specified torque.*

23.7 Retain the pump spindle with an Allen key while slackening or tightening the pulley retaining bolts

(b) *Fit a new O-ring to the pump outlet pipe union, and tighten the union nut to the specified torque.*
(c) *Refit and adjust the drivebelt as described in Chapter 1, and on completion, bleed the hydraulic system as described in Section 25.*

24 Power steering fluid cooler – removal and refitting

Removal

1 Remove the front bumper, as described in Chapter 11.
2 On models equipped with air conditioning, release the air conditioning pipes from their retaining bracket on the left-hand end of the cylinder head.
3 Release the power steering fluid reservoir from its mounting bracket, and position it clear of the working area.
4 Position a suitable container beneath the power steering fluid cooler hose connections to catch any spilt fluid, then slacken the hose retaining clips and disconnect both hoses. Plug the hose and fluid cooler ends, to prevent excessive fluid loss and the possible entry of dirt into the system.
5 Undo the three fluid cooler mounting bracket retaining bolts, and manoeuvre the fluid cooler assembly out of the front of the body.

26.4 Using a universal balljoint separator to free track rod balljoint from swivel hub

Refitting

6 Refitting is the reverse of the removal sequence, tightening the fluid cooler mounting bolts to the specified torque. On completion, bleed the hydraulic system as described in Section 25.

25 Power steering system – bleeding

Note: *Avoid holding the steering at full lock for long periods of time. Failure to do so could lead to overheating of, and possible damage to, the power steering pump and steering gear.*
1 Remove the cap from the power steering fluid reservoir, and fill the reservoir with the specified fluid.
2 Disconnect the distributor wiring at the block connector (to prevent the engine from starting), then turn the engine over for approximately 5 seconds to prime the power steering pump.
3 Reconnect the distributor wiring, then check the reservoir fluid level is between the MAX and MIN level markings on the side of the reservoir, and top-up if necessary.
4 Start the engine, and allow it to idle for approximately 30 seconds with the front wheels pointing in the straight-ahead position. After 30 seconds, turn the steering onto full lock in one direction, hold it there for a few seconds, then turn it onto full lock in the opposite direction and hold it there for a few seconds. Return the front wheels to the straight-ahead position. Repeat this procedure until air bubbles cease to appear in the fluid reservoir.
5 If when turning the steering, an abnormal noise is heard from the fluid lines, it indicates that there is still air in the system. Check this by turning the wheels to the straight-ahead position and switching off the engine. If the fluid level in the reservoir rises, then air is present in the system, and further bleeding is necessary.
6 Once all traces of air have been removed from the power steering hydraulic system, turn the engine off and allow the system to cool. Once cool, check that the fluid level is up to the MAX mark on the power steering fluid reservoir, and top-up if necessary.

26.9 Secure balljoint retaining nut in position with a new split pin

26 Track rod balljoint – removal and refitting

Removal

1 Apply the handbrake, then jack up the front of the vehicle and support it on axle stands. Remove the appropriate front roadwheel.

2 If the balljoint is to be re-used, use a straight-edge and a scriber, or similar, to mark its relationship to the track rod.

3 Holding the balljoint, unscrew its locknut by one quarter of a turn.

4 Extract the split pin, and undo the nut securing the steering gear track rod balljoint to the swivel hub. Release the balljoint shank using a suitable balljoint separator tool, taking care not to damage the balljoint gaiter (photo).

5 Counting the exact number of turns necessary to do so, unscrew the balljoint from the track rod. If the locknut is to be removed, mark its position on the track rod and count the number of turns required to remove it, so that it can be returned to exactly its original position on reassembly.

6 Carefully clean the balljoint and the threads. Renew the balljoint if its movement is sloppy or too stiff, if it is excessively worn, or if it is damaged in any way; carefully check the stud taper and threads. No leakage of grease should be visible.

Refitting

7 If necessary, screw the locknut onto the track rod by the number of turns noted on removal. This should align the locknut with the mark made on dismantling.

8 Screw the balljoint onto the track rod by the number of turns noted on removal. This should bring the balljoint to within a quarter of a turn from the locknut, with the alignment marks that were made on removal (if applicable) lined up.

9 Refit the balljoint shank to the swivel hub, and tighten its retaining nut to the specified torque setting. Use a new split pin to secure the retaining nut in position (photo).

10 Refit the roadwheel, then lower the car to the ground and tighten the roadwheel nuts to the specified torque setting.

11 Check and if necessary adjust the front wheel alignment, as described in Section 27.

27 Wheel alignment and steering angles – general information

Wheel alignment and steering angles – general

1 A car's steering and suspension geometry is defined in five basic settings – all angles are expressed in degrees, and the steering axis is defined as an imaginary line drawn through the centres of the front suspension upper and lower balljoints, extended where necessary to contact the ground.

2 Camber is the angle between each roadwheel and a vertical line drawn through its centre and tyre contact patch, when viewed from the front or rear of the car. 'Positive' camber is when the roadwheels are tilted outwards from the vertical at the top; 'negative' camber is when they are tilted inwards.

3 Camber is not adjustable on the Rover, and figures are given for reference only; while it can be checked using a camber checking gauge, if the figure obtained is significantly different from that specified, the car must be taken for careful checking by a professional, as the fault can only be caused by wear or damage to the body or suspension components.

4 Castor is the angle between the steering axis and a vertical line drawn through each roadwheel's centre and tyre contact patch, when viewed from the side of the car. 'Positive' castor is when the steering axis is tilted so that it contacts the ground ahead of the vertical; 'negative' castor is when it contacts the ground behind the vertical.

5 Castor is not adjustable, and is given for reference only; while it can be checked using a castor checking gauge, if the figure obtained is significantly different from that specified, the car must be taken for careful checking by a professional, as the fault can only be caused by wear or damage to the body or suspension components.

6 Steering axis inclination/SAI – also known as **kingpin inclination/KPI** – is the angle between the steering axis and a vertical line drawn through each roadwheel's centre and tyre contact patch, when viewed from the front or rear of the car.

7 SAI/KPI is not adjustable, and is given for reference only.

8 Toe is the difference, viewed from above, between lines drawn through the roadwheel centres and the car's centre-line. 'Toe-in' is when the roadwheels point inwards, towards each other at the front, while 'toe-out' is when they splay outwards from each other at the front.

9 At the front, the toe setting is adjusted by screwing the track rods in or out of their balljoints, to alter the effective length of the track rod assemblies.

10 At the rear, the toe setting is adjusted by slackening the front lateral link-to-body pivot bolt, repositioning the bolt in its mounting slot, and therefore altering the position of the trailing arm assembly.

11 Toe-out on turns – also known as 'turning angles' or 'Ackermann angles' – is the difference, viewed from above, between the angles of rotation of the inside and outside front roadwheels when they have been turned through a given angle.

12 Toe-out on turns is set in production, and is not adjustable as such, but can be upset by altering the length of the track rods unequally. It is essential, therefore, to ensure that the track rod lengths are exactly the same, and that they are turned by the same amount whenever the toe setting is altered.

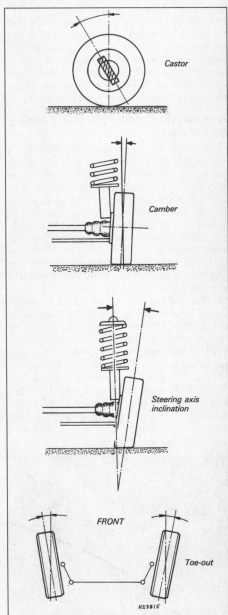

Fig. 10.11 Wheel alignment and steering angles (Sec 27)

10

Checking – general

13 Due to the special measuring equipment necessary to check the wheel alignment, and the skill required to use it properly, the checking and adjustment of these settings is best left to a Rover dealer or similar expert; note that most tyre-fitting shops now possess sophisticated checking equipment.

14 For **accurate** checking, the car **must** be at the kerb weight specified in 'General dimensions and weights'.

15 Before starting work, always check first that the tyre sizes and types are as specified, then check the pressures and tread wear, the roadwheel run-out, the condition of the hub bearings, the steering wheel free play, and the condition of the front suspension components (Chapter 1). Correct any faults found.

16 Park the car on level ground, check that the front roadwheels are in the straight-ahead position, then rock the rear and front ends to settle the suspension. Release the handbrake, and roll the car backwards 1 metre, then forwards again to relieve any stresses in the steering and suspension components.

Toe-out on turns – checking and adjusting

17 As far as the home mechanic is concerned, this can only be checked using a pair of scuff plates. Using this method, the roadwheels are rolled across a movable plate which records any deviation (or scuff) of the tyre relative to the straight-ahead position as it moves across the plate. While such gauges are available in relatively inexpensive form from accessory outlets, only an individual owner can decide whether the expense is justified, in view of the small amount of use such equipment would normally receive.

18 Prepare the car as described in paragraphs 14 to 16 above. Roll the car backwards, check that the front roadwheels are in the straight-ahead position, then roll it forwards on to the scuff plates until each front roadwheel is seated squarely on the centre of each plate.

19 Turn the steering wheel first one way until the outside roadwheel is at the specified angle; record the angle of the inside roadwheel. Next turn the steering wheel back through the straight-ahead position, and repeat the check on that side.

20 If, in either check, the inside roadwheel is not at the angle specified, check that both track rod assemblies are exactly the same length by counting the exposed threads inboard of the locknuts. If the lengths are different, this can be corrected by screwing the track rods in or out of the balljoints, but this will affect the toe setting (see below) and the steering wheel position.

21 If the angles are incorrect, but the track rods are the same length and the steering mechanism components are known from the preliminary checks to be unworn, then there is damage to, or distortion of, part of the steering mechanism, the front suspension or the body itself. This will require careful checking, preferably by an expert such as a Rover dealer, as soon as possible.

Toe setting – checking and adjusting

22 For the home mechanic, the toe setting can only be checked using a pair of scuff plates (refer to paragraph 17 above).

Front wheel toe setting

23 Prepare the car as described in paragraphs 14 to 16 above.

24 Roll the car backwards, check that the roadwheels are in the straight-ahead position, then roll it across the scuff plates so that each front roadwheel passes squarely over the centre of its respective plate. Note the angle recorded by the scuff plates.

25 To ensure accuracy, repeat the check three times, and take the average reading.

26 If the roadwheels are running parallel, there will of course be no angle recorded; if a deviation value is shown on the scuff plates, compare the reading obtained for each wheel with that specified. If the value recorded is outside the set tolerance, the toe setting is incorrect, and must be adjusted.

27 If adjustment is required, apply the handbrake, then jack up the front of the car and support it securely on axle stands. First clean the track rod threads; if they are corroded, apply penetrating fluid before starting adjustment. Release the rubber gaiter outboard clips, then peel back the gaiters, and apply a smear of grease so that both gaiters are free, and will not be twisted or strained as their respective track rods are rotated.

28 Use a straight-edge and a scriber or similar to mark the relationship of each track rod to its balljoint, then, holding each balljoint in turn, unscrew its locknut fully (photo).

29 Alter the length of both track rods (by exactly the same amount) by screwing them into or out of the balljoints one-quarter of a turn at a time, rechecking the toe setting until it is correct; shortening the track rods (screwing them into their balljoints) will reduce toe-in/increase toe-out. If the track rods are not provided with squared sections that permit the use of a spanner, they must be rotated using a self-locking wrench.

30 To ensure that the track rod lengths remain equal, always rotate them in the same direction (viewed from the centre of the car).

31 When the setting is correct, hold the balljoints and tighten the locknuts securely. Check that the balljoints are seated correctly in their sockets, and count the exposed threads to check the length of both track rods. If they are not the same, then the adjustment has not been made equally, and problems will be encountered with tyre scrubbing in turns; also, the steering wheel spokes will no longer be horizontal when the wheels are in the straight-ahead position.

32 If the track rod lengths are the same, check that the toe setting has been correctly adjusted by lowering the car to the ground and preparing it (paragraph 16 above), then re-check the toe setting (paragraphs 24 to 26); re-adjust if necessary. If the setting is correct, tighten the track rod locknuts to the specified torque. Ensure that the rubber gaiters are seated correctly, and are not twisted or strained, then refit their clips to secure their outboard ends.

Rear wheel toe setting

33 The procedure for checking the rear toe setting is the same as described for the front wheels in paragraphs 23 to 26, except that the rear wheels rather than the front wheels are rolled across the scuff plates.

34 If adjustment is necessary, chock the rear wheels, then jack up the rear of the car and support it on axle stands.

35 Mark the relative position of the front lateral link-to-body pivot bolt to use as a reference. Slacken the bolt, then, using a suitable piece of wood, lever the front of the trailing arm assembly to either move the lateral link pivot bolt inwards (to increase toe-in) or outwards (to decrease toe-in) (photo). As an approximate guide, the distance the pivot bolt should be moved is equal to the distance that the wheel is out of alignment. Note also that both bolts should be positioned at approximately the same place in their respective slot as the opposite lateral link pivot bolt. Once both right- and left-hand front lateral link pivot bolts are positioned correctly, tighten them to the specified torque setting.

36 Recheck that the toe setting has been correctly adjusted, by lowering the car to the ground and preparing it (paragraph 16 above), then recheck the toe setting (paragraphs 24 to 26).

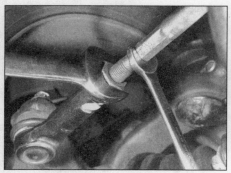

27.28 Adjusting front wheel alignment

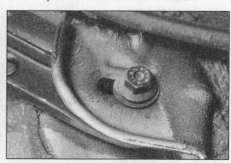

27.35 Rear wheel alignment is adjusted by repositioning front lateral link-to-body pivot bolt in its slot

Chapter 11 Bodywork and fittings

Contents

Degrees of difficulty

Easy, suitable for novice with little experience	Fairly easy, suitable for beginner with some experience	Fairly difficult, suitable for competent DIY mechanic	Difficult, suitable for experienced DIY mechanic	Very difficult, suitable for expert DIY or professional 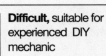

Specifications

Torque wrench settings	Nm	lbf ft
Front bumper mounting bolts	10	7
Rear bumper:		
Mounting nuts	22	16
Mounting bolt	10	7
Bonnet hinge bolts	10	7
Bonnet lock retaining bolts	10	7
Bonnet release lever mounting bolts	10	7
Wheel arch liner screws	10	7
Door glass regulator and top slide bolts	6	4
Door glass-to-regulator bolts	6	4
Door glass channel nut and bolt	6	4
Door hinge bolts	24	18
Boot lid hinge bolts	10	7
Boot lid lock retaining bolts	10	7
Boot lid lock cylinder retaining bolt	10	7
Tailgate hinge nuts and bolts	10	7
Front seat slide mounting bolts	45	33
Rear seat hinge bolts – 216 models	25	18
Rear seat back bolts – 416 models	10	7
Seat belt fasteners:		
Mounting bolts – front and rear	32	24
Front belt upper mounting nut	25	18
Inertia reel upper mounting bolt	9	7
Inertia reel lower mounting bolt	32	24
Rear side belt guide retaining bolts	32	24
Facia mounting bolts	9	7

11

1 General information

The bodyshell is made of pressed-steel sections, in three- and five-door Hatchback (216 models), and four-door Saloon (416 models) versions. Most components are welded together, but some use is made of structural adhesives; the front wings are bolted on.

The bonnet, door, tailgate and some other vulnerable panels are made of zinc-coated metal, once assembled, the entire body is given an eight-stage pre-treatment process (including a high-pressure wash) before painting. The first coat of primer is applied by cathodic electro-deposition, followed by four coats of paint and two of lacquer; an anti-stone-chip coating (finished in matt black, where exposed) is applied to the outer faces of the sills, and to the corresponding surfaces of the front and rear wings. A PVC coating is applied to the underbody followed by a coating of protective wax; all chassis members. box sections and sills are injected with liquid cavity wax.

Several of the body cavities are then filled with 'expand-in-place' foam. This process features a two-part liquid silicon foam and hardener mix, which is injected into the cavities after the body has been painted and wax-treated. The foam improves the noise insulation of the vehicle and it is also flame-retardant. On top of this, the foam is also hydrophobic (repels water).

Extensive use is made of plastic materials, mainly on the interior, but also in exterior components such as the wheel arch liners, which are fitted to improve the body's resistance to corrosion.

2 Maintenance – bodywork and underframe

The general condition of a vehicle's bodywork is the one thing that significantly affects its value. Maintenance is easy, but needs to be regular. Neglect, particularly after minor damage, can lead quickly to further deterioration and costly repair bills. It is important also to keep watch on those parts of the vehicle not immediately visible, for instance the underside, inside all the wheel arches, and the lower part of the engine compartment.

The basic maintenance routine for the bodywork is washing – preferably with a lot of water, from a hose. This will remove all the loose solids which may have stuck to the vehicle. It is important to flush these off in such a way as to prevent grit from scratching the finish. The wheel arches and underframe need washing in the same way, to remove any accumulated mud, which will retain moisture and tend to encourage rust. Paradoxically enough, the best time to clean the underframe and wheel arches is in wet weather, when the mud is thoroughly wet and soft. In very wet weather, the underframe is usually cleaned of large accumulations automatically, and this is a good time for inspection.

Periodically, except on vehicles with a wax-based underbody protective coating, it is a good idea to have the whole of the underframe of the vehicle steam-cleaned, engine compartment included, so that a thorough inspection can be carried out to see what minor repairs and renovations are necessary. Steam-cleaning is available at many garages, and is necessary for the removal of the accumulation of oily grime, which sometimes is allowed to become thick in certain areas. If steam-cleaning facilities are not available, there are some excellent grease solvents available which can be brush-applied; the dirt can then be simply hosed off. Note that these methods should not be used on vehicles with wax-based underbody protective coating, or the coating will be removed. Such vehicles should be inspected annually, preferably just prior to Winter, when the underbody should be washed down, and any damage to the wax coating repaired. Ideally, a completely fresh coat should be applied. It would also be worth considering the use of such wax-based protection for injection into door panels, sills, box sections, etc, as an additional safeguard against rust damage, where such protection is not provided by the vehicle manufacturer.

After washing paintwork, wipe off with a chamois leather to give an unspotted clear finish. A coat of clear protective wax polish will give added protection against chemical pollutants in the air. If the paintwork sheen has dulled or oxidised, use a cleaner/polisher combination to restore the brilliance of the shine. This requires a little effort, but such dulling is usually caused because regular washing has been neglected. Care needs to be taken with metallic paintwork, as special non-abrasive cleaner/polisher is required to avoid damage to the finish. Always check that the door and ventilator opening drain holes and pipes are completely clear, so that water can be drained out. Bright work should be treated in the same way as paintwork. Windscreens and windows can be kept clear of the smeary film which often appears, by the use of proprietary glass cleaner. Never use any form of wax or other body or chromium polish on glass.

3 Maintenance – upholstery and carpets

Mats and carpets should be brushed or vacuum-cleaned regularly, to keep them free of grit. If they are badly stained, remove them from the vehicle for scrubbing or sponging, and make quite sure they are dry before refitting. Seats and interior trim panels can be kept clean by wiping with a damp cloth. If they do become stained (which can be more apparent on light-coloured upholstery), use a little liquid detergent and a soft nail brush to scour the grime out of the grain of the material. Do not forget to keep the headlining clean in the same way as the upholstery. When using liquid cleaners inside the vehicle, do not over-wet the surfaces being cleaned. Excessive damp could get into the seams and padded interior, causing stains, offensive odours or even rot.

> **HAYNES HiNT** *If the inside of the vehicle gets wet accidentally, it is worthwhile taking some trouble to dry it out properly, particularly where carpets are involved. Do not leave oil or electric heaters inside the vehicle for this purpose.*

4 Minor body damage – repair

Note: *For more detailed information about bodywork repair, Haynes Publishing produce a book by Lindsay Porter called 'The Car Bodywork Repair Manual'. This incorporates information on such aspects as rust treatment, painting and glass-fibre repairs, as well as details on more ambitious repairs involving welding and panel beating.*

Repairs of minor scratches in bodywork

If the scratch is very superficial, and does not penetrate to the metal of the bodywork, repair is very simple. Lightly rub the area of the scratch with a paintwork renovator, or a very fine cutting paste, to remove loose paint from the scratch, and to clear the surrounding bodywork of wax polish. Rinse the area with clean water.

Apply touch-up paint to the scratch using a fine paint brush; continue to apply fine layers of paint until the surface of the paint in the scratch is level with the surrounding paintwork. Allow the new paint at least two weeks to harden, then blend it into the surrounding paintwork by rubbing the scratch area with a paintwork renovator or a very fine cutting paste. Finally, apply wax polish.

Where the scratch has penetrated right through to the metal of the bodywork, causing the metal to rust, a different repair technique is required. Remove any loose rust from the bottom of the scratch with a penknife, then apply rust-inhibiting paint to prevent the formation of rust in the future. Using a rubber or nylon applicator, fill the scratch with bodystopper paste. If required, this paste can be mixed with cellulose thinners to provide a very thin paste which is ideal for filling narrow scratches. Before the stopper-paste in the scratch hardens, wrap a piece of smooth cotton rag around the top of a finger. Dip the finger in cellulose thinners, and quickly sweep it across the surface of the stopper-paste in the scratch; this will ensure that the surface of the stopper-paste is slightly hollowed. The scratch can now be painted over as described earlier in this Section.

Repairs of dents in bodywork

When deep denting of the vehicle's bodywork has taken place, the first task is to pull the dent out, until the affected bodywork almost attains its original shape. There is little point in trying to restore the original shape completely, as the metal in the damaged area will have stretched on impact, and cannot be reshaped fully to its original contour. It is better to bring the level of the dent up to a point which is about 3 mm below the level of the surrounding bodywork. In cases where the dent is very shallow anyway, it is not worth trying to pull it out at all. If the underside of the dent is accessible, it can be hammered out gently from behind, using a mallet with a wooden or plastic head. Whilst doing this, hold a suitable block of wood firmly against the outside of the panel, to absorb the impact from the hammer blows and thus prevent a large area of the bodywork from being 'belled-out'.

Should the dent be in a section of the bodywork which has a double skin, or some other factor making it inaccessible from behind, a different technique is called for. Drill several small holes through the metal inside the area – particularly in the deeper section. Then screw long self-tapping screws into the holes, just sufficiently for them to gain a good purchase in the metal. Now the dent can be pulled out by pulling on the protruding heads of the screws with a pair of pliers.

The next stage of the repair is the removal of the paint from the damaged area, and from an inch or so of the surrounding 'sound' bodywork. This is accomplished most easily by using a wire brush or abrasive pad on a power drill, although it can be done just as effectively by hand, using sheets of abrasive paper. To complete the preparation for filling, score the surface of the bare metal with a screwdriver or the tang of a file, or alternatively, drill small holes in the affected area. This will provide a really good 'key' for the filler paste.

To complete the repair, see the Section on filling and respraying.

Repairs of rust holes or gashes in bodywork

Remove all paint from the affected area, and from an inch or so of the surrounding 'sound' bodywork, using an abrasive pad or a wire brush on a power drill. If these are not available, a few sheets of abrasive paper will do the job most effectively. With the paint removed, you will be able to judge the severity of the corrosion, and therefore decide whether to renew the whole panel (if this is possible) or to repair the affected area. New body panels are not as expensive as most people think, and it is often quicker and more satisfactory to

fit a new panel than to attempt to repair large areas of corrosion.

Remove all fittings from the affected area, except those which will act as a guide to the original shape of the damaged bodywork (eg headlight shells etc). Then, using tin snips or a hacksaw blade, remove all loose metal and any other metal badly affected by corrosion. Hammer the edges of the hole inwards, in order to create a slight depression for the filler paste.

Wire-brush the affected area to remove the powdery rust from the surface of the remaining metal. Paint the affected area with rust-inhibiting paint, if the back of the rusted area is accessible, treat this also.

Before filling can take place, it will be necessary to block the hole in some way. This can be achieved by the use of aluminium or plastic mesh, or aluminium tape.

Aluminium or plastic mesh, or glass-fibre matting, is probably the best material to use for a large hole. Cut a piece to the approximate size and shape of the hole to be filled, then position it in the hole so that its edges are below the level of the surrounding bodywork. It can be retained in position by several blobs of filler paste around its periphery.

Aluminium tape should be used for small or very narrow holes. Pull a piece off the roll, trim it to the approximate size and shape required, then pull off the backing paper (if used) and stick the tape over the hole; it can be overlapped if the thickness of one piece is insufficient. Burnish down the edges of the tape with the handle of a screwdriver or similar, to ensure that the tape is securely attached to the metal underneath.

Bodywork repairs – filling and respraying

Before using this Section, see the Sections on dent, deep scratch, rust holes and gash repairs.

Many types of bodyfiller are available, but generally speaking, those proprietary kits which contain a tin of filler paste and a tube of resin hardener are best for this type of repair. A wide, flexible plastic or nylon applicator will be found invaluable for imparting a smooth and well-contoured finish to the surface of the filler.

Mix up a little filler on a clean piece of card or board – measure the hardener carefully (follow the maker's instructions on the pack), otherwise the filler will set too rapidly or too slowly. Using the applicator, apply the filler paste to the prepared area; draw the applicator across the surface of the filler to achieve the correct contour and to level the surface. As soon as a contour that approximates to the correct one is achieved, stop working the paste – if you carry on too long, the paste will become sticky and begin to 'pick-up' on the applicator. Continue to add thin layers of filler paste at 20-minute intervals, until the level of the filler is just proud of the surrounding bodywork.

Once the filler has hardened, the excess can be removed using a metal plane or file. From then on, progressively-finer grades of abrasive paper should be used, starting with a 40-grade production paper, and finishing with a 400-grade wet-and-dry paper. Always wrap the abrasive paper around a flat rubber, cork, or wooden block – otherwise the surface of the filler will not be completely flat. During the smoothing of the filler surface, the wet-and-dry paper should be periodically rinsed in water. This will ensure that a very smooth finish is imparted to the filler at the final stage.

At this stage, the 'dent' should be surrounded by a ring of bare metal, which in turn should be encircled by the finely 'feathered' edge of the good paintwork. Rinse the repair area with clean water, until all of the dust produced by the rubbing-down operation has gone.

Spray the whole area with a light coat of primer – this will show up any imperfections in the surface of the filler. Repair these imperfections with fresh filler paste or bodystopper, and once more smooth the surface with abrasive paper.

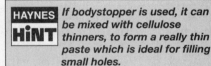

HAYNES HiNT *If bodystopper is used, it can be mixed with cellulose thinners, to form a really thin paste which is ideal for filling small holes.*

Repeat this spray-and-repair procedure until you are satisfied that the surface of the filler, and the feathered edge of the paintwork, are perfect. Clean the repair area with clean water, and allow to dry fully.

The repair area is now ready for final spraying. Paint spraying must be carried out in a warm, dry, windless and dust-free atmosphere. This condition can be created artificially if you have access to a large indoor working area, but if you are forced to work in the open, you will have to pick your day very carefully. If you are working indoors, dousing the floor in the work area with water will help to settle the dust which would otherwise be in the atmosphere. If the repair area is confined to one body panel, mask off the surrounding panels; this will help to minimise the effects of a slight mis-match in paint colours. Bodywork fittings (eg chrome strips, door handles etc) will also need to be masked off. Use genuine masking tape, and several thicknesses of newspaper, for the masking operations.

Before commencing to spray, agitate the aerosol can thoroughly, then spray a test area (an old tin, or similar) until the technique is mastered. Cover the repair area with a thick coat of primer; the thickness should be built up using several thin layers of paint, rather than one thick one. Using 400-grade wet-and-dry paper, rub down the surface of the primer until it is really smooth. While doing this, the work area should be thoroughly doused with

11

6.4 Front bumper mounting plate-to-bracket bolts

7.8 Remove rubber grommet to gain access to bumper mounting nut

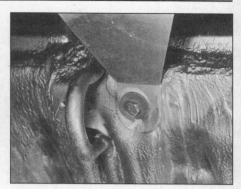

7.9 Rear bumper centre mounting bracket-to-body bolt – 416 models

water, and the wet-and-dry paper periodically rinsed in water. Allow to dry before spraying on more paint.

Spray on the top coat, again building up the thickness by using several thin layers of paint. Start spraying at one edge of the repair area, and then, using a side-to-side motion, work until the whole repair area and about 2 inches of the surrounding original paintwork is covered. Remove all masking material 10 to 15 minutes after spraying on the final coat of paint.

Allow the new paint at least two weeks to harden, then, using a paintwork renovator, or a very fine cutting paste, blend the edges of the paint into the existing paintwork. Finally, apply wax polish.

Plastic components

With the use of more and more plastic body components by the vehicle manufacturers (eg bumpers, spoilers, and in some cases, major body panels), rectification of more serious damage to such items has become a matter of either entrusting repair work to a specialist in this field, or renewing complete components. Repair of such damage by the DIY owner is not really feasible, owing to the cost of the equipment and materials required for effecting such repairs. The basic technique involves making a groove along the line of the crack in the plastic, using a rotary burr in a power drill. The damaged part is then welded back together, using a hot-air gun to heat up and fuse a plastic filler rod into the groove. Any excess plastic is then removed, and the area rubbed down to a smooth finish. It is important that a filler rod of the correct plastic is used, as body components can be made of a variety of different types (eg polycarbonate, ABS, polypropylene).

Damage of a less serious nature (abrasions, minor cracks etc) can be repaired by the DIY owner using a two-part epoxy filler repair material. Once mixed in equal proportions, this is used in similar fashion to the bodywork filler used on metal panels. The filler is usually cured in twenty to thirty minutes, ready for sanding and painting.

If the owner is renewing a complete component himself, or if he has repaired it with epoxy filler, he will be left with the problem of

finding a suitable paint for finishing which is compatible with the type of plastic used. At one time, the use of a universal paint was not possible, owing to the complex range of plastics encountered in body component applications. Standard paints, generally speaking, will not bond to plastic or rubber satisfactorily. However, it is now possible to obtain a plastic body parts finishing kit which consists of a pre-primer treatment, a primer and coloured top coat. Full instructions are normally supplied with a kit, but basically, the method of use is to first apply the pre-primer to the component concerned, and allow it to dry for up to 30 minutes. Then the primer is applied, and left to dry for about an hour before finally applying the special-coloured top coat. The result is a correctly-coloured component, where the paint will flex with the plastic or rubber, a property that standard paint does not normally posses.

5 Major body damage – repair

Where serious damage has occurred, or large areas need renewal due to neglect, it means that complete new panels will need welding-in, and this is best left to professionals. If the damage is due to impact, it will also be necessary to check completely the alignment of the bodyshell, and this can only be carried out accurately by a Rover dealer, using special jigs. if the body is left misaligned, it is primarily dangerous, (as the car will not handle properly) and secondly, uneven stresses will be imposed on the steering, suspension and possibly transmission, causing abnormal wear, or complete failure, particularly to such items as the tyres.

6 Front bumper – removal and refitting

Removal

1 Firmly apply the handbrake, then jack up the front of the vehicle and support it on axle stands.

2 Remove the headlamps as described in Chapter 12.
3 Remove the four screws securing the bumper to the right-hand wheel arch liner, then undo the three screws securing the top of the liner to the body, and prise out the screw retaining plugs. Free the right-hand wheel arch liner from the front bumper, then repeat the complete procedure for the left-hand wheel arch liner.
4 Undo the three bolts securing the bumper to the front undercover panel, followed by the four bolts securing the bumper mounting plates to the body mounting brackets (photo).
5 Release both the left- and right-hand bumper slides from their retaining studs, and pull the bumper forwards away from the vehicle.
6 If necessary, the bumper mounting plates, trim strip and number plate can be removed from the bumper, and the bumper mountings can be unbolted from the vehicle. Renew these components as necessary, and/or transfer them to the new bumper.

Refitting

7 Refitting is a reverse of the removal sequence, ensuring that the bumper mounting bolts are tightened to the specified torque.

7 Rear bumper – removal and refitting

Removal

1 Chock the front wheels, then jack up the rear of the vehicle and support it on axle stands.

216 models

2 From underneath the vehicle, undo the four screws securing the undercover panel to the left-hand side of the bumper, and remove the panel.
3 Remove the screw securing the left-hand wheel arch liner to the body, and the screw securing the right-hand wheel arch liner to the bumper.
4 Undo the bolt (situated next to the towing eye) securing the underside of the bumper to the vehicle.
5 Open up the tailgate, and from inside the

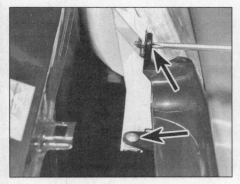

8.1 Radiator grille left-hand retaining screws (arrowed)

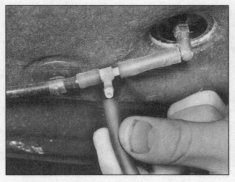

9.2A Disconnect the washer supply pipe ...

9.2B ... then support the bonnet with the aid of an assistant and remove the bonnet retaining bolts

luggage compartment, prise out the two circular grommets to gain access to the bumper mounting nuts, then undo both nuts and remove the flat washers.

6 Release both the left- and right-hand bumper slides from their mountings, and pull the bumper rearwards away from the vehicle, noting the sealing washer and two flat washers which are fitted to each of the bumper mounting studs.

7 If a new bumper is being fitted, transfer the trim strip and mounting stud washers.

416 models

8 Open up the boot lid, and from inside the luggage compartment, prise out the two circular grommets to gain access to the bumper mounting nuts (photo), then undo both nuts and remove the flat washers.

9 From underneath the car, slacken and remove the two nuts and washers securing the bumper mounting brackets to the body, and undo the bolt securing the bumper centre mounting bracket to the body (photo).

10 Remove the screw securing the left-hand wheel arch liner to the wheel arch.

11 Release both the left- and right-hand bumper slides from their mountings, and pull the bumper rearwards away from the vehicle, noting the sealing washers which are fitted to each of the bumper mounting studs.

12 If necessary, the bumper mounting brackets and trim strip can be removed from the bumper, and can be either renewed or transferred to a new bumper.

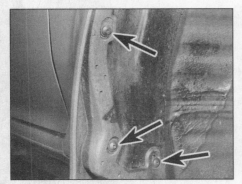

10.2 Mudflap retaining screws (arrowed)

Refitting

13 Refitting is a reverse of the removal sequence, ensuring that the bumper mounting nuts and bolts are tightened to their specified torque settings.

8 Radiator grille – removal and refitting

Removal

1 Open up the bonnet, then remove the four screws securing the radiator grille to the headlamp assemblies, and remove the grille from the car (photo).

Refitting

2 Fit the grille into position between the headlamps, and tighten its retaining screws securely.

9 Bonnet – removal, refitting and adjustment

Removal

1 Open up the bonnet and get an assistant to support it, then using a pencil or felt tip pen, mark the outline position of each bonnet hinge relative to the bonnet to use as a guide on refitting.

2 Disconnect the windscreen washer supply pipe from the T-piece. Undo the bonnet retaining bolts and, with the help of an-

10.3 Remove the right-hand wheel arch liner ...

assistant, carefully lift the bonnet clear, noting any shims which may be fitted between the bonnet and hinge (photos). Store the bonnet out of the way in a safe place.

Refitting and adjustment

3 Offer up the bonnet, position the shims between the bonnet and hinge (where fitted), and loosely fit the retaining bolts. Align the hinges with the marks made on removal (where applicable), then tighten the retaining bolts securely and reconnect the windscreen washer supply pipe.

4 Close the bonnet, and check for alignment with the adjacent panels. If necessary, slacken the hinge bolts and realign the bonnet to suit. Once the bonnet is correctly aligned, tighten the hinge bolts to the specified torque.

5 Check that the bonnet height is correct with that of the front wings and, if necessary, adjust by altering the height of the bonnet rubber stops.

6 Once the bonnet is correctly aligned, check that the bonnet fastens and releases in a satisfactory manner. If adjustment is necessary, remove the plastic lock cover, then slacken the bonnet lock retaining bolts and adjust the position of the lock to suit. Once the lock is operating correctly, tighten its retaining bolts to the specified torque and refit the lock cover.

10 Bonnet release cable – removal and refitting

Removal

1 With the bonnet open, carefully prise off the plastic lock cover, then disconnect the inner cable from the lock operating mechanism and release the outer cable from lock bracket.

2 Undo the three screws securing the right-hand mudflap to the wheel arch, and remove the mudflap (photo).

3 Remove the four screws securing the right-hand wheel arch liner to the front bumper, then undo the six screws securing the liner to the wheel arch and prise out the screw retaining plugs. Manoeuvre the wheel arch liner out from under the wheel arch (photo).

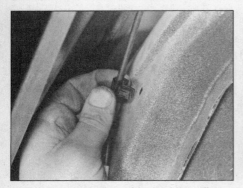

10.4 ... and release cable retaining clips from the wheel arch

11.2 Remove plastic bonnet lock cover ...

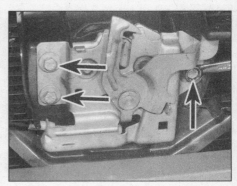

11.3A ... and undo three retaining bolts (arrowed) ...

4 Release the cable from its retaining clips in the engine compartment and under the right-hand wing (photo), then pull the cable through from under the right wheel arch.

5 From inside the car, undo the two bolts securing the bonnet release lever to the vehicle, then release the cable sealing grommet from under the facia panel. Pull the cable through from inside the car, and remove it from the vehicle.

Refitting

6 Feed the cable through from inside the car until the bonnet release lever is in position. Tighten the lever mounting bolts to the specified torque, and refit the sealing grommet.

7 From under the right-hand wheel arch, feed the cable through into the engine compartment, then fit the cable to the two retaining clips situated under the wheel arch.

8 Ensure the cable is correctly routed around the engine compartment and retained by all the necessary retaining clips, then connect the cable to the bonnet lock.

9 Refit the right-hand wheel arch liner, and press the six screw retaining plugs back into position. Refit the retaining screws and the liner-to-bumper screws, and tighten all wheel arch liner screws to the specified torque. Refit the mudflap.

10 Check that the bonnet fastens and releases in a satisfactory manner. If adjustment is necessary, slacken the bonnet

lock retaining bolts and adjust the position of the lock to suit. Once the lock is operating correctly, tighten its retaining bolts to the specified torque and refit the lock cover.

11 Bonnet lock – removal, refitting and adjustment

Removal

1 Open up the bonnet, then remove the four screws securing the radiator grille to the headlamp assemblies, and remove the grille from the car.

2 Carefully prise off the plastic cover from the lock (photo), then mark the outline of the bonnet lock on the body to use as a guide on refitting.

3 Slacken and remove the three bonnet lock retaining bolts, then withdraw the lock and disconnect the inner cable from the lock operating mechanism. Release the outer cable from lock bracket, and remove the lock from the car (photos).

Refitting and adjustment

4 Refit the release cable to the lock operating mechanism, then align the lock with the marks made on removal, and tighten the lock retaining bolts to the specified torque.

5 Check that the bonnet fastens and releases in a satisfactory manner. If adjustment is necessary, slacken the bonnet lock retaining

bolts and adjust the position of the lock to suit. Once the lock is operating correctly, tighten its retaining bolts to the specified torque and refit the lock cover and radiator grille.

12 Door inner trim panel – removal and refitting

Removal

1 Open the door, and carefully prise out and remove either the mirror inner trim panel (front door) or window inner trim panel (rear door).

2 Undo the door inner handle escutcheon retaining screw, and remove the escutcheon (photos).

3 On models without electric windows, remove the window winder handle horseshoe clip by hooking it out with a screwdriver or bent piece of wire, then pull the handle off the spindle and remove the winder escutcheon.

4 Remove the screws securing the inner trim panel and armrest to the door, noting that on certain models the armrest mounting screws may be hidden behind trim caps (photos).

5 Release the door trim panel studs by carefully levering between the panel and door with a suitable flat-bladed screwdriver. When all the studs are released, lift the panel upwards and away from the door. Note that on models with electric windows, it will be necessary to disconnect the switch wiring connector(s) as the panel is removed (photo).

11.3B ... then remove the lock and disconnect release cable (arrowed)

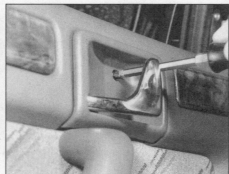

12.2A Undo retaining screw ...

12.2B ... and remove inner door handle escutcheon

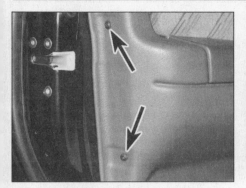

12.4A Front door trim panel retaining screws

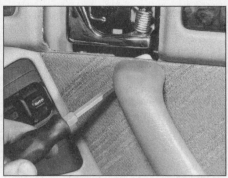

12.4B Removing front armrest retaining screw

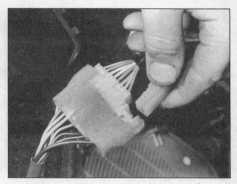

12.5 On models equipped with electric windows, disconnect wiring connectors as trim panel is removed

12.6 Fit horseshoe clip (arrowed) to manual window winder handle before refitting the handle

Refitting

6 Refitting the trim panel is the reverse sequence of removal, noting the following points.
(a) If any of the trim panel retaining studs were broken, renew them as necessary.
(b) When refitting the window regulator handle (manual windows), fit the clip to the handle first (photo), then push the handle onto the regulator spindle.

13 Door window glass and regulator – removal and refitting

Removal

Front door window glass and regulator

1 Remove the front door inner trim panel, as described in Section 12.
2 Undo the four screws securing the speaker to the door, then withdraw the speaker and disconnect its wiring connectors.
3 Undo the two armrest support bracket retaining screws, and remove the bracket from the door (photo).
4 On models with electric windows, temporarily connect the window switch wiring connector(s), and move the glass so that access can be gained to both the glass

retaining bolts via the cutaway in the door panel. If work is being carried out on the right-hand door, unplug the wiring connectors from the window control unit, then undo the control unit mounting screws and remove the unit from the door panel (photo). Release any relevant wiring retaining clips from the door.
5 On models with central locking, disconnect the wiring connectors from the door lock motor unit, and release the wiring retaining clips from the door panel. If work is being carried out on the left-hand door, unplug the wiring connectors from the central locking control unit, then undo the control unit mounting screws and remove the unit from the door panel (photo).
6 On models without electric windows, temporarily refit the winder handle, and move the glass so that its retaining bolts can be accessed through the cutaway in the door.
7 On all models, carefully peel back the polythene watershield to gain access to the regulator components (photo).
8 Slacken and remove the bolt securing the front glass channel to the door, then carefully disengage the channel from the window glass.
9 Undo the two bolts securing the window glass to the regulator, then lift up the glass and manoeuvre it out of the door (photo).
10 Slacken and remove the six regulator assembly retaining bolts, and manoeuvre the assembly out through the door panel cutaway.

13.3 Armrest support bracket is retained by two screws

13.4 On models with electric windows, the control unit must be removed when working on right-hand door

13.5 On models with central door locking, the control unit must be removed when working on left-hand door

13.7 Carefully peel back polythene watershield to gain access to regulator components

11

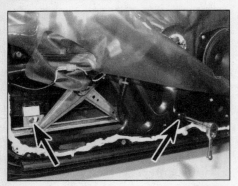

13.9 Undo window-to-regulator retaining bolts, and remove window glass

Rear door window glass and regulator

11 Remove the rear door inner trim panel, as described in Section 12.

12 Where necessary, disconnect the wiring from the central locking motor, and free any relevant wiring clips from the door panel.

13 Temporarily refit the winder handle, or reconnect the switch wiring connector (as applicable), and move the window glass so its retaining bolts can be accessed through the cutaway in the door panel.

14 Undo the two armrest support bracket retaining screws, then remove the bracket from the door and carefully peel back the polythene watershield.

15 Undo the window outer rear trim panel retaining screw, and remove the panel from the door.

16 Remove the screw securing the outer window sealing strip to the rear of the door, then carefully prise the strip out of the door panel and remove it from the car.

17 Slacken and remove the bolt securing the lower end of the rear window glass channel to the door panel, and recover the spacer (through which the bolt passes) from inside the door panel. Undo the nut securing the channel to the door, then release the rear channel from the window glass and rubber sealing strip, and remove it from the door.

18 Undo the two bolts securing the window glass to the regulator, then lift up the glass and manoeuvre it out of the door.

19 Slacken and remove the six regulator assembly retaining bolts, and manoeuvre the assembly out through the door panel cutaway.

Refitting

Front door window glass and regulator

20 Refit the regulator to the door panel, and lightly tighten its retaining bolts. Operate the regulator mechanism, either using the handle or by connecting the switch, to align the top slide, then tighten the retaining bolts to the specified torque.

21 Install the window glass, and tighten the glass-to-regulator bolts to the specified torque.

22 Refit the front glass channel, ensuring that it is correctly located, then lightly tighten its retaining bolt. Operate the regulator mechanism a few times to align the channel with the window glass, checking that the window travels up and down smoothly, then tighten the channel bolt to the specified torque.

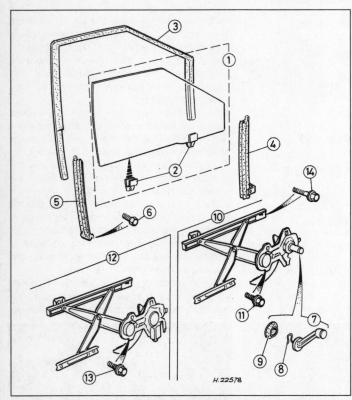

H.22578

Fig. 11.1 Front door window glass and regulator components (Sec 13)

1 Window glass
2 Window glass mounting brackets
3 Sealing strip
4 Window glass front channel
5 Window glass rear channel
6 Bolt
7 Winder handle*
8 Winder handle retaining clip*
9 Winder handle escutcheon *
10 Manual window regulator assembly*
11 Bolt*
12 Electric window regulator assembly *
13 Bolt*

* Fitted depending on model

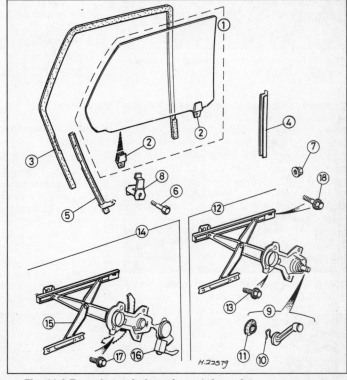

H.22579

Fig. 11.2 Rear door window glass and regulator components (Sec 13)

1 Window glass
2 Window glass mounting brackets
3 Sealing strip
4 Window glass front channel
5 Window glass rear channel
6 Bolt
7 Nut
8 Spacer
9 Winder handle *
10 Winder handle retaining clip*
11 Winder handle escutcheon *
12 Manual window regulator assembly*
13 Bolt*
14 Electric window regulator assembly*
15 Electric window regulator*
16 Electric window motor*
17 Bolt*

* Fitted depending on model

23 Refit the polythene watershield to the door, ensuring that it is securely stuck down around the edges. The remainder of refitting is a reversal of the removal procedure.

Rear door window glass and regulator

24 Refit the regulator and glass, as described in paragraphs 20 and 21.
25 Relocate the rear window glass channel with the rubber sealing strip and window glass, then refit its retaining nut. Position the spacer inside the door panel, then refit the channel lower bolt (ensuring it passes through the spacer) and tighten both the channel retaining nut and bolt lightly. Operate the regulator mechanism a few times to align the channel with the window glass, checking that the window travels up and down smoothly, then tighten the channel retaining nut and bolt to the specified torque setting.
26 Refit the polythene watershield to the door, ensuring that it is securely stuck down around the edges. The remainder of refitting is a reversal of the removal procedure.

14 Side window glass (3-door models) – removal and refitting

Removal

1 Remove the rear window parcel shelf, then fold the rear seat cushion fully forwards, and remove the rear seat back as described in Section 26. Remove the rubber seal from the rear seat back retaining catch.
2 Remove the four screws securing the rear seat side trim panel to the luggage compartment carpet, then carefully peel the front door sealing strip away from the door pillar, so that the front edge of the trim panel is freed. The panel can then be released by carefully prising it away from the body (using a large flat-bladed screwdriver to release its retaining clips) and then removed from the car.
3 Remove the single retaining screw securing the rear side window trim panel in position, then carefully prise the panel away from the body and remove it from the car.
4 Remove the upper seat belt mounting cover, then undo the retaining nut and remove the seat belt from its mounting point.
5 Undo the upper door pillar trim panel retaining screw, and peel the door sealing strip away from the front edge of the panel. Release all the panel retaining clips and remove it from the car.
6 Mark the position of the side window rear catch on the body, then remove the three hinge retaining screws.
7 Support the window glass, then undo the front hinge retaining screws and remove the window glass from the car.
8 Examine the window seal for signs of damage or deterioration, and renew if necessary. To renew the seal, first undo the two nuts securing the outer door pillar trim panel in position, and remove the panel. The

old seal can then be removed and the new seal installed. Once the seal is correctly positioned, refit the outer trim panel and tighten its retaining screws securely.

Refitting

9 Refitting is a reverse of the removal sequence, noting the following points.
(a) Align the rear window hinge with the marks made on dismantling, and lightly tighten the retaining screws.
(b) Close the window, and check that it is correctly aligned with the surrounding bodywork. Adjust, if necessary, by repositioning the hinge, then tighten all the hinge retaining screws securely.
(c) Where possible, renew any broken trim panel retaining clips.
(d) Tighten the seat belt upper mounting nut to the specified torque.
(e) On completion, ensure that all trim panels are securely retained, and that the door sealing strip is correctly located on the pillar.

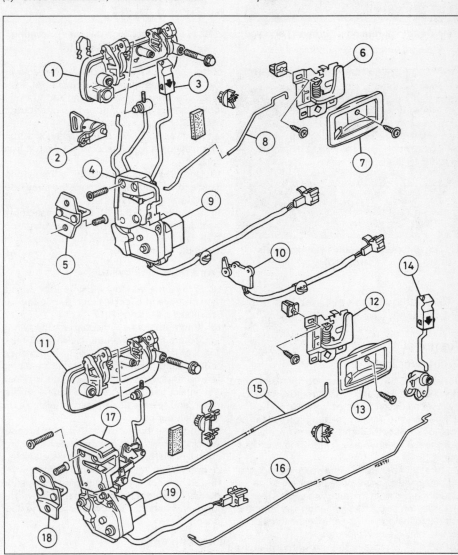

Fig. 11.3 Door lock and handle components (Sec 15)

Front door – items 1 to 10
1 Exterior handle
2 Door lock cylinder
3 Interior lock button
4 Lock assembly
5 Lock striker
6 Interior handle
7 Interior handle escutcheon
8 Link rod – interior handle to lock
9 Central locking motor – passenger door*
10 Central locking switch – driver's door*

Rear door – items 11 to 19
11 Exterior handle
12 Interior handle
13 Interior handle escutcheon
14 Interior lock button
15 Link rod – interior handle to lock
16 Link rod – interior lock button to lock
17 Lock assembly
18 Lock striker
19 Central locking motor*
*Fitted depending on model

11

15.4 Door lock retaining screws (Torx type)

15.15 Front door lock cylinder operating rod (A) and circlip (B)

15.17 Interior handle retaining screws (arrowed)

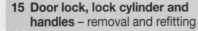

15.19 Exterior handle retaining bolts (arrowed)

15 Door lock, lock cylinder and handles – removal and refitting

Removal

Front door lock

1 Remove the front window glass as described in Section 13, then remove the lock cylinder as described in paragraph 15.

2 Position the window sealing strip clear of the lock assembly and, where necessary, release the wiring retaining clips from the door panel.

3 Remove the three screws securing the interior handle to the door panel, and free its operating rod from the retaining clips.

4 Undo the two bolts securing the exterior handle to the door, then remove the three door lock retaining screws (photo).

5 Partially withdraw the lock and handle assembly, then disconnect the interior and exterior handle connecting rods from the lock, and remove both handles from the door. Disconnect the inner lock button operating rod from the lock, and remove the button.

6 Disconnect the wiring connector from the central locking motor (where fitted), and manoeuvre the lock assembly out of the door.

Rear door lock

7 Remove the rear window glass, as described in Section 13.

8 Remove the screw securing the inner lock

button pivot to the door panel, then release the button operating rod from its retaining clips. Disconnect the operating rod from the lock assembly, and remove the inner button assembly from the door.

9 Free the interior handle operating rod from its retaining clips, and disconnect the rod from the lock.

10 Undo the two bolts securing the exterior handle to the door, then remove the three door lock retaining screws.

11 Partially withdraw the lock assembly, disconnect the exterior handle operating rod, then remove the exterior handle and lock assembly from the door.

Front door lock cylinder

12 Ensure the window glass is fully raised, then remove the door inner trim panel as described in Section 12.

13 Where necessary, disconnect the wiring connectors from the central locking (left-hand door) or electric window (right-hand door) control unit, then undo the unit retaining screws and remove it from the door panel. Disconnect the wiring from the central locking motor, and release any relevant retaining clips from the door panel.

14 Undo the two armrest support bracket retaining screws, then remove the bracket and carefully peel back the polythene watershield to gain access to the lock components.

15 Disconnect the operating rod from the lock cylinder retaining clip, then remove the circlip and withdraw the cylinder from the door (photo).

Interior handle

16 Remove the door inner trim panel, as described in Section 12.

17 Undo the screws securing the interior handle to the door, then disconnect the handle from its operating rod and remove it from the car (photo).

Exterior handle

18 Remove the inner trim panel as described in Section 12, and carefully peel back the polythene watershield to gain access to the exterior handle retaining bolts.

19 Disconnect the operating rod from the

handle, then undo the two retaining bolts and remove the handle from the door (photo).

Refitting

20 Refitting is the reverse of the removal sequence, noting the following points.

(a) Ensure that all operating rods are securely held in position by their retaining clips.

(b) Apply grease to all lock and operating rod pivot points.

(c) Before installing the inner trim panel, thoroughly check the operation of all the door lock handles and, where necessary, the central locking system, and ensure that the polythene watershield is securely stuck to the door.

16 Door – removal, refitting and adjustment

Removal

1 With the door open, peel back the wiring gaiter or remove the wiring grommet from the front edge of the door panel. Carefully withdraw the wiring from door until the wiring connector(s) emerge. Disconnect the block connector(s), and tape the 'door side' of the connectors to the door frame, to prevent them falling back into the door panel. **Note:** *If there is insufficient slack in the wiring to withdraw the wiring connectors from the door panel, it will be necessary to remove the inner trim panel as described in Section 12, and peel back the polythene watershield to gain access to them.*

2 Using a pencil or felt-tip pen, mark the outline position of each door hinge relative to the door, to use as a guide on refitting.

3 Remove the retaining clip and extract the pin securing the door check link to the door pillar.

4 While an assistant supports the door, undo the nuts which secure the upper and lower hinges to the door, then remove the door from the car.

5 If necessary, the hinges can then be unbolted and removed from the door pillar, having first marked the position of the hinge

16.5 Remove wheel arch liner to gain access to front door hinge retaining bolts (arrowed)

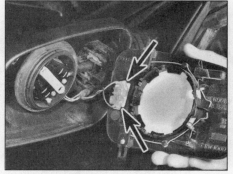

17.2 Disconnect wiring connectors (arrowed) and remove mirror glass – electric mirror

17.3 Remove the mirror inner trim panel ...

17.4A ... disconnect the wiring connector, then undo mirror retaining screws (arrowed – one hidden) ...

17.4B ... and remove mirror assembly from the door

on the pillar. To gain access to the front door hinge bolts, it will first be necessary to remove the wheel arch liner, as described in paragraphs 2 and 3 of Section 10 (photo). On refitting, align the hinges with the marks made on dismantling, and tighten the hinge retaining bolts to the specified torque.

Refitting and adjustment

6 The door is refitted using a reversal of the removal procedure. Align the hinges with the marks made on removal, and tighten the bolts to the specified torque.

7 On completion, shut the door and check that the door is correctly aligned with all surrounding bodywork, with an equal clearance all around. If necessary, adjustment can be made by slackening the hinge bolts and moving the door. Once the door is positioned correctly, tighten the hinge bolts to the specified torque.

8 Once the door is correctly aligned, check that the door closes easily, is flush with the adjacent panels, and does not rattle when closed. If not, slacken the door striker retaining screws and reposition the striker. Once the door operation is satisfactory, tighten the striker retaining screws securely.

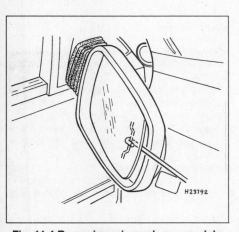

Fig. 11.4 Removing mirror glass – models with electric mirrors (Sec 17)

17 Exterior mirror – removal and refitting

Removal
Mirror glass

1 On models without electric mirrors, heat the mirror glass with a hairdryer to soften the adhesive used to stick the glass to its mounting plate. Once warm, the mirror glass can be levered out of position.

2 On models with electric mirrors, position the mirror so that access can be gained to the rear of the outer edge of the glass. Using a piece of welding rod or other suitable wire, bend the end of the rod into a hook. Locate the hook with the spring clip on the rear of the mirror glass and pull the clip outwards to release the mirror (Fig. 11.4). Disconnect the wiring connectors from the mirror heated element, and remove the glass from the car (photo).

Mirror assembly

3 Carefully prise the mirror inner trim panel out from the door (photo).

4 Disconnect the mirror wiring connector (where necessary), then slacken and remove the three screws and mounting plate securing the mirror to the door, and remove the mirror assembly (photos).

Refitting
Mirror glass

5 On models without electric mirrors, first ensure that all traces of old adhesive are removed from the mounting plate. Remove the backing from the new mirror, then press the glass firmly into place, and adjust to the required position.

6 On models with electric mirrors, connect the wiring connectors to the heated element terminals, then align the mirror spring clip with the motor mounting point. Press the mirror glass firmly onto the motor, check that it is securely retained by the spring clip, then adjust the mirror to the required position.

Mirror assembly

7 Refitting is a reverse of the removal procedure.

18 Boot lid – removal, refitting and adjustment

Removal

1 With the boot lid open, disconnect the boot release outer cable from the lock bracket, and unhook the inner cable from the lock operating mechanism.

2 Disconnect the wiring connectors from the boot lid lock warning lamp switch.

3 Remove the access cover from the left-hand side of the boot lid, and free the release cable from all its retaining clips and ties on the boot lid and hinge. Tie a piece of string to the end of the cable, then withdraw the cable from the

11

boot lid. Untie the string from the cable end, and leave the string in position in the boot lid; the string can then be used on refitting to draw the cable through into position.

4 Remove the right-hand access cover from the boot lid, and repeat the operation in paragraph 3 for the warning lamp wiring, again leaving the string in position in the boot lid.

5 Using a felt-tip pen or pencil, mark the outline of each hinge on the boot lid.

6 While an assistant holds the boot lid, undo the four hinge retaining bolts, then lift the boot lid away from the car.

Refitting and adjustment

7 Offer up the boot lid, aligning the hinges with the marks made on dismantling, and tighten the hinge bolts securely. Tie the left-hand piece of string to the boot release cable, and use the string to draw the cable through the boot lid. Repeat this procedure using the right-hand piece of string to draw the warning lamp switch wiring through the lid, then untie both pieces of string. **Note:** *If a new boot lid is being installed, it will be necessary to centralise the boot lid on its hinges, and feed the release cable and wiring through the boot lid.*

8 Connect the release inner cable to the lock operating mechanism, and refit the outer cable to its respective position on the lock. Secure the release cable to the boot lid hinge using the retaining clips.

9 Connect the warning connectors to the boot lock warning lamp switch, and secure the wiring to the right-hand hinge using the retaining clips.

10 Refit both the left- and right-hand access covers to the boot lid.

11 Close the boot lid, and check that is correctly aligned with all surrounding bodywork, with an equal clearance all around. If necessary, adjustment can be made by slackening the hinge bolts and repositioning the boot lid. Once correctly positioned, tighten the hinge bolts to the specified torque.

12 Once the boot lid is correctly aligned, ensure that it closes without slamming and is securely retained. If not, slacken the boot lid striker retaining bolts and reposition the striker. Once the boot lid operation is satisfactory, tighten the striker retaining bolts securely.

19 Boot lid lock and lock cylinder – removal and refitting

Removal

Boot lid lock

1 With the boot lid open, disconnect the boot release outer cable from the lock bracket and unhook the inner cable from the lock operating mechanism.

2 Disconnect the wiring connectors from the boot lid lock warning lamp switch (photo).

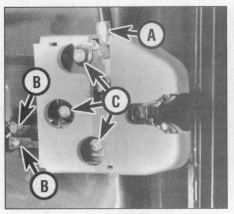

19.2 Boot lid lock release cable (A), warning lamp wiring connectors (B) and retaining bolts (C)

3 Carefully prise off the boot lid lock cover, then undo the three bolts securing the lock to the boot lid.

4 Partially withdraw the lock, then disconnect the lock cylinder operating rod from the rear of the assembly, and remove the lock from vehicle.

5 If necessary, remove the right-hand access cover from the boot lid, then disconnect the operating rod from the lock cylinder and remove it from the car.

Boot lid lock cylinder

6 Open up the boot lid, and remove the right-hand access cover.

7 Detach the operating rod from the lock cylinder, and remove the bolt securing the cylinder to the boot lid (photo).

8 Manoeuvre the lock cylinder out of the boot lid. Remove the lock cylinder gasket and discard it; a new gasket should be used on refitting.

Refitting

Boot lid lock

9 Refitting is a reversal of the removal sequence, tightening the lock retaining bolts to the specified torque. On completion, check that the boot lid closes without slamming, and is securely retained when shut. If not, slacken the boot lid striker retaining bolts, and

20.2 Remove right-hand sill finisher

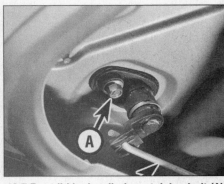

19.7 Boot lid lock cylinder retaining bolt (A) and operating rod (B)

reposition the striker. Once the boot lid operation is satisfactory, tighten the striker retaining bolts securely.

Boot lid lock cylinder

10 Refitting is a reverse of the removal procedure, ensuring that a new gasket is fitted to the cylinder, and that its retaining bolt is tightened to the specified torque.

20 Boot lid/tailgate and fuel filler flap release cables – removal and refitting

Removal

1 Remove the driver's seat and rear seats, as described in Section 26.

2 Undo the right-hand front sill finisher and carpet retainer screws, and remove the sill finisher and carpet retainer from the car (photo).

3 Remove the boot lid/tailgate and fuel filler release lever handles, then lift the flap situated on the top of the release lever cover to gain access to the retaining screw. Undo the screw and lift off the release lever cover (photos).

4 On four- and five-door models, open up the right-hand rear door and undo the two screws securing the sill finisher to the floor, then remove the sill finisher and carpet retainer. Carefully prise out the lower trim panels from the centre and rear door pillars.

20.3A Remove the release lever handles ...

20.3B ... then undo lever cover retaining screw ...

20.3C ... and remove the cover

20.8 Removing the left-hand luggage compartment trim panel – 416 model shown

5 On three-door models, remove the four screws securing the right-hand lower rear seat side trim panel to the luggage compartment carpet. Now carefully peel the front door sealing strip away from the door pillar, so that the front edge of the trim panel is freed. The panel can then be released by carefully prising it away from the body, using a large flat-bladed screwdriver to release its retaining clips, and then removed from the car.

6 On all models, remove the cap from the driver's seat belt lower anchorage bolt, then undo the bolt and free the belt from the floor. Release the trim clips securing the carpet to the floor, and peel back the carpet to gain access to the release cables.

7 Open up the boot lid/tailgate, prise out the screw caps (where necessary), and undo the screws securing the luggage compartment rear inner trim panel in position. Remove the panel from the car. Release any relevant retaining clips, and remove the luggage compartment carpet.

8 Closely examine the luggage compartment left-hand side trim panel, and remove any relevant retaining screws. Carefully prise the panel away from the body, and remove it from the luggage compartment (photo). Proceed as described under the relevant subheading.

Boot lid/tailgate release cable

9 On 416 models, detach the outer cable from the boot lid lock bracket, then unhook the inner cable from the lock/striker operating mechanism. Remove the left-hand access cover from the boot lid, and free the cable from all its retaining clips and ties on the boot lid and hinge. Tie a piece of string to the end of the cable, then withdraw the cable from the boot lid. Untie the string from the cable end, and leave the string in position in the boot lid. The string can then be used on refitting, to draw the cable through into position.

10 On 216 models, undo the tailgate striker retaining screws, then withdraw the striker and detach the release cable.

11 On all models, free the cable from all its retaining clips in the luggage compartment, then pull the cable through from inside into the car. Work back along the length of the cable to the lever, and free it from any relevant

retaining clips. Disconnect the outer cable from the release lever mounting bracket, then detach the inner cable from the lever, and withdraw the cable from the car (photo).

Fuel filler release cable

12 Detach the fuel filler release cable from the left-hand side of the luggage compartment (photo). The cable can then be removed as described in paragraph 11.

Refitting

13 Refitting is a direct reversal of the removal procedure, noting the following points.
(a) Ensure the cable is correctly routed, and secured by the relevant clips. Check that the release lever operates satisfactorily before proceeding further.
(b) Where possible, renew any broken trim panel retaining clips.
(c) Ensure all carpets and trim panels are properly located, and securely retained by all the necessary clips and screws.
(d) Tighten the lower seat belt anchorage bolt to the specified torque setting.

21 Tailgate – removal, refitting and adjustment

Removal

1 With the tailgate open, undo the two screws securing the tailgate inner trim panel to the tailgate, and carefully prise out the screw retaining plugs.

2 Using a large flat-bladed screwdriver, work around the outside of the trim panel, and carefully prise it away from the tailgate to free all its retaining clips. Once all the retaining clips have been freed, remove the trim panel.

3 Disconnect the two wiring block connectors (situated on the right-hand side of the tailgate) which connect the tailgate electrical components to the main wiring loom. Tie a piece of string around the wiring side of the block connector, then remove the grommet from the upper right-hand corner of the tailgate and withdraw the wiring. Once free, untie the string from the end of the wiring,

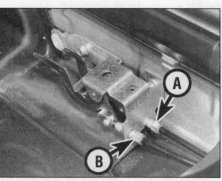
20.11 Detach the relevant cable from the release lever assembly, and withdraw it from the car

A Fuel filler release cable
B Boot lid/tailgate release cable

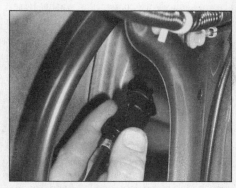
20.12 Disconnecting fuel filler release cable – 416 model shown

leaving the string in place in the tailgate. The string can then be used to draw the wiring back through into position on refitting.

4 Disconnect the washer hose from the tailgate grommet.

5 Using a felt-tip pen or pencil, mark the relative positions of the hinges to the tailgate.

6 Have an assistant support the tailgate, then raise the spring clips and pull the support struts off their balljoint mountings on the tailgate (see photo 22.2). Undo the four hinge retaining bolts, and remove the tailgate from the vehicle, noting any shims which may be fitted between the hinge and tailgate.

11

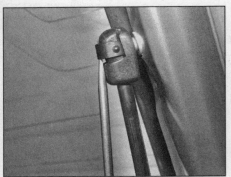

22.2 Raising tailgate support strut spring clip to release mounting

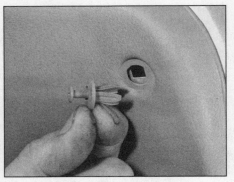

23.1 Tailgate inner trim panel retaining screw and plug

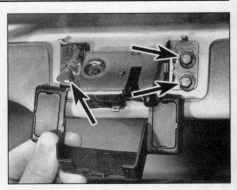

23.3 Remove plastic cover to gain access to tailgate lock retaining bolts (arrowed)

Refitting and adjustment

7 Offer up the tailgate, positioning any necessary shims between the hinge and tailgate, and refit the hinge bolts. Press the support struts firmly onto their balljoint mountings, and clip the spring clips back into position. Align the hinges with the marks made on removal, or centralise the hinges, and tighten the retaining bolts to the specified torque.

8 Tie the string around the end of the tailgate wiring, and use the string to draw the wiring back into position. Untie the string, then connect the wiring connectors and relocate the grommet in the tailgate.

9 Renew any broken retaining clips, then refit the inner trim panel to the tailgate. Ensure the panel is securely clipped in position, then refit the screw retaining plugs and tighten the screws securely. Reconnect the washer hose to the tailgate grommet.

10 On completion, shut the tailgate and check that it is correctly aligned with the surrounding bodywork. If adjustment is necessary, slacken the hinge bolts and reposition the tailgate as necessary. Once the alignment is correct, tighten the hinge bolts to the specified torque.

11 If the correct alignment cannot be achieved by repositioning the tailgate, it will be necessary to alter the hinge-to-body position. To do this, first peel away the tailgate sealing strip from the top edge of the body. Carefully prise the top of the right- and left-hand tailgate pillar trim panels, until the headlining can be peeled back sufficiently to gain access to the hinge retaining nuts. Slacken the hinge nuts, and reposition the tailgate noting that, as a guide, Rover state there should be a gap of approximately 7 mm along the top edge of the tailgate. Once correctly positioned, tighten the retaining nuts to the specified torque, then relocate the headlining, trim panels and tailgate sealing strip.

12 Adjust the height of the tailgate by screwing the rubber stop in or out, as necessary, then check that the tailgate closes easily, and does not rattle when closed. If adjustment is necessary, slacken the tailgate striker retaining screws and reposition the

striker as necessary. Once the tailgate operation is satisfactory, tighten the striker retaining bolts securely.

22 Tailgate support strut – removal and refitting

Removal

1 Support the tailgate in the open position using a stout piece of wood, or with the help of an assistant.

2 Raise the spring clip, and pull the support strut off its balljoint mounting on the tailgate (photo). Repeat the procedure for the strut-to-body mounting, and remove the strut from the car.

Refitting

3 Refitting is the reverse sequence to removal, ensuring that the strut is pressed firmly onto each of its balljoints, and that the spring clips are correctly positioned.

23 Tailgate lock and lock cylinder – removal and refitting

Removal

Tailgate lock

1 With the tailgate open, undo the two screws securing the tailgate inner trim panel to the tailgate, and carefully prise out the screw retaining plugs (photo).

2 Using a large flat-bladed screwdriver, work around the outside of the trim panel, and carefully prise it away from the tailgate to free all its retaining clips. Once all the retaining clips have been freed, remove the trim panel.

3 Disconnect the operating rod from the lock, then remove the plastic cover from the lock (photo). Using a felt-tip pen or pencil, mark the relative position of the lock assembly to the tailgate.

4 Undo all the tailgate lock retaining screws, and remove the lock assembly from the car.

Tailgate lock cylinder

5 With the tailgate open, remove the right-hand access panel from the tailgate trim.

23.7 Tailgate striker retaining screws (Torx type)

6 Disconnect the operating rod from the lock cylinder, then undo the retaining bolt, and remove the cylinder from the tailgate.

Refitting

Tailgate lock

7 Refitting is a reverse of the removal sequence, aligning the lock with the marks made on dismantling. On completion, check that the tailgate closes easily, and does not rattle when closed. If adjustment is necessary, slacken the tailgate striker retaining screws, and reposition the striker as necessary (photo). Once the tailgate operation is satisfactory, tighten the striker retaining bolts securely.

Tailgate lock cylinder

8 Refitting is a direct reversal of the removal procedure.

24 Windscreen, fixed side window and tailgate/rear window glass – general information

These areas of glass are secured by the tight fit of the weatherstrip in the body aperture; although they are not fixed by the direct-bonding method used on many modern vehicles, the removal and refitting of these areas of fixed glass is still difficult, messy and time-consuming for the inexperienced. It is also difficult, unless one has plenty of practice, to obtain a secure, watertight fit. Furthermore, the task carries a high risk of breakage; this applies especially to the laminated glass windscreen. This may not be of immediate concern, if damage is the reason for removing these areas of glass, but the inherent risks in handling broken glass are obvious. In view of this, owners are strongly advised to have this sort of work carried out by one of the many specialist windscreen fitters.

25 Body exterior trim panels – general information

The exterior body and door trim strips are held in position with a special adhesive tape. Removal requires the trim to be heated, to soften the adhesive, and possibly cut away from the door surface. Due to the high risk of damage to the vehicle paintwork during this operation, it is recommended that the work should be entrusted to a Rover dealer.

26 Seats – removal and refitting

Removal

Front seats

1 Slide the seat fully rearwards, then slacken and remove the two Torx bolts securing the front of the seat slides to the floor (photo).
2 Slide the seat fully forwards, then undo the two Torx bolts securing the rear of the seat slides to the floor, and remove the seat from the car.

Rear seat cushion – 216 models

3 Carefully prise off the hinge covers from the front of the seat cushion (photo), then undo the two Torx bolts securing the hinges to the floor. The cushion can then be lifted out of position and removed from the car.

Rear seat cushion – 416 models

4 Remove the bolt securing the rear of the cushion to the seat back (photo), then lift the rear of the seat cushion.
5 Disengage the cushion retaining clips from

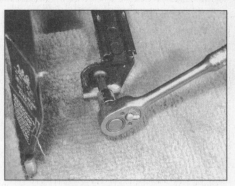

26.1 Front seat slides are secured to the floor by Torx bolts

the front of the seat cushion, and remove it from the car.

Rear seat back – 216 models

6 Remove the rear window parcel shelf, then fold the seat backs fully forwards.
7 Peel back the carpet to gain access to the centre hinge, then remove the hinge cover and undo the bolts securing the hinge to the floor (photo).
8 Disengage the rear seat back pivot pins from the body, and remove the assembly from the car.

Rear seat back – 416 models

9 Remove the rear seat cushion, as described in paragraphs 4 and 5.
10 Remove the three bolts securing the bottom of the seat back to the body (photo), then pull the seat back forwards to release it from its retaining clips, and remove it from the car.

Refitting

11 Refitting is the reverse of removal, tightening the seat or hinge mounting bolts (as applicable) to the specified torque setting.

27 Interior trim – general information

Interior trim panels

1 The interior trim panels are all secured using either screws or various types of trim fasteners, usually either studs or clips.

26.3 On 216 models, remove rear seat cushion hinge covers to gain access to retaining bolts

2 Check that there are no other panels overlapping the one to be removed; usually there is a removal sequence that has to be followed, which will become obvious on close inspection.
3 Remove all obvious fasteners, such as screws. if the panel will not come free, it is probably held by hidden clips or fasteners. These are usually situated around the edge of the panel, and can be prised up to release them. Note, however, that they can break quite easily, so replacements should be available when refitting. The best way of releasing such clips (in the absence of the correct type of tool) is to use a large flat-bladed screwdriver. Note in many cases that the adjacent sealing strip must be prised back to release a panel.
4 When removing a panel, **never** use excessive force, or the panel may be damaged; always check carefully that all fasteners have been removed or released before attempting to withdraw a panel.
5 Refitting is the reverse of the removal procedure; secure the fasteners by pressing them firmly into place, and ensure that all disturbed components are correctly secured, to prevent rattles. If adhesives were found at any point on removal, use white spirit to remove all traces of old adhesive, washing off all traces of spirit using soapy water; use a suitable trim adhesive (a Rover dealer should be able to recommend a proprietary product) on reassembly.

11

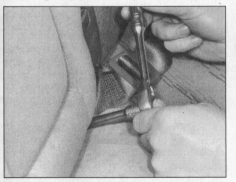

26.4 Removing rear seat cushion retaining bolt – 416 models

26.7 Rear seat back centre hinge retaining bolts – 216 models

26.10 Rear seat back retaining bolt – 416 models

28.2 Remove the cover to reveal the front seat belt upper mounting nut

28.3 Prise off the trim cap and remove front seat belt lower mounting bolt

28.4 Front seat belt inertia reel retaining bolts (arrowed)

Carpets

6 The passenger compartment floor carpet is in one piece, and is secured at its edges by screws or clips – usually, the same fasteners are used to secure the various adjoining trim panels.

7 Carpet removal and refitting is reasonably straightforward, but very time-consuming, due to the fact that all adjoining trim panels must be removed first as must components such as the seats, the centre console and seat belt lower anchorages.

Headlining

8 The headlining is clipped to the roof, and can be withdrawn only when all fittings such as the grab handles, sun visors, sunroof (if

fitted), windscreen and rear side windows (and related trim panels) have been removed. The door, tailgate and sunroof aperture sealing strips will also have to be prised clear.

9 Note that headlining removal requires considerable skill and experience if it is to be carried out without damage, and is therefore best entrusted to an expert.

28 Seat belts – removal and refitting

Removal

Front seat belt – four- and five-door models

1 Carefully prise the lower door pillar trim panel out of position, and remove it from the car.

2 Remove the cover from the upper belt mounting, undo the seat belt retaining nut, and detach the belt (photo).

3 Remove the cap from the lower seat belt mounting bolt, then undo the bolt, and detach the belt from the floor (photo).

4 Undo the two bolts securing the inertia reel to the door pillar (photo), and remove the belt and reel assembly from the car.

Front seat belt – three-door models

5 Remove the rear window parcel shelf, then fold the rear seat cushion fully forwards, and remove the rear seat back as described in

Section 26. Remove the rubber seal from the rear seat back mounting catch.

6 Prise out the lower seat belt mounting point cover, then slacken and remove the lower mounting bolt, and detach the belt from the body.

7 Remove the four screws securing the lower rear seat side trim panel to the luggage compartment carpet, then carefully peel the front door sealing strip away from the door pillar so that the front edge of the trim panel is freed. The panel can then be released by carefully prising it away from the body, using a large flat-bladed screwdriver to release its retaining clips, and then removed from the car.

8 Prise off the cover from the upper seat belt mounting, then undo the nut securing the belt to the inertia reel, and detach the belt.

9 Prise off the covers from the seat belt lower mounting bar bolts, then undo both bolts. Disengage the mounting bar from the belt, and remove it from the car.

10 Release the seat belt from its door pillar guide, then slacken and remove the two inertia reel retaining bolts, and remove the belt and inertia reel from the car.

Front seat belt stalk – all models

11 Remove the seat from the car, as described in Section 26. Undo the seat belt stalk-to-seat mounting bolt, and remove the stalk.

Rear seat side belt – five-door models

12 Remove the rear window parcel shelf, and fold the rear seats fully forwards.

13 Carefully examine the luggage compartment side trim panel, and remove all its retaining screws. If the right-hand panel is being removed, prise out the luggage compartment lamp from the trim panel, disconnect the lamp wiring, and remove it from the car. Release the trim panel, and remove it from the luggage compartment.

14 Remove the cover from the lower seat belt mounting point (photo), then undo the mounting bolt and detach the belt from the body.

15 Prise off the cover from the seat belt upper guide, and undo the two seat belt guide retaining bolts (photos).

28.14 Remove cover to gain access to rear seat belt lower retaining bolt

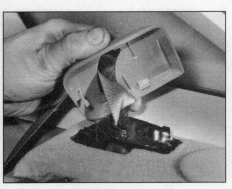

28.15A Prise off the cover ...

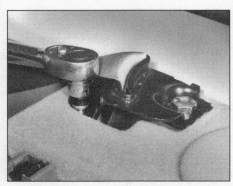

28.15B ... and remove seat belt guide retaining bolts

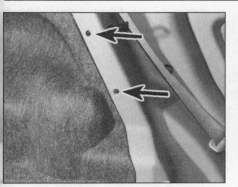

28.16A Remove rear door pillar trim panel retaining screws ...

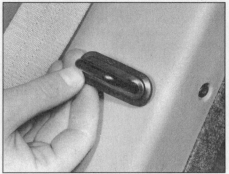

28.16B ... and remove seat catch rubber seal

28.20 Rear seat side belt lower mounting bolt ...

28.22 ... and inertia reel retaining bolts (arrowed) – four-door models

16 Undo the six screws securing the rear door pillar trim panel, and remove the rubber seal from the rear seat back mounting catch. Remove the trim panel to gain access to the inertia reel (photos).

17 Undo the two bolts securing the inertia reel to the body, and remove the belt and reel assembly from the car.

Rear seat side belt – four-door models

18 Remove the rear seat cushion and back, as described in Section 26.

19 Carefully examine the luggage compartment side trim panel, and remove all its retaining screws. Release the trim panel, and remove it from the luggage compartment.

20 Remove the lower seat belt mounting bolt (photo), and detach the belt from the body.

21 Prise off the cover from the seat belt upper guide, and undo the two seat belt guide retaining bolts.

22 Undo the two bolts securing the inertia reel to the body (photo), and remove the belt and reel assembly from the car.

Rear seat side belt – three-door models

23 Remove the rear window parcel shelf, then fold the rear seat fully forwards and remove the rear seat back, as described in Section 26. Remove the rubber seal from the seat back mounting catch.

24 Carry out the operations described in paragraphs 13 to 15.

25 Carefully peel the front door sealing strip away from the door pillar, so that the front edge of the rear seat side trim panel is freed. Release the panel by carefully prising it away from the body, using a large flat-bladed screwdriver, removing it from the car to gain access to the inertia reel.

26 Undo the two bolts securing the inertia reel to the body, and remove the seat bolt and inertia reel assembly from the car.

Rear seat centre belt and buckles

27 On 216 models, fold the rear seat cushion fully forwards, and on 416 models, remove the rear seat cushion, as described in Section 26.

28 The centre belt and/or buckle assembly can then be removed by freeing the buckle(s) from the rear seat back, and removing the mounting bolt(s).

Refitting

29 Refitting is the reversal of removal, noting the following points.

(a) *Tighten all the seat belt, seat belt guide, seat belt stalk and inertia reel mounting nuts and bolts (as applicable) to the specified torque setting.*

(b) *Where possible, renew any broken trim panel retaining clips.*

(c) *On completion, ensure that all trim panels are securely held by their retaining clips, and that the door sealing strips (if disturbed) are correctly located.*

29 Sunroof – general information

A sunroof is available as an option on all models, both an electrically-operated sunroof and a manual sunroof being available.

Due to the complexity of the sunroof mechanism, considerable expertise is needed to repair or replace sunroof components successfully. Removal of the sunroof first requires the headlining to be removed, which is a complex and tedious operation in itself, and is not a task to be undertaken lightly (see

Section 27). Any problems with the sunroof should therefore be referred to a Rover dealer.

On models equipped with an electrically-operated sunroof, if the sunroof motor fails to operate, first check the relevant fuse. If the fault cannot be traced and rectified, the sunroof can be opened and closed manually using a suitable Torx wrench or Allen key (as appropriate). Use a coin to unscrew the circular access cover in the panel (situated between the sun visors) in the headlining, and insert the wrench or key into the drive spindle. Rotate the key to move the sunroof to the required position (photo). A suitable wrench is supplied with the vehicle when new, and should be in the luggage compartment it is stowed next to the wheel trim remover.

30 Centre console – removal and refitting

Removal

1 In the rear section of the centre console, there is a cover situated just in front of the handbrake lever. Prise this cover out to gain access to the two retaining bolts (photo).

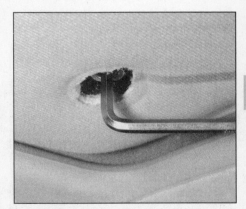

29.1 On models with an electrically-operated sunroof, the roof can be opened and closed manually via the access hole in the headlining

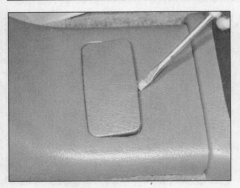

30.1 Prise out the cover ...

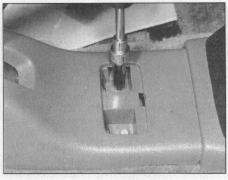

30.2A ... then undo the retaining bolts ...

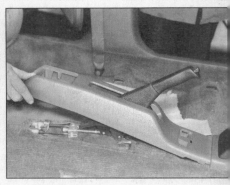

30.2B ... and remove the centre console rear section – front seats removed for clarity

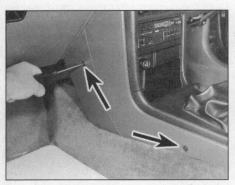

30.4A Remove front console section retaining screws (arrowed) ...

30.4B ... and remove the console section from the car

2 Undo the two bolts, then slide the rear console section backwards to free it from its retaining bracket and the front console section, and remove it from the car (photos).
3 On manual gearbox models, unscrew the gear lever knob.
4 On all models, remove the four retaining screws, then lift the front console section over the gearchange/gear selector lever, and remove it from the car (photos).

Refitting

5 Refitting is a reversal of the removal procedure.

31 Facia – removal and refitting

Removal

1 If a standard-equipment radio/cassette player is fitted, refer to the instructions supplied with the unit, and de-activate the security code. Disconnect the battery negative terminal. From within the engine compartment, unscrew the union nuts and separate the two halves of the speedometer cable.
2 Remove the centre console, as described in Section 30.

3 Slide the front seats rearwards, then remove the radio/cassette player as described in Chapter 12.
4 Working on the passenger side of the facia, remove the mat from the facia tray, then carefully prise out the clock mounting trim panel (refer to Chapter 12, Section 20). Disconnect the wiring connector from the rear of the clock, and remove the trim panel.
5 Undo the five right-hand lower facia panel retaining screws, and remove the panel (photo).
6 Remove the nuts and bolts securing the steering column assembly to the body, and remove the lower mounting clamp. Carefully lower the column assembly away from facia, releasing the wiring from any retaining clips as necessary. Rest the column on the driver's seat, taking great care that no strain is placed on any of the column wiring.
7 Slacken and remove the four screws securing the heater control panel to the facia, then undo the four screws securing the lower central panel to the facia. Partially withdraw the lower central facia panel, then disconnect the wiring connector from the cigar lighter, and remove the cigar lighter and ashtray illumination bulbs. Remove the lower central panel from the car (photos).
8 With the panel removed, disconnect the two block connectors from the relay module, and release the wiring retaining clip from the facia

31.5 Right-hand lower facia panel retaining screws (arrowed)

31.7A Heater control panel retaining screws (A) and lower central facia panel retaining screws (B)

31.7B Withdraw the central facia panel ...

31.7C ... disconnect the wiring connectors ...

31.7D ... and remove ashtray illumination bulb

31.9 Slacken two facia mounting bolts and remove relay module mounting bracket (arrowed)

mounting bracket. Use a screwdriver to release its retaining clip, and remove the relay module (refer to Chapter 12, Section 11).
9 Slacken and remove the two bolts securing the facia to the mounting bracket on the transmission tunnel, and remove the bolts along with the relay module mounting bracket (photo).
10 Open up the glovebox, and remove the door demister duct from the left-hand end of the facia. Slacken and remove the two left-hand facia mounting bolts, then close the glovebox.
11 Remove the door demister duct from the right-hand end of the facia, and undo the two right-hand facia mounting bolts (photos).
12 Slacken and remove the centre facia mounting bolt which is accessed through the clock aperture, and partially withdraw the facia rearwards, until access can be gained to the wiring block connectors situated behind the right-hand end of the facia, and to the speedometer cable (photos). Reach behind the facia, then press in the speedometer cable retaining clip and disconnect the cable from the instrument panel. Disconnect the facial instrument panel wiring block connectors, and carefully manoeuvre the facia assembly out of the vehicle.

 HAYNES HiNT *If the facia cannot be withdrawn sufficiently to reach the speedometer cable, extra clearance can be gained by disconnecting the speedometer cable from the transmission, as described in Section 22 of Chapter 12.*

Refitting
13 Offer up the facia assembly, and reconnect the four wiring connectors. Refit the speedometer cable to the instrument panel, ensuring it is clipped securely in position.
14 Manoeuvre the panel into position, ensuring that the heater control panel is correctly positioned, then refit the facia mounting bolts, and tighten them to the specified torque.
15 The remainder of the refitting procedure is a reversal of removal, noting the following.
(a) Tighten the steering column mounting nuts and bolts to the specified torque, noting that the lower clamp nut and bolt should be tightened first.
(b) On completion, reconnect the battery and check that all electrical components and switches function correctly. Where applicable, reactivate the radio/cassette player security code.

31.11A Remove door demister duct ...

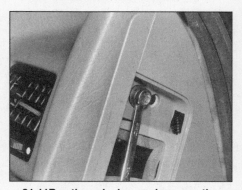

31.11B ... then slacken and remove the facia right-hand upper...

31.11C ... and lower mounting bolts

31.12A Facia centre mounting bolt is accessed via clock aperture

31.12B Removing facia assembly

11

Notes

Notes

Chapter 12 Electrical system

Contents

Degrees of difficulty

Easy, suitable for novice with little experience | **Fairly easy,** suitable for beginner with some experience | **Fairly difficult,** suitable for competent DIY mechanic | **Difficult,** suitable for experienced DIY mechanic | **Very difficult,** suitable for expert DIY or professional

Specifications

System type .... 12-volt, negative earth

Battery

Type .... Maintenance-free ('sealed for life') lead-acid
Battery code (Lucas):
  Standard equipment 063
  For cold climates 063S
Battery performance:

	Cold cranking	Reserve capacity
063	360 amps	60 amps
063S	405 amps	70 amps

Alternator

Type .... Nippon Denso
Output – @ 14 volts and 5500 rpm .... 60 amps
Regulated voltage .... 14 volts maximum
Brush minimum protrusion .... 5 mm approx (see text)

Starter motor

Type .... Nippon Denso or Mitsuba
Rating:
  Nippon Denso .... 1.2 kW
  Mitsuba .... 1.4 kW
Brush minimum length .... 3.5 mm approx (see text)

Fuses

Refer to wiring diagrams

12

Relays and control units

Component	Location
Main relay	Behind lower central facia panel
Direction indicator relay	Behind right-hand lower facia panel (square relay)
Heated rear window relay	Behind right-hand lower facia panel (circular relay)
Cigar lighter relay, foglamp relay, horn relay and headlamp main beam relay	Part of relay module, mounted on the transmission tunnel behind lower central facia panel
Electric window relay	Behind lower central facia panel
Electric window control unit	Behind right-hand front door inner trim panel
Central locking control unit	Behind left-hand front door inner trim panel
Air conditioning relays	Behind and below right-hand headlamp
Dim-dip relay	Behind right-hand lower facia panel
Windscreen wiper relay	Behind right-hand lower facia panel
Sunroof relay	Behind right-hand lower facia panel
Tailgate wiper relay	Behind right-hand luggage compartment trim

Bulbs

	Fitting	Wattage
Headlamps:		
Dipped/main beam bulb	H4	60/55
Separate main beam bulb	H1	55
Front sidelamps	Capless	5
Direction indicator lamps	Bayonet	21
Direction indicator side repeater lamps	Capless	5
Interior lamp	Festoon	5
Instrument panel warning lamps and illumination	Integral with bulbholder (except panel rear illumination bulbs, which are capless)	14V, 1.4 or 3W
Glovebox lamp	Festoon	5
Luggage compartment lamp	Bayonet	10
Reversing lamps	Bayonet	21
Tail lamps	Capless	5
Stop-lamps	Bayonet	21
Rear foglamp	Bayonet	21
Number plate lamp	Capless	5

Torque wrench settings

	Nm	lbf ft
Alternator:		
Pulley retaining nut	25	18
Pivot and adjusting link bolts	45	33
Starter motor mounting bolts	45	33
Wiper arm spindle nut	14	10
Wiper motor mounting bolts	9	7
Windscreen wiper linkage spindle assembly bolts	9	7

1 General information and precautions

Warning: Before carrying out any work on the electrical system, read through the precautions given in 'Safety first!' at the beginning of this manual.

The electrical system is of 12-volt negative earth type, and consists of a battery, alternator, starter motor and related electrical accessories, components and wiring.

The battery is charged by the alternator, which is belt-driven from the crankshaft pulley, and provides a steady supply of current for the ignition, starting, lighting and other electrical circuits.

The starter motor is of the pre-engaged type, incorporating an integral solenoid. On starting, the solenoid moves the drive pinion into engagement with the flywheel ring gear before the starter motor is energised. Once the engine has started, a one-way clutch prevents the motor armature being driven by the engine until the pinion disengages from the flywheel.

Particular care should be taken when working on the electrical system, to avoid damage to semi-conductor devices (diodes and transistors), and to avoid the risk of personal injury. In addition to the precautions given in 'Safety first!' at the beginning of this manual, observe the following when working on the system:

Always remove rings, watches, etc., before working on the electrical system. Even with the battery disconnected, capacitive discharge could occur if a component's live terminal is earthed through a metal object. This could cause a shock or nasty burn.

Do not reverse the battery connections. Components such as the alternator, fuel injection/ignition system ECU, or any others having semiconductor circuitry, could be irreparably damaged.

If the engine is being started using jump leads and a slave battery, connect the batteries *positive to positive* and *negative to negative* (see 'Booster battery (jump) starting'). This also applies when connecting a battery charger.

Never disconnect the battery terminals, the alternator, any electrical wiring or any test instruments, when the engine is running.

Do not allow the engine to turn the alternator when the alternator is not connected.

Never 'test' for alternator output by 'flashing' the output lead to earth.

Never use an ohmmeter of the type incorporating a hand-cranked generator for circuit or continuity testing.

Always ensure that the battery negative lead is disconnected when working on the electrical system.

Before using electric-arc welding equipment on the car, disconnect the battery, alternator, and components such as the fuel injection/ignition system ECU, to protect them.

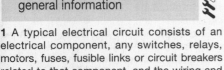

2 Electrical fault finding – general information

1 A typical electrical circuit consists of an electrical component, any switches, relays, motors, fuses, fusible links or circuit breakers related to that component, and the wiring and connectors that link the component to both the battery and the chassis. To help you pinpoint an electrical circuit problem, wiring diagrams are included at the end of this manual.

2 Before tackling any troublesome electrical circuit, first study the appropriate wiring diagrams to get a complete understanding of what components are included in that individual circuit. Troublespots, for instance, can be narrowed down by noting if other components related to the circuit are operating properly. If several components or circuits fail at one time, then the problem is probably in a fuse or earth connection, because several circuits are often routed through the same fuse and earth connections.

3 Electrical problems usually stem from simple causes, such as loose or corroded connections, a blown fuse, a melted fusible link, or a faulty relay. Visually inspect the condition of all fuses, wires and connections in a problem circuit before testing the components. Use the diagrams to note which terminal connections will need to be checked in order to pinpoint the troublespot.

4 The basic tools needed for electrical fault finding include a circuit tester or voltmeter (a 12-volt bulb with a set of test leads can also be used), a continuity tester, a battery and set of test leads, and a jumper wire, preferably with a circuit breaker incorporated, which can be used to bypass electrical components. Before attempting to locate a problem with test instruments, use the wiring diagram to decide where to make the connections.

Voltage checks

5 Voltage checks should be performed if a circuit is not functioning properly. Connect one lead of a circuit tester to either the negative battery terminal or a known good earth. Connect the other lead to a connector in the circuit being tested, preferably nearest to the battery or fuse. If the tester bulb lights, voltage is present, which means that the part of the circuit between the connector and the battery is problem-free. Continue checking the rest of the circuit in the same fashion. When you reach a point at which no voltage is

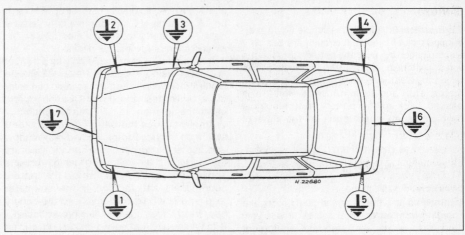

Fig. 12.1 Location of electrical system earth points (Sec 2)

1 *Behind left-hand headlamp – E1*
2 *Behind right-hand headlamp – E2*
3 *Base of right-hand front door pillar – E3*
4 *Beneath right-hand rear lamp cluster – E4*

5 *Beneath left-hand rear lamp cluster – E5*
6 *Centre of tailgate/boot lid – E6*
7 *Bonnet lock platform – E7*

present, the problem lies between that point and the last test point with voltage. Most problems can be traced to a loose connection. **Note:** *Bear in mind that some circuits are only live when the ignition switch is turned to a particular position.*

Finding a short-circuit

6 One method of finding a short-circuit is to remove the fuse and connect a test light or voltmeter to the fuse terminals, with all the relevant electrical components switched off. There should be no voltage present in the circuit. Move the wiring from side to side while watching the test light. If the bulb lights up, there is a short to earth somewhere in that area, probably where the insulation has rubbed through. The same test can be performed on each component in the circuit – even a switch.

Earth check

7 Perform an earth test to check whether a component is properly earthed. Disconnect the battery, and connect one lead of a self-powered test light (known as a 'continuity tester') to a known good earth point. Connect the other lead to the wire or earth connection being tested. If the bulb lights up, the earth is good; if not, the earth is faulty.

8 If an earth connection is thought to be faulty, dismantle the connection, and clean both the bodyshell and the wire terminal or the component's earth connection mating surface back to bare metal. Be careful to remove all traces of dirt and corrosion, then use a knife to trim away any paint, so that a clean metal-to-metal joint is made. On reassembly, tighten the joint fasteners securely; if a wire terminal is being refitted, use serrated washers between the terminal and the bodyshell, to ensure a clean and secure connection. When the connection is remade, prevent the onset of corrosion in the future by applying a coat of

petroleum jelly or silicone-based grease. Alternatively (at regular intervals) spray on a proprietary ignition sealer, or a water-dispersant lubricant.

9 The car's wiring harness has seven multiple-earth connections, each one being identified in the wiring diagrams by a reference number (E1 to E7). Each of these earth connections serves several circuits, their locations are as follows.

E1 Behind the left-hand headlamp.
E2 Behind the right-hand headlamp.
E3 Base of the right-hand front door pillar.
E4 Beneath the right-hand rear lamp cluster.
E5 Beneath the left-hand rear lamp cluster.
E6 Centre of the tailgate/boot lid.
E7 Bonnet lock platform.

Continuity check

10 A continuity check is necessary to determine if there are any breaks in a circuit. With the circuit off (ie no power in the circuit), a self-powered continuity tester can be used to check the circuit. Connect the test leads to both ends of the circuit (or to the positive end and a good earth), and if the test light comes on, the circuit is passing current properly. If the light does not come on, there is a break somewhere in the circuit. The same procedure can be used to test a switch, by connecting the continuity tester to the switch terminals. With the switch turned on, the test light should come on.

Finding an open-circuit

11 When checking for possible open-circuits, it is often difficult to locate them by sight because oxidation or terminal misalignment will be hidden by the connectors. Merely moving a connector on a sensor or in the wiring harness may correct the open-circuit condition. Remember this when an open-circuit is indicated when fault finding in a circuit. Intermittent problems may also be caused by oxidized or loose connections.

12

General

12 Electrical fault finding is simple if you keep in mind that all electrical circuits are basically electricity flowing from the battery, through the wires, switches, relays, fuses and fusible links to each electrical component (light bulb, motor, etc.) and to earth, from which it is passed back to the battery. Any electrical problem is an interruption in the flow of electricity from the battery.

3 Battery – testing and charging

1 In normal use, the battery should not require charging from an external source unless very heavy use is made of electrical equipment over a series of journeys that are too short to allow the charging system to keep pace with demand. Otherwise, a need for regular recharging points to a fault either in the battery or in the charging system.

2 If, however, the car is laid up for long periods (in excess of thirty days at a time) the battery will lose approximately 1% of its charge per week. This figure is for a disconnected battery; if the battery is left connected, circuits such as the clock (where fitted) will drain it at a faster rate. To prevent this happening, always disconnect the battery negative lead whenever the car is to be laid up for a long period. To keep the battery fully charged, it should be given regular 'refresher' charges every six weeks or so. This is particularly important on 'maintenance-free' batteries, which will suffer permanent reduction of charge capacity if allowed to become fully discharged.

3 If a discharged battery is suspected, the simplest test for most owners is as follows. Leave the battery disconnected for at least two hours, then measure the (open-circuit, or no-load) voltage using a sensitive voltmeter connected across the battery terminals. Compare the reading obtained with the following table.

Voltmeter reading	Charge condition
10.50 volts	Fully-discharged – fit new battery
12.30 volts	50% charged
12.48 volts	75% charged
12.66 volts or more	Fully-charged

4 If frequent topping-up is required and the battery case is not fractured, the battery is being over-charged; the voltage regulator will have to be checked (see Section 5 below).

5 If the car covers a very small annual mileage, it is worthwhile checking the specific gravity of the electrolyte every three months, to determine the state of charge of the battery. Use a hydrometer to make the check, and compare the results with the following table.

	Normal climates	Tropics
Discharged	1.120	1.080
Half-charged	1.200	1.160
Fully-charged	1.280	1.230

6 If the battery condition is suspect, first check the specific gravity of electrolyte in each cell. A variation of 0.040 or more between any cells indicates loss of electrolyte, or deterioration of the internal plates.

7 A further test can be made only by a battery specialist using a battery heavy-discharge meter. However, the home mechanic can carry out a similar test as follows. Disconnect and earth the ignition coil HT lead, connect a voltmeter across the battery terminals, and switch on the headlamps, heated rear window and heater blower (highest speed). Operate the starter – if the voltmeter reading remains above approximately 9.5 volts, the battery condition is satisfactory. If the voltmeter reading drops below 9.5 volts and the battery has already been charged, it is proven faulty.

8 In Winter, when a heavy demand is placed on the battery (starting from cold, and using more electrical equipment), it is a good idea to occasionally have the battery fully charged from an external source. The battery's bench charge rate depends on its code (see a Rover dealer or Lucas agent for details); for most owners, the best method will be to use a tricklecharger overnight, charging at a rate of 1.5 amps. Rapid 'boost' chargers which restore the power of the battery in 1 to 2 hours are not recommended – they can cause serious damage to the battery plates through overheating, and may cause a sealed battery to explode.

9 Ideally, the battery should be removed from the car before charging, and moved to a well-ventilated area. As a minimum precaution, both battery terminal leads must be disconnected (disconnect the negative lead first) before connecting the charger leads.

 Warning: The battery will be emitting significant quantities of (highly-inflammable) hydrogen gas during charging, and for approximately 15 minutes afterwards; do not allow sparks or naked flames near the battery, or it may explode.

10 Continue to charge the battery until all cells are gassing vigorously, and no further rise in specific gravity or increase in no-load voltage is noted over a four-hour period. When charging is complete, turn the charger off before disconnecting the leads from the battery.

4 Battery – removal and refitting

Removal

1 First check that all electrical components are switched off, to avoid a spark occurring as the negative lead is disconnected. If the radio/cassette unit has a security code, de-activate the code temporarily, and re-activate it when the battery is re-connected; refer to the instructions and code supplied with the unit.

2 Slacken the terminal clamp nut, then lift the clamp and negative (–) lead from the terminal. This is the terminal to disconnect before working on any electrical component on the car. If the terminal is tight, carefully ease it off by moving it from side to side.

3 Raise the plastic cover from the positive (+) terminal clamp, and slacken the clamp nut, then lift the clamp and lead from the terminal.

4 Unscrew the clamp bolt, and remove the clamp from the battery tray.

5 Lift the battery from the tray, keeping it upright and taking care not to allow it to contact your clothing.

6 If the battery tray is to be removed, first release any relevant wiring harness clips from the tray. Unscrew the four bolts securing the battery tray in position, and remove the tray. If necessary, undo the two battery tray support bracket retaining bolts, and remove the bracket from the car (photos).

7 Clean the battery terminal posts and clamps, and the battery tray and battery casing. If the bodywork is rusted as a result of battery acid spilling onto it, clean it thoroughly and re-paint with reference to Chapter 11.

8 Whenever the battery is removed, check it for cracks and leakage.

Refitting

9 Refitting is the reverse of the removal procedure. Ensure that the terminal posts and leads are cleaned before re-connection. Smear petroleum jelly on the terminals after reconnecting the leads. Always connect the positive terminal clamp first and the negative terminal clamp last.

4.6A Battery tray retaining bolts (arrowed)

4.6B Battery tray mounting bracket retaining bolts (viewed from underneath)

5 Charging system – testing

1 If the ignition warning lamp fails to light when the ignition is switched on, first check the alternator wiring connections for security. If satisfactory, check that the warning lamp bulb has not blown, and that it is secure in its holder. If the lamp still fails to light, check the continuity of the warning lamp feed wire from the alternator to the bulbholder. If all is satisfactory, the alternator is at fault, and should be taken to an auto-electrician for testing and repair.

2 If the ignition warning lamp lights when the engine is running, stop the engine as soon as possible. Check that the drivebelt is correctly tensioned (see Chapter 1), and that the alternator connections are secure. If all is so far satisfactory, check the alternator brushes and commutator as described in Section 7. If the fault persists, the alternator should be taken to an auto-electrician for testing and repair.

3 If the alternator output is suspect even though the warning lamp functions correctly, the regulated voltage may be checked as follows.

4 Connect a voltmeter across the battery terminals, and start the engine.

5 Increase engine speed until the voltmeter reading remains steady; this should be approximately 12 to 13 volts, and no more than 14 volts.

6 Switch on as many electrical accessories (eg the headlamps, heated rear window and heater blower) as possible, and check that the alternator maintains the regulated voltage at around 13 to 14 volts.

7 If the regulated voltage is not as stated, the fault may be due to worn brushes, weak brush springs, a faulty voltage regulator, a faulty diode, a severed phase winding, or a worn or damaged commutator. The brushes and commutator may be checked by the home mechanic, but if the fault persists, the alternator should be taken to an auto-electrician for testing and repair.

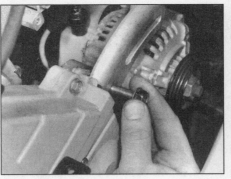

6.4 Undo the retaining bolt and remove the alternator adjusting link

6 Alternator – removal and refitting

Removal

1 Disconnect the battery negative lead.

2 To improve access to the alternator from above, undo the nut and bolts which secure the windscreen/tailgate washer reservoir to the bulkhead, then disconnect the washer pump wiring connector(s) and position the reservoir clear of the working area. Firmly apply the handbrake, then jack up the front of the car and support it on axle stands, so that access to the alternator can also be gained from below.

3 Slacken the upper alternator adjusting link bolt and the lower alternator pivot bolt, then push the alternator fully towards the engine and slip the drivebelt off the alternator pulley. Remove the alternator upper adjusting link bolt.

4 Undo the bolt securing the adjusting link to the water pump, and remove the adjusting link from the engine (photo).

5 Pivot the alternator away from the engine, and disconnect the wiring block connector from the rear of the alternator. Pull away the rubber insulating cover, then slacken and remove the retaining nut and washer, and disconnect the lead from the main alternator terminal (photo).

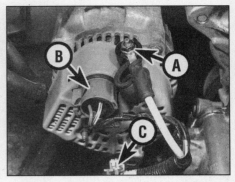

6.5 Alternator main terminal (A), wiring connector (B) and wiring harness retaining clip (C) – inlet manifold removed for clarity

6 Free the wiring harness retaining clip from the rear of the alternator, then withdraw the lower pivot bolt, and manoeuvre the alternator upwards and out of the engine compartment (photo).

Refitting

7 If a new alternator is being installed, it will be necessary to transfer the pulley from the original to the new unit. To do this, slacken the pulley retaining nut whilst preventing the pulley from rotating; either use a suitable Allen key in the end of the alternator shaft, or clamp the pulley firmly in a vice equipped with soft jaws. Remove the pulley from the old alternator and, ensuring that the pulley and shaft mating surfaces are clean, install it on the new unit. Tighten the pulley retaining nut to the specified torque, while using the method employed on removal to hold the pulley. Note that it will also be necessary to transfer the wiring mounting bracket from the rear of the original unit to the new unit, tightening its retaining bolt securely.

8 Manoeuvre the alternator into position, then insert the lower pivot bolt. Fit the pivot bolt mounting nut, noting that it should be tightened finger-tight only at this stage.

9 Refit the wiring harness clip to the bracket on the rear of the alternator, and reconnect the wiring block connector. Connect the lead to the main alternator terminal, then refit its washer and retaining nut. Tighten the retaining nut securely, and slide the rubber insulating cover back into position (photo).

10 Refit the adjusting link, and install both the adjusting link retaining bolt and the upper alternator adjusting link bolt. Tighten both bolts by hand only, then refit the drivebelt to the alternator and adjust it as described in Chapter 1.

11 Once the drivebelt is correctly tensioned and all the alternator mounting bolts are correctly tightened, refit the washer reservoir to its original position, and tighten its retaining nut and bolts securely. Reconnect the washer pump wiring connector(s) and the battery negative terminal, and lower the car to the ground.

6.6 Remove the retaining nut and withdraw the lower pivot bolt, then manoeuvre the alternator upwards and out of the engine compartment

6.9 On refitting, ensure the main terminal nut is securely tightened, then slide the rubber insulating cover back into position

12

7.2A Remove the main terminal nut and slide off the insulator sleeve (arrowed)

7.2B Undo the retaining nuts, noting the fitted position of the wiring bracket (arrowed), and remove the rear cover

7.3A Undo the retaining screws (arrowed) ...

7.3B ... and remove the brush holder from the alternator

7.4 Measuring alternator brush length

7 Alternator – brush renewal

Note: *The vast majority of alternator faults are due to the brushes. It the renewal of the brushes does not cure the fault, the advice of an expert should be sought as to the best approach; for most owners, the best course of action will be to renew the alternator as a complete unit. In many cases overhaul will not be viable, on economic grounds alone.*

1 Remove the alternator, as described in Section 6.

2 Remove all traces of dirt from the exterior of the alternator, then slacken and remove the nut from the main alternator terminal, and slide off the insulator sleeve. Undo the rear cover retaining nuts, noting the correct fitted position of the wiring harness bracket, and remove the cover to gain access to the brush holder (photos).

3 Undo the brush holder retaining screws, then remove the assembly from the alternator and remove its rubber cover (photos).

4 In most cases, the brushes will have wear limit marks in the form of a groove etched along one face of each brush; when these marks are erased by wear, the brushes are worn out. If no marks are provided, measure the protrusion of each brush from the brush holder end to the tip of the brush (photo). No dimension is specified by Rover, but as a rough guide, 5 mm should be regarded as a minimum. If either brush is worn to or below this amount, renew the brush holder assembly. If the brushes are still serviceable, clean them with a solvent-moistened cloth. Check that the brush spring pressure is equal for both brushes, and that the brushes are held securely against the slip rings. If there is any doubt about the condition of the brushes and springs, compare them with new components.

5 Clean the slip rings with a solvent-moistened cloth, then check for signs of scoring, burning or severe pitting. If worn or damaged, the slip rings should be attended to by an auto-electrician.

6 Refitting is the reverse of the removal procedure.

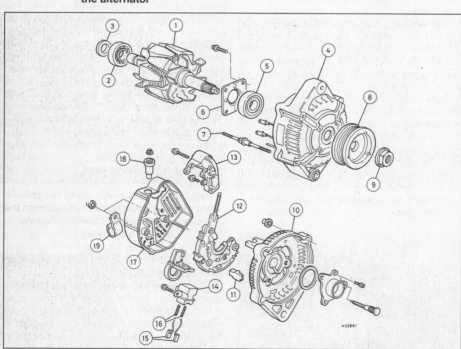

Fig. 12.2 Exploded view of the alternator (Sec 7)

1 Rotor	8 Drive pulley	14 Brush holder
2 Slip ring (rear) bearing	9 Pulley retaining nut	15 Brush
3 Spacer	10 Slip ring end (rear) bracket	16 Brush springs
4 Stator assembly	11 Insulator sleeve	17 Rear cover
5 Drive end (front) bearing	12 Rectifier	18 Insulator sleeve
6 Bearing retaining plate	13 Voltage regulator	19 Wiring harness clip
7 Stud		

8 Starting system – testing

Note: *Refer to the warnings given in 'Safety first!' and in Section 1 of this Chapter before starting work.*

1 If the starter motor fails to operate when the switch is operated, the following may be the cause.

(a) *The battery is faulty.*

(b) *The electrical connections between the ignition switch, starter solenoid, battery and starter motor are somewhere failing to pass the necessary current from the battery through the starter to earth.*

(c) *The starter solenoid is faulty.*

(d) *The starter motor is mechanically or electrically defective.*

2 To check the battery, switch on the headlamps. If they dim after a few seconds, the battery is discharged; recharge or renew the battery. If the lamps glow brightly, operate the ignition switch and see what happens to the lamps. If they dim, power is reaching the starter motor; therefore, the starter motor must be renewed or overhauled to cure the fault. If the lamps stay bright (and no clicking sound can be heard from the solenoid), there is a fault in the circuit or solenoid – see below. If the starter turns slowly when switched on, but the battery is in good condition, then either the starter must be faulty, or there is considerable resistance in the circuit.

3 If the circuit is suspected, disconnect the battery terminals (including the earth connection to the body), the starter/solenoid wiring, and the engine/transmission earth lead. Thoroughly clean their connections, refit them, then use a meter or test lamp to check that full battery voltage is available at the solenoid terminal of the battery positive lead, and to check that the earth is sound. Smear petroleum jelly around the battery terminals, to prevent corrosion – corroded connections are the most frequent cause of electrical system malfunctions.

4 If the battery and all connections are in good condition, check the circuit by first disconnecting the wire from the solenoid spade terminal. Connect a meter or test lamp between the wire end and the terminal, and check that the wire is live when the ignition switch is operated. If it is, then the circuit is sound; if not, proceed to paragraph 7.

5 The solenoid contacts can be checked by putting a voltmeter or test lamp across the main cable connection on the starter side of the solenoid and earth. When the switch is operated, there should be a reading (or the bulb should light). If there is no reading or lighted bulb, the solenoid is faulty, and should be renewed.

6 If the circuit and solenoid are proved sound, the fault must be in the starter motor, remove it and check the brushes as described in Section 10. If the fault does not lie in the brushes, the motor windings must be faulty; in this event

the motor must be renewed, unless an auto-electrical specialist can be found who will overhaul the unit (at a cost significantly less than that of a new or exchange starter motor).

7 If the circuit is thought to be faulty, check the ignition switch and wiring using the equipment and procedures outlined in Section 2 of this Chapter, referring to the wiring diagrams for full details.

9 Starter motor – removal and refitting

Removal

1 Disconnect the battery negative lead.

2 Using a pair of pliers, release the retaining clip and disconnect the vacuum pipe from the throttle housing end of the air intake hose. Slacken the retaining clamp which secures the intake hose to the throttle housing, and disconnect the intake hose. Working along the length of the intake hose, release the vacuum hoses from their retaining clips, then disconnect the intake hose from the air cleaner housing and remove it from the engine compartment.

3 Undo the wiring harness retaining bolt (photo), and free the harness from the starter motor.

4 Lift up the rubber cover, slacken and remove the nut and washer, and disconnect

the battery cable from the main solenoid terminal. Pull away the second rubber cover, and carefully disconnect the spade connector from the solenoid (photo).

5 Slacken and remove the two starter motor mounting bolts, and manoeuvre the starter motor out of the engine compartment (photos).

Refitting

6 Refitting is a reverse of the removal sequence, tightening the starter motor mounting bolts to the specified torque setting.

10 Starter motor – brush and solenoid renewal

1 Remove the starter motor, as described in Section 9.

Brushes

2 Slacken and remove the two small screws which secure the brush plate assembly to the rear end cover.

3 Using a scriber or suitable marker pen, make alignment marks between the end cover and the yoke, then unscrew the two through-bolts and withdraw the end cover, noting the fitted position of the wiring harness bracket. Remove any shims which have stuck to the rear cover, and refit them onto the armature shaft (where fitted).

9.3 Undo the retaining bolt, and free the wiring harness from the starter motor bracket

9.4 Undo the battery cable nut and disconnect the cable, then disconnect the spade connector (arrowed) from the solenoid

9.5A Remove the two starter motor mounting bolts (arrowed – one hidden) ...

9.5B ... and remove the motor from the engine

12

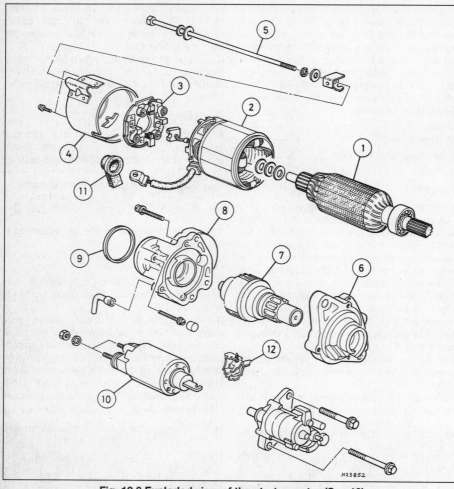

10.4A Lift the field coil brush springs with a screwdriver, then slide out the brushes ...

10.4B ... and remove the brushplate assembly

Fig. 12.3 Exploded view of the starter motor (Sec 10)

1 Armature	6 Gear housing cover	9 O-ring
2 Field coils and yoke	7 One-way clutch assembly	10 Solenoid
3 Brushplate assembly	8 Starter motor/solenoid	11 Terminal cover
4 Rear end cover	mounting plate	12 Solenoid lever
5 Through-bolt		

10.5 Measuring starter motor brush length

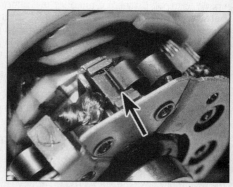

10.7 On refitting, ensure the springs are correctly seated in the brush grooves (arrowed)

4 Lift the field coil brush springs with a screwdriver, and slide both the brushes out of the brushplate. The brushplate assembly can then be removed from the end of the armature (photos).

5 In most cases, the brushes will have wear limit marks in the form of a groove etched along one face of each brush; when the brushes are worn down to these marks, they are worn out and must be renewed. If no marks are provided, measure the length of each brush. No dimension is specified by Rover, but as a rough guide, 3.5 mm should be regarded as a minimum (photo). If any brush is worn below this amount, renew the brushes as a set. If the brushes are still serviceable, clean them with a solvent-moistened cloth. Check that the brush spring pressure is equal for all brushes, and that the brushes are held securely against the commutator. If in doubt about the condition of the brushes and springs, compare them with new components.

6 Clean the commutator with a solvent-moistened cloth, then check for signs of scoring, burning, excessive wear or severe pitting. If worn or damaged, the commutator should be attended to by an auto-electrician.

7 Fit the brushplate assembly over the commutator, then lift the field coil brush springs and slot the field coil brushes back into position in their holders. With all the brushes in position, check that the springs are correctly seated in the groove on each brush, and that the brushes are free to move in their holders against spring pressure (photo).

8 Ensure that any necessary shims are in position on the armature shaft, then locate the field coil wire grommet in the end cover, and refit the cover (photo).

9 Align the cover holes with those in the brush holder, then refit the small brushplate retaining screws and tighten them securely (photo).

10 Align the marks made on dismantling, then refit the starter motor through-bolts, ensuring

10.8 Locate the end cover with the wiring grommet and slide it onto the motor

10.9 Refit the brushplate retaining screws ...

10.10 ... then install the throughbolts, ensuring the wiring harness bracket (arrowed) is correctly positioned

that the wiring harness support bracket is correctly positioned, and tighten them securely (photo).

Solenoid

11 Pull back the rubber cover, then slacken and remove the nut and washer securing the starter motor lead to the solenoid. Disconnect the lead from the solenoid terminal (photo).
12 Make alignment marks between the starter motor yoke and the starter motor/solenoid mounting plate, then slacken and remove the two starter motor through-bolts, noting the fitted position of the wiring harness mounting bracket. Carefully remove the starter assembly from the mounting plate, noting any shims which are fitted to the armature shaft (photo).
13 Undo the three screws and washers which secure the front gear housing cover to the starter motor/solenoid mounting plate, then remove the gear housing and one-way clutch assembly (photos).
14 Slacken and remove the three solenoid retaining screws (photo), and remove the solenoid and solenoid lever from the mounting plate, noting the solenoid O-ring.
15 On refitting, first ensure that the solenoid and mounting plate are clean, then apply a smear of molybdenum disulphide grease to the solenoid arm and lever. Examine the O-ring for signs of damage, renewing if necessary, and install it in the mounting plate recess (photo).
16 Engage the solenoid lever with the

10.11 Remove the retaining nut and disconnect the starter motor lead from the solenoid

10.12 Undo the through-bolts, and remove the motor assembly from the mounting plate

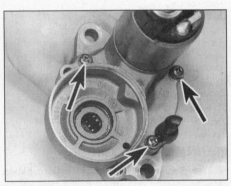

10.13A Remove the three retaining screws (arrowed) ...

10.13B ... then lift off the front gear housing cover ...

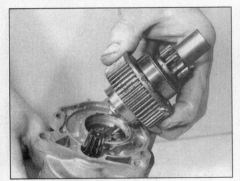

10.13C ... and remove the one-way clutch assembly

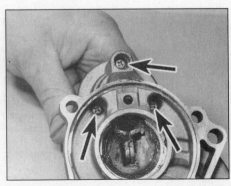

10.14 Solenoid retaining screws (arrowed)

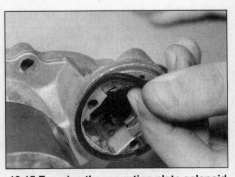

10.15 Examine the mounting plate solenoid O-ring for wear or damage, and renew if necessary

12

10.16 Lubricate the lever with multi-purpose grease, and engage the solenoid lever with the solenoid arm

11.2 Fuses can be removed using plastic tweezers supplied (arrowed)

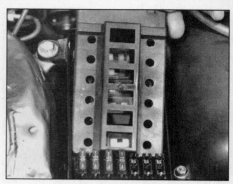

11.9A Remove the plastic cover from the engine compartment fusebox ...

solenoid arm (photo), and fit the assembly to the mounting plate. Refit the solenoid retaining screws, and tighten them securely.

17 Refit the gear housing and one-way clutch assembly to the mounting plate, then tighten its retaining screws securely.

18 Ensure that any necessary shims are in position on the armature shaft, then refit the motor assembly to the mounting plate. Align the marks made on dismantling, then refit the starter motor through-bolts and tighten them securely.

19 Connect the starter motor lead to the solenoid terminal, ensuring that the lug on the lead engages with the terminal keyway, and refit the washer and nut. Tighten the terminal nut securely, and slide the rubber cover back into position.

11 Fuses, fusible links and relays – general information

Fuses

1 Most of the fuses are located behind the panel in the right-hand lower facia panel, with a few odd fuses being located in the fusebox on the right-hand side of the engine compartment.

2 Access to the fuses is gained by removing the fusebox lid/cover. Symbols on the reverse of the lid/cover indicate the circuits protected by the fuses; five spare fuses are supplied,

together with plastic tweezers to remove and fit them (photo). Further details on fuse ratings and circuits protected are given in the Specifications section of this Chapter.

3 To remove a fuse, first switch off the circuit concerned (or the ignition), then fit the tweezers and pull the fuse out of its terminals. Slide the fuse sideways from the tweezers. The wire within the fuse is clearly visible; if the fuse is blown, it will be broken or melted.

4 Always renew a fuse with one of an identical rating; never use a fuse with a different rating from the original, or substitute anything else. Never renew a fuse more than once without tracing the source of the trouble. The fuse rating is stamped on top of the fuse; note that the fuses are also colour-coded for easy recognition.

5 If a new fuse blows immediately, find the cause before renewing it again; a short to earth as a result of faulty insulation is most likely. Where a fuse protects more than one circuit, try to isolate the defect by switching on each circuit in turn (if possible) until the fuse blows again.

6 If any of the spare fuses are used, always replace them immediately so that a spare of each rating is available.

Fusible links

7 The fusible links are located in the fusebox situated on the right-hand side of the engine compartment. Unclip the lid to gain access to them.

8 Details of link ratings and circuits protected are given in the Specifications Section of this Chapter; the links are numbered on the rear of the fusebox lid.

9 To remove a fusible link, first ensure that the circuit concerned is switched off, then prise off the small black plastic cover. Slacken the two link retaining screws, then lift the fusible link out of the fusebox (photos). The wire within the fusible link is clearly visible; if the fuse is blown, it will be broken or melted. **Note: *A blown fusible link indicates a serious wiring or system fault, which must be diagnosed before the link is renewed.***

10 Always renew a fusible link with one of an identical rating; never use a link with a different rating from the original, or substitute anything else. On refitting, tighten the link retaining screws securely and refit the link cover.

Relays

11 The Specifications Section of this Chapter gives full information on the location and function of the various relays fitted; refer to the relevant wiring diagram for details of wiring connections.

12 If a circuit or system controlled by a relay develops a fault and the relay is suspect, operate the system; if the relay is functioning, it should be possible to hear it click as it is energized. If this is the case, the fault lies with the components or wiring of the system. If the relay is not being energized, then either the relay is not receiving a main supply or a

11.9B ... to gain access to fusible link retaining screws

11.14A Use a screwdriver to release the relay module retaining clip ...

11.14B ... then slide the module out of position, and disconnect its wiring connectors

12.3A Individual combination switches can be removed by slackening their retaining screws (arrowed) ...

12.3B ... and sliding the switch out of the main assembly

12.6A Carefully prise facia switches out of position ...

switching voltage, or the relay itself is faulty. Testing is by the substitution of a known good unit, but be careful, while some relays are identical in appearance and in operation, others look similar but perform different functions.

13 To renew a relay, ensure that the ignition switch is off, then simply pull it from the socket and press in the new relay.

14 Certain relays are contained in the relay module which is situated behind the lower central facia panel. To remove this, first remove the lower central panel from the facia, as described in Section 31 of Chapter 11. Disconnect its two wiring block connectors, then release its retaining clip and slide to the left to withdraw it from the mounting bracket (photos). The complete module must be renewed, even if only one of the relays is faulty.

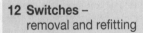

12 Switches – removal and refitting

Note: *Disconnect the battery negative lead before removing any switch, and reconnect the lead after refitting the switch.*

Ignition switch

1 Refer to Chapter 10, Section 20, for details of switch removal and refitting. A Rover dealer

will be able to tell you whether the switch can be obtained separately from the steering lock.

Steering column combination switch

2 Remove the steering wheel and steering column shrouds, then disconnect the switch wiring as described in Chapter 10, Section 18, paragraphs 1 to 4.

3 Each individual switch can be removed by unscrewing its two retaining screws, and sliding the switch out of the housing (photos).

4 To remove the complete assembly, slacken and remove the two retaining screws, and slide the assembly off the steering column.

5 Refitting is the reverse of the removal procedure, referring to Chapter 10, Section 18 for further information.

Instrument panel and facia switches

6 Check that the switch is in the 'off' position, then (taking great care not to scratch or damage the switch or its surround) prise it out using a suitable flat-bladed screwdriver. Withdraw the switch until the connector plug appears, then disconnect the wiring connector and remove the switch (photos). Tie a piece of string to the wiring connector, to retrieve it if it falls behind the facia panel.

7 On refitting, connect the wiring connector to the switch, then press the switch into position until its retaining clips click into place.

Electric window switches

8 Remove the door inner trim panel as described in Chapter 11.

9 Undo the retaining screws, and remove the switch from the trim panel (photo).

10 On refitting, tighten the switch screws securely, and refit the door inner trim panel as described in Chapter 11.

Courtesy lamp switches

11 With the door open, undo the two screws securing the switch to the body. Pull out the switch, and tie a piece of string to the wiring, to retrieve it if it drops into the body.

12 Disconnect the switch, and remove it from the vehicle.

13 Refitting is a reverse of removal.

Handbrake warning lamp switch

14 From inside the car, carefully prise out the cover from the top of the centre console rear section, to gain access to the two retaining screws. Undo the two screws, and remove the rear centre console section.

15 Disconnect the wiring connector from the switch, slacken and remove the retaining screw, and remove the switch from the handbrake lever quadrant (photo).

16 Refitting is a reverse of the removal procedure.

12.6B ... and disconnect their wiring connectors

12.9 Driver's side electric window switch retaining screws (arrowed)

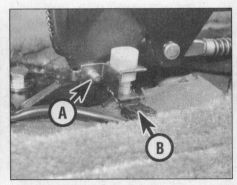

12.15 Handbrake warning lamp switch retaining screw (A) and wiring connector (B)

12

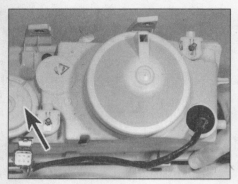

13.2 Remove large circular cover to access dip/main beam headlamp and sidelamp bulbs, and smaller cover (arrowed) to access separate main beam bulb

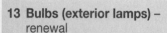

13 Bulbs (exterior lamps) – renewal

General

1 Whenever a bulb is renewed, note the following points.

(a) *Disconnect the battery negative lead before starting work.*

(b) *Remember that if the lamp has just been in use, the bulb may be extremely hot.*

(c) *Always check the bulb contacts and holder for a clean metal-to-metal contact between the bulb and its live(s) and earth. Clean off any corrosion or dirt before fitting a new bulb.*

13.12... then withdraw the indicator lamp, and twist the bulbholder free

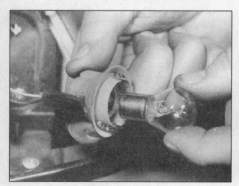

13.13 Indicator bulbs are of the bayonet type

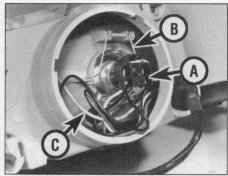

13.3 Headlamp dip/main beam bulb wiring connector (A), retaining clip (B) and sidelamp bulbholder (C) – headlamp removed for clarity

(d) *Wherever bayonet-type bulbs are fitted (see Specifications), ensure that the live contact(s) bear firmly against the bulb contact.*

(e) *Always ensure that the new bulb is of the correct rating, and that it is completely clean before fitting it, this applies particularly to headlamp bulbs (see below).*

Headlamp

2 Working in the engine compartment, twist off the relevant circular plastic cover, and remove it from the rear of the headlamp unit (photo).

3 Unplug the wiring connector, then press together the ears of the bulb retaining clip and release it from the rear of the lamp (photo).

4 Withdraw the bulb.

5 When handling the new bulb, use a tissue or clean cloth to avoid touching the glass with the fingers; moisture and grease from the skin can cause blackening and rapid failure of this type of bulb. If the glass is accidentally touched, wipe it clean using methylated spirit.

6 Refitting is the reverse of the removal procedure; ensure that the new bulb's locating tabs are correctly located in the lamp cutouts.

Front sidelamp

7 Working in the engine compartment, twist off the large circular plastic cover, and remove it from the rear of the headlamp unit.

13.15 Push indicator side repeater lamp to the right ...

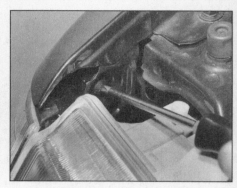

13.11 Remove the retaining screw ...

8 Pull the bulbholder from the headlamp reflector.

9 Pull the capless (push fit) bulb out of its socket.

10 Refitting is the reverse of the removal procedure.

Front direction indicator

11 Working in the engine compartment, undo the indicator lamp upper retaining screw, and withdraw the lamp (photo).

12 Twist the bulbholder anti-clockwise to free it from the lamp, and remove the lamp unit (photo).

13 The bulb is a bayonet fit in the holder, and can be removed by pressing it and twisting anti-clockwise (photo).

14 Refitting is a reverse of the removal procedure.

Front direction indicator side repeater

15 Push the lamp unit towards the right to free its retaining clips, then withdraw it from the wing (photo).

16 Pull the bulbholder out of the lamp unit, then pull the capless (push fit) bulb out of its holder (photo).

17 Refitting is a reverse of the removal procedure.

Rear lamp cluster

18 From inside the luggage compartment, remove the relevant lamp rear cover.

13.16... then withdraw the lamp, and pull out the bulbholder

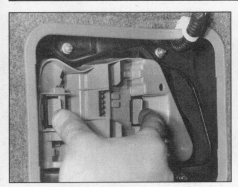

13.19 Depress the catches, and withdraw rear lamp bulb panel

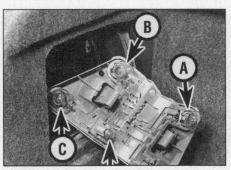

13.20A Rear lamp cluster bulbs: direction indicator (A), reversing lamp (B), foglamp (C), tail lamp (D) and stop-lamp (E)

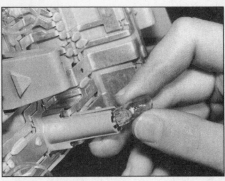

13.20B Rear cluster tail lamp bulb is of capless type ...

19 Depress the catches, and withdraw the bulb panel from the lens unit (photo).

20 The relevant bulb can then be removed from the panel, noting that the tail lamp bulb is of the capless (push fit) type, whereas all other bulbs have a bayonet fitting (photos).

21 Refitting is the reverse of the removal sequence, noting that the lamp unit rubber seal must be renewed if damaged.

Number plate lamp

22 Undo the two mounting screws, and remove the number plate lamp lens and seal.

23 Withdraw the lamp, and remove the clip from the top of the lamp body to gain access to the bulb.

24 The bulb is of the capless (push fit) type, and can be pulled out of the lamp unit.

25 Refitting is a reverse of the removal procedure.

14 Bulbs (interior lamps) – renewal

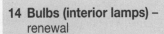

General

1 Refer to Section 13, paragraph 1.

Courtesy lamps

2 Carefully prise the lens off the light unit, then remove the (festoon type) bulb from its edge contacts.

3 Fit the new bulb using a reversal of the

removal procedure; if necessary, bend the spring contacts slightly so that they firmly contact the bulb end caps.

Glovebox lamp

4 Open up the glovebox, and undo the two switch/lamp assembly retaining screws. Disconnect the wiring connector, and remove the switch/lamp unit from the glovebox.

5 Depress the lens retaining lug, and remove the lens assembly from the unit.

6 Release the (festoon type) bulb from its contacts, and remove it from the lens.

7 Fit the new bulb using a reversal of the removal procedure; if necessary, bend the spring contacts slightly so that they firmly contact the bulb end caps.

Luggage compartment lamp

8 Carefully prise the lamp out of the trim panel, using a suitable flat-bladed screwdriver.

9 The bulb is a bayonet fit, and can be removed by pressing it in and twisting anti-clockwise (photo).

10 Refitting is a reverse of the removal sequence.

Instrument panel lamps

Warning and illumination lamps

11 Remove the instrument panel, as described in Section 17.

12 Twist the relevant bulbholder (Fig. 12.4) anti-clockwise, and withdraw it from the rear of the panel.

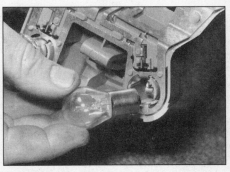

13.20C ... whereas all other bulbs have a bayonet type fitting

13 All bulbs, with the exception of the panel rear illumination bulbs, are integral with their holders. The panel rear illumination bulbs are of the capless type, and are a push fit in their holders (photos). Be very careful to ensure that the new bulbs are of the correct rating (the same as those removed) – this is especially important in the case of the ignition/battery charging warning lamp.

14 Refitting is the reverse of the removal procedure.

Selector position indicator – automatic transmission models

15 Remove the selector position indicator panel, as described in Section 18.

16 All panel bulbs are integral with their holders, and are a push fit in the indicator panel. Remove the relevant bulb and renew.

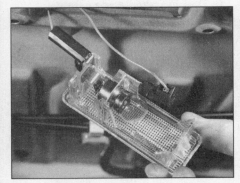

14.9 Luggage compartment lamp bulb is of the bayonet type

14.13A Instrument panel rear illumination bulbholder is a twist fit in the panel ...

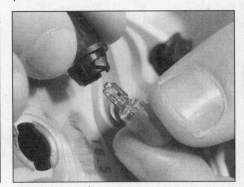

14.13B ... the bulb being of the capless type

12

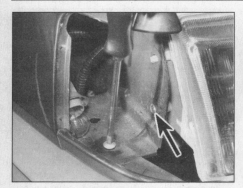

15.3A Slacken and remove the headlamp retaining screws (remaining one arrowed) ...

15.3B ... and the two headlamp retaining bolts

15.4 Disconnect the wiring connector, and withdraw the headlamp unit

17 Refit the indicator panel as described in Section 18.

Facia illumination bulbs

18 To renew the various facia illumination bulbs, it will first be necessary to remove the relevant facia panel to gain access to the bulb. Refer to Section 31 of Chapter 11 for information on facia panel removal and refitting.

Switch illumination bulbs

19 All of the facia panel switches are fitted with illuminating bulbs; some are also fitted with a bulb, to show when the circuit concerned is operating. These bulbs are an integral part of the switch assembly, and cannot be obtained separately. Bulb replacement will therefore require the renewal of the complete switch assembly.

15 Exterior lamp units – removal and refitting

Note: *Disconnect the battery negative lead before removing any lamp unit, and reconnect the lead after refitting the lamp.*

Headlamp

1 Open up the bonnet, undo the four radiator retaining grille retaining screws, and remove the grille from the car.

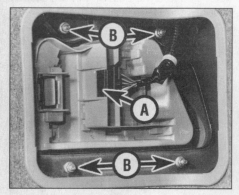

15.14 Disconnect the wiring connector (A), and remove the rear lamp unit retaining nuts (B)

2 Remove the screw securing the indicator lamp assembly to the wing, and position the lamp unit clear of the headlamp assembly.
3 Undo the two headlamp retaining screws situated behind the indicator lamp, then undo the two upper headlamp retaining bolts (photos).
4 Disconnect the headlamp wiring connector (photo).
5 Gently pull the headlamp upwards to release it from its lower retainer, then remove the headlamp and lower finisher trim panel assembly from the car.
6 If necessary, the lower finisher can be removed from the headlamp by removing its retaining screw and releasing its two retaining clips.
7 Refitting is a reversal of the removal procedure. On completion, adjust the headlamp aim as described in Chapter 1.

Front direction indicator

8 Open up the bonnet, and remove the indicator lamp upper retaining screw.
9 Withdraw the lamp unit from the wing, twist the bulbholder anti-clockwise to free it from the lamp, and remove the lamp unit from the car.
10 Refitting is the reverse of the removal procedure.

Front direction indicator side repeater

11 Push the lamp unit to the right to free its

15.15 Withdraw the rear lamp unit, noting the rubber seal

retaining clips, then withdraw it from the wing.
12 Pull the bulbholder out, and remove the lamp from the car.
13 Refitting is a reverse of the removal procedure.

Rear lamp cluster

14 Working from within the luggage compartment, remove the relevant rear lamp cover, and disconnect the lamp wiring connector (photo).
15 Undo the four nuts securing the lamp unit to the body, and remove the unit from the car, noting the rubber seal which is fitted between the lamp unit and body (photo).
16 Refitting is a reversal of the removal procedure, noting that the rubber seal must be renewed if damaged.

Number plate lamps

17 Undo the two mounting screws, and remove the number plate lamp lens and seal.
18 Withdraw the lamp unit until the wiring connector appears, then disconnect the connector and remove the unit from the car.
19 Refitting is the reverse of the removal procedure, noting that the rubber seal must be renewed if damaged.

16 Dim-dip headlamp system – general information

1 The system comprises the dim-dip unit mounted behind the right-hand lower facia panel, and a resistor situated behind the left-hand headlamp assembly.
2 The dim-dip unit is supplied with current from the sidelamp circuit, and is energised by a feed from the ignition switch. When energised, the unit allows battery voltage to pass through the resistor to the headlamp dipped-beam circuits; this lights the headlamps with approximately one-sixth of their normal power, preventing the car from being driven using sidelamps alone.

17.2A Carefully prise left-hand switch assembly out of instrument panel shroud ...

17.2B ... then withdraw assembly, and disconnect wiring connectors

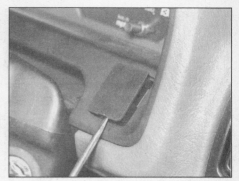

17.4 On models without an electric sunroof, remove cover from right-hand side of instrument panel shroud

17 Instrument panel –
removal and refitting

Removal

1 Disconnect the battery negative terminal.
2 Position the steering column in its lowest possible height setting, then, using a suitable flat-bladed screwdriver, carefully prise out the switch assembly from the left-hand side of the instrument panel shroud. Disconnect the switch wiring connector, and remove the switch assembly (photos).
3 On models equipped with an electric sunroof, repeat the above operation for the sunroof switch.
4 On models without an electric sunroof, carefully prise out the cover from the right-

hand lower corner of the instrument shroud (photo).
5 Remove the four instrument panel shroud retaining screws, and remove the shroud from the facia (photos).
6 Undo the four screws securing the instrument panel to the facia, and carefully withdraw the panel until access can be gained to the rear of the panel. **Note:** *If the panel cannot be withdrawn sufficiently to reach the speedometer cable, extra clearance can be gained by disconnecting the speedometer cable from the transmission, as described in Section 22.* Release the speedometer cable retaining clip, then disconnect the cable and the three wiring block connectors from the panel (photos).
7 Remove the instrument panel from the facia (photo).

17.5A Instrument panel shroud lower retaining screws are accessed through switch apertures

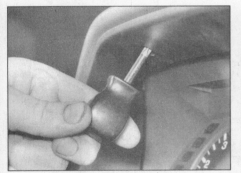

17.5B Remove upper retaining screws ...

17.5C ... then withdraw the instrument panel shroud

17.6A Remove instrument panel upper (arrowed) and lower retaining screws ...

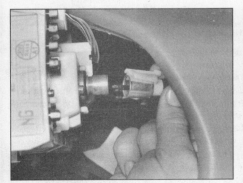

17.6B ... then disconnect the speedometer cable ...

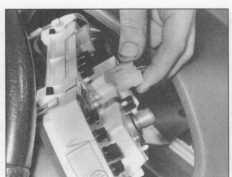

17.6C ... and wiring connectors ...

17.7 ... and withdraw the instrument panel from the facia

12

18.2A Unscrew retaining screws ...

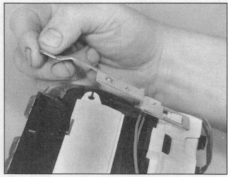

18.2B ... and remove upper mounting brackets from the instrument panel

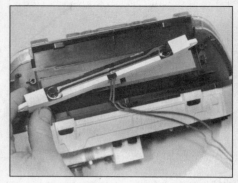

18.3 Removing instrument illumination panel

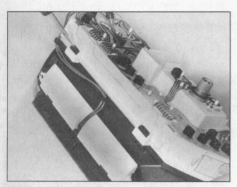

18.6 Release retaining clips and separate instrument panel case and cover

Refitting

8 Refitting is a reverse of the removal procedure. On completion, check the operation of all the panel warning lamps and instrument shroud switches to ensure that they are functioning correctly.

18 Instrument panel components
– removal and refitting

General

1 Remove the instrument panel as described in Section 17, then proceed as described under the relevant sub-heading below.

Instrument illumination panel
Removal

2 Remove the screws securing the right- and left-hand upper mounting brackets to the panel assembly, and remove both brackets (photos).
3 Release the rear illumination panel bulbholder by twisting it anti-clockwise, then remove the illumination panel from the top of the instruments (photo).

Refitting

4 Refitting is a reversal of the removal procedure.

Instruments
Removal

5 Remove the instrument illumination panel, as described in paragraphs 2 and 3.

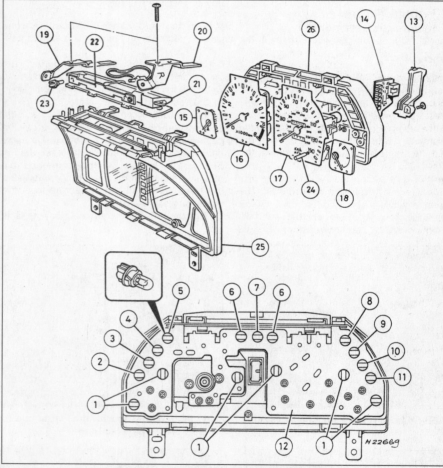

Fig. 12.4 Exploded view of the instrument panel (Sec 18)

1 Panel rear illumination bulbs
2 ALB warning lamp bulb (where fitted)
3 Boot-open warning lamp bulb
4 Hazard warning lamp bulb
5 Brake failure/handbrake-on warning lamp bulb
6 Direction indicator warning lamp bulb
7 Main beam warning lamp bulb
8 Oil pressure warning lamp bulb
9 Ignition/no-charge warning lamp bulb
10 PGM-Fi warning lamp bulb
11 Caravan/trailer indicator warning lamp bulb
12 Printed circuit
13 Automatic transmission indicator cover (where fitted)
14 Automatic transmission selector position indicator (where fitted)
15 Coolant temperature gauge
16 Tachometer
17 Speedometer
18 Fuel gauge
19 Left-hand support bracket
20 Right-hand support bracket
21 Illumination panel cover
22 Illumination panel printed circuit
23 Panel front illumination bulb
24 Tripmeter reset knob
25 Instrument panel cover
26 Instrument panel case

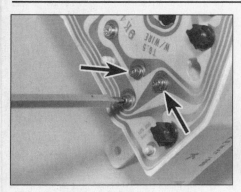

18.7A Remove retaining screws (remaining two arrowed) ...

6 Release the instrument panel cover retaining clips, and lift the cover off the instrument panel case (photo).

7 The individual instruments can then be removed separately by unscrewing their retaining screws (photos). When removing the speedometer, note the foam washer which is fitted around the base of the instrument stalk.

Refitting

8 Refitting is a reversal of the removal procedure.

Printed circuit

Removal

9 Remove the speedometer, tachometer, fuel gauge and temperature gauge from the meter case, as described in paragraphs 5 to 7.

10 Remove all the bulbholders from the rear of the case by twisting them anti-clockwise, then release the printed circuit from its retaining pins and remove it from the case.

Refitting

11 Refitting is a reverse of the removal sequence.

Selector position indicator – automatic transmission models

Removal

12 Slacken and remove the screw securing the selector indicator panel cover to the rear of the instruments, and remove the cover.

13 Carefully slide the indicator panel out from the instrument panel.

20.2B ... and disconnect clock wiring connector

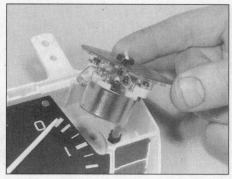

18.7B ... and remove relevant instrument from the panel case – temperature gauge shown

Refitting

14 Refitting is a reverse of the removal procedure.

19 Cigar lighter – removal and refitting

Removal

1 Disconnect the battery negative lead.

2 Remove the lighter element, then carefully prise out the metal surround, followed by the plastic body. Note the wiring connections before disconnecting them, and tie a piece of string around the connector, to retrieve it if it falls back inside the facia.

Refitting

3 Refitting is the reverse of the removal procedure.

20 Clock – removal and refitting

Removal

1 Disconnect the battery negative lead.

2 Using a suitable flat-bladed screwdriver, carefully prise out the clock mounting trim strip from the facia. Withdraw the trim, and disconnect the wiring connector from the rear of the clock (photos). Tie a piece of string around the connector, to retrieve it if it falls back inside the facia.

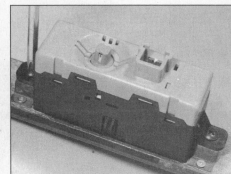

20.3 Clock is retained by two screws

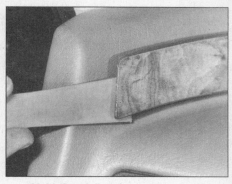

20.2A Carefully prise out the clock mounting trim strip ...

3 Undo the two clock retaining screws, and remove the clock from the trim panel (photo).

Refitting

4 Refitting is a reversal of the removal sequence.

21 Horn – removal and refitting

Removal

1 Disconnect the battery negative terminal.

2 Remove the front bumper, as described in Chapter 11.

3 Disconnect the horn wiring connectors, and unbolt the horn(s) from the body (photo).

Refitting

4 Refitting is a reversal of the removal procedure.

22 Speedometer drive cable – removal and refitting

Removal

1 Remove the instrument panel as described in Section 17, and make a note of the correct routing of the speedometer cable.

2 Working in the engine compartment,

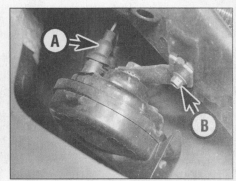

21.3 Horn wiring connectors (A) and retaining bolt (B)

12

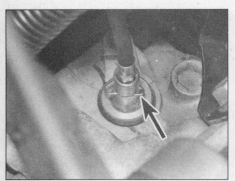

22.2 Remove the retaining clip (arrowed) and disengage the speedometer cable from the transmission

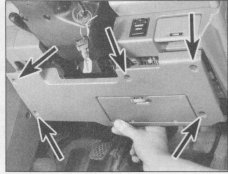

23.6 Remove retaining screws (locations arrowed), and withdraw the right-hand lower facia panel

23.7A Release the left-hand fuse panel ...

carefully displace the gaiter from the transmission end of the speedometer cable, and slide the gaiter up the cable. Remove the retaining clip from the speedometer drivegear housing, and disconnect the cable from the transmission (photo).

3 Release the cable sealing grommet from the engine compartment bulkhead, then gently withdraw the cable into the engine compartment and remove it from the car.

Refitting

4 If a new cable is being installed, transfer the sealing grommet and the lower gaiter from the old cable to the new cable.

5 Have an assistant feed the cable in through the engine compartment bulkhead, whilst checking from inside the car that the cable is following the correct route – over the demister duct and the pedal mounting bracket, and through the steering column support bracket.

6 Once the cable is correctly routed, refit the sealing grommet to the bulkhead, then draw the cable through until the coloured tape on the outer cable abuts the sealing grommet.

7 Connect the upper end of the cable to the instrument panel, and refit the panel as described in Section 17.

8 Engage the lower end of the cable with the speedometer drivegear, and secure it in position with its retaining clip. Slide the gaiter back down into position over the speedometer gear housing.

23 Multi-function unit (MFU) – general information, removal and refitting

General information

1 The multi-function unit (MFU) is mounted onto the rear of fusebox, which is located behind the right-hand lower facia panel. The unit controls the following functions.
(a) Front and rear wiper system delay intervals.
(b) Heated rear window timer.
(c) Courtesy lamp delay.
(d) Lamps-on warning bleeper.

2 The MFU also has a self-diagnostic mode, where it checks out all the relevant circuits it controls.

3 To start the diagnostic sequence, press the heated rear window switch, and turn the ignition switch on simultaneously. Release the heated rear window switch as soon as the ignition switch is turned on (the MFU should then bleep to indicate it has entered its diagnostic mode) then press the heated rear window switch for a second time. Subsequent operations of the interior lamp switches, wiper switches and headlamp switch will result in a bleep from the MFU as it receives a signal. If the unit does not bleep, a fault is indicated in the relevant circuit. A third press on the heated rear window switch will start the MFU on the

second stage of its diagnostic sequence. The MFU will now operate each of its functions in turn, starting with the heated rear window, followed by the front and rear wipers, and finally the courtesy lamp will operate for approximately two seconds if there are no faults. When all the checks are complete, turn the ignition switch off to take the MFU out of its diagnostic sequence.

4 If a fault appears in one of the circuits controlled by the MFU, check the relevant relay (where fitted) and wiring using the equipment and procedures outlined in Sections 2 and 11 of this Chapter, referring to the wiring diagrams for full details. If this fails to locate the fault, it is likely that the MFU is at fault. The MFU is a sealed unit, and must be renewed even if only one of its control functions is faulty.

Removal

5 Disconnect the battery negative terminal.

6 Undo the five retaining screws, and remove the right-hand lower facia panel (photo).

7 Release the left-hand fuse panel from the side of the main fusebox, and disconnect the two wiring block connectors from the front of the fusebox (photos).

8 Remove the two fusebox retaining nuts (photo), then partially withdraw the fusebox until the upper wiring block connector(s) can be disconnected.

9 Carefully turn the fusebox assembly around, and disconnect the block connector from the

23.7B ... and disconnect wiring connectors from front of the fusebox

23.8 Fusebox retaining nut locations (arrows)

23.9A Release the Multi-Function Unit (MFU) from the rear of the fusebox ...

23.9B ... and disconnect its wiring connector

MFU. Release the MFU from the rear of the fusebox, and remove it from the car (photos).

Refitting

10 Refitting is a reversal of the removal procedure, ensuring that all the wiring connectors are correctly refitted. On completion, reconnect the battery terminal, and check that all electrical circuits function correctly.

24 Windscreen wiper motor and linkage – removal and refitting

Removal

1 Operate the windscreen wipers, then switch them off so that the wiper blades return to the 'parked' position.
2 Stick a piece of masking tape along the edge of each wiper blade (to use as an alignment aid on refitting), then open up the bonnet.
3 Slacken and remove the wiper arm spindle nuts, and pull the arms off their spindles (photos). If necessary, the arms can be levered off their spindles using a large flat-bladed screwdriver.
4 Carefully prise out the seven trim caps from the ventilation grille, to gain access to the grille retaining screws. Slacken and remove all the retaining screws, then release the eight retaining clips situated along the front edge of the grille, and remove the grille from the car.
5 Using a large flat-bladed screwdriver, carefully lever the wiper linkage arm off the wiper motor crank arm balljoint.
6 Disconnect the wiring connector from the wiper motor, remove the four bolts securing the motor to the bulkhead (photo), then remove the motor from the engine compartment, taking care not to lose its mounting rubbers.
7 Remove the three bolts securing the right-hand wiper arm spindle in position, then, using a large flat-bladed screwdriver, disconnect the linkage rod from the spindle balljoint, and remove the spindle assembly.
8 Disconnect the two linkage rods from the

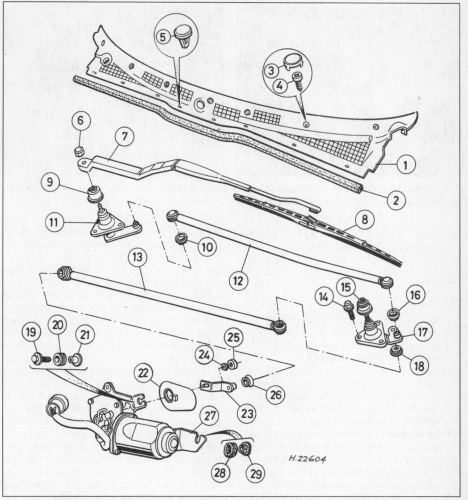

Fig. 12.5 Exploded view of the windscreen wiper motor and linkage (Sec 24)

1 Ventilation grille	11 Right-hand spindle	20 Mounting rubber
2 Sealing strip	assembly	21 Spacer
3 Trim cap	12 Connecting rod	22 Water shield
4 Screw	13 Operating rod	23 Wiper motor crank arm
5 Retaining screw	14 Bolt	24 Spring washer
6 Wiper arm spindle nut	15 Spindle cap	25 Nut
7 Wiper arm	16 Dust seal	26 Dust seal
8 Wiper blade	17 Left-hand spindle assembly	27 Wiper motor
9 Spindle cap	18 Dust seal	28 Mounting rubber
10 Dust seal	19 Wiper motor mounting bolt	29 Spacer

24.3A Slacken wiper arm spindle nuts ...

24.3B ... and remove wiper arms from their spindles

12

24.6 Windscreen wiper motor mounting bolt locations – arrowed (lower bolt hidden)

25.3 Remove cover to reveal tailgate wiper arm spindle nut

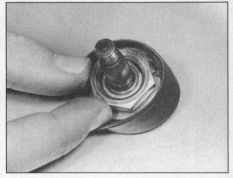

25.4A Unscrew the wiper spindle retaining nut ...

left-hand wiper arm spindle assembly balljoints, and remove the rods.

9 Undo the three left-hand wiper arm spindle retaining bolts, and remove the spindle assembly.

Refitting

10 Refitting is a reversal of the removal procedure, noting the following points.

(a) Examine the wiper motor mounting rubbers for signs of damage or deterioration, and renew if necessary.

(b) Tighten the wiper arm spindle assembly and wiper motor mounting bolts to the specified torque, and ensure all linkage balljoints are pressed firmly together.

(c) Ensure the wiper arm spindles are clean, then align the wiper blades with the tape fitted on removal, and press the arms firmly onto the spindles. Tighten the wiper arm spindle nuts to the specified torque.

25 Tailgate wiper motor – removal and refitting

Removal

1 Operate the tailgate wiper, then switch it off so that the wiper blade returns to the 'parked' position.

2 Stick a piece of masking tape along the edge of the wiper blade, to use as an alignment aid on refitting.

3 Prise off the wiper arm spindle nut cover, slacken and remove the wiper arm spindle nut, and pull the arm off its spindle (photo). If necessary, the arm can be levered off using a large flat-bladed screwdriver.

4 Undo the spindle retaining nut, then remove the toothed washer and rubber seal (photos).

5 Open up the tailgate, undo the two screws securing the tailgate inner trim panel to the tailgate, and carefully prise out the screw retaining plugs.

6 Using a large flat-bladed screwdriver, work around the outside of the trim panel, and carefully prise it away from the tailgate to free all its retaining clips. Once all the retaining clips have been freed, remove the trim panel.

7 Disconnect the wiring connector, and undo the three bolts securing the wiper motor to the tailgate (photo). Remove the motor from the tailgate, noting the three motor mounting rubbers, and the washer and rubber seal which are fitted to the wiper spindle.

Refitting

8 Refitting is a reversal of removal, noting the following points.

(a) Examine the wiper motor mounting rubbers and spindle seals for signs of damage and deterioration, and renew if necessary.

(b) Tighten the wiper motor mounting bolts to the specified torque.

(c) Ensure the wiper arm spindle is clean,

then align the wiper blade with the tape fitted on removal, and press the arm firmly onto the spindle. Tighten the wiper arm spindle nut to the specified torque, and refit the nut cover.

26 Windscreen/tailgate washer system components – general information, removal and refitting

General Information

1 The windscreen washer reservoir is situated in the rear left-hand corner of the engine compartment, with the washer system pump being mounted on the side of the reservoir. On 216 models, the reservoir is also used to supply the tailgate washer system, via a second pump.

Removal

2 To remove the washer reservoir and pump(s), unscrew the mounting nut and bolts, and lift the reservoir from the left-hand corner of the engine compartment.

3 Disconnect the wiring connector(s) from the pump(s), then disconnect the plastic tubing from the reservoir and remove the assembly from the car.

4 Empty the reservoir of any remaining fluid, then undo the retaining screws and separate the pump(s) and reservoir.

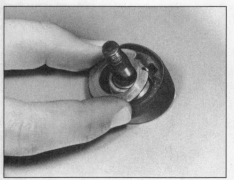

25.4B ... and withdraw the toothed washer and rubber seal

25.7 Tailgate wiper motor mounting bolts (arrowed)

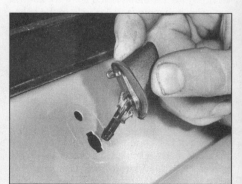

26.5 Removing tailgate washer jet – 216 models

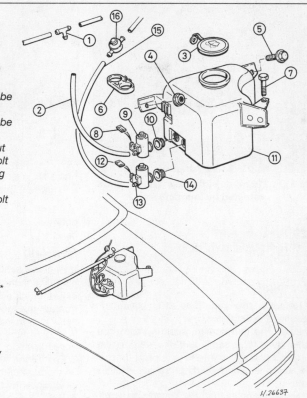

Fig. 12.6
Windscreen/tailgate
washer system
components (Sec 26)

1 *Windscreen washer tube*
  T-piece connector
2 *Windscreen washer tube*
3 *Reservoir cap*
4 *Reservoir mounting nut*
5 *Reservoir mounting bolt*
6 *Washer pump retaining*
  clip
7 *Reservoir mounting bolt*
8 *Wiring connector*
9 *Windscreen washer*
  pump
10 *Seal*
11 *Washer reservoir*
12 *Wiring connector**
13 *Tailgate washer pump**
14 *Seal**
15 *Tailgate washer tube**
16 *Non-return valve**

Fitted to 216 models only

H.26637

27.3A Use DIN tools to release retaining clips ...

27.3B ... then withdraw the radio/cassette unit and disconnect the aerial and wiring connectors

28.2A Slacken the three retaining screws ...

5 If necessary, the windscreen washer nozzles can be carefully prised out of the ventilation grille and disconnected from the tubing. On 216 models, prise the washer jet out of the tailgate and remove it (photo).
6 If trouble is experienced at any time with the flow to the tailgate washer, check that the non-return valve is not blocked; it is fitted in the tube next to the reservoir, and should only allow fluid to pass outwards, to the jet.

Refitting

7 Refitting is a reversal of removal. Ensure that the washer tubes are not trapped when refitting the reservoir, and note that the connectors for the pumps are colour-coded to aid correct reconnection on reassembly.

27 Radio/cassette player –
removal and refitting

Note: *The following removal and refitting procedure is for the range of radio/cassette units which Rover fit as standard equipment. Removal and refitting procedures for non-standard units may differ slightly.*

Removal

1 Referring to the instructions supplied with the radio/cassette unit, temporarily de-activate the security code.
2 Disconnect the battery negative lead.
3 To remove the unit, two standard DIN extraction tools are required. These are two U-shaped rods, which are inserted into the four

small holes in the front of the unit to release the unit retaining clips. The tools may possibly be obtained from a Rover dealer or an audio accessory outlet, or can be made out of 3 mm wire rod (such as welding rod). Using the tools, push back the clamps on the left and right-hand sides, then withdraw the unit and disconnect the wiring plugs and aerial (photos).

Refitting

4 Refitting is the reverse of the removal procedure. On completion, connect the battery negative terminal and reactivate the security code.

28 Speakers –
removal and refitting

Removal

Front speaker

1 Remove the front door inner trim panel, as described in Chapter 11, Section 12.
2 Undo the three speaker retaining screws, then withdraw the speaker, disconnect the speaker wiring connectors and remove the speaker from the door (photos).

Rear speaker – 216 models

3 Prise off the trim cap from the rear seat belt upper mounting point, then slacken and remove the two seal belt guide retaining bolts.

28.2B ... then withdraw speaker from the door, and disconnect its wiring connectors

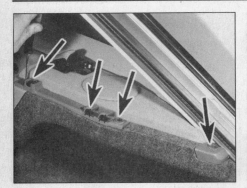

28.4 Rear speaker grille panel retaining screw locations (arrowed) – 216 models

28.5 On 216 models, the rear speakers are retained by four screws

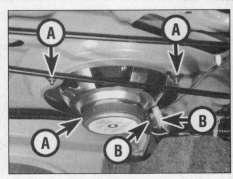

28.6 Rear speaker retaining nuts (A – one hidden) and wiring connectors (B) – 416 models

4 Open up the tailgate, remove the four screws securing the speaker grille panel in position (photo), then lift the panel clear of the speaker.
5 Undo the four speaker retaining screws (photo), lift out the speaker, then disconnect the wiring connectors and remove the speaker from the car.

Rear speaker – 416 models

6 Working from inside the luggage compartment, disconnect the speaker wiring connections, and undo the three nuts securing the speaker to the parcel shelf (photo). The speaker can then be lifted away from the parcel shelf from inside the car.

Refitting

7 Refitting is a reverse of the removal procedure.

29 Radio aerial – removal and refitting

Removal

1 Remove the radio/cassette player, as described in Section 27.
2 Undo the five screws securing the right-hand lower facia panel, and remove the panel to gain access to the relay mounting bracket. Remove the relay mounting bracket retaining bolt.
3 Trace the aerial lead back along its length, and free it from any retaining clips or ties. Tie a long piece of string around the aerial end plug.
4 Undo the two screws securing the aerial to the roof, and remove the aerial and sealing rubber. Carefully withdraw the aerial lead until the plug comes out of the aerial aperture, then

untie the string and leave it in position in the car.

Refitting

5 Securely tie the string around the aerial lead plug, and fit the rubber seal to the aerial.
6 From inside the car, gently pull the string through the radio aperture, whilst feeding the aerial lead in through the roof. When the aerial lead plug emerges on the inside of the car, untie the string.
7 Ensure the rubber seal is correctly located on the base of the aerial, then tighten the aerial retaining screws securely.
8 Refit the aerial lead to the necessary retaining clips and ties, then refit the relay mounting bracket and right-hand lower facia panel, tightening all retaining screws and bolts securely.
9 Refit the radio/cassette unit as described in Section 27.

INTERNAL CONNECTION
DETAILS

INTERNAL CONNECTIONS FOR ITEM 43

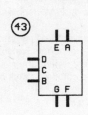

LH	B	C	A	F	G
UP	○——————○				
		○——○	○——○		
DOWN		○——○			
	○		○——○		
LEFT		○	○——○		
		○——○	○		
RIGHT	○——————○				
		○——○	○		

RH	B	C	A	F	G
UP	○——————○				
		○——○	○——○		
DOWN		○——○			
	○		○——○		
LEFT		○	○——○		
		○——○	○		
RIGHT	○		○		
		○——○	○		

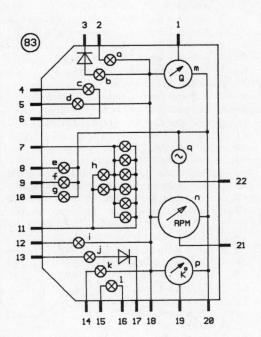

KEY TO INSTRUMENT CLUSTER (ITEM 83)

a = ALB Warning Lamp
b = Tailgate Open Warning Lamp
c = Hazard Warning Lamp
d = Handbrake/Low Brake Fluid Warning Lamp
e = RH Direction Indicator Lamp
f = Main Beam Warning Lamp
g = LH Direction Indicator Lamp
h = Instrument Illumination
i = Oil Pressure Warning Lamp
j = Ignition Warning Lamp
k = Check Engine Warning Lamp
l = Trailer Warning Lamp
m = Fuel Gauge
n = Tachometer
p = Coolant Temperature Gauge
q = Speed Sensor

WIRE COLOURS

B	Blue	R	Red	
Bk	Black	Rs	Pink	
Bn	Brown	S	Grey	
LGn	Light Green	V	Violet	
Gn	Green	W	White	
O	Orange	Y	Yellow	
P	Purple			

KEY TO SYMBOLS

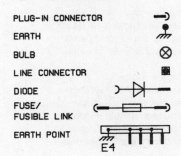

PLUG-IN CONNECTOR

EARTH

BULB

LINE CONNECTOR

DIODE

FUSE/
FUSIBLE LINK

EARTH POINT

Internal connection details, wire colours and key to symbols

WD

Engine compartment fusebox

Fuse	Amps	Circuit(s) protected
1	15A	Anti-lock braking (ALB) system
2	15A	Anti-lock braking (ALB) system
3	15A	Anti-lock braking (ALB) system
4	10A	Hazard warning lamps, engine management
6	15A	Main relay
7	15A	Main relay

Fusible links

links	Amps	Circuit(s) protected
FL1	40A	Ignition switch
FL2	40A	Anti-lock braking (ALB) system
FL3	30A	Electric window relay, electric sunroof, central locking and heated rear window
FL4	40A	Ignition switch
FL5	40A	Lighting and cigar lighter
FL6	60A	Main fusebox

Passenger compartment fusebox

Fuse	Amps	Circuit(s) protected
1	10A	Clock, instruments, direction indicators and dim-dip unit
2	10A	Starter signal
3	15A	Central locking
4	10A	Cigar lighter
5	10A	Dim-dip resistor
6	30A	Sunroof
7	10A	Right-hand sidelamps, tail lamp and number plate lamps
8	10A	Left-hand sidelamps, tail lamp and interior lamps
9	10A	Foglamps
10	10A	Left-hand headlamp dipped beam
11	10A	Right-hand headlamp dipped beam
12	15A	Radio/cassette memory, clock and interior lamps
13	15A	Windscreen washers and wipers (front)
14	10A	Engine management system
15	15A	Cooling fan, tailgate washer and wiper
16	15A	Reversing lamps, stop-lamps and electric windows
17	10A	Cigar lighter, Multi-function unit (MFU) and radio/cassette player
18	10A	Electric door mirrors and electric windows
19	15A	Headlamp dim-dip
21	15A	Right-hand headlamp main beam
22	15A	Left-hand headlamp main beam
23	25A	Heated rear window and heated door mirrors
24	20A	Heater blower motor
25	15A	Anti-lock braking (ALB) system
26	15A	Left-hand rear electric window
27	15A	Right-hand rear electric window
28	15A	Left-hand front electric window
29	15A	Right-hand front electric window

Notes

1 All diagrams are divided into numbered circuits depending on function eg Diagram 2: Exterior lighting.
2 Items are arranged in relation to a plan view of the vehicle.
3 Items may appear on more than one diagram so are found using a grid reference eg 2/A1 denotes an item on diagram 2 grid location A1.
4 Complex items appear on the diagrams as blocks and are expanded on the internal connections page.
5 Feed wire colour varies dependant on the circuit supplied but all earth wires are coloured black or have a black tracer.

Item	Description	Diagram/Grid reference
1	Alternator	1/C8, 1a/B7, 4/D8
2	Anti-lock Brake Accumulator - Pressure Switch	4/B5
3	Anti-lock Brake Compressor Pump	4/B2
4	Anti-lock Brake ECU	4/M3
5	Anti-lock Brake Fail-safe Relay 1	4/A3
6	Anti-lock Brake Fail-safe Relay 2	4/A4
7	Anti-lock Brake Main Relay	4/A2
8	Anti-lock Brake Solenoid LH Front	4/D4
9	Anti-lock Brake Solenoid Rear	4/C6
10	Anti-lock Brake Solenoid RH Front	4/D6
11	Ashtray Illumination	2b/F5
12	Atmospheric Pressure Sensor	1a/H8
13	Automatic Transmission Inhibitor Switch	1/H6
14	Automatic Transmission Lock-up Solenoid	1a/C5
15	Automatic Transmission Position Indicator	1/J3
16	Automatic Transmission Selector Illumination	2b/L4
17	Battery	1/B2, 1a/D2, 2/C3, 2a/B3, 2b/A3, 3/A3, 3a/A3, 4/C3, 5/A2
18	Central Locking Control Unit	3a/H1
19	Central Locking Motor LH Front	3a/J8
20	Central Locking Motor LH Rear	3a/M8
21	Central Locking Motor RH Rear	3a/M1
22	Central Locking Switch	3a/K1
23	Cigar Lighter	2b/F6
24	Cigar Lighter Relay	2b/E4
25	Clock	2b/D5
26	Coolant Temp Gauge Sender Unit	1/C5
27	Coolant Temp Sensor	1a/B5
28	Cooling Fan Motor	1/B7
29	Cooling Fan Switch	1/B5
33	Crank Position Sensor	1a/B2
31	Cylinder Position Sensor	1a/C3
32	Dim/Dip Resistor	2/A5
33	Dim/Dip Unit	2/J2
34	Dimmer Unit	2b/J1
35	Direction Indicator Flasher Relay	2a/F2
36	Direction Indicator LH Front	2a/A8
37	Direction Indicator RH Front	2a/A1
38	Direction Indicator Side Repeater LH	2a/C8
39	Direction Indicator Side Repeater RH	2a/C1
40	Direction Indicator Switch	2a/J3
41	Electric Door Mirror LH	3a/F8

Notes, fuses and key to wiring diagrams

Item	Description	Diagram/Grid reference	Item	Description	Diagram/Grid reference
42	Electric Door Mirror RH	3a/F1	87	Interior Lamp Door Switch LH Rear	2b/L8
43	Electric Door Mirror Switch	3a/F2	88	Interior Lamp Door Switch RH Front	2b/H1
44	Electric Window Control Unit	3a/J8	89	Interior Lamp Door Switch RH Rear	2b/H8
45	Electric Window Motor LH Front	3a/G8	90	Lambda Sensor(Cat Only)	1a/A6
46	Electric Window Motor LH Rear	3a/L8	91	Lamp Cluster LH Rear	2/M8, 2a/M8
47	Electric Window Motor RH Front	3a/J1	92	Lamp Cluster RH Rear	2/M1, 2a/M1
48	Electric Window Motor LH Rear	3a/L1	93	Light Switch	2/J4, 2a/J4, 2b/J3, 5/J4
49	Electric Window Relay	3a/E5	94	Low Brake Fluid Sender Unit	1/D2, 4/F2
50	Electric Window Switch LH Front	3aG7	95	Luggage Compartment Lamp	2b/L5
51	Electric Window Switch LH Rear	3a/L7	96	Luggage Compartment Lamp Switch	2b/M4
52	Electric Window Switch RH Front	3a/K4	97	Main Beam Relay	2/E5
53	Electric Window Switch RH Rear	3a/I2	98	Main Relay	1a/K4
54	Electronic Air Control Valve	1a/F4	99	MAP Sensor	1aG5
55	Engine Management ECU	1a/J6	100	Multi-Function Unit	2b/D3, 3/F2
56	Fast Idle Solenoid	1a/F5	101	Number Plate Lamp	2/M4, 2/M5
57	Foglamp Relay	2a/G6	102	Oil Pressure Switch	1/C7
58	Foglamp Switch	2a/J5, 2b/J4	103	Purge Valve	1A/G4
59	Fuel Gauge Sender Unit	1/M5	104	Radio/Cassette Unit	5/G5
60	Fuel Injectors	1a/E4	105	Resonator Control Solenoid	1A/A1
61	Fuel Injector Resistor Pack	1a/F4	106	Reversing Lamp Switch	2A/B6
62	Fuel Pump	1a/M4	107	Spark Plugs	1A/C4
63	Glovebox Lamp	2b/E7	108	Speaker LH Front	5/G8
64	Glove Box Lamp Switch	2b/E7	109	Speaker LH Rear	5/M8
65	Handbrake Warning Switch	1/L5, 4/J5	110	Speaker RH Front	5/G1
66	Hazard Warning Lamp Switch	2a/J5, 2b/J5	111	Speaker RH Rear	5/M1
67	Headlamp Unit LH	2/A7	112	Starter Motor	3/D5
68	Headlamp Unit RH	2/A2	113	Stop—Lamp Switch	2a/E4, 4/F4
69	Heated Rear Window	3/L5	114	Sunroof Control Switch	5/K2
70	Heated Rear Window Relay	3/G1	115	Sunroof Control Unit	5/J5
71	Heated Rear Window Switch	2b/J5, 3/J6	116	Sunroof Microswitch	5/L5
72	Heater Blower Motor	3/G7	117	Sunroof Motor	5/L4
73	Heater Blower Resistor Pack	3/G8	118	Sunroof Relay	5/H5
74	Heater Blower Switch	3/J8	119	TDC Position Sensor	1a/C3
75	Heater Blower Switch Illumination	2b/E6	120	Throttle Angle Sensor	1a/G3
76	Horn	3/A1, 3/A8	121	Washer Pump Front	3/F7
77	Horn Relay	3/G6	122	Washer Pump Rear	3/E7
78	Horn Switch	3/L4	123	Wheel Sensor LH Front	4/E8
79	Idle Mixture Sensor	1a/J6	124	Wheel Sensor LH Rear	4/K8
80	Ignition Coil	1a/B3	125	Wheel Sensor RH Front	4/E1
81	Ignition Switch	1/K2, 1a/L1, 2/J1, 2a/J, 2b/K1, 3/K1, 3a/G2, 4/J1, 5/J1	126	Wheel Sensor RH Rear	4/K1
82	Inertia Switch	1a/L5	127	Wiper Motor Front	3/D2
83	Instrument Cluster	1/H4, 1a/K3, 2/G4, 2a/G3, 2b/F3, 4/J3	128	Wiper Motor Rear	3/M5
			129	Wiper Relay Front	3/E1
84	Intake Air Temperature Sensor	1a/E5	130	Wiper Relay Rear	3/M1
85	Interior Lamp	2b/J4	131	Wiper Switch Front	3/J4
86	Interior Lamp Door Switch LH Front	2b/H8	132	Wiper Switch Rear	3/K4

Key to wiring diagrams (continued)

WD

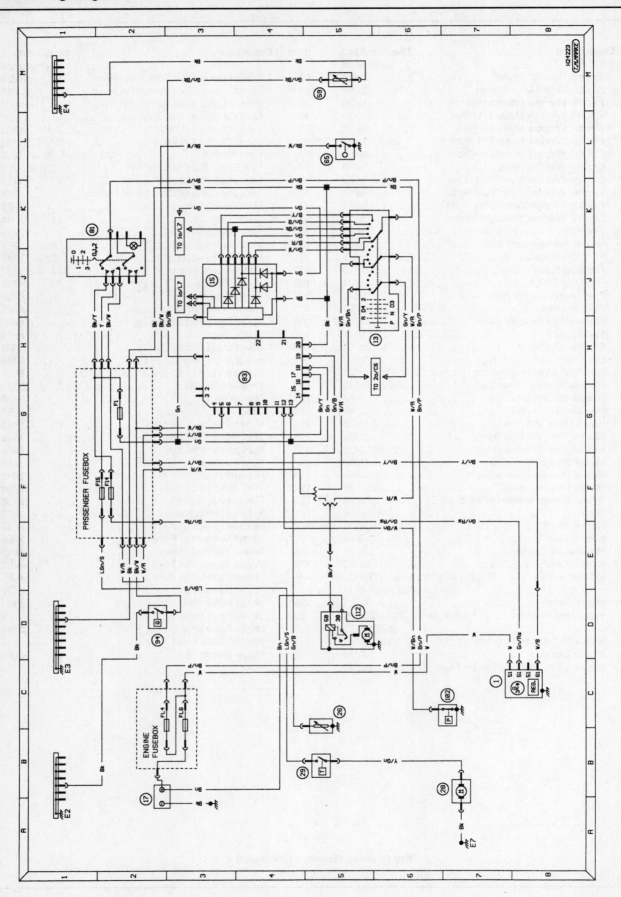

Diagram 1: Starting, charging, cooling fan, warning lamps and gauges (all models)

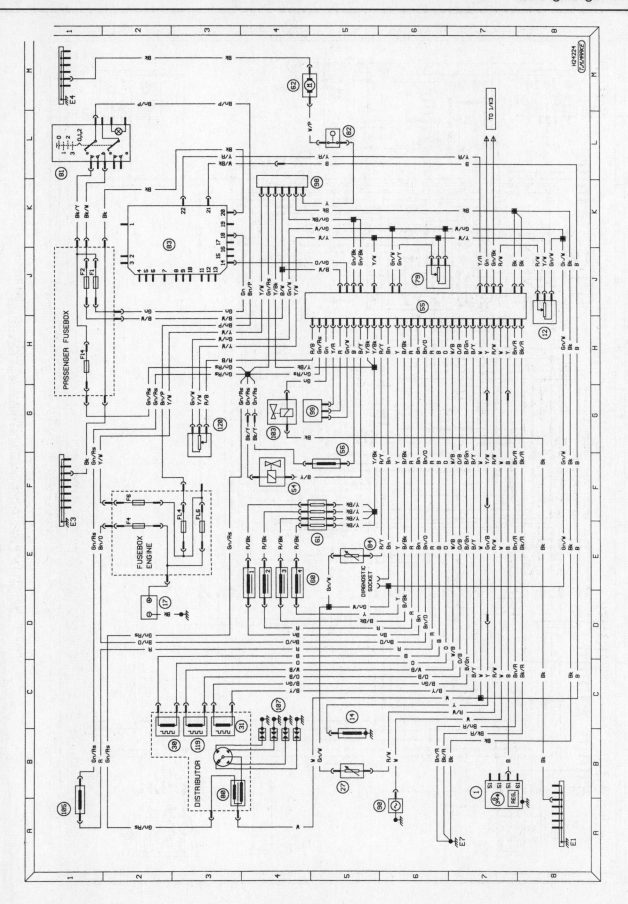

Diagram 1a: Engine management – programmed fuel injection (PGM-Fi)

WD

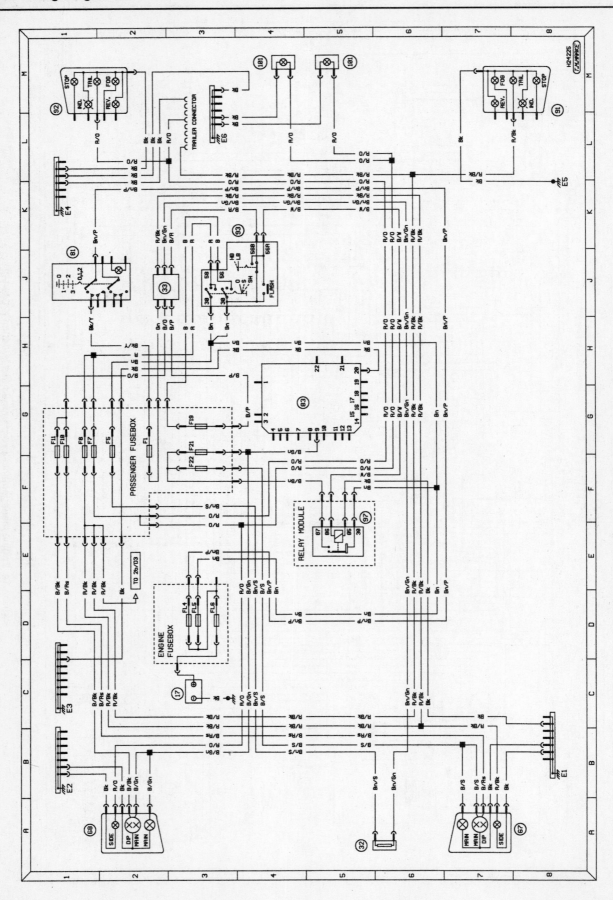

Diagram 2: Exterior lighting – side and headlamps (all models)

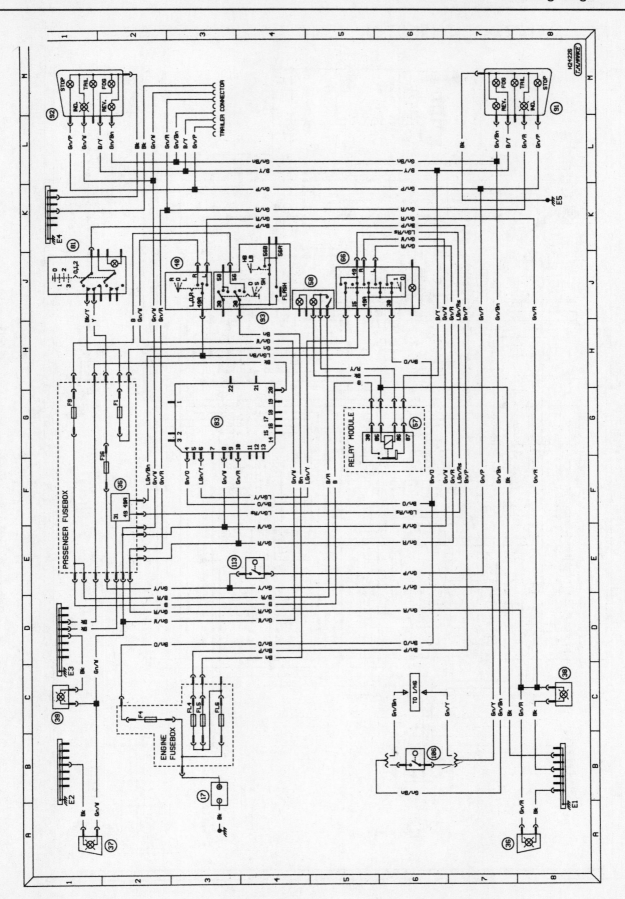

Diagram 2a: Exterior lighting – signal warning lamps (all models)

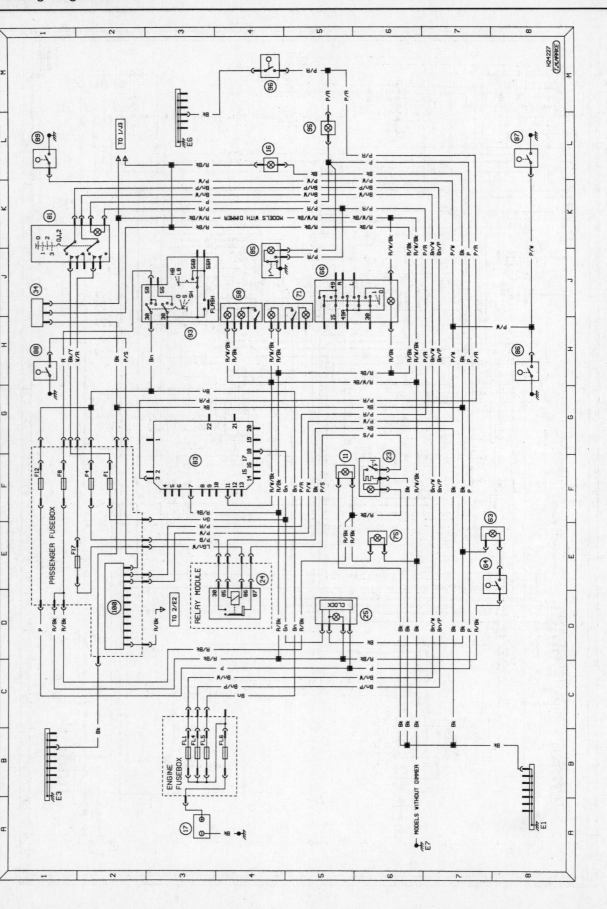

Diagram 2b: Interior lighting and associated circuits (all models)

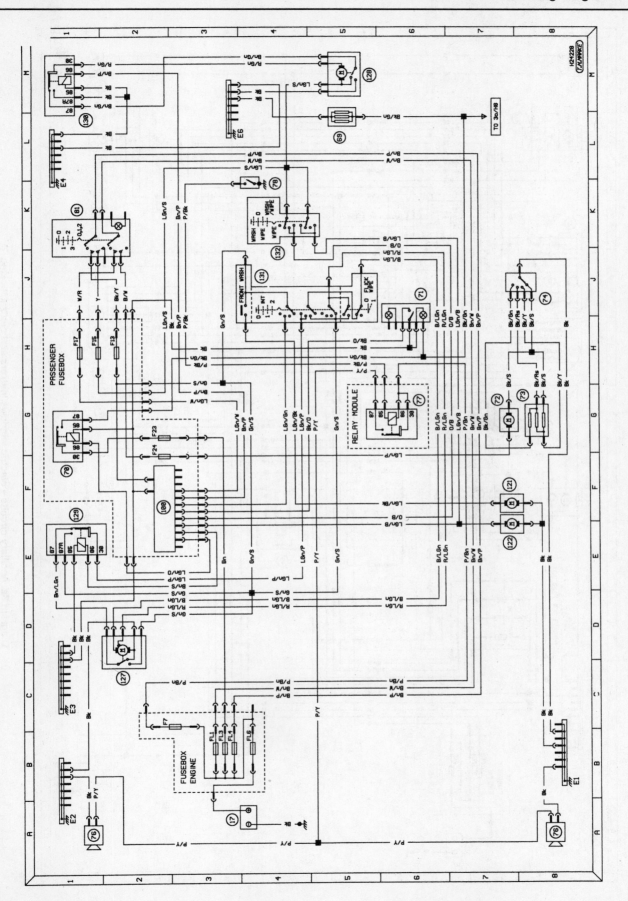

Diagram 3: Ancillary circuits: wash/wipe, blower, horn and heated rear window (all models)

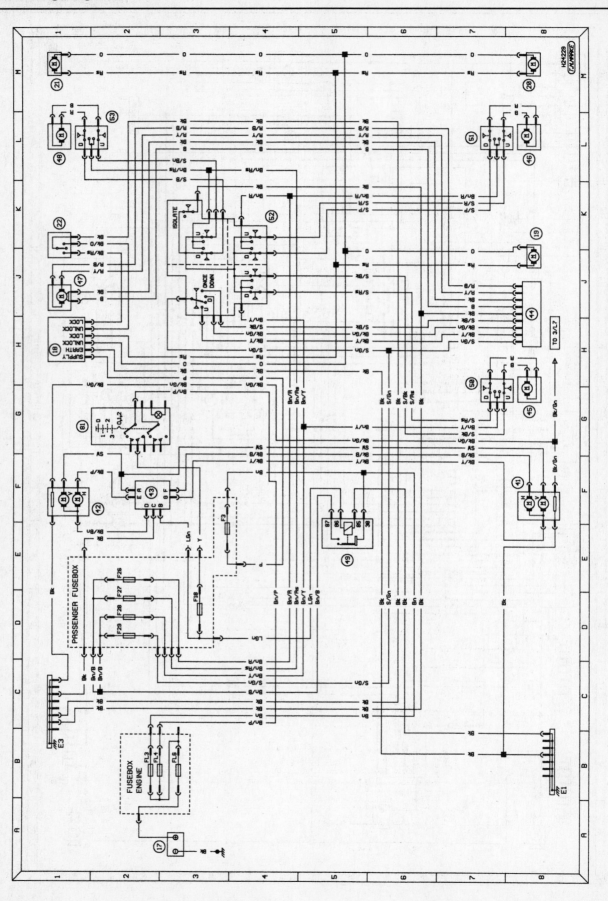

Diagram 3a: Ancillary circuits – electric windows, mirrors and central locking

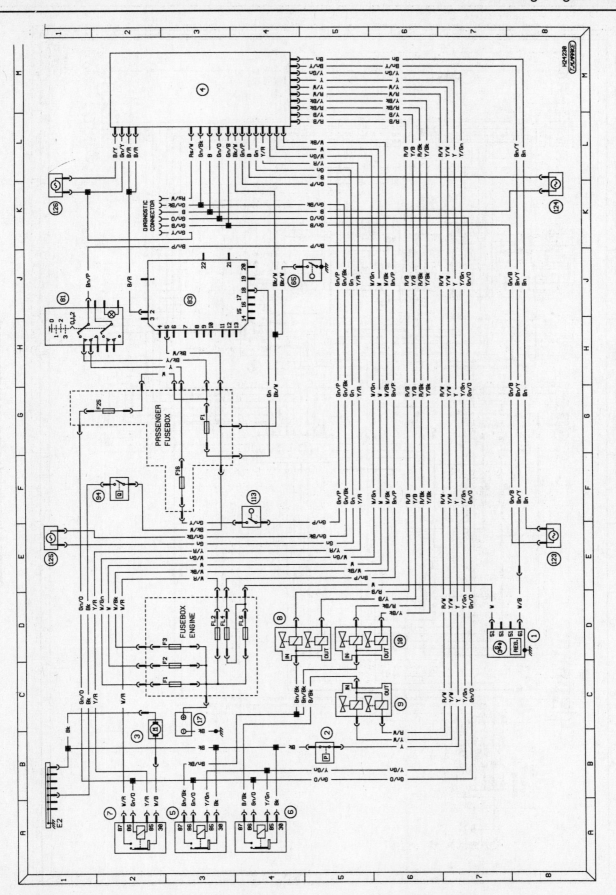

Diagram 4: Anti-lock braking system (ALB)

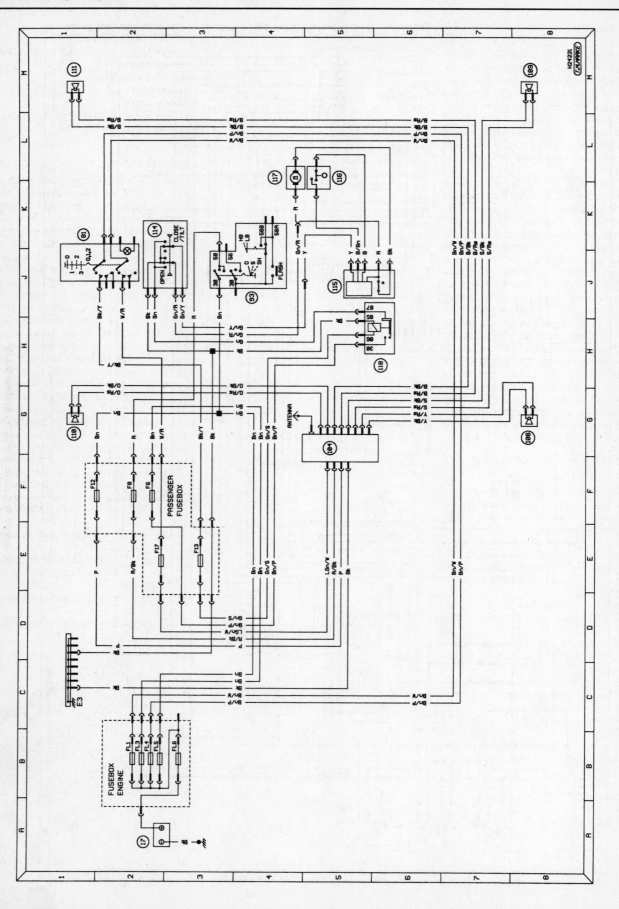

Diagram 5: In-car entertainment and electric sunroof

Tools and Working Facilities

Introduction

A selection of good tools is a fundamental requirement for anyone contemplating the maintenance and repair of a motor vehicle. For the owner who does not possess any, their purchase will prove a considerable expense, offsetting some of the savings made by doing-it-yourself. However, provided that the tools purchased meet the relevant national safety standards and are of good quality, they will last for many years and prove an extremely worthwhile investment.

To help the average owner to decide which tools are needed to carry out the various tasks detailed in this manual, we have compiled three lists of tools under the following headings: *Maintenance and minor repair, Repair and overhaul*, and *Special*. Newcomers to practical mechanics should start off with the *Maintenance and minor repair* tool kit, and confine themselves to the simpler jobs around the vehicle. Then, as confidence and experience grow, more difficult tasks can be undertaken, with extra tools being purchased as, and when, they are needed. In this way, a *Maintenance and minor repair* tool kit can be built up into a *Repair and overhaul* tool kit over a considerable period of time, without any major cash outlays. The experienced do-it-yourselfer will have a tool kit good enough for most repair and overhaul procedures, and will add tools from the *Special* category when it is felt that the expense is justified by the amount of use to which these tools will be put.

Maintenance and minor repair tool kit

The tools given in this list should be considered as a minimum requirement if routine maintenance, servicing and minor repair operations are to be undertaken. We recommend the purchase of combination spanners (ring one end, open-ended the other); although more expensive than open-ended ones, they do give the advantages of both types of spanner.

☐ *Combination spanners:*
   Metric - 8, 9, 10, 11, 12, 13, 14, 15, 17 & 19 mm
☐ *Adjustable spanner - 35 mm jaw (approx)*
☐ *Engine sump/gearbox drain plug key (where applicable)*
☐ *Spark plug spanner (with rubber insert)*
☐ *Spark plug gap adjustment tool*
☐ *Set of feeler gauges*
☐ *Brake bleed nipple spanner*
☐ *Screwdrivers:*
   Flat blade - approx 100 mm long x 6 mm dia
   Cross blade - approx 100 mm long x 6 mm dia
☐ *Combination pliers*
☐ *Hacksaw (junior)*
☐ *Tyre pump*
☐ *Tyre pressure gauge*
☐ *Oil can*
☐ *Oil filter removal tool*
☐ *Fine emery cloth*
☐ *Wire brush (small)*
☐ *Funnel (medium size)*

Repair and overhaul tool kit

These tools are virtually essential for anyone undertaking any major repairs to a motor vehicle, and are additional to those given in the *Maintenance and minor repair* list. Included in this list is a comprehensive set of sockets. Although these are expensive, they will be found invaluable as they are so versatile – particularly if various drives are included in the set. We recommend the half-inch square-drive type, as this can be used with most proprietary torque wrenches. If you cannot afford a socket set, even bought piecemeal, then inexpensive tubular box spanners are a useful alternative.

The tools in this list will occasionally need to be supplemented by tools from the Special list.

☐ *Sockets (or box spanners) to cover range in previous list*
☐ *Reversible ratchet drive (for use with sockets)* **(see illustration)**
☐ *Extension piece, 250 mm (for use with sockets)*
☐ *Universal joint (for use with sockets)*
☐ *Torque wrench (for use with sockets)*
☐ *Self-locking grips*
☐ *Ball pein hammer*
☐ *Soft-faced mallet (plastic/aluminium or rubber)*
☐ *Screwdrivers:*
   Flat blade - long & sturdy, short (chubby), and narrow (electrician's) types
   Cross blade - Long & sturdy, and short (chubby) types
☐ *Pliers:*
   Long-nosed
   Side cutters (electrician's)
   Circlip (internal and external)
☐ *Cold chisel - 25 mm*
☐ *Scriber*
☐ *Scraper*
☐ *Centre-punch*
☐ *Pin punch*
☐ *Hacksaw*
☐ *Brake hose clamp*
☐ *Brake bleeding kit*

☐ *Selection of twist drills*
☐ *Steel rule/straight-edge*
☐ *Allen keys (inc. splined/Torx type)* **(see illustrations)**
☐ *Selection of files*
☐ *Wire brush*
☐ *Axle stands*
☐ *Jack (strong trolley or hydraulic type)*
☐ *Light with extension lead*

Special tools

The tools in this list are those which are not used regularly, are expensive to buy, or which need to be used in accordance with their manufacturer's instructions. Unless relatively difficult mechanical jobs are undertaken frequently, it will not be economic to buy many of these tools. Where this is the case, you could consider clubbing together with friends (or joining a motorists' club) to make a joint purchase, or borrowing the tools against a deposit from a local garage or tool hire specialist. It is worth noting that many of the larger DIY superstores now carry a large range of special tools for hire at modest rates.

The following list contains only those tools and instruments freely available to the public, and not those special tools produced by the vehicle manufacturer specifically for its dealer network. You will find occasional references to these manufacturer's special tools in the text of this manual. Generally, an alternative method of doing the job without the vehicle manufacturer's special tool is given. However, sometimes there is no alternative to using them. Where this is the case and the relevant tool cannot be bought or borrowed, you will have to entrust the work to a franchised garage.

☐ *Valve spring compressor* **(see illustration)**
☐ *Valve grinding tool*
☐ *Piston ring compressor* **(see illustration)**
☐ *Piston ring removal/installation tool* **(see illustration)**
☐ *Cylinder bore hone* **(see illustration)**
☐ *Balljoint separator*
☐ *Coil spring compressors (where applicable)*

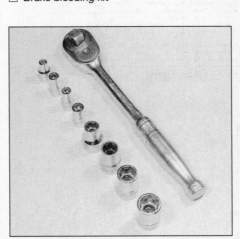

Sockets and reversible ratchet drive

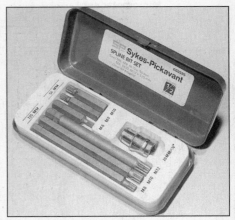

Spline bit set

Tools and Working Facilities

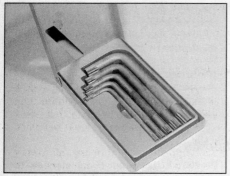

Spline key set

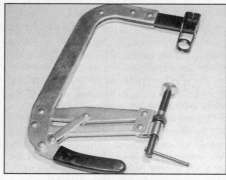

Valve spring compressor

Piston ring compressor

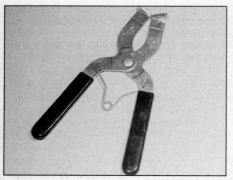

Piston ring removal/installation tool

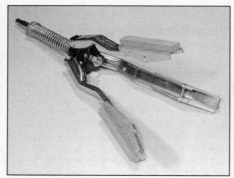

Cylinder bore hone

Three-legged hub and bearing puller

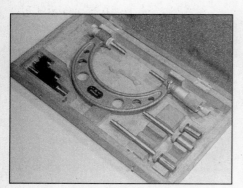

Micrometer set

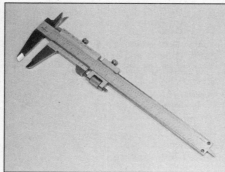

Vernier calipers

Dial test indicator and magnetic stand

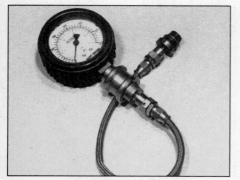

Compression testing gauge

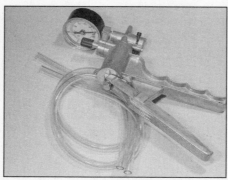

Vacuum pump and gauge

Clutch plate alignment set

❏ Two/three-legged hub and bearing puller **(see illustration)**
❏ Impact screwdriver
❏ Micrometer and/or vernier calipers **(see illustrations)**
❏ Dial gauge **(see illustration)**
❏ Stroboscopic timing light
❏ Dwell angle meter/tachometer
❏ Universal electrical multi-meter
❏ Cylinder compression gauge **(see illustration)**
❏ Hand-operated vacuum pump and gauge **(see illustration)**
❏ Clutch plate alignment set **(see illustration)**
❏ Brake shoe steady spring cup removal tool **(see illustration)**
❏ Bush and bearing removal/installation set **(see illustration)**
❏ Stud extractors **(see illustration)**
❏ Tap and die set **(see illustration)**
❏ Lifting tackle
❏ Trolley jack

Buying tools

For practically all tools, a tool factor is the best source since he will have a very comprehensive range compared with the average garage or accessory shop. Having said that, accessory shops often offer excellent quality tools at discount prices, so it pays to shop around.

Remember, you don't have to buy the most expensive items on the shelf but it is always advisable to steer clear of the very cheap tools. There are plenty of good tools around at reasonable prices, but always aim to purchase items which meet the relevant national safety standards. If in doubt, ask the proprietor or manager of the shop for advice before making a purchase.

Care and maintenance of tools

Having purchased a reasonable tool kit, it is necessary to keep the tools in a clean and serviceable condition. After use, always wipe off any dirt, grease and metal particles using a clean, dry cloth, before putting the tools away. Never leave them lying around after they have been used. A simple tool rack on the garage or workshop wall for items such as screwdrivers and pliers is a good idea. Store all normal spanners and sockets in a metal box. Any measuring instruments, gauges, meters, etc., must be carefully stored where they cannot be damaged or become rusty.

Take a little care when tools are used. Hammer heads inevitably become marked and screwdrivers lose the keen edge on their blades from time to time. A little timely attention with emery cloth or a file will soon restore items like this to a good serviceable finish.

Working facilities

Not to be forgotten when discussing tools is the workshop itself. If anything more than routine maintenance is to be carried out, some form of suitable working area becomes essential.

It is appreciated that many an owner mechanic is forced by circumstances to remove an engine or similar item without the benefit of a garage or workshop. Having done this, any repairs should always be done under the cover of a roof.

Wherever possible, any dismantling should be done on a clean, flat workbench or table at a suitable working height.

Any workbench needs a vice; one with a jaw opening of 100 mm is suitable for most jobs. As mentioned previously, some clean dry storage space is also required for tools, as well as for any lubricants, cleaning fluids, touch-up paints and so on, which become necessary.

Another item which may be required, and which has a much more general usage, is an electric drill with a chuck capacity of at least 8 mm. This, together with a good range of twist drills, is virtually essential for fitting accessories.

Last, but not least, always keep a supply of old newspapers and clean, lint-free rags available, and try to keep any working area as clean as possible.

Brake shoe steady spring cup removal tool

Bush and bearing removal/installation set

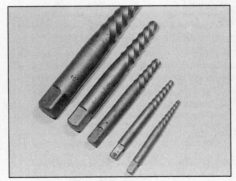

Stud extractor set

Tap and die set

General Repair Procedures

Whenever servicing, repair or overhaul work is carried out on the car or its components, it is necessary to observe the following procedures and instructions. This will assist in carrying out the operation efficiently and to a professional standard of workmanship.

Joint mating faces and gaskets

When separating components at their mating faces, never insert screwdrivers or similar implements into the joint between the faces in order to prise them apart. This can cause severe damage which results in oil leaks, coolant leaks, etc upon reassembly. Separation is usually achieved by tapping along the joint with a soft-faced hammer in order to break the seal. However, note that this method may not be suitable where dowels are used for component location.

Where a gasket is used between the mating faces of two components, ensure that it is renewed on reassembly, and fit it dry unless otherwise stated in the repair procedure. Make sure that the mating faces are clean and dry, with all traces of old gasket removed. When cleaning a joint face, use a tool which is not likely to score or damage the face, and remove any burrs or nicks with an oilstone or fine file.

Make sure that tapped holes are cleaned with a pipe cleaner, and keep them free of jointing compound, if this is being used, unless specifically instructed otherwise.

Ensure that all orifices, channels or pipes are clear, and blow through them, preferably using compressed air.

Oil seals

Oil seals can be removed by levering them out with a wide flat-bladed screwdriver or similar implement. Alternatively, a number of self-tapping screws may be screwed into the seal, and these used as a purchase for pliers or some similar device in order to pull the seal free.

Whenever an oil seal is removed from its working location, either individually or as part of an assembly, it should be renewed.

The very fine sealing lip of the seal is easily damaged, and will not seal if the surface it contacts is not completely clean and free from scratches, nicks or grooves.

Protect the lips of the seal from any surface which may damage them in the course of fitting. Use tape or a conical sleeve where possible. Lubricate the seal lips with oil before fitting and, on dual-lipped seals, fill the space between the lips with grease.

Unless otherwise stated, oil seals must be fitted with their sealing lips toward the lubricant to be sealed.

Use a tubular drift or block of wood of the appropriate size to install the seal and, if the seal housing is shouldered, drive the seal down to the shoulder. If the seal housing is unshouldered, the seal should be fitted with its face flush with the housing top face (unless otherwise instructed).

Screw threads and fastenings

Seized nuts, bolts and screws are quite a common occurrence where corrosion has set in, and the use of penetrating oil or releasing fluid will often overcome this problem if the offending item is soaked for a while before attempting to release it. The use of an impact driver may also provide a means of releasing such stubborn fastening devices, when used in conjunction with the appropriate screwdriver bit or socket. If none of these methods works, it may be necessary to resort to the careful application of heat, or the use of a hacksaw or nut splitter device.

Studs are usually removed by locking two nuts together on the threaded part, and then using a spanner on the lower nut to unscrew the stud. Studs or bolts which have broken off below the surface of the component in which they are mounted can sometimes be removed using a proprietary stud extractor. Always ensure that a blind tapped hole is completely free from oil, grease, water or other fluid before installing the bolt or stud. Failure to do this could cause the housing to crack due to the hydraulic action of the bolt or stud as it is screwed in.

When tightening a castellated nut to accept a split pin, tighten the nut to the specified torque, where applicable, and then tighten further to the next split pin hole. Never slacken the nut to align the split pin hole, unless stated in the repair procedure.

When checking or retightening a nut or bolt to a specified torque setting, slacken the nut or bolt by a quarter of a turn, and then retighten to the specified setting. However, this should not be attempted where angular tightening has been used.

For some screw fastenings, notably cylinder head bolts or nuts, torque wrench settings are no longer specified for the latter stages of tightening, "angle-tightening" being called up instead. Typically, a fairly low torque wrench setting will be applied to the bolts/nuts in the correct sequence, followed by one or more stages of tightening through specified angles.

Locknuts, locktabs and washers

Any fastening which will rotate against a component or housing in the course of tightening should always have a washer between it and the relevant component or housing.

Spring or split washers should always be renewed when they are used to lock a critical component such as a big-end bearing retaining bolt or nut. Locktabs which are folded over to retain a nut or bolt should always be renewed.

Self-locking nuts can be re-used in non-critical areas, providing resistance can be felt when the locking portion passes over the bolt or stud thread. However, it should be noted that self-locking stiffnuts tend to lose their

effectiveness after long periods of use, and in such cases should be renewed as a matter of course.

Split pins must always be replaced with new ones of the correct size for the hole.

When thread-locking compound is found on the threads of a fastener which is to be re-used, it should be cleaned off with a wire brush and solvent, and fresh compound applied on reassembly.

Special tools

Some repair procedures in this manual entail the use of special tools such as a press, two or three-legged pullers, spring compressors, etc. Wherever possible, suitable readily-available alternatives to the manufacturer's special tools are described, and are shown in use. Unless you are highly-skilled and have a thorough understanding of the procedures described, never attempt to bypass the use of any special tool when the procedure described specifies its use. Not only is there a very great risk of personal injury, but expensive damage could be caused to the components involved.

Environmental considerations

When disposing of used engine oil, brake fluid, antifreeze, etc, give due consideration to any detrimental environmental effects. Do not, for instance, pour any of the above liquids down drains into the general sewage system, or onto the ground to soak away. Many local council refuse tips provide a facility for waste oil disposal, as do some garages. If none of these facilities are available, consult your local Environmental Health Department for further advice.

With the universal tightening-up of legislation regarding the emission of environmentally-harmful substances from motor vehicles, most current vehicles have tamperproof devices fitted to the main adjustment points of the fuel system. These devices are primarily designed to prevent unqualified persons from adjusting the fuel/air mixture, with the chance of a consequent increase in toxic emissions. If such devices are encountered during servicing or overhaul, they should, wherever possible, be renewed or refitted in accordance with the vehicle manufacturer's requirements or current legislation.

OIL CARE

FOLLOW THE CODE

OIL BANK LINE
0800 66 33 66

Note: It is antisocial and illegal to dump oil down the drain. To find the location of your local oil recycling bank, call this number free.

Engine 1

- [ ] Engine fails to rotate when attempting to start
- [ ] Engine rotates, but will not start
- [ ] Engine difficult to start when cold
- [ ] Engine difficult to start when hot
- [ ] Starter motor noisy or excessively rough in engagement
- [ ] Engine starts, but stops immediately
- [ ] Engine idles erratically
- [ ] Engine misfires at idle speed
- [ ] Engine misfires throughout the driving speed range
- [ ] Engine hesitates on acceleration
- [ ] Engine stalls
- [ ] Engine lacks power
- [ ] Engine backfires
- [ ] Oil pressure warning light illuminated with engine running
- [ ] Engine runs-on after switching off
- [ ] Engine noises

Cooling system 2

- [ ] Overheating
- [ ] Overcooling
- [ ] External coolant leakage
- [ ] Internal coolant leakage
- [ ] Corrosion

Fuel and exhaust systems 3

- [ ] Excessive fuel consumption
- [ ] Fuel leakage and/or fuel odour
- [ ] Excessive noise or fumes from exhaust system

Clutch 4

- [ ] Pedal travels to floor – no pressure or very little resistance
- [ ] Clutch fails to disengage (unable to select gears)
- [ ] Clutch slips (engine speed increases with no increase in vehicle speed)
- [ ] Judder as clutch is engaged
- [ ] Noise when depressing or releasing clutch pedal

Manual gearbox 5

- [ ] Noisy in neutral with engine running
- [ ] Noisy in one particular gear
- [ ] Difficulty engaging gears
- [ ] Jumps out of gear
- [ ] Vibration
- [ ] Lubricant leaks

Automatic transmission 6

- [ ] Fluid leakage
- [ ] Transmission fluid brown, or has burned smell
- [ ] General gear selection problems
- [ ] Transmission will not downshift (kickdown) with accelerator fully depressed
- [ ] Engine will not start in any gear, or starts in gears other than Park or Neutral
- [ ] Transmission slips, shifts roughly, is noisy, or has no drive in forward or reverse gears

Driveshafts 7

- [ ] Clicking or knocking noise on turns (at slow speed on full-lock)
- [ ] Vibration when accelerating or decelerating

Braking system 8

- [ ] Vehicle pulls to one side under braking
- [ ] Noise (grinding or high-pitched squeal) when brakes applied
- [ ] Excessive brake pedal travel
- [ ] Brake pedal feels spongy when depressed
- [ ] Excessive brake pedal effort required to stop vehicle
- [ ] Judder felt through brake pedal or steering wheel when braking
- [ ] Brakes binding
- [ ] Rear wheels locking under normal braking

Suspension and steering systems 9

- [ ] Vehicle pulls to one side
- [ ] Wheel wobble and vibration
- [ ] Excessive pitching and/or rolling around corners, or during braking
- [ ] Wandering or general instability
- [ ] Excessively-stiff steering
- [ ] Excessive play in steering
- [ ] Lack of power assistance
- [ ] Tyre wear excessive

Electrical system\ 10

- [ ] Battery will not hold a charge for more than a few days
- [ ] Ignition warning light remains illuminated with engine running
- [ ] Ignition warning light fails to come on
- [ ] Lights inoperative
- [ ] Instrument readings inaccurate or erratic
- [ ] Horn inoperative, or unsatisfactory in operation
- [ ] Windscreen/tailgate wipers inoperative, or unsatisfactory in operation
- [ ] Windscreen/tailgate washers inoperative, or unsatisfactory in operation
- [ ] Central locking system inoperative, or unsatisfactory in operation
- [ ] Electric windows inoperative, or unsatisfactory in operation

Introduction

The vehicle owner who does his or her own maintenance according to the recommended service schedules should not have to use this section of the manual very often. Modern component reliability is such that, provided those items subject to wear or deterioration are inspected or renewed at the specified intervals, sudden failure is comparatively rare. Faults do not usually just happen as a result of sudden failure, but develop over a period of time. Major mechanical failures in particular are usually preceded by characteristic symptoms over hundreds or even thousands of miles. Those components which do occasionally fail without warning are often small and easily carried in the vehicle.

With any fault-finding, the first step is to decide where to begin investigations. Sometimes this is obvious, but on other occasions a little detective work will be necessary. The owner who makes half a dozen haphazard adjustments or replacements may be successful in curing a fault (or its symptoms), but will be none the wiser if the fault recurs, and ultimately may have spent more time and money than was necessary. A calm and logical approach will be found to be more satisfactory in the long run. Always take into account any warning signs or abnormalities that may have been noticed in the period preceding the fault – power loss, high or low gauge readings, unusual smells, etc. – and remember that failure of components such as fuses or spark plugs may only be pointers to some underlying fault.

The pages which follow provide an easy reference guide to the more common problems which may occur during the operation of the vehicle. These problems and their possible causes are grouped under headings denoting various components or systems, such as Engine, Cooling system, etc. The Chapter and/or Section which deals with the problem is also shown in brackets. Whatever the fault, certain basic principles apply. These are as follows:

Verify the fault. This is simply a matter of being sure that you know what the symptoms are before starting work. This is particularly

Fault Finding

important if you are investigating a fault for someone else who may not have described it very accurately.

Don't overlook the obvious. For example, if the vehicle won't start, is there petrol in the tank? (Don't take anyone else's word on this particular point, and don't trust the fuel gauge either!) If an electrical fault is indicated, look for loose or broken wires before digging out the test gear.

Cure the disease, not the symptom. Substituting a flat battery with a fully-charged one will get you off the hard shoulder, but if the underlying cause is not attended to, the new battery will go the same

way. Similarly, changing oil-fouled spark plugs for a new set will get you moving again, but remember that the reason for the fouling (if it wasn't simply an incorrect grade of plug) will have to be established and corrected. Don't take anything for granted. Particularly, don't forget that a new component may itself be defective (especially if it's been rattling around in the boot for months), and don't leave components out of a fault diagnosis sequence just because they are new or recently fitted. When you do finally diagnose a difficult fault, you'll probably realise that all the evidence was there from the start.

1 Engine

Engine fails to rotate when attempting to start

☐ Battery terminal connections loose or corroded (Chapter 12).
☐ Battery discharged or faulty (Chapter 12).
☐ Broken, loose or disconnected wiring in the starting circuit (Chapter 12).
☐ Defective starter solenoid or ignition switch (Chapter 12).
☐ Defective starter motor (Chapter 12).
☐ Starter pinion or flywheel ring gear teeth loose or broken (Chapter 12 or Chapter 2).
☐ Engine earth strap broken or disconnected (Chapter 12).
☐ Automatic transmission not in Park/Neutral position, or starter inhibitor switch faulty (Chapter 7).

Engine rotates, but will not start

☐ Fuel tank empty.
☐ Battery discharged – engine rotates slowly (Chapter 12).
☐ Battery terminal connections loose or corroded (Chapter 12).
☐ Ignition components damp or damaged (Chapters 1 and 5).
☐ Broken, loose or disconnected wiring in the engine management PGM-Fi circuit (Chapters 4 and 5).
☐ Worn, faulty or incorrectly-gapped spark plugs (Chapter 1).
☐ Major mechanical failure (eg camshaft drive) (Chapter 2).

Engine difficult to start when cold

☐ Battery discharged (Chapter 12).
☐ Battery terminal connections loose or corroded (Chapter 12).
☐ Worn, faulty or incorrectly-gapped spark plugs (Chapter 1).
☐ Engine management PGM-Fi system fault (Chapters 4 and 5).
☐ Low cylinder compression (Chapter 2).

Engine difficult to start when hot

☐ Air filter element dirty or clogged (Chapter 1).
☐ Low cylinder compressions (Chapter 2).
☐ Engine management PGM-Fi system fault (Chapters 4 and 5).

Starter motor noisy or excessively rough in engagement

☐ Starter pinion or flywheel ring gear teeth loose or broken (Chapter 12 or Chapter 2).
☐ Starter motor mounting bolts loose or missing (Chapter 12).
☐ Starter motor internal components worn or damaged (Chapter 12).

Engine starts, but stops immediately

☐ Insufficient fuel reaching fuel injectors (Chapter 4).
☐ Loose or faulty electrical connections in the engine management PGM-Fi circuit (Chapters 4 and 5).
☐ Vacuum leak at the throttle housing or inlet manifold (Chapter 4).
☐ Blocked injector(s) (Chapter 4).

Engine idles erratically

☐ Incorrectly-adjusted base idle speed and/or mixture settings (Chapter 1).
☐ Engine management PGM-Fi system faulty (Chapters 4 and 5).
☐ Air filter element clogged (Chapter 1).
☐ Vacuum leak at the throttle housing, inlet manifold or associated hoses (Chapter 4).

☐ Worn, faulty or incorrectly-gapped spark plugs (Chapter 1).
☐ Incorrectly-adjusted valve clearances (Chapter 1).
☐ Uneven or low cylinder compressions (Chapter 2).
☐ Camshaft lobes worn (Chapter 2).
☐ Timing belt incorrectly tensioned (Chapter 2).

Engine misfires at idle speed

☐ Worn, faulty or incorrectly-gapped spark plugs (Chapter 1).
☐ Faulty spark plug HT leads (Chapter 1).
☐ Incorrectly-adjusted idle mixture settings (Chapter 1).
☐ Incorrect ignition timing (Chapter 1).
☐ Vacuum leak at the throttle housing, inlet manifold or associated hoses (Chapter 4).
☐ Distributor cap cracked, or tracking internally (Chapter 1).
☐ Incorrectly-adjusted valve clearances (Chapter 2).
☐ Uneven or low cylinder compressions (Chapter 2).
☐ Disconnected, leaking or perished crankcase ventilation hoses (Chapters 1 and 4).

Engine misfires throughout the driving speed range

☐ Blocked carburettor injector(s) (Chapter 4).
☐ Fuel filter choked (Chapter 1).
☐ Fuel pump faulty, or delivery pressure low (Chapter 4).
☐ Fuel tank vent blocked, or fuel pipes restricted (Chapter 4).
☐ Vacuum leak at the throttle housing, inlet manifold or associated hoses (Chapter 4).
☐ Worn, faulty or incorrectly-gapped spark plugs (Chapter 1).
☐ Faulty spark plug HT leads (Chapter 1).
☐ Distributor cap cracked, or tracking internally (Chapter 1).
☐ Faulty ignition coil (Chapter 5).
☐ Uneven or low cylinder compressions (Chapter 2).

Engine hesitates on acceleration

☐ Worn, faulty or incorrectly-gapped spark plugs (Chapter 1).
☐ Engine management PGM-Fi system fault (Chapters 4 and 5).
☐ Vacuum leak at the throttle housing, inlet manifold or associated hoses (Chapter 4).

Engine stalls

☐ Incorrectly-adjusted base idle speed and/or mixture settings (Chapter 1).
☐ Blocked injector(s) (Chapter 4).
☐ Vacuum leak at the throttle housing, inlet manifold or associated hoses (Chapter 4).
☐ Fuel filter choked (Chapter 1).
☐ Fuel pump faulty or delivery pressure low (Chapter 4).
☐ Fuel tank vent blocked, or fuel pipes restricted (Chapter 4).

Engine backfires

☐ Ignition timing incorrect (Chapter 1).
☐ Timing belt incorrectly fitted or tensioned (Chapter 2).
☐ Engine management PGM-Fi system fault (Chapters 4 and 5).
☐ Vacuum leak at the throttle housing, inlet manifold or associated hoses (Chapter 4).

Engine lacks power

- [ ] Incorrect ignition timing (Chapter 1).
- [ ] Engine management PGM-Fi system fault (Chapters 4 and 5).
- [ ] Timing belt incorrectly fitted or tensioned (Chapter 2).
- [ ] Fuel filter choked (Chapter 1).
- [ ] Fuel pump faulty or delivery pressure low (Chapter 4).
- [ ] Uneven or low cylinder compressions (Chapter 2).
- [ ] Worn, faulty or incorrectly-gapped spark plugs (Chapter 1).
- [ ] Vacuum leak at the throttle housing, inlet manifold or associated hoses (Chapter 4).
- [ ] Brakes binding (Chapters 1 and 9).
- [ ] Clutch slipping (Chapter 6).
- [ ] Automatic transmission fluid level incorrect (Chapter 1).

Oil pressure warning light illuminated with engine running

- [ ] Low oil level or incorrect grade (Chapter 1).
- [ ] Faulty oil pressure transmitter (sender) unit (Chapter 2).
- [ ] Worn engine bearings and/or oil pump (Chapter 2).
- [ ] High engine operating temperature (Chapter 3).
- [ ] Oil pressure relief valve defective (Chapter 2).
- [ ] Oil pick-up strainer clogged (Chapter 2).

Engine runs-on after switching off

- [ ] Idle speed excessively high (Chapter 1).
- [ ] Engine management PGM-Fi system fault (Chapters 4 and 5).
- [ ] Excessive carbon build-up in engine (Chapter 2).
- [ ] High engine operating temperature (Chapter 3).

Engine noises

Pre-ignition (pinking) or knocking during acceleration or under load

- [ ] Ignition timing incorrect (Chapter 1).
- [ ] Incorrect grade of fuel (Chapter 4).
- [ ] Vacuum leak at the throttle housing, inlet manifold or associated hoses (Chapter 4).
- [ ] Excessive carbon build-up in engine (Chapter 2).
- [ ] Worn or damaged distributor or other ignition system component (Chapters 1 and 5).
- [ ] Engine management PGM-Fi system fault (Chapters 4 and 5).

Whistling or wheezing noises

- [ ] Leaking inlet manifold or throttle housing gasket (Chapter 4).
- [ ] Leaking exhaust manifold gasket or pipe-to-manifold joint (Chapter 1).
- [ ] Leaking vacuum hose (Chapters 4, 5 and 9).
- [ ] Blowing cylinder head gasket (Chapter 2).

Tapping or rattling noises

- [ ] Incorrect valve clearances (Chapter 2).
- [ ] Worn valve gear or camshaft (Chapter 2).
- [ ] Ancillary component fault (water pump, alternator, etc.) (Chapters 3 and 12).

Knocking or thumping noises

- [ ] Worn big-end bearings (regular heavy knocking, perhaps less under load) (Chapter 2).
- [ ] Worn main bearings (rumbling and knocking, perhaps worsening under load) (Chapter 2).
- [ ] Piston slap (most noticeable when cold) (Chapter 2).
- [ ] Ancillary component fault (alternator, water pump, etc.) (Chapters 3 and 12).

2 Cooling system

Overheating

- [ ] Insufficient coolant in system (Chapter 3).
- [ ] Thermostat faulty (Chapter 3).
- [ ] Radiator core blocked or grille restricted (Chapter 3).
- [ ] Electric cooling fan or thermoswitch faulty (Chapter 3).
- [ ] Pressure cap faulty (Chapter 3).
- [ ] Ignition timing incorrect (Chapter 1).
- [ ] Inaccurate temperature gauge sender unit (Chapter 3).
- [ ] Air-lock in cooling system (Chapter 1).

Overcooling

- [ ] Thermostat faulty (Chapter 3).
- [ ] Inaccurate temperature gauge sender unit (Chapter 3).

External coolant leakage

- [ ] Deteriorated or damaged hoses or hose clips (Chapter 1).
- [ ] Radiator core or heater matrix leaking (Chapter 3).
- [ ] Pressure cap faulty (Chapter 3).
- [ ] Water pump seal leaking (Chapter 3).
- [ ] Boiling due to overheating (Chapter 3).
- [ ] Core plug leaking (Chapter 2).

Internal coolant leakage

- [ ] Leaking cylinder head gasket (Chapter 2).
- [ ] Cracked cylinder head or cylinder bore (Chapter 2).

Corrosion

- [ ] Infrequent draining and flushing (Chapter 1).
- [ ] Incorrect antifreeze mixture, or inappropriate antifreeze type (Chapter 1).

3 Fuel and exhaust systems

Excessive fuel consumption

- [ ] Air filter element dirty or clogged (Chapter 1).
- [ ] Engine management PGM-Fi system fault (Chapters 4 and 5).
- [ ] Ignition timing incorrect (Chapter 1).
- [ ] Tyres under-inflated (Chapter 1).

Fuel leakage and/or fuel odour

- [ ] Damaged or corroded fuel tank, pipes or connections (Chapter 1).

Excessive noise or fumes from exhaust system

- [ ] Leaking exhaust system or manifold joints (Chapter 1).
- [ ] Leaking, corroded or damaged silencers or pipe (Chapter 1).
- [ ] Broken mountings causing body or suspension contact (Chapter 1).

4 Clutch

Pedal travels to floor – no pressure or very little resistance

- ☐ Broken clutch cable (Chapter 6).
- ☐ Incorrect clutch adjustment (Chapter 6).
- ☐ Broken clutch release bearing or fork (Chapter 6).
- ☐ Broken diaphragm spring in clutch pressure plate (Chapter 6).

Noise when depressing or releasing clutch pedal

- ☐ Worn clutch release bearing (Chapter 6).
- ☐ Worn or dry clutch pedal bushes (Chapter 6).
- ☐ Faulty pressure plate assembly (Chapter 6).
- ☐ Pressure plate diaphragm spring broken (Chapter 6).
- ☐ Broken clutch disc cushioning springs (Chapter 6).

Clutch slips (engine speed increases with no increase in vehicle speed)

- ☐ Incorrect clutch adjustment (Chapter 6).
- ☐ Clutch disc linings excessively worn (Chapter 6).
- ☐ Clutch disc linings contaminated with oil or grease (Chapter 6).
- ☐ Faulty pressure plate, or weak diaphragm spring (Chapter 6).

Clutch fails to disengage (unable to select gears)

- ☐ Incorrect clutch adjustment (Chapter 6).
- ☐ Clutch disc sticking on gearbox input shaft splines (Chapter 6).
- ☐ Clutch disc sticking to flywheel or pressure plate (Chapter 6).
- ☐ Faulty pressure plate assembly (Chapter 6).
- ☐ Gearbox input shaft seized in crankshaft spigot bearing (Chapter 2).
- ☐ Clutch release mechanism worn or incorrectly assembled (Chapter 6).

Judder as clutch is engaged

- ☐ Clutch disc linings contaminated with oil or grease (Chapter 6).
- ☐ Clutch disc linings excessively worn (Chapter 6).
- ☐ Clutch cable sticking or frayed (Chapter 6).
- ☐ Faulty or distorted pressure plate or diaphragm spring (Chapter 6).
- ☐ Worn or loose engine or gearbox mountings (Chapter 2).
- ☐ Clutch disc hub or gearbox input shaft splines worn (Chapter 6).

5 Manual transmission

Jumps out of gear

- ☐ Worn or damaged gear linkage (Chapter 7).
- ☐ Worn synchroniser units (Chapter 7).*
- ☐ Worn selector forks (Chapter 7).*

Vibration

- ☐ Lack of oil (Chapter 1).
- ☐ Worn bearings (Chapter 7).*

Noisy in one particular gear

- ☐ Worn, damaged or chipped gear teeth (Chapter 7).*

Difficulty engaging gears

- ☐ Clutch fault (Chapter 6).
- ☐ Worn or damaged gear linkage (Chapter 7).
- ☐ Worn synchroniser units (Chapter 7).*

Noisy in neutral with engine running

- ☐ Input shaft bearings worn (noise apparent with clutch pedal released but not when depressed) (Chapter 7).*
- ☐ Clutch release bearing worn (noise apparent with clutch pedal depressed possibly less when released) (Chapter 6).

Lubricant leaks

- ☐ Leaking differential output oil seal (Chapter 7).
- ☐ Leaking selector shaft oil seal (Chapter 7).
- ☐ Leaking housing joint (Chapter 7).*
- ☐ Leaking input shaft oil seal (Chapter 7).*

Although the corrective action necessary to remedy the symptoms described is beyond the scope of the home mechanic, the above information should be helpful in isolating the cause of the condition, so that the owner can communicate clearly with a professional mechanic.

6 Automatic transmission

Note: *Due to the complexity of the automatic transmission, it is difficult for the home mechanic to properly diagnose and service this unit. For problems other than the following, the vehicle should be taken to a dealer service department or automatic transmission specialist*

Fluid leakage

- ☐ Automatic transmission fluid is usually deep red in colour. Fluid leaks should not be confused with engine oil, which can easily be blown onto the transmission by airflow.
- ☐ To determine the source of a leak, first remove all built-up dirt and grime from the transmission housing and surrounding areas, using a degreasing agent or by steam-cleaning. Drive the vehicle at low speed, so airflow will not blow the leak far from its source. Raise and support the vehicle, and determine where the leak is coming from. The following are common areas of leakage.
  (a) Sump (Chapters 1 and 2).
  (b) Dipstick tube (Chapters 1 and 2).
  (c) Transmission-to-fluid cooler pipes/unions (Chapter 7).

Transmission fluid brown, or has burned smell

- ☐ Transmission fluid level low, or fluid in need of renewal (Chapter 1).

General gear selection problems

- ☐ Chapter 7, Part B, deals with checking and adjusting the selector linkage on automatic transmissions. The following are common problems which may be caused by a poorly-adjusted linkage.
  (a) Engine starting in gears other than Park or Neutral.
  (b) Indicator on gear selector lever pointing to a gear other than the one actually being used.
  (c) Vehicle moves when in Park or Neutral.
  (d) Poor gearshift quality, or erratic gear changes.
- ☐ Refer to Chapter 7, Part B for the selector linkage adjustment procedure.

Transmission slips, shifts roughly, is noisy, or has no drive in forward or reverse gears

- ☐ There are many probable causes for the above problems, but the home mechanic should be concerned with only one possibility – fluid level. Before taking the vehicle to a dealer or transmission specialist, check the fluid level and condition of the fluid as described in Chapter 1. Correct the fluid level as necessary, or change the fluid and filter if needed. If the problem persists, professional help will be necessary.

Transmission will not downshift (kickdown) with accelerator pedal fully depressed

☐ Low transmission fluid level (Chapter 1).
☐ Incorrect selector mechanism adjustment (Chapter 7, Part B).
☐ Incorrect kickdown cable adjustment (Chapter 7, Part B).

Engine will not start in any gear, or starts in gears other than Park or Neutral

☐ Incorrect starter inhibitor switch adjustment (Chapter 7, Part B).
☐ Incorrect selector mechanism adjustment (Chapter 7, Part B).

7 Driveshafts

Clicking or knocking noise on turns (at slow speed on full-lock)

☐ Lack of constant velocity joint lubricant, probably caused by damaged joint rubber gaiter (Chapter 8).
☐ Worn outer constant velocity joint (Chapter 8).

Vibration when accelerating or decelerating

☐ Worn inner constant velocity joint (Chapter 8).
☐ Bent or distorted driveshaft (Chapter 8).

8 Braking system

Note: *Before assuming that a brake problem exists, make sure that the tyres are in good condition and correctly inflated, that the front wheel alignment is correct, and that the vehicle is not unevenly loaded. Apart from checking the condition of all pipe and hose connections, any faults occurring on the anti-lock braking system should be referred to a Rover dealer for diagnosis.*

Vehicle pulls to one side under braking

☐ Worn, defective, damaged or contaminated front or rear brake pads/shoes on one side (Chapter 1).
☐ Seized or partially-seized front or rear brake caliper/wheel cylinder piston (Chapter 9).
☐ A mixture of brake pad/shoe lining materials fitted between sides (Chapter 1).
☐ Brake caliper mounting bolts loose (Chapter 9).
☐ Rear brake backplate mounting bolts loose (Chapter 9).
☐ Worn or damaged steering or suspension components (Chapter 10).

Noise (grinding or high-pitched squeal) when brakes applied

☐ Brake pad or shoe friction lining material worn down to metal backing (Chapter 1).
☐ Excessive corrosion of brake disc or drum. (May be apparent after the vehicle has been standing for some time) (Chapter 1).
☐ Foreign object (stone chipping etc.) trapped between brake disc and splash shield (Chapter 1).

Excessive brake pedal travel

☐ Inoperative rear drum brake self-adjusting mechanism (Chapter 1).
☐ Faulty master cylinder (Chapter 9).
☐ Air in hydraulic system (Chapter 9).
☐ Faulty vacuum servo unit (Chapter 9).

Brake pedal feels spongy when depressed

☐ Air in hydraulic system (Chapter 9).
☐ Deteriorated flexible rubber brake hoses (Chapters 1 and 9).
☐ Master cylinder mounting nuts loose (Chapter 9).
☐ Faulty master cylinder (Chapter 9).

Excessive brake pedal effort required to stop vehicle

☐ Faulty vacuum servo unit (Chapter 9).
☐ Disconnected damaged or insecure brake servo vacuum hose (Chapter 9).
☐ Primary or secondary hydraulic circuit failure (Chapter 9).
☐ Seized brake caliper or wheel cylinder piston(s) (Chapter 9).
☐ Brake pads or brake shoes incorrectly fitted (Chapter 1).
☐ Incorrect grade of brake pads/shoes fitted (Chapter 1).
☐ Brake pads or brake shoe linings contaminated (Chapter 1).

Judder felt through brake pedal or steering wheel when braking

☐ Excessive run-out or distortion of brake discs or drums (Chapter 9).
☐ Brake pad or brake shoe linings worn (Chapter 1).
☐ Brake caliper or rear brake backplate mounting bolts loose (Chapter 9).
☐ Wear in suspension or steering components or mountings (Chapter 10).

Brakes binding

☐ Seized brake caliper or wheel cylinder piston(s) (Chapter 9).
☐ Incorrectly-adjusted handbrake mechanism or linkage (Chapter 1).
☐ Faulty master cylinder (Chapter 9).

Rear wheels locking under normal braking

☐ Rear brake pads/shoe linings contaminated (Chapter 1).
☐ Faulty brake pressure regulator (Chapter 9).

9 Suspension and steering

Note: *Before diagnosing suspension or steering faults, be sure that the trouble is not due to incorrect tyre pressures, mixtures of tyre types, or binding brakes.*

Vehicle pulls to one side

☐ Defective tyre (Chapter 1).
☐ Excessive wear in suspension or steering components (Chapter 10).
☐ Incorrect front wheel alignment (Chapter 10).
☐ Accident damage to steering or suspension components (Chapter 10).

Wheel wobble and vibration

☐ Front roadwheels out of balance – vibration felt mainly through the steering wheel (Chapter 1).
☐ Rear roadwheels out of balance – vibration felt throughout the vehicle (Chapter 1).
☐ Roadwheels damaged or distorted (Chapter 1).
☐ Faulty or damaged tyre (Chapter 1).
☐ Worn steering or suspension joints bushes or components (Chapter 10).
☐ Wheel bolts loose (Chapter 10).

Excessive pitching and/or rolling around corners, or during braking

☐ Defective shock absorbers (Chapter 10).
☐ Broken or weak coil spring and/or suspension component (Chapter 10).
☐ Worn or damaged anti-roll bar or mountings (Chapter 10).

Wandering or general instability

☐ Incorrect front wheel alignment (Chapter 10).
☐ Worn steering or suspension joints bushes or components (Chapter 10).
☐ Roadwheels out of balance (Chapter 1).
☐ Faulty or damaged tyre (Chapter 1).
☐ Wheel bolts loose (Chapter 10).
☐ Defective shock absorbers (Chapter 10).

Excessively-stiff steering

☐ Lack of steering gear lubricant (Chapter 10).
☐ Seized track rod end balljoint or suspension balljoint (Chapter 10).
☐ Broken or incorrectly-adjusted power steering pump drivebelt (Chapter 1).
☐ Incorrect front wheel alignment (Chapter 10).
☐ Steering rack or column bent or damaged (Chapter 10).

Excessive play in steering

☐ Worn steering column universal joint(s) or intermediate coupling (Chapter 10).
☐ Worn steering tie-rod end balljoints (Chapter 10).
☐ Worn rack-and-pinion steering gear (Chapter 10).
☐ Worn steering or suspension joints bushes or components (Chapter 10).

Lack of power assistance

☐ Broken or incorrectly-adjusted power steering pump drivebelt (Chapter 1).
☐ Incorrect power steering fluid level (Chapter 1).
☐ Restriction in power steering fluid hoses (Chapter 10).
☐ Faulty power steering pump (Chapter 10).
☐ Faulty rack-and-pinion steering gear (Chapter 10).

Tyre wear excessive

Tyres worn on inside or outside edges

☐ Tyres under-inflated – wear on both edges (Chapter 1).
☐ Incorrect camber or castor angles – wear on one edge only (Chapter 10).
☐ Worn steering or suspension joints bushes or components (Chapter 10).
☐ Excessively-fast cornering.
☐ Accident damage.

Tyre treads exhibit feathered edges

☐ Incorrect toe setting (Chapter 10).

Tyres worn in centre of tread

☐ Tyres over-inflated (Chapter 1).

Tyres worn on inside and outside edges

☐ Tyres under-inflated (Chapter 1).

Tyres worn unevenly

☐ Tyres out of balance (Chapter 1).
☐ Excessive wheel or tyre run-out (Chapter 1).
☐ Worn shock absorbers (Chapter 10).
☐ Faulty tyre (Chapter 1).

10 Electrical system

Note: *For problems associated with the starting system, refer to the faults listed under 'Engine' earlier in this Section.*

Battery will not hold a charge more than a few days

☐ Battery defective internally (Chapter 12).
☐ Battery electrolyte level low (Chapter 1).
☐ Battery terminal connections loose or corroded (Chapter 12).
☐ Alternator drivebelt worn or incorrectly adjusted (Chapter 1).
☐ Alternator not charging at correct output (Chapter 12).
☐ Alternator or voltage regulator faulty (Chapter 12).
☐ Short-circuit causing continual battery drain (Chapter 12).

Ignition warning light remains illuminated with engine running

☐ Alternator drivebelt broken, worn, or incorrectly adjusted (Chapter 1).
☐ Alternator brushes worn, sticking, or dirty (Chapter 12).
☐ Alternator brush springs weak or broken (Chapter 12).
☐ Internal fault in alternator or voltage regulator (Chapter 12).
☐ Charging circuit wiring broken, disconnected, or loose (Chapter 12).

Ignition warning light fails to come on

☐ Warning light bulb blown (Chapter 12).
☐ Warning light circuit wiring broken, disconnected, or loose (Chapter 12).
☐ Alternator faulty (Chapter 12).

Lights inoperative

☐ Bulb blown (Chapter 12).
☐ Corrosion of bulb or bulbholder contacts (Chapter 12).
☐ Blown fuse (Chapter 12).
☐ Faulty relay (Chapter 12).
☐ Broken, loose, or disconnected wiring (Chapter 12).
☐ Faulty switch (Chapter 12).

Instrument readings inaccurate or erratic

Instrument readings increase with engine speed

☐ Faulty voltage regulator (Chapter 12).

Fuel or temperature gauge gives no reading

☐ Faulty gauge sender unit (Chapters 3 or 4).
☐ Wiring open-circuit (Chapter 12).
☐ Faulty gauge (Chapter 12).

Fuel or temperature gauges give continuous maximum reading

☐ Faulty gauge sender unit (Chapters 3 or 4).
☐ Wiring short-circuit (Chapter 12).
☐ Faulty gauge (Chapter 12).

Horn inoperative, or unsatisfactory in operation

Horn operates all the time

☐ Horn push either earthed or stuck down (Chapter 12).
☐ Horn cable to horn push earthed (Chapter 12).

Horn fails to operate

☐ Blown fuse (Chapter 12).
☐ Cable or cable connections loose, broken or disconnected (Chapter 12).
☐ Faulty horn (Chapter 12).

Horn emits intermittent or unsatisfactory sound

☐ Cable connections loose (Chapter 12).
☐ Horn mountings loose (Chapter 12).
☐ Faulty horn (Chapter 12).

Windscreen/tailgate wipers inoperative, or unsatisfactory in operation

Wipers fail to operate, or operate very slowly

- [ ] Wiper blades stuck to screen, or linkage seized or binding (Chapter 12).
- [ ] Blown fuse (Chapter 12).
- [ ] Cable or cable connections loose, broken or disconnected (Chapter 12).
- [ ] Faulty relay (Chapter 12).
- [ ] Faulty wiper motor (Chapter 12).

Wiper blades sweep over too large or too small an area of the glass

- [ ] Wiper arms incorrectly positioned on spindles (Chapter 1).
- [ ] Excessive wear of wiper linkage (Chapter 1).
- [ ] Wrong size wiper blades fitted, or blade rubbers perished (Chapter 1).
- [ ] Wiper motor or linkage mountings loose or insecure (Chapter 12).

Wiper blades fail to clean the glass effectively

- [ ] Wiper blade rubbers worn or perished (Chapter 1).
- [ ] Wiper arm tension springs broken or arm pivots seized (Chapter 1).
- [ ] Insufficient windscreen washer additive to adequately remove road film (Chapter 1).

Windscreen/tailgate washers inoperative, or unsatisfactory in operation

One or more washer jets inoperative

- [ ] Blocked washer jet (Chapter 12).
- [ ] Disconnected, kinked or restricted fluid hose (Chapter 12).
- [ ] Insufficient fluid in washer reservoir (Chapter 1).

Washer pump fails to operate

- [ ] Broken or disconnected wiring or connections (Chapter 12).
- [ ] Blown fuse (Chapter 12).
- [ ] Faulty washer switch (Chapter 12).
- [ ] Faulty washer pump (Chapter 12).

Washer pump runs for some time before fluid is emitted from jets

- [ ] Faulty one-way valve in fluid supply hose (Chapter 12).

Electric windows inoperative, or unsatisfactory in operation

Window glass will only move in one direction

- [ ] Faulty switch (Chapter 12).

Window glass slow to move

- [ ] Incorrectly-adjusted door glass guide channels (Chapter 11).
- [ ] Regulator seized or damaged, or in need of lubrication (Chapter 11).
- [ ] Door internal components or trim fouling regulator (Chapter 11).
- [ ] Faulty motor (Chapter 12).

Window glass fails to move

- [ ] Incorrectly-adjusted door glass guide channels (Chapter 11).
- [ ] Blown fuse (Chapter 12).
- [ ] Faulty relay (Chapter 12).
- [ ] Broken or disconnected wiring or connections (Chapter 12).
- [ ] Faulty motor (Chapter 12).

Central locking system inoperative, or unsatisfactory in operation

Complete system failure

- [ ] Blown fuse (Chapter 12).
- [ ] Faulty relay (Chapter 12).
- [ ] Broken or disconnected wiring or connections (Chapter 12).

Latch locks but will not unlock, or unlocks but will not lock

- [ ] Faulty master switch (Chapter 12).
- [ ] Broken or disconnected latch operating rods or levers (Chapter 11).
- [ ] Faulty relay (Chapter 12).

One solenoid/motor fails to operate

- [ ] Broken or disconnected wiring or connections (Chapter 12).
- [ ] Faulty solenoid/motor (Chapter 12).
- [ ] Broken, binding or disconnected latch operating rods or levers (Chapter 11).
- [ ] Fault in door latch (Chapter 11).

A

ABS (Anti-lock brake system) A system, usually electronically controlled, that senses incipient wheel lockup during braking and relieves hydraulic pressure at wheels that are about to skid.

Air bag An inflatable bag hidden in the steering wheel (driver's side) or the dash or glovebox (passenger side). In a head-on collision, the bags inflate, preventing the driver and front passenger from being thrown forward into the steering wheel or windscreen.

Air cleaner A metal or plastic housing, containing a filter element, which removes dust and dirt from the air being drawn into the engine.

Air filter element The actual filter in an air cleaner system, usually manufactured from pleated paper and requiring renewal at regular intervals.

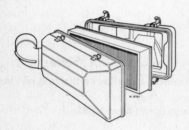

Air filter

Allen key A hexagonal wrench which fits into a recessed hexagonal hole.

Alligator clip A long-nosed spring-loaded metal clip with meshing teeth. Used to make temporary electrical connections.

Alternator A component in the electrical system which converts mechanical energy from a drivebelt into electrical energy to charge the battery and to operate the starting system, ignition system and electrical accessories.

Ampere (amp) A unit of measurement for the flow of electric current. One amp is the amount of current produced by one volt acting through a resistance of one ohm.

Anaerobic sealer A substance used to prevent bolts and screws from loosening. Anaerobic means that it does not require oxygen for activation. The Loctite brand is widely used.

Antifreeze A substance (usually ethylene glycol) mixed with water, and added to a vehicle's cooling system, to prevent freezing of the coolant in winter. Antifreeze also contains chemicals to inhibit corrosion and the formation of rust and other deposits that would tend to clog the radiator and coolant passages and reduce cooling efficiency.

Anti-seize compound A coating that reduces the risk of seizing on fasteners that are subjected to high temperatures, such as exhaust manifold bolts and nuts.

Asbestos A natural fibrous mineral with great heat resistance, commonly used in the composition of brake friction materials.

Asbestos is a health hazard and the dust created by brake systems should never be inhaled or ingested.

Axle A shaft on which a wheel revolves, or which revolves with a wheel. Also, a solid beam that connects the two wheels at one end of the vehicle. An axle which also transmits power to the wheels is known as a live axle.

Axleshaft A single rotating shaft, on either side of the differential, which delivers power from the final drive assembly to the drive wheels. Also called a driveshaft or a halfshaft.

B

Ball bearing An anti-friction bearing consisting of a hardened inner and outer race with hardened steel balls between two races.

Bearing The curved surface on a shaft or in a bore, or the part assembled into either, that permits relative motion between them with minimum wear and friction.

Bearing

Big-end bearing The bearing in the end of the connecting rod that's attached to the crankshaft.

Bleed nipple A valve on a brake wheel cylinder, caliper or other hydraulic component that is opened to purge the hydraulic system of air. Also called a bleed screw.

Brake bleeding Procedure for removing air from lines of a hydraulic brake system.

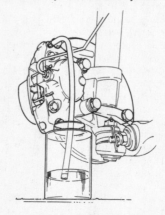

Brake bleeding

Brake disc The component of a disc brake that rotates with the wheels.

Brake drum The component of a drum brake that rotates with the wheels.

Brake linings The friction material which contacts the brake disc or drum to retard the vehicle's speed. The linings are bonded or riveted to the brake pads or shoes.

Brake pads The replaceable friction pads that pinch the brake disc when the brakes are applied. Brake pads consist of a friction material bonded or riveted to a rigid backing plate.

Brake shoe The crescent-shaped carrier to which the brake linings are mounted and which forces the lining against the rotating drum during braking.

Braking systems For more information on braking systems, consult the *Haynes Automotive Brake Manual*.

Breaker bar A long socket wrench handle providing greater leverage.

Bulkhead The insulated partition between the engine and the passenger compartment.

C

Caliper The non-rotating part of a disc-brake assembly that straddles the disc and carries the brake pads. The caliper also contains the hydraulic components that cause the pads to pinch the disc when the brakes are applied. A caliper is also a measuring tool that can be set to measure inside or outside dimensions of an object.

Camshaft A rotating shaft on which a series of cam lobes operate the valve mechanisms. The camshaft may be driven by gears, by sprockets and chain or by sprockets and a belt.

Canister A container in an evaporative emission control system; contains activated charcoal granules to trap vapours from the fuel system.

Canister

Carburettor A device which mixes fuel with air in the proper proportions to provide a desired power output from a spark ignition internal combustion engine.

Castellated Resembling the parapets along the top of a castle wall. For example, a castellated balljoint stud nut.

Castor In wheel alignment, the backward or forward tilt of the steering axis. Castor is positive when the steering axis is inclined rearward at the top.

Glossary of Technical Terms

Catalytic converter A silencer-like device in the exhaust system which converts certain pollutants in the exhaust gases into less harmful substances.

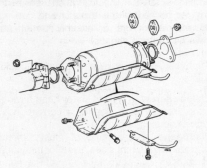

Catalytic converter

Circlip A ring-shaped clip used to prevent endwise movement of cylindrical parts and shafts. An internal circlip is installed in a groove in a housing; an external circlip fits into a groove on the outside of a cylindrical piece such as a shaft.

Clearance The amount of space between two parts. For example, between a piston and a cylinder, between a bearing and a journal, etc.

Coil spring A spiral of elastic steel found in various sizes throughout a vehicle, for example as a springing medium in the suspension and in the valve train.

Compression Reduction in volume, and increase in pressure and temperature, of a gas, caused by squeezing it into a smaller space.

Compression ratio The relationship between cylinder volume when the piston is at top dead centre and cylinder volume when the piston is at bottom dead centre.

Constant velocity (CV) joint A type of universal joint that cancels out vibrations caused by driving power being transmitted through an angle.

Core plug A disc or cup-shaped metal device inserted in a hole in a casting through which core was removed when the casting was formed. Also known as a freeze plug or expansion plug.

Crankcase The lower part of the engine block in which the crankshaft rotates.

Crankshaft The main rotating member, or shaft, running the length of the crankcase, with offset "throws" to which the connecting rods are attached.

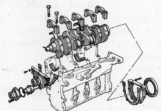

Crankshaft assembly

Crocodile clip See Alligator clip

D

Diagnostic code Code numbers obtained by accessing the diagnostic mode of an engine management computer. This code can be used to determine the area in the system where a malfunction may be located.

Disc brake A brake design incorporating a rotating disc onto which brake pads are squeezed. The resulting friction converts the energy of a moving vehicle into heat.

Double-overhead cam (DOHC) An engine that uses two overhead camshafts, usually one for the intake valves and one for the exhaust valves.

Drivebelt(s) The belt(s) used to drive accessories such as the alternator, water pump, power steering pump, air conditioning compressor, etc. off the crankshaft pulley.

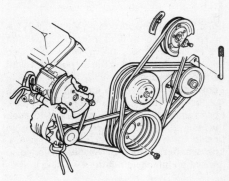

Accessory drivebelts

Driveshaft Any shaft used to transmit motion. Commonly used when referring to the axleshafts on a front wheel drive vehicle.

Drum brake A type of brake using a drum-shaped metal cylinder attached to the inner surface of the wheel. When the brake pedal is pressed, curved brake shoes with friction linings press against the inside of the drum to slow or stop the vehicle.

E

EGR valve A valve used to introduce exhaust gases into the intake air stream.

Electronic control unit (ECU) A computer which controls (for instance) ignition and fuel injection systems, or an anti-lock braking system. For more information refer to the *Haynes Automotive Electrical and Electronic Systems Manual.*

Electronic Fuel Injection (EFI) A computer controlled fuel system that distributes fuel through an injector located in each intake port of the engine.

Emergency brake A braking system, independent of the main hydraulic system, that can be used to slow or stop the vehicle if the primary brakes fail, or to hold the vehicle stationary even though the brake pedal isn't depressed. It usually consists of a hand lever that actuates either front or rear brakes mechanically through a series of cables and linkages. Also known as a handbrake or parking brake.

Endfloat The amount of lengthwise movement between two parts. As applied to a crankshaft, the distance that the crankshaft can move forward and back in the cylinder block.

Engine management system (EMS) A computer controlled system which manages the fuel injection and the ignition systems in an integrated fashion.

Exhaust manifold A part with several passages through which exhaust gases leave the engine combustion chambers and enter the exhaust pipe.

F

Fan clutch A viscous (fluid) drive coupling device which permits variable engine fan speeds in relation to engine speeds.

Feeler blade A thin strip or blade of hardened steel, ground to an exact thickness, used to check or measure clearances between parts.

Feeler blade

Firing order The order in which the engine cylinders fire, or deliver their power strokes, beginning with the number one cylinder.

Flywheel A heavy spinning wheel in which energy is absorbed and stored by means of momentum. On cars, the flywheel is attached to the crankshaft to smooth out firing impulses.

Free play The amount of travel before any action takes place. The "looseness" in a linkage, or an assembly of parts, between the initial application of force and actual movement. For example, the distance the brake pedal moves before the pistons in the master cylinder are actuated.

Fuse An electrical device which protects a circuit against accidental overload. The typical fuse contains a soft piece of metal which is calibrated to melt at a predetermined current flow (expressed as amps) and break the circuit.

Fusible link A circuit protection device consisting of a conductor surrounded by heat-resistant insulation. The conductor is smaller than the wire it protects, so it acts as the weakest link in the circuit. Unlike a blown fuse, a failed fusible link must frequently be cut from the wire for replacement.

Glossary of Technical Terms

G

Gap The distance the spark must travel in jumping from the centre electrode to the side electrode in a spark plug. Also refers to the spacing between the points in a contact breaker assembly in a conventional points-type ignition, or to the distance between the reluctor or rotor and the pickup coil in an electronic ignition.

Adjusting spark plug gap

Gasket Any thin, soft material - usually cork, cardboard, asbestos or soft metal - installed between two metal surfaces to ensure a good seal. For instance, the cylinder head gasket seals the joint between the block and the cylinder head.

Gasket

Gauge An instrument panel display used to monitor engine conditions. A gauge with a movable pointer on a dial or a fixed scale is an analogue gauge. A gauge with a numerical readout is called a digital gauge.

H

Halfshaft A rotating shaft that transmits power from the final drive unit to a drive wheel, usually when referring to a live rear axle.

Harmonic balancer A device designed to reduce torsion or twisting vibration in the crankshaft. May be incorporated in the crankshaft pulley. Also known as a vibration damper.

Hone An abrasive tool for correcting small irregularities or differences in diameter in an engine cylinder, brake cylinder, etc.

Hydraulic tappet A tappet that utilises hydraulic pressure from the engine's lubrication system to maintain zero clearance (constant contact with both camshaft and valve stem). Automatically adjusts to variation in valve stem length. Hydraulic tappets also reduce valve noise.

I

Ignition timing The moment at which the spark plug fires, usually expressed in the number of crankshaft degrees before the piston reaches the top of its stroke.

Inlet manifold A tube or housing with passages through which flows the air-fuel mixture (carburettor vehicles and vehicles with throttle body injection) or air only (port fuel-injected vehicles) to the port openings in the cylinder head.

J

Jump start Starting the engine of a vehicle with a discharged or weak battery by attaching jump leads from the weak battery to a charged or helper battery.

L

Load Sensing Proportioning Valve (LSPV) A brake hydraulic system control valve that works like a proportioning valve, but also takes into consideration the amount of weight carried by the rear axle.

Locknut A nut used to lock an adjustment nut, or other threaded component, in place. For example, a locknut is employed to keep the adjusting nut on the rocker arm in position.

Lockwasher A form of washer designed to prevent an attaching nut from working loose.

M

MacPherson strut A type of front suspension system devised by Earle MacPherson at Ford of England. In its original form, a simple lateral link with the anti-roll bar creates the lower control arm. A long strut - an integral coil spring and shock absorber - is mounted between the body and the steering knuckle. Many modern so-called MacPherson strut systems use a conventional lower A-arm and don't rely on the anti-roll bar for location.

Multimeter An electrical test instrument with the capability to measure voltage, current and resistance.

N

NOx Oxides of Nitrogen. A common toxic pollutant emitted by petrol and diesel engines at higher temperatures.

O

Ohm The unit of electrical resistance. One volt applied to a resistance of one ohm will produce a current of one amp.

Ohmmeter An instrument for measuring electrical resistance.

O-ring A type of sealing ring made of a special rubber-like material; in use, the O-ring is compressed into a groove to provide the sealing action.

Overhead cam (ohc) engine An engine with the camshaft(s) located on top of the cylinder head(s).

Overhead valve (ohv) engine An engine with the valves located in the cylinder head, but with the camshaft located in the engine block.

Oxygen sensor A device installed in the engine exhaust manifold, which senses the oxygen content in the exhaust and converts this information into an electric current. Also called a Lambda sensor.

P

Phillips screw A type of screw head having a cross instead of a slot for a corresponding type of screwdriver.

Plastigage A thin strip of plastic thread, available in different sizes, used for measuring clearances. For example, a strip of Plastigage is laid across a bearing journal. The parts are assembled and dismantled; the width of the crushed strip indicates the clearance between journal and bearing.

Plastigage

Propeller shaft The long hollow tube with universal joints at both ends that carries power from the transmission to the differential on front-engined rear wheel drive vehicles.

Proportioning valve A hydraulic control valve which limits the amount of pressure to the rear brakes during panic stops to prevent wheel lock-up.

R

Rack-and-pinion steering A steering system with a pinion gear on the end of the steering shaft that mates with a rack (think of a geared wheel opened up and laid flat). When the steering wheel is turned, the pinion turns, moving the rack to the left or right. This movement is transmitted through the track rods to the steering arms at the wheels.

Radiator A liquid-to-air heat transfer device designed to reduce the temperature of the coolant in an internal combustion engine cooling system.

Refrigerant Any substance used as a heat transfer agent in an air-conditioning system. R-12 has been the principle refrigerant for many years; recently, however, manufacturers have begun using R-134a, a non-CFC substance that is considered less harmful to the ozone in the upper atmosphere.

Rocker arm A lever arm that rocks on a shaft or pivots on a stud. In an overhead valve engine, the rocker arm converts the upward movement of the pushrod into a downward movement to open a valve.

Rotor In a distributor, the rotating device inside the cap that connects the centre electrode and the outer terminals as it turns, distributing the high voltage from the coil secondary winding to the proper spark plug. Also, that part of an alternator which rotates inside the stator. Also, the rotating assembly of a turbocharger, including the compressor wheel, shaft and turbine wheel.

Runout The amount of wobble (in-and-out movement) of a gear or wheel as it's rotated. The amount a shaft rotates "out-of-true." The out-of-round condition of a rotating part.

S

Sealant A liquid or paste used to prevent leakage at a joint. Sometimes used in conjunction with a gasket.

Sealed beam lamp An older headlight design which integrates the reflector, lens and filaments into a hermetically-sealed one-piece unit. When a filament burns out or the lens cracks, the entire unit is simply replaced.

Serpentine drivebelt A single, long, wide accessory drivebelt that's used on some newer vehicles to drive all the accessories, instead of a series of smaller, shorter belts. Serpentine drivebelts are usually tensioned by an automatic tensioner.

Serpentine drivebelt

Shim Thin spacer, commonly used to adjust the clearance or relative positions between two parts. For example, shims inserted into or under bucket tappets control valve clearances. Clearance is adjusted by changing the thickness of the shim.

Slide hammer A special puller that screws into or hooks onto a component such as a shaft or bearing; a heavy sliding handle on the shaft bottoms against the end of the shaft to knock the component free.

Sprocket A tooth or projection on the periphery of a wheel, shaped to engage with a chain or drivebelt. Commonly used to refer to the sprocket wheel itself.

Starter inhibitor switch On vehicles with an automatic transmission, a switch that prevents starting if the vehicle is not in Neutral or Park.

Strut See MacPherson strut.

T

Tappet A cylindrical component which transmits motion from the cam to the valve stem, either directly or via a pushrod and rocker arm. Also called a cam follower.

Thermostat A heat-controlled valve that regulates the flow of coolant between the cylinder block and the radiator, so maintaining optimum engine operating temperature. A thermostat is also used in some air cleaners in which the temperature is regulated.

Thrust bearing The bearing in the clutch assembly that is moved in to the release levers by clutch pedal action to disengage the clutch. Also referred to as a release bearing.

Timing belt A toothed belt which drives the camshaft. Serious engine damage may result if it breaks in service.

Timing chain A chain which drives the camshaft.

Toe-in The amount the front wheels are closer together at the front than at the rear. On rear wheel drive vehicles, a slight amount of toe-in is usually specified to keep the front wheels running parallel on the road by offsetting other forces that tend to spread the wheels apart.

Toe-out The amount the front wheels are closer together at the rear than at the front. On front wheel drive vehicles, a slight amount of toe-out is usually specified.

Tools For full information on choosing and using tools, refer to the *Haynes Automotive Tools Manual*.

Tracer A stripe of a second colour applied to a wire insulator to distinguish that wire from another one with the same colour insulator.

Tune-up A process of accurate and careful adjustments and parts replacement to obtain the best possible engine performance.

Turbocharger A centrifugal device, driven by exhaust gases, that pressurises the intake air. Normally used to increase the power output from a given engine displacement, but can also be used primarily to reduce exhaust emissions (as on VW's "Umwelt" Diesel engine).

U

Universal joint or U-joint A double-pivoted connection for transmitting power from a driving to a driven shaft through an angle. A U-joint consists of two Y-shaped yokes and a cross-shaped member called the spider.

V

Valve A device through which the flow of liquid, gas, vacuum, or loose material in bulk may be started, stopped, or regulated by a movable part that opens, shuts, or partially obstructs one or more ports or passageways. A valve is also the movable part of such a device.

Valve clearance The clearance between the valve tip (the end of the valve stem) and the rocker arm or tappet. The valve clearance is measured when the valve is closed.

Vernier caliper A precision measuring instrument that measures inside and outside dimensions. Not quite as accurate as a micrometer, but more convenient.

Viscosity The thickness of a liquid or its resistance to flow.

Volt A unit for expressing electrical "pressure" in a circuit. One volt that will produce a current of one ampere through a resistance of one ohm.

W

Welding Various processes used to join metal items by heating the areas to be joined to a molten state and fusing them together. For more information refer to the *Haynes Automotive Welding Manual*.

Wiring diagram A drawing portraying the components and wires in a vehicle's electrical system, using standardised symbols. For more information refer to the *Haynes Automotive Electrical and Electronic Systems Manual*.

Conversion Factors

Length (distance)

Inches (in)	25.4	= Millimetres (mm)	x 0.0394	= Inches (in)
Feet (ft)	0.305	= Metres (m)	x 3.281	= Feet (ft)
Miles	1.609	= Kilometres (km)	x 0.621	= Miles

Volume (capacity)

Cubic inches (cu in; in^3)	x 16.387	= Cubic centimetres (cc; cm^3)	x 0.061	= Cubic inches (cu in; in^3)
Imperial pints (Imp pt)	x 0.568	= Litres (l)	x 1.76	= Imperial pints (Imp pt)
Imperial quarts (Imp qt)	x 1.137	= Litres (l)	x 0.88	= Imperial quarts (Imp qt)
Imperial quarts (Imp qt)	x 1.201	= US quarts (US qt)	x 0.833	= Imperial quarts (Imp qt)
US quarts (US qt)	x 0.946	= Litres (l)	x 1.057	= US quarts (US qt)
Imperial gallons (Imp gal)	x 4.546	= Litres (l)	x 0.22	= Imperial gallons (Imp gal)
Imperial gallons (Imp gal)	x 1.201	= US gallons (US gal)	x 0.833	= Imperial gallons (Imp gal)
US gallons (US gal)	x 3.785	= Litres (l)	x 0.264	= US gallons (US gal)

Mass (weight)

Ounces (oz)	x 28.35	= Grams (g)	x 0.035	= Ounces (oz)
Pounds (lb)	x 0.454	= Kilograms (kg)	x 2.205	= Pounds (lb)

Force

Ounces-force (ozf; oz)	x 0.278	= Newtons (N)	x 3.6	= Ounces-force (ozf; oz)
Pounds-force (lbf; lb)	x 4.448	= Newtons (N)	x 0.225	= Pounds-force (lbf; lb)
Newtons (N)	x 0.1	= Kilograms-force (kgf; kg)	x 9.81	= Newtons (N)

Pressure

Pounds-force per square inch (psi; lbf/in^2; lb/in^2)	x 0.070	= Kilograms-force per square centimetre (kgf/cm^2; kg/cm^2)	x 14.223	= Pounds-force per square inch (psi; lbf/in^2; lb/in^2)
Pounds-force per square inch (psi; lbf/in^2; lb/in^2)	x 0.068	= Atmospheres (atm)	x 14.696	= Pounds-force per square inch (psi; lbf/in^2; lb/in^2)
Pounds-force per square inch (psi; lbf/in^2; lb/in^2)	x 0.069	= Bars	x 14.5	= Pounds-force per square inch (psi; lbf/in^2; lb/in^2)
Pounds-force per square inch (psi; lbf/in^2; lb/in^2)	x 6.895	= Kilopascals (kPa)	x 0.145	= Pounds-force per square inch (psi; lbf/in^2; lb/in^2)
Kilopascals (kPa)	x 0.01	= Kilograms-force per square centimetre (kgf/cm^2; kg/cm^2)	x 98.1	= Kilopascals (kPa)
Millibar (mbar)	x 100	= Pascals (Pa)	x 0.01	= Millibar (mbar)
Millibar (mbar)	x 0.0145	= Pounds-force per square inch (psi; lbf/in^2; lb/in^2)	x 68.947	= Millibar (mbar)
Millibar (mbar)	x 0.75	= Millimetres of mercury (mmHg)	x 1.333	= Millibar (mbar)
Millibar (mbar)	x 0.401	= Inches of water (inH$_2$O)	x 2.491	= Millibar (mbar)
Millimetres of mercury (mmHg)	x 0.535	= Inches of water (inH$_2$O)	x 1.868	= Millimetres of mercury (mmHg)
Inches of water (inH$_2$O)	x 0.036	= Pounds-force per square inch (psi; lbf/in^2; lb/in^2)	x 27.68	= Inches of water (inH$_2$O)

Torque (moment of force)

Pounds-force inches (lbf in; lb in)	x 1.152	= Kilograms-force centimetre (kgf cm; kg cm)	x 0.868	= Pounds-force inches (lbf in; lb in)
Pounds-force inches (lbf in; lb in)	*x 0.113*	*= Newton metres (Nm)*	*x 8.85*	*= Pounds-force inches (lbf in; lb in)*
Pounds-force inches (lbf in; lb in)	x 0.083	= Pounds-force feet (lbf ft; lb ft)	x 12	= Pounds-force inches (lbf in; lb in)
Pounds-force feet (lbf ft; lb ft)	x 0.138	= Kilograms-force metres (kgf m; kg m)	x 7.233	= Pounds-force feet (lbf ft; lb ft)
Pounds-force feet (lbf ft; lb ft)	x 1.356	= Newton metres (Nm)	x 0.738	= Pounds-force feet (lbf ft; lb ft)
Newton metres (Nm)	x 0.102	= Kilograms-force metres (kgf m; kg m)	x 9.804	= Newton metres (Nm)

Power

Horsepower (hp)	x 745.7	= Watts (W)	x 0.0013	= Horsepower (hp)

Velocity (speed)

Miles per hour (miles/hr; mph)	x 1.609	= Kilometres per hour (km/hr; kph)	x 0.621	= Miles per hour (miles/hr; mph)

Fuel consumption*

Miles per gallon, Imperial (mpg)	x 0.354	= Kilometres per litre (km/l)	x 2.825	= Miles per gallon, Imperial (mpg)
Miles per gallon, US (mpg)	x 0.425	= Kilometres per litre (km/l)	x 2.352	= Miles per gallon, US (mpg)

Temperature

Degrees Fahrenheit = (°C x 1.8) + 32   Degrees Celsius (Degrees Centigrade; °C) = (°F - 32) x 0.56

* It is common practice to convert from miles per gallon (mpg) to litres/100 kilometres (l/100km),
where mpg (Imperial) x l/100 km = 282 and mpg (US) x l/100 km = 235

Note: *References throughout this index relate to Chapter•page number*

Haynes Manuals – The Complete List

Title	Book No.
ALFA ROMEO	
Alfa Romeo Alfasud/Sprint (74 - 88)	0292
Alfa Romeo Alfetta (73 - 87)	0531
AUDI	
Audi 80 (72 - Feb 79)	0207
Audi 80, 90 (79 - Oct 86) & Coupe (81 - Nov 88)	0605
Audi 80, 90 (Oct 86 - 90) & Coupe (Nov 88 - 90)	1491
Audi 100 (69 - Sept 76)	0162
Audi 100 (Oct 76 - Oct 82)	0428
Audi 100 (Oct 82 - 90) & 200 (Feb 84 - Oct 89)	0907
AUSTIN	
Austin Allegro 1100, 1300, 1.0, 1.1 & 1.3 (73 - 82)	0164
Austin Ambassador (82 - 84)	0871
Austin/MG Maestro 1.3 & 1.6 (petrol)(83 - 95)	0922
Austin Maxi (69 - 81)	0052
Austin/MG Metro (80 - May 90)	0718
Austin Montego 1.3 & 1.6 (84 - 94)	1066
Austin/MG Montego 2.0 (petrol)(84 - 95)	1067
Mini (59 - 69)	0527
Mini (69 - 95)	0646
Austin/Rover Diesel Engine 2.0 litre (86 - 93)	1857
BEDFORD	
Bedford CF (petrol)(69 - 87)	0163
Bedford HA Van (64 - 83)	0607
Bedford Rascal (86 - Oct 94)	3015
BL	
BL Princess & BLMC 18-22 (75 - 82)	0286
BMW	
BMW 316, 320 & 320i (4-cyl)(75 - Feb 83)	0276
BMW 320, 320i, 323i & 325i (6-cyl) (Oct 77 - Sept 87)	0815
BMW 520i & 525e (Oct 81 - June 88)	1560
BMW 525, 528 & 528i (73 - Sept 81)	0632
BMW 3 Series (sohc, petrol)(81 - 93)	1948
BMW 5 Series (sohc, petrol)(81 - 93)	1948
BMW 1500, 1502, 1600, 1602 & 2000 (59 - 77)	0240
CITROEN	
Citröen 2CV, Ami & Dyane (67 - 90)	0196
Citröen AX (petrol & diesel)(87 - 94)	3014
Citröen BX (83 - 94)	0908
Citröen CX (75 - 88)	0528
Citröen GS & GSA (71 - 85)	0290
Citröen Visa (79 - 88)	0620
Citröen Xantia (petrol & diesel)(93 - Oct 95)	3082
Citröen ZX (diesel)(91 - 93)	1922
Citröen ZX (petrol)(91 - 94)	1881
Citröen Diesel Engines 1.7 & 1.9 litres (84 - 94)	1379
COLT	
Colt 1200, 1250 & 1400 (79 - May 84)	0600
Colt Galant (74 - 78) & Celeste (76 - 81)	0236
Colt Lancer (74 - 77)	0419
DAIMLER	
Daimler Sovereign (68 - Oct 86)	0242
Daimler Double Six (72 - 88)	0478

Title	Book No.
DATSUN (see also Nissan)	
Datsun 120Y (73 - Aug 78)	0228
Datsun 1300, 1400 & 1600 (69 - Aug 72)	0123
Datsun Cherry (71 - 76)	0195
Datsun Cherry (79 - Sept 82)	0679
Datsun Pick-up (75 - 78)	0277
Datsun Sunny (Aug 78 - May 82)	0525
Datsun Violet (78 - 82)	0430
FIAT	
Fiat 124 (66 - 75)	0080
Fiat 126 (73 - 87)	0305
Fiat 127 (71 - 83)	0193
Fiat 500 (57 - 73)	0090
Fiat 850 (64 - 81)	0038
Fiat Panda (81 - 95)	0793
Fiat Regata (84 - 88)	1167
Fiat Strada (79 - 88)	0479
Fiat Tipo (88 - 91)	1625
Fiat Uno (82 - 93)	0923
Fiat X1/9 (74 - 89)	0273
FORD	
Ford Capri II & III 1.6 & 2.0 (74 - 87)	0283
Ford Capri II & III 2.8 & 3.0 (74 - 87)	1309
Ford Cortina Mk III 1300 & 1600 (70 - 76)	0070
Ford Cortina Mk III 1600 & 2000 (70 - 76)	0295
Ford Cortina Mk IV & V 1.6 & 2.0 (76 - 83)	0343
Ford Cortina Mk IV & V 2.3 V6 (77 - 83)	0426
Ford Escort (75 - Aug 80)	0280
Ford Escort Mk II Mexico, RS 1600 & RS 2000 (75 - 80)	0735
Ford Escort fwd (Sept 80 - Sept 90)	0686
Ford Escort (Sept 90 - Feb 95)	1737
Ford Fiesta (inc. XR2)(76 - Aug 83)	0334
Ford Fiesta (inc. XR2)(Aug 83 - Feb 89)	1030
Ford Fiesta (Feb 89 - 93)	1595
Ford Granada (Sept 77 - Feb 85)	0481
Ford Granada (Mar 85 - 94)	1245
Ford Mondeo (93 - 95)	1923
Ford Orion (83 - Sept 90)	1009
Ford Orion (Sept 90 - Feb 95)	1737
Ford Sierra 1.3, 1.6, 1.8 & 2.0 (82 - 93)	0903
Ford Sierra 2.3, 2.8 & 2.9 (82 - 91)	0904
Ford Scorpio (Mar 85 - 94)	1245
Ford Transit Mk 1 (diesel)(65 - Feb 78)	0418
Ford Transit Mk 1 (petrol)(65 - Feb 78)	0377
Ford Transit Mk 2 (petrol)(78 - Jan 86)	0719
Ford Transit Mk 3 (petrol)(Feb 86 - 89)	1468
Ford Transit (diesel)(Feb 86 - 95)	3019
Ford Diesel Engines 1.6 & 1.8 litre (fwd)(84 - 95)	1172
Ford Diesel Engines 2.1, 2.3 & 2.5 litres (77 - 90)	1606
Ford Vehicle Carburettors	1783
FREIGHT ROVER	
Sherpa (74 - 87)	0463
HILLMAN	
Hillman Avenger (70 - 82)	0037
Hillman Minx & Husky (56 - 75)	0009
HONDA	
Honda Accord (76 - Feb 84)	0351
Honda Accord (Feb 84 - Oct 85)	1177

Title	Book No.
Honda Civic 1200 (73 - 79)	0160
Honda Civic (Feb 84 - Oct 87)	1226
JAGUAR	
Jaguar E Type (61 - 72)	0140
Jaguar MkI & II, 240 & 340 (55 - 69)	0098
Jaguar XJ6, XJ & Sovereign (68 - Oct 86)	0242
Jaguar XJ12, XJS & Sovereign (72 - 88)	0478
LADA	
Lada 1200, 1300, 1500 & 1600 (74 - 91)	0413
Lada Samara (87 - 91)	1610
LANCIA	
Lancia Beta (73 - 80)	0533
LAND ROVER	
Land Rover Series II, IIA & III (petrol)(58 - 85)	0314
Land Rover Series IIA & III (diesel)(58 - 85)	0529
Land Rover 90, 110 & Defender (diesel)(83 - 95)	3017
Land Rover Discovery (diesel)(89 - 95)	3016
MAZDA	
Mazda 323 rwd (77 - Apr 86)	0370
Mazda 323 fwd (Mar 81 - Oct 89)	1608
Mazda 626 fwd (May 83 - Sept 87)	0929
Mazda B-1600, B-1800 & B-2000 Pick-up (72 - 88)	0267
Mazda RX-7 (79 - 85)	0460
MERCEDES-BENZ	
Mercedes-Benz 190 & 190E (83 - 87)	0928
Mercedes-Benz 200, 240, 300 (diesel) (Oct 76 - 85)	1114
Mercedes-Benz 250 & 280 (68 - 72)	0346
Mercedes-Benz 250 & 280 (123 Series) (Oct 76 - 84)	0677
MG	
MG Maestro 1.3 & 1.6 (83 - 95)	0922
MG Metro (80 - May 90)	0718
MG Montego 2.0 (84 - 95)	1067
MG Midget & AH Sprite (58 - 80)	0265
MGB (62 - 80)	0111
MITSUBISHI	
Mitsubishi Shogun & L200 Pick-Ups (83 - 94)	1944
Mitsubishi 1200, 1250 & 1400 (79 - May 84)	0600
MORRIS	
Morris Ital 1.3 (80 - 84)	0705
Morris Marina 1700 (78 - 80)	0526
Morris Marina 1.8 (71 - 78)	0074
Morris Minor 1000 (56 - 71)	0024
NISSAN (See also Datsun)	
Nissan Bluebird 160B & 180B (rwd) (May 80 - May 84)	0957
Nissan Bluebird fwd (May 84 - Mar 86)	1223
Nissan Bluebird T12 & T72 (Mar 86 - 90)	1473
Nissan Cherry N12 (Sept 82 - 86)	1031
Nissan Micra K10 (83 - Jan 93)	0931
Nissan Primera (90 - 95)	1851
Nissan Stanza (82 - 86)	0824
Nissan Sunny B11 (May 82 - Oct 86)	0895
Nissan Sunny (Oct 86 - Mar 91)	1378
OPEL	
Opel Ascona & Manta B Series (Sept 75 - 88)	0316

Title	Book No.
Opel Kadett C Series (Nov 73 - Nov 79)	0395
Opel Kadett D Series (fwd)(Nov 79 - Oct 84)	0634
PEUGEOT	
Peugeot 106 (petrol & diesel)(91 - 94)	1882
Peugeot 205 (83 - 95)	0932
Peugeot 305 (78 - 89)	0538
Peugeot 306 (petrol & diesel)(93 - 95)	3073
Peugeot 309 (86 - 93)	1266
Peugeot 405 (88 - 95)	1559
Peugeot 405 (diesel)(88 - 96)	3198
Peugeot 504 (68 - 82)	0161
Peugeot 504 (diesel)(74 - 82)	0663
Peugeot 505 (79 - 89)	0762
Peugeot Diesel Engines 1.7 & 1.9 litres (82 - 94)	0950
Peugeot Diesel Engines 2.0, 2.1, 2.3 & 2.5 litres (74 - 90)	1607
PORSCHE	
Porsche 911 (65 - 85)	0264
Porsche 924 & 924 Turbo (76 - 85)	0397
RANGE ROVER	
Range Rover V8 (70 - Oct 92)	0606
RELIANT	
Reliant Robin & Kitten (73 - 83)	0436
RENAULT	
Renault 4 (61 - 86)	0072
Renault 5 (72 - Feb 85)	0141
Renault 5 (Feb 85 - 95)	1219
Renault 6 (68 - 79)	0092
Renault 9 & 11 (82 - 89)	0822
Renault 12 (70 - 80)	0097
Renault 14 (77 - 83)	0362
Renault 15 & 17 (72 - 79)	0763
Renault 16 (65 - 79)	0081
Renault 18 (79 - 86)	0598
Renault 19 (petrol)(89 - 94)	1646
Renault 19 (diesel)(89 - 95)	1946
Renault 21 (86 - 94)	1397
Renault 25 (84 - 86)	1228
Renault Clio (petrol)(91 - 93)	1853
Renault Clio (diesel)(91 - 95)	3031
Renault Fuego (80 - 86)	0764
ROVER	
Rover 213 & 216 (84 - 89)	1116
Rover 214 & 414 (Oct 89 - 92)	1689
Rover 216 & 416 (Oct 89 - 92)	1830
Rover 820, 825 & 827 (petrol)(86 - 95)	1380
Rover 2000, 2300 & 2600 (77 - 87)	0468
Rover 3500 (76 - 87)	0365
Rover Metro (May 90 - 91)	1711
Rover Diesel Engine 2.0 litre (86 - 93)	1857
SAAB	
Saab 95 & 96 (66 - 76)	0198
Saab 99 (69 - 79)	0247
Saab 90, 99 & 900 (79 - Sept 93)	0765
Saab 9000 (4-cyl)(85 - 95)	1686
SEAT	
Seat Ibiza & Malaga (85 - 92)	1609
SIMCA	
Simca 1100 & 1204 (67 - 79)	0088
Simca 1301 & 1501 (63 - 76)	0199
SKODA	
Skoda 1000 & 1100 (64 - 78)	0303

Title	Book No.
Skoda Estelle 105, 120, 130 & 136 (77 - 89)	0604
Skoda Favorit (89 - 92)	1801
SUBARU	
Subaru 1600 (77 - Oct 79)	0237
Subaru 1600 & 1800 (Nov 79 - 90)	0995
SUZUKI	
Suzuki SJ Series, Samurai & Vitara (82 - 94)	1942
Suzuki Supercarry (86 - Oct 94)	3015
TALBOT	
Talbot Alpine, Solara, Minx & Rapier (75 - 86)	0337
Talbot Horizon (78 - 86)	0473
Talbot Samba (82 - 86)	0823
Talbot Sunbeam (77 - 82)	0435
TOYOTA	
Toyota 2000 (75 - 77)	0360
Toyota Celica (78 - Jan 82)	0437
Toyota Celica (Feb 82 - Sept 85)	1135
Toyota Corolla (rwd)(80 - 85)	0683
Toyota Corolla (fwd)(Sept 83 - Sept 87)	1024
Toyota Corolla (Sept 87 - 92)	1683
Toyota Hi-Ace & Hi-Lux (69 - Oct 83)	0304
Toyota Starlet (78 - Jan 85)	0462
TRIUMPH	
Triumph Acclaim (81 - 84)	0792
Triumph GT6 (62 - 74)	0112
Triumph Herald (59 - 71)	0010
Triumph Spitfire (62 - 81)	0113
Triumph Stag (70 - 78)	0441
Triumph TR2, 3, 3A, 4 & 4A (52 - 67)	0028
Triumph TR7 (75 - 82)	0322
Triumph Vitesse (62 - 74)	0112
VAUXHALL	
Vauxhall Astra (80 - Oct 84)	0635
Vauxhall Astra & Belmont (Oct 84 - Oct 91)	1136
Vauxhall Astra (Oct 91 - Oct 92)	1832
Vauxhall Carlton (Oct 78 - Oct 86)	0480
Vauxhall Carlton (Nov 86 - 93).	1469
Vauxhall Cavalier 1300 (77 - July 81)	0461
Vauxhall Cavalier 1600, 1900 & 2000 (75 - July 81)	0315
Vauxhall Cavalier (fwd)(81 - Oct 88)	0812
Vauxhall Cavalier (Oct 88 - 94)	1570
Vauxhall Chevette (75 - 84)	0285
Vauxhall Corsa (Mar 93 - 94)	1985
Vauxhall Magnum (73 - 77)	0294
Vauxhall Nova (83 - 93)	0909
Vauxhall Rascal (86 - Oct 94)	3015
Vauxhall Victor & VX4/90 FD Series (67 - 72)	0053
Vauxhall Viva HC (70 - 79)	0047
Vauxhall Diesel Engines 1.6 & 1.7 litres (82 - 94)	1222
VOLKSWAGEN	
VW Beetle 1200 (54 - 77)	0036
VW Beetle 1300 & 1500 (65 - 75)	0039
VW Beetle 1302 & 1302S (70 - 72)	0110
VW Beetle 1303, 1303S & GT (72 - 75)	0159
VW Golf 'Mk 1' 1.1 & 1.3 (74 - June 84)	0716
VW Golf 'Mk 1' 1.5, 1.6 & 1.8 (74 - 85)	0726
VW Golf 'Mk 1' (diesel)(78 - June 84)	0451
VW Golf 'Mk 2' (Mar 84 - 92)	1081
VW Golf 'Mk 3' (petrol & diesel)(Feb 92 - 95)	3097

Title	Book No.
VW Jetta 'Mk 1' 1.1 & 1.3 (74 - June 84)	0716
VW Jetta 'Mk 1' 1.5, 1.6 & 1.8 (74 - 85)	0726
VW Jetta 'Mk 1' (diesel)(78 - June 84)	0451
VW Jetta 'Mk 2' (Mar 84 - 92)	1081
VW LT vans & light trucks (76 - 87)	0637
VW Passat (73 - Sept 81)	0238
VW Passat (Sept 81 - May 88)	0814
VW Passat (May 88 - 91)	1647
VW Polo & Derby (76 - Jan 82)	0335
VW Polo (82 - Oct 90)	0813
VW Santana (Sept 81 - May 88)	0814
VW Scirocco 'Mk 1' 1.5, 1.6 & 1.8 (74 - 85)	0726
VW Scirocco (82 - 90)	1224
VW Transporter 1600 (68 - 79)	0082
VW Transporter 1700, 1800 & 2000 (72 - 79)	0226
VW Transporter with air-cooled engine (79 - 82)	0638
VW Type 3 (63 - 73)	0084
VW Vento (petrol & diesel)(Feb 92 - 95)	3097
VOLVO	
Volvo 66 & 343, Daf 55 & 66 (68 - 79)	0293
Volvo 142, 144 & 145 (66 - 74)	0129
Volvo 240 Series (74 - 93)(2nd Edition)	0270
Volvo 262, 264 & 260/265 (75 - 85)	0400
Volvo 340, 343, 345 & 360 (76 - 91)	0715
Volvo 440, 460 & 480 (87 - 92)	1691
Volvo 740 & 760 (petrol)(82 - 91)	1258
YUGO/ZASTAVA	
Yugo/Zastava (81 - 90)	1453

NEW TECH BOOKS	
Automotive Brake Manual	3050
Automotive Electrical & Electronic Systems	3049
Automotive Tools Manual	3052
Automotive Welding Manual	3053

SPECIAL INTEREST AUTOMOTIVE BOOKS	
Automotive Fuel Injection Systems	9755
Car Bodywork Repair Manual	9864
Caravan Manual	9894
Dishwasher Manual (New Edition)	9866
Ford Vehicle Carburettors	1783
Haynes Technical Data Book ('87 to '96)	1996
How To Keep Your Car Alive	9868
In-Car Entertainment Manual (2nd Edition)	9862
Japanese Vehicle Carburettors	1786
Kitcar Builder's Manual (2nd Edition)	H898
Pass the MOT!	9861
Small Engine Repair Manual	1755
Solex & Pierburg Carburettors	1785
SU Carburettors	0299
Weber Carburettors (to '79)	0393
Weber Carburettors ('79 to '91)	1784

All the manuals featured on these pages are available through good motor accessory shops and book stores. In case of difficulty, contact Haynes Publishing on 01963 440635

Preserving Our Motoring Heritage

< *The Model J Duesenberg Derham Tourster. Only eight of these magnificent cars were ever built – this is the only example to be found outside the United States of America*

Almost every car you've ever loved, loathed or desired is gathered under one roof at the Haynes Motor Museum. Over 300 immaculately presented cars and motorbikes represent every aspect of our motoring heritage, from elegant reminders of bygone days, such as the superb Model J Duesenberg to curiosities like the bug-eyed BMW Isetta. There are also many old friends and flames. Perhaps you remember the 1959 Ford Popular that you did your courting in? The magnificent 'Red Collection' is a spectacle of classic sports cars including AC, Alfa Romeo, Austin Healey, Ferrari, Lamborghini, Maserati, MG, Riley, Porsche and Triumph.

A Perfect Day Out

Each and every vehicle at the Haynes Motor Museum has played its part in the history and culture of Motoring. Today, they make a wonderful spectacle and a great day out for all the family. Bring the kids, bring Mum and Dad, but above all bring your camera to capture those golden memories for ever. You will also find an impressive array of motoring memorabilia, a comfortable 70 seat video cinema and one of the most extensive transport book shops in Britain. The Pit Stop Cafe serves everything from a cup of tea to wholesome, home-made meals or, if you prefer, you can enjoy the large picnic area nestled in the beautiful rural surroundings of Somerset.

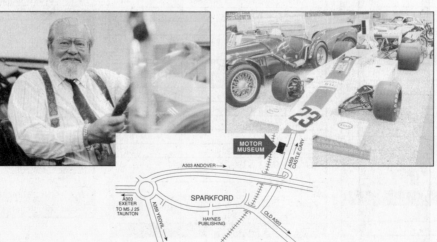

> *John Haynes O.B.E., Founder and Chairman of the museum at the wheel of a Haynes Light 12.*

< *Graham Hill's Lola Cosworth Formula 1 car next to a 1934 Riley Sports.*

The Museum is situated on the A359 Yeovil to Frome road at Sparkford, just off the A303 in Somerset. It is about 40 miles south of Bristol, and 25 minutes drive from the M5 intersection at Taunton.

Open 9.30am - 5.30pm (10.00am - 4.00pm Winter) 7 days a week, *except Christmas Day, Boxing Day and New Years Day*

Special rates available for schools, coach parties and outings Charitable Trust No. 292048